Labor's Text

Labor's Text
The Worker in American Fiction

LAURA HAPKE

Rutgers University Press
New Brunswick, New Jersey, and London

Library of Congress Cataloging-in-Publication Data

Hapke, Laura.
    Labor's text : the worker in American fiction / Laura Hapke.
      p.   cm.
    Includes bibliographical references (p.   ) and index.
    ISBN 0-8135-2879-8 (alk. paper)—ISBN 0-8135-2880-1 (pbk. : alk. paper)
    1. American fiction—History and criticism.   2. Work in literature.
  3. Working class writings, American—History and criticism.   4. Labor
movement in literature.   5. Working class in literature. I. Title.

PS374.W64 H36 2001
813.009'3523317—dc21

                                        00-039031

British Cataloging-in-Publication data for this book is available from the
British Library

Manufactured in the United States of America

Frontispiece: Detail, William Gropper, *Automobile Industry*. Mural Study, Detroit,
Michigan, post office, 1940–1941. Oil on fiberboard, 20 1/8 × 48 in. National Museum of American Art, Smithsonian Institution.

Jude remains obscure.

—DAVID JOSEPH (1995)

Contents

Illustrations

Preface

A decade ago, I began my research on American labor fiction by revisiting my immigrant father's novella, serialized in a radical journal of the early 1930s.[1] In his pages workers were never written into silence or hidden in a subplot. What laboring people thought and did, resented and combated, planned and carried out, was the lifeblood of his story of the itinerant organizer Max Harris, Cliff, the hobo Wobbly, and a cast of straight-talkers. I realized that every one of them would be as out of place in the labor fiction of the looming new millennium as a Damon Runyan figure.

Turning reluctantly to the modern scene, I looked in more timely venues for inheritors of the concern my father shared with his era for the "working stiff." I sought out references to today's workers by sorting through political speeches, newscasters' pronouncements, sociological surveys, and "soft news" pieces on the decline of middle-class affluence or the weakness of trade unionism. My father, whether prisoner of doctrine, thirties realist, or both, had kept his eyes firmly fixed on what used to be called the proletariat. I found this could not be said of the opinion pieces of the last ten years. The op-ed page of the *New York Times,* for instance, featured a spirited defense of the 1995 baseball strike. It located millionaire ballplayers (though not the hundreds with less glamorous jobs thrown out of work by their job action) in the tradition of the "hard-fought strikes and legislation of the New Deal," the bloody Homestead, the crushed Pullman strikes.[2] Truer to the tradition of Homestead than it knew, another op-ed page on the same day called for city workers to increase their work week "just . . . to 37 and 1/2 hours": the old cry of Taylorism, Fordism, and the speedup.[3]

As I pored over all this, I found a sad contrast between today's refusal to understand the one who labors and the Depression era's profound respect for this figure. My father's stories were of "little guys" storming the factory, fearful of the company guards and elated when victorious—a tale told often, and sometimes truly enough, of the hardscrabble 1930s. If, save for an occasional walkout, no one really storms the barricades in new millennium imaginings, it is because not only has the labor novel largely ceased to exist, but so, to judge by the current climate, has the laborer.

I doggedly teach the Depression era's preeminent social protest novelists Mike Gold and mining-town bard Agnes Smedley, the despondent postmodern work novels of Russell Banks, the up-from-poverty memoirs and occasional novels by the new African American, Latino, Native American, and Asian authors. My students, when asked who makes up the working class, tell me it includes anyone who works for a living. There is some truth to this view. From those who survive by piecing together minimum-wage jobs to the vast numbers filling the lower rungs of the burgeoning service and ill-paid manufacturing sector to the college-educated children of the old lower middle class, there is no longer an expectation of bourgeois security.

My father, though long gone, again supplements my understanding: the *UA Journal*, his union's publication, explains that fourteen million workers—almost one-eighth of the full-time civilian workforce—earn full-time wages below the poverty line.[4] But in the 1990s, when rampant downsizing had pushed so many Americans into low-wage or part-time work, the irony was that 95 percent of those interviewed in a recent survey, including those whose income qualified them for the subproletarian one-fifth, called themselves middle class.[5]

Admittedly, "working class," not to mention "proletarian," is vague terminology in a country where class boundaries are supposed to be fluid. Paul Lauter, the veteran analyst of the literature of labor, includes as working class those who sell their labor for wages, have relatively little control over the nature of their work, and are neither managers nor professionals. Daniel Walkowitz and Stanley Aronowitz, in contrast, envision a white-collar proletariat, comprising, among others, professors, social workers, and even midlevel managers. The new code words for "working class"—"poor," "minorities," "service-sector employees," or "lower-level white collar"—may describe but do not clarify these different interpretations. Even the government no longer uses the occupational designation "blue collar," and a highbrow magazine like *The New Yorker* only muddies the waters with the term "middle-class working stiff."[6] In sum, it does not take a sociologist to notice the tremendous confusion in America about class terms, although it does take one to sort it out.[7] One such observer, Richard Sennett, notes that "class has been the dirty secret of American history, denied by promises of individual freedom, by dreams of upward mobility—memories that prove on inspection only to be recovered-memory fantasies."[8] Whether we revert to the term "working class" or not, in an officially classless society a working-class identity is an ambiguous gift.[9] Not many seem ready to accept it.

There is much opprobrium directed at—and defeatism in—workers' struggles, and great ambiguity about what, if anything, distinguishes co-opted or poverty-line workers from the vast American middle class. In such a visual age, of course, the images disseminated by film and in cyberspace are excellent popular-culture sources for students of important media-manufactured attitudes toward working people. To probe more deeply, though, literature tells us how our culture's perception of workers and their perceptions of themselves became this fuzzy. It is as crucial to chart the antebellum predecessors of a Terry McMillan novel of a marginally employed welfare mother as it is to examine Herman Melville's tale of wraithlike paper-mill girls. In these texts, as in the many in between, the imagined lives of workers have mapped the tensions between moving up and falling down, between the price of acculturation and the cost of staying put.

However much today's fiction now explains why no one wants to be called working class anymore, a survey of its predecessors can show us when it was in the popular imagination that the worker began the long hunt for the ever-elusive good life. Uncovering the literary iconography of sweat can tell us whether our nation's social protest authors ever found workers noble and proud, and whether these creators urged them to remain true to what they were.

Concern about American attitudes toward workers and work underlies my goals in writing this book. On a more personal level, I do not want to see my father's life erased from the laborscape. In clambering up twenty floors, summer and winter, to fit pipes on a skyscraper not yet graced with elevators, he joined the people of the steel towns, mining towns, sweatshops, and electronic sweatshops in building this country. Nor do I want to see his concern with social justice snuffed out in a general scramble to disavow the proletarian novel.

My history of worker representations in American literature charts what workers, real or imagined, have told and been told about themselves for 150 years. If, in the act of restoring knowledge lost and scattered, I cast a particularly critical eye on the erasures, harmful distortions, and unjust stereotypes in that discourse, it is in service to that goal.

I extend my thanks to the English Department and my chair, Sherman Raskin, to the former dean of the Dyson College of Arts and Science, Charles Masiello, and to the current dean, Gail Dinter-Gottlieb, for supporting this project through released time and summer research grants. My gratitude goes out as well to the staff of the Pace University Library, particularly the director, Mel Isaacson, and to Elisabeth Birnbaum, Amernel Denton, Michelle Fanelli, Luz Gonzales, Mary Habstritt, Alicia Joseph, Rey Racelis, and Tom Snyder, for their dedication in tracking down sources and ensuring I could gain access to them. I thank Andrew Lee of the Tamiment Library, and Debra Bernhardt and Gail Malmgreen of the Wagner Archives, both collections located at the Bobst Library of New York University. My gratefulness goes as well to the staff of the Reference Center for Marxist Studies for invaluable access to archival materials on the labor left.

I am grateful to the editor-in-chief of Rutgers University Press, Leslie Mitchner, for her unwavering support during this lengthy project. Cindy Buck, my meticulous copyeditor, is patience on a monument. Fulsome praise as well for the expert editorial assistance provided by Elizabeth Gilbert and Martha Whitt.

My profoundest thanks must go to one of the founders of the new field of working-class studies, Janet Zandy, who has guided, empowered, and inspired me for almost two decades.

I thank too the estimable scholars in the allied fields of labor history, American studies, African American studies, the literature of the American Left, and working-class studies. Among the numerous generous individuals who discussed my project with me are Eric Arnesen, Rosalind Baxandall, Paul Buhle, the late Constance Coiner, Shelley Fisher Fishkin, Henry Louis Gates, Jr., Timothy Gilfoyle, Miriam Gogol, Roger Keeran, Paul Lauter, Sherry Lee

Linkon, Bill Mullen, Bob Niemi, Wendell Ricketts, Eric Schocket, Jon-Christian Suggs, Alan Wald, Seth Widgerson, Will Watson, and David Yamada.

My collegial thanks to my scholar-colleagues Antonia Garcia-Rodriguez, Mark Hussey, Karla Jay, Elizabeth Lott, Mary Ann Murphy, Bernard Newman, Mary Ellen Oliverio, Michael Rosenfeld, Roger Salerno, and Walter Srebnick for their bibliographical suggestions and research leads.

The staff at Pace's Design and Development Office, especially the director Jackie Womack and her assistant Ursula Shand, were wizards at zip drives and transcription. In the project's early data-processing stages, Sam Drukman was efficient and engaged. I owe my able graduate student helper, Ursula F. Nigrelli, an enormous debt of gratitude for helping me see the project through from midpoint to completion. Her keyboard skills, precision, and enabling presence remain impressive. That "I knew her when" she was a student struggling to decode Mike Gold, Frank Norris, and Agnes Smedley makes her contribution even more meaningful.

My respectful gratitude goes as well to those who shared their experience of U.S. radicalism with me. I thank my father, the late Daniel Horwitz, and my mother, the late Frances Gutglass, and Priscilla Alexander, Phillip Bonosky, Dorothy Doyle, Marcia Folsom, Lottie Gordon, Melvin Henriksen, Charles Keller, and Marty, Miriam, and Elliott Kotler. Accomplished oral historians all, they took me over the rough terrain of the New Deal and cold war years with a tolerance for the children of affluence that can only be called enlightened.

Brooklyn, New York, Labor Day, 1999

Labor's Text

Raphael Soyer, *Sixth Avenue,* c. 1933–1934. Oil on canvas. Wadsworth Atheneum, Hartford. Gift of Mr. and Mrs. James N. Rosenberg.

Any Saturday, the aisles of literary supermarkets are filled with those bent on purchasing the new John Grisham or Danielle Steele, the latest diet, self-help, or emotional recovery guru, the most recent ghostwritten Hollywood memoir. Other readers, wanting more substance, pass by impatiently, knowing that Poetry and Philosophy, and through the next doorway Psychology, Literary Criticism, and African American History, await them. But it is only by accident that interested readers find Labor Studies, much less the American work novels that are integral to this field. In a dark corner of the bookstore, obscured by a display on computer games, work occupies the slenderest of spaces in the American mind.[1]

When, in August of 1997, the *New York Times* covered a UPS strike, and followed with articles on an early-winter UAW strike, both soon settled without major worker concessions, such reportage seemed a departure from the prevailing cultural amnesia.[2] There had been sporadic job protests in the 1990s by autoworkers and coal miners, but they were transient and soon erased from public awareness. The very fact that the Teamsters' strike was their first since 1979 demonstrated that labor news was elsewhere. Work truth resided instead in the stern *Times* headline: "Accepting the Harsh Truth of a Blue-Collar Recession: Old Way of Work, and Life, May Never Return."[3] It inhabited the occasional article on the dearth of union membership (a low 13.5 percent as the new millennium drew near) or the brief, unimpassioned piece on the extreme dangers of mining work. It had a home too in the breezy relegation to the Style Section of a piece on the trend among the unjustly affluent to underpay and verbally abuse their domestic help.[4] It lay in piece after piece on the troubled recent history of the AFL-CIO, in the *Crain's Business Weekly* headline that yet another industry was leaving New York City. It shaped the news reports about American workers who stifled their anger at management restoration of company unions; even the news item on the booming construction trades minimized the fact that skilled building tradesmen were solidly unionist.[5] The truth about work resonated as well in the "human-interest" pieces on the newly jobless, middle-class specialists in data processing, banking, or middle management, all on their way to deskilling and part-time or menial jobs.[6] Even as the economy of 1999 seemed very much on the rebound, productivity, which is closely tied to economic growth, was far below the rates of the blue-collar golden age of the 1950s and 1960s.[7]

John Steinbeck's hard-pressed Okies, Mike Gold's sweated immigrants, Agnes Smedley's mining-camp drudges, Richard Wright's ghettoized Chicago blacks, and Meridel Le Sueur's sororal community of poverty-stricken mothers have all but vanished from the artistic and social landscape. A new working class with its own tales of downward mobility and class stagnation, such as the overworked or unemployed bourgeoisie of Michael Dorris's story collection *Working Men* (1993), now dwarfs the blue-collar masses. Absent are novels and stories that give voice to those losing the post–Taft-Hartley battle against NAFTA, the people who still suffer from the striker replacement acts, the erosion of the manufacturing sector, and a pervasive popular indifference. Those still slaving in the sweatshops of urban America, tending the gardens of the rich, picking beans for agribusiness bosses, or finding in urban crime a seductive alternative to minimum-wage work have become a new generation's forgotten men and women. Where are their bards?

In a recent homage to Mike Gold and the neglected proletarian fiction of the 1930s, Morris Dickstein comments that "the poor may always be with us" but American writers and audiences "seem to notice them only at thirty-year intervals."[8] His comment may easily be extended to the men, women, and children of the industrial, manual, and migrant workforce as well as to nonindustrial, low-level sales, clerical, and service workers, among other laboring groups.[9] Yet the lives of such toilers have been chronicled by American writers of every stripe, from the politically insurgent to the genteelly traditional, for over 150 years. Once controversial, this mass of works, save for a resurgent interest in the proletarian 1930s and scattered feminist and African American authors with labor sympathies, is now forgotten.

At the core of my inquiry will be the attempt to recover these worker representations. They date from the birth of the Gothic "mysteries and miseries" novel of class stratification and the factory novel of the Lowell textile mills to the fiction of the troubled postindustrial present. This is not to argue that such texts form a composite homage to the American workforce. Far from it. Prior to the Progressive Era (1900–1917), outside of the insular world of the radical small presses, most fiction on labor included diatribes against or idealizations of the white workingman and, less often, the workingwoman. It was as if blacks, Asians, Latinos, and Native Americans inhabited a workless sphere of their own. And in the HUAC-infused climate of the McCarthy years, it was hardly fashionable for literature to offer the kind of Heroic Worker who had so briefly graced New Deal murals and Great Depression novels. Nor, again, was that figure usually representative of more liminal workers such as women and African Americans.

In spite of such lapses from verisimilitude and erasures of the lived history of the other half of American workers, novelists did pay their respects to the American at work. Their roster ranges from Rebecca Harding Davis to David Graham Phillips, Stephen Crane to John Steinbeck, Anzia Yezierska to Fannie Hurst, the radical John Dos Passos to his later conservative reincarnation. Also audible were the voices of African Americans, those on the margins of the margins. Such writers included Harriet Wilson, who pictured northern female indentured servitude, and Martin Delany, who told of slavery in terms of class as well as race. It was not until the Harlem Renaissance that the perennial post–Civil War theme of racial uplift—whether extolled, challenged, or rebuked—was linked with scrutinies of the black proletariat, as Langston Hughes, William Attaway, Zora Neale Hurston, and Ann Petry did in their novels. Later still, in the post-Vietnam era, Denise Chavez's Latino, Leslie Marmon Silko's American Indian, and Fay Myenne Ng's Chinese personae were rescued from the subplot shadows in which minority Americans of labor-class origins have dwelled for decades.

All of these authors engage in narratives or counternarratives of classlessness. Despite this nation's history of sharp labor-capital antagonisms, it remains Americans' ideology of "exceptionalism" that class boundaries seem fluid in a country of such unlimited economic possibility. The authors of *The American Perception of Class* (1987) are wise to observe that defining American exceptionalism more precisely has become an academic cottage industry.[10] The factors that produced the exceptionalist ideology and weakened the labor movement are diverse enough. Suggestions include the lack of a feudal past, political suffrage, racial and ethnic divisions, and even the two-party system. In the broadest sense, however, the term connotes a certain specialness based upon material abundance and consensual values.[11] As construed by U.S. authors, social protest or not, the pervasive exceptionalist text or subtext is the myriad of workerist battles with the bourgeoisie, more often than not to pry open a collective entry into the middle class and seize the American Dream.[12]

Faced with the limits of ascension ideology, antilabor authors, particularly turn-of-the-century Social Darwinians, have been quick to blame not the dream itself but the mass of workers they deem unworthy or incapable of attaining it. Conversely, echoing through the most passionate literary defenses of labor activism and the militant collective is the cry of the self-made man. The irony is that, whether banished by the anti- or prolabor text, the Way-to-Wealth ghosts of Ben Franklin and Horatio Alger return again and again to haunt labor fiction.

To be sure, a series of literary counterthrusts, from the pens of the firebrand labor writers of the Great Depression to those of the cynical post-Depression authors of the 1940s onward, form a composite challenge to the exaggerated emphasis on embourgeoisement. Debunking the "land of opportunity" theme, they offer versions of socialism or, their worker figures trailing clouds of disappointment, deplore the exclusions of capitalism. Some argue that the very fact of selective ascension makes the success ethic difficult to challenge. Whatever their perceptions of the vanished American Dream, these radical texts revise but do not dismantle individualism.

It is important at this point to distinguish between working-class and (implicitly pro-) labor fiction. Janet Zandy observes that a "working-class text centers the lived, material experiences of working-class people."[13] Attentive to the physicality of suffering, such a text challenges dominant cultural assumptions about working people, including the conflation of stereotyped masculinity and working-class manhood. (Laboring men are routinely described as "burly" and "beefy," adjectives rarely used for the bourgeoisie.)[14] There are problems with this definition, as its author acknowledges: contradictory voices in working-class texts are as prevalent as collective ones.[15] The Zandy definition also compels us to clarify the differences between the overlapping categories of worker-writer and working-class writer.[16] And finally, we must consider whether middle-class writers can produce working-class texts, a burning issue in the 1930s Proletcult debates (see chapter 9).

To explore these arguments, I have not confined this study to working-class fiction. Depression era authors, seizing the proletarian moment, were almost simultaneously serialized in Left journals and published by mainstream ones. Otherwise, working-class fiction, largely a twentieth-century phenomenon, has been fragmentary at best. This situation is due in part to material restraints on worker-writers rather than their literary choice.[17] My survey does not emphasize writing for working-class consumption available through the labor or radical press. I do contrast such proworker fare with the imaginative literature more readily available to nonunion readers. What trade unionists, Socialists, or laborite anticapitalists read, and the extent to which they recognized themselves in it, are more properly subjects of other studies.[18] My purpose, rather, is to understand what the worker has meant to American fiction, much of which, though only loosely radical in nature, has been a source of information for readers whose knowledge of strikes and sweatshops, child labor and sitdowns, was not firsthand. To be sure, the literary heritage of a century and a half of the fiction of work is a panoply of labor figures. Yet these invented sons and daughters of labor reveal less who is being looked at than who is looking. Among the observers, only a minority wears the two hats of worker and writer.

As Peter Conn acutely observes, fiction is "expressive of ideological transactions within a society and may offer insights otherwise less accessible."[19] Accordingly, my study poses the very questions asked by the texts themselves, taken as a whole. How did literary perceptions of the morality and humanity of the laboring man and woman alter over the broad sweep of one and a half centuries? What kind of lens onto the larger world of workers, of labor protest, of workplace and after-hours gender, racial, and ethnic relations, did a broad range of American authors provide? How, according to observers from divergent class origins and political allegiances, did workers view one another? What is the evolution in literary depictions of the workingman and -woman? What literary cruxes and historical controversies inform those depictions and attempts to insert women, blacks, Asians, Latinos, and Native Americans into a white, male labor-literature tradition? In sum, to what public rhetoric did the myriad of workforce fiction contribute?[20]

Whether in direct or coded form, much of the U.S. fiction on workers refers to key labor events. Cultural studies and New Historicism have by implication included the long sweep of labor history in the extraliterary concerns welded to an understanding of texts. Yet despite the turn toward history evident in American studies, African American studies, and women's studies, "history" is a highly disputed term. This is especially so in the New Historicist criticism of naturalism and realism, the two most common schools of work literature.[21] In the reestablishment of links between manual labor and fiction, neither realism nor naturalism is an accurate, objective record of social conditions. A series of deconstructions of the determinist model traditionally used to characterize realism and naturalism is clearly in order. It is equally crucial in that regard to locate the plurivocal textual voices—that is, the ways in which the voice of power in the text also records other voices.[22]

To analyze the power relations encoded in the very production of a labor text as pro- or anticapitalist, however, is not my mode of resuscitating fiction in relation to the historical experience of workers. This book, rather, is an alternative contribution to the emerging field of working-class studies. The compass I use for my border crossings is the acknowledgment that while there is no unitary working-class experience, there are observable lived histories of workers, from the seminal events of unionism to the everyday stories of the "apolitical" communities and work cultures shaping the outlooks of working people. I recognize that each generation reinterprets the labor-literary text. Nor in situating literature within a chronological and historical context do I minimize the mentoring and other formative influences on the individual writer. But my assumption throughout is that labor novels and stories originate in a specific time, place, and ideological milieu that shape their meaning. My aim is thus to provide as much labor historical background as possible, and to that end I have also made the notes interdisciplinary and full.

There is an allied (and more potent perhaps) reason to provide historical contexts for work-related fiction. Despite a resurgence of interest in the left-wing or proletarian novel of the Great Depression, modern theorists advocating multiculturalism and a more inclusive literary canon still minimize what the historian John Higham terms the broader inequalities of class.[23] If class is linked with organized labor, there is more than a little truth to C. Wright Mills's 1945 observation that the postwar liberal left was unsympathetic to (organized) labor because it did not present the image of the downtrodden.[24] But when the definition of the worker is more accurately expanded to include the vast numbers who have taken no part in the trade union movement, it remains puzzling that there has been so little rediscovery of the fiction of work. One compelling reason is that work fiction invokes a naturalistic tradition that embraces a sociological vision with vaguely leftist biases.

Carla Cappetti positions these biases against naturalism in a larger dispute that "exiled the whole urban sociological tradition from the hall of fame of American letters."[25] She correctly ascribes hostility to naturalist fiction to the fallout from the ideological landscape of the cold war. Such formulations may no longer be fashionable but their effects are still with us. Yet that bias alone cannot completely account for a critical predilection untouched, as Nelson Algren noted, by working-class life in America.[26] Paul Lauter finds a "renewed interest in literary study [paralleling] the shift in history from an overwhelming emphasis on political, diplomatic, and military study to a new regard for social history, especially history 'from the bottom.'"[27] To be sure, some major academic publishers are reissuing "lost" proletarian novels and fiction on and by radicals with multiple allegiances—to labor and feminism, civil rights and socialism.[28] However, as Elaine Scarry remarks of the British in a comment even more applicable to U.S. scholarship, work as a subject of critical writings on the novel is neither "a major category of thought, nor a rubric in most indexes, nor a way of perceiving literature taught in the classroom, nor a subject surrounded by a richly elaborated, shared vocabulary."[29]

Recent scholarship by Alan Wald, Michael Denning, Bill Mullen and Sherry Lee Linkon, and others has expanded the multicultural scrutiny of traditional American literature to proletarian and working-class writing by pointing to the diversity of radical writing itself.[30] Paula Rabinowitz reminds us that the term "proletarian literature" to define fiction about the working class was used as early as 1900; Julia Stein pinpoints modern writers who continue the proletarian literary tradition.[31] In broader terms, the multicultural scholarship of the last decade and a half has altered and revised the definition of both American working-class and American labor literature. There is important work in integration and synthesis yet to be done. It has been over forty years since the publication of Walter B. Rideout's classic *The Radical Novel in the United States, 1900–1954* (1956). Daniel Aaron's *Writers on the Left* (1961) appeared four decades ago. More than twenty-five years have passed since Fay M. Blake's *The Strike in the American Novel* (1972) and more specialized studies such as David Madden's essay collection, *Proletarian Writers of the 1930s* (1968), were published.[32]

Michael Denning's *The Cultural Front: The Laboring of American Culture in the Twentieth Century* (1996) has recently widened the Depression era proletarian literary tradition. Denning not only considers novels from the 1930s and 1940s, among many other art forms, but also argues for the enduring effect of these artworks in reshaping American literature and post-1930s culture.[33] Alan Wald's forthcoming noncanonical history of Marxist writers from the 1930s through the 1960s promises to continue the reevaluation of left-wing literary tradition. It will recover the multicultural red traditions of African American, Jewish American, socialist-feminist, Native American, and mass-cultural (Communist producers of period science fiction, detective fiction, and the like) writers.[34] Douglas Wixson has aided the timely reappraisals of texts noted in Rideout and Blake by making an exhaustive study of the proletarian writer Jack Conroy and his relation to midwestern literary radicalism. The contributions of Barbara Foley and Paula Rabinowitz have been searching feminist revisions of 1930s texts. Paul Lauter has probingly written on, and Janet Zandy has thoughtfully anthologized, working-class women's writings.[35] The same has been done for leftist women's writings, fictive and otherwise, of the 1930s by the editors of *Writing Red* (1987).[36] By applying labor perspectives, Nicholas Bromell and David Herreshoff have reinvigorated the classic authors of the antebellum era. And Denning has taken a mass-cultural approach to the politically ambiguous subgenre of dime novels, which features but defuses violent strikers, tramps, and other controversial labor figures.[37] The mighty contributions of Foley, Rabinowitz, the late Constance Coiner, and others have revised our understanding of representations by and of women writers.[38] And a number of still unheralded dissertations have filled in the literary-historical gaps by addressing such subgenres as the procapitalist industrial novel of the 1870s and 1880s, the turn-of-the-century working girl's romance, and the fiction of prolabor, Depression era black writers.[39]

Even as late as the dawn of the year 2000 the issue of class is much more repressed in gay labor literature than in any other genre.[40] The more tradition-bound labor movement has only gingerly embraced the issue of job bias against gays and lesbians, and it was not until 1997 that an independent film festival aired *Out at Work,* a documentary about gay men and lesbians on the job.[41] Class raises parallel issues of denial and the ambition to reinvent oneself economically. But to date, except for well-researched social histories like John Loughery's *The Other Side of Silence: Men's Lives and Gay Identities* (1998), with its citations to novels of the 1930s, only a curiously sparse body of work has utilized a limited rhetoric of gay and lesbian class issues.[42] Omitted from labor multiculturalism and studied separately by experts in the field, gay literature is marked by classism in the queer movement, which runs up against what working-class lesbian scholars protest is that the "word queer captures not only sexual identity but class identity as well."[43] It is to be hoped that future scholars of gay work and gay red fiction will build on the initiatives of the writer John Gilgun to examine linkages between and remove the veils from the two fields.[44] As it is, fine labor authors such as Dorothy Allison continue to produce separate texts to talk about sexuality and about (white-trash) class (see chapter 12), while important small presses like Firebrand Books often subordinate labor to sexuality.[45]

My effort to piece together the wider American literary response to wage earners, both unionist and underclass, stoutly probourgeois and itinerant, builds on the valuable scholarship described here and in the notes. I am wary, however, of a trend, even in some of this fine criticism, to defend manual toil by intellectualizing it.[46] Janet Zandy's brilliant essays, providing a more useful approach, explore the very synecdoche "hired hand" to uncover the truth that working-class "language" is more than oral or textual.[47] The pressure to contextualize work-related literature has rightly resulted in studies that analyze the relation between literary and other forms of labor. This is particularly so, as in the case of Jack Conroy, Sanora Babb, and others, where the workers in question labored by day and drafted fiction by night.[48] The boundary between adjunct teachers and other kinds of wage laborers seems porous enough, but problems arise in likening, for instance, true-crime "journalistic labor" to "police labor."[49] Furthermore, the aestheticizing of manual work implied in making a philosopher-king of the cowboy or in referring to the workingman's pain and exhaustion as the "problematics of embodied labor"[50] risks distancing laborers from what they do. And particularly in U.S. fiction, the psychological world of the worker, even more than the jobsite world, has proved an immensely elusive subject. Indeed, if "all people who work with their hands are only partly visible," as George Orwell sagely observes, a student of the fiction of manual toil need seek no larger task than to understand the many ways in which literature has expressed, enhanced, or resisted that invisibility.[51]

Yet to make the worker visible is to remember, as the historian Lise Vogel points out about the antebellum workingwomen of the Lowell mills, that at "no time were [workers] a monolithic mass sharing a single consciousness. The consciousness of individuals does not conform in any simple way to the usual categories of political analysis."[52] Workers who are skilled or unskilled, organized or unorganized, leftist or nonleftist, Communist, Socialist, or "pure and simple" trade unionist, Protestant or non-Protestant, native or non-native born, European immigrant or non-European immigrant, white or black, male or female have historically been uneasy allies and frequent adversaries. Moreover, the very term "work culture"—or labor's response to jobsite requirements and restrictions—is far from unitary. The new labor historians, speaking a language of culture, gender, and race, have widened the locus of struggle from the strike to include the social group. In their vision of labor history, work culture can be traditionalist and militant; leisure-time, workplace, and picket-line; capitalist and anticapitalist.[53] Moreover, the new women's historians are providing ample evidence of the divisions that have characterized 150 years of American work: the gendered separation of labor in mills and factories, steeltowns and coaltowns, laundries and restaurants, fruit fields and auto plants, department stores and canneries, and traditionally feminine and masculine work venues.[54]

The interpretations of John R. Commons, the famed chronicler of official trade union history, are greatly at odds with the work of the eminent cultural historian of the rank and file and the laborite Herbert Gutman. Whatever angle of vision addresses working-class events should not obscure the rich lived history of American laborers, who have struggled, at times against one another, for control of the workday, the wage, the shop floor, the health benefit, and the pension.[55] Most important, they have repeatedly proclaimed their right of access to fairly paid work. Antebellum slaves bargained for pay when farmed out to bonded work in craft and industrial labor. The efforts of the journeymen of the pre–Civil War North, drawn to the fledgling worker federations, have proved the cornerstone of the labor movement, however that movement has been delineated by historians.[56] Moreover, workers, often at odds with one another, have fought and lost corollary battles over the right to define their own morality. As successive temperance, antivice, social hygiene, assimilationist, and, most recently, politically dismissive ideologies have arisen to regulate the lives of the working class, there has been a corresponding struggle for control over everything from the saloon to the Fourth of July picnic to the immigrant family diet.[57]

To what degree these events represent the working masses is still the subject of lively debate among labor historians. Similar events include: the slave revolts of the antebellum South; the mechanics' institutes serving ambitious pre–Civil War apprentices; the popularity of melodramas of the streetwise Bowery b'hoy among antebellum working-class men; the 1872 shoeworkers' protests by the Daughters of St. Crispin; the National Colored Labor Union manifesto of 1871; the secretive 1886 Knights of Labor ritual; the folk poets of the 1892 Homestead Strike; the genteel WASP arbiters on the 1911 New York City Committee on Amusements; the Paterson Strike Pageant of 1913; the Chicago Vice Commission of 1915; the biracial coalminers' strike of 1927; the Harlem Jobs Boycott of 1934; the Communist Party Women's Commission's 1936 Mother's Bill of Rights; the Ladies' Auxiliary of the Flint, Michigan, 1937 sit-down strike; the ineffective labor opposition to the Taft-Hartley Act; the rise in the late 1960s and early 1970s of the United Farm Workers; and the American Indian Movement push for jobs in the same period. What should be made clear, however, is the extent to which the nation's writers, regardless of political affiliation, have consistently traded a consciousness of class relationships for literary refigurings of the labor-linked phenomena mentioned earlier and, particularly after the Great Depression, of labor defeats.[58] In so doing, American authors have responded to the cultural anxieties generated by workers. Indeed, with the exception of the strike- and Hooverville-centered novels of the economically famished 1930s, our national fiction has demonstrated a curious resistance to proletarian art. Even in novelists with liberal sympathies, anxious fantasies of worker upheaval generate, almost ritualistically, literary defenses of individualism, both economic and personal. From the gentleman worker of nineteenth-century stories to the narcissistically alienated blue-collar man of modern fare, workers in American fiction do not easily submerge the self in the Cause.

Exceptions obviously occur in what Rideout bills as the 1930s strike and conversion novelists, who strove to reverse American literary ambivalence toward laboring folk and substitute mass action for self-propelled activity.[59] But Depression bards could not escape what one astute *New Republic* reviewer at the time called the difficulty of "writ[ing] in terms of the mass, of whole classes of people caught up in the [economic] circumstances of their time."[60] Such difficulties notwithstanding, 1930s radical fiction has received much new notice among scholars.[61] These proletarian and Communist authors have been resurrected by associating them with a revisionary politics, whether or not fully realized aesthetically in a true worker's art.

Nevertheless, when 1930s Left writers officially extol the collective, their own narrative methods typically reveal ambivalence. One has only to compare American literary proletarianism with, say, the 1925 Fyodor Gladkov novel *Cement*, translated to great international fanfare in 1928. U.S. authors are far more likely to focus on the consciousness of the solo hero, however extensive his travels among the courageous syndicalists or the politically unaware. Exceptions occur. A protagonist transcends the creator's emphasis on the drama of his or her conversion. Le Sueur's welfare mothers are politicized. Wright's murderously violent Bigger Thomas relinquishes his rage. Such exceptions, though, must be placed squarely in the context of gender or race, as if awareness of class oppression alone could not sustain such new visions.

Whether one looks to the "working stiff" 1930s or eras less friendly to laborite heroes, choosing key worker texts, much less those that bear out my contentions, is an interpretive act in itself. The British critic Carol Snee, updating the Depression era controversy over "true" revolutionary literature, rejects A. E. Schachner's view that proletarian fiction "reflects the life of any typical cross-section of the proletariat and need not be more revolutionary than the proletariat . . . at the time." To her the crucial difference between proletarian and working-class writing is that the former foments rebellion, while the latter describes worker life.[62] Nicholas Coles makes another useful distinction. He sees in authors who are themselves working class an awareness of writing from within that life, whether or not their literary products are proletarian. And unlike Snee, he further argues for including middle-class authors such as Upton Sinclair and Jack London in any reading list on the worker.[63]

Marxism in U.S. fiction might be broadly defined as an explicit or implicit belief that collective struggle will humanize the work experience through a work-floor democracy that would mark a crucial alteration in capitalistic political and economic institutions. U.S. labor fiction exhibits the recurrent Marxist belief that a revolutionary consciousness is needed if such a transformatory experience is to make work meaningful again to workers. At this writing, the debate continues on whether U.S. novels ever sustained a solid Marxist presence, especially in the cold war years (see chapter 10).[64] Furthermore, it is beyond the scope of this study to define the ideal fiction of blue-collar experience, other than to suggest that it would be opposed to conventional elitism.[65]

My task is to explore the changing and unchanging characteristics of imagined workers and of worker fiction, from the antilaborite consciousness permeating pre-1930s novels to the push toward authenticity that Great Depression authors left as their legacy. My aim is to move more or less chronologically over 150 years of fiction about paid toil, from the earliest industrial fiction of the Lowell factory school of writing through recent efforts by Russell Banks, Raymond Carver, Dorothy Allison, and other masters of the blue-collar anomie narrative.

The periodization approach, however, has distinct limits when applied to the four basic subjects of work-related U.S. fiction: (1) white Euro-American workingmen, (2) enslaved and postbellum African American workingmen and -women, (3) low-paid workingwomen of all races and colors, and (4) the recent arrivals on the American scene, marginalized non-Europeans. Boundaries between these categories blur, and the novels and stories that depict each obviously overlap. Particularly in narratives of women's wage earning, gender often, though not inevitably, transcends race and ethnicity. To discuss the divergent histories of these four groups, however, certain chapters separately trace the work populations that do not constitute the highly visible "male and pale" labor force.[66]

While it could be argued that any American text that erases the worker even from its subplot shadows is by that very fact relevant to working-class experience, any survey following such an argument would surely founder in the attempt to be all-inclusive. Literary perceptions of the workforce can be more carefully studied through prominent representations, which, in the case of the white industrial worker, have existed from the burgeonings of a paternalist factory system up until yesterday's job action. But representations of other workers live on in fiction. Harriet Wilson gives a brilliant 1840s portrayal of a northern family's oppression of their "nig" servant. John Hay sneers at "foreign" agitators. Henry James is repulsed by the vulgar shopgirl. Stephen Crane indulges in turn-of-the-century asides on the "lazy" blacks of small-town New York State. Edward Anderson provides a memorable Depression chronicle of those most forgotten men, the hoboes. Sanora Babb takes a long overdue place of honor with her 1938 ode (only recently published) to California fieldhands. Sapphire (the pseudonym of Ramona Lofton) excels in modern characterizations of teenaged New York City welfare mothers, thwarted rather than empowered by workfare, who seek an escape from a life of horrendous sexual abuse.

As these examples indicate, my definition of the workforce is a revisionary one. It includes slave and nonindustrial labor, poorly compensated "women's" work, and veterans retreating into mindless jobs, topics often excluded in modern critical discussions of the fiction of work. Yet finding treatments of these subjects often entails what the historian Ardis Cameron, in a related context, terms locating the "scattered bits and pieces of working-class . . . lives," particularly in fiction that is not usually presented or perceived as blue collar.[67] In such texts, race, ethnicity, and gender intersect with class, even if narrative references to marginalized, jobless, or itinerant laboring protagonists as laborers are limited to a passage or a few pages.[68] Yet it is even more important that in such texts the loud silences—authorial or otherwise, deliberate or not—be heard. Gayl Jones's rootless, black barroom women, laid off from tobacco farm or factory work, perceive themselves in relation to loveless men, not as tired workers. Also lacking in labor awareness are Leslie Marmon Silko's alcoholic Indian youths. Only after they find spiritual meaning do they search for sustaining work.

This survey divides naturally into three sections: fiction before, during, and after the Depression. All too often, prior to the 1930s, American authors, invoking the gospel of self-betterment, limn workers not as they are but as they should be. These writers hold workers accountable for their circumscribed lot, appoint outsiders to speak for them, and for the most part deny them a voice. Anticity biases, faceless slum dwellers, laboring masses, and emigration schemes mark virtually every antebellum storyteller's attempt to fictionalize working people. Even before the Civil War, fiction was already engaged in the pattern that would mark so much of American literature up to the Great Depression: imposing cherished ideas about the work ethic and the morality of useful toil on the complexities of a diverse workforce.

Doubts about the laborer's probity and adherence to the work ethic inevitably found their way into literary refigurings of the "honest mechanic." The resultant white labor figures and their black work counterparts constitute antebellum fiction's imposition of order and ideology on the laborscape. The authorial message was that Franklinesque ideals must hold sway over a welter of conflicting ideologies.

From antebellum times to the crash of 1929, class antagonism surfaces and resurfaces even in the fiction of the most passionate advocates of the dignity of labor—Dreiser, London, and Sinclair. These professional literary men either repudiated their humble origins or never knew any. In the 1930s the worker-protagonist and, to a lesser extent, the worker-writer are, however briefly, the new hero-experts. A more egalitarian treatment of workers, though one still informed by a muted individualism, is forged in some texts by crushed hopes, in others by a solidarity ethos.

Whether Depression era fiction displays unalloyed respect for unreconstructed working-class life is problematic. Indeed, this decade's fictional heroes are often blanketed with scorn. Yet in its search for the authentic proletariat, 1930s fiction bequeathed a crucial legacy to those who portray postwar worker disillusionment. For more than a century, those writers have chronicled setbacks among the less entrenched subgroups (their leaders having been ejected or turned into fat cats) on the waterfront, in the fruit fields, in the factories, in the low-paying industries. The new blue-collar writers, themselves frequently at war with their origins, must defend the laboring—and jobless—protagonist to society as well as to himself or herself. Cynical about upward mobility without a corresponding faith in labor activism, these writers speak to the dilemma of the modern labor author.

Over the broad sweep of 150 years, American writers have envisioned workers as human scenery and mob men, anarchists and artisan republicans, individualists and ciphers, yeomen and grotesques, gentlemen and militants, dolts and students and experts. All too often inaccurately portrayed as either falsely conscious or too fully conscious, laboring folk have been demonized, sanitized, co-opted, erased, infantilized, mythologized, depoliticized, politicized, and anesthetized. Workingmen have been called both democracy's linchpin and its enemy, and workingwomen are either duty-bound but secondary wage earners or rootless vixens. More, if less honorable, roles have been available to working people of color: sinister plotters or subnormal drudges, luckless menials or manipulative cheats, "low-down folks" or incendiary outcasts.

Whatever the type or antitype, writers, whether addressing middlebrow readers, liberal or radical sympathizers, or, far less often, the proletariat itself—look at the worker through the lens of upward (or selective) mobility. Depending on the author's political allegiance, such portrayals either vindicate the success myth or attempt to overturn or reshape it, particularly in proletarian fiction, with limited effectiveness. But for a century and a half, worker depictions have remained married to the ideology of American exceptionalism. Comments Alan Trachtenberg in a related context, "This exceptionalist vision of society [is] governed by a rhetorical Dream flexible enough to serve alternate and even opposing social ideologies."[69] Where labor's imaginers differ is in their perspective on universal economic ascension, not in a refusal to acknowledge the pervasiveness of this myth.

Acknowledging the difficulty of representing the laboring body in literary texts, "work itself resists representation," Michael Denning has written.[70] In charting the evolving yet remarkably consistent fictive representations of Americans at toil, I locate them all in the ideological battlefield between the recognition of class inequality and the belief in upward mobility. I do not, of course, believe that American workers as individuals should not aspire to a better material existence. But in what Janet Zandy has called the problem of "hegemonic two-ness," being in two worlds and belonging to neither, I too find that working people are often caught between philosophies of collective and individual success.[71]

Finally, in this attempt to make a contribution to the reevaluation of writers on and from the working class, I also hope to make visible that host of laboring figures often obscured by literary critics, to synthesize the masculinist and feminist, as well as the white and African American, critiques of both female and male authors. Most of all, though, my wish is to capture the American dreaming embodied in the neglected labor fiction of a nation that is so hard at work and so relentlessly devalues its working people.

PART I

From the Antebellum
to the Progressive
Era

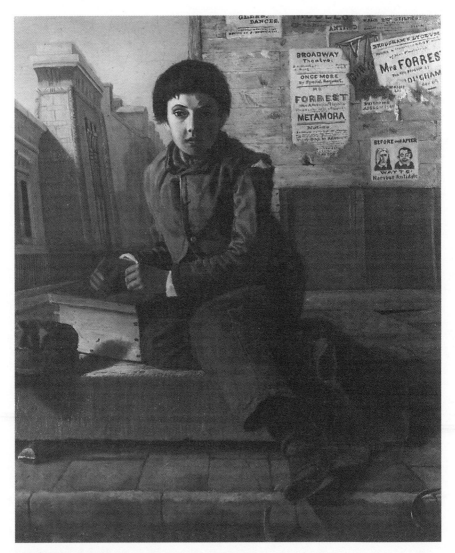

George Henry Yewell, *The Bootblack,* 1852. Collection of The New-York Historical Society.

The machine truly entered the working-class garden in the two decades prior to the Civil War.[1] The United States began to move in earnest from an agricultural and handicraft economy to one increasingly fueled by proletarians likely neither to become master workmen nor to realize the yeoman dream of self-employment in other ways.[2] By 1840 Longfellow's sentimental ode to the village smithy helped mark the beginning of the end for the old artisans and independent small producers, as well as the modest entrepreneurship both groups embodied. His fellow authors surveyed the new landscape of burgeoning cities, sweated outwork, and large textile mills. They lamented the expansion of unskilled immigrant labor and the shrinkage at the top of the largely native-born "honorable trades." They sought to understand what the transformation of the old order meant to the cherished ideology of the self-made man.[3] Looking back to the rural village and forward to the industrial future, American imaginers of work, accustomed to traditional categories like the "laboring poor" and the "lower orders," slowly began to notice that a new class was in the making. They were less sensitive to the fact that its members, wedded to hierarchies of skill, race, and ethnicity (and, the subject of chapter 3, gender), did not always acknowledge or welcome the appellation.[4]

Denying their looming obsolescence, white artisans and small craftsmen reasserted their economic independence, nonunionist ambitions, and the republican heritage of the freeborn toiler.[5] Stubborn subscribers to the adage "today's journeyman, tomorrow's master," they recycled the Franklinesque credo of self-transformation.[6] With some success, they implicitly demanded that fiction join the "improving literature" that elevated self-madeism—though not collective ascension—into a laborite philosophy.[7]

By the beginning of the 1840s, however, this class-crossing role model for the "mechanic," or skilled journeyman, was under challenge by workerist groups whose status was being eroded by capitalist expansion and who had little hope of becoming self-employed entrepreneurs.[8] These "free laborites," clinging to their faith in broadened opportunity and the freedom of contract (labor's right to determine the length of its working hours and, in some quarters, wage value), invoked their dream of membership in bourgeois society.[9] With limited success, they challenged employers to provide better conditions and in general sought changes in their relations with owners. Yet they did not extend their plaint to capitalism itself. Sparse were the era's indictments of private property.

Those criticisms, in fact, were the province of a minority of German-born

Marxist emigrants in the skilled trades, transcendentalist philosophers removed from the workplace who romanticized the exhaustions of manual labor, and small groups of secular utopians who espoused the communal ownership of Fourierism and Owenism.[10] The Germans' rare, diluted socialist novels were largely unavailable to English speakers.[11] The transcendentalists neither reconciled their theories of self-culture and self-reliance with the operative class they viewed from afar nor, while claiming to "embrace the literature of the common," ever produced it.[12] The most visible early radicals were more interested in applying the labor theory of value that traced the true origins of wealth to farmers and artisans.[13] Sounding an alternately hopeful and desperate note, these other theorists preferred new settlements to industrial dystopias. All were more likely to generate political tracts than fiction.[14]

Their movement to the West and "free land" was hailed outside of trade union quarters as a solution to the problem of the discontented or underpaid mechanic. Such a mass exit even began to appear in finales of numerous fictive texts with labor subplots. Workingmen not resigned to the economic mire surface repeatedly in the stories of the avidly read popularizers George Lippard, Elizabeth Oakes Smith, T. S. Arthur, the clergyman Sylvester Judd, and, in his futile quest for mass appeal, Herman Melville.[15] But novels and tales on strikes and organized labor protests were another matter entirely, and all but absent from the literary landscape.[16] In real life, fledgling associations of skilled trade unionists, and antebellum working-class radicalism, both manifested in the workday-regulating Ten-Hour Movement and sporadic strikes in the "conflict trades" such as tailoring, carpentry, shoemaking, and masonry, continued to ebb and flow. The 1850s in particular witnessed the early stages of trade unionism, confined to a tiny nonimmigrant or German-born minority. But there are no emergent litterateurs to commemorate these events.[17]

Labor's other half, most notably Irish immigrants in the denigrated occupations of railroad and canal building, and dock and hauling work, generated strikes but built only tentative connections to the craft aristocracies, much less to the sweated trades of the large cities.[18] The butt of nativism, they were associated with what one traveler called "the lowest stations of the hardworking classes."[19] One group they joined by default was the alien poor, working and jobless, massed in the metropolitan slum. Caricatured or otherwise rendered grotesque, rarely pitied, they all inspired urban storytellers' transient sympathy.

Blacks' minimization by more empowered laboring men was reflected in their marginalized role.[20] In a parallel development, they appeared in white labor texts, with few exceptions, as villainous or job-shirking go-betweens and in more extended portrayals—save those, arguably, of the *Uncle Tom's Cabin* (1852) school—as mindless or mutinous slaves.[21] Black-authored narratives (novels were extremely rare) employed techniques of fiction to "place discernible patterns on [their creators'] lives" and to challenge racist stereotypes, though without suggesting cross-race labor action.[22] Whether they parsed the slave tale or not, enlightened leaders of the white labor force joined abolitionist authors to respond to the plight of the southern slave. Labor took up the cause of the northern fugitive, though not to argue for freedmen's entry into jobs held by the skilled native-born workers.[23] Vocal unionist and laborite organizations and periodicals feared that their own jobs were becoming waged versions of southern imprisonment. Cognizant of the skilled workman's wages pocketed by the masters of plantation blacks, they directed their attention elsewhere.

In sum, the fledgling labor movement was skilled, white, and stung by what it saw as the status and pay loss occasioned by the transformation of the workshop into the factory, and the handworker into the operative. It tried to reconcile its fading industrial independence with both the land reform and the Ten-Hour Movement radicalism of the day, as well as with a lingering hope in Franklinesque credos.[24] Those like the editor of the short-lived *Voice of Industry*, the 1845 journal of the craft-based New England Workingman's Association, reasserted the right of free (white) men to full economic and political citizenship. And they deplored, though offered no real program to deter, "unfeeling capital, and destructive competition."[25] In columns both scornful and fearful of the hireling title "wage workers," labor journals, long before the birth of the Knights of Labor, attempted to inspire their constituencies. "A peer of the realm might well envy [you]," declared the *Voice*.[26]

If this aristocratic language suggested that labor did protest too much, it had reason to do so. This bold new rhetoric was clearly devised to shore up an artisanal ascendancy belief under siege by the new technology and the rise of the factory system. The same issue of the *Voice*, invoking support for the Ten-Hour Movement, worried that mechanics and factory operatives were being sneered at.[27] Unlike the old master craftsmen, the new workingmen could not be certain that waged labor was a step along the way to dignified self-employment. But they could substitute a vague white egalitarianism, informed by quasi-militant labor-cooperative ventures and associations, and in general respond to the denigration of the crafts by reinforcing the idea of the skilled worker as what one newspaper, the *Mechanic's Free Press*, typically labeled "the nobleman of nature."[28]

Yet mechanics' "nobility" was clearly under siege outside laborist circles. Challenges to the heroism of the average manual worker permeated what can only loosely be called the antebellum labor novel. Consistently depicted as an exception to rather than an exemplar of the common man, the ennobled mechanic appeared in virtually every piece of fiction, whether produced by bourgeois authors or sometime radicals who were seeking—though seldom finding—a vocabulary of real working-class heroism.

Nevertheless, most of the (middle-class) creators of this early fiction instructed apprentices bent on exiting the worker class in the myriad possibilities of mercantile capitalism. Of transient literary but important cultural value, their works were among the earliest mass disseminators of imagery about laboring whites. They provided middle-class or literate workingmen audiences with the titillations of cross-class exposé or the pleasures of money-linked escapism. They lambasted and, very occasionally, heralded any character who doubted the upward struggle myth or threatened the solidity of the burgeoning factory world. And they sought in various ways to reconcile cultural shibboleths about work with the obvious condescension society directed at those actually performing it.[29]

Given white fears of disenfranchisement, freed blacks were provided adequate literary space only in the slave novel and narrative, which bolstered abolitionism by fashioning what a rare Frederick Douglass novel extolling the Underground Railroad called the "noble fugitive," the enslaved black fleeing imprisoned work.[30] Attention to this minority within a minority was necessarily more circumscribed as long as the bulk of the African American labor force remained in southern chains. Still, the images of the black work experience wrought by black authors counterpointed black bonded drudgery with rebellion through flight, intelligent cunning, and abolitionist self-elevation. Their slave and runaway heroes, longing to work free, both challenged and reflected white labor-class aspiration.

Whatever inequities and dangers of downward mobility plagued masculine labor were heightened for women. They entered the mass-production factory in large numbers and dominated the sweated clothing trades. They also suffered the implications of the "pin money" theory that women were transients in the paid workforce—and potential victims of seduction in it—rather than needy laborers themselves. Their roles were restricted both in the job market and as protagonists of the Lowell factory novel.[31]

As Marcus Klein observes in his iconographic study of late nineteenth-century popular literature, "sheer presence has a meaning."[32] Pre–Civil War authors consistently responded with three tropes, all centered on morality and character as much as on job status. In this primitive taxonomy, the white laboring man is (1) the urban jobholding tough, individuated in Mose the "Bowery B'hoy"; (2) the dying or disappearing craftsman, moribund pawn of the merchant banker, workshop master, or his own self-destructiveness; or (3) the gentleman in disguise, or accidental worker, en route to another class. Not only are such tropes fixated on native-born protagonists, as if recent immigrants offered possibilities too anarchic, but each is informed by—or unable to find alternatives to—a bourgeois ethic. Whether deliberately or not, they reflect the dislocation wrought on a wide range of laborers by both the transition to an industrial environment and the increasing limitations of the ideology of ascension. Still, this triad of workers—those holding their economic own, plummeting, or ascending—reveals much about the attitudes that different antebellum American authors brought to the laboring man. This was at a time when terms like "craft unionism" and "strike for closed shop" applied to very limited populations, and "proletarian consciousness," much less "subversion of capitalism," were not terms in the labor glossary.[33]

We now turn to these literary rearrangements of the labor landscape, to their cultural value and cost, what they include or exclude about the antebellum work map, and the extent to which African American toilers, enslaved and free, could either counter or redefine such figurings.

Proletarian Fragments: The Bowery B'hoy

Almost a century before the Great Depression inspired the attempt in earnest, no period had taken on the mighty task of finding a white male workingman to symbolize the industrial wage laborers who predominated in the 1840s. That labor world comprised skilled craft workers, textile hands, home or out-workers, and unskilled, immigrant, or free black laborers.[34] Fiction on the male work experience was most interested in the first category, particularly in the setting of the venerable metropolitan trades. If urban authors did not always place the skilled workman in the center of the narrative and either gave him one chapter or wove him in and out of a labyrinthine subplot, they at least associated him with the rewards of toil. Literature responded to the economic forces altering the old relation of journeyman to master, shrinking the expectations of ascension. From this figure emerged a form of proletarian portraiture that posed the issues and problems of class stratification that infiltrated depictions of the semi- and the unskilled and would mark American literature from then on.

The figure who best symbolizes the shifting images of the new young workingman is Mose the Bowery B'hoy (an affectionate era variant on "boy," though meant to connote a young man). The real-life Mose Humphreys of the Lady Washington Fire Company was a late 1830s anti-Irish street brawler and gang member.[35] By the 1840s, still street-wise and a saloon habitué, he reenters popular mythology in a labor-class guise: worker by day and civic-minded fire company volunteer by night. He takes on a comic particularity in the figure made famous in the Benjamin Baker play *A Glance at New York* (1848) and a decade's worth of "Mose" dramas.[36] An immense favorite with working-class audiences, the stage Mose challenged ascension ideology by remaining vernacular, proud of his after-hours finery, unambitiously self-supporting (his occupation is never fleshed out), and scornful of any encroachments on his leisure-time pursuits.[37] Thumbing his nose at the "upper ten" (a fairly inaccurate term for the city's elite) by parodying their dandyish attire, he amalgamated the street smarts of the have-not with the economic security of the one who can always find work. Although he socialized with Bowery toughs, he distinguished himself from the gangsterism of the main branch of New York's Bowery scrappers by his membership in the volunteer fire companies, a social club for many nonimmigrant urban journeymen.

The late 1840s witnessed the rise of the urban exposé novel, a formulaic subgenre recycled from a sophisticated pair of Continental novelists then in vogue, Eugene Sue and G. M. Reynolds.[38] As plied by E.Z.C. Judson (a k a Ned Buntline), George G. Foster, and their less-practiced colleagues, the New York version reflected the strains and anxieties a home-grown proletarian figure generated. In the officially classless society of America, there was considerable literary confusion surrounding his occupation and status. Was he skilled or marginally so, a hard-working journeyman or a shiftless jobsite junior? He was called everything from a master workman to a butcher (or his boy) to a printer to a stonecutter to a carpenter to an out-of-work apprentice.[39] The confusion was not resolved in novelistic treatments of him. A fleeting type who brought his name recognition to the plot, he was a volatile and uncontrollable character in Judson's *The Mysteries and Miseries of New York* (1848). He makes a madam-taunting visit to a brothel, hardly the venue or behavior for the civic-minded workman in his previous incarnations.[40]

Foster well understood the cultural need to erase Mose, a worker refusing to be work-involved (we never see him at or even alluding to work) but contemptuous of the nonworking elite. As if alarmed at even Judson's take on so much anarchic potential, Foster altered the Mose of his own semifictional *New York in Slices* (1849).[41] The early Mose was given to the grog shop and "mobs and gangs who conspire against the public peace" (*Slices*, 44). In *New York by Gaslight* (1850) he is considerably sanitized. Content with his social and economic place—like Judson, Foster is ambiguous on Mose's workplace identity—Mose redirects his disruptive impulses. He no longer drinks and has an ambitious shopgirl fiancée, Lize. This rehabilitated man is fearless where the old one was rowdy; cheerful and patient where his evil twin was angry and volatile. Foster did not so much graft the honest mechanic onto the anarchic urban tough as banish him entirely. In so doing, he inaugurated an enduring American hostility to working-class identity.[42]

The portrait at this point, though it papered over the real Mose, seems calculated to square him with a bourgeoisie skittishness about the dangerous classes and the Revolution of 1848 echoing from across the Atlantic. In a further logic shift, Foster made the figure a western individualist. Living clean, he becomes one with the Hoosier, the trapper, the gold miner. But remembering the old Mose he had disguised, Foster offered a final solution to the problem of the rowdy metropolitan worker. He invokes the return to the land that was supposed to solve the economic difficulties and reverse the moral lapses of low-rung urban workers. Mose goes west.

By the time Foster had reinvented the Bowery B'hoy he was having the era's last novelistic word on a once vital and distinctive figure, now completely fragmented. Neither civilized nor tamed, rebellious nor conformist, skilled mechanic nor brawling apprentice, easterner nor westerner, he is an ill-assorted composite of all these qualities.[43]

Foster's literary cleanup job does suggest an attempt to make the Bowery tough palatable to bourgeois society. Imposing ambitions, associations, and tractability of the type that neither the Mose figure nor, by all accounts, the real-life antebellum "working stiff" actually possessed, Foster defused the anxieties that Mose provoked in a city where workingmen's riots—nativist, antiabolitionist, and the like—were not uncommon.[44] Originally drawn as a member of a laboring subculture who refutes bourgeois and evangelical pieties by his affiliation with the barroom and a pugilism both enacted and observed, Mose had been rendered middle class without portfolio. Having cast out Baker's and Judson's hard-drinking blue-collar Mose, Foster's proletarian everyman, thus atomized, ends up no one at all.

Devalued: Labor's Pawns

If the limited antebellum imagining of labor-class resilience that Bowery Mose personified was one of blurred and shifting images, the type himself was no economic casualty. Whatever the contestations over his labor-class persona, none of Mose's interpreters doubted his ability to survive. He was unaffected by the economic depressions of 1837–1843 that destabilized craft workers in the tailoring and shoe trades and others employed in producing for large markets.[45] With characteristic feistiness, Mose remained immune to the effects of increased mechanization.[46] The same trend toward increasing the division of labor caused journeymen to become low-wage earners. Working conditions worsened, pay fell, and "the journeyman's hopes of one day joining the ranks of independent masters grew dimmer."[47] When novels shifted from the scrappy Mose to the industrious workmen unable to support themselves, they fashioned an iconography of labor reduction to deathlike passivity. Rather than use the down-and-outer to indict the mobility ideal, writers from the status quo conservative to the socialistic Jeremiah offered the victimized worker. As an extreme type of labor passivity, no Workingmen's Party, Owenite community, or free-land emigration scheme could reverse his decline.

Cornelius Mathews's *The Career of Puffer Hopkins* (1842) subordinates urban Gothic to a mixture of metropolitan picaresque and political satire. The novel features a scene between a master tailor and his wretched employee, Fob, exiled to outwork in his garret. The piece was unusual in the period for its focus on the tenement home of a bachelor with no band of clinging children or invalid seamstress wife. It conforms to the city novel's emphasis on the extreme differences between the employer and employee classes. Having arrived to pick up some finished work, the master exhorts Fob to sew until he dies— "overwork yourself, Fob"—and receive a handsome burial.[48]

In lieu of sharpening the lens to focus on the horror of the tailor's plight, Mathews chooses to fuse Dickensian satire with pastoral nostalgia. Fob himself, in thrall to the vicious mercantilism of his employer, is an addled, dithery figure. He responds to his labor woes by invoking a preindustrial past and, in the ubiquitous plot device of antebellum city novelists, a stolen inheritance. He reminisces about his own arcadian early life, all the while exhibiting the serio-comic eccentricity of character that is the hallmark of Dickens's run-down employees, from Sydney Carton to Stephen Blackpool. Fob is a Dickensian clerk. His days and nights are spent making clothes for gentlemen "till [his] needle grew so fine [he] couldn't see it" (95). The portrait, focused for a time on Fob's sweated circumstances, might have been an early delineation of a real urban casualty of deskilling, but the Mathews glance keeps wavering. As an adaptee to metropolitan hardship, Fob is in an early Victorian time warp.[49]

If fiction was wary of giving much attention to the fallen and marginally employed artisan, when he drank there was a similar reluctance to detail his psyche. To be sure, the labor-class drunkard is a stock type in the city tour, though of less sensationalist interest than the alcoholic middle- or lower-class girl who goes wrong, of whom more later.[50] If the laboring inebriate did claim some part of the subplot, no author attempted to portray his workplace drunkenness or the "drink culture" that characterized many urban workshops until well into the Civil War period.[51] Yet considering the wealth of period exhortations by workingmen's journals and mechanics' institutes warning workmen to raise themselves, surprisingly few writers pay extended attention to temperance heroes of this socioeconomic level.

Walt Whitman's tyro novel *Franklin Evans; or, The Inebriate* (1842), commissioned by the American Temperance Union, moves only tentatively toward this figure. His cautionary title character, the son of a hand-to-mouth carpenter, begins his own work life as a farmworker. His creator soon swerves into the problem of the rural-laboring alcoholic.[52] The eponymous hero's period as a drunkard occurs when he is a New York lawyer's clerk, and his unsavory barroom companions are also firmly established in the white-collar bookkeeping ranks.[53] T. S. Arthur expresses the same concern with reforming the educated worker, though he makes more allusions to deskilling, in his tear-jerking *Ten Nights in a Bar-Room* (1854). Immensely popular, it is situated, unlike Whitman's tale, in the likelier home of worker drunkenness, the industrial city. The story centers on Joe Morgan, a mill owner and a forerunner of Frank Norris's drink-sodden Vandover. Arthur reverses the trajectory that the era's pulp novelists (and its savvy playwrights like Dion Boucicault in his 1857 play *The Poor of New York*) used to sustain plots of switched births, orphan heirs, and recovered estates. The fact that Morgan is reduced to odd jobs powerfully links his self-propelled fall into alcoholism with his economic descent.[54] Joe's rejection of the gospel of "useful work" was central to the credo of the mechanic and aspiring classes. Once abandoned, it unleashed in him the passions of the laboring ranks.[55] Not surprisingly, when Joe renounces drink, he reclaims his position as a mill owner. Still, as with the Fobs and Evanses, the redeemable bourgeois man remains a stand-in for his socioeconomic inferiors.

Typically, neither Mathews nor Arthur gave much thought to the links between the journeyman fallen but not mired in financial misfortune and the oppressed factory operative who expected nothing else. The instability of working-class life in America[56] was usually condensed into affecting tales of luckless or misguided individuals who confuse temptation with opportunity. Antebellum factory tales—capped in early wartime by Rebecca Harding Davis's "Life in the Iron Mills" (1861)—combine analyses of depressing conditions with anticapitalist exhortations. These stories were (as chapter 3 will clarify) largely the province of women authors and feminine subjects.

George Lippard, a Philadelphia newsman, "wicked city" novelist, and frequenter of industrial congresses, was a rare exception. Though also known as an exposer of urban woes, he was far more the maverick than Judson or Foster. He was certainly more engaged than they in describing labor's indignities, even if that concern was subordinated to his semipornographic novels of the city.[57] The editor of a weekly with labor sympathies, Lippard in his editorials attacked the merchant, land-owning, and professional classes. He revealed his stripes as an apostle of a diffused pre-Marxian socialism amalgamating historical allusions to class struggles. He praised workers' associations, secret brotherhoods, land reform, and a vague plan for every worker to become a capitalist.[58] He peppered his columns and nonfiction with references to the war of labor, the sweat, blood, and tears of the workers, and even, though apparently he had not read the *Communist Manifesto* (1848), the workmen of the world.[59] And he announced that a national literature should work for reform, to "picture the wrongs of the great mass of humanity."[60]

Lippard's urban Gothic novels became part of the first subgenres to place a variety of skilled laboring and subproletarian characters, squeezed by the wiles of corrupt merchants, satanic financiers, and bloodless politicos, in the background of a recognizable, if melodramatic, city setting. In these early texts, juxtaposing what Lippard called the "lower million" with the "upper ten," sympathy for the deserving poor joined that for the victim of the factory system as well as the disenfranchised journeyman.[61] In the glancing fashion of his day, Lippard produced sketches of the economic conditions that were ripe for unified proletarian rage. *The Nazarene* (1846) portrays both a textile factory and a Philadelphia tenement subworld where weavers slave in fetid air. *Adonai* (1851) presents an allied vision of factory hands chained to the machine. Expanding the imagery of the dying workman is Lippard's most extended sketch, a mini-chapter in his vastly successful *The Quaker City; or, The Monks of Monk Hall* (1844).[62] Particularizing a representative labor figure, Lippard has the carpenter John Davis step out of workerist anonymity and accost the venal banker whose house he has helped build and in whose stocks he has invested. In beseeching the corpulent representative of the economic elite, this once-proud member of the skilled trades begs first for reimbursement of his lifetime savings, then for money to buy wood and bread, and finally and pathetically, for a dollar for his sick child. In the finale to a scene filled with images of maddened, debilitated labor, the refused Davis, borrowing the final body language of the fallen woman of mid-Victorian fiction, takes his rage out on himself in suicide.

Yet if, added to this, Lippard's fiction briefly tours, in his semisequels laid in New York, the huts and dens of the once-"industrious mechanic" (*Quaker City*, 407), it is to enhance the image of the dying workman. Lippard does not posit the firebrand alternatives alluded to in his nonfiction. No doubt this deathlike reduction of worker characters to wraiths and suicides is Lippard's signal that the city has unfairly excluded the working masses. Lippard's historical fiction set in American revolutionary times had no difficulty in creating "poor protagonists manifesting verve, healthy rebelliousness, and concrete political knowledge."[63] Moreover, the metaphor of the walking dead was subsequently used as a radical critique by every muckraker of labor from Maxim Gorky in *The Lower Depths* (1902) to recent American labor literature.[64] In Lippard's hands this disempowering imagery revealed the gaps in an antebellum radical's attempt to provide a literary antidote to what he viewed as workerist suppression.[65] When his fiction seeks a language to describe radical self-help for workers too wretched to form food cooperatives and too debilitated or benighted to attend industrial congresses, he has no image of militancy. Joining his fellow imaginers of the mechanic hero, when he cannot elevate, he can only cast down.

Gentility Disguised: Labor Noblemen

Given the long American literary tradition of Emersonian self-reliance, it would be surprising if one voice, of an American Adam, did not sing out from the laboring chorus. Neither the buffoon, the faceless proletarian, the drunkard, nor the suicide, the honest mechanic variously claims, "I gain my bread by the work of my hands," "It is work that makes the man," and "I seek a snug operative's berth."[66] In 1840s texts, including Lippard's, the honest mechanic walks the wicked city otherwise inhabited by laboring and underclass grotesques and eccentrics. In the next decade, moving toward center stage, he survives the city-, sea-, and factoryscape without suffering moral degradation or incurring his creator's ridicule. Yet the very strategy employed to keep the worker in focus—portraying him as nature's nobleman—blurs the lens through which he is viewed.

Lippard himself counterbalances the wraithlike mechanic with an energetic, indeed herculean one. The carpenter John Davis fades away. Arthur Dermoyne, a shoeworker who also appears in *New York: Its Upper Ten and Lower Million* (1853), becomes stronger in the course of *The Quaker City*. Like Davis, he has been swindled by the banking class and claims to be a workman above all else. Where Davis meets the fate of the worn-out wage slave, Dermoyne reasserts the triumphant labor alternative: artisanal pride and self-sufficiency. Echoing the rhetoric of the labor journals, he claims to be "nobly descended" (*New York,* 109) from wheelwrights, cobblers, and carpenters. Applying the radical labor theory of the day espoused by Seth Luther, William Heighton, and others, he explains that the laboring classes are better than the educated ones because they produce. Labor's gentlemen are not idle; there is no other kind to be.

Proclamations of equality in antebellum labor portraits inevitably invoke their antithesis. The more Dermoyne expounds his labor theory of value and proclaims his kinship with the people, the more he sounds like the labor superman who would flourish fifty years later as Jack London's Martin Eden or David Graham Phillips's Victor Dorn (see chapter 5). As Dermoyne, in elegant periodic sentences, harangues a snobbish representative of economic privilege, he reveals that he has studied for years and could take up a profession if he wished, provided his republican ideals did not prevent him. Physical excellence complements his intellectual abilities. Without exertion, he bends in two an iron candlestick and, an urban John Henry, confides that he has the strength of two men. In the novel's final passages, he leads a group of working folk to a Fourierite community in the West and gives the worker nobility ideal a new definition. He claims his place as a natural leader, not one of the sweating masses. If he has wrenched the spotlight away from the debate on the right of labor to its fruits, he has, in so doing, fixed another one on the problem of labor representation, a debate that would be carried on well past the Great Depression.[67]

Obsessed with but unable to apply ascension myths to a swelling urban workforce living hand-to-mouth, Lippard's "radical" wicked city fiction both sees and does not see those marked by diminished opportunities. As he moves toward an indictment of the free market system, Lippard injects pre-Algerian rescues from poverty via recovered legacies and defeated villains, or emigration schemes. Furthermore, when one teases out the strand of Lippard's characteristic blend of erotic seduction tale, Gothic romance, and sermonizing about "how the rich and their henchmen amuse themselves with the money they have sweated from the laboring man," what is left is a Christian dystopia. There, to avoid destruction, workers must in effect cease to be workers and become pioneers and settlers.[68] Lippard's own wavering support for the workingmen's strikes of his day did not extend to his fiction. In his plots, the noble worker is simply out of place in a city determined to impose greed and inhumanity on dealings between human beings. Those who reclaim their rightful wages are as rare as those claiming a family legacy from which they had been excluded. The moral superiority of the honest mechanic does not infuse him with the proletarian energy of the Revolution of 1848, which Lippard supported in theory. In Lippard's fictions he is in a brave new world, not on the barricades in the corrupt old one.

Although it envisioned a noble laborer only to offer him a metropolitan and industrial dead end, Lippard's *The Quaker City* was still selling well a decade later.[69] Readers, including the lower middle class who formed part of the audience for cheap urban fiction, may not have found a recognizable class representative. But they continued to enjoy the heady brew of muckraking and eroticism, Riisian peeps at working-class squalor and despondency, and the showy juxtaposition of classes.[70] Significantly, that same year Elizabeth Oakes Smith, an author whose religious and political sensibilities were almost diametrically opposed to Lippard's, saw in the urban workingman "competence and repose." Such rewards were earned "by the sweat of the brow" (*Newsboy*, 12) and thus offered a revision of Lippard's labor nightmare and the rare noble figure who awakes from it. Read by some of the same plebeian readers who swallowed up the excitements of Lippard's *New York*, Smith's fiction sanitized his vision of economic evil. She did so without challenging the mercantile hegemony that generated psychic and social dislocation among the children of the working poor. She produced a Christian variant on the Lippardian wicked city tale, one that neither sent the superior working-class hero into exile nor acknowledged the glimmerings of class conflict.

Smith's *The Newsboy* (1854) was as much a manipulation of popular subgenre as any by Lippard. It used the improbable strive-and-succeed tale of an orphaned street hawker. After an adolescence among the marginal, he rescues a wealthy merchant's kidnapped daughter. In an atypical plot twist, he renounces her so that she can marry a man of her own class. He nevertheless wins a place in the merchant's firm. A respected poet and intimate of the New York literati, Smith, who had also penned Indian captivity narratives, took the clever tack of grafting the "woman's" or sentimental romance onto the dime novel. The result was a mixture of Christian sentimentalism and the urban boy-adventure novel that opposed Lippardian apocalypse with a rather vague redemption for the legions of "unskilled poor, who lack the faculty of steady work" (*Newsboy*, 12).

Separating the reader, modern or period, from the optimism in *The News-*

boy is the authorial gaze averted from the cruelty of poverty, the improbability of the plotting, and the very reduction of the conditions of New York laboring and workless life to a painted backdrop for virtue's triumph. What clearly lured period readers was the will to gentrify the morally superior urban worker. But all antebellum authors spinning workerist plots and subplots faced their own distrust of urban influences on laboring men. Such distrust propelled Lippard to thrust Arthur Dermoyne into the wide open spaces, and Smith to another stratagem. In a city where, increasingly, the adult journeyman exhibited little of the gentrification central to antebellum imaginings of the noble worker, Smith simply looked to the innocent child.

Smith's pre-Algerian newsboy is far more relevant to period concerns about the laboring man than is at first apparent. "Newsboy" was a catch-all term for the "street arabs" later to be photographed by Jacob Riis. They variously survived by doing odd jobs, blacking boots, or hawking papers.[71] In 1854, the very year Smith wrote *The Newsboy,* ten thousand homeless boys, the majority orphaned or cast out by their indigent immigrant parents, roamed, and, depending on the observer, developed character or criminality on the sidewalks of Gotham.[72]

Rejecting the implications of those statistics, what developed around them, particularly in the art of the period, was an idealization of street children. It enabled their creators to avoid depictions of the adult homeless and omit all "actualities of the urban context in which the impoverished and displaced resided."[73] Twenty years later, the philanthropist and founder of the Children's Aid Society, Charles Loring Brace, in his history of the lodging house, was still idealizing these children. They were "impetuous little tradesmen," "embryo professionals" (not mere proletarians in the making). By selling newspapers for a living instead of "pilfering or vagabonding," Brace opined, they demonstrated "their desire to do right."[74] In favor of child labor as character building, as were many period reformers, Brace predicted that those who were rescued by Christianizing influences would rise not only to become lower-level mechanics but, more likely, respectable merchants—exactly the fate of Smith's hero.

This trajectory from up-against-it child laborer to solid burgher was all the more important viewed against the context of those whom, next to the criminal elements, reformers feared most, the marginally employed and jobless poor. A year after the Smith novel was published, the Children's Aid Society annual report linked children with the lowest class of working poor who must not be corrupted by the shiftless underclasses forming around them.[75] Still shuddering in the shadow of the European revolution, Brace was loath to think of what the dangerous classes, if thrown out of work, might resort to. Seeing in child rescue a defusing of underclass tensions, he hoped child workers would indeed be the fathers of proletarian men.[76]

Smith went Brace one better. In her portrayal of the virtuous newsboy, she rehabilitated the image of at least a subsection of New York's deserving poor. She made a bow to the vaudeville theater frequented by the boys—a shorthand recognition of the plebeian culture of the actual newsboys. And she acknowledged that, as period accounts bear out, the boys, if no churchgoers, did exhibit a rough fraternal ethic, a remarkable resilience, and a street code that provided mutual protection. But with the individualizing tendency that was second nature to American imaginers of working folk, Smith's Bob was the exceptional working boy. Her sentimental approach to childhood precluded the invective other commentators hurled at the youngsters of the notorious Five Points District. She was more interested in selectively applying the mid-Victorian cult of the sinless child (the title of one of her poems) to a shining member of the lower orders.[77] Certainly the urban vice novel, like the Indian captivity tales Smith also produced, required a morally superior hero who rises above squalor. An alleyway innocent, her title character anticipates Stephen Crane's own, the 1890s slum flower Maggie, though Bob avoids her sordid fate, prostitution and suicide. In this feminization of American culture, many of the era's women novelists, such as Catharine Maria Sedgwick, Susan Warner, and even Harriet Beecher Stowe, called for a reassertion of feminine values. They preached extending domestic virtues to the larger society, not only by extending charity to sufferers but by Christianizing them, inculcating patience and resignation.[78] Smith, however, applied her own brand of non-Calvinist Protestantism. Bob the street boy is already noble enough (*Newsboy*, 9) to teach his economic betters.

Modern interpreters have satirized the angelic qualities Smith imparts to the newsboy. In a primitive version of the brotherhood of working people, Bob shares whatever he has with the other newsboys.[79] If he comes close to a type of Christ, Smith's is not an allegory of Christian street socialism. Far from it. For if *The Newsboy* magically Christianizes those deemed at risk of corruption, it overlays the piety with the Franklinesque advice that would repeatedly surface in American imaginings of the workforce. Anyone, from poor boys like Bob to the very ragpickers in the city gutters, can "grow rich at their toil, as everybody can who will" (*Newsboy*, 146).

Smith averts her authorial gaze from the harshness of the street-level work experience. While she provides surface details on where Bob sleeps, the catch-all meals he eats, and the strong drink he scrupulously avoids, she does not in fact describe Bob's "work" in even the off-the-cuff manner characteristic of most antebellum authors. Yet this lapse is not without design. When, as a well-off young man, Bob reflects on his past life, Smith offers this remarkable passage:

This was a great change for the Newsboy, from the confined streets and alleys of his childhood, houseless and friendless, to the deck of a ship as agent of a wealthy house, the companion and friend of the rich merchant of New York. [Bob] did not see that the trappings of wealth conferred any dignity on him. He had always done heart work and head work; and now that wealth superseded the necessity for anxious toil for daily bread, he was apt to undervalue its utility. (480)

For all her discussion of the potential for converting the transient and homeless class from which the newsboy sprang, Smith's Christianity was detached from any revivalist program in the slums and oblivious to the issue of child poverty. It proved no panacea to the turbulence of economic depriva-tion. Her perspective was no better than a fantasy in light of the misery of the seething urban underclass as well as the political assertiveness of the factory workers who were fighting the initial labor battles. Too, rather than give the vast and diverse workforce a believable urban surrogate, she simply produced a literary sermon. She spiced her homiletic with a dime novel plot of villains, kidnaps, and plutocratic daughters in peril to smooth over the fissures be-tween the degrading conditions and the innate goodness of some who toil. Notwithstanding her "sweetness and light," Smith produced her own version of the Lippardian escape from labor history.[80]

Novels did address the new realities of the urban and factory workforce then undergoing struggles for control of the workday and the industrial morality connected with it. Such fiction, offering its own Christianizing solu-tion, was rare enough prior to the Civil War. In the pulpiest of antebellum and wartime fiction, Frances McDougall's *The Mechanic* (1842), Day Kellogg Lee's *The Master Builder* (1853), and Mary Howe's *The Merchant Mechanic* (1865), "a dying economic order was frozen into a living reality." Such writers fueled an antebellum dream factory in which the honest mechanic, passing an evening at the mechanic's library, could aspire to mercantile success, or the carpenter or mason, the last of the labor aristocrats, could enjoy a rags-to-riches mobility.[81]

The clergyman Sylvester Judd in his novel *Richard Edney* (1850), though embracing his own success mythology, registered the shift to a factory econ-omy. A well-known period addition to the ideology of the ennobled worker, *Richard Edney* attempts to balance a thinly disguised elitist hero with the growing national realization that the industrious mechanic is no longer a privileged or important part of the workforce. Judd's title character is one of the few antebellum characters positioned in the new, changing, and recog-nizable workplace environment, a New England sawmill. There artisan values give way to the "ascending ideology of industrialism."[82] At this labor cross-roads, with laborers less directly supervised by and in less contact with the owner than in the antebellum workshop, a workman finds his opportunity. Rallying coworkers, he organizes grievance committees to change the nature of the workplace.

More documentary in a sense is that Judd layers this sawmill with the two most important workplace issues of the 1850s, industrial morality and con-trol of the workday.[83] The kind of mill Richard enters was central in the struggles to control the workday under the resurrected Ten-Hour Movement. It is a place that employs semiskilled workers who are taking the place of the old craftsmen. But it is also one in which workers are defending their prein-dustrial right to drink on the job, an eighteenth-century work tradition.[84]

To this potentially explosive situation Richard brings neither Mose's volatility nor the Christian self-transformation of the orphan newsboy. In fact, he is a figure who represents the transition from the old Franklinesque philosophies to the new realities of the permanent wage. He is a hybrid: he may not be an artisan, but neither was he born to be a factory operative. The disenfranchised yeoman, he must "find a snug operative's berth" (12) if he is to survive economically. But as the son of a onetime farmer, he is still the masculine counterpart of the Lowell factory girls, drawn to the factory by the hope of wages and social betterment.

In Richard, Judd is attempting nothing less than the codification of what Montgomery calls the industrial Christian soldier, that new, willing workman who follows the rules of industrial productivity at work and outside of it as well.[85] But for Judd to forge that ideal worker means that Richard must inspire a workplace Great Awakening. It not unlike that Second Great Awakening sweeping over sections of New England at the time Judd was writing, a movement spearheaded by clerks and small tradesmen exhorting their operative brothers.[86] Various New England and northeastern towns in the 1840s saw a push from tradesmen's societies, factory owners, artisans, and, to a lesser degree, journeymen and operatives themselves toward a kind of secular revival. It was aimed not so much at elevating workingmen as at keeping them in moral harness.[87]

Offering a version of preconversion shop-floor unregenerates, Judd portrays Richard's coworkers as comic cousins to T. S. Arthur's Joe Morgan before his conversion. They are updates on Shakespeare's rude mechanicals in *A Midsummer Night's Dream*: loud, confused, and drunken, they deny the moral preeminence of work. In this scenario, working-class agitation becomes a drunkard's undisciplined ravings. Registering the philosophy of the temperance movement itself, for the factory worker to be a new soldier, an outsider must be the knight. Accordingly, not long after starting the job, Richard "broke the bottles of the liquor-peddler with a righteous zeal" (81). He is thus "nature's nobleman" (271) not because he echoes the *Voice of Industry* call for respect for labor but because, a Sir Gawain of the factory, he commands respect. Egalitarianism slips into elitism in a trice.

If Richard enters the work world, as Judd's alter ego, to reform it, his relation to the workplace is a transient one. As a workman in an antebellum fiction, a figure overlaid with images of downward or upward mobility, Richard is a millplace drudge only long enough to convert his unruly coworkers to a new submissiveness. He takes on a worker's disguise to redeem the sinners and then, his duty done, moves on.

Richard Edney is one of the few antebellum novels to articulate a practical management approach to labor relations. Important as a powerful response to the new radical language of organizers and strikes, job actions and unions, the novel served as a mouthpiece for the paternalistic management response to strikers that would obtain past the Civil War. Indeed, the popularity of the novel was such that it was reprinted as late as the era of the Knights of Labor (1880). One reason was the perennial appeal of the worker who rises to marry the heiress and throw off his proletarian disguise to emerge as the prince, a plot that later would be modified in the Knights of Labor novels to include the real blue-collar worker who ascends. But there is another clue to *Richard Edney*'s significance as a cultural product. A novel published less than three years later, *The Master Builder* by Day Kellogg Lee, helps contextualize this importance. In the Lee book, a foundling becomes a carpenter and finally a master builder. He is able to throw off his humble origins because he never really possessed them: he is the kidnapped son of a well-to-do couple. By the 1850s, however, the disguised gentleman was too much of an interloper on the factory floor. Judd, who recognized the rising ideology crucial to combating labor solidarity and the specter of the strike, conflated gentlemanliness with something new. To give a counterthrust to worker solidarity, he offered moral conversion (214).

Far more than Arthur or Smith, Judd crafted a revivalist narrative that, like the "most individualistic and deferential wage earners" who embraced it, shunned the labor radicalism of the early trade unions and the old antitemperance thinking of the traditionalists.[88] Judd's sobered-up workforce may be more efficient, but it reaps no reward in wages or work-floor control. Judd helped lay the groundwork for Taylorism and Fordism, but he failed to extend its promise of personal advancement.

The second subtitle of Herman Melville's *Redburn, His First Voyage* (1849), *The Son of a Gentleman in the Merchant Service*, appears to signal a departure from the era's gentrification plotting. But Melville did not so much extract the gentrified workman, in this case an impoverished gent, from his hoi polloi surroundings as plunge him into them. (Even Melville's inscrutable Bartleby, while a veteran of deadening office jobs, is well spoken and has an aura of gentility. He is certainly many cuts above his Dickensian fellow clerks.) With the avowed purpose to write for the millions, Melville fictionalized the quasi-Brahmin teller of Richard Henry Dana's well-known apprenticeship autobiography *Two Years before the Mast* (1840).[89] To be sure, prior to his shipboard realization that the sailor is a "slave," Dana craves the restoration of health and the thrill of adventure augured by life at sea. Melville's Wellingborough Redburn, like his creator before him on the New York–Liverpool 1839 packet *St. Lawrence,* needs the money.[90] But straitened finances mark him less than his class-based resemblance to the real-life Dana and Melville. All three have been finely educated and, to survive the brutish life of those Redburn calls the "refuse and off scourings of the earth," adopt a tourist perspective in the "barbarous country" (76) of merchant seamen.[91]

In Melville's day, despite a gradation in job duties that distinguished shipboard laborers from one another, skill levels had declined, and sailors were among the most downtrodden of workers.[92] It is not surprising that, notwithstanding his antiflogging sermons, Melville dismisses them as "underlings" in *White-Jacket* (1850). He tosses a line to the crew and whole chapters to the military hierarchy of the officer class. The effect is to separate the antiflogging message from the pain of those flogged. And he reduces sailors to mindless servitors in the grip of Ahab's obsessional will in *Moby-Dick* (1851). They certainly cannot defy or individuate from their "employer," who has productivity goals, but for an insane purpose.[93] Moreover, in these post-*Redburn* works, even when he describes work activities, Melville separates the actions from the toilers themselves. He is not the last American work imaginer to do so.

Melville displays a grudging verisimilitude in his accounts of the wretched lot of the common sailor, in part the product of his own matriculation in a harsh seagoing college. And he makes gestures toward undercutting the language of class superiority in which Redburn and the narrative are steeped.[94]

Though not without its distancing images, *Redburn* delineates the habits and attitudes of the despised nautical proletariat in some detail. But they are carefully and repeatedly counterpointed with those of the superior Redburn and of the "rough fellows" (25) who people the situation he so resents. He has little but disdain for the sailors' improvidence, ignorance, and sexual depravity (152). He scorns their impotence and passivity in the face of inequities, as when they are cheated out of wages or pensions (18, 25). He vents his spleen by scornfully calling them "gentlemen" (335) because they so little merit the term.

As if oblivious to Melville's overriding preoccupation with the ungentlemanly (*Redburn*, 295) sea worker, period reviewers commented on the entertainment and lively portraiture the novel provided. Most agreed that the sailors were humorous grotesques and found no scorn in the encounters between elitism and the people.[95] What they did not observe was that, in refusing to be his shipmates' colleague but apparently being the chronicler of their work lives, Redburn/Melville is really providing a bitter catalog of what indignities a talented, educated, well-born, but poor man—a gent in laboring disguise—must suffer among the poor. On one level, of course, *Redburn* is an allegory of his own situation as an underrated, underread antebellum artist. (*Moby-Dick* did not sell well.) On another, it establishes the jobless gent who looks forward to the journalist-hoboes of the 1930s, talented men who adopt a philosophical irony that insulates them from coarsening influences. His shipmates' jibes serve to prove that Redburn, the lowliest cabin boy, is above them.

Despite its "wisps of class struggle," *Redburn* is Melville's most complete repudiation of lumpen proletarians.[96] Their ascension has been preempted by inferiority. As evidenced by his letter to a fellow gent, shipmate Harry Bolton, Redburn can effortlessly resume his class post, all the more magically in that he has not earned a penny. The wonder of it is not how altered he is by his voyages, but how little he has changed. An unpleasant apprenticeship among the inmates of a nautical sweatshop has not convinced him of their worth, but it has certainly convinced him of his own.

"Nigger Work": Mose in Blackface

To read Melville is to be convinced that gentlemanliness, however rare among sailors, was a white labor prerogative. His sea fiction responded to the widespread conviction that, from the transcontinental oceans to the northern whaling towns to the southern forced-labor plantations, blacks were meant for what white labor called "nigger work."[97] Melville's attitudes toward African Americans, his dislike of colonialism notwithstanding, were certainly ambivalent. Nevertheless, he offered a more optimistic assessment of the black work spirit than did white culture (such as with *Moby-Dick*'s Steelkilt), or than he himself did for white sailors in the crowd-pleasing *Redburn*.[98] The antebellum period, as one whaling historian observes, actually saw a decrease in black seafaring opportunities. Veteran documenters of black labor describe atrocious conditions for black sailors at this time.[99] If Melville's own tales did not clearly register these perceptions, he was certainly attuned to shipboard racism. Despite his skilled harpooners Dagoo and the Indian Tashteego, preindustrial nobility was greatly at odds with the negative personae of his other black workers: the murderous slave mutineer Babo; the schizoid Pip; the compliant Fleece, "Baltimore," and Mungo.[100]

On land, Melville's white colleagues were reluctant or unable to clothe the black workforce in the kind of precapitalist dignity represented by the imperial, if primitive, Dagoo. In fact, their rhetoric of black toil seemed rooted in a black Mose. Far from being an African American counterpart of the rowdy white urban jobholder, the black Mose represented the sum of racist stereotypes available to the culture.[101]

The African American Mose, a blackface fixture of the minstrel shows so popular with working-class Bowery b'hoys themselves, was a combination of the shiftless, if fatherly, plantation darky and the ludicrous urban dandy.[102] The dandy, linked to the high style of his white counterpart, satirized parasitic white fops and their upper-class pretensions. Yet new research on blackface minstrelsy and the American working class suggests that Mose and other figures were more than vessels of white workers' anxieties or rage. Rather, whites projected their (anti-industrial) desires onto the blacked minstrel as a form of displaced protest.[103] Nevertheless, whatever Mose represented in terms of white self-affirmation, as an urban comic type he had no artisan or mechanic identity. Most of all, he lacked any connection to the minuscule number of blacks in the skilled trades.

Viewed as a reduction of the more representative black work experience of enslavement, the Mose persona bypassed what one recent study calls the other slaves. They included the assorted miners, ironworkers, operatives at tobacco and hemp factories, foresters and lumbermen, saltworkers, and even, in the supreme irony perhaps, railroad workers.[104] The southern novelist Thomas Nelson Page, writing in the mid-1860s on decades of slave work, exaggerated only somewhat when he said that blacks held "without rival the entire field in industrial labor throughout the South."[105]

Not all white workers who guiltlessly enjoyed the debased black Mose chose to join their more violent labor brothers in race riots such as occurred in 1844 Philadelphia or mid–Civil War 1863 New York.[106] There were the rare defenders of interracial cooperation during strikes.[107] Even Frederick Douglass, who elsewhere details the racism of the American shipyard, includes an anecdote in his *Narrative* (1845) about his Irish coworkers on the Baltimore docks who advise him to run north.[108] Yet despite a fear that their own waged work might degenerate into a version of southern slavery, white workers rarely attended antislavery meetings. Although a significant number of mechanics and shoe and textile workers supported abolitionism, no distinct labor wing of abolitionism developed.[109] In *Uncle Tom's Cabin,* the celebrated white abolition novelist Harriet Beecher Stowe may have joined some of the prominent black slave narrators and novelists of the day, among them Josia Henson (wrongly said to be the prototype for Uncle Tom) and Martin Delany.[110] In the works of white authors not committed to sending ex-slave artisans like

Stowe's George Harris to Liberia (or Lippard's disinherited half-black *New York* character to European exile), the era's black Mose trope fuses with a host of condescending or malevolent novelistic depictions of uneducated blacks (*New York in Slices*, 25).

The robotically faithful servant, literally or emotionally bound to a white master, seemed omnipresent in white period imaginings. In Solon Robinson's alternately lachrymose and lurid *Hot Corn: Life Scenes in New York* (1854), Peter the wood sawyer is more admirable than those who despise him. He decorates his humble apartment with religious imagery, saves little girls from street peril, and patiently binds himself in slavish obedience to whites. More writers, however, joined Lippard, who was privately sympathetic to abolitionism and in *New York* includes a heroic mulatto, Black Randolph. All of these writers layered the servitor stereotype with master-fueled criminality. Thus the thick-lipped, flat-nosed Glow-worm has teeth like boar tusks; scarcely human too is the bulging-eyed Musquito, also in *The Quaker City* (52). Crime, an alternative to work, was also linked to the shiftless-Mose stereotype. Among the many whom the wicked city form satanized were blacks stalking drunkenness in Foster's beer cellars in *New York by Gaslight* (125) or thievery and worse outside them (42, 41).

In contrast to racist white literary perceptions of blacks, slave narratives reveal a human landscape of labor oppression. There were a handful of white abolitionist texts; Stowe's George Harris works in a bagging factory and even invents a machine. But the era's only recognizable black workers, from illiterate southern field hands to self-educated slave artisans whom their masters rented out to Baltimore shipyards, were in black-authored slave narratives or novels. Among the more celebrated accounts, the *Narrative of William Wells Brown, A Fugitive Slave* (1848) provided an umbrella term for the bonded experience: "unrequited toil."[111] Just as Henry Bibb did with sugarcane work, Solomon Northup, another notable fugitive autobiographer, filled out the image with pages of details of an ordinary day's oppressive plantation work.[112] Retrospective accounts included Frederick Douglass's *Narrative* (his 1845 text the first of a number of versions) and J. W. Pennington's *The Fugitive Blacksmith* (1850). Both men expanded the definition of enslaved labor to include the skilled blacks whose escape was belied by their inability to reap the limited job rewards of their freed brothers. Even the Brown novel *Clotel* (1853), more concerned with the tragic mulatta theme, mentions "slave mechanics" and includes a job interview between a slave and a prospective buyer.[113]

By its very focus on toil, the figure of the industrious black worker was a refutation of black Mose in all his guises, particularly that of mindless plantation menial or his more sinister urban equivalent. That figure did not represent a viable freed black worker. In fact, the reticence of black fiction and narrative about freed black labor history paralleled the white authorial silence about whites, though for different reasons. African American authors, confronted with the cultural disbelief in a productive black working class, turned to the trope of natural nobility. If blacks could not be journeymen, they could be gentlemen.

Slave Pawns and Fugitive Nobles

In *The Afro-American Novel and Its Tradition,* Bernard Bell speaks of the "irre-pressible bravery" of the slave narrative protagonists, "articulate activists committed to the struggle for justice and freedom."[114] That struggle was much on the minds of the narratives' abolition-minded readers, who termed the fugitive selves in the Douglass, Bibb, Northup, Brown, and Henson autobi-ographies the heroes of the age.[115] Heroic and noble they no doubt were. Their dignity graces the very letters they wrote to their former employer-masters after they had variously seized or bought their freedom. Naturally these documents, like the narratives that contain them, subordinate economic ill-treatment to dehumanization. More dramatic as well is the corresponding self-elevation. The male slave narrator (a discussion of bondswomen's more vexed ascension occupies a part of chapter 3) moves from skilled bond-work to emigrant communal leader or abolitionist lecturer. He becomes an advocate of industrial training schools and of the American League of Col-ored Laborers, whose (thwarted) aim was promoting black artisanal self-employment. The whipped slave was reborn as a leader exhorting his people, as did Frederick Douglass, to find new methods of obtaining livelihoods. "The colored men must learn trades," he urges. "Learn trades or starve!"[116]

The narratives and novels respond to this idea after a fashion. Josia Hen-son's account narrates the real-life relocation of southern slaves to a farming and mill community in Ontario.[117] On how to make the transition from non-factory to factory work Henson is silent. In the fiction by Douglass, Delany, and Brown, however, the problems created by the idea of seeking a new land result in various proposals. Delany calls for rebellion in all lands where blacks reside, from Canada to Haiti. *Clotel* makes a passing reference to land pur-chased in Ohio.[118] Two things are noticeable. As in whites' wage-liberation schemes, these commentators view the land as salvation, and the issues of training and literacy are not addressed. The black in these accounts does not sue for membership in the American workforce. He becomes an ex-slave seek-ing safe haven.

The most noted ex-slave activist of his time, Frederick Douglass, explored in his fiction and famed slave narrative the options available to the skilled black runaway. His narrative, published in 1845, revised in 1855, and again in the 1880s, straddles the entire antebellum period during which white authors conceptualized the white worker. The *Narrative* easily outsold *Redburn* and *Moby-Dick* put together.[119] To be sure, Douglass agitated in other venues for freed blacks' labor rights. He helped propose an industrial college (which never eventuated) and preached to the more than 480,000 freed blacks living in the United States.[120] But he did not address, in either his slave narrative or his novel, the situation of the freed black laborer.

His reasons clearly are anchored in the urgencies of abolitionism. Four mil-lion blacks remained in southern slavery as 1860 approached. As Douglass well knew, exclusion from the fruits of the free labor market was as much a re-ality for runaway defiers of the Fugitive Slave Act of 1850 as for the less than

5 percent of blacks living in the North.[121] Yet Douglass's depictions of his run-away protagonists in both the *Narrative* and *The Heroic Slave* (1853) suggest the possibilities as well as the limits of the black laboring experience in ante-bellum fiction.

The *Narrative,* while not fiction, shares with its period the rhetoric and themes of self-help and personal success. In Douglass, the rich plantation owner, a racist southern version of the urban merchant, torments his bonds-men. Like urban artisans in debt to the banks, his vassals must give up their pay to their masters. Obviously, Douglass's childhood experience as a field hand on Captain Anthony's and Colonel Lloyd's plantations was far removed from the labor world of the newsboy Bob, much less Richard Edney's. He is soon bonded in situations where he can arduously acquire literacy. As a young man with shipyard skills, he can command the high pay given to the most experienced calkers (*Narrative,* 103). Yet he is always aware of his sepa-rateness from his white counterparts, workers who rebuff and castigate him. In a sentence ringing with outrage at workplace exploitation, he observes that he is unable to earn a fair wage that will urge him on to seek freedom. He pro-claims himself a bona fide workingman. "I contracted for it; I earned it; it was paid to me; it was rightfully my own; yet, upon, each returning Saturday night, I was compelled to deliver every cent of that money to Master Hugh" (104). In this culminating injustice, the paid white mechanic becomes in a sense both inspiration and enemy, a paradox that would face all black au-thors on emancipation.

Douglass in his enslaved state no doubt spoke for many of the bonded skilled blacks of the day. When he had won his liberty, he did not land a job with the skilled, white New Bedford workforce. Characteristically, Douglass transformed this hard labor fact into a Franklinesque occasion for redoubled effort. "There was no work too hard," he concluded, "none too dirty" (*Narra-tive,* 118).

In his rhetorical support of the myth of America and minimization of racism in the closing pages of the *Narrative,* Douglass determinedly preaches uplift despite his private pessimism about integrating black workers into the labor force.[122] Too, Douglass's gracious refusal to complain about his treatment bol-stered the nobility of his fugitive status. Such nobility, a rising above the racist treatment of freed blacks, also characterizes his fictive treatment of the slave fugitive in *The Heroic Slave.* The articulate Madison Washington, a for-mer Virginia millworker characterized as the "noble fugitive" (33), is a slave who toils in the mill rather than at abject plantation labor. Dignified and elo-quent, Washington's mere presence can convert a former slaveholder to ar-dent abolitionism. But he solves the problem of employment only through flight to Canada, a land removed from the industrial centers of the U.S. North.

Martin Delany, onetime coeditor with Douglass (of *The North Star*), a fellow abolitionist, was an apostle of self-help for his people—flight for the enslaved, and good industrial and professional jobs for the freed. Delany sought to ex-pand the search for a black nationality beyond Canada to Central America, and possibly to Africa. Delany's novel *Blake; or, The Huts of America* was serialized first in 1859 in the New York City–based *Anglo-African Magazine* and, by 1861, in the *Weekly Anglo-African*. Delany covered the ideological ground of many black thinkers of the time, who suggested emigration as an outlet for blacks, whatever their job status under the plantation system.[123]

In his emigrationist tracts, essays, and parts of his novel, Delany airs fears about newly arrived immigrants pushing blacks out of jobs. Racism denied him a Harvard medical education and produced his alienation from white abolitionists unwilling to confront the issue of economic discrimination. Both sets of experiences found artistic form in a far more militant version of Douglass's heroic slave.[124] The very title of Delany's work refers to the self-transformation of a Louisiana escapee, Henry Holland, who conducts a lengthy insurrectionary tour through the South, raising the awareness of plantation workers and forest runaways. West Indian born, Holland rechristens himself Blake when he arrives in Cuba to become general of a black revolutionary force with plans to wrest political power for the slave population there. Delany lauds in Blake the intelligence, courage, ferocious militance, and, to a lesser degree, bloody-mindedness of a Nat Turner. Although a man on the run, Blake is less in flight than in constant movement. He exhorts his rapidly growing band of followers to declare war against their oppressors and kills the white overlords who chase him—though most often in self-defense. Violent though he may be, his intellect is keen and his rhetoric so elegant that, unlike the illiterate dialect characters he exhorts, he became the ennobled intellectual of much antebellum abolitionism.

The creation of so magical a character is an important achievement.[125] Yet Delany's silence on the black laborer in his extended works mirrors that of other activists. Delany has Blake appropriate his wages as a response to job exploitation (and has many minor characters do the same). But Blake's creator, even more than other writers, was painting a revolutionary canvas, and worker images blur.

In African American work writings, fictive spokesmen for former slaves exhorted, inspired by example, or visited the few black manual labor schools in the United States. But what they could not render artistically was entry into the ranks of skilled, native-born American men. From the mutinous militants of the fiction to the job and education seekers of the narratives, a postslave life as a menial worker is unthinkable.[126] Yet personal elevation is won at the price of flight. The noble fugitive, transformed from runaway to man of stature, replaces the white workplace aristocrat whose transit is from shop floor to management, not from chains to Canada. To be sure, abolitionist literature, in its concern with uplift, implicitly addresses the idea of workplace ascension through self-help. But what Douglass realized, in an oft-quoted remark to his son, that it was easier for a black man to be a lawyer than a blacksmith, resulted in a dearth of black labor images.[127] The reasons for this gap are dissimilar from those informing white portrayals. But the message complements those portraits. In antebellum imagining, once legally free to labor, the black worker remained labor's fugitive: nowhere at home.

To the Worker: Rise, Conform, or Die

On the eve of the Civil War, whether the worker-hero was plugged into a sensationalist urban world, courting alcoholism and disgrace, or elevated out of his class, literature by and for white readers, informed by a lingering nostalgia for the Franklinesque artisan, was re-forming and reforming the American workingman. No antebellum novelist could sustain a narrative about the work or inner life of the honest mechanic, much less the semiskilled, unskilled, transient, or child laborer, unless he ascended to ownership or fell to penury. Formulaic fare on the thwarted amours and machinations of the affluent and the mercantile crowded all of these labor figures, WASP or otherwise, from the storytelling stage.

But these economic and narrative outsiders always return for reckonings with—or disappearance into—the economic elite. Though construed as problems in and of themselves, by their very presence they revealed the cultural anxieties about the evils of the factory system, the dangers of the immigrant, the challenges posed by the disgruntled trade unionist, the chaos inherent in the swelling underclass. Each plot tries, often uneasily, to resolve such problems by applying myths of selective economic ascension and competitive individualism. In the name of personal mobility, factory workers are elevated to owners, cabin boys to gentlemen, shoemakers to leaders of workers' relocation to the West.

In this fixation on rising, antebellum American writers had a labor vision, however limited, that their successors would adapt, modify, and reshape, but not radically revise until the early decades of the next century. Their fictive landscape, with few exceptions, did not embrace militant class discord or preach that the working and the owning classes were inevitably at odds. If anything, their rhetoric resolved the contradiction between the idea of a permanent force of white wage earners and the antisocial implications of a volatile proletariat. And it did so by invoking the unlikely panacea of crossing class boundaries. There remained, in the midst of this mobility mythicizing, the disturbing vision of labor's dismay at diminishing opportunities and the impoverishment that threatened those thrown out of work, exploited, or replaced by cheaper hands. But this antebellum version of magic realism was not completely at odds with what the labor movement itself would embrace for many years to come: the American Dream. It would fall to the next literary generation to refashion without abandoning ascendancy thinking. Its members would examine the tension between the burgeonings of proletarianism and the increasingly constricted opportunities for embourgeoisement; between the much-vaunted work ethic and the thralldom of the factory; between the constantly invoked self-made man and the ideological alternative, working-class mutualism.

Refiguring the labor gentleman to meet a far more elitist aim than labor intended, antebellum fiction, rarely if ever using the term "class," conveyed the subtler message that workers needed to understand the rules of class society. Invisibility for many was the price of ascension for the talented few. Thus the worker-hero could not be a class representative, much less have a class identity. To reinforce that message, white authors discussed the working class via stand-ins for it, mediated between disdain and documentation, and compassion and distaste.

In a variety of ways, they sealed the frightening fissures of class division and the real threat of workingmen's riots, presocialistic or not. Michael Denning reminds us that white fiction had not yet found a way of representing the character who remains working class, and the literary preference for raising up the singular workman evidences that.[128] Yet the three tropes discussed in this chapter, if perceived as ideological restructurings of white laboring men, illuminate how the formal properties of art both organized and covered over working-class unrest.

For blacks, flight was for Douglassian noble runaways. He and other African American writers may have consciously or unconsciously translated Mose figures, labor pawns, and labor gents. But what transcended these characterizations was an understanding of the realities of imprisoned southern labor and northern job discrimination. In their fictions and narratives, a fuguelike insistence on self-reliance and self-transformation does challenge the slavery system that made a mockery of the black work ethic. (Ironically, slave novels and narratives contain some of the most detailed descriptions of antebellum manual workers.) To the extent that these narrators evince ambivalence toward the untutored masses still enmeshed in oppression, these too are upward-mobility narratives.[129] Still, the ersatz proletarian who wasn't, a staple of white imaginings of natural nobility, becomes the bondsman on the run in black imaginings, his flight, however courageous, a metaphor for his insubstantial place in the labor force.

In all of these sources, the workingman who remains who and what he is, an elusive type for American authors, continues to wait in the wings. Perceived as a living reproach to Franklinesque ideology, he is variously defused, deadened, or elevated from his laborer role. His literary coming-of-age, much less that of the worker-writer, is far off. Soon a wave of postbellum strikes and protests would accompany the rise of the first national labor organization, the Knights of Labor. They would inspire authors of many stripes to redouble the search for proletarian worth that their antebellum predecessors, however ambivalently, had begun.

CHAPTER 2

I'm Looking through You
Working Men from Status Quo
to Knights of Labor Fiction

"These miners are as unreasonable as children. . . . Laborers, as a class, have just sense enough to see when their employers are in a tight place, and losing money. Then they get up their confounded strikes. It's so with all the trades."

—C. M. CORNWALL, *FREE, YET FORGING THEIR OWN CHAINS* (1876)

"I'm going to stick to the Knights. I'd rather be a Master Workman than own a mill, any time."

—FREDERICK WHITTAKER, *LARRY LOCKE, MAN OF IRON*
(SERIALIZED 1884)

A stranger to the South might say: "Ah, I see. The negro is the same everywhere—a hewer of wood, a peddler of vegetables, a wearer of the waiter's apron."

—WILLIAM WELLS BROWN, *MY SOUTHERN HOME* (1880)

John George Brown, *The Longshoremen's Noon,* 1879. Oil on canvas, $33\frac{1}{4} \times 50\frac{1}{4}$ in. Collection of the Corcoran Gallery, Washington, D.C. Museum Purchase, Gallery Fund.

During the late 1860s and early 1870s, the miners' Workingmen's Benevolent Association, the Iron Moulders' Union, and the National Labor Union began to flex a new unionist muscle.[1] Although labor lobbies, boycotts, and profit-sharing factory ventures did not produce widespread public awareness of a labor movement, they began to set the agenda for it.[2] By the early 1870s the creation of a public labor image was well under way.[3] Theoretically, the mainstream of labor advocated fair wages for those white, native-born women in sex-segregated work. Many of them, like urban seamstresses, were without male economic mainstays after the Civil War. But, with exceptions such as the bi-gender alliances between Troy's male ironworkers and the women in "female occupations," the masculinist mainstream rigorously excluded "intruders."[4] Labor also ignored or opposed the job needs of recently freed blacks and newly arrived Slavic and Mediterranean immigrants.[5] It was loud in vilifying the Chinese, perceived in most quarters as strikebreaking or otherwise wage-deflating immigrants.[6] And it was unmoved by a federal Indian policy that turned detribalized Native Americans into reservation-based laborers.

Moreover, the thirty newly founded or strengthened national unions did not represent the marginalized or even the mass of unaffiliated white male toilers, particularly semi- and unskilled immigrants. Nevertheless, in (white) labor's name, these unions demanded attention, forged a certain visibility, and pointed repeatedly to their exclusion from the American Dream.[7] At the same time, nonunion craft workers, even in the increasingly militant carpentry, iron, and steel industries, applied the old artisanal ethic to industrial autonomy.[8]

The majority, though, had little opportunity to profit from a labor-class version of acquisitive individualism in the industrial trades. From the late 1860s to the depression of 1873, what they saw as their economic exclusion from the rewards of capitalism provoked rebellious responses in the 300,000-strong membership of national and local unions.[9] From the labor press to the union meeting, these organizations forged a language of quasi-militant cooperation.[10] As the Knights of Labor's self-naming suggests, the new diction did not so much replace as expand the old craft-based rhetoric of natural nobility (see chapter 1). By the postbellum era, a cross-trade fraternalism pervaded the *Workingman's Advocate,* the *National Labor Tribune,* and the various trade journals. They plastered their front pages with defiant notices of strikes, and called with some success for like action from workers in other trades.[11]

Nevertheless, until the late 1870s the gains of the first postbellum phase of the industrial trades' self-strengthening, including the birth of the 1870s labor novel to give them artistic form, were forestalled by a lengthy depression. That event in turn fomented a militant second phase, represented by the Railway Strike of 1877, also called "the Uprising" or "the Great Upheaval." The nation's first general strike, it was a violent reaction to economic dissatisfaction.[12] Emphatically stamped out as interference with property rights, even in defeat it marked a revival of the labor movement.[13]

Perhaps the first strike to generate a novelistic exchange on class rage in America, the Uprising of 1877 inspired both status quo tales excoriating labor's methods and a loosely radical fiction that took antilabor thinking to task. Taken together, this politically variegated group of novels also explicated the early 1880s rise of the cross-trade Knights of Labor. The Knights were the only national worker group to generate their own literary propagandists, T. Fulton Gantt included. Until the antilabor fallout from the 1886 Haymarket incident, in which a bomb thrown during an eight-hour-day rally "turned nervousness into the full-blown hysteria of an anarchist scare," theirs was the most powerful labor organization of their time.[14] Numbering as many as three-quarters of a million at their height, the Knights challenged the capitalist wage system.[15] As a consequence, they attracted so wide a range of workers that the listing in each issue of the Knights' journal was pages in length.[16] Long on radical impulse and universal brotherhood, if short on detail, they officially opposed but locally supported a fair number of the thousands of strikes between 1880 and 1887.[17] Their demise in the wake of a tenuous association with Haymarket anarchism marked the end of a labor history period, even as the less visionary American Federation of Labor (AFL), which pragmatically excluded the unskilled to consolidate union gains, was about to symbolize organized labor.

Like its AFL rival and successor and so many of the smaller Gilded Age unions, the Knights' rebuttal of the "by one's own bootstraps" myth was born from workers' opposition to the human cost of amassing great fortunes.[18] As in antebellum times, Marxist socialism could not be said to have penetrated the consciousness of the myriad and often disorganized strike groups.[19] The Knights were never American Marxists, although Marx looked favorably on them. But the Knights and allied groups applauded the short-term successes of scattered profit-sharing ventures such as the foundries in Troy, New York.[20] Yet all of these attempts to unite craft unionism and political socialism—nativistically reformulated in antilabor fiction as the machinations of repellent foreign agitators—were weak enough in this period to be reversed after Haymarket.

Far beyond its actual power over or appeal to the mass of workers, socialism, alongside the upheavals, and the Knights' potential to disseminate a philosophy empowering labor, interested divergent labor imaginers. They ranged from those laudatory of its workingman's democracy credo to management bards who were suspicious of its secrecy and cross-trade appeal. Such apparent recognition of the new realities of labor unrest altered the promise of worker ascension so haltingly extended by the novels of the 1840s and 1850s.

Yet much of this new paternalist fiction concealed the very fears it tried to allay.

Procapitalist fiction of the early Gilded Age also had its literary armor in place to repel an imagined proletarian onslaught. Less fearful that workers' solidarity—or anger—would undermine American individualism, Knights of Labor and utopian socialist writers strove to reconcile individualism with a mutualist ethic. We shall examine how well this labor knight personified that rebuttal of European working-class consciousness known as American exceptionalism.

As white authors debated whether labor-class compliance led to self-improvement or more disenfranchisement, in texts on the African American labor experience, antebellum bondage continued to imprint the discussion of work. The postbellum black worker was predominantly a sharecropper or strikebreaker. Dim racial prospects were fitfully brightened by the short tenure of the National Colored Labor Union (NCLU) and instances of biracial cooperation and in the pronouncements of the Knights of Labor.[21] But with the wages paid to black farmworkers in 1867 lower than those paid to antebellum slaves, blocked mobility was an even more urgent issue for freedmen than for white workers agitating for the eight-hour day.[22]

In such a labor climate, black authors gave "conformist" and "rebellious" new literary meanings. The retrospective slave novels and semifictional narratives of the 1880s by Frederick Douglass, William Wells Brown, and lesser lights attempted to forge a viable African American labor model for a post-Reconstruction era. How did these authors indict a restrictive white labor movement in such revisioning?

Native Americans, another oppressed minority, were attracting literary notice. It followed in the wake of the Battle of Little Big Horn (1876), the swift humiliation of Crazy Horse and Sitting Bull and, from the late 1870s to the end of the next decade, the expansion of federal Indian policy. To make sense of what they saw as this transit to labor debasement, rare novels like Helen Hunt Jackson's *Ramona* (1884) imagined the Native American labor experience of a detribalized racial minority.

Finally, the Chinese, organized labor's hated "coolie" interlopers, were invariably accused of thwarting the progress of white workers. Did fiction like that of Bret Harte mirror labor movement sinophobia or view Asians as fellow aspirants in an American struggle to realize working-class ambition? Returning to the "mainstream" labor novels of the time, we ask of what did proletarian ambition consist?

Paternalist Narrative and Proletarian Ambition

As the American workforce acquired an increasingly urban and company-town hue, literary defenders of the status quo, most notably C. M. Cornwall (Mary Abigail Roe), Thomas Bailey Aldrich, John Hay, and Charles Bellamy engaged in their own form of Gilded Age agitprop. These writers offered veiled or minimizing responses to the era's plentiful labor turbulence. A year before the coal strike novel of the pseudonymous C. M. Cornwall, *Free, Yet*

Forging Their Own Chains, the violent six-month Anthracite Coal Strike of 1875 went down in defeat in central Pennsylvania.[23] It is not clear if Cornwall drafted her novel after the 1875 strike. It is certain that her novel found ample literary material in the region's recent unrest following the mine-collapsing Avondale disaster of 1869.[24] Despite her reduction in scale of the visible coalfield protest movement in America's largest mass industry, Cornwall was one of the earliest postbellum writers to provide a sustained acknowledgment of worker-management struggles.[25]

Yet, inheriting the antebellum literary tendency to look away from the oppressed worker just when he seems most real or human, Cornwall used an approach-avoidance method emblematic of the entire novel.[26] Mining-town wretchedness, acknowledged as a group plight, merely infiltrates her narrations. She limits labor-class dialogue to malcontents' scheming, crowd-pleasing rabble-rousing, and rhetorical chicanery.

The unfree work world of *Free* is hidden in a narrative concern with gentry-based responses rather than worker grievances. The novel's panacea for labor unrest comes in the form of John Graham, a management-allied, Christianity-spouting mine manager opposed to strikes but allegedly in sympathy with the impoverished miners. If he can achieve enlightened supervision of the mine, he can satisfy the labor masses for whom mobility has been preempted and retain the company loyalists who worked during the strike to help defeat the hotheads.

The most interesting aspect of the Cornwall novel for modern readers is that Graham mouths a mobility thinking in which the novel simply does not believe. His question "Who are your boss miners and engineers, but men who by industry and skill worked their way up?" (34) and his exhortations to starving miners to go to school to rise (34) are offered not as true labor alternatives but as the proper sentiments for a managerial hero. Graham is too old to be Mark the Match Boy. Yet Algerian or not, it is Graham alone who achieves the upward climb he has publicized to the strikers.

In the constricted Cornwallian labor landscape, not surprisingly, the good scab merely retains what he has—in this case, a job as colliery boss. Thus Andrew Fuller, who with formulaic predictability is the son of a hard-pressed bourgeois, regains his position, and his father, similarly restored, is rescued from debt. In antebellum fiction, where, as we have seen, distinctions between conservative and radical approaches to labor shifted and blurred, the ambitious Fuller's credentials would have propelled him into mercantile and marital ascension, or at the very least placed him at the rudder of a quasi-socialistic workers' community. In the more polarized labor-literary climate of the 1870s and 1880s, the conservative novelists cannot empower a have-not to marry the heiress and buy the factory.

A final component of Cornwall's fantasy of the "reformed" coal worker is the idea that the abolition of corrupt owners will automatically subdue the violent leaders of workers in turmoil.[27] However short on logic, she joins her colleagues in ending up with a contented worker, one who knows his place and understands his fate.[28]

The most disturbing aspect of this representative antilabor novel is not the demonizing of the Molly Maguires and their followers. Rather, it is Cornwall's conviction that Graham's capitalist activism is the only kind that matters.[29] Many period authors, particularly Christian ones appalled by trusts and oligarchies, condemned upper-class chicanery along with labor-class mobocracy.[30] Cornwall does overlay the novel with a number of ruthless financiers who use corrupt "walking delegates" to further their elaborate scams. Both sets of miscreants lose power and ill-gotten gains by novel's end. In *Free* and allied texts, the blame for workingmen's economic defeats falls most squarely on their own inability to wait for the good labor boss.

In *Free,* Cornwall subdues her authorial voice by the adoption of a gender-ambiguous pseudonym.[31] Thomas Bailey Aldrich, who shared her repressive attitude toward strikes and also based his fiction on actual events, was a more visible literary figure than the shadowy Cornwall. While publishing *The Stillwater Tragedy* in 1880, he was climbing the journalistic ladder that would land him the editorship of the prestigious *Atlantic Monthly* the same year and help identify him to a middlebrow public anxious about labor unrest.

His novel was probably informed by a notable but disastrous job action—the iron moulders' strike of 1877 in Troy, New York.[32] Aldrich may also have known of ironworkers' strikes in Chicago in the years prior to his book's appearance. He was certainly aware of the kind of labor solidarity evidenced in the famous events of 1877 and shared Cornwall's impulse to censor the irresponsible, volatile workers. Yet shared strategies of minimization apart, he paid far closer attention to the methods that ironworkers had by the late 1870s evolved in their search for power and authority.

As the novel opens, the marble workers of New England's fictitiously named Stillwater are stirring in sympathy with the ironworkers in a neighboring town. Essaying what in reality the iron moulders in the larger Troy had done, they seek control over the number of apprentices on the shop floor.[33] Throughout the late 1860s and early 1870s, Troy's moulders thus had the ability to safeguard their craft against deskilling.[34] Attempts at workers' control in various skilled trades by the early 1880s, including ironwork, found a movement from spontaneous to planned collective action.[35]

Aldrich rightly sensed that the apprentice issue was symbolic of a coming resurgence of labor in the 1880s. He decided against privileging the Amalgamated Association of Iron and Steel Workers (AAISW) and the Sons of Vulcan locals, which were again trying to create a resurgent trade unionism. In a vague melding of local ironworkers' protests like Troy's and the nationwide Railway Strike of 1877, his novel backgrounds the events of 1877. It emerges instead as a strike restricted, unlike that of 1877, to New England. He refashions events by placing militance in the hands of a foolish group of marble cutters who inhabit a latter-day antebellum workshop rather than place workers in a heavily technological factory. There is some labor violence injected into the plotting. One resident foreign agitator, Torrini, flashes a knife to attack the manufacturing scion Richard Shackford. In a further parable of labor's unwarranted attack on capital, Richard's Uncle Lemuel is murdered by one Durgin, the Molly Maguire of Stillwater. In New England's Stillwater, the marble workers enter the narrative swaggering. They leave as penitents beseeching employers for a return to the old paternalism.

In Aldrich's reading, the men foolishly hold the owner ransom when, to keep wages high, they forbid him to hire more workers, a reference to the era's hotly contended apprentice issue. Such labor sins swiftly generate punishment. The men who ungratefully exit when the owner resists return contritely when they lose the strike.[36] The middle-management protagonist, Richard Shackford, seizes Torrini's knife, boots out the Irish lazies, and ends up as co-owner of the marble works. Before this labor gent is rewarded, Aldrich calls on dime novel formula. Richard for a time takes the role of the unjustly accused, held as the killer of a rich relation when it is the labor-class Durgin who did the deed. In the hands of a prolabor novelist like Martin Foran, the acquittal of the wronged workman heralds his opportunity to rise to a worker-owned factory trustee. In the hands of Aldrich, the accusation is final proof of labor's bad faith.

The antistrike novel that transformed the violent into the humbled was fashionable well into the late 1880s.[37] But no novel from the early 1870s to the next decade's end exacted labor penitence more than *The Bread-Winners* (1884), a late response to the events of 1877. It was the handiwork of President Rutherford B. Hayes's former assistant secretary of state, John Hay, who was to figure in several more administrations. Hay prudently safeguarded his diplomatic career prospects while increasing book sales by keeping silent about his authorship.[38] Thus protected, he represented workingmen's unreasonable demands to rise as the desperate acts of venal men who, their rampage curbed by capitalist paramilitary heroism, were destined for punishment or the silence of the defeated.

Hay rewrites labor unrest by trading a few rough Molly Maguires or a trio of agitators for an Irish deadbeat turned schemer, Offitt, and his mindless henchman, Sleeny. The two lead an entire union local composed in equal parts of the disgruntled and the malleable. With queer rituals and surly followers, the "brotherhood" is thus a satirical combination of the Brotherhood of Locomotive Engineers so instrumental in the 1877 strike and of the Knights themselves.[39] Hay also makes vague allusions to allied strikes elsewhere in the state. (The 1877 strike involved many more.) They are all as quickly quelled as the one in Cleveland, a railroad center integral to the strike.[40]

Images of labor's moral and physical squalor transcend those of its evil mischief in depictions of the "brothers." But the narrative takes them seriously enough to empower a cadre of militia comprising imported Good Workmen, former employees of Arthur Farnham, a local patrician whose financial interests are imperiled by the strikers.[41] Again Hay's is a fictive embroidering on the melding of mercantile and military force. In his response to the destruction wrought by real-life strikers and their sympathizers, Hay, rather surprisingly for a former (and future) government man, consolidates authority in Farnham. He musters a private army to squelch the 1877 disturbances, not bothering to claim even the limited legal justification of the actual troops.[42] As

Hay weaves in and out of actuality, strikers in the vaguely designated "south" (*The Bread-Winners,* 240) take over railway stations. Local strikers set up an encampment near a common roadway to block traffic as well as to try to mobilize to storm factories (240).

Here Hay is on solid historical ground. Looting, rioting, and marching on stockyards, mills, factories, and docks, though more linked to angry mobs than to organized labor, did characterize railway centers. Yet, when he might have given artistic force to a delineation of the domestic-insurrectionary nature of the Railway Strike, Hay, his nose pushed in class struggle, responded by deflating the importance of the threat. He finds a more hortatory version from actual events in a ridiculous deus ex machina. "[E]very woman went for her [striking] husband and told him to pack up and go home, told 'em their lazy picnic had lasted long enough, that there was no meat in the house, and that they had got to come home and go to work" (241). Hay's plot thus negates the familial solidarity that midwestern women, Chicagoans who struck in sympathy during the actual 1877 Uprising, offered their men.[43]

In his movement between deflating and acknowledging the lessons of the Railway Strike of 1877, Hay sets out the terrain of conservative labor fiction for many decades to come. The fear was that labor would only become more confrontational, but its threat could be defused by the enfeeblement and compliance plot. Yet Hay himself argued in an anonymous letter to the *Century* in March 1884, signed "Author of 'The Bread-Winners,' " that "no important strike had ever been carried through without violence."[44] In fictional terms, this conviction produces not, as its author claimed, a novel of misguided laborites sinking to the mob level to do their leaders' bidding but a shifting laborscape in which labor protesters are ineffective and menacing. By the time Hay's laboring fools crawl back to their bossy wives, they are all but invisible.

A paternalistic novel about a New England mill strike by Charles Joseph Bellamy, *The Breton Mills* (1879), provides some final insight into the relation between the Hay school's class revulsion and novels proving that the labor movement merited only repression. Ironically enough, the book was popular with labor readers, perhaps because it features a romantically doomed labor organizer who marries above himself and suffers for it.[45] It was one of the few completely antistrike novels to invoke a profit-sharing plan. It provides an alternative to what its lawyer-creator and mill-owner hero, Philip Breton, views as a worker outbreak about to erupt into violence against mill property. But both in the workers' response to the reforms and in the romance plotting that would be a staple of much fiction on laborers for decades to come, Bellamy offers only pessimism.

In a formulaic way, the menace of the strikers is symbolized by those who manipulate them. Though, like a servant, Curran is not accorded a Christian name, he threatens to usurp both Breton's management control and his emotional life. When Curran, who has whipped up the strike, actually marries Breton's well-born love interest, the social chaos is complete. Breton pardons Curran the agitator and the rival alike. In a fantasy of labor's ideal relation to management Breton's offered reorganization of the mill and of dividends based on skill level are met with wild enthusiasm.[46]

In a work world gone awry, however, "the glad shouts of the poor ringing in his ears" cannot put things right. In a moment of verisimilitude Breton points out that workers will see little raise in pay or shortening of hours. But rather than look to Breton's noble patience, they visit Breton's home to complain about their conditions. Perhaps worse in the Bellamy worldview, they leave dirt marks on the carpets and curtains.

In this conservative vision of providence, Curran, punished by fate for aspiring to cross-class union, weakens and dies. He leaves the members of an "inert" (439) and presumably pliable workforce to keep their dirty feet off the carpets of their betters. In the status quo writers, workers' very anger, reformed as a kind of mass temper tantrum, reveals no cracks in the attempts to substitute a rhetoric of compliance for one of rising. Neither strikebreakers nor scabs who have sprung from labor's ranks, in fact, ascend. The new message was that industrial obedience in a factory economy assured the swelling members of the factory force that self-support now meant simply having a job at all.[47]

The Hay school imagined workers as failures at an ascension that remains no less Franklinesque for being so elusive. In novels more respectful of collective aims, does an urgent new labor theme, mutualism, shift the focus away from exceptionalism altogether?[48] Perhaps now it was not the laborer who had to comply, but the capitalist.

Surrogate Paternalism or Labor Fraternalism?: "Radical" Fiction's Assenting Workforce

Writing of what he called the "slow dissemination of Marxist thought" in the 1870s and 1880s, Walter Rideout found no Uncle Tom's Cabin of Capitalism. *Das Kapital* was not even translated by the late 1880s.[49] Adopting a touristic viewpoint in vignettes of factory towns, Henry F. Keenan's *The Money-Makers: A Social Parable* (1885), titularly concerned with the welfare of the workmen, seems embarrassed by them as well.[50] How else to explain the three brief scenes in which workers figure? They riot, they meet in a union hall that, the property of the "moneymaker," collapses and kills many of them, and, an anonymous mass, they cheer a misguided labor leader.[51] Otherwise, Fred Carew, an antistrike journalist with inexplicable power over unnamed union leaders, stands firmly on the Keenan podium.

In the utopian novel, another stream of economic fiction, American attempts to help labor by putting an end to the need to strike through a futuristic cooperative commonwealth are emblematized by Edward Bellamy's *Looking Backward* (1888). Though popular enough with middle-class "opposition forces," Bellamy and his colleagues again reduced the worker to a cipher in his own world, whether the strike-torn Boston of 1887 or the brave new world of 2000.[52]

The novels that did make thrusts toward including characters from organized labor—what the author, former cooper, and trade union leader Martin

Foran called the "other side"—concentrated their energies defensively. Thus the Arthur Farnham character, who in *The Bread-Winners* leads an armed militia to crush the Railway Strike rioters, in Harriet Boomer Barber's re-formation (*Drafted In,* 1888) descends to financial misfortune. He is befriended by workers and, back on his mercantile feet, purchases a coal mine to run. His plan is "co-operative, upon a broad platform of philanthropy."[53] Reviving the Philip Breton plan that workers should receive a percentage of the profits according to the labor performed, he views their suspicion not, as in the Charles Bellamy scenario, as the primitivism of the dirty, but as the "result of grinding oppression in the past" (*Drafted In,* 347). In *The Other Side,* Foran's mouthpiece Richard Arbyght, a Chicago meatpacker, receives a windfall inheritance at novel's end but needs no deus ex machina to bolster his leadership. In early scenes fictionalizing the 1877 upheaval, he calms an angry crowd of strikers: "You will not feel at home in a thieves' carnival."[54] Foran's alter ego thus preaches arbitration, negotiation, and working self-reliance instead of "the promises of politicians or the advice of hot-headed leaders" (*Other Side,* 439).

Foran's quasi-radical fiction is joined by novels such as Amanda Douglas's *Hope Mills* (1879), Beverley Warner's *Troubled Waters* (1885), and, to some degree, William Dean Howells's philanthropy tale, *Annie Kilburn* (1887). Capitalists are now receptive to laboring men, and charismatic spokesmen are elevated to leadership positions. But labor's own voice is reduced to a mass assent, a group willingness to obey an allegedly proworker mandate. The man entrusted with cooperative planning is no grassroots type. Like Foran himself, Richard Arbyght quickly replaces his work-floor tenure with a position in administration. But the rank and file's own conflicts between group solidarity and upwardly mobile individualism are not the concern of these novels. If anything, they suggest that the U.S. workforce has not yet learned self-rule.[55] The men do not so much adopt a wage system loosely based on the period's actual experiments in profit sharing as accede to their labor surrogate's agenda. Not only is there no clear model for class-based decision making, but the workers must be encouraged, "as children are" (*Drafted In,* 345).

The message, then, that workers must learn to be cooperative, in both senses of the word, undercuts the rhetoric of communalism. Labor harmony is constructed as a workforce delegating responsibility to affluent representatives. Compared with a Cornwall or a Bellamy, these authors respond to the nonrevolutionary unionism of the craft workforce and, to a lesser degree, the union-favoring discontent in the era's slaughterhouses, mines, cigar factories, and steel mills. Yet the recommended trustee-run cooperatives do not herald a future of worker-run ventures. They seem imposed on plots that offer as palliatives to labor violence and employer bad faith either a Christian socialism or the personal diplomacy of the superior-workman-turned-exceptional-leader. Too, such novels are implicitly restricted to the enlightened or self-educated— not the Mediterranean, eastern European, and/or "communistic" immigrants viewed suspiciously in all quarters.[56] As worker-fraternal ideals struggle with management-paternal ones, the crowd of workers who readily agree to the organizers' plans remains voiceless and undifferentiated (*Other Side,* 459). Only the labor surrogate emerges as the victor.

Surrogacy Revisited: Knights of Labor Novels

The cooperatively run factory was embraced by Christian socialists like Barber and, to a lesser extent, Warner, and erstwhile trade unionists like Foran.[57] It found favor with the U.S. labor commissioner, the editor of the *Nation*, and a wide range of reformers and members of the governing classes seeking a panacea for labor unrest.[58] Whatever the cooperative concept signified to each novelist, all of this fiction used it to sweep aside matters of unifying workers along class lines, or explaining how the labor movement would awaken a sense of cross-trade solidarity.[59]

Nor was most fiction in the cheap-story papers read by workers, some of it reprinted by august publishing houses for middle-class consumption, any more radical. Working-class readers seeking not self-education through improving literature but a kind of entertainment and escape not provided by the hortatory labor poetry of their trade journals seemed content to escape with the old accidental worker plot of Daniel Doyle. Or they applauded the justice-served scenario in works by Albert Aiken, in which the dangerous Molly Maguires are brought to trial.[60] Even the Knights of Labor's Frederick Whittaker, a workingman's press regular whose most grassroots hero, Larry Locke, rejects a managerial job to stay with his fellow workers, usually preferred to extol a more ambitious type. A Knight on the rise, his 1884 title character in *Job Manly* starts out in a carriage factory. He owns it by the end of the *Beadle's Weekly* serial.[61]

A minority of serial fiction about the Knights of Labor did not sacrifice mutualism to financial self-transformation but attempted to realize the Knights' motto "Organize, Agitate, Educate" in fictional terms. These tales depicted a workforce involved in an active program of cross-trade labor assemblies and boycotts. As a character from Gantt's *Breaking the Chains* explains, workers must rest hope of self-improvement with their own class (113). Nor is this improvement facilitated by the rise of managerial affluence that rewards Foran's labor representative. True to the Knights' focus, industrial, intellectual, and moral probity is the goal. But how well did two Knights authors through their respective protagonists realize such ideas in fiction?

Outside the pages of *Larry Locke,* his most radical production, Whittaker, a veteran dime novelist, was certainly adroit at the Alger plot. But Larry, a craneman in a Pittsburgh steel factory who has been working his way up to the skilled job since youth, is a departure. He embraces, at least theoretically, a labor-democratic philosophy and pride in a workman class. A lengthy and complicated plot involves him in leading a strike, dealing with union-busting owners, being accused of a murder, and monitoring strikes in every way from telling workers not to settle to cautioning them not to destroy property. Does this make him, as Denning and others contend, "a hero of mutualism and solidarity," perhaps American labor fiction's first?[62]

The way Whittaker has chosen to characterize him belies that claim. Though in some ways the plot decenters the superior workman, in others it makes him more central than ever. Whittaker's novel is less strike fiction than the Labors of Hercules in the satirically named Skinner Steel Mill. In the opening chapters, Larry well merits his epithet, "boy of iron." He defeats a much larger bullying apprentice, and significantly, one who resurfaces as a capitalist's long-lost son. Winning the job, miraculously strong and cunning, Larry is a boy with iron in his soul as he comes to manhood. Drawn to the Knights, he quickly moves from district representative to strike fomenter as the morally sordid capitalist owner cuts men's pay—retroactively. Earning his author's approbation as the "shrewdest and boldest of the lot" (171), he holds sway over a strike force that is alternately uncertain and enraged. Even had Whittaker not known of a series of Pittsburgh steel strikes in the early 1880s, this fearful, destructive mass is not too far from the anarchic band John Hay so scorned.

With so volatile a strike band, it is Larry's iron will that must dominate events. In scene after scene, as he exhorts wilting protesters and faces down his scheming employers, he seems less the leader of the strike than the strike itself. In teaching by example, this Knights' John Henry espouses Algerian sentiments. The more militant Larry becomes, even taunting the Skinners, "I don't mind a lock-out, if you don't" (172), the more he speaks to his followers on education and self-improvement, which become his religion. All things to all Knights, he juggles fistfights with management thugs, beatings, and one-man recruitment drives at the steelworks with Franklinesque orations.

In addition to succumbing to the idealization of a labor superman, the problem that Whittaker encountered was one that would dog many imaginers of the American workforce for decades to come, how to realize in novelistic terms the less pacific aspects of laborite philosophy. The vigilant shop committees, the drive toward autonomy rather than simply higher wages on the shop floor, and the campaign for the eight-hour day all find expression when the strike is won, but largely in Larry himself.

Whittaker looks no further for role models than to a dime-novel version of Terence Powderly, the Knights' Grand Master Workman. T. Fulton Gantt moves in the other direction entirely, toward the skilled workmen who constituted the core of the Knights' membership. Harry Wallace of Gantt's *Breaking the Chains* is so much the mouthpiece for an inclusive Knights philosophy, inclusion that is careful to focus on native-born whites, that he has no fictive personality at all. He is interchangeable with the labor leader Jack Nolan, and with unnamed other thirsters after the truth of the order. His grammatical speech, skilled job description (he is a plumber, soon to found one of the more venerable craft unions), and aspiration to enter the civil service may separate him from the many less articulate or literate unskilled workers the Knights sought to recruit.[63]

In the course of many didactic scenes, Maud wonders if there will ever be a labor literature for them (71). Gantt offers a plot that satirizes Hay. Captain Arthur Barnum, now an opium addict who is one of the novel's enthusiastically corrupt business types, tries unsuccessfully to seduce Maud. By novel's end, labor receives justice. In Knights' terms, the cross-trade boycott so favored by the Powderly leadership, though it occurs offstage, has brought the merchants to their knees. Barnum and his vile cohorts are defeated, and—formula as resolution—Harry has a mortgage-free home where the Knights can always meet. Owning but sharing, rising but leaving no one behind him, Harry's mutualism has neatly met his self-improvement.

In his valuable study *The Colloquial Style in America* (1966), Richard Bridgman points to a new turn-of-the-century interest in managing vernacular speech among authors dealing with dialect characters, an effort to catch the rhythms, pauses, and stresses of speech.[64] On the rare and brief occasions when any of the above-mentioned novels quotes labor-class speech, it is in either the patois of the stage Irishman or, a common variant, a fractured combination of Irish-sounding slang and standard English: "We wuz only goin' to hev a bit of fun wi' him, ye know. We wouldn't hurt a hair of his delicate head for the world" (*The Money-Makers*, 275). When the well-spoken Larry wants to rouse steelworkers, he uses a similarly peculiar blend: "I wouldn't like to put sich a good-looking man to so much trouble" (215). Ironically, a novel so concerned with spreading Knights gospel has no vernacular voice at all. In the name of solidarity, Gantt's is the only voice from the assembly platform.

Looking Up by Looking Back:
Gaps in Black Labor Representation

Despite the Knights of Labor's supposed biracial platform (blacks were admitted as members, though not without controversy), their representative—read white—authors were scornful about the "job-stealing" Chinese and silent on the blacks. If they offered no African American Larry Lockes, the omission was not surprising in a time when three-quarters of the black population still sweated in the agricultural South in a system with elements of peonage.[65] Black authors, not surprisingly, omit the Knights and their officially enlightened labor policies and offer minimal representations of black organized labor or the struggle for entry into the trades.

Frederick Douglass, from his 1871 presidency of the National Colored Labor Union to his 1883 support of the Knights of Labor's titular biracialism, obviously considered black access to the labor movement of immense importance.[66] But few labor observers, black or white, fictionists or not, could deny that the battle against postbellum job discrimination was slowing by the 1880s. In 1886, a year before Gantt's novel was serialized, blacks numbered sixty thousand of the Knights' membership in four hundred all-black—that is, segregated—locals.[67] Yet they benefited at most ideologically from the Knights' upper echelon's exhortations to end color discrimination among workingmen. Steel, the stalwart worker-hero Larry Locke's profession, was a case in point. The Amalgamated Association of Iron and Steel Workers in Larry's home city of Pittsburgh, for instance, had paid lip service to black workers as early as 1876.[68] By the end of the decade, despite some tentative efforts toward solidarity with white workers and biracial unionism in that town, the Amalgamated, like the Knights, had done little to help black steelworkers overcome the lily-white policy of the trade unions.[69]

In a parallel development in 1887, the year that Gantt's novel appeared, almost ten thousand striking African American sugar workers on Louisiana plantations refused to settle with employers until they recognized the Knights as their bargaining agent, only to be betrayed by the order. Fearful of white southern fallout, it refused to defend black leaders from imprisonment and lynching.[70]

For black industrial laborers, then, the gains of the early postbellum period, including the manifestos of the short-lived National Colored Labor Union and other black workingmen's associations, seemed minimal. By 1880 in post-Reconstruction Detroit, whose freed black population had a venerable antebellum history, there were still no blacks in industries as diverse as brass and shipbuilding, and a minute twenty-one blacks among over fifty-eight hundred tobacco, stove, iron, and shoe workers.[71] Whether traduced by the only truly national labor organization that admitted them or, like the mass of freedmen, disconnected from organized labor entirely, blacks, particularly those outside the recently slave-training South, formed a minuscule part of the skilled manufacturing workforce on which the Knights and lesser organizations drew.[72] Even by the end of the 1880s, fewer than seventy-five hundred southern blacks worked industrially rather than rurally, and those who did, like Alabama's steel and coal workers, were given the dirtiest, most dead-end jobs.[73]

Booker T. Washington, the linchpin of the Hampton Normal and Industrial Institute, had a horror of strikes.[74] Even the periodical *Southern Workman*, the Hampton organ, tried to ensure that blacks entering the workforce subscribed to an industrial program. The *Workman* thus exhorted character building for the new semiskilled, or artisanally skilled, black workforce; the school focused on training black freedmen in self-sufficient farming, home construction, and the use of agricultural machinery. Absent were the newer technologies that would have moved them into the skilled trades and the labor movement.[75] In a similar vein, the rare black newspapers to address the skilled labor issue, in the 1870s the *National Anti-Slavery Standard*, and in the 1880s, the *Globe*, focused on the fact that blacks could find paid work of any kind.[76]

Subsistence rather than empowering work was clearly not the ideal of the novelist and activist William Wells Brown, who was trying to place slavery within the broad sweep of a racial history that had as recently as Toussaint L'Ouverture bred fierce resistance to colonial rule. He not only revised *Clotel* a fourth time by the end of the Civil War—to acknowledge his heroine's altered circumstances as a slave emancipated—but continued to reclaim an extra-American black past. His postbellum *The Rising Son: The Antecedents and Advancement of the Colored Race* (1874) was both a book-long homage to prominent blacks from pre-Christian times through the present and a semi-fictional account of black workers from the plantation era to mid-Reconstruction. Joining in this retrospective assessment, though restricting it to the slavery and immediate postslavery experience, were the eminent Frederick Douglass, who revised not his antebellum novel but his better-known autobiographical *Narrative* in 1881, and one of the few black novelists of the Reconstruction period, James Howard, the author of the tellingly titled 1886 *Bond and Free*.

Yet representing the race's upward struggle as a mass effort proved problematic. Douglass, his own best racial model, continued to extol and lecture on the self-made man rapidly climbing out of waged labor. But his praise for such a figure alternated with his tacit realization of the discrimination awaiting ill-equipped ex-slaves unable to profit from the Reconstruction or post-Reconstruction rural labor market.[77] Despite his belief in black unionism, Douglass's *Narrative* omits any mention of the difficulties that beset black workers when they were denied access to white workingmen's organizations and work opportunities beyond the menial.[78] On how he, much less his fellow black caulkers, would have fared had he remained in the trade, or in the Reconstruction era Colored Calkers' Trade Society, he is silent. A parallel silence informs his surprisingly nostalgic return to the plantation where he suffered such misery, and where, nearby, he might have seen semislave conditions for bondsmen working the master-turned-employer's land.[79]

Douglass's colleagues were similarly unfocused on labor, industrial or agricultural. Brown's 1867 version of *Clotel* added a passage in closing in which the title character, born in slavery, founds a school for freed blacks in Tennessee. He does not, however, address whether whites would train them, what they would learn, and what work they would find upon graduation. In his novel *Bond and Free,* Joseph Howard, though writing many years later, also returns to the early days of emancipation to underscore that slavery developed life skills for those who survived it. But his freed Virginian, William McCullar, for years an illiterate field slave, is more a variant on than a revision of the antebellum Douglassian Noble Fugitive. Joy at his release overshadows his bewilderment about the kind of new work life.

Hope alternates with ambivalence about what Douglass himself called the possibility that newly freed "colored men" had to be schooled to "serious thought and effort."[80] Determined to extract a serious work type from the ruins of the slavery era, Douglass and his fellow chroniclers offer not the successor to the self-forging Noble Fugitive so much as the progress-report autobiography.[81] Although it is an uplifting approach to racial issues, in limning the "black proletariat," in W.E.B. Du Bois's phrase for Reconstruction workers, representation falters.[82]

In Brown's *My Southern Home* (1880), reprinted a number of times in the early 1880s, the labor dilemmas engendered by this approach are most vivid. Revisiting the work life of the imprisoned 1840s at first provides for strong material. The first part of his book, virtually a slave novel in itself, overlays the tragic slave plotting of *Clotel* with a postbellum awareness of the slave's legal deliverance from slavery. Brown's own narrative persona has an ambiguous status that symbolizes the changed work times. He is an educated black observer or even a white plantation guest rather than a fugitive slave. The tone describing the plantation is also laced with postfreedom anger. The orchard bears substandard fruit, the master is a phony F.F.V. (First Families of Virginia) member, and the mistress is a hypocritical fool.[83] And most important, Brown offers a cast of survivalist slaves, contemptuous enough of their exploitive masters to call them "white trash."[84] There is great emphasis on their power struggles with those in titular command of them, as if they had been sent by the Freedman's Bureau to negotiate labor contracts.

Having stressed the hidden power of the African American slave laborer in part one, however, Brown, with unconscious irony, worries at the self-chaining of the freedman. In a series of transition chapters, Brown laments the persistent superstition of the otherwise canny slave-time black in the Reconstruction era that had recently come to a close. But having retraced the steps taken by black labor from pre–Civil War times to the confusing labor present, his narrative provides no coherent image, semifictional or otherwise, of the new black worker. Instead of a world with the vivid personalities of the book's first section, the narrative presents conflicting ideas of the black labor force. Passages on the new agricultural peonage and descriptions of the onset of Jim Crow transect affectless summations of the racist conviction that blacks are a servant class. There are the predictable sermons on self-reliance and attending night schools that teach trades and a few vague references to the minority of skilled black "mechanics."[85] But whether such men transferred skills they had acquired in slave times or entered trade schools is not clear.[86]

If Brown's workingmen are ambivalent about entering the industrial age, in this they mirror their chronicler. Urging blacks to learn trades, Brown reverses himself and advocates farm work. He praises the black who ascends to a profession, but wonders whether Boston's blacks are not "better fitted for farm service, mechanical branches, and driving an ash cart."[87] Brown's message is redolent of the "Hampton thinking" he affected to reject.

On one level, the inconsistencies in *My Southern Home,* and in the postbellum disavowal of the industrially immobilized black workman, suggest the interest of black ideologues in the more pressing issue of agricultural enfranchisement.[88] Yet the retrospection brought by slavery's end seemed unresponsive to black labor's problems. Neither Brown nor his colleagues could connect with the fragmented black strikes of the day. Nor could they energize a muckraking narrative, fictional or not, with a new labor type. Nor, even well after Reconstruction's "black codes" and other mistreatments of freedmen, could Howard's updated bondsman, the unlettered son of a field hand, be given voice to decry the new second-class status of southern workmen, the labor failures of the Freedman's Bureau, or the rise of Jim Crow. The "progress-report autobiography," absent a period cadre of black labor tales, served as the Gilded Age equivalent of the white labor novel. Yet whether by design or default, the subgenre largely provided enfranchisement polemic. African American economic aspiration was denied both particularity and poignancy by a postbellum narrative that looked backward rather than upward. By so doing, it offered a proletarian—and literary—dead-end.

Vanished or Too Visible:
Work Fictions of Native Americans and Chinese

Blacks were not the only racial minority whose real-life oppression contributed to an accommodationist plotting that, in one form or another, marked the period's labor tales. Scanty, white-authored fiction on Native Americans, most notably Helen Hunt Jackson's *Ramona* (1884), shared both

black texts' retrospection and their difficulty in reconciling racial acculturation with equitable treatment of minority laborers.

Ramona differs, though, from *My Southern Home* or *Bond and Free* in its romanticized vision of her subject's communal, and laboring, past. It is set in
antebellum California at the beginning of the American annexation of Mexican aristocrats' and Native Americans' lands after the Mexican War of 1849.
Jackson chose a retrospective narrative, aware that by the mid-1880s the government was vigorously carrying out a plan to counteract Indians' "wildness"
and other "alien" qualities.[89] *Ramona* is less a historical novel than an allegorical version of Jackson's earlier tract *A Century of Dishonor* (1881). Like Sarah
Winnemuca Hopkins's less ambitious *Life among the Piutes* (1883), it inveighs
against federal double-dealing with a variety of Indian tribes.[90]

On the surface, the novel traces a love affair between a chief's son, Alessandro, and the orphaned title character, who was raised in a hacienda but is
spiritually tied to her lost Indian mother's people. On a deeper level the novel
is not a cross-class, cross-race romance but an indictment. For one thing, it
provides an occasion to contrast Mexican employers' semirespectful treatment of their seasonal Indian farmworkers with the duplicitous behavior of
Euro-Americans profiting from U.S. "Indian policy." For another, through the
inexorable economic disempowerment of the hardworking, Christianized
Alessandro, the novel documents racial prejudice. By contrasting the hacien-
das' treatment of their transient Indian farmworkers, who are free to return
after the harvest to their villages, with the brutal land seizure and racial contempt of the Yankee interlopers, Jackson provides a lament for the dissolution
of Indian cultures. Even the bellicose desperation of Sitting Bull ended pathetically, three years before the Jackson novel, in his surrender to Dakota
authorities.[91]

Above all, Jackson's novel dramatized the first phase of Indian policy, assimilation through menial labor. As would North American tribes like the
Lakota Sioux, the Nez Perce, and the Poncas, Alessandro and his people, the
Temecula Mexicans, plummet from self-supporting migrant workers and
semicommunal landowners to beggars. Forced to work at horse-breaking for a
Yankee employer when once he had owned horses himself, Alessandro, who
has by now wed Ramona, can neither support her and their infant son nor
bear the indignity of his lot. When their son dies because a white doctor will
not treat him, Alessandro sinks to disorientation. He moves in and out of a
self-protective trance anticipating that of the 1890 Wounded Knee Ghost
Dancers and is killed by a sadistic employer "to teach you damned Indians" a
lesson (*Ramona*, 316). With poverty and despair her future as a tribal remnant, Ramona sadly returns to Mexican culture.

Three years after *Ramona* appeared, the Dawes Allotment Act of 1887 enacted a second phase, implementing labor-class versions of Ramona's assimilation. Yet Jackson's novel had well anticipated the evils of what came to be
known as the Vanishing Policy.[92] This was a federal plan to acculturate Native
Americans by inculcating in them an individualist agrarianism and a rudi-
mentary knowledge of agricultural machinery, the idea being to bring an end
to reservations entirely. In charting Alessandro's mental deterioration and

death and Ramona's loss of family and folkways, Jackson offered a vision of dispossession that challenged the very foundation of period thinking on making Indians good workers.

Although Jackson did not allude to them, there were parallels between the government's assimilationist plans for Native Americans and those for post-bellum African Americans.[93] If the mission school system embodied in the 1890s by the Carlisle Indian-Industrial School was not yet in place, Hampton was already experimenting with the education of Indian students. Some were trained as interpreters and teachers. Others were enrolled in low-level agricultural and artisanal programs designed to return them to the reservation, dissolve tribal customs, and eventually abolish the reservation. Even though charges grew in the 1890s that blacks were being trained for a new slavery, the Hampton method of inculcating rural-artisanship and promoting Anglo-Saxon character building was only one of many options available to literate blacks.[94] For the little more than one-quarter of a million Indians left, the thrust to civilize through manual labor schools was central to the larger Vanishing Policy.

As *Ramona* rendered into art, the vanishing Native Americans experienced the abolition of their communal work identity as a slavelike acculturation to the white world. Labor fiction about the all-too-visible Chinese fantasized a far less civilized racial diaspora. As the stereotyped tales of Chinese working-men attested, they were too alien a presence to be viewed outside the fixed labor identities that the culture attached to them. Bret Harte did satirically suggest in his poem "The Heathen Chinee" (1871) that, far from impenetrably heathenish, they were understandably inscrutable in a land of card cheats and uncouth miners.[95] His colleague and fellow miners' storyteller, Joaquin Miller, found even less to praise when he positioned "Washee Washee" the launderer among the grotesques of a California mining camp in *First Fam'lies of the Sierras* (1876). And even that cliché was an improvement on the murderous fantasies of Ambrose Bierce's stories. The latter's "Mortality in the Foothills" (1872) opined that Chinese should join Native Americans in a mass grave.[96]

"Yellow peril" xenophobes were another white authorial subgroup unequal to the task of making sober analyses of the Chinese labor threat. They wrote novels like *Last Days of the Republic* (1880), in which a monolithic mass with a common ambition overruns the labor market and, eventually, the nation itself.[97] Labor papers such as John Swinton's quasi-radical publication constantly accused Chinese workers of a group-think racial infiltration into the railway, mining, and cigar and shoe manufacturing sectors, considered the province of whites.[98] Outside the editorial pages, such sentiments erupted in the San Francisco anti-Chinese riots, a by-product of the Railway Strike of 1877, which symbolized a hatred on the part of white labor that affected even the inclusive Knights of Labor. T. Fulton Gantt himself put the imprimatur on a portrait of an opium-dealing Chinese servant in *Breaking the Chains*. Even selling drugs to his plutocratic master, thereby destroying him, earns him no labor praise. Gantt's vitriolic portrait of Li Hung injected a powerfully divisive tone into the otherwise pacific labor vision that the Knights novel preaches.

With the majority of Chinese workers herded into the dangers of scabbing or self-chained in sweltering hand laundries, their numbers increased until, in large part owing to labor movement agitation, the passage of the Chinese Exclusion Act of 1882. Barely had American fiction, in service to the labor movement, linked these workers to the ideology of sinister rising than Asian racial workplace otherness, squelched by the act, abruptly ceased to arouse the passions of literary imaginers.

Looking at as Looking through: Work Fiction before the Gilded Age

In the 1870s and 1880s, literary portraitists of various political stripes filtered the white labor history of their time through the lens of workerist cooperation combined with enlightened trusteeship. Literary socialism was still quite adulterated. It was no match, in fact, for the conservatives who responded to charges of destructive capitalist practices with a fierce rhetoric of agitational foreigners and labor minimization. Such authors constricted everything, from the character of the protest leaders to the varied, and occasionally biracial, nature of labor unrest, to the degree of protesters' triumphs. Hay and his colleagues moved beyond blaming the victim to a philosophy of humble compliance as atonement for conduct at once dangerous and childish. Faced with the danger that group man would not separate from his fellows, the status quo labor novel looked through him.

While the counterculture strike novel in its mature form had yet to be born, the rather mild and pacific semisocialist productions of the anti-Hay school, including Knights' fiction and novels of utopian experiments, offered not atonement but truce. In this interim time for labor fiction, Gilded Age novels air crucial labor issues. Their divergent political philosophies apart, however, all of these attempts to depict white and thus assimilable workers rest on trading the upward bound, eccentric proletarian or moribund worker of antebellum fare for the tractable breadwinner, a white, native-born, Protestant master workman who leads by example. The type bore little resemblance to the German, Irish, and British workers in the mines and the iron and steel mills toiling seven twelve-hour days a week. Furthermore, there is virtually no description of the rigors of heavy industrial work, described by one Homestead worker as the closest thing to hell.[99]

Most important, though, the novels discussed in this chapter, despite strong differences about profit-sharing allocation, were not ready to muster a strong rebuttal to American exceptionalism. Rising is unchallenged as an ideal; those who cannot achieve it must still be at fault. Even fledgling delineations of worker culture other than the mechanics' institute model of self-education—would have to await the attentions of 1890s authors.

For labor's racial others, retrospection was meant to provide clarity about their ongoing disenfranchisement. But authors of black fiction and narrative with fictive elements touching on labor themes, both scarce enough, seemed uninvolved in giving a social protest novel form to these new problems. They offered odes to the self-made theme that privileged racial role models but outlined a vague moral self-reform for an illiterate black proletariat. Thus the Brownian exhortations for field hands to rise above their circumstances adulterated by regret for their sorry state or bolstered by portraits of Great Men whose labor-class days are well behind them.

The literary posture of self-madeism was not available to novelists and storytellers of the Native Americans or Chinese, whose economic ascension was neither predicted nor culturally desired by their white imaginers.[100] Representations of Chinese workers, labor's most hated scabs, range from the vitriolic to the occasional attempts to redress the balance, but Gantt's Li Hung, Harte's Ah Sin, and others are such paper Chinamen that they seem more like mouthpieces for labor's ire than literary explorations of the Chinese laboring experience.

In sum, before a more probing representation of all laborers could inform American labor literature, much in the relationship between the "working stiff" and the ascension myth still had to be worked out, particularly the implicit idea that it was un-American to picture hellish labor. And if, as the revisionist labor history *Who Built America?* (1989) contends, "working people survived the rigors of urban-industrial life by relying on group identity as much as on individual effort and initiative," still missing were the novels and tales of that survival. In all of the above texts, there is no sense that white workers' history includes more than compliance or solidarity during a labor-management dispute. Moreover, neither white fiction nor the labor history of racial minorities had yet acknowledged that to understand the workers we must study the workers—their own institutions and beliefs, not the projections of authors removed by birth and predilection from proletarian life.

CHAPTER 3

Labor's Ladies
Work Fiction and True Women from Antebellum Lowell through the Gilded Age

It is good for every girl, rich or poor, to spend a year in a mill.

—DAY KELLOGG LEE, *MERRIMACK; OR, LIFE AT THE LOOM* (1854)

Women with peculiar bleached yellow faces passed by. . . . They looked like beautiful moving corpses. . . . Miss Kelso had noticed them since she first came [to visit her textile mill].

—ELIZABETH STUART PHELPS, *THE SILENT PARTNER* (1871)

She learned that in some towns in Massachusetts, girls make straw bonnets—that it was easy and profitable. But how could *she*, black, feeble and poor, find any one to teach her?

—HARRIET WILSON, *OUR NIG; OR, SKETCHES FROM THE LIFE OF A FREE BLACK* (1859)

Song of the Shirt, cover, *Every Saturday,* October 29, 1870. Collection of The New-York Historical Society.

Until the "discovery" of the working poor in the 1890s, American fiction haltingly reflected, determinedly sanitized, angrily negated, or selectively reconstructed workers' struggles for economic inclusion. Yet in these stories of white male toil, however divergent in other ways, working-class characters were recognized by lifetime effort, subsistence if not ample wages, and the inexorability of their breadwinning role. "Women's work" evoked the unmanly, menial, domestic task, the transient's or intruder's status, and the family, pin money, or otherwise substandard wage.[1] Texts about and usually by black men, cognizant of the slave woman's bonded labor and forced-sex roles, joined most black women's ante- and postbellum accounts in work distinctions based more on race than on gender. But such important differences notwithstanding, African American male authors shared their white colleagues' vision of women toilers.

By the early decades of the nineteenth century, native-born white women formed a significant portion of the workforce in textile New England, with Lowell, Massachusetts, the jewel in the region's manufacturing crown.[2] Moreover, well before the Civil War, a female seamstress and laundress workforce was a fixture of shoe factories in New England, collar manufacturers of New York State, and the piecework clothing trade in New York City. These women's hopes were evident in organizations like the Ladies' Shoebinders, the United Seamstress Society, and the New York Working Women's Labor Union.[3] By the 1880s and 1890s, Italian immigrants from southern Europe and Jewish ones from eastern Europe began to infuse a limited women's labor movement with the stirrings of the next century's garment-trades socialism. Until the turn of the century, however, female radicalism was more likely to be the province of well-off intellectuals defending women's rights, from the antebellum Fanny Wright to the 1870s suffragist publishers of the journal *Revolution* or the anarchist-spiritualists of *Woodhull and Claflin's Weekly*. With fewer resources than men to build unions, a minority of nonsocialist laboring women, whether native-born Protestants or Catholic emigrants, preferred to balance family-wage goals with sporadic work stoppages in the large industrial cities and company-town mill villages.[4]

Freeborn African American women, as Frederick Douglass was quick to point out, neither reaped such rewards nor engaged in such job actions, whether at Lowell or the other female factory venues often connected to the sewing trades.[5] By midcentury there were still no black women employed in northern factories, and none admitted to trade unions. They were not even counted in the census as workers, a tacit assumption that their lot in some way mirrored that of their enslaved southern sisters.[6] In the wake of the Civil War, African American women's wage earning was still largely restricted to southern field work, the region's segregated tobaccories, or to metropolitan domestic servitude in the South or North.[7] Too, these bottom-rung workers were three times as likely to be wage earners as white women toilers.[8] Particularly in the cities of the South, the region where most blacks still lived, more than half of all adult black females were gainfully—read menially—employed at least part of the year around the turn of the century. Moreover, these women were far more likely than their white counterparts to remain workers

after marriage.[9] Still, black women, particularly those in servants' jobs demanding seamstress skills, had a bond of oppression with the sweated white clothing-trades women of the Northeast. Though rarely viewing themselves as sister toilers, these women all formed a cheap labor pool for whom the ideology of survival replaced sisterly militance or Franklinesque individualism.

Not all was survivalist acquiescence in workplace exploitation. The new social historians question the traditional vision of wage-earning women, whether contributors to the family wage or self-supporters, as either removed from labor militancy or mere auxiliaries to activist men.[10] Punctuating the early to midcentury were quasi-feminist white women's protests, even in smooth-running, paternalistic Lowell. Labor sparks flew, thanks to the Daughters of St. Crispin, in Massachusetts among skilled shoe factory workers at Lynn agitating before and after the Civil War and among Lawrence's textile women as early as 1860 and as late as 1886; and among carpet weavers in Philadelphia in the early 1880s.[11] In late 1880s Chicago the Illinois Women's Alliance, a socialist-feminist workingwomen's group rare for its time, helped mobilize against sweatshops and for factory inspections.[12] Black women were more isolated when initiating gendered protest, particularly given the southern caste system. Yet they benefited somewhat from Knights of Labor recruiting drives, at least in selected venues, and they initiated their own protests, as striking laundresses in Jackson, Mississippi, in 1866; and in Galveston, Texas, in 1877.[13] By 1881 the washerwomen of Gilded Age Atlanta were exhibiting the activism of seasoned protesters, even if, without a place in a local or national labor movement, they were no match for the legal maneuvers of the white city fathers.[14]

Women's labor activism, white or black, also informed the men's strikes of the early labor movement. Before the Civil War, members of the Lowell Female Labor Reform Association, including Lowell's fiery Sarah Bagley, supported the Ten-Hour Movement, and, both before, during, and after the war, they endorsed the Eight-Hour Movement and had ties to the New England Workingman's Association.[15] Troy, New York, women struck in sympathy with the iron moulders' strikes and were, in a rare labor development, aided by them in the 1860s and 1880s.[16] Midwestern women participated as workers and workers' wives in the Great Upheaval's 1877 events; became (Lady) Knights of Labor, sixty-five thousand strong by the late 1880s; and, unfortunately, shared the racism and sinophobia of their laboring brothers throughout the century and well into the next.[17] Black women seeking cross-gender solidarity could occasionally find it by joining Reconstruction's other landless laborers, their black male coworkers. Their fervent, ineffective job actions were expressions of a common anger at long hours and poor pay in South Carolina and Georgia.[18]

Such female agricultural militance, bi-gender or otherwise, was predictably rare. Thus black women were simply paid less for the same field work or, like child laborers, restricted to nonrural lower-skilled work.[19] If anything, the sexual division of labor that had characterized the black family during slavery became even more sharply focused in the mass of African American field-working families after its decline. Whether women sharecropped alongside male relatives or not, husbands reinforced gender divisions in two crucial ways. Like white workingmen, they controlled the slim monetary rewards of their women's labor. And even outside rural areas, where their women secured work and they could not, there were chores to be done after the wage-earning workday.

While the response of organized labor to the sexual division of paid work was not always consistent, in the main, "the pressure to keep women out of certain jobs was [perceived by union men as] the only way to keep their own."[20] Thus labor's allegiance to egalitarianism "was at odds with the prevailing notions of domesticity and women's sphere."[21] Whether a convenient defensive strategy or a heartfelt belief, or both, the widespread labor movement maxim was that good women did not work.[22]

The white workingwoman was subject to the same patriarchal ideology that informed antebellum artisan culture and its factory-floor successors. She could appear as the impoverished title character of a seamstress narrative, the grimy mill-girl interlocutor of a mill-owning heiress, a well-born daughter reduced temporarily to paid work, or the object of an elitist devaluation of working folk. In such fiction, as in the wider culture, the spectacle of a (not yet immigrant-dominated) female proletariat generated questions about womanliness. To the answers ambiguously provided by the first schools of fiction to essay portraits of blue-collar women, we now turn.[23]

"Nobler Womanhood": Morality as Vocation in Lowell Fiction

The lineaments of antebellum women's work fiction can be discerned in preindustrial novels of sentiment such as Susanna Rowson's best-selling *Charlotte Temple* (1791) and Martha Read's *Monima, the Beggar Girl* (1802).[24] Though not daughters of the people, the native-born, white title characters of these metropolitan fictions are the first in a long line of women to stare poverty in the face.[25] Their successors are the heroines of works like Ariel Ivers Cummings's *The Factory Girl; or, Gardez La* [sic] *Coeur* (freely translated, *Watch Whom You Love*) (1847)—"O Factory Girl. Virtue shall enable you to win the prize."[26] By retaining their virtue, the imaginary mill girls of the 1840s and 1850s find marital rescue from their loom exertions or, the family mortgage paid off, an early retirement to the New England homestead. The Lowell girls' more exploited sisters were the starving operatives and pale-faced seamstresses of tales such as *The Seamstress* (1843), penned by the temperance zealot T. S. Arthur, a fiction popular enough to be reissued in the 1850s. Both keep their vow to remain virgins in a climate where "lust [was] a better paymaster than the mill-owner or the tailor."[27]

In addition to retaining the old Virtue Imperiled plot, the new working-girl fictions of the 1840s and 1850s also belonged to the "melodramas of beset womanhood" representative of so much of the period's domestic fiction.[28] (Even Fanny Fern's famously successful 1855 *Ruth Hall,* in which a widowed mother climbs from piecework seamstress to noted journalist, is a tribute to the adaptable heroine's ability to support her children.) The new novels of workplace womanhood tried to reconcile what a protagonist in Day Kellogg Lee's *Merrimack; or, Life at the Loom* (1854) called the "nobler womanhood I resolved to attain" with "the toils and trials of factory life" (32). The new tales located women in technological or urban-sweatshop settings rather than in the early nineteenth-century outworker's home. More important, they joined the lively period debate on the moral appropriateness of women's nondomestic paid work.

In the beginning Lowell, extolled by so much period fiction, seemed to answer these questions. By 1840 it was the nation's largest textile manufacturing center, the site of ten textile corporations with thirty-two mills and eight thousand largely female factory operatives. The city initially drew a workforce of farmers' daughters with the "home training" that sixty years later, the naturalist author Theodore Dreiser would lament, the Sister Carries of the cities sadly lacked.[29]

Features of Lowell so reordered the factory experience that the term "factory lady" seemed an 1840s possibility. The economic benefits to manufacturers helped bolster the idea. For the factory system, by "substitut[ing] the temporary and carefully supervised work force of New England farm 'girls' for that of a permanent proletariat," could, it was thought, ensure a tractable workforce.[30] Lowell inculcated an industrial work ethic in this population of girls that could be framed as enhancing, not undermining, their womanhood. Thus it offered a management alternative to the more militant philosophy of the Factory Girls' Association, the Lowell Female Industrial Reform Society, and like-minded, if short-lived, organizations of the 1840s. To complete the metaphor of the industrial family, some visitors to Lowell imposed the cult of domesticity on the factory.[31] In these influential accounts, women tending their looms were perceived as extending homelike nurturing to the factory floor. But as early as that decade, Lowell's profactory defenders had invoked the trope of the Happy Mill Girl: in harmony with her environment, cultivating her feminine virtues as she tended her spinning jenny.[32]

Such formulations, of course, often ran up against the improbability of gentrified factory work. New England manufacturers required women who applied for factory work at Lowell to sign a "regulation paper" and promise moral conduct, church attendance, and residence in a corporation boardinghouse.[33] But the very web of rules was the corporate response to fears about and complaints among the industrializing female workforce. Though a fledgling insurgency, by 1840 the labor movement in Massachusetts had come of age, with women workers in the Lowell mills at its heart.

Literary defenses of Lowell swept past these admittedly limited women's struggles for control of the work floor and updated the preindustrial *Charlotte Temple* novel. The spindle room was mentioned only as a backdrop. And its morally superior heroine who, though she contributes to the millworkers' journal the *Lowell Offering*, embraces not the operative's wage or potential for self-reliance but the self-sacrifice requisite in period heroines, whatever their social class. In *The Factory Girl,* written by a New England physician, Ariel Ivers Cummings, the Lowell factoryscape—an increasingly immigrant one— is thus recast for its novel-of-sensibility heroine, Calliste.[34] The name disguises the Vermont girl's middling rural origins, as does the novel's florid, archaic style. "The personal charms of Calliste," the reader learns, "would have graced the palace of nobility" (42).

Entangled in the formulaic framework—the novel ends, predictably, with an upscale marriage for its heroine—is a management-allied defense of woman's work. *The Factory Girl* contends that industrial surroundings have no effect on the superior individual, whose real labor is to perfect her character through a feminized combination of the work and sacrifice ethics.

Even on the pulp literature level, defending the Lowell woman meant recasting her worker days as a prologue to domesticity. Three years before *The Factory Girl,* the Gothic sensationalizer Osgood Bradbury, the author of numerous anti-urban diatribes about the "mysteries of the city," reversed his profitable literary exploitation of the theme of "female depravity" (the title of his 1857 novel) to demonstrate that the opposite was true in Lowell. In a familiar literary assertion of what constituted nobility for worker characters, Bradbury unveils the "humble, although honest and respectable" mill girl as one born to the better classes and thus a marriageable prospect for a wealthy husband (Bradbury, *Mysteries of Lowell,* 8).

Popular male writers, from middlebrow to dime novelists, made a lady out of the factory girl, dismissed the breadwinning hoydens who were not genteel exemplars, and moved virtuous women's aspirations from the workplace to the marital arena. The worker-writer contributors to the *Lowell Offering* provided alternative perspectives. The journal was their own literary product, though published under the stern eye of the corporations that owned the various Lowell mills. Billed as a "Repository of Original Articles, Written Exclusively by Females Actively Employed in the Mills," it was variously lauded by advocates of factory women's gentility and criticized by the "radicals" of the Ten-Hour Movement.[35] Chief among the detractors was a former contributor, Sarah Bagley, who contended that the essays and fiction merely disseminated official truths to garner the patronage of the Boston merchants who subsidized the magazine.[36]

The title character of the anonymously authored 1841 "Susan Miller," appearing in the *Lowell Offering,* is, on the surface, a testament to the moral orthodoxies surrounding virtuous Lowell workers. Lowell provides a way to act out her "noble and cherished purpose" (181), pay her father's creditors, and return to her home role. After the typical four years at Lowell, she has won the "success of her noble exertions, the affection and gratitude of her relatives, the esteem of her acquaintances, and the approbation of conscience"

(181). Back home, where she had resolved to return, she "now always thinks of Lowell with pleasure" (182) but with no further ambitions to work in the wage-earning world.

A closer reading of "Susan Miller" uncovers a subtext in which the mill-girl experience is a lesson in the underside of duty. Mill work is a decision born only of disappointment. She had first looked to a profitable marriage to a suitor she loved and had counted on to solve her late father's financial difficulties, but he spurns her. The unpleasantness of her plight is further heightened by her former lover's father, the deacon, who, in a plot twist, is her late father's creditor. Another rejecting paternal figure, he expects swift repayment but warns Susan against going to Lowell to earn money to pay him off. Some of the deacon's warnings about Lowell—for instance, that she will be "boxed up fourteen hours a day, among a parcel of clattering looms, or whirling spindles, whose constant din is of itself enough to drive a girl out of her wits" (176)—prove correct. The work is very tiring and hard, and though Susan may find a kind of comfort in self-abnegation, she also finds a "life of toil and privation" (180) in a factory boardinghouse with no privacy: the underside of duty. Finally, success on the homefront brings no wedlock: her jilting suitor marries a woman who has not had to spin for a living. Far from returning to reap the domestic rewards of work well done, Susan "think[s] she will be an old maid" (182), posing questions about whether financial self-subordination for family rightly replaces personal ambition.

"Tales of Factory Life, No. 1," by the future firebrand Sarah Bagley, was another sketch appearing in the *Offering* in 1841. As if heralding what would lead her to repudiate the *Offering* altogether, it is a tribute to the womanliness of paid work. Unlike her creator, this namesake protagonist is socially inferior, a fatherless, barefoot servant girl fleeing a harsh and physically abusive employer. Whereas Susan Miller's Lowell decision was made by default, Sarah is eager to earn a relatively higher wage. In the years to come, and with wages falling, Bagley, a cornerstone of the Lowell Female Labor Reform Association and an ardent supporter of the Ten-Hour Movement, would revise her "Tales" vision. But this early vignette applauds Sarah T.'s vision of spindle toil as she reflects, "I shall be paid for what I do now" *(Lowell Offering,* 69).

To still controversy, the narrative voice reminds the reader that Sarah's proclamation reveals that she has learned usefulness. If such plot devices deflect attention from Sarah's Bagleyesque consciousness of herself as a woman and worker, at story's end she has her savings in a (company?) bank. At a time well before even middle-class women could sign a check or retain their own property, this is a significant achievement.

This last WASP labor force in America, idealized in *The Factory Girl* and *Merrimack,* romanticized in *The Mysteries of Lowell,* variously experiencing signs of alienation or gesturing toward individualism in the *Lowell Offering,* changed in the next decades.[37] By the mid-1850s, the Susans and Sarahs, whether they left for health reasons or wedlock, out of protest or to take less proletarian jobs elsewhere, were replaced by an Irish immigrant labor force, many of whose members, working for their families' subsistence, had neither the energy, time, nor education to produce fictive autobiography.[38] Wage cuts and speedups were entrenched; and militant discontent, however minoritarian, had marked labor relations there for decades.[39] Lowell had seen its best days as that improbable entity, an industrial finishing school.

Whether he understood the rebellious subtexts hidden in the *Lowell Offering* or was alarmed by women's interaction with mass industry, Herman Melville was perhaps the only fiction writer of stature to satirize Lowell. "The Paradise of Bachelors and the Tartarus of Maids" (1855) is correctly perceived as a rebuttal to Lowell's factory-lady iconography. Melville cleverly threw back in the literary propagandists' faces the very images they anachronistically continued to ply. Yet he too exhibited the very fears about workplace waywardness that the Lowell girl was supposed to allay.

Industrial womanhood, wayward or otherwise, is deliberately absent from the story's opening. The introductory section is set in the pampered world of London lawyers and their bachelor dinners. It thus contrasts with the unhappier—and more ominous—gendered world of the tale itself. Moving thus from contented to forced "bachelorhood," Melville attacks the Lowell novel's contented female industrial celibacy. The factory he creates, where only "maidens" can be hired, so far from an extension of woman's proper sphere, is a "large whited building . . . like some great whited sepulchre."[40] A grotesque inversion of the woman-staffed New England mill, it is a venue where pristine paper, a symbol superior to the unruliness of threaded cloth, superficially stands for the vaunted order and cleanliness of the enlightened work floor. The Melvillian mill is thus a twinned nightmare of industrial over-efficiency and working-class exploitation.[41] Melville's implicit excoriation of Lowell's claims to protect its operatives while nurturing their womanliness was part of a growing social perception of factory dehumanization for men and women. The story's added insistence on the operatives' nunlike asexuality as well as their maternal machine-tending isolates them as gendered workers faced with the choice of wage earning (displaced womanliness) or true mothering (real womanliness). Yet the paradoxical yoking of workplace celibacy and mothering forms more than an allegory of feminine exploitation.

Taken together, the images indicate that the feminine dedication to the machine has become more than self-destructive; the very procreative powers of these women are being perverted. Wage-earning women's reproductive dangers preoccupied not only literary moralists but industrial physicians and opponents of women's work, their views emblematized in C. W. Webber's tellingly titled *Spiritual Vampirism* (1853).[42] From this cautionary perspective, Melville's women, "blank looking . . . blankly folding blank paper" ("Paradise," 220), are empty vessels.

Melville's key description is of girls strapped into a machine with a scythe-like blade that shreds rags mixed with water from the Red River and delivers blank paper after a few minutes. It merits the extended sexual metaphor, comments Michael Rogin, of "crotch, phallus, 'germinous particles' of semen, vagina dentata, umbilical cord, and birth."[43] In fact, the mill girls' redirected sexuality, more than solely painful or symbolically linked with a kind of monstrous birth, bears out the fears at the heart of the Lowell system itself. But if these young-old women are barren, it is because they are "in the grip of a sexualized, mechanical power."[44]

Far less obliquely than Melville, midcentury French social scientists and physicians surveying the morality of the female working classes found the woman-staffed European work floor a sexual hothouse. They claimed that everything from the forced monotony to the confinement in crowded and often overheated rooms contributed to "a state of sexual excitement." On one level, such commentators viewed, or fantasized, textile and sewing tradeswomen as lesbians, an observation they also made of prostitutes. On another, they saw these women as indiscriminate sexual agents.[45]

In early Victorian America, these theories were not fully articulated. American medical practitioners joined their Continental colleagues, however, in the conviction that women, though innately chaste, once aroused were carnally uncontrollable. As Mary Poovey has remarked of the allied British "discourse of prostitution," such one-false-step thinking "incited fears that every woman" might be a prostitute at heart.[46] The growth of the factory only fed such anxieties. Thus the New York City physician William Sanger, the noted midcentury interviewer of prostitutes, was distressed that so many of his subjects, including former factory girls, cited "inclination" as the reason for leaving respectable work. He deplored the jobsite ennui and, in an unwitting allusion to single-sex relations, the "insidious influence [of corrupt women] in every factory throughout the country," an influence, he posited, that helped propel unwary women to commercialized sex.[47]

Melville's sisterhood of the technologically damned offered a countervision of laboring womanhood that subtly played on period associations between factory work and prostitution. His tale was the culmination of a tradition of factory-girl literature extolling the patient endurance of the woman toiler.[48] Through these opportunities Melville articulated the fear of feminine sexual waywardness at the heart of American's Patient Griselda literature. Instead of its nun, from the Lowell onward, the woman breadwinner risked becoming industry's harlot.

Sewing, Not Sinning: Seamstress Fiction before the Civil War

Another major group of native-born women wage earners gained fictional attention in the antebellum era, one far more likely than the female Lowellians to suffer the exploitation Melville warned against. While the last of the New England Protestant Lowell girls saved their earnings for a brother's education or their own impending marriages, twice as many urban seamstresses were, reported the *New York Daily Tribune*, seeking "fair employment for wages."[49] Whether the widows of artisans or seamen or single females with dressmaking skills, they evoked the sympathy offered to respectable white women forced to make their way in the world. In 1845, as the early muckraking journalist Horace Greeley lamented, "their frames are bent by increasing and stooping toil, their health destroyed."[50]

In contrast to Melville's vision of Lowell, however, the seamstress's physio-

logically taxing work did not inevitably mean moral debility. Fifty years before Jacob Riis concluded that the sewing girl was in the main virtuous, writers applied to these sweated heroines a special rhetoric of gentility. The
historian Christine Stansell's provocative discussion of New York City's factory girls and seamstresses highlights the alleged sexuality of the former
group. The antidomestic factory girl contrasted with the seamstress, the
"'true' woman of the bourgeoisie."[51] While Melville's colleague Nathaniel
Hawthorne touched on a similar theme in his portrait of the childlike Priscilla
in *The Blithedale Romance* (1852) and, in more allegorical ways, the pilloried
Hester Prynne of *The Scarlet Letter* (1850), most period authors retold the Lowell story of nobler womanhood in an urban milieu. As early as 1840 Harriet
Beecher Stowe polished the myth. Her sketch "The Seamstress" pictures a
"delicately reared" young woman at home with her mother. The dyad is surrounded by "memorials of former times" and genteelly engaged in sewing
work.[52]

It was the rare period author who created a clothing-trades heroine who
supported herself, was not enmeshed in or impoverished by family duty, and
conducted relations with men that were lively without being sinful. In journalistic and theatrical treatments, such a girl was Lize. The girlfriend of the
Lower East Side's colorful workingman/gadabout Mose, she was the Bowery
g'hal to his Bowery b'hoy. George Foster, who briefly envisioned her in her
work and after-hours milieus in his semifictional "Mose" vignettes in *New
York in Slices* (1849) and *New York by Gas-Light* (1849), lamented that neither
Mose nor Lize was accorded literary respect. Yet Mose was a fixture in the era's
subliterary fare; it was Lize who received short shrift.

Foster's short sketch reveals why. The Lize whom he describes, variously a
capmaker, semiskilled printer, and bookbinder, rejects the ideology of True
Womanhood. Neither a Franklinesque figure nor a militant one, she lives
out a third alternative to the reductive (and management-fueled) vision of
Lowell's docile moral exemplars. "As independent in her tastes and habits as
Mose himself," she is "perfectly willing to work for a living," writes Foster, but
"never feels herself at home but at the theater or the dance" (*New York by Gas-
Light*, 175). She is given to clothing that, in a challenge to period censure of
finery-loving workingwomen, ensures her an "exhilarating appearance"
(176). High-spirited, garrulous, slangy, but respectable, she works hard by day
and explores what Christine Stansell calls the social "possibilities of working-
class life" by night.[53] Compared with the patient, scrimping mill and sewing
girls of other fictions, Lize has already realized her greatest ambition: to be
her own person.

She thus handily bypasses the era's literary categories for female wage earners. Though without family moorings, neither at the worksite nor in the
dance hall is she a body at risk. She pragmatically views her job as a necessity,
though a monotonous one, a sentiment that generations of blue-collar
women would share with her. Nor, in another realistic touch, does her socializing with Mose automatically expose her to the perils of seduction. She represents the young pleasure-seeking workingwomen of the antebellum Bowery
"who understood themselves in social and aesthetic terms" but whose Bower-

iness did not extend to part- or full-time sexual favors for money.[54] Yet if by her brand of Jacksonian self-reliance Lize repudiated the anxieties raised by self-supporting or subsistence-earning workingwomen, she did not tranquilize them. Capmaking, one of the chief occupations with which Foster associates her, was often linked to promiscuity in period literature. A few years before Foster wrote, the *New York Tribune* had wondered why all women pursuing starvation sewing work did not become "degraded and brutalized in taste, manners, habits, and conversation."[55] Conversely, bookbinding and printing, other trades Lize was said to ply, drew women from a better class and commanded good pay: the same woman could not have gained entry to such divergent professions. Moreover, Lize, for all her self-assertion, is out of step with her time. The woman in any job, skilled or menial, able to live on her earnings in a time of plummeting wages was a vestige of the 1820s and 1830s, when a tiny minority of women artisans were fairly well paid.[56] Finally, compounding his confusion about workingwomen's occupations, Foster chooses not to locate Lize in a credible workplace identity or future. He cannot imagine her five or ten years later at a toilsome job, subject to wage fluctuations and mass firings, much less spearheading the militant New York City women typesetters of 1855.[57] Just how working class was this woman anyway?

The question of the workingwoman's proletarianism would continue to vex the next generation of industrial authors. But given the status and vocational contradictions in the Lize portraiture, it is not surprising she had little part in the new labor fiction of Davis, Phelps, and Alcott.

Where Is the True Woman?:
Women's Labor Fiction during and after the Civil War

"The Civil War," explains the labor historian Alice Kessler-Harris, "provided the background against which [white, native-born] wage-earning women began to reevaluate their condition."[58] Hardly before the war had drawn to an end, even a nostalgic mill novelist like Charlotte Hilbourne in *Effie and I* (1863) was repudiating the Lowell school's standard denouements by sending her heroine back to that venue from a bad marriage. Late 1860s seamstress fiction also withdrew the marital rewards of a workplace apprenticeship: Wirt Sikes, in *One Poor Girl: The Story of Thousands* (1869), chronicled a genteel but supposedly typical sewing woman who neither was guaranteed nor benefited from an eleventh-hour rescue. Yet Sikes's popular potboiler, like his subtitle, was more sensational than documentary.

It fell to a new group of women authors, sympathetic to the female workforce, to portray the woman born to labor or thrust into a permanent life of subsistence pay. Refusing to cosmeticize waged work or load it with grand claims for character building (or, in its seamstress variant, martyrdom), Rebecca Harding Davis, Elizabeth Stuart Phelps, and, to a lesser degree, Louisa May Alcott were the first serious novelists to explore how industrial wage earning deformed rather than elevated the feminine character.

Davis and Phelps in particular treated the physical and psychic toll of factory work on women, a theme that, apart from covert *Lowell Offering* plaints and formulaic vignettes of emaciated sewing girls, had been largely absent from women's labor fiction. Davis's "Life in the Iron Mills" (1861) and Phelps's *The Silent Partner* (1871) replaced the Lowell school's factory ladies with victims of moral and physical debility; Alcott depicted a seamstress turned streetwalker to drive a similar point home. Yet these authors also repudiated Melville's vision of debased, sexualized wage slaves. Advocates of cross-class sisterhood, the trio were not outright foes of capitalism. They sought to join traditional Christian values and woman's "innate" selflessness rather than advance a solution to feminine industrial suffering. Sooner or later, they believed, women's efforts to build a more just society would ameliorate the unfair work conditions that weighed on workingwomen with families to care for. These early social protest authors were reluctant to implement radical change, however, and lacked a clear definition of working-class self-activity. For them too the myth of True Womanhood on the work floor would die hard.

The industrial stories of Rebecca Harding Davis, the daughter of a businessman–city official, were the unlikely product of a woman bred to cosseted womanhood. To research the working classes, she apparently toured the foundry and textile mills of Wheeling, the West Virginia town where she was raised and where her most enduring tale, "Life in the Iron Mills," is set.[59] In the years before she wrote the lengthy story, despite such unorthodox sorties, Davis conformed outwardly to the precepts of mid-Victorian womanhood, returning from a seminary to help care for her siblings. Yet as a woman of letters, she was preoccupied by what the era reduced to the term "the Woman Question."[60]

Her novel *Margret Howth* (1862), which contains descriptions of mill women's sufferings and a portrait of an enfeebled mulatta mill child turned peddler, centers on a gentrified bookkeeper who eventually weds her employer. "Life in the Iron Mills" reworks Davis's struggles with the problems of thwarted vocation, feminine longing, and the alienation of an immigrant (and in an allusion to a textile mill, an interracial) industrial proletariat.[61] The story centers on two tormented laboring figures. One is a the near-hunchbacked textile mill picker, the pathetic Deborah, who lives to serve her emotionally elusive cousin, Hugh Wolfe. Symbolic of her deprived life, she is not even given a last name. The other is Wolfe himself, a Jude the Obscure precursor, brooding, self-involved, alienated. He endures his furnace-tending by day only to remain at the foundry and fashion from its refuse statues of elemental working-class women by night. Responding unconsciously to women's work sufferings through art in a way he cannot in life, Wolfe sculpts a "Korl woman." Spiritually starved but physically powerful, she is his cousin Deborah transformed.[62]

Given the uncertain position of the woman artist in mid-Victorian America, it is not surprising that Davis published the tale anonymously in the *Atlantic Monthly* and chose an unnamed male narrator from her own class to legitimize her tale. He projects her frustrations onto both a male protagonist, reduced to an amateur artist status, and an obsessively devoted female one, unappreciated by her family and society.[63] Davis's is not only a dual projection of resentments at her own domestic and artistic oppression but also an ambitious bi-gender proletarian narrative. The story first traces a working-woman's steps from her mill—as her female coworkers, much like their menfolk, troop off to a saloon—to her tenement and then to her male relative's foundry worksite. It is a transit in which men's and women's worlds both intersect and diverge. For its detailed heavy-industrial setting, the story gained a good deal of notice in its time as an exposé of mass production and is still often characterized as a muckraking novel of heavy industry.[64] Nevertheless, the authorial decision to use dual protagonists highlights even more greatly the sexual division of industrial labor, the social relations between workingmen and workingwomen that it produced, and the very nature of the female work character.

Davis opens with trenchant descriptions of "the flames and poisonous stench of the iron works, [in which] bodies crack and lives drain away in the service of the new industrial order."[65] She envisions "a [hellish] manufacturing town known by the vast machinery of a system by which the bodies of workmen are governed . . . unceasingly from year to year."[66] Nor did Davis, who had considered entitling the work "The Korl Woman," mean "workmen" to be gender specific.[67] Both sexes inhabit the iron mills after the workday is over by snatching needed rest near the work floor itself. Davis, confronting the problems of representation that would inform worker narratives for a century and a half, attempts to balance the theme of gendered labor-class oppression with that of sexual subordination. Deborah is also more of a victim than Hugh, a victimization that Davis presents as representative. Deborah's textile factory tasks are not described, in part because, like many workingwomen of the day, she perceives her work, the lowliest in the textile mill, less as a means of self-support than as a contribution to the family economy.

Davis daringly moves to redefine notions of the workingman and the workingwoman. The consumptive Hugh, the titular breadwinner, is nicknamed "Molly" by his coworkers and otherwise viewed as enfeebled and feminine. On one level, he is Davis's surrogate aesthete, the febrile Hawthornian artist of the beautiful. Later in the narrative, jailed for a theft a woman really committed, he chooses suicide rather than self-defense. In a society that, Davis makes clear, is oblivious to the limitations of the manly self-help credo, Hugh's feminine sensitivity is a liability rather than an avenue of upward movement.[68] In this he is contrasted with both the masculinized Korl woman and the crippled but survivalist Deborah.

Momentarily breaking out of her submissiveness in her devotion to Hugh, Deborah takes decisive, if ill-fated, action. It is at the point that she acts for Hugh that the narrative experimentation with proletarian gender roles becomes the most complicated, and Davis's own ambivalent relation to the cult of True Womanhood is made manifest. If Deborah is both manly and womanly, decisive and self-subordinating, her conflation of gendered attributes underscores the problem of the narrative as a whole. Davis is caught between her sympathy for worker sufferings, particularly those of women, and her own classed convictions about lower-class behavior, again, especially about the women's "unwomanly" conduct. These contradictions are present in the narrative all along. To reconcile them, Davis employs the antebellum literary device of singling out the "better" working character. While Hugh, though a true artist, is contradictorily characterized as "by habit, only a coarse, vulgar laborer" (25), consumed by his own sorrows, the uncomplaining Deborah, in Davis's bold formulation, is a type of "heroic unselfishness" (21). Yet Deborah, no Lowell girl or genteel seamstress, is still a member of the immigrant classes Davis nativistically describes as brutish and unwashed. Even punishment, three years in prison, proves a more elevating influence than continuing to live among her own kind.[69]

Deborah was not the only Davis character to essay a reconciliation of domestic ideology and industrial womanhood. Lois, a secondary character in *Margret Howth,* is another onetime factory woman crippled by overwork, denied the traditional status of wife and mother, and further marginalized by her mulatta status. Yet she too forms a "quintessential True Woman" to embody women's "special" altruism and propensity for spirituality.[70]

Davis had begun to lay out the new terrain of the woman worker as an individuated figure, stirred by passionate longings and the frustrations of the poor. Deborah's passions, however, do not extend to the mill women's real-life push for better conditions that transiently activated a number of northeastern mills around the time of the Civil War.[71] In *The Silent Partner,* Elizabeth Stuart Phelps, without disavowing Davis's belief in religious transcendence, tried to do just that.

Phelps had been an investigator of women wage earners' lives well before she wrote her 1871 novel. Like Davis, whom she had read, she stressed affinities between talented middle-class and industrial lower-class women: lack of opportunity or choice, little or no respect, poor pay. Where there were gaps—in *The Silent Partner,* the affluent woman's bane is idleness, the worker's, exploitation. Phelps enacted her own intersection of the genteel and the laboring by conducting interviews about the Pemberton Mill fire, resulting in a short story, "The Tenth of January" (1868). She taught mill children and worked with "fallen women" at a shelter. Addressing Boston workingwomen's conferences, she concurred with their charge that they were the "white slaves" of the New England factory system.[72]

Phelps transforms herself into a kind of privileged surrogate in the figure of Perley Kelso, the title character and the mill's "silent partner" in both senses of the word. Soon Perley propels the narrative with a philanthropic interest in her factory hands. A Deborah figure, Sip, debilitated by cotton cough, practices family sacrifice. Yet Phelps's portraiture extends Davis's industrially crippled figure: Sip, despite her ailment, is a figure of strength. It is her father, killed in an accident, her mother, dead of overwork, and her retarded sister Catty who pay the physical cost of mill-town capitalism.

Phelps's world, like Davis's, includes crippled operatives, drinkers, decay, flighty mill girls, industrial diseases, and oppressed and oppressing workingmen. It is also a world in which operatives testify before Senate committees and single heads of households like Sip address strike rallies and, by the denouement, are no better off economically than at the beginning. A life financed by a Quaker sect is impossible for this mass of workers.[73] Phelps, as if in response to Davis, even emphasizes that Quakers would not have accepted Sip (294).

In Phelps's hands, Sip is a more suggestive figure than her counterpart in Davis. "A little rough, brown girl . . . talking fast" (294), Sip, unlike the tongue-tied Deborah, gains in rhetorical power what she lacks in physical stature. An earnest worker convert who spreads God's word (300–301), she is a throwback to the midcentury Second Great Awakening, when New England's evangelized workingmen became temperance advocates urging their coworkers to abandon drink and allied wickedness.[74] Sip earlier in the novel had scorned the foreigners (50) she worked with, but later she resembles antebellum labor evangelists who accepted the new Irish Catholic mill workers into the fold. In her new persona, she fits Bruce Laurie's definition of the apolitical labor-class preacher who gives "a message of deliverance . . . at odds with political radicalism or class antagonism"; she even recalls the abstinent Washingtonians of the 1840s.[75]

Phelps swerves around a literary problem that would plague labor authors for decades: how does a workingwoman enter male labor history? Sip must provide a remedy for labor pain that is consonant with acceptable womanly behavior in sustaining orderly and stable families and provokes no confrontation between labor and capital. She thus remains remote from what Herbert Gutman calls the post–Civil War "labor evangel," who urged workers to make Christ real to themselves while holding the industrialists accountable.[76] By advocating moral improvement based on New Testament principles, labor evangels formed "a crucial part of the labor movement." Though not Marxists, they implicitly urged justice for the oppressed.[77] In contrast, in Phelps's hands, Sip's Christianity is no metaphor for class unrest or Christian socialism but symbolizes the search for a wider social family by a woman who has lost her own. Complementing the workers' self-help society that Perley, apparently without irony, hopes to develop, Sip offers a nurturing that is consonant with the community caretaker role she has adopted.

Too, Sip's power as a laboring version of True Womanhood rather than a masculinized labor agitator must be taken in the context of woman's limited militance in the novel as a whole. This point is made explicit in a strange scene in which the strikers gather to revolt but, with the appearance of "the young leddy" (252), go peaceably back to work. Prefiguring Sip's conversion, Perley effects a near-magical transformation of her militant mill hands. They mass to storm the mill, but their anger over wage cuts disappears when she walks among them. Labor's true woman as true virgin, she need only express her compassion for them. Phelps mixes Christ-like images with Victorian notions of woman's moral suasion; the touch of Perley's cloak causes the workers to tremble. In the aftermath of this scene, it is not surprising that Sip continues Perley's work rather than disseminate a labor-militant message.

The Silent Partner is only in part a disobedient narrative.[78] Its challenge to the ideology of feminine domestic nurturance remains muted. Phelps's book has links to the 1870s–1880s labor compliance novel of her ultraconservative contemporaries John Hay, Beverley Warner, and Mrs. C. M. Cornwall. Sip Garth herself is a female version of their Good Worker, who learns to be content with her wretched lot. Her drunken sister Catty, though a victim, is erased from the narrative, like the Hay school's male malcontents, because she undermines stability and moral order. Moreover, Phelps, unlike the labor-class compliance authors, sympathizes with industrial discontent. Yet in her narrative, class wounds inevitably heal. From a labor-militant perspective, the text's true silent partner is Sip herself.

Perhaps no period writer was more concerned with resolving the political and economic dilemmas generated by what her novel *Work* (1873) calls the attempt to form a "loving league of sisters" than Louisa May Alcott.[79] Alcott herself was the daughter of the transcendentalist Bronson Alcott, whose household was marked by a philosopher's refinement but complete financial improvidence. She of necessity abandoned the spectatorial role of Davis and Phelps to teach, sew, do domestic service, and even Civil War nursing. In a kind of feminist riposte to the domestic sentimentalism of successful girls' books like her own *Little Women* (1868), Alcott has her heroine shed family duties through these and other dead-end jobs as a seamstress, governess, companion, and, improbably, actress. Alcott never trumpets, in the person of Christie, either the factory-floor gentility of Lowell writers or the proletarian uplift of a Davis or Phelps. Yet her heroine manages to fuse the lady and the worker without disrespecting either the former's "fine instincts [and] gracious manners" or the latter's "skill and courage" (430).

It is true that Alcott uses Christie's awakened bonds with ex-slaves, laundry-women, and streetwalkers to repudiate the stifling aspects of the leisure-class feminine sphere.[80] Yet only a windfall marriage enables Alcott's lady at work to sustain herself economically and, in widowhood, only a windfall inheritance enables her to rescue a group of similarly hard-pressed women from the menial's lot. Another labor surrogate managing these women's self-help, much as Alcott herself ran her father's hapless communal experiments, Christie now envisions a cross-racial, quasi-socialistic women's work community, from which cutthroat competitiveness and racism have been eliminated.

Praised for its inventive plans for cross-class sorority, Alcott's vision still limits female breadwinning to those too refined to stand it for long. Hers is a sisterhood of distressed gentlewomen with Ladies Bountiful that all but excludes labor-class women. Even a redeemed prostitute seems preferable to a sweating Irish mill worker or another representative of female labor en masse. Thus Rachel, a former streetwalker Christie befriends in a sewing shop— shades of T. S. Arthur—is unmasked as the daughter of a good family. Other than an adolescent runaway factory hand, the novel's only actual worker figure is the washerwoman Cynthie Wilkins, who is not so much individuated as coded as a Dickensian eccentric. Moreover, she is explained away as Sip Garth with a husband and family, always preaching charity and compliance. Cynthie apart, in the novel's closing pages a strange hostility to the feminine rank and file, presumed to be impossible to reach through an enlightened version of Bronson Alcott's communal Fruitlands experiment, enters the text. Considering large groups of women in subsistence jobs, Alcott scoffs at what she sees as the "myth" of starving needlewomen (427). And she is so put off by the vision of a feminine factory that she omits those who fuel it from her utopian collective, relegating the lives of the factory force to a martyrdom for which there seems no remedy.

Ironically, Davis, Phelps, and Alcott, by allying the interests of heiresses, governesses, religious women, and factory or fugitive slaves, reconcile lower-class women to capitalism. Ideologically, they thus shore up the cultural certainty that women must have no permanent place in industrial settings. Going beyond the confines of antebellum True Womanhood thinking, they all remain anchored in it as well.

Up from (Gendered) Slavery: Black Women's Narratives

White women authors, anxious to include white workingwomen at moral risk in the universal community of women, chastened a Deborah, tamed a Sip Garth, redeemed an erring Rachel. Alcott and Davis gave this community an interracial dimension by offering black subplot figures who do not need a moral conversion. Alcott's fugitive Hepsey, a cook who preaches humility, is eagerly welcomed into the new women's community that closes the novel. The freeborn, crippled Lois Yare, a minor mulatta character in *Margret Howth*, is a type of Christian forgiveness. (Such transcendence, it should be noted, is denied the drunken mulatta mill girls in "Life in the Iron Mills" or in an 1862 Davis tale, "Blind Tom," with its barely glimpsed, apathetic slave field hand mother.)

Writing in the Civil War era, black women authors revised the white authorial narrative of black women's work, making the heroines of their narratives slave, fugitive, and freeborn wage earners. Their own experiences, whether slave or freeborn but living in poverty, were the stuff of their semificional narratives or novels, whose proceeds helped sustain them. In different ways, Harriet Jacobs, Elizabeth Keckley, and Harriet Wilson challenged rather than rewrote True Womanhood, arguing that it inevitably excluded African American women. Yet only Wilson, in the first novel published by a black woman in English, embraced a female proletarian vision that rejected the dialectic of workers and ladies.

Incidents in the Life of a Slave Girl (1861) is Harriet Jacobs's veiled autobiography with melodramatic elements and sentimental diction. The book is permeated with the realization that slave women were excluded from feminine behavior. Published pseudonymously under the name Linda Brent, its heroine, taught to read as a plantation girl, is as literate as any *Lowell Offering* contributor and skilled enough with her needle. She carves out a terrain quite separate from that of the white women of the factories and mills—where white women routinely refuse to work alongside slave operators.[81]

Superficially, *Incidents* follows what one recent explicator has termed the formula of the slave narrative: the birth in slavery; the life under it; the lowly status; the plan for and eventual escape; the adversities of the fugitive; the call to abolitionists when free.[82] Redefining this form in terms of gendered difference, however, reveals that Jacobs displays the female slave narrator's interest in maintaining her family relations rather than playing the Noble Fugitive of a Frederick Douglass or a Martin R. Delany.[83] Black men's narratives often cast bonded women as tragic heroines. *Incidents* reverses that trope. Like the title character of novelist William Wells Brown's novel *Clotel*

(1853), Jacobs's protagonist joins the elite 5 percent of slave women who worked as house servants. Such women certainly understood the thirteen-hour field day they were spared by this status, attracted the uncertain economic favors of white masters, and sometimes won or bought freedom for themselves and their children.[84] Clotel pays for her victory with a shortened life. Jacobs's slave girl survives and finds work in the North with an abolitionist family.

What is striking about *Incidents'* self-representations, however, is also what allies it to the white workingwomen's fictions of the day. Unlike a Bradbury or Davis heroine, her alter ego does succumb to sexual liaisons with the employer class and even bears children out of wedlock. Her sexual transgressions occur under the slave system in which white owners annex black women. But by castigating the sexual bondage of the plantation South, the narrator reasserts the wider cultural emphasis on feminine virtue, whether for black or white women.

Jacobs/Brent resists explicitly yoking her most arduous duties to her sexual slavery, though at one point she says she would prefer field work "from dawn till dark" to concubinage.[85] That Brent's oppressed work involves sexual as much as domestic servitude invokes her narrative scorn for her hard-hearted employer. Aptly named Dr. Flint (in real life James Norcom), he offers her the alternatives of being a "lady" by becoming his mistress (*Incidents,* 56) or being cast down to field work if she does not capitulate. To avoid Flint's advances, she must accept those of another man, the fittingly named Sands (in Jacobs's own life, the attorney Samuel Tredwell Sawyer), who promises no more secure a footing. (Sawyer himself never made good on his promise to emancipate the children Jacobs bore him.) In a landscape of such odious employers, her agreement with Sands, she remarks, at least does not extinguish her spirit as would a liaison with Flint.[86]

Brent's attempts to reverse the association of black women with forced and thus unnatural sexuality redouble in the second part of the narrative. Jacobs prepares for that section by reversing the death-as-punishment finale experienced by wayward womanhood in clothing-trades fiction.[87] She does not seek suicide as atonement. Instead, having staved off Flint's various attempts to sell her children, she flees him and hides in a garret for seven years. In this maternal purgatory, where she can hear but not see her children, she is both dead and alive, exile and stay-at-home, slave woman and impassioned mother.

In contrast to the emotional penitence or the cut-your-losses pragmatism of many slave narrators, Jacobs creates a vision of black womanhood that reconciles cultural and literary contradictions between pure and fallen workingwomen. Rather than acknowledge her exclusion, as an African American slave servitor, from the period debate on Lowellian purity, she joins it. She validates herself within a maternally domestic rather than a self-directed and labor-class framework. It seems appropriate that after she leaves her work as a governess for a northern antislavery family, she becomes a Quaker, aiding the poor, sick, and orphaned. Thus Jacobs extends but never abandons the super-mother identity.[88]

Not so Elizabeth Keckley, who desired self-definition above all. Three years after the war's end, a freed Keckley authored a slave narrative–cum–eyewitness history as Mrs. Lincoln's dressmaker/confidante, *Behind the Scenes; or, Thirty Years a Slave, and Four Years in the White House* (1868). While economic struggle occupies the bulk of all these narratives, Keckley differed from Jacobs and her writing sisters in developing an entrepreneurial persona under the lash. In the Franklin/Douglass self-reliant tradition, she struggles upward from life as a serving girl who endures whippings and sexual mistreatment, doing the work of three. She becomes an urban slave dressmaker who garners enough to support her bonded family.[89]

She soon carves a meaning from the role of what William L. Andrews, contrasting her to Harriet Jacobs, calls a superworker.[90] Not only does she spiritedly follow a work ethic under slavery, but in her belief in paid labor as a lodestar, she elides indenture and self-employment. Although here she is describing her post-1855 life as an unwed mother under slavery, she might as well be alluding to the period inaugurated by her triumphant subtitle, "four years in the White House."

Jacobs refigures, and Keckley bypasses, True Womanhood. In the indentured servant novel, Harriet Wilson's autobiographical *Our Nig* (1859), an African American worker-writer and a "working-class black woman" makes clear its complete futility as a labor-class ideology.[91] Wilson's title and authorial self-naming evidence the biting indictment of the work to come. Appearing as the literary product of "Our Nig," and lengthily subtitled *Sketches from the Life of a Free Black, in a Two-Story White House, North, Showing that Slavery's Shadows Fall Even There*. If Keckley hopefully recasts slavery as a sewing woman's labor apprenticeship, Wilson, a freed black, revisions her heroine Frado's life as a servant under time-limited indenture and, later, as an alternately vilified and patronized hatmaker, as enslavement itself.

As a kind of prologue, the early chapters chronicle the waywardness of "Nig's" white mother, Mag Smith. Making cultural fears realities, Mag, like Alcott's Rachel after her, cannot withstand seduction, does not die of shame or childbirth, and even returns to domestic service and laundry work after her baby is born dead. Yet Wilson's bold novel explores frontiers forbidden to Alcott and her colleagues. Mag does leave the workplace, but only in a kind of parody of white bourgeois domesticity. She marries a black man, bears his daughter, and, on his death, no grieving widow, abandons her to an indentured labor fate at the Bellmonts', where she herself once worked unhappily. Wilson, writing autobiographically, creates a novel devoted, unlike a Jacobs or Keckley narrative, to descriptions of meanly paid labor, in childhood and young womanhood: farm work, kitchen work, house work. Leaving harsh employment leads only to a mockery of marital salvation: Frado does domestic work for another white family, teaches herself sewing, marries a fugitive slave, bears him a child, but experiences only spousal abandonment, not economic support. The white community that supported Jacobs and made Keckley prosperous variously sneers at, refuses to apprentice, or is indifferent to Frado. The message is that no blacks need apply.

Wilson offers a tragic proletarian mulatta, but the character is one who shifts the Jacobs/Keckley focus from the concubinage of the kept woman to hardscrabble wage earning. Thus if hers is an allegory of a slave narrative, as most commentators have argued, it also operates as African American women's labor fiction of a quite prophetic kind.[92] As an indentured servant in the Bellmont home, suffering racist comments, starvation, and other forms of employer abuse until she has "paid out" her toil, her lot replicates that of many black New York workingwomen denied even the limited opportunities of the white seamstress. Furthermore, neither slave nor economically free, Wilson's Frado is barred from developing the transient working-class militance of Lowell, Lynn, and Troy; she is barred from working alongside whites. Dependent on the largesse of strangers to buy her wares, she lacks the web of friendly relations with affluent whites of the dressmaker Elizabeth Keckley. Yet neither can she become part of a white workforce that does not use a home workshop.

A veiled autobiography, *Our Nig* has two endings, one ideal, one real. The fictive one concludes with Frado, denied the vocation of bonnet-making more open to white women. Instead she creates and sells "a useful article for her maintenance" (358), left vaguely delineated perhaps because the trades into which black women could enter were so circumscribed. The narrative ends there, with Frado in hopes of a prosperous white clientele. But the novel's author was not as optimistic, a point implicit in the biographical "Appendix" by a white friend hoping to raise funds for Wilson, who by the time of publication was in an impoverished state. Whether included at Wilson's behest or not (her preface had already appealed to readers to purchase her book), the Appendix contains poignant excerpts from Wilson's letters on her life in the county poorhouse. When seen as an alternative conclusion to *Our Nig*, it suggests a tragic end to Frado's dreams as well. Even without this depressing finale, by narrative's end the title character has found neither secure employment nor a place in an affluent white home. Thus the novel, though it precedes the narratives of Jacobs and Keckley, already interrogates their beliefs in interracial and cross-class sorority.

In the decades before what Henry Louis Gates, Jr., calls the turn-of-the-century "Black Woman's Era" of African American literary history, Wilson stood almost alone in her willingness to take a hard-eyed look at black women's labor and the thwarted struggle to attain marketable vocational skills.[93] Nor did the author of *Our Nig* look to quasi-industrial training of what a decade later would be called the Hampton type, as if sensing that such schooling would be yet another form of domestic servitude.

Ladies No More: The Demise of the Lowell Myth

By the 1860s and 1870s, the Hampton Institute had begun a new uplift mission that sought to enable manual laborers to acquire what Booker T. Washington called "the independence and self-reliance that the ability to do something that the world wants done brings."[94] Pragmatically bypassing the white factory world, with its founding in 1868 the Hampton Institute admitted a pilot group of freed black women. This Women's Labor Department, if rooted in uplift, also recalled the domestic servitude and spartan living quarters allotted the more privileged antebellum slaves.[95] Soon the institute's journal, *The Southern Workman,* was even acting as a "situations wanted" exchange for graduates.[96] In this early period, Hampton women seeking self-elevation, much less teaching careers, underwent a peculiar training in housework and teaching. By the late 1870s, the school's industrial education for black women joined its programs for Native American women, although it offered no place for women like Iron Teeth, the Cheyenne horse-breaker and eyewitness to battles between her people and U.S. soldiers.[97] Her experience of resistance to government reservation and assimilation programs would have alienated her from the Hampton code.

In the mind of Hampton's white principal, Gen. Samuel C. Armstrong, women of color were not ladies, nor were they expected to marry up. Hampton remained true to the cult of domesticity in other ways. Well before an 1890s Hampton annual report listed "married and in good homes" as a common "occupation" of its graduates, their work paths "remain[ed] within the boundaries dictated by the proscriptions of women's separate sphere that cut across the boundaries of race and class."[98] By the 1880s, when the black press was formally urging black women to be ladylike, educated black women joined their white counterparts in acknowledging the social distance between the working and middle classes.[99] The mass of women of color remained poor and underskilled, the segregated of the female factory world.

The 1870s and 1880s that followed witnessed the rapid growth of women and girls in the nation's paid labor force. Yet the increasingly multiethnic factory was a hopeful place neither for the new immigrants nor for the Yankee women whose own mothers had been at Lowell. Industrial work thus joined sweatshop sewing and domestic service as no longer (if ever) a badge of respectability: Harriet Beecher Stowe herself in *We and Our Neighbors* (1875) devoted many pages to anxieties about the morality of Maggie the Irish serving girl, as did, less generously, male foes of labor like Charles Joseph Bellamy in *The Breton Mills* (1879).

The daughters and granddaughters of the Lowell generation had turned away from sewing and spinning to sales and, to a lesser degree, clerical work. But such new positions, with mistaken reputations for light work, also seemed to turn working-class True Womanhood into a sham. George Ellington's misogynist taxonomy, *The Women of New York: The Under-World of the Great City* (1869), reprinted twice by 1878, included a careful chapter on ladylike occupations and let readers draw their own conclusions. A more scientific study, the prestigious Massachusetts Labor Survey of 1884, found poor conditions in former and current jobs with ladylike associations, clerking and department store work among them.[100] As worrisome to these analysts as the economic exploitation (of white girls) was the immoral career switch. The fears about prostitution haunting the factory since before Civil War were now realized in case histories of streetwalkers.

In fiction such as the genteel author Alice Rollins's *Uncle Tom's Tenement* (1880), what should have been a new scrutiny of the burgeoning feminine workplace seemed a recycling of stereotypes, with thrusts toward naturalism. The New York City reformer Helen Campbell's own *Mrs. Herndon's Income* (1886) and *Miss Melinda's Opportunity* (1886) in radically divergent ways skewed the implications of her own research on the vulnerabilities of feminine lower-class life. The former, a Lady Bountiful text, seeks in a subplot to empower one workingwoman by marrying her to a German revolutionary. The latter offers a genteel circle of accomplished bachelor maidens a housing and recreation center.

As late as 1887, the job-seeking protagonist of Lillian Sommers's *For Her Daily Bread,* a novel for middlebrow readers, could list sewing next to teaching as "within the bounds of womanly accomplishments."[101] Yet by this decade such work was no longer commensurate with gentility. Norma essays seamstress work, only to have a needle pierce her finger. Teaching provides little more benefit, and she turns to business training instead, soon marrying her employer. She resolves her status ambiguity by reentering the privileged classes to which she belongs.

Knights of Labor literature, disseminated by that important AFL precursor during its heyday, was also tardy in relinquishing the ladylike ideal. A case in point is W. H. Little's *Our Sealskin and Shoddy* (1888). Mamie Symington, a Cincinnati manufacturer's daughter and a Perley Kelso type, befriends Lizzie Knowlton, a factory girl, though (unusual for a Knights tale) one from a well-bred background. All the while, true to the Knights' credo, she works for a cooperative plan for operating the factory that will preclude future strikes. She also stirs the romantic interest of another well-born labor surrogate, Hal Hinston, who advises and acts as physician to the striking factory girls. With Hal installed as president, Mamie as his wife, and Lizzie as a forewoman, and company reading rooms and restaurants established, the bargain is apparently complete.

In his allusion to a Sewing Girls Protective Association, Little's book touches on the new militance that was informing sewing work. But the group is a far cry from the Illinois Women's Alliance, which espoused left-wing thought and depended on a coalition of lower- and middle-class women. When Hal achieves the presidency of the company, there is no more talk of female unionism. Like woman's labor-class communitarianism in other Knights novels, such as T. Fulton Gantt's *Breaking the Chains* (1887), feminine militance mid-1880s style is circumscribed.

Even read as Knights of Labor characters, the Mamie/Lizzie/Hal trio raises questions about the democratic representation of labor and the fictional representation of feminine labor. Little's factory workers are no New York State Joan of Arc Assembly of fiery "collar girls" or Yonkers carpet weavers but a group of women content with delegating authority to their betters in exchange for profit sharing and welfare capitalism. Linked to the more conservative wing of their labor "brotherhood," they are further traditionalized as Lady Knights. Both equal and not, they are thus tied to a family wage economy and helpmeet ideology.

As the sewing job became the province of Euro-American immigrants, alternative cultural constructions of the lady arose. The department store acquired the patina of upward mobility that the early Lowell mill had possessed. Despite a long-lived countertradition that linked selling work to sexual availability, in the Gilded Age the very term "saleslady" excluded non-

English speakers and suggested a closed society of genteelly ambitious young women. Stores like Macy's, founded in 1858 and venerable even by the mid-1880s, provided outwardly attractive work environments. Management took pains to hire daughters of the better classes, whom it underpaid and only occasionally elevated to the more promising position of buyer.[102]

Yet, building on decades of distrust of urban workingwomen, novelists of the late 1870s and the 1880s increasingly associated the sales job with gold-digging ambition. Less often imperiled than morally suspect, this self-propelled shopgirl surfaced in dour, didactic novels such as *Against Fate* (1876), by Mrs. M. L. Rayne, or filled out the scheming antiheroine's role in John Hay's similarly cautionary *The Bread-Winners* (1884). The new type was further personified by the flamboyantly self-confident Millicent Henning in Henry James's *The Princess Cassamassima* (1886) (set safely in London). And she dominated the shop-to-gutter portraits as the tawdry Lily Luttrell and the pathetic Cora Strang in the society-and-slum novel of the James imitator Edgar Fawcett, *The Evil That Men Do* (1889). Sexual opportunists all, these allegedly vulgar women either come to their senses and marry into their own class or, still rashly seeking self-madeism, they languish in the shop or fall into the harsh streets outside it.

To the Workingwoman:
Act Like a Lady Lest You Drudge Like a Prole

From antebellum times to the 1890s, the literary iconography of wage-earning woman depicted the white, native-born worker who wasn't. Neither militant nor complaining, not black, ethnic, widowed, old, or, above all, sexually wayward, this factory lady was described in the same rhetoric of accidental worker, bourgeois aspirant, and, after the Civil War, worker's surrogate that permeated fictions of male work for most of the nineteenth century. Yet for laboring men, such strategies of authorial and cultural control purveyed a stringent new industrial morality. Laboring men were variously Franklinesque or uncooperative, thwarted or selectively realized, guided or replaced by a labor surrogate.

The compliance that the earliest U.S. labor authors wished to impose on the male workforce changed when applied to laboring women. "Woman worker" remained a contradiction in terms. From cheap fiction's antebellum male authors to mainstream feminine professionals of the Civil War era to mouthpieces for the Knights of Labor, white imaginers of working-class women reinforced the gendered divisions between men's paid and women's domestic labor. In the more feminist work novels, womanly labor-class tribulations were leavened by Christian piety and a cross-class sorority with veiled socialist elements. Davis, Phelps, and Alcott did challenge marital domesticity. Yet, seeking to "save" the laboring woman, these three inadvertently minimized or erased the very institutions such women were forming on their own.

As refigured in U.S. fiction from the Lowell loom to the city shop floor, the social dream of actual workingwomen depended on their virtue.[103] In such imaginings of the wage-earning experience, personal ambition shorn of family devotion conjured up the sexually predatory; woman's marital self-madeism was her brand of American exceptionalism. Furthermore, while in labor and capitalist quarters alike the strong bodies of skilled male workers symbolized manliness, sewing and serving women's very vulnerability defined their womanliness.

Most African American women writers, creators of narratives or novels of their own or others' real or figurative slavery, consciously revised racist assumptions that a black woman was no woman at all. Those like Harriet Jacobs reconciled ideological contradictions between slaves and true women by constructing the fugitive slave as the ideal mother. Success-oriented ex-slaves like Elizabeth Keckley created an entrepreneurial narrative that omitted the problem of the unfeminine black menial woman. Only Harriet Wilson, a solitary voice, cut through the womanhood debate to remind the culture of what grinding work meant for black women and all women. It was a subject that would be neglected by male narrators and bypassed in odes to motherhood or acquisitive individualism by female narrators for some time to come.

As armies of non-English-speaking women joined foreign-born men in the expanding industrial workplace, the sanitized seamstresses of Lowell faded from cultural memory, although the old urge to gentrify took on new forms. By the mid-1890s, public discourse on the working class, from Crane's slum shocker *Maggie: A Girl of the Streets* (1893) to the driest labor survey, had to acknowledge that real workingwomen were here to stay.

Out of other developments, in the wake of nativism, the rise of restrictive craft federations, the setbacks to industrial unionism, the proliferation of the immigrant slum, and the joblessness occasioned by the depression of 1893, there arose a literary sociology of labor's most recent and least assimilated arrivals (while largely excluding people of color). The journalist-storytellers Jacob Riis, Stephen Crane, William Dean Howells, and Abraham Cahan joined the many whose tenement forays probed the complicated new intersections of working-class ethnicity with American ascension.

CHAPTER 4

Taking to Their Streets
Ethnic Cultures and Labor Texts in the Sociological 1890s

The historic subculture of workers was evident as significantly in their homes and neighborhoods as it was at work or on the picket line.

—DAVID MONTGOMERY, "TO STUDY THE PEOPLE: THE AMERICAN
WORKING CLASS" (1980)

"Say, you know me friend de barkeep? Well, he's no dead tough mug. . . .
[H]e's right people. Sure; he's just as right people as dere is on de Bow'ry."

—E. W. TOWNSEND, *CHIMMIE FADDEN* (1895)

The last act was a triumph for the hero, poor and of the masses, the representative of the audience, over the villain and the rich man. . . . Maggie always departed with raised spirits from the showing places of the melodrama.

—STEPHEN CRANE, *MAGGIE: A GIRL OF THE STREETS* (1893)

The Station: Incident of the Homestead Steel Strike, c. 1892. Photograph. Collections of the Library of Congress.

In the 1890s skilled white native-born workers, allied with British, Welsh, German, and Irish "old immigrants," refused to let their awesome new adversaries define them. They agitated against the monopolistic Carnegies, Fricks, Pullmans, and other corporate magnates of the foundries, railways, and mines. As these union men asserted the dignity, if no longer the nobility, of heavy-industrial labor, they rekindled the militancy dashed in the red scare, antilabor climate generated by the Chicago Haymarket Affair of the mid-1880s.[1] Together with the old brotherhoods of the building trades, they even scored some modest early victories under the aegis of the Eight-Hour Movement.[2] But in what an eminent labor historian has called the fall of the house of labor, they encountered more numerous and more telling defeats.[3] In one of the most notable, the Homestead Steel strikers of 1892 tried to combat a mechanization made ominous to them by influxes of cheap "new immigrant" labor, union-busting tactics, and economic depression. When the rollers, puddlers, and molders of the Amalgamated Association of Iron and Steel Workers stormed Andrew Carnegie's huge, Bessemerized Pennsylvania mill, they were broken, in a crucial setback, by Pinkertons, the state militia, and the increasingly concentrated power of industry.[4]

In the barely unionized coal mines, the old-immigrant majority acted out a wavering biracialism. But in most other heavy industries, Homestead-like strikes were aided not by limited numbers of black migrants from the South but by Poles, Slavs, and Italians not permitted in the craft unions.[5] It is not surprising that the decade saw little cross-ethnic working-class unity. To the trade union imagination, the newest ethnics were inarticulate, swarthy, and relegated to the slums; in many labor quarters they were cast as the "poor, ignorant Poles and Italians [living] in 'the dens' by the brickyards."[6] The depression of 1893, which extended workplace sufferings to millions of non-unionist whites, deepened skilled-labor combativeness and enlisted half a million strikers from rail and coal unions. But it forged neither cross-trade nor interethnic bonds.[7] The next year too saw widespread Midwest agitation, this time by the American Railway Union. Led by the soon-to-be-jailed socialist tribune Eugene V. Debs, this strike also was not successful.[8]

Whatever bitter organizing lessons the strike taught Debs's chastened English-speaking followers, it gained the recent Slav arrivals, who played very little part in the protest, only cultural resentment of foreigners. They were tarred with the anarchist brush of Alexander Berkman, who had vainly attempted to assassinate Henry Clay Frick during the Homestead Strike.[9] A vocal but faction-ridden minority of garment-trades workers on the Lower East Side of New York City belonged to more politically viable groups such as the largely skilled-trades Jews of the Socialist Labor Party (SLP), led by Daniel DeLeon. Many of these groups espoused socialism, although, as Irving Howe points out, there was no mass socialist movement in the East Side or elsewhere.[10] The SLP succumbed by decade's end to fragmentation and to Samuel Gompers's ascendancy among more centrist AFL socialists who were committed less to industrial than to craft-based democracy. Confined to essentially segregated unions, Jews battled masters of their own ethnicity in the needle trades, as isolated from the Homestead and Pullman militants as if they were still in the Pale.[11]

The new century retained the cherished ideologies of self-propelled worker mobility and cross-trade fraternalism, which had been central to the once potent Knights of Labor (rehearsed or recast in a wide range of labor-gent and labor-surrogate fiction). Yet such ideas were increasingly inapplicable to established workers who were antipathetic to corporations and recent immigrants alike.[12] By the mid-1890s, an unprecedented number of failed strikes prompted organized labor to a pragmatic redefinition of worker ascension and the exclusionary solidarity needed to achieve it. Supplanting the broad liberality of the Knights, Samuel Gompers, despite his philosophical adherence to socialist syndicalism, led his survivalist American Federation of Labor in a restrictively prudential unionism. Fed by high dues, the AFL stressed skilled trades and set an agenda to "bind . . . a strong and aggressive labor movement to the bourgeois social order."[13] From the AFL to the Immigration Restriction League, the farmer-dominated Populist Party to the anti-Catholic American Protective Association, there was no place for the untrustworthy new ethnic, anarchistic or lumpen.[14]

Yet growing east European and Mediterranean immigrant influxes reasserted to working people, affiliated or otherwise, as well as to the wider culture, a new subaltern rootedness. The tenement house became all but synonymous with the foreign born, whether in a backyard section of a company town or the "Jewtown" of a metropolis, to use the phrase of the photojournalist Jacob Riis.[15] Whatever the ethnics' vicissitudes at the lowest end of the job (or criminality) market, their tenement stasis was not perceived as stability, fostering habits of cleanliness and order, but instead made them the constant butt of criticism for intemperance and immorality, infection and crime. As waves of new immigrants arrived, they occupied an underclass habitat perceived, in the words of Riis's 1890 watershed text, as the terrain of how the other half lives. The slum revision of the American work ethic required that its adherents live in the mire, close to the job supply on docks and in warehouses, factories, and business streets, in an unprecedented crowding into American cities. By 1890, to cite a prime example, New York City's thirty-five thousand tenements contained an overwhelming number of the total population of a million and a half.[16] To influential cultural commentators like Riis, Jewish, Slavic, and Italian survivalism had little in common with the craft-based self-reliance still invoked by Gompers or the strike-torn industrial unions in their negotiations and confrontations with corporate expansionism.[17]

In their swelling numbers, unfamiliar customs, unsanitary lifestyles, and frequent association with criminality, urban immigrants pointed to the cultural crisis of the acculturation experience.[18] In actuality, the city, particularly New York City, altered the new foreign laborers more than they altered it by inexorably incorporating them into their adopted society.[19] It is risky to generalize about the social fluidity of laborers, tailors, and peddlers. Nevertheless New York's numerous Jews and Italians began the 1880s at the bottom of the social order and by the 1890s had moved in significant numbers out of manual labor or into jobs with some long-run amelioration.[20] Yet the many investigators who studied them and other newcomers were poised between ethnic stereotyping and ethnographic inquiry. (They christened some groups of foreign toilers the "well-paid working poor," the odd phrase suggesting typical period confusions about ethnicity and economic struggle.)[21] In alleged revolt against the traditional view that impoverishment was the fault of those suffering it, a fledgling sociology researched the city's Lower East Side. It found environmental determinism, a vision made haltingly manifest in a spate of studies on sweated toil, child labor, and the tenement as the hub of working-class life.[22]

Reformist studies with sentimentalized case histories that made immigrants more human, journalistic exposés of sweatshops making them more bestial, and the fiction that drew on both subgenres explored how ethnics lived, or subsisted, rather than where they worked. All suggested that even the most tractable of the new multiethnic workforce donned a workday compliance only to shed it after hours. It was habitat, furthermore, that was crucial to the comprehension of immigrant oddity. When the regionalist author Hamlin Garland was dispatched to poststrike Homestead, he focused on the squalid communities surrounding it, ignoring both the steel mill experience and the more prosperous skilled workers' dwellings a short distance from the mill, even those that housed the militant strikers of 1892 themselves. "To give these folk power would unchain strange beasts," he concluded of the newest ethnics.[23] Other visitors, both to a sullen Homestead and to a passive Fall River, Massachusetts, a textile town, further decried what they perceived as the squalor of the ethnic inhabitants.[24] The Socialist A. M. Simons's more sympathetic study of immigrant-intensive industries like Chicago meatpacking was titled *Packingtown* (1899), to focus on the straitened work community as much as on the slaughterhouses that supported it.

Far more common than prejudiced or semiobjective sorties into depressed heavy-industrial neighborhoods or paternalistic company towns were those into the swarming proletarian street. Theirs were august assessments of working-class misery and joblessness, like the anthology edited by tenement expert Robert A. Woods, *The Poor in Great Cities* (1895). The anecdotal *Darkness and Daylight: Lights and Shadows of New York Life* (1897) was written by a group of slum missionaries finding more underclass silt than upper-class glitter. The alarmist tenement survey *Civilization's Inferno: Studies in the Social Cellar* (1893) was the brainchild of the *Arena* editor B. O. Flower. This fledgling sociology of lower-orders ethnicity was played out for public consumption in the new fiction, deplored by gentrified critics and variously termed the fiction of "low life" and the "lower depths."[25] In this timely literary landscape of the ethnic Other, dwellings and leisure activities, kinships and friendships, street accidents and alliances were all subjects of pseudo-scientific, horrified, or satiric fascination.

This near-obsessive tenement tourism was especially central to the journalistic tales, novellas, and novels of New York City, home, by 1890, to the largest immigrant labor force in the world.[26] The impressionistic newsman Stephen Crane informed readers in the subtitle that his Irish American seamstress Maggie, doomed to Bowery prostitution, was "of the streets" in both senses of the term. Similarly alert to borderline poverty and ethnic survival, Crane's fellow journalist Julian Ralph anchored workers in their habitat by calling his popular collection *People We Pass: Stories of Life among the Masses of New York* (1896). There were other newsmen who gained notice, from the genteelly educated E. W. Townsend in *A Daughter of the Tenements* (1895) to the Gompers ally James W. Sullivan, author of *Tenement Tales of New York* (1895). Even the muckraking photographer and journalist Jacob Riis, who, like Ralph, had worked as a *New York Sun* reporter, tried his hand at Bowery fiction in *Out of Mulberry Street: Stories of Tenement Life in New York City* (1898). Joining him in interpreting garment-trades Jewishness were the eponymous *Yekl: A Tale of the New York Ghetto* (1896) by the socialist explicator and future *Jewish Daily Forward* editor Abraham Cahan. Important too was *Joseph Zalmonah* (1893), a tenement roman à clef by the Scottish American Edward King about the early United Hebrew Trades organizer Joseph Barondess.

Authors' fictive forays outside New York, though less plentiful, extended the inquiry beyond the decayed tenement, often focusing on lodging-house transients or members of the more respectable lower middle classes. The New York school was joined by practitioners in Boston, such as Alvin Francis Sanborn in *Moody's Lodging House and Other Tenement Sketches* (1895), and Chicago, such as I. K. Friedman in his saloon-tale collection *The Lucky Number* (1896). A coda to the tenement tale was Frank Norris's *McTeague: A Story of San Francisco* (1899). Primarily a Zolaesque novel about the fall of a self-taught dentist with mining-camp origins, its subplot, concerning a bizarre and avaricious Jewish junkman, recalls the more mean-spirited of the New York tales. Its sense of place, though, was anchored in working-class Polk Street, its lodging houses, saloons, passersby, and inhabitants.

All of these writers developed an ethnically selective literature of the new American workforce that made visible the deepening clashes between assimilation and ethnicity.[27] They bypassed the old Euro-American workers, who despite reversals at Homestead and Pullman had developed a whole system of institutions, "from the most informal pub to the more formal workingmen's club, lodging, benefit society, cooperative, and union."[28] These 1890s slum tellers were for the most part ambitious journalists with genteel credentials. The venerable *Atlantic Monthly* editor William Dean Howells in his cross-class novel *A Hazard of New Fortunes* (1890) alluded to an old-immigrant traction strike, modeled on late 1880s events. But he buried the labor action in the narrative as a curiosity of slum life (against the contrasting normality of the middle-class city dweller). Frank Norris's *McTeague* relegated coal miners to atavism rather than National Mine Workers' unionism and tossed off disapproving references to the Pullman Strike and its predecessor, the Upheaval of 1877. And the iconoclastic Stephen Crane, whose own family owned coal stock, implicitly reproved them. His brief piece on an oppressive Pennsylvania coal mine, "In the Depths of a Coal Mine," was published in the reformist *McClure's* in 1894. But the sketch played no part in his naturalistic fiction of laboring subcultures.[29]

Still, from Riis to Howells to Crane, the ethnic thoroughfares, back alleys, "barracks" dwellings, and stale-beer dives inspired labor texts of a crucial kind. The texts reverse, question, or adapt the exceptionalist-ascension work and strike stories to tell new ones of slum immigrants. In so doing, they exhibit the first true interest in the artistic uses of working-class subject matter.

Until the Progressive Era (1900–1917), little fictive attention was paid to the ambitions of working-class female ethnics or of the blacks migrating from the peonage of the Jim Crow South, be they male or female. The influx of immigrant womanhood into urban sweatshops only solidified earlier literary attempts to decouple femininity from workplace and leisure culture. Tenement writers did link the white immigrant woman's individuality with her supposed propensity to sexual excess. But in a variety of ways they narrated her, and her desires, out of the story. Moreover, in the heyday of the slum tale, the number of slum-dwelling blacks in northern cities, though still no Great Migration, had seen a 75 percent increase over the previous decade.[30] Recognition of, much less respect for, this migration, though, was limited to racist asides. "See here, dingy," asks one patron of a lowbrow Chicago saloon, "can you play this tune?"[31] (Similarly, Chinatown Asians, alluded to as "Chop Suey, the neighborhood laundry man," operated or patronized opium dens.[32] The admittedly small Native American Bowery population merited only a tenement author's allusion to "red men.")[33] In regard to the black women migrants consigned to paid cleaning service from Pittsburgh to Harlem, excluded in the North, as they were back home, from the hard-driving industrial sector, there is literary silence. Or there is the occasional prostitution reference, as in the Riis story "Nigger Martha's Wake" (1898). In sum, the turn-of-the-century urban literary preoccupation with the tenement-dwelling new American constructed him as white and male.

Whatever the gaps in these formulations of the (im)migrant labor force, the clash between "respectable" and "un-American" labor, between genteel notions of public conduct and the realities of proletarian (mis)behavior, widened a U.S. labor literature previously wed to a gospel of personal choice and upward rising. By far the largest group of new writers exploring the unruliness of ethnic individualism was the "local color" tenement school.

The Tenement Show:
The Skewed Individualism of the Other Half

The conventional tenement tale, distinct from the disturbingly maverick art of a Stephen Crane or an Abraham Cahan, was part of a larger literary movement dubbed regionalism or local colorism. Seeking simple, honest, and sharp impressions of American subjects, the regionalists stressed the importance of localized environment to verisimilitude by situating their genre-painting plots in small towns or on endurance-oriented farms.[34] Their steady, yeomanlike characters stoically traverse the main-traveled roads of Hamlin Garland or the farmhouse parlors of Mary Wilkins Freeman and Sarah Orne Jewett. A possible exception is Garland's novel *A Spoil of Office* (1892). His careerist lawyer hero begins as a hired hand with Farmers' Alliance views but does not end as one. Regional folk protagonists, always toiling, have little class identification with either the Populist Party or their real-life counterparts, much less a swarming immigrant proletariat.

The urban story successfully offered its hyperactive inner-city ethnics to Garland's middlebrow audience, to whom the working, marginal, and criminal poor, all embodied in the immigrant, were exotic.[35] Sharing with this book-buying readership a moralism about the metropolitan "lower orders" central to the genteel practitioners of so much pre-1890s portraiture, tenement authors never rejected ascension or the rags-to-riches credo outright. The Social Darwinism of their slum tales implicitly reasserted their own Protestant values. But mirroring their bourgeois readers, they were fascinated by those who neither saw ambition as triumph over adversity nor engaged in the Franklinesque struggle upward. In tenement fare, the very disorder of ethnic laboring life is a tourist attraction.[36] The perceived descent into the immigrant city generates a taxonomy of types. Substituting eccentricity for aspiration, these tales "cloud the conditions and dynamics of poverty by an unfailing reduction to moral individualism, the picturesque, or the dangerous classes."[37]

Few authors put the Lower East Side laboring ethnic on parade to transform the working and borderline poor into an exciting slum show with more popular success than E. W. Townsend. He struck publishing gold in the early 1890s with the Chimmie Fadden stories. They were a regular feature of the *New York Sun* and in eponymous book form sold two hundred thousand copies.[38] All that had repelled a John Hay or a Thomas Bailey Aldrich about working people—their rough ways, lack of ambition, unrestrained emotion, and slangy inarticulateness—became the stuff of comedy in the person of the truculent Irish street kid Chimmie.[39]

If Chimmie's monologues and his observations of the pretensions of the elite Four Hundred generate a comedy based on unbridgeability of class gaps, he is as harmless as a stage Irishman. He peddles newspapers, hangs around the settlement house observing the Ladies Bountiful, and accepts tips from the rich for escorting them on saloon tours. "Mr. Paul often says t'me dat he's stuck on de Bow'ry,"[40] he observes. In all ways he is a sidewalk gamin asserting his class identity for humorous ends: "Listen. De old mug calls me 'a unregenerate heathen!' Did ye ever hear such langwudge?" (11). To milk the cross-class comedy, Townsend soon has Chimmie gain the patronage of a society employer, trading his newsie's route for a valet's post (103). But he remains the court jester returning to his old haunts for new material.

Chimmie took the tenement stage at a time when vaudeville houses hosted amateur nights in which young working-class people auditioned (the subject of an Ashcan Group painting, George Luks's 1899 *The Amateurs*). On other evenings, the stagily Irish J. W. Kelly entertained vaudeville audiences with his monologues about cadging drinks and generally living by his wits.[41] Vaudeville's creative roots lay largely in vernacular satire and a world of tenements, immigrants, and street corners.[42] With his grab bag of "say," "see," "dese," and "dose" and wry commentaries on the "swells," Chimmie has links to the ethnic stage vaudevillian who "captured the relationship between the rough and the refined."[43] Moreover, as a self-appointed showman with a store of jokes about the teeming immigrant street, he enables his creator to acknowledge and deny socioeconomic barriers. As if on an urban plantation, calling his employers "Mr. Paul" and "Miss Fannie," Chimmie upholds class stratification: a Bowery performer who knows his place.

Published the same year as the first book version of the Chimmie Fadden tales, Townsend's novel *A Daughter of the Tenements* (1895), now remembered chiefly because of Crane's ironic praise of it as tenement realism, also features an immigrant in performance.[44] The book replaces the Irish amateur with a professional, the Italian danseuse Carminella, the daughter of a philandering ne'er-do-well and a lowly ballet girl. Unlike Chimmie, who remains a servant, this good-hearted Lower East Side Cinderella makes a class leap to stardom. Although with a mother to guide her and an upwardly mobile suitor she can bypass the moral compromises that would mark Theodore Dreiser's money-hungry title character in *Sister Carrie* (1900), Carminella, like the Dreiser heroine, defies the odds against chorus-girl anonymity.

Read as a novel whose protagonist is less Carminella than the tenement scene, Townsend's novel has a titular heroine who is only the most gifted performer in the pageant of the urban labor class. Townsend sanitizes what Crane and Cahan would recognize as signs of oppositional cultures: the dirt and crowds, the omnipresent drinking, the Babel of languages and curious sidewalk occupations, the slumming narrator who sees what he himself creates, "the gay companionship of the market-place" (59–60). The noise level of the neighborhood becomes the melodious "piping of museum and concert-hall orchestras" (92); the unregulated gutter activity of Riis's latchkey adolescents and street Arabs, "the scurrying games of thousands of children" (92). All is working-class disorder made orderly by genteel formula. The want and misery of the Other Half become side excursions into the freak shows of sweaters' dens, uncovering stunted (Jewish) creatures blinking at the light. Yet such dark day trips soon cede to a string of assertions about the cheery mentality of the masses (33). Dockworkers, peddlers, ragpickers, street-sweepers, and fruit and fish vendors are strolling players in a Shakespearean play: entertaining oddities all, contented with their parts on the slum stage. Even so, such skewed individualism cannot guarantee more than a servant's lot. Carminella's tenement days are soon a memory, and easily trading ethnicity for fame, she rises to a culturally acceptable finale as a star.

Of the many newsman storytellers who tamed the energies of tenement life by evoking the tenement show, Jacob Riis was one of the few to overlay Townsend's Slum That Never Was with naturalistic observation.[45] Perhaps he could do so because he was no stranger to semipoverty or the manual trades.

In his 1870s youth he had been an ironworker, coal miner, and peddler.[46] After taking an Algerian path by enrolling in business-school telegraphy and becoming a reporter, first for the *New York Tribune* and later the *Evening Sun,* he became distanced by his profession from the work he once sweated at. All of his professional life Riis agitated vigorously to clean up worker habitat, reduce infant mortality, and upgrade living conditions and open up leisure space by replacing substandard housing with more habitable buildings graced with playgrounds. Yet like his fellow narrators of otherness, a fear and hostility underlay his motivations for saving the slums.[47] Whether consciously or not, Riis always differentiated between the slum dwellers, jobholding or otherwise, and the fading artisanal workforce he had joined and then single-mindedly transcended. It is almost as if he wanted to clean up the slum so that immigrants would stay put there. In his short stories, vacillation between a desire to aid poor workers and repulsion at their alleged debasement is at its most evident.

The stories in *Out of Mulberry Street* foreground heroic victims, sentimentalized toughs, and holy street kids in tales proving the tenement child is the father of the man. Like so many of their deadbeat, criminalized, or oppressed fathers, Riis's children are doomed figures. The title character of "Paolo's Awakening" is an altruistic eight-year-old pants presser who studies at night. Yet while there are a few sentimental moments in Riis's collection (the "shiny-eyed" children of "Merry Christmas in the Tenements"), no slum Lincolns, studying by candlelight, live to realize their ambitions. Paolo, the very day of his high school graduation, dies in a transit mishap. Such occasions for pathos are extended to others besides the "good" assimilants denied their reward. The belligerent adolescent tough grows up to become the atavistic escaped con of "The Kid," but he risks certain recapture to do a noble act.

Drawing and embellishing on stories he covered as a crime reporter, Riis sketched dialect protagonists who are killed in gun battles with one another. They are crushed in railway accidents, hit by trucks, burnt up in sweatshop conflagrations, launched into insanity by accumulated troubles, or sent to prison in childhood only to escape and be caught once more. Riis had another reason to rewrite Townsend's Chimmie as snuffed-out little Paolo or starving little Ben, the Jewish tailor's son ("The Slipper-Maker's Fast"), besides his familiarity with their real-life counterparts. Beneath the sentimentalizing, his message is that all of these figures are at not only environmental but ethnic risk. The numerous nativist slurs of *How the Other Half Lives* (1890) are realized in these sketches in the characters' failure to transcend their own identities despite the fact that the majority have jobs, lodging, and kinship relations. The parsimonious Jew, the improvident, hotheaded Italian, the drunken-criminal Irishman, and, in brief allusions, the lazily derelict black act out immigrant scripts. These figures' obsessive cheapness ("The Slipper-Maker's Fast"), intemperate vendettas ("The Christening in Bottle Alley"), or self-defeating drunkenness ("In the Mulberry Street Court") imprison them as much as their depressing habitat. Townsend's landscape is cheerily industrious, filled with characters busy hawking fruit or their own colorfulness. Riis responds with the picturesque made tragic, or at least pathetic, by the grime of ethnicity. If for these penned-in people Mulberry Bend and Bottle Alley afford neither relief nor exit, they are no less on display.

Riis repudiated happy poverty but retained the narrative authority to sentimentalize or blame the ethnic victim. The former *New York Times* columnist and quasi-socialist James W. Sullivan attempted to overturn the spectatorial point of view altogether. Reluctant to abandon the vantage point of the educated outsider, some of his *Tenement Tales of New York* do echo the ethnic clichés of *Mulberry Street*. But the haunting "Not Yet: The Day Dreams of Ivan Grigorovitch" focuses on an alienated sweatshop tailor who is the spectator of his sufferings and the interpreter of his own life. Through Ivan's daydreams, his power to control his own world, however illusory, reveals his dissatisfaction with life in the sweatshop. As the sketch opens, Ivan is the butt of cruelty from his coworkers. Their scorn for his abnormality is underscored by their inhumanity to their own children, whom they have required to lie about their ages and set to work at age eleven. However out of touch with his surroundings, Grigorovitch longs to take his own children to the "big new dime museum," in search of the new mass entertainment pleasures increasingly pursued by city workers who represent emerging biculturalism, blending the old world and the new.[48]

Ivan's search for escape holds a mirror up to the labor-class inhumanity a sweated life can generate while Sullivan replaces the slumming narrator with the worker expert. The narrative increases in power as an implicit contrast is drawn between Ivan the local eccentric and Ivan the silenced voice of social protest. Charged with everything from picking through garbage to incompetence, Ivan, if viewed by the standards of the rapacious shop, is indeed a dreamer. Yet when the point of view shifts to Ivan's tortured consciousness, all that is odd about him becomes reasonable: plans for empowering workers through voting, for collective ownership, for improving the infrastructure of the poorer districts. By the standards of the tenement tale Ivan is a "mild lunatic" (176), and thus yet another ghetto oddity. By his own standards, he is a labor thinker who realizes that workers need the pleasure of spectacle for themselves, not to provide it for bourgeois audiences. In his visionary imagination, working-class leisure is part of a larger socialistic vision. Sullivan, a friend of Samuel Gompers, may have been influenced by Gompers's essay on leisure and the eight-hour day. In any case, Ivan dreams of a better workplace with "earnings not reduced by monopoly . . . [and of] workingmen in . . . fine houses" (192).

In the end, having communicated with neither his fellow workers nor the larger society, Ivan is a martyr to a cultural indifference that either typecasts or rejects the immigrant laborer. The poor tailor dies exhaustedly on a city sidewalk and is shipped off to Potter's Field, buried, in a final irony, by rough laborers unable to appreciate a proletarian utopia.

In denying picturesqueness to this labor-class antecedent of Walter Mitty, Sullivan challenged his colleagues' reduction of ethnic individualism to comic or pathetic oddity. But he reasserted the tenement writers' reductionism in the psychic segregation he imposes on his workingman victim. In the ambiguity of the story's close, Ivan's very strangeness, his inability to adapt, destroys him as much as the harshness of his avaricious subcontractor and oxlike coworkers. In his desperation, Ivan has willed himself out of the immigrant work world. Embracing neither an unlikely assimilation nor a soul-destroying survival, Ivan ultimately finds that there is no place on earth for the oddest Jew in the shop.[49]

Unlike the depiction of white male ethnics as cheerfully industrious, harmlessly deviant, and prone to misguided actions or fatal illusions, blacks in tenement fiction were dismissed in racist asides or otherwise consigned to literary invisibility.[50] In *How the Other Half Lives,* where he attempted a broader survey, Riis includes a chapter on "The Color Line in New York," which, had he chosen to revise it, might well have formed a vignette for *Out of Mulberry Street.* In it he distinguishes the respectable working class comprising "the new settlement of colored people . . . in Harlem" from the shiftless black tough of the mixed-race beer dives, who went "to the ball with a razor in his boot-leg."[51] Extending Riis's inquiry, W.E.B. Du Bois in *The Philadelphia Negro* (1899), using urban ethnography, social history, and descriptive statistics, offered a true sociology of class structure in the African American Seventh Ward.[52] Yet when he meets those he and fellow members of the Talented Tenth called the Submerged Tenth, he returns to Riisian tenement conventions. He deplores the "libertine" amusements and "larcenous" habits of these wily, lower-rung desperadoes of whom, together with the allegedly unprincipled new foreigners, he disapproved. In brief passages on "rough black pleasureseekers" who "do not work" and often form part of "the more desperate class of criminals," Du Bois applies the slum-story perspective to a violent episode:[53]

> A few [black] loafers [are] on the corners, a [black] prostitute here and there, and the Jew and Italian plying their trades. Suddenly there is an oath, a sharp altercation, a blow; then a hurried rush of feet, the silent door of a neighboring club closes, and when the policeman arrives only the [black] victim lies bleeding on the sidewalk; or at midnight . . . comes the sharp, quick crack of pistol shots—a scurrying in the darkness, and only the wounded man lies awaiting the patrol-wagon.[54]

The black-authored Harlem tenement tale, exchanging the vignette from a safe distance for a probing study of southern migrant social dislocation, awaited 1900s works like Paul Laurence Dunbar's *The Sport of the Gods* (1902). But despite its spectatorial viewpoint, Du Bois's excursion into the black street would also prove prophetic.

The Other Other: Ethnic Womanhood in Tenement Texts

By the last decade of the nineteenth century, new technology that broke up processes previously performed by men allowed unskilled women to enter the labor market in record numbers. Four times as many women worked outside the home in the 1890s as in the 1870s.[55] From the sweatshops of the Lower East Side and the paper-box factories of Brooklyn to the packinghouses of Chicago, the laundries of Buffalo, and the textile mills of Atlanta and the industrializing South, single white women under twenty-five put a collective stamp on the term "working girl." By the time Riis included his essay "The Working Girls of New York" in *How the Other Half Lives,* more immigrant female industrial workers toiled in that city than in any other. Of the nation's four million women wage earners, 350,000 lived and worked in the world's greatest ethnic enclave, the majority of them foreign-born clothing workers or their first-generation daughters.[56]

Predictably, this army of feminine workers provoked ambivalence even among its titular defenders. Riis's representative essay sentimentalizes the seamstresses as it praises their sad lives, their valor in the face of starvation wages, and their refusal to become sexual chattel.[57] Yet the same essay that approves a sewing woman who threw herself out a window rather than resort to streetwalking called it a miracle that more young women did not replace sewing and starving in an Elizabeth Street attic with a vocation of commercialized sex.[58] Like so many decade observers deploring the feminine exploited, the protection Riis really offered the seamstress was from herself.

In or outside the tenement tale, these women's presence added a new dimension to the half-century-old debate on the propriety of white women's work. The ethnic female majority, less skilled and educated and not so culturally malleable as the Yankee daughters of Lowell, suggested the outmodedness of the factory lady without weakening the imperatives that produced the trope. Instead, the old impulse to impose chastity took new forms, heightened by a perceived link between working girls' recreation, whether in workplace gossip or after-hours pleasure seeking, and sexual waywardness. To most tenement authors, white ethnic females were imperiled less by a decline in factory conditions (although that too was noted) than by a new sexual expressiveness that both marked and confirmed them as what Magdalena Zaborowska calls the "oversexed ethnic female" who "work[ed] half-undressed . . . with [sweatshop men]" (*Daughter of the Tenements,* 115).[59]

Although the prurient fantasy indicted the observers rather than the observed, the historian Kathy Peiss has found much evidence of "frank discussions of sexuality among [immigrant] laboring women" on the shop floor. This new affirmation of heterosexuality was further acted on in the dance halls that by 1900 appeared every two or three blocks on the Lower East Side and in mixed-sex resorts like Coney Island amusement parks.[60] Lengthy descriptions of the language, clothing, and social and workplace rituals associated with these assertive new sexual identities were still schematic before the Progressive Era. Yet, particularly in tenement tales, immigrant women foster one another's flighty conduct on the job, reveling in a personal style that mistakes the flashy for the self-assertive.

In spite of the grim experience of work-floor oppression they depict, the authors of these cautionary tales preach the familiar American sermon of nothing else but hard work (Ralph, "Dutch Kitty," 137). There are no feminine Chimmie Faddens, exculpated for rebelliousness by comedy. Nor did Riisian sentiment leaven portrayals of women victimized by their moral frailties and tenement-world determinism the way it did for thugs with hearts of gold. Instead, from Riis to Sullivan, writers regulated immigrant femininity through a suitor who demonstrates his acculturation not so much by a journey upward as by saving the daughter of the tenements. (An apparent exception, Townsend's Carminella, whose English is completely unaccented, is too good for a tenement peer. Buttressed by a watchful mother and her own considerable talent, she needs no saving anyway.) In his *People We Pass,* Julian Ralph's coquettish shopgirl in the eponymous "Dutch Kitty's White Slippers" is chastised for and saved from dancing too much by her stolid German suitor. In Ralph's created work world, Lewy Tusch rightly tells her that her (Irish) girlfriend, Rosy Stelling, is not "straight" (144), a possible allusion to prostitution. In this didactic tale, fear does what warnings cannot. Kitty, who had "danced as much as any working-girl in New York" (138–139), finally runs from the dance hall to the arms of her Dobbin-like suitor. True to ethnic cliché, Irish salvation is more problematic. The sewing-shop title character of Sullivan's "Minnie Kelsey's Wedding," avid for dancing and ripe for corruption, experiences an eleventh-hour rescue, and that by a neighborhood man with a dubious reputation. Presumably they will redeem each other. Brander Matthews's "Before the Break of Day" in *Vignettes of Manhattan* (1894) features Terry the saloonkeeper, who sets an already wayward girl, Maggie O'Donnell, toward marriage and housekeeping, above rather than of the barroom.

Even the naive Ernestine Beaulefoy of Sullivan's "Cohen's Figure" in *Tenement Tales of New York* has but to request a modeling job in a sweatshop, where the other models are "cheap . . . talking and laughing with the men, unconscious of immodesty" (83), to inspire the greasy proprietor to run his hands over her body. While remaining a virgin, she plunges out a window to acknowledge her taint and avoid further manhandling. But beneath the death-over-dishonor moral is the linkage of wage-earning womanhood and sensuality. Another plummet is the fate of the Jewish cloakmaker Rosie Baruch of the "harum scarum ways" and "animal spirits" in the *Mulberry Street* story "The Cat Took the Kosher Meat." Heedless of neighbors' warnings about tenement-building dangers, Rosie in a similar vein stays out late and comes home noisily to proclaim the liberty denied her in the Old World.[61] It is not long before she falls down an air shaft, Riisian poetic justice for all Lower East Side sexual roustabouts.[62]

These tales of women headed for a fall alternately provide last-minute rescues of foolish virgins and kill off those whose carnal knowledge had morally doomed them. Black laboring women in their rare appearances were denied any such salvation. Jacob Riis, one of the few to fictionalize an African American woman of the Bowery, chose not to explore the impact of discrimination, although he was well aware of it. The title character of "Nigger Martha's Wake" was an accepted member of the multiethnic streetwalking group that gathers at her funeral. But like her cohorts Cock-Eyed Grace and Sheeny Rose, they are "tigers," "fiends," "disheveled hags" (*Out of Mulberry Street,* 112). Martha, a suicide, is one sullied representative of a troublesome minority who will trouble the police or look for a "night's catch" (107). Yet her act does not signify her victimization by a racist society unwilling to hire black women over a Kitty or a Rosie. The preference of death over continued degradation that for other minorities would have earned praise here does not.

There is no evidence that Riis had read the ex-slave narratives extolling hard work or *Iola Leroy* (1892), by the racial uplift advocate Frances E. W. Harper, a novel that positively portrays sharecropping southern women during Reconstruction.[63] Yet if he had, it is unlikely that he would have applied Harper's insights about Iola's experiences in the northern labor market, which excluded black women from industrial and clerical jobs. A refined mulatta, Iola is still denied employment in white businesses. With Martha paid to be promiscuous and nothing else, it is clear that the black woman's tenement world is the most morally constricted of all.

To return to the dominant tenement narrative of white ethnics, a curious exception to the linkage of ethnicity and promiscuity, whether thwarted or enacted, is provided by *Tom Grogan* (1895). It was a popular novel by a scion of Philadelphia gentility, Francis Hopkinson Smith, about a rough female stevedore with two children to raise. Though not strictly a tenement tale, it contains scenes in which "Tom," who forswears femininity to run a Staten Island hauling concern almost single-handedly, contrasts with the hard-pressed labor-class women of the teeming Lower East Side. Tom's ability to ride the streets as a teamster rather than walk them as a sweatshop drone en route to the job or a prostitute on the stroll suggests a manlike capability that liberates her from the strictures of tenement-tale womanhood. Going Chimmie Fadden one better, she is a walking show, the last word on quaint proletarians. To the approval of period audiences, Smith loaded descriptions of Tom with apparent praise for her muscular figure.[64] Best of all to an audience fearful of foreign agitators, she commands respect among everyone but the slackers of the union, who, unlike anti-union Tom, work hand-in-glove with thieving businessmen.

Tom's version of ethnic comedy is to act out everything an American workingman ought to be.[65] Smith thus erased her hero(ine)'s ethnic identification, for the Irish had dominated carting for decades in the city. But the novel's more important message was built on bourgeois assumptions about the problematic sexuality of ethnic working women. Through Tom, Smith neatly recasts and solves this culturally vexing problem. Her workplace cross-dressing curbs Tom's life as a woman and thus revokes the sexual free agency of the Dutch Kittys and Minnie Kelseys. Given the ideologies of ethnic laboring otherness that governed cultural debate and tenement fiction alike, it did not matter that the decade's most colorful woman worker was no woman at all.

The Tenement (Re)cast:
Ethnic Misbehavior in Crane, Cahan, and Norris

From the pathos-driven Riis sketch to the contrived Smith novel, the commercially successful story of the tenement offered a uniform vision of ethnic oddness. It is not surprising that in the heyday of this subgenre, Stephen Crane, the young bohemian journalist, incognito Bowery rover, and interviewerbefriender of teamsters and prostitutes, had to publish his counterversion of the immigrant worker, the unexpurgated version of *Maggie: A Girl of the Streets,* at his own expense.[66] Analysts concur that Crane "transform[ed] the beatitudes of the Protestant ethic [into his characters'] idle contempt and aggressive longings." His vision of Irish American plebeian street life is more elusive.[67] For over one hundred years critics have attempted to classify the unique approach Crane takes to the effect of community and social factors upon working-class behavior and consciousness, from child rearing and family networks to sexual conduct and barroom culture.[68]

On the surface, *Maggie* employs the conventional frame of a girl who worked in a shirt factory and was ruined by a strangling work life, a hard-drinking labor-class family, a neighborhood seducer, a love of pleasure, and her own considerable naïveté.[69] The less conventional elements, principally the profanity (hells and damns) and a fallen Maggie Johnson's solicitation of an unsavory waterfront man, were edited out when Appleton and Company reissued the novella in 1896 on the strength of Crane's reputation from *The Red Badge of Courage* (1895). Yet such excisions mattered little. Most period reviewers labeled it an overly sympathetic sweatshop-to-streetwalker story despite its titular heroine's river suicide. Condemning the self-sustaining slum types as much as the failed prostitute, Crane's contemporary Hamlin Garland (who had visited "hideous" Homestead two years before) found in the novella the atmosphere of the jungles, "where outlawed human nature rebels against God and man."[70] Its few defenders, making a virtue of its supposed flaws, commended it for reversing romantic tenement fiction. William Dean Howells, though privately shocked by the prostitution theme, elevated *Maggie* to Greek tragedy.[71]

In fact, the novella does something more subversive than opponents of its amorality or proponents of its realism or elemental truth realized. Maggie herself, though more a period cliché than a fully realized character, is part of a landscape of misbehaving Irish Americans. They are men and women who both appropriate and buy into the era's nativism by calling one another "micks" (3) and whose childhood, tenement, workplace, and after-hours misconduct Crane privileges over the civilities of the dominant culture. Crane's bellicose proletariat in its Irish enclave probes neither itself nor its status; instead, it relentlessly violates the norm. Thus in an oft-quoted line, a neighbor, hearing another fracas inside the Johnson apartment, opens the door to ask of little Maggie, "Is yer fader beatin' yer mudder, or yer mudder beatin' yer fader?" (10). Stripping away the mediating conventions of his colleagues, Crane places his readers uncomfortably close to the live melodrama of the tenement classes. His many scenes in the city's saloon venues, where laboring folk further act out their desires, fantasies, and resentments, dramatize "the seductions of a self-interested and hedonistic urban ethic."[72] In Crane's reenvisioned tenement world, such behavior drives as much as it taints the Rum Alley and Devil's Row people who engage in it.

Crane was uniquely qualified to reject the pieties of the tenement school's Bowery. A self-styled "One in Rebellion" and in flight from a pietistic temperance upbringing and emotionally unstable family, Crane consulted police court records, lived experimentally as a derelict, interviewed "chorus girls" in barroom surroundings, and both patronized and went to court for some of them.[73] He walked the Lower East Side streets looking as unkempt and the worse for drink as his fictional creations Jimmie the teamster, his abusive father, his friend Pete the bartender, or, the subject of a later tale, a Johnson neighbor, the young workman George Kelcey. For all his experimentation, Crane never relinquished his vision of the lower-rung working class as cordoned off both emotionally and financially from a bourgeois normality he understood if rejected. In *Maggie,* he offers an invented Lower East Side of "frantic quarrels" (10) and of traumatizing overcrowdedness. He then infuses this portrait with his conviction that for the working poor the slum was also a state of mind. Their isolation from respectability was in part self-imposed. It dampened their ambitions and imprisoned them in defensive fantasies of self-importance, but it did not lessen their energetic rebuttal of the work ethic.

Crane did not work out a true sociology based on these notions of working-class and borderline-class fears of inadequacy.[74] But he did give artistic expression to the struggle between enraged frustration and pleasure seeking experienced by his Lower East Side wage earners. In *Maggie* and in "George's Mother," written in 1896 but concerning events prior to the novella, his is a surrealist sociology of anarchic children and monster parents, and the obsessional, self-defeating ways they all pursue gratification. Crane paved the way for the inner-city naturalism of James T. Farrell's *Studs Lonigan: Judgment Day* (1935), Nelson Algren's *Never Come Morning* (1942), and Richard Price's *Bloodbrothers* (1976).

Crane's labor-class characters solidifed nativist prejudices about the anarchic Irish even though the Johnsons' Irishness is of less importance than their intractability.[75] Precursors of a long line of workers at odds with themselves, Crane's brawling working poor defy and vilify, waging battles that scar them. Including the masochistic Maggie, his personae live on impulse. Jimmie Johnson, whose childhood street brawls open the novella, is an updated Mose. Where the antebellum figure prided himself on his fire-company allegiance and wage-earning abilities as much as his streetwise savvy, Jimmie's hallmark is an alienated truculence—Chimmie Fadden unbound. Through saloon forays, shouting matches as he drives his team through the streets, profane battles with his brawling, Medusa-like mother, and callous affairs with local girls, he appeases and unleashes the hostile energies created by his lower-class status.

His sister Maggie, also viewed from her battered childhood on, is the capmaker Lize in a constricted economic and psychic landscape. Though the eternal victim of her bullying family and Pete, her jilting bartender lover, she too restlessly seeks pleasure. She certainly finds no group identity in a sweatshop work culture of gossiping women. There is evidence of the intensity of this Irish American working girl's immersion in popular-cultural fantasy in one much-analyzed scene. In it she communes with and mistakes the hiss-the-villain plots of the concert hall for the possibility of triumph (28) in her own sad life. The Bowery melodrama may well have peddled conservative cultural messages and, by implication, a false consciousness for working people.[76] Certainly Maggie's inarticulate response to the painted backdrops and contrived plotting of Virtue Triumphant scenarios is Crane's indictment of her refusal to acknowledge the oppressions of her life and her hunger to appropriate middle-class virtues and attitudes.

Yet Maggie is no different from the countless working-girl readers of Laura Jean Libbey. Her dime novels use the same plotting as the Bowery melodrama Crane disdained. Michael Denning, in his study of Libbey books such as *Only a Mechanic's Daughter* (1894), contends that they played on fantasies of climbing upward without repudiating a working-class identity.[77] Maggie may well be too thinly realized to make such distinctions. The craving she shares with other frustrated Bowery dwellers for rescue from drabness does not undercut her connection to the Lower East Side world. There the popular theater she adores, as well as the dime museums she frequents, was born and flourished. Whatever Crane suggests about the cheap theater represented as a way to colonize the working-class imagination, he also allows Maggie to "rejoice" in it (28) far more than other period authors did. Together with her bartender lover, Maggie is a willing member of the concert saloon audiences. She is certainly part of those who, Crane writes pointedly, worked with their hands (22). What in Townsend or Smith simply provides entertainment for the slummer (relegated in the Crane tale to Freddy, a drunken fool jettisoned by Nell, a clever streetwalker) in this environment regales the worker crowd. Through Maggie's fervent need to submerge herself in the melodramas she attends, Crane, however tentatively, approaches the issue of mass culture in a way his colleagues do not.

Nor does he merely juxtapose the inauthentic fare of the Bowery stage, where virtue inevitably triumphs and the good prosper, with the alcoholic blue-collar father and the out-of-control, abusive mother who substitute manipulation, cowardice, and illusion for parenting. Whether his characters frequent the cheap theater, sit on the bar stool, rant at the judge, or hurl whiskey bottles at one another, their lives are permeated with a chaotic intensity that has nothing of the safely picturesque. They may, as Alan Trachtenberg contends, view their lives melodramatically. But as Peter Brooks explains in *The Melodramatic Imagination*, melodrama "offer[s] . . . a refusal of the dailiness of the everyday . . . refus[ing] to content itself with the . . . disappointments of the real."[78] Moreover, though mired in rather than actualized by their own rebellion, Crane's workers project their dissatisfaction onto an outside world that does not share their value system. In this their creator was moving toward the insight that alienation can fuel cultural expression, that "deviant" ways structure lives, quite separate from either conformist acquiescence or Homestead-like militance. The exaggerations and grotesqueries in which Crane indulges should not obscure his attempt to enter the enraged psychic landscapes, alienated labor worlds, and insular enclaves of the working poor. In a halting way, *Maggie* is an experimental unleashing of Bowery culture in that Crane all but permits the Johnson family to wrest control of the narrative. Their closing platitudes about the dead Maggie remind the reader of the toll of street life on young working women, particularly when combined with a dysfunctional family. "I'll fergive her!" yells Mary Johnson (58) in Crane's satiric thrust at his own religious parent. Tenement survivors, they live to scream another day. The last word remains theirs.

After *Maggie*, Crane continued to be torn between denying his blue-collar Irish Americans' behavioral violence and celebrating the energy it unleashed. In "George's Mother" (1896), continuing to probe temperance as a class issue, he again gave voice to drink culture as an oppositional response to the pressures particularly felt by ethnic groups unused to factory routines.[79] The imposition of industrial conformity on Bowery escapism is personified in a figure reminiscent of Crane's own mother, and no more successful at imposing Protestant morality.[80] The story centers on the steel magnolia churchwoman Mrs. Kelcey. She is engaged in a psychological tug-of-war to "save" her worker son George from the "little smiling saloon," the political and recreational hub of many real-life workingmen.[81] Unlike in *Maggie,* the moral arbiter, not the scapegoat, perishes. An increasingly alcoholic George is left at story's end rudderless but free. Again, though, the only worker politics is one of sensation, and his search for self is a dead end. Benedict Giamo, a close student of the tale, sees in the death of George's mother a retreat from an authentic exploration of plebeian culture. A bewildered George is left with nothing but spiritual and material impoverishment.[82]

Given his conviction of the entropic nature of working-class mores, Crane had gone as far as he could with the counterculture theme. He brought to his invented after-work culture only barrooms and phony religiosity. Thus he could not find in the furies of the Bowery laborer any of the real-life significance that an older ethnic culture invested in the lodges, burial societies, and political groups that Francis Couvares has found in pre-Homestead Pittsburgh.[83] Having located an outlaw culture on the working-class Bowery, Crane's art could not infuse it with possibility.

Also criticized for "sordid" tenement tales of waywardness among the Lower East Side dialect-ridden, Abraham Cahan, like Crane, produced stories in the name of Lower East Side working-class authenticity.[84] Crane, always in search of fresh wartime landscapes, saw his Bowery days in that fashion. For Cahan, a Russian-Jewish immigrant and onetime cigar worker, this was the beginning of a lifelong political and literary immersion in the socialistic trade union circles of the downtown (east European) Jews. By the time *Yekl* appeared in 1896, Cahan, soon to edit the *Jewish Daily Forward,* the largest Yiddish-language paper in the nation, was already established as a cultural leader and moral authority in New York's Lower East Side ghetto.[85]

If Crane's Lower East Siders are at a dead end caused by their own ungovernable volatility, Cahan's are at a cultural crossroads. Addressing in his fiction Jewish garment-trades workers' responses to assimilation, biculturalism, and the lure of new moralities and popular entertainments, Cahan made visible the gaps in Crane's artistic sociology. Despite his innovations, Crane was wedded to stereotypes of wild Irishness that two disparaging references to money-mad Jewishness did little to dispel (*Maggie,* 25, 26). Cahan, though critical of new cultural practices among his ambitious Jewish subjects, re-shaped the discourse of the "odd ethnic" in ways that none of his contemporaries could have imagined.

All of Cahan's garment-shop characters are hard workers, and Yekl is no exception. In a rejection of Sullivan's and Riis's tragic toilers—and, for that matter, Crane's oily, enigmatic subcontractor who bosses Maggie around—Yekl is determined to become a real "Yankee," learning English, saving money, and generally moving up. Again his aspirations are emblematic of enterprise. Many Jews traded a sewing machine or pushcart for a clothing shop or real estate holdings.

Like his sweatshop coworkers, Jake turns the Lower East Side into a school. He improves his English while attending boxing matches or following betting scores. English is spoken even at the dancing academy where he seeks a more American wife; he hums popular songs at the machine. In describing Professor Joe Peltner's dance school, Cahan adds significantly that the sweatshop workers learning the new dances look like they are working more than playing. Though, like the ambitious, diamond-hard Mamie Fein, he is enticed by clothing and amusement, bent on enjoyment as well as ascension, Yekl has entrepreneurial ambitions that, with Mamie's savings, he will realize.

Yet the irony is that Yekl, renaming himself Jake, is a misbehaving ethnic, and all in the name of becoming a real American. The title character's quest to slough off the greenhorn label includes a swaggering boastfulness not unlike a Jimmie Johnson's and, with a shabby wife and child not yet arrived from the old country, also provides a version of Jimmie's philandering. Yet Cahan, while challenging tenement tale pieties, gives the issues of pleasure clubs and ethnic immoderateness a far more searching scrutiny. What period reviewers denounced as immorality, Jake's dance school flirting, is meant to be symbolic of the new self-directed immigrant who works at forsaking Jewishness by cutting his hair, changing his clothes, and joining the new consumer culture. Cahan implies that Jake himself ascribes less importance to his threat to strike unless he is better paid than to his courtship of the shrewd, modish, and salary-saving Mamie Fein. All of this culminates in his forsaking his unfashionable wife for Mamie, immigrant immorality garbed in New World clothing. And the fact that they will buy a dance academy to further similar aspirations among Jewish newcomers perpetuates Jake's morally irresponsible assimilation.

What was hedonism in Crane has a way of turning into discipline, for these workers crave the settled respectability characteristic of older immigrant groups and even of the uptown German coreligionists still wary of them. To Cahan, however, there is no greater misconduct than this way of mounting a search for self. The *Forward* campaigned against the "unbridled desires" the dance craze embodied, chiding workers for indulging in a frivolous use of leisure as well as aping bourgeois customs to desert the working class.[86] Such a charge was ironic given middle-class disapproval of working-class dance halls, but telling from a socialist perspective. Jake and Mamie's plan to open a dancing school is proof that they want nothing more than to forsake the involuntary labor community of the shop to cash in on a new mass need for amusement. In this they can be juxtaposed with more attractive figures such as David and Beile in Cahan's "A Sweatshop Romance" (1898), principled workers who strike rather than abandon the idea of a true workers' culture.

Cahan was one of the few tenement writers to use the problems of class to address those of culture. Thus working-class culture in his fiction is a choice between an enlightened Jewish Americanism dedicated to industrial democracy and a frivolous self-interest melded to the new mass amusements and commercialism. Casting a cold eye on Yekl's zealous conversion to capitalism, Cahan suggests that assimilation without conscience is the most eccentric choice of all.

While Cahan was worrying over the costs of assimilation, a disturbing novel of working-class San Francisco's established immigrants was preaching that ethnic inferiority was so strong that no change, whether of climate or fortune, could weaken its dangers. The era's darkest portrait of immigrant strangeness, Frank Norris's *McTeague* initially focuses on assimilated and fairly prosperous lower-middle-class figures, bringing in an avaricious Polish Jew and a demented Hispanic servant as dim reminders of the tenement tale. The novel overhauls the slum tour in sections on the "little" life of Polk Street (187), a bustling thoroughfare where the native-born workers ply their trades. As with the Townsend school, sidewalk culture is again amusing, but in this improved version, there are old Germanic and native-born Polk Street clerks, railway conductors, and political club devotees, the very bedrock of a solid American workforce least likely to rebel. Even the rough-hewn title character has climbed out of his Irish mining past and ascended to a Polk Street (unlicensed) dentist's status and a romance with a daughter of established German immigrants, Trina Sieppe. Her ambition is made firmer when she wins a lottery and brings a dowry to the union.

This daughter of Polk Street soon becomes something quite different. Norris loosely based his plot on Patrick Collins, a real-life Jimmie Johnson character run amok. A brutal, alcoholic Irish laborer, he stabbed his cleaning-woman wife to death when she refused to give over her wages.[87] Norris sees degeneration of the Collins kind in the lives of working people whose prospects are initially much brighter. The disintegration of the McTeagues' marriage into Trina's miserliness and Mac's alcoholic sadism is this early eugenicist's sweeping indictment of the lower classes. Well before that disintegration, Norris has racialized the working class via the dirty Polish Jew Zerkow, Polk Street's sole ragman (though a common figure of the New York Bowery), and the crazed Hispanic Maria Macapa, a thieving cleaning woman similarly given to fantasies of wealth. (When they marry and produce a child, it is a "strange, hybrid little being" [240] and thus perishes quickly, apparently deprived of the superior strength of the white race.)

The grotesque behavior of these two Darwinian failures only foreshadows that of the McTeagues: Mac, like Zerkow, will steal and eventually murder his own wife, a woman, like Maria, who has become increasingly demented as her self-control erodes. Tracked down by Trina's cousin, Marcus Schouler, another workingman ruined by greed, McTeague flees, appropriately, to Death Valley, where he kills Marcus and soon perishes himself.

By this nativist narrative's end, atavism taints Jew and Spaniard, German and Irishman alike, even bubbling up from the souls of those like the once-disciplined, fastidious Trina. This skilled toy worker and her worker-intellectual cousin Marcus had once enjoyed the prudent materialism and urban pastimes of the lower middle classes. They soon join the other Norris types devoured by their passions, their ambitions corrupted by miserliness, greed, or drunkenness. Norris thus sounds the alarm about ethnicity that would help fuel the quotas and restrictive immigration laws in the next century. In this repudiation of tenement local color, he provides the decade's ultimate morality tale about the immigrant street world: ethnic strangeness as self-destruction.

Not on My Street:
Some Notes on Strike Fiction's Absent Ethnics

The model town of Pullman, Illinois, was founded outside Chicago by the Pullman Palace Car Company in 1880. A site of industrial protest by its native-born workers in the mid-1890s, it had been planned to make the dirty worker clean by controlling every aspect of employees' lives.[88] The most conservative labor novels of the 1890s advocated similar controls on workers or harked back to an idealized craftsman's past. In James M. Martin's *Which Way, Sirs, the Better?* (1894), the neat streets of Beldendale, named after the local mine owner, are sanitized of crime, violence, and all references to ethnic workers. So too Alice French's stories in *The Heart of Toil* (1898), peopled by abstemious, hardworking Anglo-Saxon yeomen.[89] Even when this labor force erupts in Pullman-like strikes, they are a faceless horde rather than a foreign one. Such is the case in Harry Perry Robinson's *Men Born Equal* (1895) and Charles King's *A Tame Surrender* (1896), respectively set in Pittsburgh and Chicago. Particularly in the novel by King, a military man, the workers are easily quelled when they cravenly invade Chicago's wealthy neighborhoods. A band of similarly misguided ironworkers storms a New York State iron magnate's mansion to demonstrate their might in *The Lawton Girl* (1890), by the literary naturalist Harold Frederic. But when told to disperse by a local defender of the status quo who promises no foreigners will take their jobs, they return docilely to their side of town.

Even the period's rare socialist texts preferred the skilled native-born or old-immigrant worker to the unruly ethnic. Mrs. Nico Bech-Meyer's 1894 novel *Pullmantown* thus privileges a German machinist and an American-born carpenter. Both men doubt whether the unskilled new workforce can achieve political awareness. Other socialist fiction supposedly defending recent immigrants only underscored their irrelevance to "American" labor events like Homestead and Pullman. One has but to look at Edward King's sympathetic garment-strike novel, *Joseph Zalmonah*, modeled on an 1891 United Hebrew Trades' strike involving Joseph Barondess. It sensationalized the militance of "all these types of Hebrews."[90] They are so emotionally uncontrolled and consciously theatrical that King's many comparisons of Zalmonah/Barondess to a biblical Joseph turn the narrative into an Old Testament story more than a strike tale.

In contrast, William Dean Howells's *A Hazard of New Fortunes* was a rare attempt to merge the old-immigrant strike novel with that of the tenement ethnic. Howells draws on several railway strikes of the late 1880s with Pullman-like elements and constituencies. But, recalling the Brooklyn traction protest of 1889, he places his imagined Manhattan strike near poor immigrant neighborhoods.[91] That Howells does not attempt to integrate analysis of the customs and mores of the immigrant ghetto into his short section on organized labor's protest suggests the marginalized position of immigrant labor even in his own city. While the novel remains politically enigmatic, variously billed as quasi-socialistic and conservative, it makes clear that have-not challenges to traditional authority were proliferating, soon to encompass the picturesque poor as well as the skilled trades.[92] Nevertheless by novel's close, Howells trivializes his own perceptions. Throughout the novel he had presented the newer ethnics as "interesting shape[s] of shabby adversity" integral to the "reckless picturesqueness of the Bowery" (159). Despite their disorderliness, his patrician spokesman Basil March finds them as harmlessly colorful as his American strikers are violent. Yet as the strike mounts in intensity, March sanitizes the foreign born. Now they walk the immigrant streets as respectable Sunday strollers who have no relation to the labor unrest of the day. While these ethnic folk are a departure from the rigid typing of the novel's opening sections, their presence in the strike section has another meaning. Having raised the possibility of a multiethnic militant labor movement, Howells now rewrites the ethnic in the name of accommodation. In so doing, he makes visible the problem hanging over all tenement tales: immigrants cannot inhabit their streets on their own terms.

A story by Crane published at decade's end highlighted the dilemma of writers with vague worker sympathies but no literary will to take immigrant labor seriously. The tenement child of "An Ominous Baby" is reminiscent of a young Jimmie Johnson. He stumbles into a wealthy neighborhood and steals a toy when his request to share it is refused. With his usual ambiguity, Crane withholds censure while casting doubt on the boy's cooperative spirit. In allegorical terms, the story asks if a disciplined ethnic labor movement, manned by the sons of the immigrant streets, can ever create itself.

The Incomplete Sociology of the Literary 1890s

In the early ethnographic fiction of the 1890s, a tenement typology replaced the religion of rising central to the labor fiction of previous decades. Where ascension was possible, it remained problematic. Despite formulaic treatments of success stories, such as in *A Daughter of the Tenements,* most 1890s urban writers saw ethnicity and upward rising as at odds. In more thoughtful authors, the gospel of materialism was associated with immigrant self-betrayal, as in Cahan, or seen as a catalyst in the fall of the atavistic ethnic, as in Norris.

Yet in all of these texts the challenge to competitive individualism remained muted. The tenement tale's reiterations of behavioral oddity marked the boundary between working-class and middle-class behavior. The New York local colorists produced slum-dwelling deviants from self-help whose escapist yearnings ranged from harmlessly colorful to pathetically self-defeating. Their laborers' rogues' gallery comprises anything but men and women at recognizable American toil: amateur vaudevillians, tourist attractions, troublemakers, curiosities, ethnic schemers, overwrought sufferers, menacing atavists, girls who go wrong—skewed identities all. And they all stay in their own slum, apparently too bizarre for the nativist conservative labor novel, whose intruders into genteel neighborhoods are at best a faceless mob.

In a more radical text like *Pullmantown,* immigrant militance is also dissipated in otherness metaphors or rendered invisible in a dominant narrative of native-born labor. Even when the slum story attempts to meet the strike novel, authors have enormous difficulty, of their own and their culture's making, integrating the spirit of the immigrant ghetto into portrayals of (skilled and unskilled) labor unrest. Like King, they portray ethnic histrionics or, in the Howells mode, eccentricity. Whatever the immigrant representation, authors adulterate rather than explore ethnic oppositionalism. Immigrant laborers remain literally and figuratively ghettoized.

Crane's characters, who are more self-born than Irish American, submerge or repudiate the work ethic. His Rum Alley working people have no commitment to being other than what they are. By minimizing narrative didacticism (though not irony) and focusing on the primacy of his characters' desires, Crane dramatizes a turbulent, escapist working class that rejects homogeneity and propriety. Their truculence, however, produces no empowerment. Like his fellow authors, with the partial exception of the rather rigid Cahan, Crane had little feel for the stronger, more stable elements of working-class life, even in the volatile slum, much less for the ethnic labor networks and enclaves that were forming in and outside ghettoized areas.[93] Slumming through the streets of the poor, he recognized neither diverse patterns of collective behavior nor cultures of solidarity, whether of ethnic affiliation or labor-class grievance.

In the early 1890s, Edward and Eleanor Marx Aveling wondered why American fiction had no real studies of workers, including the many in city tenements.[94] The authors who were loosely grouped as students of the working and borderline poor tried to fill this gap. They made attempts at a literary sociology, for their characters did swim in a plebeian sea.[95] But their tour-guide approach, while imposing a reassuring order on the unassimilated immigrant street, exposed far more about their ideologies of ethnicity, race, gender, and social mobility than about the lived experience their sociological art claimed to understand.[96]

CHAPTER 5

Beastmen and Labor Experts

Fiction and the Problem of Authority from 1900 to 1917

He was the human slag of the mills. . . . He . . . overworked, overdrank, and lived like a beast. . . . And yet was it *his* fault?

—JAMES OPPENHEIM, *PAY ENVELOPES* (1911)

I had looked for a [dockworker] army. I saw only mobs of angry men . . . picketing the docks. . . . [They were] jamming into barrooms, voicing the wildest rumors, talking, shouting, pounding tables with huge fists. And to me there was nothing inspiring but only something terrible here, an appalling force turned loose, sightless and unguided.

—ERNEST POOLE, *THE HARBOR* (1915)

"Bad luck?"

Chucky was silent. His past was not vivid. Hunger, cold, the cough,— these were the chief memories.

—MARY FIELD, "BUMS—A STORY," *THE MASSES* (MAY 1913)

Benjamin Messick, *Main Street Café Society,* c. 1938. Oil on canvas, $30\frac{1}{8} \times 23\frac{3}{16}$ in. Los Angeles County Museum of Art. Gift of Velam Hay-Messick.

By 1900, in an unprecedented yoking of workforce ethnicity and mass production, new forms of scientific management had accelerated the process of deskilling under way since the birth of the factory system. Corporate employers could now hire vast numbers of cheap immigrant laborers to feed the new industrial assembly lines. Three-quarters of the jobs in Pittsburgh's basic industries were manned by unskilled or semiskilled workers that very year.[1] By the time of Upton Sinclair's explosive best-seller *The Jungle* (1906), Chicago meatpackers employed one-third of the nation's packinghouse workers, many of them unskilled Slavs laboring at the giant Swift's and Armour's factories, and even they were outnumbered by the Bohemians, Italians, and Jews of that city's garment industry.[2] Three years later, twenty thousand people, one-fifth of Youngstown's population and the majority of them Slavs, Poles, and Lithuanians, were working in that Ohio city for Carnegie Steel and Youngstown Sheet and Tube.[3] By the next year, 1910, New Hampshire's Amoskeag mills employed whole families in the world's largest textile plant, seventeen thousand hands, in an ethnic diversity unheard of in the antebellum Lowell days of a "Yankee" workforce.[4]

The beginning of the next decade saw the growth not only of meatpacking, textiles, and steel but the garment trades, coal, iron, and construction; recent ethnic arrivals constituted one-half of the workers in these industries although they made up 14 percent of the population.[5] Whereas during the 1890s an average of less than half a million newcomers arrived each year, more than one million immigrants arrived in each of the six years between 1905 and 1911. (In a related development in these years prior to the Great Migration, one million African Americans worked by 1910 in mines, on railroads, and as urban day laborers.)[6] By that decade's end, too, Mexican Americans and Asians, though the majority were relegated to migratory labor in California, worked in the Southwest's coal and metal mines.[7]

This remaking of the American working class enabled common laborers and low-level factory operatives, often as unskilled in English as in the trades whose lowest jobs they filled, to "enter history," in the words of Irving Howe.[8] Although the new foreigners were apt to be more pliable than the strike-prone "old-immigrant" workforce, they were capable enough of sustained militance to be at the center of the period's so-called Hunky Strikes,[9] the derogatory ethnic label applied to all Slavs, Hungarian or not. A Chicago packinghouse workers' strike a few years before Sinclair's blockbuster, for instance, included polyethnic mass meetings and union literature printed in six languages.[10] Lawrence alone, the site of a successful 1912 Massachusetts strike—and one shunned by the skilled-trades American Federation of Labor—had twenty-five nationalities speaking fifty languages working and protesting at the mill.[11] And in nonurban venues such as the mining town of McKees Rocks, the end of the century's first decade saw an unlikely if failed alliance between skilled America-born workers and the Slavs and Italians, in the first in a series of industrial conflicts in western Pennsylvania.[12]

Although the mass of new arrivals, barred by language and a multitude of other cultural factors, were not involved in rank-and-file protest, by 1910 big, demonstrative strikes of foreign-born laborers had become commonplace.[13] Moreover, though many of the strikes were unsuccessful, they all demonstrated new forms of immigrant self-activity.[14] Nor was ethnic labor action limited to the picket line. While the Socialist Party had offered limited appeal to most immigrants, particularly in the century's first decade, unskilled immigrant workers made up an increasingly large proportion of the membership during the 1910s.[15] This was particularly so in the garment-trades unions such as the International Ladies' Garment Workers Union (ILGWU) and the Amalgamated Clothing Workers (ACW), virtually created by the Jews of New York's Lower East Side and in cities from Chicago to New York. In the "Golden Age of Yiddish Socialism" these needle-trades unions became synonymous with the Socialist Party.[16]

Socialist or not, all of this activity signaled a protest not only against employers determined to fire strikers and ban all except company unions but against a rigid unionism. Such failings were personified in industries like coal and steel by the craft-based American Federation of Labor. With a few key exceptions, such as the Amalgamated Meat Cutters of North America, and a foothold in the coal industry, the AFL had all but abandoned attempts to organize mass industry.[17] Indeed, strengthening its associations with Americanism and "guild unity," the burgeoning labor organization officially barred most "new" immigrants from membership. It viewed immigrant groups with horror as bastions of doctrinaire Marxists or anarchists.[18] Such sentiments were echoed by nonunionist craftsmen in texts such as the epistolary narrative *Letters from a Workingman* (1908), which minutely detailed the skill-based social strata in a big-city machinist's shop.[19] Yet there were complications in this intersection of nativist politics and craft insularity. The AFL, for example, was supported by and often proclaimed its fidelity to (right-wing) socialism, which in turn had considerable influence in many unions, including those of the machinists and mine workers.[20]

At the other end of the union spectrum were the agrarian and migrant labor bodies created by the disenfranchised whom the (left-wing) socialist Industrial Workers of the World (IWW) labeled the "true proletarians." Such ad hoc groups created scattered, transient locals of poor-white tenant farmers, or of Mexican and even Japanese field hands.[21]

Politically invisible African Americans, a far larger minority than Hispanics or Asians, constituted an impressive 12 percent of all laborers as the new century began.[22] But with exceptions such as the West Virginia coal industries and the more constricted work world of the Pullman porter, they were permitted far more participation on the wrong than on the right side of the picket line. Until the wartime era they were not only barred from survivalist alliances with native-born whites but denied equal entrée to a mill town and foundry workforce in the throes of political self-transformation.[23]

In sum, the period from 1900 through the "decade of strikes" was marked by sectional conflicts between trade unionists of varying political hues and by more pervasive battles between employers, skilled "old" immigrants, and less-skilled ethnic and racial minority workers. All of these conflicts would find echoes in the imaginative literature of the day. Fiction would also hear other labor voices.

Observers of rather than participants in the labor-political fray, so-called Progressives or social engineers were far more interested in doing battle with corrupt politicians, exposing trusts, and in general reordering society along more "scientific" lines than they were in industrial democracy and the workingman. But a substantial stratum of the reform element was forging its own ideologies of American labor by charting the lives of the ethnic newcomers of the Other Half and their responses to the unrestricted power of the new corporations. These surveyors, drawn from universities, philanthropies, settlement houses, investigating commissions, and the Protestant ascendancy, were appalled that industries like steel were so unregulated and deaf to the tragedy of industrial accidents and the strains of speedups.[24] Their Progressive mission was nothing less than to ensure social progress by regulating industrial capitalism, using laws, social agencies, and Americanization—all administered by the new social professionals.

Problem solvers and social engineers, these earnest worshipers of expertise were also data gatherers who wished to codify the complexity of the American working class.[25] (A notable exception, Lewis Hine, commissioned by various reform organizations to enlarge the narrative by providing visual documentation, shared a working-class background with his subjects.)[26] It is true that the forces of Jane Addams, the Women's Trade Union League (WTUL), and "a social and industrial Progressive elite" lent aid to long-running, highly visible ethnic urban strikes.[27] Yet even these advocates of industrial democracy were more involved in municipal and factory reform than in partnering the striking worker. It was as people to be examined that the workingman and workingwoman became the subject of University of Chicago sociological research on the social organization of Packingtown, data on which the author of *The Jungle* partly drew. A similarly careful tabulation appears in Louise Boland More's representative *Wage Earners' Budgets: A Study of Standards and Costs of Living in New York City* (1907), William Lauck's *Conditions of Labor in American Industries* (1917), and—with a muckraking subtext—Sophonisba Breckinridge and Edith Abbott's "Housing Conditions in Chicago," serialized in the 1911 *American Journal of Sociology.*[28] Blue-collar values, politics, religion, and leisure time were assessed in Mary K. Simkhovitch's *The City Worker's World in America* (1917) and Grace Abbott's *The Immigrant and the Community* (1917).[29]

Though less numerous, Progressive texts on black workers included a book by Mary White Ovington, then executive secretary of the NAACP, *Half a Man:*

The Status of the Negro in New York City (1911) and William A. Crossland's *Industrial Conditions among Negroes in St. Louis* (1914). Although none of these texts adopts the sociological condescension of Riis's *How the Other Half Lives* (1890), all of them do once again instruct the working-class subject on his lived experience.

Of the avalanche of such titles, the Pittsburgh Survey was the quintessential product of the new scrutiny. As such, it embodied the religion of expertise preached everywhere from the settlement house to the city planning commission to the platform committee of the Socialist Party to the key muckraking, Socialist, and antilabor fiction of the day. Funded by corporate philanthropists, the Pittsburgh Survey was the first extensive study of a major industrial city.[30] It was in all ways intended "to connect the reformist purpose with all the newest methods of scientific inquiry, and [to list] and coordinat[e] a variety of methodologies and academic disciplines in the quest for the totality of the social fact."[31] A massive research enterprise, between 1907 and 1914 it produced six volumes with 525 photographs, drawings, and charts. Compared with the highly selective ghetto and sweatshop sorties of the previous century, its scope was vast. The six volumes, prominent among them *The Steel Workers* (1911) by John A. Fitch and *Wage-Earning Pittsburgh* (1914), edited by the survey director, Paul U. Kellogg, scrutinized that city's industrial relations, workplace accidents and legal redress, blue-collar stratification in the mill, the panorama of urban women's jobs, and the lives of their domestic counterparts in the mill towns.

Taken in totality, such Progressive studies by experts established a new seriousness about the lives of working people. Yet there was a tension between the ambitious social accounting of the Pittsburgh Survey and the mission to speak for the skilled or unskilled worker denied access to a national forum. Fitch's tome, which deals with every aspect of the steel industry, did give voice to steelworkers.[32] Yet, like Theodore Roosevelt's Progressive Party itself, the Kellogg group was wedded to regulating rather than abolishing the capitalist system, a far cry from the view of the more militant men at the foundries owned by Carnegie and Frick. Moreover, because the surveyors were reluctant to engage in a class analysis, their new "Social Gospel" often fit those viewed and interviewed into the mold of social-scientific spokesmanship.

Despite socialists' perceptions of the Progressives as too middle class and disconnected from the lived experience of overworked ethnics, no less a figure than the IWW powerhouse Bill Haywood was impressed by the amplitude of the survey.[33] The most popular period novelists who addressed working-class experience applied the heightened documentary approach to their fiction on Ludlow mining protest and Lawrence textile mill upheaval, picketline militance, and other working-class self-activity. These authors included those like the sometime Socialist poet and settlement worker James Oppenheim, whose short-story collection *Pay Envelopes* (1911) focuses on skilled and unskilled workers. Joining them was Upton Sinclair in the Ludlow, Colorado, strike novel *King Coal* (1917), appending Industrial Commission findings on "Bloody Ludlow" to the novel itself. And a more surprising contributor was the American author Winston Churchill, a disillusioned upholder of genteel values who produced a Lawrence strike novel, *The Dwelling-Place of Light* (1917). A broadened and heightened interest in accuracy about labor, skilled and unskilled, craftsmen and menials, informs these texts, evident particularly in the careful attention to detail and the use of journalistic observation.[34] These authors, most of socialist persuasion, were the first generation to balance a close scrutiny of workers' lives with a critique of capitalism. As novelists, they broke free of the strike-centered novels of the 1870s and 1880s and the local-color approach of the 1890s.[35] As ideologues opposed to corporate paternalism or embourgeoisement, and often pessimistic about the fruits of assimilation, they all in one way or another gave the idea of rising an eastern European immigrant point of view.

Turning the spotlight on workers, however, was one thing. Relinquishing literary authority to them was another. For this generation of authors, few of whom came from the working class themselves, to take immigrant working people seriously, a tradition of literary ambivalence about workers was not easily jettisoned. The literary love affair with the tenements may have ended, but not the debate about the worker's maturity and stability. Old arguments resurfaced, even in relatively advanced literary quarters. Thus the atavistic brute-as-laborer, heralded in titles such as *Vandover and the Brute* which, though written years before, appeared in 1914, is the controlling metaphor and book title of *The Jungle*. The trope was played out in other texts by Sinclair and his fellow Socialists Ernest Poole and Jack London in antiestablishment pieces in *The Masses* (1911–1917). It informed the vacillating Progressivism of David Graham Phillips and the anguished conservatism of American author Winston Churchill. And it even appeared in edited "life stories," the autobiographies of immigrants—rare narratives by Asians, Native Americans, and others—told to Poole and others writing for the general-interest magazine *The Independent*.[36]

All of these representations in one way or another addressed brutish industrial poverty by indicting the degraded worker for lacking the tools to analyze the class relations that produced his debasement. In some texts the indictment took a Jekyll/Hyde form, tracing a descent from skilled work to brutishness. In others it followed a reverse trajectory, the beast of burden achieving worker consciousness and Socialist education or the nonworker being converted to labor's cause. All these period attempts to produce a discourse of polyethnic labor, however, were marked by a disbelief in its mass possibilities. Even as the new social protest authors relied more heavily than did their nineteenth-century predecessors on the authority of experience, they filtered the work voice through an authority all their own.

The issue of authorial expertise surfaces as well in fiction about and by African Americans. It is necessary to understand why white social protest fiction represented black laborers, glimpsed in the asides of Sinclair or Poole, as even more degraded than the ethnic whites they worked with—or supplanted. The few African American imaginative writers to discuss the problem of the black workforce—Charles Waddell Chesnutt, Paul Laurence Dunbar, and Oscar Micheaux chief among them—positioned their discussions in the context of race more than class. Yet this was an era when there was a "revival of scientific attempts to prove the [black] a degraded being,"[37] when European immigrants were preferred over black migrants in the South, and when race riots burgeoned anew. The tensions between atavism and advancement that occupied black texts now need renewed scrutiny. How effectively did these texts give voice to the labor menial? Did black Progressives like Chesnutt entertain the kind of doubts about black working-class self-activity that white Progressives did about ethnics and nonwhites? And to what extent were Dunbar and Micheaux taking on the mantle of labor expertise to distinguish themselves from "low" or unambitious blacks—providing as classed a view as any white author's condemnation of the great unwashed?

Researching the Real:
Literary Socialism and the Beast in the Jungle

Four years after the Socialist Party was formed in 1901, espousing common ownership and an end to capitalism, Upton Sinclair, beginning work on *The Jungle,* joined it.[38] Cementing his political allegiance, he published a serialized version of the novel in the periodical *The Appeal to Reason,* which had a large Socialist readership and gave him an advance to research the Chicago stockyards. The paper, which, like radical trade union journals, was read by literate workingmen with socialist leanings, was a good choice for the Sinclair installments. It had a wide circulation, 150,000, although its readers hardly equaled the million who would read the work in book form by the end of 1906.[39] And its philosophy seemed to accord well with the newly converted Sinclair's: gradual abolition of capitalist ownership, and until then a more equitable distribution of goods while building a mass base for socialism.[40]

The novel's radicalism, however, was more open-ended than suggested by its appearance in *The Appeal,* which did not publish the book in its entirety. In converting Jurgis Rudkis, his brutish Slavic meat cutter, sometime steelworker, and alcoholic tramp, into a committed Socialist, Sinclair may have been attempting to mend the party divisions between immigrant and native born, between strict Marxian socialism and a socialism that did not subordinate immediate reform to revolutionary ideology.[41] Many sections of *The Jungle* exemplify the uplift approach embraced by the conservative and dominant wing of the Socialist Party. Sinclair embraced ethnic education in the broadest sense, from night school to party propaganda, political rallies, and electoral work. Such schooling occurs under the aegis of mentors like the Lithuanian intellectual Ostrinksi, a benevolently Socialist Svengali who leads the atavistic Jurgis out of the psychic ghetto of inarticulate rage. Yet the novel's controlling metaphor, made explicit in the title, also points to a workforce trapped in a jungle from which it must hack its own way out. This is a more class-based view of social struggle than that suggested by charismatic leaders or by the novel's own conclusion in which electoral victories send Socialist leaders to Washington. Seen as a veiled agitational tract in which the victory of the party at the polls heralds an anticapitalist era inaugurated by trust-busting and the death of oligarchy, the novel can be read as Debsian. It foreshadows the real-life ethnic Socialist political activity of immigrant Packingtown or the related grassroots-level agitation of the vast Chicago garment uprisings a few years later. Debs had written: "The workers themselves must take the initiative in uniting their forces for effective economic and political action; the leaders will never do it for them."[42] Even the maverick IWW, founded two years before the Sinclair novel (only to split in 1912 from a Socialist Party it soon found elitist), could find hope for its "trade unionism of the dispossessed" in Jurgis's transit.[43]

Yet a close reading of Sinclair and fellow literary Socialists, from the dedicated James Oppenheim to the celebrated Jack London, uncovers the same dilemma at the heart of the split between Socialists and Wobblies, between advocates of selective unionism and those of mass unionism. Despite their dedication to researching those underrepresented by the party's mainstream, the literary Socialists were much like their party brothers. They "sought to substitute themselves for a political working class that did not [yet] exist."[44] Far from resolving the right-left schism by giving voice to the ethnic newcomers' emerging constituencies, they novelized their ambivalence about spokesmanship and authenticity. In so doing, they revealed the radical author's difficulty with rewriting individualist ascension as rising with one's class.

From the viewpoint of earlier literary schools, however, Sinclair's achievement is particularly stunning. His array of Packingtown woes is impressive reportorial spokesmanship rather than slumming. Unlike the local colorists and even the literary naturalists, he wrote with a new thoroughness about working people's exposure to environmental pollution, at home and on the job, substandard housing, and health risks. At a time when Progressive scrutiny of daily budgets was meticulous but dry, Sinclair captured the terrors of workers. These people lived in a world imperiled by an illness or a sick child or an unmet mortgage payment, their ignorance of political process played on by industrialists, foremen, political bosses, and liberal candidates. In a tour of the packing factory that is at once scientific and harrowing, Sinclair provides what he calls "an exact and faithful picture."[45] He draws the reader into an awareness of what it is like to arrive in the Golden Land and take filthy work knee-deep in entrails in a freezing room.

Titularly Socialist contemporaries of Sinclair's were inept at giving a Socialist gloss to Pittsburgh Survey–like data. Leroy Scott's anachronistic *The Walking Delegate* (1905), while it describes the New York City construction worksite, particularly union infighting and ethnic tensions, reinvigorates the old John Hay conservative novel. The message is that corrupt leaders alone sabotage the American work ethic and the workers who should follow. Walter Hurt's *The Scarlet Shadow* (1907), published by the Socialist Appeal to Reason Press, was billed as a truthful novel of the famed 1904 Cripple Creek coal strike. Yet it crumples into part ode to Eugene Debs and part daredevil journalist whose globe-trotting extends to the Colorado coal fields. Such attempts to prove the existence of a militant workforce ended up muddled and trite, offering industrial relations as the province of a charismatic leader.

In contrast, consonant with its message that menial laborer and bourgeois reader alike must be re-educated to realize the oppressive nature of modern capitalism, *The Jungle* was drenched in the data of the Slavic newcomer's work world. The brilliance of this detailed proof that modern capitalism had created an industrial jungle also reveals the novel's limits. Comments James Barrett, "Today most scholars and students still pay surprisingly little attention to the workers whom Sinclair intended to be the focus of his book."[46] This is another way of saying that the book's excessive focus on degradation has a dulling effect. Even the opening scene of the wedding between Jurgis Rudkis and the doll-like Ona quickly moves from folkishness and community to a chaos of brawling and drinking. Although Sinclair manifests a certain sympathy for people who earn forty cents an hour for boning beef, risking mutilation and blood poisoning, he does not withhold moral judgment. He reiterates that few could prevent being brutalized by this life. Yet when he observes that "men who have to crack the heads of animals all day seem to get into the habit, and to practice on their friends, and even on their families, between times," documentary is at war with irony and condescension.[47] The language is elevated to describe people who are not. In many passages Sinclair, who had been reared on the evils of self-indulgence and was torn between his father's sensuality and his mother's Puritanism, loses his stance of impartiality completely.[48]

More important, the proliferation of beast images casts doubt on workers' ability to climb out of the mire. In Sinclair's vision, workers must be atavists if he is to reveal the rottenness of the system that enchains them. But when their souls are no longer "asleep" (165), they experience conversion in as frightening a way as they hack the carcasses of enormous beasts.[49] Too backward to speak for themselves, they can only scream. Even when Jurgis is moved to political fervor, he retains his bestial persona. Thus it is difficult to believe in Jurgis's conversion.[50] Surely the Jurgis who is converted by elegant oratory and eventually makes a speech himself bears no resemblance to the worker mired in thwarted rage. It is no accident that in the 1913 film version of *The Jungle* Sinclair reclaimed Jurgis's fleeting authority by acting the part of the Socialist orator who first introduced Jurgis to political action.[51]

Fellow Socialist James Oppenheim in *Pay Envelopes* tries to subordinate his spokesman role to working-class ethnic activity in a way that Sinclair does not. Oppenheim's stories concern a variety of low-paid workers, male and female, native born and newcomer, in the North and the Midwest. The titles and plots, such as that of "The Cog," in which a skilled worker, his spirit ravaged by overwork, drunkenly beats his wife, drinks, reveal continuities with the Sinclair subject. Oppenheim's story "Slag," set in Pittsburgh's steel mills and centered on the Hungarian Jo, condenses the Jurgis story while retaining the salient elements. Possessed of hope and astonishing physical strength, Jo has been used as a dray horse, "pure iron drained from his soul, and only the slag left," his evil self rising to the surface in violence, drink, and marital jealousy.[52] As with Jurgis, conversion is through an educated emissary, in this case a schoolteacher whose interest is in English lessons, not socialism. Oppenheim's unstated assumption may be that an English-speaking Jo can stand on soapboxes and tell the mainstream what it is like to be bestialized. Still by story's end he is a far cry from even the IWW's native-born hobo poets who wrote for *Industrial Worker* in iambic pentameter.[53]

The irony of the story's conclusion, in which Jo practices simple English phrases in front of the wife with whom he has reunited, affirms working-class spokesmanship only to undercut it. If Jo's childlike simplicity—"I unlace my shoes," he "shout[s] gloriously" (128)—is a prelude to empowerment, he is still as mentally undeveloped as his English. Erasing the frustrations that led him to be bad, he expresses his desire to reform as a schoolboy might. Kneeling down in front of his wife, he tells her that he will be good (128). (Jo's solo climb from alcoholism to grade-school grammar is allegedly more proactive than Jurgis's falling under the spell of Ostrinski, but it is even less sophisticated.) That Jo's political development could have already begun in his own language is not suggested. Rather, ethnic stereotypes of the beastman speaking a foreign tongue are subtly reinforced. Given the mainstream Socialist emphasis on an immigrant workforce that could assimilate to party policies in a variety of ways, Oppenheim in the final analysis is even more doctrinaire about uplift than Sinclair. Baby steps toward literacy accomplish little of a political nature; a docile ironworker is a domesticated version of the wild animal rather than a mature man.

It is no accident that the redeemed brute title character of Jack London's *Martin Eden* is a more complex persona than Sinclair's Jurgis or Oppenheim's Jo. By the late 1890s, London had lived Martin's work life. His hero too was a California-based sailor, laundryman, tramp, a would-be author and newly converted Socialist. Both Martin and London brought a double consciousness to jobs customarily assigned to foreigners and women. It was that consciousness that distinguished worker-writers from their workmates, an awareness, writes one London scholar, of "difference within sameness . . . of being [simultaneously] joined and divided."[54]

By the time *Martin Eden* appeared in 1909, London had achieved extravagant fame by "offering himself as the ever present, energetic subject of his writing."[55] His roman à clef about his climb from laborer to literary man offers an extended section that reads like a diary of his menial years. But his protagonist lives out his creator's dual consciousness by laboring mindlessly while registering a profound disgust at the circumstances of his life. At the height of his celebrity, letters from London, who dreaded the possibility of returning to his working-class origins, sound the same rueful note taken by Martin when he acknowledges that he is "a beast, a work-beast."[56]

Whether despite or because of London's preoccupation with his laboring past, the beast sections of the novel are among the most sensitive treatments of workers' responses to brutalizing toil produced in the period. Its thirty pages could stand alone as an account of a worker who begins as "ceaselessly active" (194). Soon he is no better than a "human motor, a demon for work" (197). Although London writes in the third person, his passages on a man who is losing his grip on himself have the feel of a memoir:

A fifth week passed, and a sixth, during which he lived and toiled as a machine, with just a spark of something more in him, just a glimmering bit of soul, that compelled him, at each weekend, to [flee]. But this was not rest. It was super-machinelike, and it helped to crush out the glimmering bit of soul that was all that was left him from his former life. At the end of the seventh week, without intending it, too weak to resist, he drifted down to the village with [his coworker] Joe and drowned life and found life until Monday morning. (203–204)

In sections such as this, the line blurs between Martin's comprehension of his plight and London's imaginative reenactment of his past.

When Martin escapes from the pit of proletarian toil and learns to embrace socialism, he prefers to distance himself from that experience completely. In this he follows Ernest Everhard, the smithy-turned-theorist of the utopian novel *The Iron Heel* (1907) and London himself. In a key speech late in the novel (392–393), Martin is an orator whose political expertise has made him unrecognizable to his onetime bestial self. Rather than build on the lessons of his laundry toil, he makes no reference to his lived oppression, calling his listeners slaves (391) and working-class socialists a "miserable mass of weaklings and inefficients" (390). This taking on of authority involves a class betrayal that opens the way for the labor *Übermensch*.[57] Again it is the jungle, but Martin is the lion king.

Conversion Fiction versus the Labor *Übermensch*: The Prewar Decade

When Ernest Poole reworked spokesmanship in his dock-strike novel *The Harbor* (1915), he seemed to be advocating a conversion the reverse of the one at the center of the London novel. Like his semiautobiographical narrator, the well-born but socialistic Poole translated his expensive education into socially concerned journalism. (Sinclair drew on Poole's 1904 *Outlook* and *Independent* pieces on the Chicago stockyards.) Perhaps the protagonist joins his creator when he remarks, "I found that by making friends with 'Micks' and 'Dockers' . . . you find they are no fearful goblins, bursting savagely up among the flowers of your life, but people as human as yourself."[58] Prefiguring the 1930s plot, Poole's fictional surrogate balances socialist ideology with in-strike training. But to hear the strikers' voices is not to lessen doubts about their self-governing talents. In an era when social protest authors ended up worshiping raw power and money, the convert risked becoming as power hungry as the corporate types he defied.

The Harbor does invert the Martin Eden story to an extent. Poole's journalist, Bill, already the competent writer the young Martin wished to become, seeks wisdom through downward mobility. He soars in admiration for the unadorned life of the working class, becoming a denizen of the strike-filled hiring hall as the narrative unfolds. A best-selling text, Poole's *Harbor* is based on Sinclair's original idea for *The Jungle* of a nonworker converted to the worker cause.[59] The book keeps trying to give voice to the strikers but always circles back to the educated figure who draws socialist conclusions from their waterfront activities. Labor spokesmen abound. There are no less than three converts: the journalist Bill; Joe Kramer, a Bill Haywood type but with college credentials; and Marsh the orator. One scene, late in the novel, is a partial exception in that an Elizabeth Gurley Flynn–like figure exhorts the workers, but she too has a white-collar background. Indeed as the narrative increases in sympathy, it engages in a hydra-headed proliferation of educated socialists. To an extent, the trio of Billy, Marsh, and Kramer reflects currents in the Socialist Party itself: leaders must not be foreign and must be literate. Poole may also have been courting a middle-class audience alarmed by unrest but compassionate toward foreigners. But by privileging the conversion plot he allows the reader no more opportunity to hear the rank and file than do Oppenheim and the young Upton Sinclair.

In *King Coal* (1917), Hal Warner, Upton Sinclair's patrician stand-in for the socially conscious son of the oligarch mine owner John D. Rockefeller, wants to experience life down below.[60] Yet his improbable goal thoroughly disrupts his conversion experience, making it even more problematic than those in *The Harbor*. Sinclair's announced intention was a dual one. Not only did he want to "picture the life of the workers in unorganized labor camps," but he wished to bombard the reader with information gathered in Ludlow during the failed coal strike of 1913–1914.[61] The novel is best in the opening sections when Hal plays an incognito Colorado version of a Pittsburgh surveyor. These chapters enable Sinclair plausibly to expose the mine owners' noncompliance with state mining laws, abuses vehemently protested in Ludlow the year of the 1913 strike by the Western Federation of Miners. Yet introducing the allegedly charismatic Hal into the camp converts miners to admiration for him far more than the other way around. A daughter of the people falls in love with him, and grassroots socialist miners look to him for guidance. Management negotiates only with him, and he even dresses down a group of slumming plutocrats, erstwhile friends, for their absentee ownership philosophy.

With so heavily laden a plot Sinclair chose not to relate the worst abuses of the actual Ludlow strike, particularly the fact that corporate gun thugs set strikers' tents on fire and gunned down immigrant leaders. The focus returns to Hal, who leaves the camp after the strike is lost. His change of heart is at best a philanthropic one, witnessed by his return to the moneyed world from which he came and his unrealized plans to help the workers from afar.

The *Übermensch* separates himself in another way from the conversion experience in a novel by the journalist whom Theodore Roosevelt called "the man with the muckrake." Departing from his usual essays and stories on sinister corporate wealth and venal congressmen, David Graham Phillips in *The Conflict* (1911) wrote a story of the successful rise of a midwestern urban reform party. Phillips experiments with giving voice to at least a section of the working class. He imagines a workingmen's league that publishes journals, leads public meetings, and exhorts its skilled worker constituency to great effect.[62] Phillips was no Socialist, but he apparently admired Debs's appeal to a number of constituencies: the old, skilled tradesmen, the Socialist intelligentsia, and the unorganized ethnics. Yet in the novel, it is almost a foregone conclusion that, as Victor Dorn, an ambitious and curiously antistrike Socialist whom Phillips delights in praising, laments to his upper-crust reform friends, "[o]nly a small part of the working class as yet is at the heart of the working class" (140). Illustrating the view that workers are not a constituency until they are educated, the novel no sooner has Dorn address a crowd of followers than a member of the vast unconverted hits him with a rock that leaves him unconscious. As one of a vast gang of unskilled laborers, this unknown brute joins the shadow masses deplored by the very education army (269) that is setting out to convert them.

In the final analysis, there is very little difference among the labor saviors envisioned by Poole, Sinclair, and Phillips. Whatever the proffered sympathy for a small band of their enlightened followers, all view atavistically the mass of proletarians who do not heed their Socialist leadership. Ironically, it was a conservative novelist, responding to one of the era's most important multiethnic strikes, who gave a face to this crowd. In *The Dwelling-Place of Light* (1917), Winston Churchill responded to the important Lawrence Textile Strike of 1912. As much of a cause célèbre as Ludlow, it was much better organized and, in the short run, more successful. Ten thousand men, women, and children, representing the welter of nationalities employed in that Massachusetts city's mills, demonstrated large-scale ethnic solidarity and a commitment to wage and hour reforms before IWW leaders like Haywood and Flynn even arrived to direct them. The rage of the manufacturing establishment is personified by Ditmar, whose "atavistic beasts" strike his Chippering Mill (in the real strike the American Woolen Company).[63] He too is uncivilized: as in the actual strike, he sends his henchmen to dynamite the houses of the more militant employees. In fact, the ethnic rage of Lawrence eventually topples the key nonethnic characters in the novel. Ditmar is killed by enraged strikers; and the book's symbol of the native-born workforce, Janet Bumpus, dies bearing Ditmar's illegitimate child.

Interestingly, although the novel recoils from the charismatic orator Leonard Rolfe, a combination of the actual strike leaders Carlo Tresca and Bill Haywood, and demonizes the enraged immigrants, Churchill is that rare period novelist who recharges the favored image of the alien horde (284) of striking ethnic laborers. His enraged picketers act for themselves and with a plan. They need no Tresca to remind them that, as an Italian immigrant woman says of the scabs, "they take the bread from our mouths" (323).[64] Rather, the foreigner is any immigrant on strike who, as one of them says triumphantly, is "for the cause . . . [against] the capitalist" (323).

As period reviewers pointed out, Churchill retires from the problems the novel poses by forsaking the industrial Babel the Lawrence strike symbolized for him.[65] He takes refuge in an Arcadian finale in which Janet's infant daughter will be raised by latter-day Brook Farmers opposed to modernity. Yet the more resonant meaning of the novel, despite its watery denouement, is that in a battle between the beasts of trade and those of labor neither side garners authority, and indeed, neither deserves it. If the vengeful strikers are not socialized enough to speak for themselves, there is no moral authority left who can speak for them.

Whose Bestiality?: Abraham Cahan and the Paradox of Rising

Perhaps no period writer was better equipped to reverse the negative association of immigrant labor than the veteran editor of the *Jewish Daily Forward*,
Abraham Cahan. He was trusted by the Socialist Party, the Jewish needle
unions, the United Hebrew Trades, and the Jewish fraternal organizations of
New York City. A leading light of the massive 1913 New York Garment Strike,
and ever sensitive to the subtlest nuances of Jewish immigrant culture,[66] he
also embraced a more universal proletarianism by publishing *The Jungle* in
the *Forward* in full.[67] He was far less ambivalent and far more pro-union about
those whose lives consisted of endless submission to toil than fellow Socialists Sinclair and Oppenheim. Yet for all that, even this onetime garment-
trades organizer, who inspired the very workers who would people his finest
novel, could not escape the elitism of his spokesman's role.

The title character of his 1917 novel *The Rise of David Levinsky* willfully
repudiates the workers under his authority. Like Cahan himself, Levinsky
the cloak manufacturer quickly climbs from difficult labor circumstances on
the Lower East Side. Yet the very struggles that Cahan commemorated in the
pages of the *Forward* excite Levinsky's contempt. A shop-floor Svengali, he engages in a battery of tactics at once seductive and arrogant. When a feeble
strike looms in the trade, he hires away the best workers and manages to de-
flate the militance of the others, confiding in a fellow manufacturer that
union leaders lack brains or the desire to work.[68] He finds no apparent contradiction between his paternal concern for his overworked tailors and cutters
and the belief that "a working-man, and every one else who was poor, was an
object of contempt to me—a misfit, a weakling, a failure, one of the ruck"
(283).

Levinsky, in fact, makes it seem that crushing the many potent strikes
that erupted with the rise of the ILGWU in 1909 and allied organizations
like the United Garment Workers in the years that followed was a successful
combination of superior will and intelligence. He glories in cheating the
union and inverts the righteousness of his Old World religious upbringing.
In the world of the novel his success implies the failure of socialism and
heralds the enduring oppression of the workers he so cynically controls. It is
no wonder that his moral deadness, meant to be the hallmark of the ruthless moneyman novel already produced by Frank Norris in *The Octopus*
(1901) and *The Pit* (1903), instead provoked criticism of the novel as an
anti-Jewish portrait.

One of Cahan's most important interpreters points out that Levinsky's creator never steps beyond his protagonist's angle of vision.[69] The novel stands
in contrast with New York City Jewish labor fiction by Bruno Lessing (*Children
of Men*, 1903), who praised the silent sufferings of the sweatshop, and Elias
Tobenkin (*Witte Arrives*, 1916), who focused on an educated Socialist title
character. Cahan reinforces doubts about the virtue of capitalist individuality
without offering a viable political alternative to the worker. The title character's spiritual bankruptcy links Cahan to the muckrakers. Yet by the time he

wrote the novel, Cahan himself confessed to an increasing guilt over his abandonment of youthful revolutionary fervor, which he termed "the tragedy of [his] success."[70] But *Levinsky* is more than a stern critique of the immigrant rush to success, just as Cahan's ascension was more than merely representative.[71] A nightmare alter ego, the Levinsky character points to Cahan's own fears of a rank and file inadequate to the task of self-activity. It is as if the "complex sustaining web of Jewish affiliation, social formation, and collective identity" cannot withstand the force of corporate will.[72] There will be no proletarian upsurge without an elite cadre, the very message that permeates *The Jungle, Pay Envelopes,* and *Martin Eden.* Cahan's workers may not be brutes, but such mute presences are not fully human either.

The Authority of the Underling: *The Masses*

Observe that [*The Masses* does] not enter the field of any Socialist or other magazine now published, or to be published. We shall have no further part in the factional disputes within the Socialist Party; we are opposed to the dogmatic spirit which creates and sustains these disputes. Our appeal will be to the masses, both Socialist and non-Socialist, with entertainment, education, and the livelier kinds of propaganda.[73]

Between roughly 1911 and 1917, when wartime censorship closed it down, the oppositional arts magazine *The Masses* supported the IWW in the name of seizing the narrative reins of class struggle. The feisty periodical defended the underdog in Ludlow and Paterson, in Passaic and Youngstown, in the red-light district and the Jim Crow railway car. John Reed himself not only covered the hotly contested 1913 Paterson Silk Strike for *The Masses* but wrote and directed the Paterson strike pageant, performed by IWW-organized silk workers in Madison Square Garden in June of that year. No workers, however, were given lines to speak, and even choral pieces were written by strike leaders.[74] Joining Reed, contributors included reporters of the ilk of Max Eastman, and artists such as John Sloan and George Bellows. The sociological advocate of the African American, Mary White Ovington, and the ghetto Cinderella Rose Pastor Stokes (a Lower East Side girl who became the wife of a millionaire Socialist), even appeared in the journal's pages. Most of the other Socialist magazines, with the partial exception of the anarchist *Mother Earth* and the illustrated social journal, *The Comrade,* had little political patience for the arts.[75] The cultural rebels of *The Masses,* in contrast, found no contradiction between a radical commitment and imaginative literature.[76] But if the magazine's reportage, sociological essay, and artwork painted a broad canvas of labor-class injustice, fiction by Reed, Mary Field, Helen Forbes, and Ovington favored the flamboyant vignette. An anticapitalist spin-off of Jacob Riis's cautionary but sentimental portraits in *Out of Mulberry Street* (1898), with elements of O. Henry and Jack London, this fiction suggests the ongoing artistic difficulties of imagining labor without allying it to brutishness.

For one thing, these stories offer no vision of the era's defining moments of labor unrest corollary to that of the magazine's nonfictive selections. Instead, the subjects of *Masses* stories concern jobless laborers and derelicts, cleaning women, and trod-upon southern blacks, not the Paterson silk strikers en masse. Rather than proletarian foot soldiers in a fictive army of walking wounded, these characters, while meant to represent the oppressed groups from which they hail, and though about to be jailed, humiliated, fired, or traduced, seem as jaunty and energetic as their creators.

A fine sense of irony and moral outrage animates *Masses* graphics and reportage on the crucial Ludlow, Colorado, mining strike of 1913.[77] John Sloan's June 1914 cover illustration portrays a miner on the barricades who grasps a gun in one hand as he holds his dead child in the other. Sloan thus shares the outrage of Max Eastman's journalistic piece in the next month's issue, "The Nice People of Trinidad." Both pulsate with the conviction that even workers who defend their rights will be pilloried by the forces of the state. In such selections, labor is defended but not spoken for. Yet the authority of spokesmanship founders in the journal's short fiction. Rather than interchanges between intellectuals observing and workers enacting, they are the projections of Village bohemians fascinated by the imagined unconventionality of the laborer. John Reed's "Another Case of Ingratitude" (*Masses*, July 1913) places his own theories of class difference in the mouth of a derelict seeking a handout. Initially Reed satirizes his own tendency toward an inverted snobbery about the jobless and homeless. His foolish narrator is enchanted by his ability to give a meal to a genuine working-class person.[78] He delights in the hungry man's uncouth manners as he eats. And Reed reverses a standard stereotype when he writes that the starving man "had been a beast" but when he slopped his bread roughly he "was a man!" (17). The narrator's delight at defending the manly vulgarity of a real worker drops away when the object of his charity becomes a mirror image of himself. Initially the man had used vernacular in refusing to be grateful: "I'm thankin' my luck—not you—see?" Such freshness of response, which the narrator links to true proletarianism, no sooner appears than it vanishes. The derelict now taunts: "You just had to save somebody tonight" (17). Apparently his slang has disappeared along with his authenticity.

A reverse process, but one governed by a similar principle, occurs in Mary Field's "Bums—A Story" (*Masses*, May 1913). In it her surrogate's meeting with a hard-luck laborer, Chucky, prompts him to "unconsciously reflect . . . [the] rhetoric of the proletarian."[79] Moreover, Chucky, though completely unaware of political theory, ends up preaching anyway, heatedly inveighing against the capitalist.

In his analysis of left-radical poetry both in *The Masses* and elsewhere, Cary Nelson has pointed to the way in which genteel values battle with socialist or Marxist ones.[80] Yet the sense of a dialogue between political radicalism and literary traditionalism operates in *The Masses* stories to highlight John Reed and his Greenwich Village colleagues. They remain curiously remote from the working and workless people they observed and portrayed.

"I Ain' No W'ite Folks' Nigger":
Bestiality as Choice in Chesnutt, Dunbar, and Micheaux

Although in 1907 W.E.B. Du Bois described socialism as the "one great hope of the Negro in America," few Socialist authors outside the pages of *The Masses* took up the black worker's cause.[81] In her story "The White Brute" (1915), Mary White Ovington, one of the founders of the NAACP, expressed compassion for the southern black field hand faced with being a "dead man or live cur" if he defied the Jim Crow South.[82] And the pages of the anarchist journal *Mother Earth* carried the impassioned Voltairine de Cleyre's short story "The Chain Gang" (1907), though it is more a Shelleyan lament than a portrait of the convict labor used in southern states to undercut pay rates for white union members. In any case, in the hands of white writers the African American workforce was subject to insulting portraits. They ranged from that of the best-selling and racist Thomas Dixon, Jr., in *The Leopard's Spots* (1902) and *The Clansman* (1905) to Stephen Crane's in his *Whilomville Stories* (1900).[83] Upton Sinclair neither criminalized the allegedly oversexed black male, as did Dixon, nor rendered him grotesque, as did Crane. Yet Sinclair offered a common response of even "enlightened" white Socialist authors. In *The Jungle* blacks are intruders, the basest of the base, avid for scabbing and vice. He would modify this view in his later novel *King Coal,* in which blacks work with white miners, albeit in a silent, helping capacity. This characterization was a reduction of the actual, if limited, status of many black miners by the Progessive Era.[84]

Whatever blacks' circumscribed gains in heavy industry, black authors knew that an African American version of Jurgis would not be perceived as educable or redeemable by white society. Aware of blacks' continuing agricultural peonage and exclusion from the labor movement, they seemed reluctant to devote a novel to redressing the black proletarian balance. Nor did they portray a laboring community like the one that was already beginning to occupy parts of industrial, steel, and mining towns. Black workers in such communities had recently made the transition in the South from factory labor as slaves to employees.[85] From fiction acknowledged by the white literary establishment to popular stories catering to the black readership of the New York–based *Colored American Magazine,* black authors were far more concerned with different strata of the African American community, particularly a small, newly respectable middle class.[86] In their secondary plots and minor characters, they both repudiated and bought into period assumptions about lazy, sensual, ungovernable blacks.[87]

Still, as part of their recovery of black manhood, Charles Waddell Chesnutt and Paul Laurence Dunbar presented alternatives to the scabbing, vice-ridden stockyard blacks of Upton Sinclair.[88] Dunbar's Harlem character in *The Sport of the Gods* (1902) is a skilled barber, and Chesnutt's North Carolina dockworker in *The Marrow of Tradition* (1901) an honorable person who takes no man's job. Although these men ply trades both open to and regionally manned by blacks, they also echo Sinclair's disturbing black personae. Dunbar's southern-born figure, out of his rural element, falls prey to city snares.

Chesnutt's, afire with vengeance for southern wrongs, dies in a racial vendetta fueled not only by the Klan but also by his own obsessions. Well before the Civil War, Frederick Douglass in the many versions of his autobiographical *Narrative* (1845) had vowed to raise himself up from the baneful demoralization of slavery.[89] Novelizing their own reservations about postbellum black laborers, Chesnutt and Dunbar create figures who exhibit the same uncontrolled behavior lamented by Douglass.

Josh Green, though a minor character in *The Marrow of Tradition,* is highly important in terms of Progressive Era portrayals. Chesnutt himself has been termed one of the few who fought for the civil rights of blacks, an issue that the Progressive movement largely ignored.[90] This fight had both a journalistic dimension, in his reports on southern peonage, and a literary one, as in his novel *The Colonel's Dream* (1905), on black sharecroppers denied whites' mill jobs and industrial education. Josh Green, however, represents a new kind of southern black worker. A stevedore, he is involved in the nonrural labor that was akin to that of northern and midwestern blacks even prior to the Great Migration. Black dockworkers in another southern city, New Orleans, had long been involved in sporadic militance. At various times they had formed alliances or done battle with white trade unionists.[91] While Josh lacks both these men's political savvy and the benefit of New Orleans' relative racial liberalism, he does lead a band of cotton hands in a defensive revolt during a white race riot. Chesnutt himself does not make this point, but Josh is attempting the kind of organizing that the Populist Party was trying with white farmworkers in other rural sections of the country.

Chesnutt's focus, however, was on the violent racist behavior with which the new century had opened in the South. There had been hundreds of lynchings by the time the novel was published.[92] Summoning the very qualities that Sinclair had scorned, Josh is described as a "black giant, famed on the wharves for his strength" (357), when he tries to prevent a lynching. Joined to his resentment of past injustice is a family history of Klan outrages. Josh, in fact, is caught at a crucial moment of racial history, the 1898 riot in Wilmington, North Carolina. The black majority of the town was attacked by white mobs who swarmed over the black sections, killing and destroying property.[93] Because Josh refuses to remain passive in the face of the white aggression unleashed by the riot, some critics have seen revolutionary potential in him.[94] Yet Josh himself is no leader of workers, a fact he recognizes when he asks for an educated black to lead them (431). The more sophisticated urban Louisiana dockworkers would have repudiated this position; Josh, aptly termed an "illiterate folk hero," cannot.[95] Caught up in a potentially modern moment of labor unrest, Josh sees only the racial strife of the past. He dies while killing the white man who had tormented his father and thus suggests the political limits of "the lower-class cultural ideal of the 'bad nigger.'"[96]

Like Chesnutt, Dunbar contextualized the black workforce in the heritage of southern racism.[97] As with Chesnutt his characters suffer the lingering effects of a white antebellum mindset. Thus in the opening chapters of *The Sport of the Gods,* Berry Hamilton, the servitor of a bigoted plantation family, is falsely accused of theft and given a long prison term. Yet unlike Chesnutt,

Dunbar acknowledges the early stages of the Great Migration. He moves his ex-convict retainer character to the bewildering modernism of Harlem street life. In the "free" North he is unable to find anything but janitorial jobs, decides to return south, and is pensioned off by the guilt-ridden masters he once served. Yet the rest of the novel concerns Berry's even more thwarted son, Joe. Indeed, Joe's story is the novel's counterpart of Josh Green's. Dunbar completed the book soon after the Harlem Race Riot of 1900, set off by whites angry that Arthur J. Harris, a hot-tempered, high-living onetime carpenter and cook, had allegedly killed a white policeman.[98] Dunbar himself, by 1900 a well-known poet, visited frightened Harlem residents, attempting to calm them and telling them to refrain from doing anything to incite a riot. Joe Hamilton is clearly as vulnerable as was Arthur Harris, even though, unlike in *The Marrow of Tradition,* no direct reference is made to a historical race riot. Both were transplanted southerners from fragmented families, sons of the South denied work there. Both were literate, a cut above menial laborers, and unable to cope with the white North.

Yet complicating the story is its fidelity to then-current theories of labor-class degeneration. Dunbar himself, the son of ex-slaves, was no stranger to debasing work. As a high school graduate in the Midwest, the only job he was offered was as an elevator operator.[99] Dunbar soon turned himself into a literary spokesman for the "lowly," winning the favor of William Dean Howells (who would soon aid Chesnutt's reputation as well) and Howells's introduction to his poetry collection *Lyrics of Lowly Life* (1896). With this boost, Dunbar became a successful literary man. His Joe Hamilton, however, did not fare as well. Although he is able to find work as a Harlem barber he collaborates in his own destruction by taking on dubious friends, frequenting local night clubs, and becoming an alcoholic. Dunbar himself echoed the Progressives who cautioned black urban communities in the Midwest and North to avoid the sporting subculture. Yet Joe symbolizes the heedless young black men whose "false ideals" and "unreal ambitions" plunged them into depravity.[100] (Alice Dunbar-Nelson, in a 1914 labor story rare for both the author and the NAACP journal *Crisis,* echoed her husband' s views. The urban waiter-hero of her "Hope Deferred" is a model of rectitude, contemptuous of white working-class immorality. Still, his is the bourgeois probity expected of one who has trained to be an architect but, as a black, cannot find work.)

For Chesnutt and Dunbar the social changes needed for black workers to lead lives of dignity in white society included a program of self-transformation to infuse them with discipline and purpose. In the next decade Oscar Micheaux outlined such a program in the opening section of his autobiographical novel *The Conquest* (1915). As the participant-observer of a variety of black labor experiences, he toils at jobs in manufacturing, mining in a black mining town, stockyard labor, steel work, coal heaving, shoe shining, and Pullman portering—the last one of the more lucrative jobs held by working-class blacks of the time.[101] All of these jobs make him restive, annoyed at the passivity of his coworkers, but all too aware of the economic frustrations that push them into dishonesty. The Pullman job earns his particular scorn: "Thousands of black porters continue to give their service in return for starvation wages and are compelled to graft the company . . . for a living" (50). In passages such as this, though rare in the narrative, Micheaux voices African American labor-class discontents that he himself had experienced. Yet his work biography section is but a segment of a lengthy novel and one dedicated, significantly, to Booker T. Washington. It is soon clear that the remedy for his protagonist's debasement is ambition. In the world of the novel, it is the only alternative to group oppression before the founding of A. Philip Randolph's Brotherhood of Sleeping Car Porters. Thus he reverses the era's black migration to large cities in order to homestead in South Dakota, where the real-life Micheaux took over a small farm and eventually did rather well.

In this narration of personal exodus, farming is viewed not so much as a community answer to white oppression or a haven from Jim Crow— Micheaux's hero is satisfied to be the only black in the territory—as a route to financial security. Nor does Micheaux ever depict the rigors of farming as anything less than the price of achievement. While he makes no direct reference to southern sharecropping, the transcendence of peonage implied by a successful "Negro pioneer" (the subtitle of the novel) is clear. Yet the price of success is a disconnectedness from those whom Micheaux calls not "competent" (17) or ambitious enough to escape "the very roughest kind of work" (27). He was pulled between his conviction that a black man could be anything (145) and his counterbelief that the majority of his race was "lacking guts" (146). In the end his practice of the principles of Booker T. Washington is reserved only for pioneers like himself.

Editing the Undistinguished:
Asian and Native American Work Stories

Except for sporadic IWW organizing attempts among them, as in the previous century Asian minorities also endured proletarian and labor-movement resentment. The Chinese were particularly subject to exclusionary policies, and the Japanese were often ostracized by other ethnic groups with whom they worked.[102] The AFL president, Samuel Gompers, was particularly vocal against both ethnic groups. They remained restricted to seasonal employment in agriculture and canneries or to ethnic enterprises such as laundering for Chinese and house service for the Japanese. Native Americans followed the patterns set by the Hampton Institute model of the nineteenth century. They experienced ghettoization on the reservation or a missionary school upbringing fitting them for domestic service or the lower rungs of teaching and the professions.

For all the era's case-study scrutiny, the workforce experiences of all three groups would have been largely unavailable to American readers had not the *Independent,* a secular, liberal journal of general interest edited by the New England patrician Hamilton Holt, addressed them in a fashion.[103] Beginning in the early 1900s, for over a decade the journal published heavily edited interviews with working people. In 1906 autobiographical sketches of nineteen of these interviews were published under the title *The Life Stories of Undistinguished Americans as Told by Themselves.*

Reviewers singled out the stories, or lifelets, of an Italian bootblack, a Lithuanian stockyards worker (read and used by Sinclair), and a Swedish peasant, but they bypassed those of ethnic nonwhites.[104] Like the Europeans' accounts, the ones with Asian subjects shared a period approach. There was collaboration between interviewer and subject; questioning to reveal the muckraking layer of their job experiences; and balancing resentment with an agenda for self-transformation. The Chinese lifelet is as authoritative as any of the European sketches. It embellishes a knowledge of varieties of Chinese occupation born of a picaresque work experience with commentary on Chinese customs, manners, and foodways. And like the European life stories, each of the three sketches on a racial minority encapsulates certain experiences associated with that group. Yet differences appear as well, differences that expand the scope of what, from the Pittsburgh Survey to *The Jungle,* the era defined as labor expertise.

For one thing, more than the other sketches, the minority stories comment directly on and rebut period prejudices. They attempt to speak to an audience familiar with exclusion acts and American Indians' internment/education at the Hampton Institute, and the like. And with the earned authority of suffering, they express resentments and angers for themselves and for their ethnic labor brothers not given such a forum.

Theirs, then, are inside stories of humiliation, discrimination, and living with the perception of their backwardness. (Even the Socialist Party spoke of "backward Orientals.")[105] At least one of the sketches, "The Life Story of a Japanese Servant," by retaining an awkward syntax and poor grammar, gives the feel of transcription rather than edited prose. Each figure tells his own story in order to tell an ethnic one. The lifelet thus raises the issue of whether the editorial voice of expertise—sometimes Hamilton Holt's, sometimes Ernest Poole's—subverts that of the worker.

As with so many of the era's real-life stories, whether transposed into fiction or presented as a case study, the subtext of resentment is in tension with the carefully crafted story of struggle and ascension (or Socialist re-education).[106] The Chinese story is particularly telling for the way it displaces class onto ethnicity. Account after account of ethnic mistreatment is given with a Progressive taste for dates, sums, and budgets. In more spirited passages, the narrator blames other ethnic groups, among them the Irish and the Italians, for the poor treatment he has received. The labor movement was instrumental in keeping Asian labor-force participation low. The narrator makes little connection between that fact and the need for a Chinese labor solidarity.[107] Rather, he repudiates both workers and the ethnic labor movement in America, choosing instead to "take [his] money and go back to [his] village in China."[108] The same praise for reverse migration back to China after American success appears in an *Independent* essay by Sui Sin Far (Edith Eaton). Her "Chinese Workmen in America," was published seven years after its predecessor. Yet unlike that by the anonymous former worker himself, Eaton, though opposed to sinophobia, implicitly approves the association of America and rising. Thus she blames Chinese laundrymen who never attained wealth, citing their lower-class origins as evidence of shiftlessness, a class bias shared by Eaton's fiction and essays on North American Chinatowns.[109]

The Native American life story, whose narrator is proud of his separation from his "scalp-taking ancestors," can be juxtaposed with the Chinese man's autobiography, and Eaton's as well. All three suggest the importance of returning to one's roots.[110] The unnamed Indian subject would have had little in common with Edward Goodbird who, in *Goodbird the Indian: His Story* (1914), remained outside assimilationist circles, as did other Progressive Era Indian memoirists.[111] He was quite separate from the industrial work world (by that period Native Americans were erecting urban skyscrapers), and highly critical of "the white man's way."[112] Ironically, the Indian of *Life Stories*, a Hampton Institute graduate, realizes his continuing ethnic separateness. Rather, when he writes that he has suffered many times from having been mistaken for an Asian, he underscores the rightness of the Chinese man's return home.

Viewed less as working-class narrative than as fragmentary, edited tales of the Asian and Indian labor experience, the sketches thus raise a series of tantalizing questions. If there is what Werner Sollors calls the problem of authorship, there is a problem of resentment too.[113] To what extent was the bitterness emended by ghostwriting? Why was there so little deviation from the strive-and-succeed formula? To what extent did the editors let these minority workers be experts on their own lives?

Brute or Not?: The Work Tales of the Progressive Era

Between 1900 and 1917, a variety of Socialist, Progressive, status quo, and African American authors wrote a new chapter in the literary effort to connect the "sullen, angry, rebellious worker and his alienating, uncreative work."[114] Boundaries between skilled and unskilled workers began to blur, and the nineteenth-century stereotypes of accidental workers and surrogate leaders were finally dispensed with. Nevertheless, even as authors advocated political and cultural education as collective advancement, they offered a claylike rank and file that belied that possibility. It is true that figures like Sinclair's atavistic Jurgis remake themselves, as does London's laundry worker and sailor Martin Eden. Oppenheim's beastman goes to night school, and Reed's vernacular down-and-out suddenly acquires Greenwich Village eloquence. Yet in the posture of the Socialist platform, all of these authors express disapproval of the brutalized ethnic.

There had been a nineteenth-century tradition of associating the working class with bestiality.[115] But not until the Progressive Era were recurrent themes of degeneration, animality, substandard intelligence, and even self-defeating passivity played out in a wide variety of political novels and stories. That spokesmen became spectators suggests the unresolved difficulties in the new literary scrutiny of working folk. Texts devoted to uncovering the truths of white ethnic industrial poverty are unwilling to relinquish authority about proletarian suffering to those experiencing it. In texts on and by African Americans, authors were similarly reluctant to give voice to the laborer. In venues other than fiction, Chinese, Japanese, and Indian laborers were all but nonexistent. But, at least to judge by the *Independent* lifelets, which provide a rare period forum for other minority laboring groups, vocal resentments were both filtered through and diluted by genteel editing.

Commenting on the unfinished agenda of the period's labor writers, Walter Rideout points out that novels centered on a strike were few. The new radical novelist, because of his middle-class background, "was more likely to feel at home in a political party than a labor union."[116] In sum, the prewar period in American labor literature offered a renewal of the long-lived national ambivalence toward working folk and the reality of class struggle. At the core was an unresolved doubt: had the American Dream failed the working class or they it?

It would not be until the 1930s that social protest authors recharged or refocused the idea of the worker as beast, turning it to their own leftist or liberal purposes. All-encompassing novels, ambitious tales of the collective, and claims of collective rising had to await that bonanza for worker literature, the Great Depression. Until expertise and authenticity were no longer antitheses, the worker, whether as group man or little guy, could not be heroic.

CHAPTER 6

Facing the Unwomanly

Sweatshop and Sex Shop in Progressive Era Labor Fiction

When Leonora [O'Reilly] stopped [speaking], little Clara [Lemlich] rose and I felt mighty proud of that simple Jew girl. She told them point blank that she came there to ask for help, but added that it wasn't for us present, only for the thousands of young girls who've been working since they were big enough to turn a wheel.

—THERESA S. MALKIEL, *THE DIARY OF A SHIRTWAIST STRIKER* (1910)

"It's a business, then, ain't it?" Violet asked. "A regular business," nodded Evelyn—"fifty cents and up. . . . There are hundreds of young chaps all over the country who make their living by selling girls to places like this—and worse than this; and there are more who make better livings by making one, two or even three girls walk the street for them. Just now, in New York, the street's the main thing."

—REGINALD WRIGHT KAUFFMAN, *THE HOUSE OF BONDAGE* (1910)

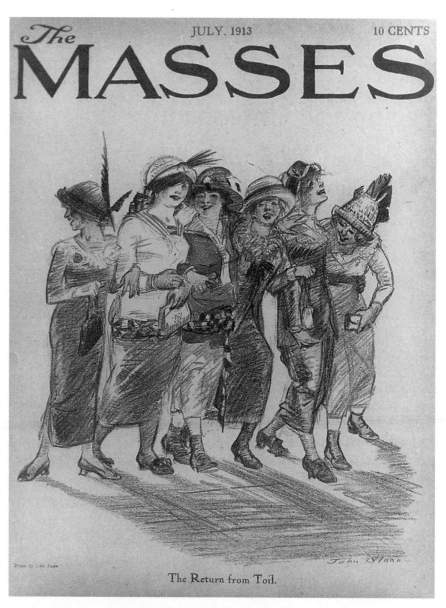

JULY, 1913   10 CENTS

The Return from Toil.

John Sloan, *The Return from Toil*, cover, *The Masses*, July 1913. Tamiment Institute Library, New York University.

In the winter of 1909, an irate New York City magistrate was faced with unrepentant clothing-trade strikers, Jewish and Italian women arrested for allegedly disturbing the peace. They came before him as members of or sympathizers with an ILGWU local that had called a general strike of shirtwaist makers. It became known as the Uprising of the 20,000, a landmark of women's labor history. Before handing down a stiff sentence, he told them they were "on strike against God and Nature."[1]

However factually inaccurate, the statement revealed much about social disapproval of female militants and the tactics they employed. The first two decades of the new century saw women striking in greater numbers than ever before. Strikes proliferated particularly in the clothing trades, and for causes other than a family wage or the "pin money" thought to be their reason for working since the antebellum Lowell and "factory lady" days. In the Progressive Era, the Spindle City still employed masses of women in the textile industry. Yet it was now visited by the IWW organizer Elizabeth Gurley Flynn, the "rebel girl." She urged them to follow her example, and they did, striking a year after the Uprising of the 20,000.[2]

In a broader sense, the magistrate's statement about the rebel girls of the Great Shirtwaist Strike suggests the intense preoccupation with women breadwinners' behavior that characterized the Progressive Era. Both in and out of U.S. labor fiction, an overzealous concern with working-class women's morality prevailed well before 1900. But immigrant women flooding into textile jobs and an influx of single working girls into the cities, combined with burgeoning prostitution, heightened the previous century's crusade to regulate feminine virtue.[3] To be sure, Progressive surveyors and economists praised the resilience implied in the title of Mary Van Kleeck's *Working Girls in Evening Schools* (1914) or reexamined the kind of depressing labor landscape embodied in Edith Abbott's *Women in Industry* (1910), Louise Montgomery's *The American Girl in the Stockyards District* (1913), and two key Pittsburgh Survey volumes, Elizabeth Beardsley Butler's *Women and the Trades: Pittsburgh, 1907–1908* (1909), and Margaret Byington's *Homestead: The Households of a Mill Town* (1911). Dedicated labor statisticians accounted in a similar fashion for "The Condition of Woman and Child Wage-Earners in the United States," the title of Helen Sumner's 1910 report for the Bureau of Labor. They were concerned with overextended ethnic housewives (the majority of whom kept lodgers) or "the unskilled and underpaid drudges of the industrial world," who routinely received less pay than men, even when, as in the garment trades, their work duties overlapped.[4]

Economic records of self-supporting women, life histories, interviews, and a variety of other investigative reports remained, as in the previous century, fixated on sexual waywardness.[5] In the new century, however, this fixation was part of a shift in direction away from the social purity campaigns to elevate morality and to abolish prostitution and the sexual double standard spearheaded in the 1890s by middle-class women and clergymen and aimed at many social classes. By the 1900s, the narrower crusade for moral order was enthusiastically supported by women and church groups. Yet it was managed by male municipal politicians, professional reformers, and civic investigations and directed particularly at procurers and the wanton daughters of the lower orders. In the Progressive battle against vice and immorality, social hygienists and criminologists were in the forefront, arguing that prostitution, though a grave danger to impressionable, sensual, or lazy young working women, was basically a business in which women's activities supported male networks of pimps and other profiteers. Didacticism was thus uneasily mixed with the language of the laboratory, and the "social evil" was now termed a "modifiable phenomenon."[6] By the 1910s, social-scientific studies of the sex trade encoding that mixed message proliferated. From Syracuse to Kansas City, New York to Chicago, titles like *Commercialized Prostitution in New York City* (1913) and *The Social Evil in Chicago: A Study of Existing Conditions* (1911) sought to erase the biblical condemnation of harlots while shying away from categorizing prostitution as another form of women's work. The Chicago civic investigation, the era's preeminent study, even employed a Pittsburgh Survey approach to brothels, owners, numbers, ages, former occupations, places of birth, family background, economic class of occupants, and, suitably bowdlerized, the types of sexual services rendered. Censored as well were the actual words of routinely profane interviewees. Instead, their postlapsarian views echoed those in corollary studies of respectable wage-earning women. Their constant refrain was said to be, "I can't live on hopes and virtue."[7]

The boundary between fallen and virtuous eroded further when the term "women adrift" arose to describe even women who, as the century began, were alarming reform elements by traveling alone to urban centers to live in boardinghouses and furnished rooms.[8] The phrase was often applied to the three out of four white single women who made up the Progressive Era feminine labor force.[9] As early as 1900, of the one-quarter of the urban female population who worked in factories and shops and as domestic servants, the majority were immigrants and their daughters. At the very least, these women were the targets of a widespread hostility toward ethnic and lower-class women, who were considered more sexual than middle- and upper-class white women.[10]

Black women, though no more than one-quarter of the female population, were half of all city laundry workers and, by 1920, nearly 40 percent of the urban servant population, unofficially segregated in those unenviable jobs.[11] Documentation of their plight, whether in southern or northern domestic servitude, appeared in the pages of the Hampton Institute's *Bulletin* from the early 1900s, in the short-lived *Voice of the Negro,* and in the NAACP journal *Crisis,* launched in 1910 by W.E.B. Du Bois.[12] In the social work journal *Charities and the Commons,* Helen Tucker's 1909 article "The Negroes of Pittsburgh" gives women short shrift, and there was no mention of black women at all in Butler's lengthy *Women and the Trades.* Save for sections of Mary White Ovington's *Half a Man: The Status of the Negro in New York City* (1911), studies by other white reformers centered on the status of or migration of poor black women from the South.[13] Ironically, even the working-class organizer Clara Lemlich, rallying white ethnic women strikers in the Socialist daily the *New York Call,* chose to compare their lot to that of black slaves in the antebellum South. It was as if she was deliberately oblivious to the fact that her own Local 25 followed ILGWU policy and excluded black members.[14] In fact, although African American female workers were rarely discussed in any of the reformist studies and labor fiction about white women, they were thought to have more potential for immorality. Soon a key African American writer tried to defend the maligned figure. Pauline Hopkins was the contributing editor of the *Colored American Magazine* and the author of the novel *Contending Forces* (1900). She prophesied that "Negro women [would] be held responsible for all the lack of virtue that is being laid to their charge today."[15]

African American women were indeed excluded from northern white middle-class reformers' concern with the sexual dangers and temptations that surrounded working-class women in American cities. The anxiety over black female waywardness coexisted with the era's refusal to acknowledge the existence of interracial houses of prostitution in New York City's seamier red-light areas.[16] Also so excluded, to judge by the prevailing view, were California's Chinese women. While silent movies like *The Yellow Menace* (1916) were busy linking white women's sex slavery to villains of the "yellow peril," the Chinese women who were forcibly recruited to satisfy the needs of Chinese men were ignored.[17] Their customers ungratefully dubbed such a woman *bakk hakk chai,* the "hundred men's wife," adding their ridicule to that of American nativists.[18] Little evidence is available on Mexican and Chicana prostitutes in the period, although the early 1900s saw the beginnings of an influx of Mexican migrants, some of whom even took their daughters to court to prevent their sexual and social autonomy.[19] A Mexican bordello girl does appear in the African American author William Attaway's *Blood on the Forge,* a 1941 proletarian novel about Progressive Era Pittsburgh, and no doubt Latina women did enter the trade. Despite a tacit acknowledgment of the polyethnic nature of the sex trade, then, outside the pages of the *Southern Workman* and *Crisis,* articles on the dangers to black girls migrating north, or the records of San Francisco crusaders against Asian vice rings like Donaldina Cameron, white slaves remained white.[20]

Yet for their burgeoning anger at slavelike industrial conditions, thousands of white ethnic women—by 1910 over thirty thousand in more than six hundred New York City garment shops—were frequently branded with the censorious terms "prostitute" and "whore."[21] Clothing manufacturers considered them bad women whose assertiveness made them "little better than streetwalkers."[22] When, in the Great Shirtwaist Strike of 1909–1910 they agitated for a fifty-two hour week and an end to making workers pay for materials and electricity, a number of the more vocal picketers were classified by the police and courts as streetwalkers.[23] This punishment was more than an attempt to demoralize them, although that was surely a motive. It was also the cornerstone of a discourse on promiscuity that permeated descriptions of "the daughters of the poor," the title of an avidly read series of muckraking articles in *McClure's* magazine from 1907 to 1909.

The respected journalist George Kibbe Turner subscribed to the widespread theory that most young prostitutes were the involuntary recruits of a traffic in "white slaves," as did other magazines usually more immune to sensationalistic reportage.[24] Agitation against this supposedly forced prostitution even resulted in the 1910 passage of the Mann Act to prevent the interstate transportation of women for immoral purposes. More dubious period investigators observed that "this white slave joke is certainly the biggest that was ever invented," calling white slavery "nothing more than a myth."[25] Among political radicals, the Socialist Party adopted a resolution that white slavery had an economic base. They were in rare accord with Emma Goldman who, in an essay for the anarchist journal *Mother Earth,* "The White Slave Traffic" (January 1910), saw prostitution, like marriage, as contracted for economic reasons under the "merciless Moloch of capitalism."[26]

For all the theorizing from diversified quarters, modern historians have found that at most a small percentage of these women were coerced into the trade.[27] But like the Chicago prosecutor Clifford Roe's *The Great War on White Slavery* (1910) and Theodore Bingham's *The Real Facts about the White Slave Traffic* (1911) (both complete with phony pictures of entrapments), Turner painted an alarming picture of the men in the vice business. They allegedly scoured the industrial towns of New England and Pennsylvania, "where they obtained supplies from the large numbers of poorly paid mill girls."[28] While the deliberate commodification of his word *supplies* is meant to be ironic, it also suggests the way working women were routinely thought of as nubile or lustful bodies.

In the previous century's fiction, the Christian conversion or the marital rescue were favored ways to remove a girl from the factory's corrupting influence. The Progressive Era author, whatever his or her political philosophy, had to acknowledge what otherwise liberal-minded *Everybody's Magazine* called the "invasion" of young women into the workforce.[29] This mass female entry inevitably transformed many young women into "agents of sexual innovation and cultural change." By frequenting the new dance halls, parks, movie houses, hotels, department stores, public streets, restaurants, and theaters, they were "putting on style" and opening up possibilities, however limited, for pleasure seeking and autonomy.[30] These recent developments both alarmed reformers and caused them to conflate the sweatshop and the brothel.

In the recurrent hostility to working women demonstrated by trade union journals, particularly those of the skilled trades, the anonymous author of one 1901 article, "Marry the Women," asserted: "Work is for men."[31] Given that by 1910 more than one out of every five gainfully employed workers was female, statements of this kind created a crucial debate about the nature of women workers' ambition. There already existed what the historian Alice Kessler-Harris calls the "self-imposed social restrictions" on the kinds of jobs women were prepared to take.[32] Moreover the majority of blue-collar women, a tiny percentage of whom were unionized by 1910, might well have concurred that only marriage, even if it did not provide mobility, could release them from industrial oppression.[33] Yet that did not silence the chorus of dissenting voices both in and out of fiction. They ranged from right-wing apostles of the home to Progressive regulators of working women's after-hours amusements.[34] Included as well were publicity-courting theorists of the alleged white-slave traffic in working-class women. Socialists preached that politics, not prostitution, was the working woman's only chance for decent wages, even if their responses ranged from the sobering argument that capitalism prostituted all women to the lurid headline "Girls Fed to Ghouls."[35]

Women from southern and eastern Europe joined their "new immigrant" male coworkers and relatives on picket lines, in parades, and in confrontations with strikebreakers and authority. Among such women's female and male defenders were the more enlightened members of the Socialist Party of the mainstream press, and the interclass circles of industrial-feminist groups such as the WTUL. Inevitably they provided conflicting interpretations of this volatile feminine mass. Thus, in the fiction, new issues of militance and empowerment collide with old ones of imperiled workplace innocence. Such works included Theodore Dreiser's kept-woman novels *Sister Carrie* (1900) and *Jennie Gerhardt* (1911), Arthur Bullard's Shirtwaist Strike novel *Comrade Yetta* (1913), and David Graham Phillips's prostitution saga *Susan Lenox: Her Fall and Rise* (1917). The pressing question was whether any form of feminine independence, whether political or sexual, whether it led to a crossing of class boundaries or a life of tenement toil, was appropriate womanly behavior. As the corrupted working girl became the feminine counterpart of the atavistic workingman, a corpus of working-girl fiction emerged to defend, explain, or repudiate her. Some subgenres, such as James Oppenheim's socialist strike novel of the Lower East Side, *The Nine-Tenths* (1911), dealt with ethnic women. The rural or native-born small-town girl came under scrutiny in the cross-class novel, such as Marie Van Vorst's *Amanda of the Mill* (1904). Predictably irreverent, John Reed peopled his *Masses* vignettes like "Where the Heart Is" (January 1913) and "A Taste of Justice" (April 1913) with defiant hometown girls who became career streetwalkers. And rare references to African American female breadwinners in a novel like Pauline Hopkins's *Contending Forces* and its companion pieces in the Boston-based *Colored American Magazine* (1900–1904) provided a challenge both to contemporary racist thinking and to cultural disapproval of women who worked.[36] But such challenges appropriated the trope of the ladylike wage earner, thus joining white authors in the attempt to reconcile female sexuality and political dissent.

Rising before the Uprising:
Imagining the American Factory Girl, 1900–1909

The earliest years of the new century did not look favorably on female immigrant labor volatility. The most prominent writers to take up the textile trade striker, if anything, looked backward. Concentrating on native-born women, they invoked the anachronistic Lowell factory lady, although they placed her in a traumatizing workplace where the conditions threatened to defeminize her and completely preclude her ascension. Yet unlike the antebellum fiction of the New England mill, early twentieth-century fiction, in this case by women writers, was part of an effort to ameliorate the sufferings arising from the poor employment conditions and limited education of working women. As such, it was a literary corollary to women's journalistic forays into canneries, glove and hat factories, and waitressing.[37] But unlike these pieces, which bore witness to the feminine working-class self-activity that by 1900 was an important aspect of the bookbinding, textile, hat, and cap trades, among many others, fiction writers extolled cross-class sisterhood.[38] Although in *The House of Mirth* (1905) the literary grande dame Edith Wharton pictured Lily Bart's "fall" from socialite to milliner as a great tragedy, even Wharton approved Lily's prelapsarian generosity to a working girls' club. Writers like the long-neglected Marie Van Vorst and the rediscovered authors Mary Wilkins Freeman and Dorothy Richardson sought to inspire nonimmigrant working girls by imbuing them with middle- or even upper-class culture. But as those miserably exploited by the manufacturing class were too legion to reach en masse, texts like Van Vorst's were centered on individualized female interactions across the class divide. However restricted the likelihood of the mill-girl protégé, it would be a favored trope in women's labor fiction throughout the Progressive Era, even appropriated by the Socialist and labor press. But fiction was slow to focus on the female militant; in the early 1900s novelists, particularly women, awoke to the idea that the working woman was not only the unsavory pleasure seeker or virgin craving marital rescue pictured in 1890s tenement fiction. To depict a woman who voiced dissatisfaction with conditions and even for a time challenged her employer, the wealthy Marie Van Vorst and her sister-in-law Bessie posed as workers. They gathered data on the privations of female mill and cannery labor. A year after the copublished *The Woman Who Toils,* a quite popular exposé based on their experiences, Marie published her novel *Amanda of the Mill.* In it, rather than build on the class lessons of her incognito investigations, she chose to look backward by fusing a factory girl and a lady. Van Vorst's contemporary Mary Wilkins Freeman was known to her wide American audience as a regionalist whose stories centered on self-sufficient rural women. In 1901 she departed from her standard subject matter to produce *The Portion of Labor,* which begins as a labor saga of a young shoe-factory operative who leads striking men and women when the employer cuts their wages and ends, as does *Amanda,* with a labor Cinderella.

Van Vorst, Freeman, and their contemporaries created such fiction not because they were blind to social divisions but because they were all too aware of them. They chose to see the female proletariat en masse from a middle-class perspective.[39] Thus while they provided descriptions of strike meetings, they deemed it necessary to separate their refined heroines from the uncouth, wayward types who constituted the female workforce. Despite a sympathy with women who, with Van Vorst's title character Amanda, sweltered in southern mills for fourteen hours a day from childhood on, the dominant thrust of this fiction was to extract the heroine from the milieu that damned the others. *Amanda of the Mill* is a rare period attempt to treat the rural woman; the opening sections concern the poverty of isolated mountain farm folk who are forced to relocate in mill towns. Yet once the title character becomes a mill child, her creator emphasizes her superiority to the transplanted colony that peoples the mill. Soon the owner's wife, her self-appointed capitalist protector, removes Amanda in childhood from her brief working life. When, years later, Amanda tries to help striking mill women, even attending meetings and giving anonymous donations to the cause, Van Vorst emphasizes that she is, rightly, a Lady Bountiful. She is in distinct contrast to her "barbarian" older sister Lily Bud, who after years of work has degenerated into a promiscuous drunkard.[40] It is only proper that Amanda marries the man who inherits the mill, although Van Vorst does add that he will run it along enlightened lines. Similarly, although in *The Portion of Labor* Mary Wilkins Freeman's Ellen Brewster toils at making shoes and even organizes workers for a walkout, a strike action she later recants, she is too refined to socialize with her crude, man-obsessed female coworkers. She is the only working woman her patrician employer considers his peer—and soon makes his wife.

The very Lady Bountiful novels that claim to counter Ellen's story actually underscore it. Working girls' clubs sponsored by the wealthy proliferated in the early 1900s to offer culture and conduct guides to poor working girls. Yet, like the novels written about them, the clubs joined the more rarified settlement house ventures in disguising the possibility of economic power by a program of "inducing . . . ladylike behavior."[41] The Wellesley professor Vida Scudder set *A Listener in Babel* (1903) in the kind of settlement house she often visited. The novel confirms the power of the trope by puzzling over why young women who work in steam laundries all day do not appreciate the classics of literature by night.

Paralleling the rise of working girls' clubs and settlement house education, the middle of the decade saw other incognito investigators. Dorothy Richardson was then a *New York Herald* reporter. Her anonymous and novelistic *The Long Day: The Story of a New York Working Girl* barely touched on collective action. In the Epilogue she opined that working women were not ready for trade unionism (289). (Curiously she had published a more favorable analysis the year before, including descriptions of lady "walking delegates" and striking scrubwomen.)[42]

The 1906 issue of the scholarly *Annals of the American Academy of Political and Social Sciences* published another Richardson piece, on the difficulties and dangers facing New York workers. Richardson's joined an article by Rose Pastor Stokes, the rags-to-riches wife of the philanthropic James G. Phelps Stokes, "The Condition of Working Women, from the Working Woman's Viewpoint."[43]

Stokes was one of the many admiring reviewers who approved this allegedly inside story of habits, mores, and escape reading, of slang and more genteel speech, among women in the Broadway sweatshops, paperbox, hat, and artificial flower factories, steam laundries, cheap rooms, and philanthropic "working girls' homes."[44]

Despite its air of verisimilitude—reviewers alternately described it as a true story or a novel—Stokes was reading her own version of the book, glossing over her political and philosophical divergences with Richardson. Stokes, who had garnered praise from *Socialist Woman* and Elizabeth Gurley Flynn, had consistently argued that uplifting the working girl meant not picking out protégés but granting inclusion to the female masses. If anything, *The Long Day* embodies many of the class biases of Van Vorst and Freeman regarding female blue-collar vulgarity and sensuality. Observes Richardson: "The average working girl is even more poorly equipped for right living and right thinking than she is for industrial effort."[45] Like Van Vorst and Freeman, she brought her nonlabor perspective to the alleged "loose living and inherent vulgarity" of native-born female breadwinners; non-English-speakers, presumably even more suspect, did not receive her attention (*Long Day*, 282). Stokes's *Annals* piece condemned that "patronizing, condescending type of interest shown so often by rich women . . . [their] attempting to encourage the so-called unfortunates by visiting them and telling them what they should do."[46]

Yet if the era saw memoirs like Mary Antin's *The Promised Land* (1912) and Rose Cohen's *Out of the Shadow* (1918), by labor-class Jewish immigrants thankful for the scholarship and the settlement house, respectively, these contained subtexts of resentment that subverted the official version of their stories.[47] Antin inflated her educational attainments: she claimed to have graduated with honors from Barnard, but she only attended for a time. While her improved success story reveals her bowing to assimilationist and class-based pressures, Antin undercuts her own exaggerations by concealing beneath their surface "[an]other story of Americanization," the coercion to, in her words, "learn to think in English without an accent," to become both genteel and Gentile.[48] Rose Cohen's resentments surface in a quite different fashion: she shifts the focus to the educational and professional opportunities awaiting her younger brother, an erasure of her own longings that implicitly registers suppressed rebellion at her disappearance from her autobiography.

From her maiden days as a writer for the *Jewish Daily Forward*, Stokes, in contrast, exhorted labor-class women to be proud of belonging to the working class. It is all the more ironic that one of the few voices of a marginalized subgroup soon spoke from the podium of the millionaire's wife—albeit the "socialist millionaire" Stokes. The AFL journal *American Federationist* would have scorned Richardson's suggestion that parlors for receiving male visitors solved the working woman's most pressing problems. However, AFL fiction, focused, like Richardson, on native-born women, did little to implement Stokes's suggestion that ethnic laboring women's voices should be heard.[49] Even pieces in the Wobbly press invoked a genteel, nonethnic firebrand, wrongly arrested on sedition charges.[50] It remained for "new immigrant" women from eastern Europe and their daughters to play out a script in which the comrade and the philanthropic lady found themselves on the same picket line.

Whose Strike Was It?:
Fictions of Lemlich and the Great Shirtwaist Strike of 1909–1910

In the three years immediately following the Great Shirtwaist Strike of 1909–1910, prominent clothing and textile strikes in which women participated occurred in Massachusetts mill towns like Lowell and Lawrence (both in 1912), Cincinnati (1911), and Chicago (1910–1911). But it is noteworthy that in the New York City Shirtwaist Strike, 70 percent of the strikers were twenty thousand women, resilient enough to take the lead in boycotting their work for an unprecedented thirteen weeks. Outside male labor circles, contemporary accounts, from sympathetic reportage in mainstream journals like *Collier's* to case histories of Jewish and Italian "girl strikers," to impassioned defenses in Socialist newspapers, left no doubt that it was a women's strike.[51] In fact, comments one of the new revisionist women's historians, it was "the largest strike by women workers the United States had ever seen."[52] Although it was an incomplete victory producing limited employer concessions, by the time it was over, it had radicalized thousands of young women factory workers. It had also put the finishing touches on twenty-three-year-old Clara Lemlich's early education in organizing, contested the claim that immigrant seamstresses were incapable of sustained militance, and enlisted in their aid the *New York Call* and other Socialist journals. Furthermore, it had marshaled the support of the well-funded Women's Trade Union League and Leonora O'Reilly, its liaison between affluent and working women. Last but not least, it laid the foundation for the city's 1910 cloakmakers' general strike, which ushered in a new era of industrial democracy in the needle trades.[53] Most crucially, it enabled workingwomen to carve a new identity for themselves that would provide a model for later women strikers.[54]

Before the Uprising of the 20,000, male unionists like Samuel Gompers, the powerful head of the AFL, considered women neither "organizable [n]or dependable."[55] Yet the dominant view, crafted by male historiographers, is succinctly put in Irving Howe's "What the girls began, the men completed."[56] In point of fact, the men to whom Howe refers struck five months after the conclusion of the women-fueled Shirtwaist Strike. Many of the women strikers were quite young, of course. But Lemlich was already a woman with formidable agitational experience who had organized the walkout of Local 25 of the ILGWU that stimulated the 1909 strike. To garner public sympathy, she too called the walkout a "girls' strike." But she herself, a "woman" to equal Howe's "men," was no girl.[57] Nor did she disappear into marriage and motherhood after the protest, as another myth of the strike would have it. Furthermore, unlike her sister activists Elizabeth Gurley Flynn, Mother Jones, Kate Richards O'Hare, and Leonora O'Reilly, Lemlich was a working member of the garment center labor force she helped rally. While she was joined by three other "forceful historical actors" of the "1909 vintage" of Jewish female clothing-trades activists, Fannia Cohn, Pauline Newman, and Rose Schneiderman, only Lemlich was so closely identified with the strike as to become a symbol of the fiercely determined women of the Uprising.[58] When, on 22 December 1909, she rose to address a meeting of garment workers in New York's Cooper Union Great Hall, she did so as a worker's representative who interrupted the formal program.[59] Speaking in Yiddish and English, she cut through the talk of the Socialist Party, the AFL, and the affluent women seated on the podium. "I have listened to all the speakers," said she. "I have no further patience for talk. I am one who feels and suffers from the things pictured. I move we go on strike."[60]

The novels of the Shirtwaist Strike school, all published during or immediately after the strike, charted new territory for labor literature by visualizing Lemlich and the women strikers. Until then women agitators were perceived either as demons or ciphers, not surprising in a period when women made up less than 5 percent of Socialist Party membership, and only a minority of those were foreign-born, working-class women.[61] Thus May Beals, though a Socialist Party organizer, built on her experiences in the fields of Louisiana and the mines of Tennessee and concentrated on male figures in her collection of stories *The Rebel at Large* (1906). Novels otherwise as disparate as the prolabor Isaac Kahn Friedman's *By Bread Alone* (1901) and the archconservative Thomas Dixon, Jr.'s *Comrades* (1909) depict the anarchist Emma Goldman, next to Lemlich the most visible female radical in period fiction, as a malicious incendiary who comes to a bad end. Even writers like Upton Sinclair had been inattentive to women's workplace agitation. In *The Jungle* (1906) he glosses over the fact that women accounted for more than 10 percent of meat workers, had their own local, and supported male strikers.[62] In thrall to a literary tradition that erased female labor activity, Sinclair denies this enlightenment to Jurgis's wife, Ona. Though also an oppressed stockyard worker, she is cast as incapable of political awareness. Jurgis finds the political light; she falls victim to employer seduction and remorseful death.

All of these writers, regardless of political affiliation, failed to anticipate the next decade's images of politicized women workers, the Rebel Girl and the Union Maid.[63] The former, taken from a 1915 song by the IWW martyr Joe Hill and dedicated to Elizabeth Gurley Flynn, became synonymous with a dedicated proletarian woman aiding her mate and comrades in the battle to form the Wobblies' visionary One Big Union. Another such Wobbly exemplar was Kate McDonald. Arrested on sedition charges in 1917, she was known for balancing revolutionary zeal with "gentle courteousness, refinement and womanliness," as the IWW organ, the *Industrial Worker*, put it.[64] Even by the end of the Progressive Era, however, this figure found little fictional embodiment in that paper's short stories. Like so much of the period labor fiction, the *Industrial Worker* pieces subordinated Flynn-like radicalism to her domesticity.[65]

The Socialist fiction of the second decade, in effect launched by *The Diary of a Shirtwaist Striker*, Theresa Malkiel's 1910 Shirtwaist Strike novel, serialized in the *New York Call*, also subscribed to notions of woman's subordinate comradeship. Despite its commitment to trade-based unionism and its advocacy of an evolutionary movement to socialism, Socialist fiction tempered its depictions of the radicalized working woman. Such is the case with Gertrude Barnum's fiction in the AFL's *American Federationist* and the ILGWU's *Ladies' Garment Worker*. In allied stories in trade union journals, if women rose up to defy bosses, foremen, and foreladies, to walk out and shut down, to vocalize resentment at sweated conditions, they did not sustain their commitment by story's end. In this they joined the varied fictional portraits of Clara Lemlich in novels by James Oppenheim, Arthur Bullard, Theresa Malkiel, and other writers to open up the literary discussion of working women's political involvement. The ways in which these Shirtwaist Strike authors empower their heroines by reinventing Clara Lemlich reveal much about the attempt to reconcile the female firebrand's right to political action with heartfelt notions of antithetical destiny as a woman.

Typical of superficially radical but commercially viable treatments of the working girls' bildungsroman were those by male authors, like Arthur Bullard's *Comrade Yetta,* praised in the *New York Times* as a "timely human document."[66] In the years prior to its 1913 publication, Bullard edited the *New York Call,* which serialized Malkiel's *Diary* a few months after the strike was settled. During the strike the paper printed special editions to raise funds for the out-of-work shirtwaist makers and to pay homage to leaders like Clara Lemlich.

Early in *Comrade Yetta,* Yetta Rayefsky, an orphaned Jewish immigrant unused to questioning her treadmill existence as a Lower East Side vestmaker and a boarder with relatives whose greed is exacerbated by poverty, finds enlightenment. Bullard's handling of the scene marks a rejection of the seduction thinking pervasive in treatments of the female naïf from the tenement tale through the white-slave novel. Yetta, who "had never heard the life of the working class discussed before," goes to a skirt finishers' ball, unaware that it is a strike meeting as well.[67] As a series of WTUL, Socialist, and garment union speakers illuminate the oppression of her life, including her misperception that because she is a "speeder," or quick worker, she profits accordingly, she eagerly receives the new truths. Although she enters the "ball" a vulnerable sweatshop girl whose craving for dance hall romance makes her prey for a prowling local cadet, Harry Klein—Bullard's bow to white-slave thinking—she leaves an incipient activist. Shedding Klein and decades of American seduction literature, the awakened working girl rises to speak, the very "champagne which was to have been [Yetta's] utter undoing [giving] her courage": "If there's a union in my trade, I'll join it. I'll try not to be a slave. I can't fight much. I don't know how. . . . That's all I got to say! . . . I'll try not to be a slave" (83–84).

Like her sisters in militance who people the narrative, Yetta moves from the sexually vulnerable sweatshop girl to the self-strengthening woman whose dual drive is to "fight" and to "know." Soon a labor ball of fire, she inspires a shop walkout, as did Lemlich in 1906 when she formed Local 25 of the ILGWU. Like Lemlich, she takes classes at the Socialist Rand School. When, in 1909, the strike gains force, again like Lemlich, Yetta becomes a WTUL organizer.[68]

During the strike Bullard's Lemlich figure expands her contacts with politicized working women and their supporters. She encounters a host of impassioned girl picketers—young Jewish and Italian women ready to go without food or warm clothing and intent on following the rules for pickets, chief among them the order to "plead, persuade, appeal, but . . . not threaten" the scabs entering the boycotted factories.[69] As she embraces the spirit of martyrdom lauded by contemporary observers friendly to strikers, Yetta welcomes affluent women reformers, as did Lemlich with WTUL luminaries.[70] But in a break from such philanthropic influence, again in the Lemlich mold, she throws it off to advocate change in her own way. Before that break, she drums up support from women's organizations whose air of privilege she resents. She pickets, is violently harassed by hired thugs, is arrested—though not, as Lemlich was, seventeen times. Like Lemlich and another prototypical striker, Yetta Ruth, she is sent to the workhouse. Yetta Rayefsky emerges a celebrity of sorts and rededicates herself to the strike action.

What the real-life Yetta experienced afterward has not been recorded. When the clothing manufacturers offered a settlement and helped force the strike to a close, many women did go back to a shorter workweek and increased wages. But the employers blacklisted Lemlich and others deemed troublesome. Some of those awakened to the power of collective action may well have found themselves worse off economically than when the strike began. It is known that Lemlich, through her Socialist affiliations, found political work, but she had difficulty making a living and lost her job with the suffrage forces in an unknown dispute. New research has revealed that rather than fall into obscurity, she simply shifted her activism to other arenas, including cost-of-living protests, tenants' unions, and above all the Communist Party.[71]

Rather than envision Lemlich's poststrike organizing, Bullard sidesteps the issue, unsure of how to depict the romantic and workplace experiences of sisters in militance once the excitement has died down. He turns the novel into a tract on Socialist woman as helpmeet, a role in which he casts Yetta, who joins the staff of the *Clarion*, Bullard's version of the *New York Call*, and the party as well. She finds her romantic identity in marriage to a lawyer sprung from her own class, the *Clarion*'s editor, Isadore Braun.

The alliance cements her dedication to the nonviolent agenda espoused by party regulars, who sought to "make socialism relevant to the existing problems of American workers."[72] Though there were fierce internal divisions in the major unions over Socialist influence, the party remained a power until the coming of World War I. Furthermore, in a presuffrage age, no other political party "fought as consistently for the full enfranchisement of women," and in its heyday around the time of Bullard's novel, one-tenth of the party's 120,000 dues-paying members were women.[73] But if in theory the party was more enlightened than trade unionists, it remained opposed to all-women organizations outside party subsections and generally refused women full political acceptance.

The fate that Bullard has in store for Yetta is representative of this refusal. Exchanging her interest in industrial unionism and in editing the newspaper's "Labor Page" for a socialist version of domestic womanhood, she becomes the editor of the *Clarion*'s "Mother's Column," as if a woman's acceptance of that role denies her participation in all but a woman's club version of socialism. In her assessment of the book, the author of *Women and the American Left* (1983) finds Yetta in every way her husband's comrade.[74] Yet to this reader Yetta inhabits a Socialist separate sphere much tamer than the domain of the women of the Socialist Party's Women's National Committee, themselves excluded from high-level party councils.[75] In defusing Yetta's militance, Bullard employs a sexual division of intellectual labor. Though with her husband she is a delegate to an international Socialist convention, domestic concerns have become her political platform. Not even suffrage, which her sister Socialists agitate to include in the party platform, interests her now. It is not that woman's concerns with home and child are narrower, but that Bullard is fixated on keeping political womanhood womanly.

Bullard defends Lemlich's activism only to close by Victorianizing her. Much of *The Nine-Tenths*, by the onetime social worker and utopian Socialist James Oppenheim, appears to be on a reverse trajectory, although he ultimately resolves the split between contending types of womanhood in a manner similar to Bullard's. He allows the prim schoolteacher Myra Craig to be drawn into the Shirtwaist Strike long enough to imbibe the heady spirit of feminine freedom. But he is careful to distinguish her from the militant women she meets and to shunt her into marriage to Joe Blaine, a printing-plant owner turned radical editor. It is Blaine who registers events. He distracts the reader from the seasoned professional organizer, Sally Heffer, or Oppenheim's Lemlich persona, Rhona Hemlitz, whose trial Blaine covers.

That Oppenheim highlights male consciousness of a largely female labor event has gone unremarked by period and modern reviewers alike. They prefer to interpret the book, to cite Walter Rideout, as the "most nearly complete fictional account of the Uprising."[76] Missed by those who have commented on the novel as "photography"[77] of female activism is that Joe Blaine rejects the "easy comradeship" of Sally Heffer. He chooses the ultrafeminine and fitfully political Myra, who would provide "peace, relaxation, diversion" (290).

Even as Oppenheim's surrogate Blaine reports on the admirable actions of those like Rhona-Clara, whose workhouse "martyrdom . . . could be used as a fire and a torch to kindle and lead the others" (279), he distinguishes between true women and the zealots who "man" the barricades. In the novel Rhona-Clara's fervor cuts her off from the feminine options available to the narrative's more conventional female strike supporters. Oppenheim reasserted the same conviction in a story in his collection *Pay Envelopes,* published the same year as *The Nine-Tenths*. There the title character of "Joan of the Mills" trades her role as a self-appointed mill-town agitator, a "free, strong, almost masculine" figure, for marriage to one of the burly workers whose consciousness she has awakened with her political saintliness.[78] That Oppenheim sees no such possibility for Rhona-Clara suggests his gendered response to both: their unnaturalness is the measure of their passionate commitment to the strike.

In contrast to Oppenheim and his male colleagues, women strike novelists refashioned female militance by refusing either to domesticate the female picketer or to associate her with a kind of abnormal womanhood. In *The Children of Light* (1912) by the WTUL advocate Florence Converse, the marriage of Bertha Aarons, the Lemlich surrogate, to a radical Russian (Lemlich herself would wed a Russian printer and radical, Joe Shavelson, in 1913) does not lessen her involvement. For most of the otherwise unbelievable labor romance, Bertha is a viable enough figure. Yet palliating the historical reality, Converse sends Bertha off to join the WTUL just at the moment in the actual strike when Lemlich broke with the women's organization as middle class and condescending to the strikers. A former garment worker and cloakmakers' union organizer, and a more politically radical woman than Converse, Theresa Malkiel called Lemlich by name in the novel *The Diary of a Shirtwaist Striker;* Clara joins other crucial historical actors such as Mother Jones, Rose Phelps Stokes, and Leonora O'Reilly. The novel is further distinct from those of Converse, Bullard, and Oppenheim in that it is the "diary" of "Mary," a working woman herself, one who moves from initial apathy to so intense an involvement in the strike that she defies her father, her fiancé, and, commenting that "picketing ain't half so bad as I thought it would be," the state itself.[79] "Now," she writes, on being arrested for picketing, "I'm a real striker—felt the grip of a policeman's hand, had a free ride in a patrol wagon, spent a few hours at the police station and was arraigned in court" (26).

Furthermore, Malkiel, a former shop worker herself, was faithful to the chronology of the Shirtwaist Strike, described by Mary as the "first real girls' strike" (35), the unwarranted accusations of immorality endured by the girls, and the warm bonds between leaders like Lemlich and the young women themselves. Yet she uses strategies that rein in the women strikers even as they restrict Lemlich's actual potency. Three-quarters of the strikers were Jewish, and Italians made up much of the remaining number. Mary is native born and, save for the occasional colloquialism, unusually literate for an oppressed sweatshop worker. As Francoise Basch explains in her introduction to the recently reprinted text, Malkiel hoped that using a native-born speaker would widen the appeal of the narrative to a middle-class WASP readership.[80] Whatever her motive, the novel sidelines the many female immigrants radicalized by the 1909 protest, particularly Lemlich herself. While her Cooper Union speech is briefly summarized and praised, it is done sketchily. Nor does the reader hear Lemlich deliver it. In any case, her reported remarks are completely overshadowed by Mary's stirring talk, which immediately follows that of "little Clara" (120).

Mary, in effect, becomes a culturally acceptable Lemlich. When, after the strike is settled, she speaks of plans to marry her fiancé, whom she has converted to socialism, the novel tidily resolves the contradictions posed by a labor protest of unmarried ethnic females and the cultural imperative to be assimilated and married off. In contrast to the other writers of the Shirtwaist Strike school, this is less a strategy of banishment than of reconciliation. As a fictional homage to Lemlich and her sisters, though, it joins other period novels to rewrite whose strike it was.

That the Shirtwaist Strike school had shaped the representation of the girl striker for the rest of the decade was evident in 1910 and the years immediately following, when the veteran ILGWU organizer Gertrude Barnum and others published short fiction like "At the Shirt-Waist Factory" (1910), "The Pig-Headed Girl" (1912), and "In the Jacket Shop" (1912) in the union's official paper, *Ladies' Garment Worker*. In such directive tales, women join the union, close down the shop, and otherwise negate the assumption that women workers cannot organize. Yet once again, political maturity is transient, modified by the marriage that returned women still committed to the labor movement to an adjunct activism.

Theodore Dreiser and the Counternarrative of Working Womanhood

If the chroniclers of the Shirtwaist Strike had to defuse Lemlich in order to pay homage to her, their treatment of female labor-class solidarity inaugurated a counternarrative of working womanhood. From a non-Socialist political perspective, Theodore Dreiser joined the antitraditionalists. He too chronicled the twinned urban industrial dangers of women's sexual harassment and their dubious "escape" from sweated work through sexual favors to middle- or upper-class men. In *Sister Carrie* and *Jennie Gerhardt*, by offering laboring women who bartered their sexuality while they lived with their families, Dreiser repudiated as manipulative and ineffectual the guardianship model of Richardson's *The Long Day*. New data about Dreiser's lifelong philandering and his midlife pursuit of young, even underage, girls, compel further feminist rereadings of these early novels.[81] Thus his message that family control matters little in a society that underpays and overstimulates impressionable urban women wage earners seems hypocritical, even prurient, in light of recent biography. Nevertheless, Dreiser complicates the debate on the moral regulation of working girls. For one thing, he highlights the inattentiveness of salt-of-the-earth working-class parent figures: Carrie's sister and brother-in-law see her as a useful boarder; the Gerhardts are too mired in their own misery to see Jennie at all. For another, he portrays the proletarian home as a mirror of societal tensions about female promiscuity.

Dreiser's well-paid contemporary O. Henry (William Sydney Porter) was silent on such family influences. In Sunday paper and periodical stories like "The Skylight Room," "Elsie in New York," and the somber "An Unfinished Story," he commiserated with young workingwomen to point out the difficulties and dangers confronting them. Yet while O. Henry lacked the profundity to endow a worker heroine with interiority, much less the consciousness of economic injustice, Dreiser was alive to those issues, and virtually alone in his careful respect for the emotional hungers and legitimate desires of his representative title characters. He paid serious attention to the factual realities of salary, work conditions, restrictions, and social relations. Nor did he scant bons vivants like Drouet, Hurstwood, and Lester Kane, men who pay for sex and live with women outside of wedlock. In that daring mix, his novels provide fictive counterparts of key sections of Progressive Era documentary classics like Butler's *Women and the Trades: Pittsburgh, 1907–1908*.

That work, including many case studies, appeared under the aegis of the ambitious Pittsburgh Survey. Butler's massive industrial study "virtually documented the absence of [non-sex-trade] occupational mobility among wage-earning women" in an early twentieth-century sister city to Chicago and New York.[82] Her ambitious examination ranges from scrutinizing the physical characteristics of factories to outlining the sexual division of labor in leading industries, subjects treated in Dreiser's two "kept woman" novels. Butler matter-of-factly provides many capsule histories of women who bartered sexual services for the possibility of ascension. Butler includes her own "Jennie," a small-town Akron girl unable to ascend as a Pittsburgh salesgirl, who "consented to be kept in an apartment."[83] A number of her other subjects even send money home from their new jobs in houses of prostitution.[84]

What is implicit in Butler is explicit in Dreiser, for he mounts a situational ethics argument that all but transforms the sexual "falls" of the Chicago shoe factory worker Carrie Meeber and the hotel laundress Jennie Gerhardt into self-protective feminine economic activity. It is important to note that, like the era's prostitution and white-slave novelists, Dreiser emphasizes both the sexual vulnerability and the suggestibility of the working girl. Thus Carrie is not long on the wearisome job before a male coworker prods her in the ribs, a rude harbinger of what she can expect if she remains. Given the combination of naïveté and longing with which she arrived in Chicago—she allowed a flashily dressed stranger to flirt with her and even gave him her address—Carrie is unlikely to find conditions in other factory jobs more to her liking. In the unpromising world of low-level work, it is her good fortune that Drouet, the stranger on the train whom she moves in with, treats her better socially and economically than she has ever known. Indeed, he elevates her at the price of a moral compromise she quickly makes—quite unlike the brutal gigolos who peopled the memoirs of turn-of-the-century streetwalkers. Carrie, in any case, quickly understands that she is ill equipped to descend to the alternative survival of her female coworkers, who seem to welcome the unsavory socializing of their male colleagues.

Even Carrie's coworkers, uncouth as they are, would have looked down on laundresses, who were viewed through period stereotypes as louche and sexually available. Such prejudices were only bolstered by Degas's sensual paintings and Richardson's satiric portraits in *The Long Day*. By 1906 laundresses, though rarely achieving the notice of garment workers, were throwing off such cultural clichés by rebelling against their notoriously low wages.[85] But Dreiser guards Jennie Gerhardt, who docilely works with her mother cleaning and laundering in a large hotel, from both sexual slurs and feminist politics. A gentle soul who loves domesticity (in direct contrast to Dreiser's own sisters), Jennie desires only to replicate domestic duty outside the home, a wish granted at the cost of sexual bartering.

Arguing for fallen womanhood as true womanhood, Dreiser sanctifies Jennie's love affairs, first with a hotel guest, Senator Brander, and then, after his death, with another affluent male predator, Lester Kane, in the name of self-sacrifice. He sustains the argument that Jennie, whose illegitimate daughter Vesta (like her mother a kind of vestal virgin) dies young, is tragically maternal.[86]

In symbolic attempts to shield the labor-class woman from a habitat deemed sexually corrupting, Dreiser makes the subversive point that even the most refined of workingwomen can ascend only as the mistress of an affluent capitalist man. If he removes working-class womanhood from the labor fray, and thus from the possibility of a political culture with feminine institutions and networks, he is making a point similar to that made by the Shirtwaist strikers themselves: women are vulnerable under industrial capitalism, and those without economic independence are in danger of sexual exploitation. Dreiser explodes cultural fantasies of and hostilities to proletarian womanhood first by revising marriage to include affairs and then by casting these "marriages" as punishment, not reward. Still, his is a compromised radicalism that decouples women and work.

Intersections: The Sex-Trade Novel as Working-Class Narrative

The era's various subgenres of working-girl fiction were divided between acknowledgment and denial of their characters' positive qualities. Whether it was refinement, chastity, or the ability to agitate, doubts of working-class women's moral probity or political effectiveness clouded otherwise affirming portraits. A similar collision between affirmation and condemnation informed the era's fiction of the "Girl That Goes Wrong," the title of the Socialist Reginald Wright Kauffman's own 1911 collection of vice-trade stories. Kauffman was the period's most famous novelist-investigator of the white-slave trade at a time when everyone from Progressive journals like *Social Hygiene* to big-city mayors, women's clubs, and ghostwritten memoirs by prostitutes themselves were speaking out against prostitution and attempts to close down red-light districts were proliferating.

His 1910 best-seller *The House of Bondage,* its seriousness belied by its sensational title, was *the* novel of prostitution in the decade and a half prior to World War I. It went through printing after printing and was still selling well three years after it appeared.[87] The product of ten years of interviews in the vice districts of major American cities and an extensive knowledge of local and national reports on the "social evil," it tried to do with the sex trade what a few years before Sinclair had done with the meatpacking industry.[88]

The novel is titularly the abduction and coercion story of a restless, small-town, lower-class girl, Mary Denbigh. Lured to the city, she is quickly renamed "Violet" by her Jewish procurer and madam and virtually imprisoned in a brothel, only to escape and fall economically even lower, to streetwalking, after briefly trying respectability. The white-slave plot is not Kauffman's only device to palliate Violet-Mary's moral fall. She also serves as a Progressive orator, the kind of informed eyewitness whose edited testimony appeared in so many vice commission reports. She becomes expert in the economic benefits to recruiters, types of houses, fees charged, and machine politicians who reap the profits (320). She is even poised to testify at a white slavery hearing, but her resentment that the world of decent work is closed to her pushes her back to the sex trade.[89] Kauffman's testifier is outdone by the prostitute Marguerite Howard in Walter Hurt's *The Scarlet Shadow* (1907), who peppers her speech with Socialist rhetoric, biblical references, classical allusions, and even quotations from Charlotte Brontë.

The forced bordello recruits of most white-slave novels were not viewed in lower-class terms. When, as in James H. Brower's *The Mills of Mammon* (1909), published at the height of the furor, a seventeen-year-old girl pleads with her captor, she is described as a daughter of the church whose diction matches her religiosity.[90] Kauffman, though, seeks to focus more on the classed nature of "recruits." A recent historian labels Kauffman the premiere white-slave ideologue, but a careful rereading uncovers another dimension to the novel's representation of the vice trade.[91]

Although Kauffman both shares and trivializes Dreiser's vision of a sexualized female world, *The House of Bondage* is not just a veiled recital of the traffic in poor women. Kauffman casts a cold eye on the middle- and upper-class women who were spearheading social purity legislation aimed at closing vice districts and rescuing their female inmates.[92] Instead, Kauffman creates interactions between respectable working-class and "fallen" women that place the two types in closer contact than most period novelists were willing to put them. In one section, a feisty Irish shopgirl, Katie Flanagan, joins a Lithuanian garment worker, Carrie Berkowicz, to help Violet-Mary escape from the brothel. The strong-minded Katie approves when her Socialist boyfriend lectures the girl on capitalist oppression. When Mary cannot find any respectable work to sustain her, though, she turns not to socialism but to selling herself on the street. Another segment briefly addresses the Shirtwaist Strike. However, because he views it through the prism of the sex trade, Kauffman cannot take Carrie's commitment to ILGWU activism seriously. Wearying of her participation in the strike, she cedes to the procurer and enters a brothel, finding the wages, if not the work, an improvement over the picket line.

However improbable Katie's rescue or Carrie's transit from picket line to red-light district, Kauffman circled truths unwelcome to the mainstream antivice crusader. One was that labor-class women, and not necessarily those in the poorest jobs, found "illegitimate means to achieve the socially acceptable goals of economic security and social status."[93] The other was that the prostitute was less the ruined child or passive victim than the alienated worker who, whether delusively or not, chose another way of earning. Kauffman covered over these insights with typical period punitiveness.[94]

After the Progressive Era and the American entry into the Great War, when successful attempts to squelch red-light districts made the prostitute a less toxic figure, there appeared the anonymous autobiography *Madeleine* (1919). The book chronicles a onetime labor-class woman who experienced fifteen years of brothel life in the cities of the Midwest and on the Canadian frontier. A decade earlier, in Kauffman's time, anyone looking for a survivalist narrative of this type could have read it only in manuscript form. (Even a partial exception, Lydia Pettengill Taylor's 1913 *From under the Lid,* an autobiography probably heavily aided by a ghostwriter, veered between fury at former customers and sentimental appeals for understanding.) Although Kauffman purportedly spoke with veterans of the sex trade, absent from his novel are the kinds of sentiments expressed in "My Story: The History of a Prostitute's Life in San Francisco" (c. 1910). This manuscript of Margaret von Staden, a San Francisco streetwalker in the early 1900s, joins the writings of Maimie Pinzer, who, in a series of letters to a female benefactor, recounted her impressions of plying the trade in Philadelphia around the same time. Interestingly, in a paragraph appended to the von Staden manuscript, an anonymous author, identifying von Staden as a real person, lamented that she had "tried to get it published [b]ut Reginald Wright Kauffman's *House of Bondage* had made much trouble."[95] Yet whatever antiprostitution sentiment the Kauffman novel provoked, efforts to publish either the memoir or the Pinzer letters would have been in vain.

Von Staden demythifies Kauffman's invented world by anchoring her life in the vice trade in a pragmatic working-class context. She details her origins as a longshoreman's daughter and the sister of ironworkers and describes her own jobs as a shirt-factory worker and department store clerk. Not only does she downplay her loss of virginity and subsequent pregnancy, but she describes returning to respectable work after these experiences. When, after a time, she turns to casual prostitution, she continues to downplay her "fall." And in her most unorthodox statement, she suggests that prostitution be unionized "like other trades."[96] Even her admission that, as work, it is drudgery too (148) cements the connection between prostitutes and other nonunion labor. The manuscript, circulated with the comment that von Staden had died of venereal disease, also disclaims its job language by burying it in lengthy homiletics on the cruelty of pimps and the hypocrisy of respectable society. But these scattered vocational assertions are more memorable than either the mini-sermons or the catalogs of insider's facts and complaints.

Maimie lived to be penitent in a way that von Staden did not. Her remorse tempers her own matter-of-factness because she has left the trade and is partly dependent on her benefactor's largesse. Yet she is frank enough in her frequent admission that having tried department store work before her "fall," she was certain that prostitution was easier work than any other she could have found.[97] In contrast, the paradox of white-slave fiction is that it acknowledged prostitution as a business while it denied that the supposedly enslaved women who engaged in it did a form of labor. Though unreliable in other ways, the writings of participant-observers implied that working women did not see prostitution as purgatory. Rather, they chose to float in and out of it from a combination of economic need, alienation from respectable work, and a certain sexual waywardness. But the labor press, whether a Socialist publication or even the Wobbly organ, *Industrial Worker*, was largely silent.[98] The stories in the ILGWU organ, *Ladies' Garment Worker*, shrank from the subject.[99] Perhaps cognizant of the strikebreaking role played by veteran streetwalkers in the Shirtwaist Strike, where they were hired to disrupt the picket line, Malkiel and Oppenheim portray prostitutes as hardened, uninterested in decent work, and hostile to the women who do it (*Diary*, 183–184; *Nine-Tenths*, 210). Red-light women continue their harassment of female strikers in prison, where they taunt those arrested for protesting as fools who could earn more money in the sex trade.

There were, however, those sympathetic to socialism, the prostitute, or both, who found her neither sex slave nor labor foe. They reasserted her defiant working-class authenticity in the pages of *The Masses;* in Hutchins Hapgood's political novel *An Anarchist Woman* (1909), later serialized in the 1916 *Masses;* in *Edna: A Girl of the Street,* a 1915 novella by Alfred Kreymbourg; in the reform politician Brand Whitlock's story "The Girl That's Down" (1912); and in David Graham Phillips's *Susan Lenox: Her Fall and Rise,* completed in 1911, the year of his death, and published six years later. Although none of these authors controlled the sexuality of working women in the cautionary manner of white-slave narratives, in one way or another they all balked at the idea of sex work. The heroine of John Reed's 1913 *Masses* vignette "Where the Heart Is" is a "reckless-mouthed" woman "insolently swinging her hips" who represents the "life-force indomitable."[100] A cheerful siren in tight clothing and a yellow-plumed hat, proud of her popularity with the college boys, Martha, the voluble dance hall woman of the sketch, is romanticized as a proletarian bon vivant. Even her Parisian counterpart Marcel in "A Daughter of the Revolution" defends herself with ferocity. (Her revised speech patterns, those of her educated creator, are similar to those of the edited workingmen and derelicts of Reed's labor sketches in *The Masses.)* "'Regret my life?' she flashe[s]. . . . 'Damme, no, I'm free!' "[101] At the very least, *The Masses'* literary message is that she and her red-light sisters have lived more fully than the self-denying working girl at the heart of Adriana Spadoni's June 1916 piece, "A Hall Bedroom Nun."

If Winslow and fellow *Masses* contributor James Henle ("Nobody's Sister," *Masses*, January 1915) mix a British Magdalen plot with *Masses* heroinizing, *An Anarchist Woman* casts Marie, a former factory girl and servant, as propelled to prostitution by the quest for excitement and remaining there as a matter of principle, proclaiming herself one of the "brave girls" who withstand life's trials.[102] Politics proves for a time more legitimate, but she eventually rejects anarchism in her search for pleasure and meaning. Even so she is more serious-minded than a labor-class protagonist uninterested in speaking in class terms, Edna, the slangily youthful title character of a short novel by John Reed's Village acquaintance Kreymbourg. Since the work includes a hotel room scene in which she expresses contentment with her life, the Vice Society of New York immediately confiscated the 350 copies of the story and hauled the editor and publisher off to court for selling obscene material. If Kreymbourg's novella is mentioned now at all, it is as a victory over American censorship (the obscenity case was dismissed) rather than as the depiction of an antitype of the white slave. As in the Reed sketches, prostitution brings a liberty more personal than economic. Edna proclaims: "It'd be hell to sleep with the same fellow every night."[103] Mace, her equally tough counterpart in a Brand Whitlock tale, "The Girl That's Down," provides a Progressive literary alternative: emerging from night court as disgusted with her trade as at the legal system that incarcerates her but not her clients, the protagonist decides not to be the "fall guy" anymore.[104]

David Graham Phillips, in contrast, understood that the bohemianism of New York City's streetwalkers was limited and certainly paled in comparison with their economic self-interest. Phillips was an urban reporter in the Midwest, a London correspondent for the *New York World,* a seasoned journalist, and a muckraking novelist of corrupt senators, society adulterers, and parasite wives. He subordinated his Reed-like admiration for the lower-class sex rebel to that curious fascination with the strong-willed social climber common to so many naturalist and Progressive authors. His hybrid novel *Susan Lenox: Her Fall and Rise* is a massive story of an illegitimate small-town Indiana girl who spends years in dead-end factory, sweatshop, and sales jobs. As an economic alternative, she is kept by a number of men. Soon she descends to drug addiction and streetwalking, only to rise improbably to fame on the New York stage.

A combination of Progressive Era documentary, hard-boiled reportage on urban corruption, working-girl dime novel, and Scarlet-Woman-as-Horatio-Alger tale, the book offers a heroic prostitute who is streetwise, resilient, and contemptuous of efforts to control her. Nor is her entry marked by a decisive moment or a vicious seducer, as it is for the pathetic white slaves or maddened streetwalkers of most prostitution fiction, though not for the former shopgirls and seamstresses of Progressive case studies. Susan selects prostitution after her $4 a week as a hat trimmer and her $3 as a paperbox folder prove insufficient to live on. She simply moves from casual prostitution to supplement her workday to "make the bargain she could and accept the world's terms" (II, 104).

Yet if Phillips was the rare social protest novelist to reward a gutter prostitute with upward mobility, he too defends the working prostitute by erasing her sexuality. Over and over the narrative defends her against charges of sexual profiteering by insisting on her innocence and essential purity; a pimp she takes up with, Freddie Palmer, who sleeps with and then beats her, taunts her with being "Sunday-schoolish."[105] The portraitist and illustrator Howard Chandler Christy, famed for his drawings of blooming womanhood, lent his talents to ads and illustrations when much of the text was serialized in *Hearst's* in 1916. Described in one as the "heroine," Susan wears a bonnet and looks demure.[106] Such cosmeticizing did not prevent the Society for the Suppression of Vice from forcing *Hearst's* to stop publishing it and Appleton and Company to issue a bowdlerized version months after it had issued the original text.[107]

To play out his ambivalent fascination with people of power, Phillips, as in his political fiction prior to *Susan Lenox,* mythifies his title character's talent to rise. In fact, Susan oddly resembles Phillips's good friend Albert J. Beveridge, who had climbed from a logging camp to become a U.S. senator—in *The Plum Tree* (1905), Beveridge's fictional representative becomes President. While Phillips retains gendered notions of what women can achieve politically, he does propel Susan to the Broadway stage and, as a famed actress, to an "upper ten" social success that Dreiser's Carrie Meeber could only long for. Thus Susan ends up neither immoral, proletarian, nor unwomanly. What should have been a subversive text on the working woman and the American urban sex trade was as much a Progressive Era fairy tale as any white-slave tirade.

"Oh, I Like the Work Very Well": The African American Woman's Plot

In 1903 Pauline Hopkins became the literary editor of the *Colored American Magazine,* located in Boston. It placed her in a position of authority, as it was the first black magazine founded in the twentieth century and one whose African American writers, artists, and spokespeople appealed greatly to a predominantly black audience seeking to reconstruct its heritage.[108] Three years prior, when she was writing women's columns for the periodical, Boston's Colored Co-Operative Publishing Company published Hopkins's *Contending Forces: A Romance Illustrative of Negro Life North and South.* The narrative was a historical romance tracing the lives of several generations of an African American family from Caribbean enslavement to a free life in turn-of-the-century Boston. The bulk of the novel joined most of the literary contributions to *Colored American* in airing issues of racial discrimination, mixed-race love affairs, and the evils of a system in which blacks were constrained to pass for white. Yet Hopkins's lengthy book also joined these pieces in minimizing the hard truths of the African American labor experience, whether in New England, the Midwest, or the Deep South. In many of these stories by Hopkins and her colleagues that updated the tragic mulatta of William Wells Brown (*Clotel,* 1864) and other black authors of the Civil War era, protagonists were often female; the quadroon heroine in *Contending Forces* is Sappho Clark (born Mabelle Beaubean).

For most of the second part of the novel Sappho tries to live down the sexual tragedy of her past. As a beautiful, light-skinned New Orleans girl she was raped by her white uncle, placed by him in a brothel, and finally rescued and taken to a convent, where she gave birth to a son. Revising *Clotel,* Hopkins empowers Sappho and weds her to a black civil rights activist who accepts both her past and her illegitimate child. In so doing, Hopkins rejects the clichés of the "tabooed seductress . . . damaged wom[a]n" accepted by the most modernist of white authors, such as the expatriate Gertrude Stein, in her privately published *Melanctha* (1909). In it, Stein's oversexed African American title character, however much her vernacular self-expression appeals to period readers in search of African American authenticity, comes to the expected bad end.[109]

However, largely overlooked even in recent feminist discussions of Sappho is that she is an educated woman skilled in office work, who is able to support herself as a freelance typist and "like[s] the work very well" (*Contending Forces,* 99). The sections of the book in which she does this work constitute an important transition between a past she keeps secret from the other boarders in the Boston lodging house and her new life as the respected wife of an African American professional. Hopkins deliberately constructs Sappho's transitional identity as that of a wage earner who is many cuts above laundry or domestic work. Implementing her own suggestion in her later editorials for the *Colored American,* she permits Sappho the beginnings of a business career while denying the unattractive realities facing Sappho's real-life sisters.

As late as a decade after the Hopkins novel, Chicago, considered a more attractive job mart for southern migrants, employed only twenty black teachers in the entire school system, and those in all-black venues.[110] That city's largest employer of clerical workers, Montgomery Ward, no doubt sent a widespread cultural message when it kept its black female office workers in mail-order jobs where they were invisible to the public.[111] The would-be Boston clerical worker Addie W. Hunter, though a high school graduate with the proper training, echoed the lament of Chicago breadwinners who found office work "closed to the Negro girl."[112] Progressive Era stories of highly educated black women condemned to a lifetime of menial work proliferated.[113]

Sappho's labor situation, however, is not ideal either. Although she can pass for white, her employer, knowing of her mixed-race background, will only give her work to do at home. (In this she fares better than most "assimilated" Native American women. In real life, they were consigned to teaching at the Carlisle Indian-Industrial School or, like Mourning Dove, a half-Okinagan Indian, they discovered that an education in a government Indian school secured an Indian woman no work at all.)[114] Because Sappho acknowledges her African American lineage, she is banished from the kind of workplace interview dramatized in Dreiser's *Sister Carrie*. Seeing that Sappho is white and native born, a prospective employer asks routinely: "Are you a stenographer or [a] typewriter?" (21). As Maimie Pinzer's letters record, in 1912 even this reformed prostitute, half-blind and socially awkward, a few months after her stenography course found a number of acceptable jobs in the New York City area and started her own business two years later in Montreal.[115] Thus the same woman who fears exposure as a fallen woman and unwed mother will not conceal her racial identity. Hopkins reconciles such contradictions in her heroine's veracity by contrasting the involuntary sexuality with a newfound self-reliance untarnished by posing or passing. Furthermore, as a ladylike typist, Sappho, Hopkins insists, is rightly welcomed in a sewing circle that includes the kind of privileged black clubwomen who spearheaded antilynching and uplift campaigns at the turn of the century.[116]

Nevertheless, for all that, Hopkins rightly termed her work a romance. Sappho's psychic and economic journey from the sexual chattel of southern white men to convent penitent to respectable northern wage earner, much less to the wife of a member of the Talented Tenth, is a fantasy of ascension. Sappho's vocational success, when joined to that of other women in the book, extends the vision of ambition realized to black female entrepreneurship. As Hopkins well knew, few heavily vernacular Boston inhabitants, represented by characters such as the former cook Ophelia Davis and the maid Sara Anne White, could profitably run a laundry business. The fantasy expands when the two join an equally successful boardinghouse keeper and her educated daughter in their group resolution not to be, as Ophelia Davis puts it, "livin' in white folkses' kitchens" (105). In a representative variant such as Ruth D. Todd's "The Octoroon's Revenge" in *Colored American* (March 1902), the title character, a serving woman, dwells in poverty for most of her life. The romance mode reasserts itself when her daughter marries a mulatto. It is noteworthy too that the New York acting success of the rural southerner Kitty Hamilton, a secondary character in Paul Laurence Dunbar's *The Sport of the*

Gods (1902), a somber novel of Harlem's effect on southern migrants, is viewed as a moral decline, not an economic ascension.

White authors from the working girls' favorite, Bertha M. Clay, to the naturalistic Theodore Dreiser also elevated the servant heroine. Yet to the extent that their heroines move smoothly across the class divide, their plots of ascension are no less romances. Thus however much these works are what Hazel Carby terms "cathartic responses" to U.S. racism, the fact that Hopkins and her widely read peers turned to fairy tales of vocational affluence and fantasies of feminine agency meant that hard-headed explorations of the black work experience had to await another literary decade.[117]

Unacceptable Behavior:
Women, Texts, and U.S. Labor Fiction in the Progressive Era

From colonial times onward, the reading habits of lower-class women were the subject of debate. Novel reading, from its inception, was considered a woman's pastime. As such it was morally suspect. The habit could "keep the poor from being good workers," whether the servant who read her mistress's books or the factory girl who eagerly responded to a seduction novel like *Charlotte Temple* (1791) (which was, after all, subtitled *A Tale of Truth*).[118] But the rise of the affordable dime novel and the escapist desires of working girls in monotonous jobs joined Progressive Era fears about the moral pitfalls of the workplace to intensify the controversy over what working women should read. Concern over breadwinning women's choice of literature surfaces repeatedly in the texts with labor themes. Dorothy Richardson devotes a satiric chapter to the tastes of those like her more refined heroine's uneducated coworker Phoebe, who "hold[s] forth upon music and literature" that to Richardson's mind is vulgar, crudely written, and completely unreal in its reiteration of feminine virtue triumphant (*Long Day,* 75). While aware that the Phoebes would scorn such fare, she concludes by recommending *Robinson Crusoe* and *The Vicar of Wakefield* (85). Theodore Dreiser, more attuned to though no less judgmental of the cheap fiction devoured by many working-women, marks Carrie's rise in the world with her new appetite for serious reading; by story's end she is making her way through a Balzac novel. Hopkins's Sappho, ever ladylike, is well versed in the Bible as well as great, if romantic, poetry. And the Progressive surveyor Louise Montgomery sounds a similar note in her 1913 Chicago slum study by including a case history of a girl who, having quit the soap factory to attend Hull House classes, asks not for a novel but for a serious book on "how poor girls became famous."[119] Finally, Malkiel's newly politicized Mary would have rejected all of the above readings for an account of injustice in the *New York Call.*

Yet even as they lauded the working girl who strives to elevate herself through reading, the authors discussed in this chapter knew that the mass of laboring women were caught up in more immediate problems. Moreover, even as they advanced a genteel code in their novelistic defenses of the worker heroine, their subtexts were concerned with her propensity to prostitution or kept womanhood. Too, because the chastity of the labor-class woman was suspect, most authors rejected their own implication that sex work was on a continuum with other low-paid labor. The period novel depicted commercialized sex not as a form of paid work but as the feminine counterpart of the bestiality of *The Jungle*. Even the Socialist labor text's message that blue-collar women could learn to be radical collided with the suspicion that such a lesson was unwomanly.

Yet the most visible workingwomen of the time, the organizers and strikers, mocked the Victorianism that prevented women from breaking the boundaries between the male and female work worlds. Cast aside as well was the relevance of an ideology that insisted on the superiority of the lady to the mass of women workers, a staple of the backward-looking texts of Van Vorst, Freeman, and Richardson. In 1912 the garment-trades organizer Rose Schneiderman spoke up, disgusted at the inaction following the Triangle Shirtwaist Factory Fire of 1911 in which 146 perished, 126 of them women. Women who toiled were not "regarded as women," she stormed, because the ideologues of ladyhood "talk[ed] all this trash of theirs about finer qualities."[120]

Schneiderman, like Lemlich and other mainstays of the women's labor movement, may have been more radical than the workers who staged walkouts and boycotts only to return to jobs little improved and life goals defined by marriage rather than continued paid work. In a wide variety of texts, neither the political education nor the self-help lessons these women received as strikers formed part of the period vision of the feminine rank and file. Indeed, even Clara Lemlich, their most ardent representative, is subdued: elevated, isolated, and domesticated by Bullard, cameoed by Oppenheim, sidelined by Malkiel and Converse, and displaced onto a seamstress-turned-prostitute in Kauffman. It is true that in the early sections of Bullard's *Comrade Yetta* and Oppenheim's *The Nine-Tenths,* she reveals an energy absent in the literature of previous decades. Gertrude Barnum's *Ladies' Garment Worker* piece, "The Pig-Headed Girl," even reconciles her union activity with her restless search for better employment. Yet, in light of the real-life achievements of empowered types like Elizabeth Gurley Flynn at Lowell and Lawrence, Mother Jones in the coal fields of Cripple Creek, Colorado, and Lemlich in the garment trades on the Lower East Side, the response of fiction to (white) women on the labor barricades was a vacillating one.

There were no literary representations of Rebel Girls and Union Maids in fiction by and about black women, and very little on the kind of manual work such women were permitted to do for pay. Yet that was because they were excluded from garment shops and clothing union locals alike, including ILGWU Local 25.[121] Given their awareness of stereotypes about black women wage earners, black writers invoking the ascension plot did not so much combat the images of the happy or sexual domestic as maintain a vigilant silence about them. Not until the Harlem Renaissance would fiction detail the lives of maids and prostitutes in Wallace Thurman's *The Blacker the Berry* (1929) and Claude McKay's *Home to Harlem* (1927), respectively.

The mass-industrial experience of the first two decades of the twentieth century inevitably reshaped cultural and literary representations of the female laboring classes. The old workplace exits and marital ascendancies were dislodged by plots of self-directed ethnic women wage earners refusing to be sweatshop drones, a decision these authors did not extend to women of color, Asians, or Native Americans. Still, the new visibility of the ethnic factory girl joined the notoriety of the streetwalking prostitute, whether country girl or immigrant, to prompt U.S. labor authors to the halting realization that neither woman would survive, much less rise, without repudiating Victorian stereotypes of self-sacrifice and moral frailty. Whether U.S. worker stories would successfully challenge the old models of the genteel or morally imperiled factory girl, the victimized or bestial sex slave, and even the domesticated comrade was a task left for the next two decades.

PART II

The Road to 1930

CHAPTER 7

The Hungry Eye
Desire and Disaffection in 1920s Labor Fiction

[Clyde] . . . wandered on, essaying one small job and another, in St. Louis, Peoria, Chicago, Milwaukee—dishwashing in a restaurant, soda-clerking in a small outlying drug-store, a grocer's clerk, and what not; and [was] discharged and laid off and quit . . . because he did not like it.

—THEODORE DREISER, *AN AMERICAN TRAGEDY* (1925)

Floppin' is done by the best people. . . . Where does a stiff find any more high-class sensations than comes to him just after rollin' in to a fine well-thrown together bunk . . . in a bugless paradise?

—WILLIAM AKERS [RALPH WINSTEAD], "TIGHTLINE JOHNSON GOES TO HEAVEN," *INDUSTRIAL PIONEER* (JULY 1923)

All art is Mammonart save Communist art. . . . [In] the Proletcult theaters [of the Soviet Union]. . . . the bourgeois . . . is shown the gutter, and the healthy worker running his beloved machine, conqueror of famine, poverty, and want is given the center of the stage.

—ROBIN E. DUNBAR, "MAMMONART AND COMMUNIST ART," *DAILY WORKER* (MAY 23, 1925)

George Luks, *Pottstown, Pennsylvania*, late 1920s. Oil on canvas. Wadsworth Atheneum, Hartford. The Ella Gallup Sumner and Mary Catlin Sumner Collection Fund.

The ten years between the "decade of strikes" and the Great Crash of 1929 saw renewed corporate attempts to foster a mass-work, postcraft mentality. Giants like Ford Motor, International Harvester, and Swift and Company led the way in offering white ethnic immigrant and native-born workers a management vision of industrial democracy. These companies lured workers with group insurance, benefit plans, paid vacations, overtime, and profit sharing (albeit based on workplace loyalty). The decade also saw company sports competitions and family picnics—far from paltry affairs when the heavy-industrial workforce often represented a sizable percentage of the payroll.

To further ensure working-class cooperation and the loyalty on which it was based, the Ford Company had successfully "placed a new kind of freedom so tantalizingly close to the wage earner that most workers were willing to accept their tenuous lot."[1] With their bonuses and overtime pay, Ford workers could purchase automobiles on time. They joined other assembly-line toilers in buying tract houses and furniture on the installment plan. And they were also prime customers for the mass of goods and entertainments newly available to the working class.[2]

When Theodore Dreiser wrote *An American Tragedy* (1925), a novel concerned with the exaggerated desires fostered by consumerism, he was presciently commenting on the entire Fordist decade. Integrating his research on the rewards and monotonies of the new kind of factory into the novel, he marveled at the high wages for experienced hands, the on-site employment bureau, and the company doctor and hospital.[3] Dreiser's novel, however, was a mammoth case study of a man who lacked the work ethic and resented his workload. Dreiser realized that, however benevolent, 1920s welfare capitalism served what one business executive admitted was "cold-blooded Ford efficiency." This philosophy, sometimes called Taylorism, was also dubbed Fordism after that motor magnate's success. Throughout the 1920s, Ford's motor empire both compelled and inspired worker output on the completely standardized production line and demoted skilled craftsmen to specialized machine operators.[4]

In an overview of the period, labor historians have dubbed it the "backsliding 1920s." It was a time when workers were dazzled by glitzy consumerism, and outbreaks of militancy lacked the concentrated force of the previous decade.[5] Despite the fact that wages advanced modestly in the postwar era, the 1920s version of the American Dream was one of affluence and institutionalized incentives for well-behaved, white mass-production workers. In the battle against the Ford mystique, the radical organizer Steve Nelson found it frustratingly hard to rally that company's workers to the Communist Party. Six decades later he still remembered how the "Ford idea of individualism held many under its spell. . . . The propaganda of the rugged loner was in their mothers' milk, and it [also] hit them in the papers and at the movies."[6]

By the mid- to late 1920s, layoffs and cutbacks were ominous harbingers of 1929.[7] After wartime replacements were no longer needed, not even the promise of affluence was extended to blacks and Latinos, the cheapest immigrant labor of the decade. They were the black menials at Ford and tenant farmers in Kentucky, or the Mexican migrants in the lettuce fields of California's Imperial Valley and the citrus region of Orange County.[8] Moreover, for many white, Euro-American workers, material living standards in basic industry were higher than before the war, but the working-class struggle for economic security did not abate.[9] Nor were most workers connected in values to corporate employers or, if ethnics, inevitably Americanized.[10] And among a minority of Euro-Americans, both in and outside basic industry, there was embattled activism of the kind described by the anarchist Bartolomeo Vanzetti.[11] Why, then, was labor radicalism—and its fictive embodiments—so slow in reawakening? To find the answers, one must backtrack to the "red scare" years between 1919 and 1923.

"Reds," Rising, and Narrative

The "red scare" spanned the years between the 1917 American entrance into World War I and 1923.[12] Nineteen seventeen was also the year the Russian czar was executed and the U.S. Immigrant Act penalized anyone teaching the overthrow of the American government. At war's end, Russian revolutionary factions struggled for national supremacy. From 1919 to 1923, the Bolsheviks, a party of professional revolutionaries espousing the dictatorship of the proletariat, consolidated their power via the Red Army. Such events fed U.S. anxieties about what the *Times* predicted would be the end of capitalism if the "reds" triumphed in America.[13]

Visitors to "Red Russia" included the benevolently skeptical garment trades and mining union leaders David Dubinsky and John Brophy and the Communist literary devotee Mike Gold.[14] Whether these groups' admiration for the early years of the Soviets' New Economic Plan was vocal, muted, ambivalent, or nonexistent, in the United States itself "communistic" literature and militancy were swiftly repressed.[15] Deportations, spurred by a rash of anarchist bombings, increased. Reporting on these early 1920s raids that often bore the last name of Attorney General Mitchell Palmer, who termed radicals the "criminals of the world," the *New York Times* routinely ran headlines such as: "500 Reds at Ellis Island: Prisoners Taken in Raids Hurried to This Port for Deportation."[16] In 1920, at the height of the scare, two Italian anarchists, Nicola Sacco and Bartolomeo Vanzetti, were arrested (and later executed) for allegedly robbing and shooting down a Massachusetts paymaster and his guard.[17] In his Sacco-and-Vanzetti novel *Boston* (1928), Upton Sinclair retrospectively deplored the "deportations delirium" for creating the climate that ultimately doomed the two men.[18]

Nevertheless, in the first half of the decade, protest activity did occur on the railway in the Great Strike of 1922. It erupted on the waterfront, in heavy industry, and in a series of maritime and loggers' strikes from 1923 to 1925, demanding freedom for imprisoned labor figures who had opposed the country's entry into the war.[19] (In the early 1920s, the future proletarian novelist Mike Gold wrote "Free!" detailing the psychic dislocation of newly released leftist prisoners, who, as in real life, had been incarcerated at Fort Leavenworth for the duration of the war.)[20] And just after the war, the Automobile Workers' Union, a left-allied radical group cast out by the conservative American Federation of Labor, was able to rally fifteen factories doing business with Ford Motor Company to strike for industrial unionism.[21]

Gold's story "Reds," seeking to appeal to workers' unionist strivings, in the early 1920s fought the perception that radicalism was marginal to American labor, and attempted to form alliances within the business-unionist AFL. The AFL mission had been clarified and strengthened by the Bolshevik Revolution—producing a "real workers' republic," wrote the 1919 steel-strike luminary William Z. Foster—and the formation of the Communist International (Comintern) in 1920 and of the Workers' (later Communist) Party (CP) in 1921.[22]

In this early phase, the CP advocated mass action, political strikes, and demonstrations.[23] But it vacillated between accepting and rejecting American exceptionalism. Given the lack of socialist consciousness among American workers, Party members worried that Marxism had to be reshaped to meet "special American conditions."[24] Whatever the ideological vicissitudes, the desire to implement revolutionary doctrine in the face of American suppression of radicals remained steady. The veteran Socialist Upton Sinclair, though dubious about the Communist Party, gives it a backward look. He casts one of his sympathetic college-bred activists in *Oil!* (1927) as a California organizer enamored of the Russian Revolution. Sinclair doctrinally ends his schisms when the novel's socialist hero is fatally wounded in an early decade "red scare" raid on his headquarters.[25]

By the waning years of the red scare, the fallout had severed the ties between the CP and trade union, Farmer-Labor Party, and left-wing socialist politicians. Such proactive antileftism dashed hopes that the CP could organize a labor party, amalgamate the craft unions, and in general mobilize the left wing of the American labor movement.[26] The Communists formed a brief, fragile alliance with the similarly militant Industrial Workers of the World. Certainly Party members would have concurred with T-Bone Slim, one of the most famous and popular IWW writers. Preaching to the converted Wobbly readership of the *Industrial Worker*, he warned: "You're not a worker but Henry Ford's tool."[27] If the Party gained the allegiance of one IWW notable, Big Bill Haywood, the loose-knit Wobblies soon rejected Soviet communism and Comintern rigidity.[28] Yet in a Fordist time, the Wobs too went the way of all radicals.

With this diminution of the CP and IWW, the corporate fear of "reds" in Russia or in U.S. trade unions and factories clarified the corporate countervision of contented, or at least docile, U.S. workers, whose increased earnings canceled out the need for labor unity.[29] The era's left-wing literature no sooner attempted to keep pace with Russian developments through espousing a proletarianism that advocated an American version of the radical text than it too was marginalized. Such literature was confined to small sketches in a few radical periodicals and exchanges of correspondence, or contained by the era's intense antiradical, anti-immigrant sentiment.[30] At the other end of the genre spectrum was the left-wing Socialist Elias Tobenkin's lengthy work, *The Road* (1923), a rare novel praising the Soviet way of life. In an appeal to radical readers, he sends the heroine into voluntary exile at book's end.

To counter the constrictions of the era, while searching for a true proletarian literature, Mike Gold produced a landmark February 1921 *Liberator* essay, "Towards Proletarian Art." As one of the first to call for a distinct working-class literature and culture, the piece has been widely discussed.[31] In elevating the art of the masses, Gold rejected earlier definitions that negatively associated it with the slums and poverty.[32] Instead he lyricized the common man and expressed certainty that a new art would spring from him: in the "Russia of the workers, the proletarian culture has begun forming its grand outlines against the sky."[33]

Not only in the early years but throughout the 1920s, Gold produced earnest reportage and fictive pieces about "how clean and brave it is in Russia" in the *Liberator*. In the decade's second half he reiterated this idea when he wrote for, and later edited, the *New Masses*.[34] For the length of the decade Gold energetically corresponded with critics and writers interested in fostering proletarian writing, adapting Russian constructivist theater to left-wing plays in this country, conducting worker-writer workshops, and using the *Liberator* and *New Masses* as an organ for radical literature.[35]

If Gold was laying a Proletcult foundation, he was using the enemy's tools, for he was in an embattled position in the 1920s. Gold and his fellow left-labor authors were kept to gather anecdotal evidence to refute the "managerial narrative," that range of pro-efficiency literary and extra-literary stories told in the centrist periodicals and books of the day.[36] In that narrative, workers rightly embrace or succumb to Taylorism, lured by the possibility of social mobility and chastened by the perils of corporate reprisals. Whether consciously or not, by the late 1920s, when he was on surer literary ground, Gold captured the pull between Taylorism and communism in his 1928 *New Masses* story "Love on a Garbage Dump." In it, he rescues his tempted protagonist from the seductions of capitalism—symbolized by a desirable Back Bay, Boston, woman—and propels him to a Party meeting, on a wave of proletarian anger.[37] Yet those seductions remain real enough.

In contrast to Gold and his male colleagues, the decade's fiction by women was more imbued with rising than with communism. While aware of women's underpaid and transient work, these postsweatshop novels responded to the new possibilities in clerical work. The era's more pragmatic women organizers either acquired office skills or improved their oratorical abilities in summer workshops held by the ILGWU. The most probing of these authors was Anzia Yezierska. Though she spent the entire decade cautioning would-be ghetto Cinderellas to be careful what they wished for, her own rise as a professional writer belied the warning.

Until the Depression, no solid body of works cast off American exceptionalism or protested the waste of human potential under capitalism. Yet 1920s texts did mount an assault on U.S. ascension ideals and Fordist truisms.[38] For the first time, radical vignettes rejected economic mobility as a goal for the masses of workers, not because they were flawed but because it was. However dronelike, jobs were still plentiful at both the center and the margins. In this transitional era before the rise of proletarian fiction, labor authors challenged the Gospel of Wealth and its managerial disciples. But they did so not by proposing a dictatorship of the proletariat but by dramatizing the gospel's effects on those who believed in, scorned, and warred against it. A useful approach to the work fiction and semifictive narratives of the 1920s is through the pull between working-class satisfaction and discontent. The notion of attaining one's desires, whether defined in consumerist or syndicalist terms, marked a swath of texts including Yezierska's once-popular *Salome of the Tenements* (1923), made into a Hollywood film. Working-class longing is central to Sinclair's *Boston* and to the rural-drudgery novels *Weeds* (1923) by Edith Summers Kelley and *The Swamp Angel* by Dorothy Langley, though the latter two are sensitive renderings from an insider's perspective. The theme was further explored in articles and sketches, known in left circles as "workers' correspondence" pieces, in the anticapitalist *Daily Worker Magazine* or the *Haldeman-Julius Quarterly*.[39] The *Quarterly* was partial to worker-generated pieces by casual laborers, who both spoke vernacularly and, as in other period writings, focused attention on the dissatisfied wage earner. Establishing the era's thematic opposition between boundless desire and thwarted longing, two of the era's most established writers considered whether it was better to pursue Fordism or collectivism, money or revolution.

To Die For: Labor and Belief in Theodore Dreiser and Upton Sinclair

In the mid-1920s, the proletarian novel was embryonic. The rare assembly line–ennui novel, the little-known *Temper* (1924), by Lawrence H. Conrad, bowed to the Fordist sentiment that its Italian American protagonist's failure to rise in the auto factory was due to his limitations, not the company's. Even the average man lampooned in Sinclair Lewis's *Babbitt* (1924) was solidly middle class. But Theodore Dreiser's *An American Tragedy*, which made Sherwood Anderson's novel *Poor White* (1920) look tame, was a shocking and unorthodox text with a worker-protagonist. The massive novel is the story of Clyde Griffiths, hungry to put behind him a past of lowly jobs, and of his factory girlfriend, Roberta Alden, whom he abandons. It was inspired by the sensational 1906 Cortland, New York, trial and execution of Chester Gillette for murdering Grace Brown, his pregnant girlfriend.[40] Like the social-climbing Gillette, Clyde drowns his drab rural girl when she presses for marriage. What made the trial so sensational, and Dreiser's version a best-seller, was that the man accused and put to death was both a poor nephew and a favorite employee of the upstate town's leading factory owner.[41]

Altering crucial aspects of the Gillette story, Dreiser created a radicalized version that criticized the American justice system and the power of wealth. In a romance between Clyde and a wealthy young local woman, Dreiser supplies just the damning circumstances needed to squelch reasonable doubt and demonize the alleged murderer. All the while, he clouds the issue by reiterating Clyde's frenzied despair as a crucial factor in Roberta's death. The mainstream press, responding with surprising approbation to this dark novel, called it quintessentially American, always a loaded word, but even more so in that antiradical time.[42]

To the most influential reviewers, Clyde's is an odyssey from a disgruntled poor relation dreaming of recognition to a willing if pathetic victim of the American ideology of ascent. Nor did Dreiser correct that critical half-truth. He fed the public's conception of him as a great American novelist by separating himself from collective heroes and revolutionary thought.[43] However disingenuously, even a year before he began to flirt with communism and five years before his 1927 visit to the Soviet Union, Dreiser was proclaiming: "I don't care a damn about the masses. . . . It is the individual that concerns me."[44]

The left-wing press drew alternative conclusions. It pointed out that Dreiser's "individual" was clearly outlawed by the class-based capitalist system that ultimately put him to death. Louis Adamic, the future surveyor of 1930s proletarian fiction, wrote an appreciation of the writer as "radical, yet intensely patriotic," for the January 1927 issue of the *Haldeman-Julius Quarterly,* praise that subtly claimed Dreiser for the Socialist ranks rather than the Communist ones.[45] Mike Gold, who had corresponded respectfully with Dreiser, considered only him and Sinclair worthy representatives of an older literary generation, although he found both short on strategies for combating the American capitalist system.[46]

Dreiser's ambivalence about the success and consumption ethic make the more radical sections of the novel, those fleshing out the management pecking order, spatial separation of male and female employees, and largely ethnic "basement world" (*American Tragedy,* 190), seem ultimately anecdotal.[47] Even the extended attention that Dreiser gives the class divisions in the Chicago hotel where Clyde Griffiths first finds work is lost in the wealth of detail about Clyde's consumer urges and romantic reversals. Such ideological vagueness suggests Dreiser's old fascination with and distrust of ascension thinking from the *Sister Carrie* (1900) days. His 1920s depiction of a character obsessed with climbing, who only feels hungrier, not more satisfied, with each step upward, complicates the earlier plot. In Dreiser's most probing study of the rigidly stratified world of the assembly line, the controlling irony is that his antihero is at once obsessed with class and classless.

Clyde is born to a family of street and storefront missionaries, a shiftless father so uninspiring that his own father had disinherited him, and a mother who tries to keep the family afloat. After false starts, Clyde moves from a drifter's life in the Midwest to Lycurgus (Gillette's Cortland, New York) at the behest of his successful uncle, head of the Griffiths Company. Allegorically, he is so near and yet so far.

Traditional Dreiser criticism looks at Clyde as a man whose wish is his doom, a tragic Aladdin obsessed with success and barred by class and snobbery.[48] To these critics, Clyde is the victim of those whose values he had embraced.[49] Dreiser seemed to bolster this argument by making some of the facts of Clyde's life fit his own life, rather than Chester Gillette's. Of the three, only Gillette had known privilege as a youth. Furthermore, Clyde's social climbing could be contextualized by Dreiser's view that his own eventual success as a writer enabled him to join the "class to which I properly belonged."[50]

Regardless of the autobiographical correspondences noted above and the sentimental-novel trappings, this is not what Clyde is like. "What a wretched thing it was to be born poor and not to have anyone do anything for you" (*American Tragedy*, 18) is hardly a self-help sentiment. Nor has Clyde an artisan ethos or the desire to repudiate his uncle's Fordism.[51]

Although Dreiser argues for Clyde as an ideological victim (or a victim of his own ideology), Clyde identifies with the aggressor. He expresses nativist distaste that an Asian (and probably not an affluent one) is on death row with him. It is a distaste he would have extended to an Italian anarchist fish peddler and shoemaker had he encountered them. His working-class lover Roberta may be culturally acceptable to him, but his dislike of her is based in part on his conviction that she is an economic inferior. Moreover, xenophobia has widely infected this work world, from the clerks with whom Clyde comes in contact at his rooming house to Roberta herself. She considers her foreign coworkers "ignorant, low, immoral, un-American!"

In Clyde Dreiser created, whether deliberately or not, a pre-Depression era figure caught up in the irrelevance of work to belief or desire. He is too much the alienated worker to toil at rising, and too much the materialist to stop working altogether. Usually read only as a condescending comment, his cousin Gilbert's summation of Clyde is accurate: "You haven't had either a commercial or a trade education of any kind" (*American Tragedy*, 230). If ascension rather than a modest living is all, Clyde by his desperate act in a sense dies for his beliefs. But contrasted with the radical protagonist at the center of Upton Sinclair's novel, who proclaims, "I never loved money" (*Boston*, 416), Clyde's beliefs were not even worth living for.

Bypassing Dreiser, Walter Rideout remarks that "the radical novel did not die in the twenties, but it barely kept alive. . . . the only obvious continuity . . . given by the lonely but indefatigable figure of Upton Sinclair."[52] Sinclair's socialism, though quite in tune with the *Haldeman-Julius Quarterly*, in which he published opinion pieces, occasioned ambivalence in the Party press. But the Sacco-Vanzetti case itself was a CP rallying cry, and Sinclair's well-researched account was politically correct, to use a current phrase.[53] The trial was pivotal for the period's radical writers.[54] Sacco and Vanzetti, arrested in 1920, sentenced in 1921, and executed six years later, were in left and liberal quarters perceived as martyrs to their politics and ethnicity. Modern historians like Paul Avrich, a leading authority on anarchism, also point to the

repressive environment of the trial, even if they are not certain of the inno-
cence of the two men. But, save for a brief mention in the nonlabor novel
Manhattan Transfer (1925), by John Dos Passos, who also wrote the pamphlet
Facing the Chair (1927), only Sinclair novelized this cause célèbre prior to the
Great Depression.[55]

As with *An American Tragedy*, Boston newspapers responded negatively to
Boston, reacting this time to "obscene" passages on contraception and, showing their bias, against the two Italian figures at the center of the book.[56] Just as
predictably, the more liberal New York reviews termed *Boston* masterly. None
of the era's prominent reviewers, whether left, liberal, centrist, or conservative, noted that Dreiser and Sinclair based their respective novels on notorious court cases of working people.[57]

Both writers also wove in information about workplace duties, after-hours
peer groups, pay scales, daily expenses, and lodgings, humanizing the defen-
dants and palliating their alleged crimes. There, of course, the resemblances
end. The Dreiser novel never suggests that Clyde make common cause with
other workers to refute the paternalistic management philosophy of the ruling classes. In the world of *Boston's* working-class, Italian anarchist subculture, proactive management behavior is in counterpoint to that community
(and its tacit allegiance to the IWW through the foreign-language periodical
Il Proletario). Many of these labor-class men and women had brought their
militant politics with them from Sicily, as Sacco and Vanzetti did.

Like most nonfictional accounts of the case, *Boston* shows the intersections
of class tensions in the Boston region through the lives of Sacco and Vanzetti,
although the novel privileges the more articulate Vanzetti. To frame this
story, Sinclair juxtaposes scenes of proper, nativist Boston, exemplified by
the fictive Thornwell clan, with those of Italian working-class culture and
political activity in and around the New England textile mills. The wealthy,
unpleasant Thornwells were a composite of the politically prominent New
Englanders who helped create the antianarchist atmosphere surrounding the
trial. The family fights over inheritance, even spiriting out the valuables to
spite one another. At the same time, the Italian company-town community
surrounding the Plymouth Cordage Company, where Vanzetti had worked, is
pictured as generous and upright, a challenge to the nativist Thornwells.

This nativism is enunciated when Abner Thornwell comments on the
Braintree robbery, before the culprits are identified: "two bandits in an automobile. . . . It's these foreigners! . . . First Irish, then Jews, then Dagoes, then
Hunkies, then God knows what. They've taken the country from us" (*Boston,*
198). Though this patrician would have scorned a visit to Plymouth, Sinclair
provides a sympathetic section on the multiethnic presence there and their
"gruppi autonomi" (65), Italian political clubs in which Vanzetti participated.
"Such was Vanzetti's solution of the labor problems," Sinclair observes, "the
'gruppi autonomi,' was his phrase; each of these gruppi would decide what it
wanted and appoint a representative to meet with others from the Por-
tuguese, the French-Canadians, the German, the Irish" (65).

To dramatize the class divide, Sinclair uses Cornelia Thornwell. In real life,
she was a composite of the wealthy Mrs. Gertrude L. Winslow and Mrs. Eliza-

beth Glendower Evans, key members of the Sacco-Vanzetti Defense Committee.[58] In the novel, Sinclair goes farther. Disgusted with her grasping plutocratic family, she poses as a factory worker, a clear throwback to the educated observer who peoples so many of his other novels. If she is looked at through the prism of a Dreiser novel, her preoccupation with her own unhappiness is lifted when she crosses class lines.

Vanzetti and his landlords, the Brinis, who in real life did have him as a lodger, teach how to forswear wealth and to enjoy a life free of pretension and hypocrisy. Whether talking politics or voting with their feet, the Brinis and many of the Plymouth Cordage Company ethnics are as animated as those in the Griffiths Company are automatons: "living presence of class struggle" (*Boston*, 69), particularly when scabs threaten their jobs. In contrast, the Griffiths Company's passive employees, who are almost as mechanized as the factory in which they work, seem to have no awareness of the upheavals in their home state's textile industry spearheaded in New York City by the Amalgamated Clothing Workers of America (ACWA). Nor would they have known of the fervent campaign many Italian workers in the ACWA waged throughout the early and mid-1920s for Sacco and Vanzetti.[59] The Griffiths themselves, who could not "tolerate socialistic theory" (*American Tragedy*, 176), might well have kept abreast of such events in order to maintain a system in which the workers "know their place and keep it" (159). In *Boston*, though, as in the actual Plymouth Cordage Company strike of 1916, workers erupt spontaneously, sans tutelage by Socialist Party intelligentsia. The ethnic laborer has come of age, as heavily accented agitators like Vanzetti proclaim, "What for is reason for treat poor people such way?" (103).

Four years before *Boston*, and two years before Sacco and Vanzetti's appeal for a new trial was turned down, Sinclair had favorably reviewed Vanzetti's *Story of a Proletarian Life*.[60] Sinclair's version relies heavily on the real Vanzetti's account of both his life as an Italian-born worker living in crowded rooming houses and his experience with underpaid jobs like ditch-digging and construction.[61] Like his prototype, Sinclair's Vanzetti uses his outsider status as a way of understanding the sufferings of other immigrant workers. Both in his jailhouse pamphlet and in Sinclair's rendition, he is as caring as Clyde is narcissistic and uninvolved. As he awaited execution, Vanzetti was described by supporters as selfless, dignified, and intelligent.[62] Sinclair largely accepted Vanzetti's self-portrait as a lover of humanity.[63] Yet he was also alive to contradictions in Vanzetti's nature. Bomb diagrams were found among Vanzetti's papers when he was arrested, and he was clearly dedicated to revolutionary militance.[64]

As that rare figure in Sinclair's fiction, a self-taught worker ideologue, Sinclair's Vanzetti very much resembles the martyred figure of the extensive protest literature surrounding the trial and 1927 execution. There was coverage of what Sinclair called the "class-war case" (283) in the *New Masses* and the *Labor Defender*, also a CP journal, and by others in the leftist press.[65] Yet like all of these admirers, Sinclair does not relinquish authority to his worker figures. Vanzetti reputedly wrote every night in his cell, carrying on a voluminous correspondence that merited extensive republication. But only a few letters, to the Brinis, his kind-hearted Plymouth landlords, and to the wealthy Mrs. Winslow, are fictionalized in the novel (*Boston*, 195–196, 226–227).[66] Elsewhere, too, Vanzetti's voice hardly dominates. Nevertheless, Vanzetti enabled Sinclair to bridge the literary divide between worker and thinker in a way that Dreiser could not.

However divergent in other ways, both *An American Tragedy* and *Boston* respond critically to the paternalism of 1920s factories. Clyde Griffiths and Bartolomeo Vanzetti both wanted what employers could not provide: equality. For Clyde, of course, labor is unrelated to desire. For Vanzetti, it was the cornerstone of social justice. Clyde's is a rootless, superficial self, and Vanzetti's a revolutionary one, rooted in fanatical adherence to an outlawed political code. That two characters so antithetical should embody the most dramatic worker portraits of the period suggests not so much the dearth of portraiture in that time as the difficult path to a proletarian fiction. Thus Clyde, a social cipher driven by status insecurity, and Vanzetti, propelled to international fame and notoriety, are not as opposite as they appear. In the doomed battle with their own social inferiority, their life scripts embody the dominant culture's thinking on the perils of unseemly working-class desire.

The warning that life is perilous for those who reject the limited largesse of a commodity culture would echo in the short fiction of the era's left-wing male writers. Before we turn to them, however, an added context can be provided by the female authors of women's labor texts. A crucial question is whether, as these women wrote to combat their historic marginalization, they are more likely to envision workers whose yearnings energized instead of destroyed them.

Be Careful What You Wish for: Anzia Yezierska and the Perils of Aspiration in Women's Work Fiction

From the money-worshiping Clyde Griffiths to the anarchist apostle Bartolomeo Vanzetti, no working-class male in 1920s fiction imposes his will on events or lives out his desires like the alter egos of Anzia Yezierska, a Jewish immigrant working-class writer and onetime servant, factory hand, and sweatshop worker. Yezierska was, above all, a storyteller of ambitious women's labor. "Great hopes beat in my breast, like wings of flying things," proclaims one of her fictive selves in her most famous novel, *Bread Givers*.[67]

In the world of women's work, the decade prior to the Depression saw a parallel flowering of female ambition in response to wartime vocational empowerment and the rise of clerical work as an alternative to women's unskilled factory work. By 1920, for the first time, the largest percentage of white women workers held clerical positions rather than jobs in manufacturing or domestic service.[68] If wages did not keep pace with expectations, there was a widespread cultural perception that women were "invading" all sorts of jobs.[69] In Dreiser's and Sinclair's texts, the more ambitious working-class female characters fare well enough, if they are not sidetracked by romance. Dreiser's grasping shopgirl Hortense Briggs, not shackled by Roberta's marriage-centered morality, successfully pursues golddigging. In *Oil!* Sinclair's Rachel Menzies, torn between radical trade unionism and the culturally approved social feminism of professional social work, decides in favor of the latter. She thus avoids the fate of both *Oil!*'s "red," Paul Watkins, who dies as a result of injuries sustained in a Palmer raid, and *Boston*'s fictive versions of Sacco and Vanzetti, who, convicted for crimes they may not have committed, also die at the hands of the law.

But in the force of their desire for and will to power, their sheer hunger for a better life, all of Dreiser's and Sinclair's worker figures, male or female, pale by comparison to Yezierska's Lower East Side Jewish heroines. In the postsweatshop novel by her colleague Samuel Ornitz, *Allrightniks Row* (1923), a satire on the vulgarity and unscrupulousness of Jewish ambition, female aspirants are either ethereal fantasy figures or uncouth seekers of Gentile husbands.

Unlike Ornitz, Yezierska seemed to be fascinated with the degradations of ethnic women's work. She certainly surveyed a swath of occupations without sacrificing verisimilitude or breadth. Her immigrant everywomen work in paperbox factories (*Bread Givers*), as janitors ("Hunger," 1920), laundresses ("Soap and Water," 1920), and household help, both paid and unpaid ("Wings" and "The Lost 'Beautifulness,' " both 1920).[70] She exposes Jewish women to bad lodgings, nasty landlords, grasping employers, tyrannical rabbinical fathers, manipulative and self-subordinating mothers, and snobbish charity workers and women's deans. Although it is true that her great subject is herself in all her "hoarse-throated orality," she upholds the primacy of feeling.[71] This self-preoccupation may blot out the possibility of unionism or collectivity; nevertheless, she was one of the first U.S. labor writers to capture the urgency, agency, and postsweatshop regrets of the immigrant ghetto.

Yezierska, who published articles in women's magazines relating her own harsh ghetto experiences, was closely identified with her stories as well. Her master narrative was always the desire-driven but disciplined quest for acceptance by "the icebergs of convention."[72] In 1925, the same year *An American Tragedy* appeared, she was already forty-five when her semiautobiographical novel *Bread Givers* came out. By that time, unlike its heroine Sara Smolinksy, who reconciles with her misogynistic Old World father, Yezierska was unrepentant. A veteran of clashes with her repressive family, she remained estranged from her religious father. Married and divorced twice, the second time she left her little daughter with her second husband. To be sure, her Sara, who climbs from factory to professionalism, resembles her creator and many other Yezierska characters in other crucial ways. Impatient with sweatshop and factory jobs, she reinvents herself as a successful, if dissatisfied, professional. There are further similarities. In the mold of the Yezierska type, she conflates knowledge and desire in the person of the elusive, educated WASP male.[73]

Yezierska's autobiographical fiction and autobiography were rooted in the Jewish immigrant Lower East Side, but her life and art lived out an updated ethnic Horatio Alger fantasy. As in Alger, disciplined ambition pays off, but pluck becomes the courage to endure humiliations and the luck to access to education. Even the sewing women's plot resolution of the previous century, upscale marriage, is revamped: the heroine uses romantic longing for an assimilated upper-class man to further stoke her ambitions. In a development that could not have occurred in earlier labor fiction, Yezierska cast off her marginal status by spinning culturally acceptable tales of figures whose whole lives are devoted to casting off theirs.

Though she has been accused, with some justice, of always writing the same upward mobility story, ongoing controversies about her fictional proxies' self-absorption and the degree of her radicalism have obscured Yezierska's reputation as a worker-writer.[74] Feminist critics, finding contradictions in her work between feminine proletarianism and an ethos of personal ambition, continue to debate the extent of Yezierska's radicalism. In an era in which Ford was providing Americanization programs for his employees, she shrewdly gave interviews to *Good Housekeeping* in which she spoke of her recently realized immigrant longing to be part of America.[75] Despite her self-promotion as an upward struggler who rose to write Hollywood scripts and live on Fifth Avenue, Yezierska was not writing a managerial narrative. She understood that enviable work became proletarianized when women were hired to do it.[76] Her outpouring of fiction subverted the conformity of the sweatshop. As the title *Arrogant Beggar* (1927) suggests, she particularly detested paternalism masquerading as philanthropy. In a time of rising hopes for women in fields like selling and schoolteaching, her Adele Lindner and Sara Smolinsky find only postsweatshop tedium.

If Yezierska responded to the contradictory circumstances of women's work in the 1920s in a covertly radical way, she also knew the ravages of guilt. In story after story, she dramatizes the punishments of attainment and the limitations of success. She adds richness to the plot of the hardworking tenement Jewess, like the dress entrepreneur Sonia Vrunsky, who breaks through what was later called the glass ceiling only to find a spiritual void. Making similar discoveries are characters like Hanneh Breineh, the newly affluent mother of an arriviste son, who removes her from the ghetto and places her in an arid luxury home ("The Fat of the Land," 1920), imprisoned in the superficiality of American money.[77] In the end, Yezierska could only challenge the era's favored narrative of working-class desire by "placing alternative subtexts into her tales beneath their commercial happy endings."[78]

This truth is underscored in the work of her contemporary, Bella Cohen, whose escape from obscurity lasted longer than Yezierska's. She was another transplanted daughter of the Russian Pale who found American fame for her writing (she coauthored the 1948 musical *Kiss Me, Kate*). Had Cohen completed her memoir, *Streets*, written in 1922 but published only recently, Yezierska's shadow sister might have been a rival. As it is, only a few watered-down excerpts, most notably the short story "Hands" (1920), published in a little-known, short-lived women's magazine, *The Touchstone*, both reasserted and altered the attainment plot. Again the central character is a Jewish girl, avid for escape through education, who resents her invisibility as a waitress and a chambermaid. Sharing Yezierska's literary melancholy, she, too, filters her dissatisfaction with the raw truth of the Lower East Side through a prose style at once lyrical and vernacular. Her 1920s published stories either pay homage to prevailing ideologies of ambition or are set in the Old World where diminished expectations were the norm for the Jewish poor.[79]

Streets, in contrast, is a bitter indictment of the real America (21). Bella defies the rich, proclaiming, "I'm not a maid! Don't you dare call me that" (*Streets*, 151). The memoir sharpens the humiliations described in "Hands," in which a teacher relegates her to the back row out of dislike (389). In *Streets* she is publicly insulted and banished from a schoolroom for allegedly smelling of onions (21). The story mutes the bitterness of the unfinished memoir as if Cohen knew that, even had she completed the book, it was too pessimistic to find a publisher. To sound like a ghetto voice, her defeatism can only be a whisper.

It is ironic that female labor novelists whose heroines were not striving Jewish women could recount the death of aspiration represented by dead-end domestic service and the unpaid drudgery of the sharecropping wife. Fannie Hurst's *Lummox* (1923) poignantly illustrates the oppressions of Bertha, a New York City hired girl, and Edith Summers Kelley's *Weeds* (1923) details those of a Kentucky one, Judith Pippinger. The oppressive circumstances of servants, urban or rural, had never generated popular U.S. fiction, but such subjects seemed particularly out of tune with the 1920s achievement plot.[80]

Still, both books received applause from important quarters. Trotsky himself responded warmly to the Hurst novel.[81] Kelley was praised, though not supported, by Mike Gold, Sinclair Lewis, and Upton Sinclair, who perceived the proletarian novel as masculine.[82] Nor were these texts of working-class women denied the legitimate fruits of their toil popular with middlebrow readers. Out of step with their time, they have remained in literary limbo until recently, unjustly forgotten as precursors of Olsen, Le Sueur, and Smedley.[83]

The downwardly mobile heroine of *Weeds* shifts from a hired girl who can keep some of her earnings to a poor tenant farmer's wife who has no money of her own. Her community, like the Census Bureau, lumped female home and field workers together and did not recognize as real work the unpaid labor of farm wives.[84] No wonder that Hurst's passive servant seeks the consolations of near-saintly altruism. Working harder the older she becomes, Kelley's once-spirited rural wage earner concludes it is useless to struggle and vanishes into the drained, poor-white wife/mother (*Weeds*, 330).

Like his colleague Louis Wirth, who authored *The Ghetto* (1928), a study of a lower-class Chicago Jewish neighborhood, William Isaac Thomas, the coauthor with Florian Znaniecki of *The Polish Peasant in Europe and America* (1918–1920), was an important member of the University of Chicago school of sociological writing. Both men predicted that assimilation and upward mobility would address the psychic fragmentation of uprooted Old World ethnic groups. When Thomas published *The Unadjusted Girl* the same year as the Hurst and Kelley novels, he turned to the same solution. Though at heart a Progressive who believed in social engineering, Thomas gave a psychological dimension to the approach exemplified by Elizabeth Butler's pioneering Pittsburgh case-by-case study *Women and the Trades* (1909). Many of his case histories focus on recent immigrants or girls who have run away from mid-western farms, figures close enough to the subjects of *Lummox* and *Weeds*. In yet another narrative that pigeonholed working-class longing into a bourgeois mold, Thomas's case studies of servants and shopgirls drew on a long literary tradition of promiscuity (see chapters 3 and 5). While yoking discontent to sexual deviance, Thomas argued that such waywardness resulted from a quartet of human wishes: for new experience, security, response, and recognition.[85] When these wishes were not regulated, they found outlets in female sexual maladjustment. Interestingly, Hurst's and Kelley's heroines might well have merited mention in *The Unadjusted Girl*. Both have sex out of wedlock, one with her employer, and the other before marriage to her husband and, during marriage, adulterously with a local preacher. Moreover, these women attach no taboo to their actions; Hurst's Bertha even tenderly befriends Helga, a maid turned prostitute. What Thomas's interpretation might have omitted was that women, so ruled by the need for pleasure, were also self-denying. Lacking the puritanical ambition necessary for the upward climb, they could not, in Thomas's schema, distinguish between ambition and desire.

Like their fictive selves, Yezierska and Cohen were too iconoclastic to join the diminished women's labor movement of the 1920s. Though less disposed to imprint their personalities onto their hard-luck heroines, Hurst and Kelley also saw themselves as separated from the rank and file. With female suffrage newly won, the distance between affluent activist women and their working-class counterparts reasserted itself. It is not surprising, therefore, that this quartet of authors, their sights set on female empowerment, omitted women's labor militance from their fiction.

Although recent research has unearthed a 1920s "industrial feminism," it was in the form of campaigns for labor laws, neighborhood women's tenant organizations, and schools for women workers.[86] The Labor Department's Women's Bureau, studying women's union membership, found that only one out of every thirty-four women was a member of organized labor (compared with one out of nine men).[87] Yet women trade unionists found a home and publication of sorts in *Shop and School*, the journal of the Bryn Mawr Summer School for Working Women. A program established in 1921 by the college president, M. Carey Thomas, and enrolling hundreds by the end of the decade, it was the first of the resident workers' colleges for women.[88] More important, it was an educational haven for women factory workers. They could study public speaking, economics, political science, and English, returning to the ILGWU or the ACW as more polished organizers.[89]

The teaching staff wisely stressed that the workers' own experiences should be central to their writing, and these young workers, both native born and ethnic, also produced autobiographical narratives of their political coming of age. The titles seemed experiential enough: "My First Arrest," "An Experience with a Sweatshop Boss," "The New York Elevator Strike," and "The Funeral of Sacco and Vanzetti."[90] But however much these young women agreed with Yezierska and her colleagues that the American Dream was hollow, they never elevated separateness, consumerism, or assimilation. They discarded the hungry I, whether self-proclamatory or patient. Their writings reveal personae neither trapped in a value system they despise nor making their way in a flawed and sordid world. They moved beyond a "static, limited version of the self."[91] For the summer at least, they found joy in mass identity denied Yezierska's and Cohen's scripted achievers and Hurst's and Kelley's valiant failures. For if such narratives described spiritual hunger, the Bryn Mawr amateurs told how they were fed.

Crossing the Bar: Mike Gold, the *Liberator,* and the Beginnings of the *New Masses*

Like Yezierska and Cohen, Mike Gold was tenement-bred on the Lower East Side and determined to write his way out of the ghetto. But he would not have seen self-involvement and desperate ambition as the road to working-class art. Nor did the Hurst and Kelley texts offer the "rebel chambermaids," whether native or foreign born, whom he briefly extolled as subjects for proletarian women's fiction.[92] His decade-long immersion in "red" politics was one reason it took him so long to finish his own immigrant novel-as-memoir, *Jews without Money* (1930).

Gold's progress as a writer had been as halting as Yezierska's was sure. Throughout the twenties he was trying to work out problems of characterization and narration that she had solved by elevating individualism. Searching for a more radical bildungsroman, he experimented with a collective worldview, a repudiation of the ethic of rising, and a reversal of the capitalist money-eyed ending. Ironically, the pessimism over personal liberation that characterized his early 1920s stories would provide the transition to the revolutionary euphoria that was the finale of his Depression best-seller.

In the years before and in the early part of the 1920s, Gold was on a search to connect with "all the younger writers with a proletarian tendency."[93] Despite some apprentice work at the old *Masses* and the new, pro-Bolshevik *Liberator,* which he helped edit, he could not yet render urban ghetto life artistically.[94] Part of the problem was the lack of models. By the early 1920s, aside from the letters rather than the finished essays that were the favored leftist genre, only scattered Russian texts by British translators were available. The Comintern journals *World Literature* and *Literature of World Revolution* provided at best a few non-English stories in translation.[95] Proletarian literary magazines that published American authors were virtually nonexistent, and the little magazines with modernist artistic agendas were not hospitable to a working-class art still reliant on traditional forms.[96]

Furthermore, the work by Gold's *Liberator* colleagues Alfred Kreymbourg and Elmer J. Williams that did appear between 1920 and 1925 retained the old Progressive Era trope of the bestial, wordless worker. The unnamed Teamsters in Kreymbourg's "Truck Drivers" (April 1923) are simply versions of the belletristic author himself.[97] Another literary man, Floyd Dell, favorably reviewed Charles Rumford Walker's *Steel: The Diary of a Furnace Worker* (1922) in the February 1923 issue, implying it was authentic worker art. Walker was in reality a 1919 Yale graduate and an ex-army officer who spent a summer in a steel mill.[98] Again following Progressive formula, the half-bull, half-man of

Williams's "The First Born" (May 1923), is a ditchdigger named only Ivor, reminiscent of Jurgis Rudkus in *The Jungle* (1906).[99]

With his colleagues producing fiction that had little relation to their Party-line reviews and essays, in the years following the red scare, Gold became a one-man Proletcult factory. What he was proselytizing for needs some clarification. Briefly, the term "Proletcult" referred to art produced by the workers and dedicated to the world of revolutionary labor. Rarely mentioned in the 1920s outside of U.S. Communist journals and correspondence, Proletcult was generated in the Soviet Union as a workers' movement for cultural production through study groups. These members would ostensibly develop a revolutionary art "true to their own experiences and needs and integral to their everyday lives."[100] As a cultural movement spawned by the Russian Revolution, Proletcult supposedly had 450,000 members in the Soviet Union by 1920.[101] Its chief architect, A. A. Bogdanov, gained widespread acceptance among Bolshevik intellectuals with his vision of literary studios where worker-correspondents would write and teach. Interestingly, Lenin and Trotsky opposed Bogdanov, doubtful that one group alone could produce proletarian or people's art. Such dissension, joined to policy shifts within the Comintern itself on proletarian art and the function of the worker-correspondent, early alienated authors. John Dos Passos for one, shunned Gold's argument to adapt Russian models to American scenes.[102]

Gold's own fiction in the early 1920s began the Proletcult mission haltingly. A short story for the *Liberator,* "The Password to Thought—to Culture" (February 1922), an early version of *Jews,* is set on his own home ground but rings false because he is unsure of how to articulate an antiascension credo. He had not yet succeeded in turning his autobiographical fiction into something other than a vernacular saga of disappointed Jewish garment workers, who alternate between defeatism and shrillness. His joyless fictive representative, David, battles with harping ethnic parents and a bleak labor environment. He takes refuge in a pessimism that detests moneymaking but can find no valid alternative. His oppressive boss tells him he doesn't need culture to work in a sweatshop. The subtext is clear: proletculture is all he needs, as a worker and a searcher. Yet "The Password to Thought—to Culture" does not offer a sense of the humanity of Jews as an alternative. The parents are also oppressors, and the formal language of the narrator undercuts the Yiddish American authenticity.

By the middle of the decade, in "Faster America, Faster!" (*New Masses,* November 1926), written shortly after he returned from Moscow in 1925, Gold continued to wrestle with an American Proletcult. "On a Section Gang" was published in the same journal two years later (July 1928). A comparison of the two pieces highlights the dilemma facing Gold during a period when American prosperity had not yet been called into question by the Great Crash. In "Faster America" are all of the precepts of Russian ideology as explored in *Daily Worker* columns on "Mammonart" (money-worshiping cultural production).[103] The piece, subtitled "A Movie in Ten Reels," unsuccessfully attempts to amalgamate a Bolshevik shooting script with the newsreel-vignette method of Dos Passos's *Manhattan Transfer.* In the oddest passage, the peasant class, which is to join with the industrial one in the final overthrow of money, is pictured thus: "A pale farmer came running from the dark. He had a sickle in his hand. A pale worker in overalls came up, with a hammer. They soberly began the rescue work. Dawn grew. The red morning star appeared."[104]

Two years after this skewed homage to Eisenstein, "On a Section Gang" proved that Gold could be the worker-correspondent he had been praising since his *Liberator* days. Gone is the humorlessness pervading all of his early sketches and tales. In this piece of leftist Americana, which blurs the boundary between short story and reportage, even the Marxism is witty. "Pay day— pay—it's the opium of the masses," the unnamed narrator, a migratory worker, remarks. "And the gang spent most of it by the next morning."[105] "On a Section Gang" is little more than a series of related anecdotes on a multi-ethnic track-laying group whose members sweat, curse, play the harmonica, hate the foreman, briefly unite, and blow their pay at Carney's speakeasy-hotel. There is no workers' revolution, only a penniless proletariat with a mass hangover.

Subordinating the doctrine of collectivity to the eccentric and individualizing acts of Ed Bass, the farmer, Sven the Swede, old Tony the Italian, Mexicans, Poles, and a "Negro named Harry" (8), Gold had found a way to go left in the United States. The decade from the founding of the *Liberator* to his editorship of the *New Masses* had been a study in the difficulty of filtering U.S. working-class deprivation through Russian precepts about art in a country Gold saw as deprived of the revolutionary exuberance central to Soviet cultural production. Escaping from portrayals of the U.S. proletariat that veered uncertainly between depressive responses to capitalism and inapplicable Proletcult scenarios, he was finally ready to go home a novelist and produce *Jews without Money*.

Go West, Young Wobblies:
The *Industrial Pioneer,* the *Haldeman-Julius Quarterly,* and the Vagabond Narrative

In the early years of the Great Depression, Gold, Agnes Smedley, and James T. Farrell were skillfully integrating ethnic and American colloquial speech patterns into their novels. They were joined by Jack Conroy's "rebel poets" (the title of a magazine Conroy edited beginning in 1931). But in the decade after the founding of the CPUSA in 1919, literary leftists struggling to implement Proletcult had few indigenous literary sources on which to draw. A small group of *Liberator* authors, and, later, *New Masses* authors, Gold included, however, found inspiration in the short fiction and narrative, songs, and graphic art of the IWW, which celebrated the counterculture of migrant laborers. In the red scare era, literary schisms among embattled proletarian authors were not as impassioned as they would become. These writers amicably shared a social-protest interest in the marginal workforce with the editors of the socialistic midwestern *Haldeman-Julius Quarterly*. They had much in common as well with the sometime Wobbly Jack Conroy's unpublished "rebel poets" (who would find print after 1931 in Conroy's magazine). The attempts of Gold, Floyd Dell, the non-CP writer Carl Van Vechten, and the playwright Eugene O'Neill to imitate or employ Wobbly approaches and themes were less successful than those of IWW adherents. The short stories of Ralph Winstead and O. W. Cooley, the vignettes of Harry Clayton, the poems of T-Bone Slim, the cartoons of Ernest Riebe, and the republished songs of the Wobbly bard and martyr Joe Hill all captured the spirit of native-born radicalism far more authentically. The attention that all of these writers directed at the vagabond proletarian of the IWW ensured that the Wobbly legacy would be passed on to Depression era writers. To understand the unheralded role played by the pro-IWW author in the formation of working-class literary radicalism, both Communist and not, a brief discussion of the organization itself is in order.

By 1920 the IWW could look back on fifteen years of labor protest, free-speech fights, trials, and an "extensive literature and lore all its own."[106] Close to sixty official and semiofficial IWW periodicals had also seen print by that date, many in foreign languages. Among those journals, the *Industrial Pioneer,* the *One Big Union Monthly,* and *Solidarity* featured poetry, prose, and visual art. This body of work was both created and enjoyed by the lumber, mining, building, hoboing, farm, ranch, and seafaring workers, primarily in the Pacific Northwest, the West, and California, who carried the IWW "red card" and preached the message of revolutionary industrial unionism.[107] Whether they carried the card or not, these Wobblies were syndicalist militants who believed in the tactics of direct action, in the abolition of "wage slavery," and in "striking on the job" and stronger expressions of industrial sabotage. In the wake of the red scare, after 1920 they were variously harassed, imprisoned, exiled, and, if ethnics, deported.

As Gold well knew, the Wobblies were scattered and embattled throughout the 1920s, but they were still alive. Thus when he wrote "Go Left, Young Writers!" (*New Masses,* January 1929), he was doing more than punning on Horace Greeley's nineteenth-century injunction. Greeley had seen the West as a place of enrichment. Gold went west for literary material and largely found it in Wobbly prisoners newly freed from Fort Leavenworth, Kansas, and the adventure-seeking, floating workforce of casual laborers who had never heard of the Lower East Side. One of his stories, "Free!" published in *The Damned Agitator and Other Stories* (1926), was a tribute to IWW prisoners jailed for opposing the American entry into World War I. Written between 1919 and 1921, when the federal government was releasing these prisoners, the story takes an activist trio through a series of bewildering encounters. The dollar-driven world into which they are catapulted seems no more just than Leavenworth.

The solemnity of most of Gold's writing prior to 1928 mars this tribute to the Wobbly, but *The Damned Agitator* is far superior to the output of his contemporaries like the poet Lloyd Thompson, "A Vag in College" (*Liberator,* July 1923), who longed to be in the hobo jungles and mines "singing Wobbly songs."[108] Where Thompson romanticized, Patrick and Terence Casey in "The Road Kid" (*Liberator,* July 1921) tried to give mythic significance to a Wobbly betrayed by a derelict-mentor. The story seems false, as does "Hallelujah, I'm a Bum" (*Century*, June 1925) by Gold's former *Liberator* colleague, Floyd Dell. Dell romanticized the Wobbly in his story, its title taken from the famous IWW song.[109] Nor did O'Neill write dialogue from a serious working-class perspective. He sanitized the speech of a minor IWW character in his play *The Hairy Ape* (1921), rendering him far less vivid than the atavistic protagonist, Yank Smith (his name a further swipe at the American workingman).

In authentic Wobbly art, the successful representation of "hobohemia" was the true beginning of the radical worker-writer. In their fiction and narrative, authors like Winstead and Cooley made their autobiographical protagonists into "prophet[s] in [their] own li[ves]."[110] These writers' narrative authority issued as much from their experiences as from their verbal facility. In fact, in contrast to their successors, the 1930s "on the road" novelists Jack Conroy, Tom Kromer, and Edward Dahlberg, the best IWW authors were vagabonds first and social-protest writers second. (The Wobbly martyr Joe Hill's popular song, "The Tramp," was a mainstay of the 1923 *Little Red Song Book*.)[111] Nor did this dual expertise separate them from the Wobbly rank and file, who were in the main quite literate and whose reading included IWW journals as well as *Hobo News*, written and edited by hoboes.[112] As veterans of the floating workforce, they experimented with hobo autobiography. Winstead and Cooley obviously refashioned the world of the male vagabond-radical. Yet these authors infused their eyewitness reportage and social realism with that mixture of literacy and orality, storytelling sense and tall tale, so common in that era to Wobblies and hoboes alike.

In this transitional time, not all Wobbly writers freed the narrative of the wage-earning itinerant from doctrine. Harry Clayton's semifictional "The IWW on a Full-Rigged Ship" (*Industrial Pioneer*, September 1926) details the sailors' radicalization by the brutal shipboard regime on the Tacoma-registered *Star of Washington* and subsequent conversion to the Wobbly creed. While Clayton preaches that the conversion is theirs, he belies that argument by speaking on their behalf.[113] The IWW had its own Sacco-Vanzetti Defense Committee. The veteran IWW organizer Matilda Robbins, who had been jailed in 1920 for her opposition to World War I, published an interview with Vanzetti in prison (*Industrial Pioneer*, July 1924).[114] Curiously, she also dispensed with the worker's voice, although Vanzetti was a voluble conversationalist, even if his command of English was limited. Robbins allots him little more than the fluent "I am so pleased to see you, comrades! . . . That is why I am still living."[115]

In contrast, the worker is the narrator in a series of anecdotal short stories by Ralph Winstead, who also wrote under the pen name William Akers. Dotted with labor terms, these stories were vastly popular with the readers of the Wobbly magazine *Industrial Pioneer*. Self-educated, Winstead learned the proletarian ropes on construction sites, in mines, and as a lumber workers' union leader. Between 1920 and 1923 a series of his stories featured his Wobbly hero Tightline Johnson, a clever, if homespun, lumber worker. Johnson was a master of the deadpan, which humorists like Mark Twain had used to narrate impossible exploits in a frontier or rural setting.[116] But there was a crucial difference. In a typically exaggerated piece, "Tightline Johnson Goes to Heaven" (tightline was a logging term for a cable rigging device), the title character brings tears to God's eyes with his account of IWW work conditions. "Was you ever in a fix like that?" he asks the Creator, pictured as an "old geezer." Glorying in his own irreverence, Johnson challenges God to act any differently than a Wobbly who rebels against "the slave-drivin' system."[117] In other stories, Johnson whips a coal-mining camp into IWW shape ("Light Exercise and Change," *Industrial Pioneer,* January 1922). He quits a section gang in disgust after doing the work of five men ("Chin-Whiskers, Hay-Wire, and Pitchforks," *Industrial Pioneer,* January 1921). Ejection from a logging camp for complaining about the contract only hardens his Wobbly resolve ("Johnson the Gypo," *Industrial Pioneer,* September 1921).

Comic and savvy, the Johnson character skillfully blended native American humor and radical politics in a way that few other period characters could emulate. Consider the title of former Wobbly Gerald Morris's semifictional "On the Skidroad: What One Sees on Los Angeles' Street of Forsaken Men." It was published in the September 1928 issue of the *Haldeman-Julius Quarterly,* a journal friendly to a variety of socialist and radical causes. The sketch cleverly introduces Four Penny Slim, IWW newsboys, and soapboxers decrying the Criminal Syndicalism Law. Morris's acute observation, however, peters out when he reveals how he had come "up from the depths."[118] Far closer to Tightline Johnson is another tale, from the spring 1928 issue of the *Haldeman-Julius Quarterly.* As with the Winstead series, O. W. Cooley's "The Damned Outfit: A Pair of Apple Pickers Fall into a Haywire Dump" is told completely from the inside.[119] While Cooley does not mention the IWW by name, he spins a typical Wobbly plot and gives further clues as well. The title term "haywire dump" (suggesting a dismal, fenced-off enclosure for the workers) was routinely used in the *Industrial Pioneer.* Also familiar was the fact that the narrator of the story, told in the first person, was "Slim." The name is both an allusion to the Wobblies' favorite road poet, T-Bone Slim, and is one of their most common nicknames (and one later used for characters in proletarian fiction of the 1930s).[120] As in this passage, worth quoting at length, Cooley's Slim, joined by his pal Horace (Wobblies often took classical names), is about to hop a freight:

> [I asked,] "Where is White Salmon?"
> "Down the line, [Horace answered.] Why?"
> "Some bird there is advertisin' fer pickers."
> Horace squinted his eyes and pursed his dirty mouth.
> "Sounds haywire," he said, "but what-ta-hell."
> We bumped south toward White Salmon, lived on apples and pears, breathed air that was keen, cooled by the ice-topped mountains and pungently flavored by the pines it blew over. I was ravenous.
> The second day we got a ride with [Dorsey,] a thick-set man in a touring car. There was a box of juicy pears in the back seat. He turned out to be the man who wanted pickers and took us right to his ranch. He looked Horace over doubtfully and Horace looked him over.

"Think you can pick apples?"

"Do you know," said Horace slowly, "you're just my idea of a sweet old puke." He walked genially over to old Dorsey and reached up and thumped him on the back, cackled, and stuck out his hand. ("Damned Outfit," 160–161)

As if the language is the experience itself, there is a new sureness of tone born of the authority of the vagabond. Despite some poetic flourishes, this representative passage conforms to what Richard Bridgman, in his important book *The Colloquial Style in America* (1966), defined as colloquial prose marked by an internal coherence. Like Twain before him, and Hemingway after, Cooley produces a language of slangy freshness and immediate experience through a series of simple interchanges and declarative sentences.[121]

There is no editorial intrusion, a stylistic omission that bolsters the disdain for bourgeois morality at the center of the story. In the person of Dorsey, property owning becomes unscrupulous greed, as he feeds his workers badly, houses them shamefully, tries to cut their wages, and cheats them. To underscore the story's vague reference to revolutionary plans, as the tale closes Slim and Horace are threatening assault if they are not paid fairly. It is a version in miniature of the IWW resistance to bossism. The wages they pry out of Dorsey symbolize Wobbly syndicalism, not the reward for honest labor prized by the capitalist ascension plot.

In the decade to come, the worker-writer would displace the vernacular narrator of the Wobbly sketch. Wobbly art would fade, a victim of the limitations of its fragmentary literary traditions and of the encroachments of the CP cultural front. Forgotten as well would be the laborer as a figure of survival in the midst of plenty, a proletarian troubadour who could always get by. The 1930s economy of scarcity would reconfigure Tightline Johnson's self-assertion, Slim and Horace's direct action, and the scornful willingness to quit at a moment's notice central to the Wobblies and their bards. But the Wobbly contribution has been greatly undervalued. By capturing their own lives as militants and forgotten men, they set the stage for both the Depression era workers' correspondent and the proletarian novel itself.

Objects of Desire: Labor Texts and the 1920s

In left-wing circles working-class writers were taking halting steps to the full-length novel. In liberal and mainstream ones there was a continuing reluctance to grant literary authority to working people. A defeatism about labor militancy recycled the genteel worker of the nineteenth century to meet the poor-white and ethnic longings of the new decade. The results were equivocal: psychically or politically, anarchic figures who worshiped self-improvement were caught in the net of their own desires. Within certain texts, and sometimes intertextually, there was continuing confusion about labor-class values, lifestyles, and collectivity. The confusion was evident as well in the literary attempts to make protagonists both exceptional and unexceptional. Though lackluster and uninspiring compared with Sinclair's (and the real-life) Vanzetti, the alienated radical is now the one with emotional greatness.

Taking a Bartolomeo Vanzetti's hopes more seriously than ever before tied Sinclair to the Wobbly literature of the "other twenties."[122] The IWW used ethnic organizers in New England strikes, and Vanzetti's marginal, peripatetic existence prior to his arrest could have found its way into a vignette in *Industrial Solidarity* or the *Haldeman-Julius Quarterly*. Yet Sinclair changes to the plot of the elitist observer. Without literary models for "how to make Marxism about form as well as content,"[123] CP practitioners of a radical aesthetic could only martyr their heroes or present them as impulsive, directionless, living in the moment, remote from ethnic radicalism if not from plummeting postwar wages for itinerant workers.

With the exception of Upton Sinclair, who was termed part of the "middle generation" by Gold, the sustained literary work voice of the 1920s, then, came not from the still-fragmentary output of those "writing red" but from those like Anzia Yezierska and, to a lesser extent, Theodore Dreiser. In tune with their era, these 1920s writers used coded ways of criticizing U.S. labor exploitation and welfare capitalism alike. The strikes and labor landmarks that had inspired Progressive Era work novels ceded in theirs to plots of obscure workers elevated to success or notoriety. Thus Yezierska's subversive countermessage was ignored, and she herself rewarded with Hollywood contracts. Dreiser's Clyde became a pathetic version of Fitzgerald's self-born millionaire bootlegger Jay Gatsby, sharing the hunger for success and the Golden Girl with no real ability to attain either.

But the labor psychodramas played out in Dreiser and Yezierska also register the toll taken by bourgeois longings, whether realized or thwarted by a selectively rising living standard. In Yezierska, the Dreiserian hunger for capitalist success feeds not so much on the object of desire as on itself. Yezierska was, by rights, a worker-writer. She was familiar with the shtetl, the sweaty trades, and her own sense of class exclusion. In her fiction, the old cultural fixation on the worker as man, and now woman, on the rise is reinvented once again. Now the daughter of the people is a loner who climbs by keeping separate. That figure is unable to reconcile an outraged social consciousness and a post–red scare avoidance of left-wing affiliations, a horror of poverty and a contempt for materialism. In her social climbing and egalitarianism, she never reconciles the American Dream to subversive realities.

Outside fiction in some way representative of the dominant culture, leftist authors tried to close the gap between observer and observed, between workers and writers, that had defined American labor literature since before the Civil War. The stories by Gold and his CP literary colleagues had not yet energized the depiction of labor in chains; Gold's stronger stories emanate from the Wobblies, not Proletcult. Sinclair and the contributors to IWW journals, if anything, celebrated the socially marginal persona. Their characters' disdain of materialism, whether resulting in the martyrdom of Vanzetti or the defiant itinerancy of the Wobbly narrator-hero, recast but did not Bolshevize the cult of personality.

In the months closest to the Great Crash of 1929, when strikes reasserted themselves and wages fell, the *New Masses* reiterated the call for worker-writers that would become the cornerstone of their editorial policy until the Popular Front's CP "Americanism" of the mid-1930s. By December of 1928, the journal's new worker-correspondents like Ed Falkowski and H. H. Lewis had already traded their IWW allegiance for short, politicized pieces from the mines and factories at home and in the Soviet Union.[124]

Yet even as these new worker-writers carved new narrative space, the old era's doomed outcasts provided its most famous epitaph. Bartolomeo Vanzetti, speaking in 1927 in Dedham prison to the journalist Phil Strong, in an interview published in the *New York World* on May 13, 1927, and widely reprinted (including in *Boston*), gave closure to the old era and heralded the best labor fiction of the next decade.[125] His eloquence is both his own and the voice of oppressed labor:

> If it had not been for these thing . . . I might have live out my life talking at street corners to scorning men. I might have die, unmarked, unknown, a failure. Now we are not a failure. This is our career and our triumph. Never in our full life could we hope to do such work for tolerance, for joostice, for man's understanding of man as now we do by accident. Our words—our lives—our pains—nothing! The taking of our lives—lives of a good shoemaker and a poor fish-peddler—all! This last moment belongs to us—that agony is our triumph.

Anticipating Tom Joad, Casey the Preacher, Mikey, Anna Holbrook, and Bigger Thomas, Vanzetti, like them, was reshaped in the "artist's" hands. It was Strong who added the famous phrases "good shoemaker" and "poor fish-peddler" and strengthened the rhetoric as well. Yet it is no less Vanzetti's voice for that. In the following decade, such proletarian eloquence was earnestly sought, and sometimes achieved. Even as the Depression dawned, *Jews without Money* had already moved to resolve its author's 1920s conflicts. A younger generation of labor writers now began to face the challenge of making workers heroic for rising with their class, not dying to escape it.

CHAPTER 8

From Black Folk to Working Class

African American Labor Fiction between the World Wars

[Whites considered] Negroes rather ugly but serviceable fixtures, devices that happened to be alive, dull instruments of drudgery.

—RUDOLPH FISHER, *THE WALLS OF JERICHO* (1928)

The ordinary Negroes hadn't heard of the Negro Renaissance. And if they had, it hadn't raised their wages any.

—LANGSTON HUGHES, "WHEN THE NEGRO WAS IN VOGUE," *THE BIG SEA* (1940)

Proletarianism takes a different shape when it intersects with race.

—PAUL LAUTER, "AMERICAN PROLETARIANISM" (1991)

Jacob Lawrence, "Migrants left. They did not feel safe." Panel 22, *The Migration Series,* 1940–1941. Tempera on gesso on composition board, 12 × 18 in. The Museum of Modern Art, New York. Gift of Mrs. David M. Levy. Photograph © 1995 The Museum of Modern Art, New York.

Black Folk, White Labor, and the Great Migration (1916–1929)

By 1916, anticipating wartime needs for replacement workers and lured by recruitment agents and advertisements in black newspapers like the *Chicago Defender*, by kinship networks, and by an exaggerated picture of northern racial tolerance, the Great Migration of working-class and impoverished blacks proceeded northward. Although the economic devastation of the early 1930s still produced more migration from the South than to it, the Great Migration was a pre-Depression phenomenon: a million and a half southern blacks had moved to northern cities by the end of the 1920s.[1] As pragmatic as it was idealistic, this African American mass journey was marked by a determination bordering on desperation: the bulk of the black rural sharecropping class was abjectly poor.[2] Beneath a surface discourse of job opportunity, the aim was escape from a rural South infested with the boll weevils that lowered cotton production and inhabited by the impoverished sharecropping tenantry (more than three-quarters of tenant farmers were black) held down by Jim Crow laws.[3]

At the end of the Great Migration, though more than three-quarters of the country's eleven million blacks remained in the South, the majority lived in cities, where they could earn more than on the sharecropper's rented soil. There was some leverage—and even transient unionization—on the docks of New Orleans and a large if unorganized labor force in the shipyards of Norfolk and Richmond and the coal mines of Alabama and Tennessee.[4] Yet throughout the Great Migration period, the plantation ethos still controlled the economics of southern life. Bearing witness are the Georgia sawmill of Jean Toomer's *Cane* (1923) and the Eatonville, Florida, home laundries of Zora Neale Hurston's short story "Sweat" (1926).

Throughout the postwar South, black male farmhands made one dollar per day, females even less. In the southern urban industrial centers, such as segregated Birmingham, where iron and steel work was plentiful and thus pay was higher, male blacks earned less than three dollars a day.[5] Black women doing paid work faced a similarly bleak wage outlook, whether in their customary maids' jobs or in the textile mills; a small percentage held down the worst southern manufacturing jobs, for which they could expect two-thirds less pay than poorly paid white women received.[6]

When migrants, the majority of them young men between twenty and twenty-four, formed a sizable industrial labor presence in the northern and midwestern cities, they fared better than in the 1920s South.[7] By the middle of the decade, in "The New Negro" (1925), the Harvard-educated aesthete Alain Locke, the man most associated with the interwar cultural and literary movement known as the Harlem Renaissance, though he rarely alluded to manual work, urged migrants to leave the "medieval South" for the North, where African American laborers could "brush elbows" with whites at work. Within a year of Locke's essay, the Ford Motor Company was employing ten thousand blue-collar blacks, almost one-tenth of its Detroit-area workforce.[8]

Ford's River Rouge plant implemented an aggressive recruitment policy, interracial pairing on the line, apprentice schools for blacks, and occasional access to supervisory jobs.[9] These black workers no doubt strived as hard as their white coworkers to fit the Fordist mold of super-efficiency, consummate loyalty, and "proper" conduct, at least to judge by the proud "I work for Henry Ford" buttons some African Americans affixed to their Sunday best. If African Americans were, as usual, given the most dangerous jobs, Ford paid them almost as much as whites.[10] As blacks too gained access to a new consumer culture, southern blues songs contained lyrics like the late 1920s "I'm goin' to get me a job, up there in Mr. Ford's place."[11]

But if Ford's progressive hiring policy was cementing the loyalty of a new black male urban proletariat, the migrant entry into industrial democracy predicted by Locke was minimal. Ford himself believed in residential and social separation.[12] Thus at Ford as elsewhere, African Americans tasted only the fruits of segregated welfare capitalism, from quotas on "black" apprentice slots to "Black Belt" recreational centers.[13] Blacks found a similar racial policy, though fewer benefits, in other basic-industrial venues like Homestead. By decade's end, the mills of Pittsburgh and its environs employed one-fifth of all black steelworkers in western Pennsylvania.[14] Yet, more typical of the African American lower-class work situation, Chicago's International Harvester, Swift, and Armour used hiring limits for blacks, while at Detroit's Willys-Overland the job assignments were based on race.[15]

From Detroit to New York City, this factory-floor ghettoization was replicated throughout the pre-Depression era in neighborhoods as well. Representative in this regard was Chicago, after New York and Philadelphia the U.S. city with the third densest population of blacks, and the most notable for providing industrial livelihoods for migrant men and women.[16] By 1922, over 100,000 blacks lived in Chicago. One-third of them, mostly male, worked in the stockyards, registering a significant black presence in most packing centers.[17] Of the female migrants to Chicago, less numerous proportionally than their male migrant counterparts, recent feminist readings of the Great Migration decade have contended that their reasons were complex: many women were not only hoping for economic betterment but fleeing abusive families or husbands. But they replicated black male work patterns when they retained their segregated work in hotels, commercial laundries, restaurants, and stockyards and, invisible to white customers, in mail-order departments, earning lower wages than their white female counterparts and barred from sharing facilities and job space with them.[18] Most commonly, whether in New York or Philadelphia, Detroit, Chicago or Washington, D.C., two-thirds of servants in the 1920s were black women who had traded a southern job as a domestic for a better-paying northern one.[19]

Black men or women in Chicago, as in other industrial cities, joined a smaller and, by the Depression, more transient group. Recruited for and discriminated against by Rust Belt industries, Mexicans replaced European immigrant labor in the menial work associated with steel and auto factories and with stockyard and railroad labor.[20] In the field-as-factory world of California migrant labor, racial policies circumscribed Mexican, Japanese, and Filipino farmworkers in ways that mirrored the African American experience in the cotton-producing South. To underscore this "hierarchy of color," Filipinos were also used by the Pullman Car Company as racial stand-ins for striking black porters, though without the intense cultural and literary scrutiny that black labor now provoked.[21]

Numbering anywhere from a few thousand to tens of thousands in key industries, African Americans of the Great Migration inspired a sociology that surpassed in degree and quality the previous decade's, including the condescending chapters in the books written for the Pittsburgh Survey. A number of the new publications, first produced as graduate research on the years of the postwar Great Migration, were published under the powerful aegis of the University of Chicago's Sociology Department. Notable among them were such surveys of the pre-Depression work experience as Lorenzo J. Greene and Carter C. Woodson's *The Negro Wage Earner* (1930). Alma Herbst produced *The Negro in the Slaughtering and Meatpacking Industry in Chicago* (1932), and E. Franklin Frazier, *The Negro Family in Chicago* (1932). The sections on women in these texts joined *Negro Women in Industry* (1922) and Mary V. Robinson's *Domestic Workers and Their Employment Relations* (1926), both published with the imprimatur of the Labor Department's new Women's Bureau. Such studies amplified the picture of the benefits and risks of the northern workplace provided by two prominent Harlem-based journals, the NAACP's *Opportunity* and *Crisis*, by word-of-mouth migrant networks and letters home, and by fiction loosely associated with the Harlem Renaissance.[22] Joining blues songs, longings for a return southward are eloquently reiterated in Jean Toomer's lyric novel *Cane*. As a young migrant who must stay in stockyards Chicago looks longingly out of his rooming-house window, he remembers the scent of a "pine-matted hillock in Georgia."[23]

Whether feeling lonely, bought, or cheated, benefiting from welfare capitalism, or resenting the label of a "scab race," these migrants also experienced, however haltingly, a process of proletarianization that was firmly rooted in their migrant influx into heavy industry.[24] This included limited new interactions with white trade unionism from the early years of the migration to the Great Crash. In a decade when as many as 10 percent of miners in states like West Virginia were black men, the United Mine Workers responded to a postwar influx of blacks into that region from states like Alabama. The UMW widened efforts to halt racial strife in its locals, increase the paltry number of black organizers, and curb the power of antiblack hate groups like the Ku Klux Klan.[25] Black unionists did play roles in UMW strikes. They even battled scabs of their own race in the failed coal strike in Mingo County, West Virginia, in 1921 and in the strikes of the western Pennsylvania and central Appalachian region in the mid- and late 1920s.[26]

These and other attempts at interracial unionism, however, provided no models outside the industries in question. In response to employers' creation of interracial jobsites to train blacks in case of white strikes, Chicago's stockyards union, the Amalgamated Meat Cutters and Butcher Workmen, recruited blacks—the most prominent of only four labor organizations in Chicago to do so.[27] But despite the efforts of the rare black organizer who tried to unite black and white in meat-processing centers, the union could not offer equality of treatment or opposition to the standard practice of separate black locals.[28] In fact, blacks assigned to mixed work gangs were segregated socially and given the dirtiest jobs. In another highly unionized field, railroad work, blacks labored as track layers, firemen, brakemen, and repairmen with white apprentices. Still, the railroad brotherhoods, in unison with a recalcitrant American Federation of Labor, were intransigent about blacks belonging to integrated unions or working in "white men's" jobs. The small countertradition of independent African American unions, such as those in the South among longshoremen and workers in the building trades, did not prevent intense hostilities. Nor did it forestall the actions of bigoted white trade unionists, such as those who participated in the Chicago Race Riots of 1919.[29]

Despite the Industrial Workers of the World's authentic commitment to integration, and the Socialist Party (SP) and Communist Party official if less trustworthy policies, throughout the 1920s these left-radical organizations also had little appeal. In the aftermath of the red scare, the entire Left unsuccessfully preached a militant biracial unionism at odds with the negritude radicalism of Marcus Garvey's United Negro Improvement Association (UNIA) nationalism. Leftists were further blocked by the prevalence of black migrant religiosity as well as by black resentment of any white labor organizers, whom black workers may have associated with the workers who participated in race riots, such as those in East St. Louis in 1917 and in Chicago in 1919. Thus by the new decade, the modest IWW southern influence on black Louisiana lumber workers through the Brotherhood of Timber Workers, like that of the Wobbly Ben Fletcher on his fellow Philadelphia dockers, had faded with Palmer raid incursions.[30] The Harlem branches of the SP and the CP were always small. Henry Ford, who made little distinction between radicals, hated socialists for "trying to Bolshevize the Negro,"[31] yet even in the leftist Auto Workers' Union, fears of blacks going "red" in the relatively prosperous 1920s were groundless. In Detroit and iron-industry Birmingham, home to the black CP organizer Hosea Hudson, the CP foundered.[32] During its brief tenure, the pro-Communist *Liberator* (1917–1924) had one black member on the editorial board, Claude McKay, and he was critical of its inattention to race issues. The Party itself had at most one thousand African American members (over half of whom worked in the stockyards and automotive industry of Chicago). Communism did gain a limited following in the black nationalism of the secretive, Harlem-based African Blood Brotherhood (ABB), to which

McKay belonged. But few followed McKay's example of balancing ABB membership with an enthusiasm for the revolutionary Soviet Union.[33] Among socialists, Frank Crosswaith, a leading black SP member, formed the black Trade Union Committee for Organizing Workers in New York in 1925 (possibly to offset the CP's titularly interracial Trade Union Education League), but it was financially strapped and ineffective.[34]

Recent scholarship on rural blacks migrating to the Northeast and Midwest as well as to the urban industrial South of Richmond, Virginia, and Birmingham has pointed out that migrants had been no more passive in the Jim Crow South than they were in the New North.[35] Calling these unorganized migrants a "grassroots social movement" may be an overstatement. The migrants did engage in a covert resistance to racism by deliberately remaining apart from any organization that could not further their goals.[36] This resistance affected black unionism too. Aside from modest organizations of Pullman waiters and cooks, A. Philip Randolph's Brotherhood of Sleeping Car Porters shunned the AFL. The BSCP termed it the "most wicked machine for the propagation of race prejudice in the country." Randolph's was virtually the only association to challenge the intransigence of the lily-white labor movement and anti-union blacks alike.[37]

Randolph's socialist *Messenger* (1917–1928) outlived other Harlem-based socialist periodicals such as *The Crusader* (1919–1922). *Messenger* articles and cover illustrations featured black coal miners (March 1927), steelmen (October 1927), street pavers (February 1928), stevedores (September 1927), and the Pullman porter's friendly rival, the dining car worker (August 1927). Given the relative insularity of the journal and the many setbacks to the BSCP, the claim of Randolph's ally Frank Crosswaith that the unionized Pullman porters were "the real proletariat of America" was exaggerated.[38] Nevertheless, in and outside the pages of the *Messenger* Randolph was attempting to transform the BSCP into a cross-trade voice of black industrial unionism, defiant of entrenched white craft and business unionism. Whether porters and their less culturally visible coworkers, the parlor-car waiters, responded to lily-white unionism through job actions or apathy, their lived experience in this "black man's job" would mark African American labor culture and fiction for some time to come.[39]

Home at Pullman:
The "Black Man's Job" and the 1920s Labor Novel

Faithful to a self-interested post–Civil War tradition posing as philanthropy, the Pullman Company remained the largest single employer of blacks in the 1920s.[40] Although it was far less industrial than stockyards or steel mills, its employees now formed part of the first wave of black urban workers.[41] Even more than working on the often segregated Ford line, Pullman service meant job security. Moreover, the railroad itself had long been a symbol of freedom in the oral tradition of African Americans.[42] That freedom certainly lured a variety of people, from the many unskilled to the few educated men who could not find more suitable work or were working their way through law or medical school.[43] In many black communities, including the more settled parts of Harlem, a Pullman job enabled a man to marry, raise a family, and gain respect from working- and middle-class blacks (if not from the Talented Tenth). Like their fellow Pullman waiters, porters enjoyed an elevated status in the black community and were often homeowners and pillars of the church.[44] With considerable irony, Wallace Thurman captures the pious type in a minor character from his Harlem novel *The Blacker the Berry* (1929): "an ex-preacher turned Pullman porter because, since prohibition times, he could make more on the Pullman cars than he could in the pulpit."[45] He even sends his son to college on his savings.

Pullman work was also, however, an emblem of the black as menial, for, in the words of one veteran, T. T. Paterson, the porter was treated like a "piece of furniture."[46] Dependent on tips, he had a grueling schedule at substandard wages and could not advance to more highly skilled and paid positions. Frank Crosswaith deplored the porter's "destiny": "once a porter always one."[47] In Pullman's own brand of Fordism, the porter was required to comply with passenger requests cheerfully and to answer routinely to the name of "George" (the founder Pullman's first name).[48] An incensed McKay, who wrote for the *Messenger* and was a former Pullman waiter well versed in the porter's world, detested "George's 'Yessahboss.' "[49] Stormed W.E.B. Du Bois in his utopian tract *Dark Princess* (1928), complete with an undercover politico posing as a porter: "A [white] scullion . . . achieving a sleeping-car berth proclaim[s] his kingship to the world by one word: 'George!' "[50] When Hollywood needed a comic "darky," it often found one in a Pullman porter.[51]

The Pullman experience was even more contradictory for women. As maids on the cars or in the yards, they earned more than their sisters in domestic service outside Pullman. Yet their lot reflected not only feminine job segregation but a political invisibility for those who joined the union. Well before achieving union status in the 1930s, Randolph's BSCP tried to rectify gender exclusion; its full name, in fact, was the Brotherhood of Sleeping Car Porters and Maids. Yet this stab at inclusion was soon dropped.[52] Despite the presence of women workers on the cars and in the yards, when the cars returned home, even in the most pro-Pullman articles the "activist" women praised were the wives of porters, who published "odes to the Brotherhood" in the *Messenger* proclaiming their support.[53]

Whatever the views of its female members, the BSCP gained enough force that by 1926 half of all porters had joined its 5,000-strong membership; two years later its attempted "strike" was preempted by the company.[54] Nor should one forget the members of another proto-union, the 4,000-strong Brotherhood of Dining Car Employees (BDCE). Although it comprised almost half of those employed in the service, this organization lacked the proactive reputation of the larger body.[55] For all its energy, the BSCP, the shakiest union in America as late as the FDR administration, would not win formal recognition until the labor-friendly New Deal. Nevertheless, Randolph and allies swayed hearts and minds with 1920s slogans like "Join the Brotherhood and Be a Man!"[56] The organizers blasted management's company union plan as "contemptible." "The new Pullman porter," Randolph thundered, is a "rebel against all that 'Uncle Tom' suggests."[57] Fighting his own disillusionment with the white labor movement, he optimistically urged blacks to join unions and whites to admit them, in his *Messenger* news pieces and proactive organizing drives. At the same time, he hammered away at the paternalism of the Pullman Company. Bending the dominant rhetoric of the Harlem Renaissance to a prolabor end, he called the porter who joined his union the "New Negro."[58]

Randolph obviously found allies in Claude McKay and Wallace Thurman, who published poetry and fiction in or helped edit the BSCP's *Messenger* and included porters in their Harlem novels. (The "New Negro" luminary W.E.B. Du Bois devoted an entire section of his fictive *Dark Princess* to the porters' agitational activities in Harlem and Chicago.) The Pullman porter's real importance, though, is as a gauge of the transitional nature of the African American work experience. For the job symbolized the situation of the transplanted migrant torn between northern mechanization and southern servitude, between militance and compliance, between buying into white racist stereotypes and developing an independent identity; in short, the North was a site of both opportunity and crisis. In McKay and, to an extent, Wallace Thurman's *The Blacker the Berry* and Rudolph Fisher's 1925 *Atlantic Monthly* story "The City of Refuge" (reprinted the same year in Alain Locke's anthology *The New Negro*), the Pullman experience intersects with the Harlem one. Toomer, Marita Bonner, and others variously expand or recast the Pullman-Harlem plot to include other jobs in other northern cities. McKay and his contemporaries allied themselves with, redefined, or rejected the Harlem Renaissance outright. All criticized the embourgeoisement ethic and the narrow parameters of the "black man's job."

Renaissance Renegades: McKay and His Contemporaries

The Harlem Renaissance was a brilliant upsurge of creativity in literature, music, and art within black America that spanned roughly the postwar years to the early years of the Great Depression, reaching its zenith in the second half of the 1920s. It flowered in *The New Negro*, the 1925 anthology lauded as a touchstone for the movement.[59] Its many belletrists, artists, and cultural commentators represented a composite affirmation of negritude through a search for the essential identity of the black common folk and its culture. Under Alain Locke's aegis, this important circle of writers, artists, and thinkers celebrated the qualities of the African spirit and promoted oneness with nature, freshness of response to experience, and rejection of the mechanization and vapid materialism of the 1920s.[60] Celebrating the southern heritage while recasting the migrant experience (in Lockean terminology) contributors lauded the urban pioneers with their new ideals and aspirations toward self-determination.[61]

Locke and his circle were reluctant to scrutinize the southern labor experience of the "ordinary man," the "folk," the "migrant masses," or the "masses," all terms used interchangeably in Locke's writings.[62] On the rare occasions he alluded to northern laborers, he mirrored his contributors in the belief that the black bourgeoisie provided more interesting material than the "black proletariat."[63] In his view, this "New Negro" could best thrive as a cultural being, not a political force. Locke defined the figure as part of a folk with a new sense of racial pride, whose voice could best be heard through a Talented Tenth artist expressing what the less articulate could not. Furthermore, this "folk" persona, though a singer of spirituals, a teller of tales, and an ancestor of African artists, was only occasionally, as in brief *New Negro* contributions from Hughes and others, a participant in the blues culture of Harlem's Jazz Age nightclubs and the sensuality of the rural South.

The newest readings see Locke's "cultural nationalism of the parlor" as a way of securing legitimacy for the black bourgeoisie and intelligentsia by minimizing, idealizing, or otherwise circumscribing lower-class blacks.[64] Thus William Stanley Braithwaite's "The Negro in American Literature" deftly upholds an ideal of "Negro poetic expression" by severing it from the vernacular trickster whose rapid-fire jests, insults, and verbal pyrotechnics are rooted in African systems of thought.[65] For all the *New Negro* references to the need for a new racial idiom reflective of the American Negro, Locke's own allusions to the "man farthest down" are typically sparse and uncomfortable. He is far more at ease in suggesting that even such a man may become a black professional. Omitted from his class-based anthology are the sexual radicalism and musical innovations of the cross-class jazz clubs and buffet flats, the radical "people's" politics of Caribbean Harlem, and, last but not least, Randolph's pro-unionist writings in the *Messenger* and other radical-socialist journals.[66]

Seeking to establish an African American literary tradition, Locke did include Rudolph Fisher's Harlem story "City of Refuge," in which an unscrupulous cabaret owner fleeces and ruins a credulous North Carolina migrant. Certainly if read as sympathetic to the uprooted southern black, it echoes a classic black novel, Paul Laurence Dunbar's *The Sport of the Gods* (1902). Sympathetic to the southern folk or not, many works were deemed too radical. Among them were bitter "black work" and sex-work poems. Their very titles were too explicit for the Locke anthology: McKay's "Alfonso, Dressing to Wait at Table," and Langston Hughes's eponymous "Elevator Boy," "Mulatto," "Ruby Brown," and "Red Silk Stockings." Locke did choose the stirring, if conventional, McKay sonnet "If We Must Die." Perhaps he had not read the oblique satire published a few years before in which the same poet disdained "convention-ridden and head-ossified Negro intelligentsia."[67] Locke also included Hughes's "I, Too, Sing America," with its mixture of defiance and patriotism. But within the context of the McKay and Hughes poems that Locke included, these selections are muted, whether by formal language or a guarded optimism.

A similar dilution occurred when Locke changed the highly charged title of Jean Toomer's poem "The White House," to "White Houses," angering the author. Toomer was further put off by Locke's decision to include only the lush early sections of his *Cane* with their softened eroticism. He preferred selections from his more controversial scenes of the lynching of a black laborer by affluent white racists ("Blood-Burning Moon"), of segregated southern schools ("Kabnis"), or of the chaotic work and nightlife of a Washington,

D.C., version of Harlem ("Theater"). A surprising inclusion is Zora Neale Hurston's seriocomic story "Spunk," which cleverly offers dueling explanations—industrial accident or hex—for the death of a Herculean sawmill worker. Yet the didactic overlay (the worker was, after all, a murderer) resolves complexities of conduct that her other pre-Depression stories do not.

Locke's choices and exclusions demonstrate that the New Negro cultural resurgence, though emanating from black urban intellectualism, was not easily amalgamated with the city novel, much less with the African American labor thrust of Toomer, McKay, Fisher, Hurston, Bonner, or Thurman. Where they celebrated spirituals, he saw "sublimated bitterness." He was willing to be labeled a "hog rooting in Harlem."[68] Locke's renegade contributors (or outright foes, such as Thurman) did found their own journal *(Fire!!)* or seek out established ones such as the *Crisis* magazine.

The noble fugitive plot, anachronistic even by the Dunbar period, seemed inapplicable to the interracial city and the labor complexities of the Pullman porter and waiter, as well as the Harlem janitors, elevator operators, longshoremen, and chauffeurs. Some, like McKay, described their work as proletarian. Others, like Fisher and Thurman, though recognizing the racist obstacles, infused their fiction with an ethic of upward mobility. Drawing on elements of the Noble Fugitive slave narrative and the ethnographical fiction of an Upton Sinclair, they created the Great Migration narrative of the postwar decade. Capturing what both the geographical and the symbolic Harlem meant by the African American "home" and "work" would prove a formidable labor-literary task.

The earliest "renegade" of Harlem Renaissance novels with working-class themes, *Cane* has the fewest Harlem references. Indeed, Toomer replaced Harlem with Black Belt Philadelphia, Washington, D.C., and Chicago. Prior to the writing of the novel, he had migrated through many personae and regions, among them a disaffected New York University student, a Chicago Ford salesman, a Washington socialist shipyard organizer, the Georgia headmaster of a rural industrial and agricultural school, and a Harlem aspiring belletrist.[69]

Experimenting with a subversion of the Uncle Tom myth of a happy-black-folk culture, Toomer made his southern black characters three-dimensional by punctuating the text with subversive spirituals, antilynching ballads, and other ambivalently nostalgic poems. *Cane's* first sections are set largely in rural-industrial Georgia and feature male and female day workers and local shopkeepers. As people attuned to the rhythms of southern (and even African) time, Toomer implies, they possess a sensuality and spirituality that intellectual Harlem can only read about. Yet the rhythm of each sketch is broken by harsh modernity, resulting in a psychic fragility that keeps them focused more on failed relationships than on migration. Many of the women domestics and store clerks become stay-at-homes by default. Their immersion in their own needs, their hunger for something, prompts a comparison to *Winesburg, Ohio* (1919) and the white aspiration theme of so much 1920s work fiction. On the surface, this migration text seems, if anything, stopped in languid southern time.

When unified with the later sections, the Georgia sketches reveal a subtext of dreamers caught in the class, race, and gender snares of black work. Beginning in the migrants' home county rather than in the "free North," Toomer first fleshes out a drab Georgia laborscape—sawmills, cotton fields, kitchen work, low-level teaching in segregated schools, and pick-up maintenance jobs. In some sections he interposes a black bourgeoisie, glimpsed mainly through the thwarted longings of its well-socialized daughters.

Toomer projects his uncertainty about his own class and race affiliations onto the principal male figures of the novel, particularly the half-white, dissatisfied Ralph Kabnis, the eponymous center of the final section. Earlier in the book, various male and female aspirants flee to Washington, D.C., Chicago, Philadelphia, and New York, only to realize that their dreams have become as tawdry—or ruled by mindless acquisition (see the "Rhobert" section)—as their Black Belt surroundings. Kabnis, a more educated man, has even higher expectations of the "free North" but is humiliated enough to return south. There he seeks company in pain with local craftsmen whose refrain about whites is: "They like y if y work for them" (*Cane*, 100). A typically modern protagonist, he is caught between contempt for the racial obeisance of the South and the moral maelstrom of the North. Whichever place he is in, he is nostalgic for the other one.[70]

As a migration text, whether to the North or "home" again, the novel elides the geographical and spiritual journeys. An early Harlem Renaissance renegade, Toomer was searching for modernism as much as for his own African roots. (The sociological portions of *Cane* appeared in the *Liberator*, and the avant-garde ones in the "little magazine" *Broom*.) A Toomer sketch always begins with a migration, whether through fantasy or flight, from the racial, or racist, certainties of the South. In a dialectic between the burden of the real and the search for the desired, the Toomer persona often simply retreats inward, sometimes at the cost of physical survival. And most revisionary of all in a labor-migrant text, at journey's end there is no sanctuary. The black South remains a place where folk creativity and the danger of lynchings coexist, as do religious fervor and sexual longing. But in the spiritual void of the North, from D.C. to Harlem, there is nobody home.[71]

Moving the plot of *Home to Harlem* in and out of the Harlem that Toomer so distrusted, Claude McKay constructed "work" as ceaseless movement. A transplanted West Indian familiar with the black meccas of the States, McKay spent most of the 1920s in Russia, Europe, and North Africa, finding in migration a form of control over experience. Similarly, in *Home to Harlem* Jake Brown exercises the wanderer's privilege of leaving and returning at will. Ignoring the onerous aspects of his job as a Pullman waiter, he is glad to be in motion rather than rooted in what McKay called taking "Miss Ann's old clothes for work-and-wages."[72] Harlem enables him to remain in movement as he changes lodgings, lovers, and friends.

Constructing Pullman work as a form of self-expression, however, proves difficult. In his Pullman stopovers, Jake seeks out the safe Black Belt neighborhoods in places like Pittsburgh, by the mid-1920s a milltown venue for southern refugees.[73] Rather than bear witness to the southern migrants' adaptation to the strictures of urbanization, he scorns the quarters that the Pullman Company provides for black employees.

From the novel's beginning to the end, Jake's virtue and flaw is the personal nature of his rebellion. Proud of his break with the Locke circle, McKay cast it in terms of *Home to Harlem* as a "real proletarian novel," an unintentional irony in that his unruly work found wider acceptance, at least to judge by sales, than Harlem Renaissance texts.[74] Jake declares to an IWW organizer trying to rouse black workers that he will never "scab it on any man" (*Home,* 45). On the job he engages in friendly taunting of the porters as "chambermaids" (174). But Jake appears not to have heard of the BSCP, despite years of widening unrest among sleeping car porters in New York and other cities over working conditions.[75] Nor does he seem aware of the organization he could have joined, the Brotherhood of Dining Car Employees.[76]

Politically the most radical of the authors in flight from Locke's aesthetics of negritude, McKay used terms like "class struggle" and "interracial solidarity" throughout the early 1920s.[77] When his insistence on more coverage of racial issues caused a rupture with his former white left colleagues on the *Liberator,* he broke with them but strengthened his pro-Bolshevik stance. And for years after the novel appeared, he averred that Jake was "class-conscious."[78] Yet the decision not to radicalize Jake beyond his announcing that he will not cross a picket line or live off a woman results in an ideological impasse. Jake's decision to leave Harlem with Felice for a presumed job mecca, Chicago, may be an act of self-definition, although the reader cannot ignore the symbolism of the city as the home base for the Pullman Company. In any case, moving to another town hardly constitutes the working-class self-awareness that Jake's creator claimed to believe in.

Of all the authors of the Harlem Renaissance era to acknowledge the work culture of Harlem, Rudolph Fisher came from the most privileged background. He was a graduate of Brown University, an M.D. in 1921 at age twenty-four, seven years before his Harlem novel *The Walls of Jericho* was published. He did not have the odd-job experience of McKay and Hughes. Still he demonstrated the most ironic attitude toward the North's opportunities for rising. He found racial blockage by everyone from do-gooder whites to middle-class blacks to a con man—cast in an earlier story, "The City of Refuge," as a former Pullman porter. In the novel, by contrast, his protagonist, a furniture hauler called Shine, but only by his black peers, has legitimate if unlikely business aspirations. The real ascension, Fisher suggests, is toward self-knowledge. In order to deny the implications of his racist nickname, this African American Joshua must fight himself. When he drops his streetwise, violence-prone façade and acknowledges his own humanity, he conquers his modern Jericho, a brutalized Harlem. Recognizing the bonds of race over class, however, Fisher also uses the novelistic podium to chastise well-off blacks who admire the attempts of white "slummers" to either wallow in or redeem Jazz Age Harlem.

In an attack on the white literary storytellers of "uptown" life, Fisher aims his sharpest arrows at writers like Carl Van Vechten. Fisher had a point. However much he thought he was giving black characters narrative authority, Carl Van Vechten, though defended by prominent black writers like Richard Wright and Wallace Thurman, appended a glossary of "Negro words" to his novel *Nigger Heaven* (1926). Van Vechten also treated the Harlem plot more satirically, as did Eugene O'Neill, both writing before McKay and most of his colleagues. To them should be added the Left-futurist tract play of McKay's erstwhile colleague Mike Gold, *Hoboken Blues* (1927), its good intentions subverted by racist stereotyping not palliated by its Marxism.[79] Before embracing a CP vision at play's end, Gold's Harlem, envied in black Hoboken, is awash in hucksterism and fixated on the money chase. Sharing Gold's satirical attitude toward Jazz Age Harlem but not his radical politics, Van Vechten's *Nigger Heaven* follows the Harlem amours of a former bootblack in a Memphis barbershop. It joins *Home to Harlem,* to which it is sometimes compared, in an attention to black dialect, nightlife, and male sexual unscrupulousness. O'Neill's *Emperor Jones* (1921) finds pathos in the fall of Brutus Jones ("ten years on de Pullman ca's"). This was despite the fact that he seeks out Harlem as a chain-gang escapee who has murdered a man in a crap game, ends up a self-proclaimed ruler on a Caribbean island, and dies, apparently by his own hand, rather than give himself up to colonial authority.[80] Though they could not condone Gold's leftist minstrel show, McKay, Hughes, and others defended the Van Vechten and O'Neill texts against charges of racism. At the very least, the two shifted the dialect venue from the caste-ridden Catfish Row of the white South Carolina novelist Du Bose Heyward's *Porgy* (1925). To modern readers, however, Gold, Van Vechten, and O'Neill all promulgated the uptown slum-visit perception of primitivism against which the Harlem Renaissance authors, mainstream or rebellious, were reacting.

Using the Pullman job and a host of other menial ones, black writers like McKay and Fisher variously displaced or racialized the 1920s plot of disappointed expectations, unfocused rebellions, and lack of commitment to a worker community. In conveying a labor response about "proletarian Negroes" (*Blacker,* 139), these writers struggled with the meaning of literary proletarianism, given the white-dominated labor movement. Others, seeking to restore an African heritage to characters with southern slave genealogies, struggled with the racist overtones of primitivism. David Levering Lewis, perhaps exaggeratedly, called the type a Lenox Avenue version of the Noble Savage.[81] Restoring dignity to the male workforce in *The Blacker the Berry,* Thurman's sometime pair Alva and Emma Lou view their menial work as transient, as does Nella Larsen's Helga Crane in *Quicksand* (1928). But to the degree that these texts are successful "racial art," they hardly embrace embourgeoisement. Instead, they dramatize the odysseys of laboring figures who struggle between the need for freedom and the search for a spiritual home. For women, whether stay-at-homes or migrants, the quest for a stable identity vies, often unsuccessfully, with the geographical and sexual rootlessness and defeated expectations generated by the Great Migration.

The Shadow over Them:
Sexuality, Migration, and Women's Work from *Cane* to "Sweat"

As men were exploring jobs in basic industry in Chicago and elsewhere, the *Chicago Defender,* the most influential black newspaper distributed nationwide, was also luring women to that city by running advertisements for domestics. Servant's work, while it paid two or three times more than in the South, was still compensated at well below what the Women's Bureau deemed subsistence wages. Women who could left domestic service rapidly as they found the better-paid jobs available just after World War I.[82] Still, in the postwar era domestic service in Chicago remained women's largest single occupation, as in other major cities outside the South. More than most urban centers, Chicago also offered predominantly segregated work in stockyards and candy factories, and, occasionally, in commercial laundries and the garment trades, provided immigrants were not available or men had refused the low pay.[83] Some women with more education became that rarity, the black clerical worker, always in black-owned firms.[84] Such positions, as well as the more prestigious work available to a small upper tier of college-trained professional women, did little to alter the fact that by 1930 two-thirds of black female breadwinners still worked in unskilled occupations.[85]

Just as in the Progressive era the white prostitute symbolized the panic over the displacements and dislocations of modernism, the black woman migrant represented the fears of societal disintegration generated by the Great Migration.[86] Black reformers joined white ones to warn of the midwestern and northern cities as gateways to black laboring women's immorality.[87] In an era when the segregated YWCA perceived its mission among blacks as solving the moral "problem" these women posed, white agencies and institutions, black organizations, and sectors of the black bourgeoisie tolled the alarmist bell about the un-Christian lodging house successfully luring single women away.[88] By lodging in places under minimal supervision, such varied groups warned, these African American women, like the white rural and small-town girls far from or without any family, merited the label of the "woman adrift."[89] The distrust of white lower-class women's sexuality was pervasive, yet these women did not have to face the associations with southern promiscuity or concubinage that inevitably marked the discourse on black female migrants. Implied rather than stated, the trope of the black woman as overly sexual permeated sociological studies of young black women.[90]

The sexual associations were extended to those on the fringes of commercialized sex who plied trades in the new consumer culture of entertainments—theaters, dance halls, and picture houses. Working in cabarets particularly blurred the border between performing and commercialized sex, both potentially lucrative employments.[91] The young blues singers who worked as brothel entertainers and sang lyrics that dramatized the defiance and anger of the prostitute's life represented a brazen sexuality also associated with prostitutes: indeed, these singers moved in and out of the sex trade themselves.[92] Finally, in relation to their numbers, a disproportionate number of black women were associated with and encoiled in the sex business.[93] No wonder that in the Locke anthology the sole woman essayist, the rather proper Elise Johnson McDougald, wrote of the "shadow hanging over" black women. While there is no evidence that she read Langston Hughes's satiric fable of the sultry "Luani of the Jungles," published the year after, the story would only have deepened her concern.[94]

If the Locke circle, with its nostalgic vision of the southern rural folk and its celebration of primitivism, had difficulty with the male proletariat of Pullman and Harlem, its difficulties with breadwinning women were even greater. In their minimal contributions to the Lockean vision women also urged blacks to enter professions but said little about the difficulties involved in such a status climb. In its limited selections on the black matriarch, such as Jessie Fauset's playlet "The Gift of Laughter," *The New Negro* carefully extolled her courage and endurance. Instead of the cry for justice at the heart of Langston Hughes's "Song of a Negro Wash-Woman" (1925), Locke chose the pedestrian message of the undistinguished Anne Spencer poem entitled, without irony, "Lady, Lady." Its very old-fashioned structure and formal diction work against its allusion to the work-bleached hands of the black laundress.

It was not only the woman imagined by the *New Negro* who bore little relation to the restless or ambitious women either fleeing the South or marking their discontents within it. The renegade male imaginers of the Harlem Renaissance displayed some of the same ambivalence about black women breadwinners as the watchdogs of the reform element. In eponymous sketches, *Cane* had made a point of eliding the sensuality and essential worth of women like Fern and Karintha, and suggested that the thwarted sensuality of Esther was destroying her. Rural sensuality could eventuate in the tragedy of "Blood-Burning Moon," in which white and black lovers fight to the death over the maid Louisa. Yet, though not without a modern element (the black man rises up and kills the white), the story harks back to the tragic mulatta stories of *Clotel* and women's slave narratives. Southern women are too easily led by emotion; but those who migrate north corrupt themselves.

A Toomer surrogate in *Cane*, as if prophesying the poems of Hughes and the fiction of their contemporaries, claims to want an art that would open the way for women the likes of "those who left the South" (46). But in the lingering Victorian formula, the women who are his northern refugees are either puritans or sluts. Thus Toomer can moralize about women who take "life easy" (*Cane*, 44) in the North. In this he builds on Victorian strictures about prostitutes summed up in the subtitle of Henry Mayhew's classic study of street crime, *London Labour and the London Poor* (1851), as *Those Who Do No Work*. Toomer makes little distinction between the woman for hire on Chicago's State Street and the married woman, dissatisfied but financially supported, who inhabits a Harlem tenement (15). Toomer extends the castigation to women entertainers like Dorris ("Theater"), who eyes the rich men in the audience.

Wallace Thurman, another chronicler of migrant women's sexuality, extended and deepened Toomer's observations. He established his political radicalism as a managing editor of the *Messenger* in 1925 and as a literary editor of *Fire!!* (1926), the short-lived counterthrust to *The New Negro,* to which he also contributed a short story, "Cordelia the Crude." Still jousting with the Harlem Renaissance group, he offered a biting satire on the Locke circle in the novel *Infants of the Spring* in 1932.[95] His contribution to *Fire!!* is of particular interest, both in fleshing out Toomer's observations about female migrants and in anticipating his own most fully realized Harlem novel, *The Blacker the Berry* (1928).

"Cordelia the Crude" sketches a discontented teenage girl minding the siblings of her disorganized Harlem migrant family. Her work choices, as Thurman represents them, are a white kitchen or a black brothel. Already a living embodiment of the "girl problem," in a year or two of promiscuity, drugs, and drink, she may join those lamented in the sociologist William Isaac Thomas's *The Unadjusted Girl* (1928) and E. Franklin Frazier's *The Negro Family in Chicago* (1932). These studies catalog cases of young black women whose paid promiscuity was punctuated by appearances in night court and stays in New York State's Bedford Hills Reformatory. Again, like them, once released Cordelia may sink deeper into the sordid business of selling sex.

In *The Blacker the Berry,* Emma Lou, older than Cordelia, more level-headed, more educated, and from a stable family in Indiana, receives a more positive portrayal, perhaps because her work history intersects at points with Thurman's own. Like Emma Lou, Thurman went to college, though he did not finish, and he also lived in Harlem working at low-level jobs, despite his college training. Like her creator, Emma Lou expects to mingle with "the right sort of people" (*Blacker,* 79) and has class prejudices about the lower element in migrant Harlem (90). Thurman, who wrestled with his own racial identity, identified with the frustration that builds up in Emma Lou because of her dark skin. She is passed over even for a "stenographic position in some colored business or professional office" (69) and jilted by the light-skinned men she craves (79). Furthermore, Thurman implies that she projects vocational disappointments onto her quest for love and sex. Having by novel's end climbed from debasing experiences and relationships to teaching in the schools, she experiences the spiritual hollowness of many of the white-collar strugglers in the works of the ethnic novelist Anzia Yezierska.

For the bulk of the novel, though, Emma Lou has a good deal in common with Cordelia. Even in college prior to Harlem, she is restless and antagonistic, unwilling to meet family obligations. Arrived in the black mecca, she becomes promiscuous, scorns the "lifting as we climb" thinking of the local YWCA, and is thrown out of her furnished room for not being a "respectable woman" (196). Thurman even plays on the idea that the "lodger evil" of taking a room without appropriate guardianship contributed to her downfall.[96] Returning to her senses by reclaiming her middle-class attitudes, she jettisons her "sweetman," whom she has supported on a servant's wages, finds a room at the Y, a teaching job in Harlem, and "salvation within [her]self" (225). Significant to the Toomer-Thurman perception of women workers, Emma Lou throws off identification with other exploited women as forcefully as she does promiscuity. Escape from drudgery, then, means renouncing the female working class as well.

Read in the context of Toomer and Thurman, McKay, ostensibly less prudish about both "street floaters" (*Home,* 83) and women who are servants by day and sexual by night, reveals a similarly negative confluence of sex and class. He extolls Felice for returning money to Jake Brown, a client she loves, but despises the cook Susy for searching out a man to support and sleep with, and throwing him out when he is unfaithful. It is no accident that McKay dubs her the "hideous mulattress" (*Home,* 69). Even in Rudolph Fisher's "Blades of Steel" (*Atlantic Monthly,* August 1927), the Harlem beauty-parlor employee who gives her lover a razor to fend off another lover fares better: she may be carrying a concealed weapon, but she is standing by her man.

Of the black women writers who provided alternative voices of black female labor, Zora Neale Hurston, whose story "Sweat" appeared in the sole issue of *Fire!!,* is the most interesting. Like her earlier *New Negro* tale "Spunk," "Sweat" builds on the folklore research she conducted in the South, Jamaica, and Haiti. Yet it is distinct from the 1925 tale in drawing, however obliquely, on her observations of women's jobs in Eatonville, Florida, and on her own early 1920s work life in city jobs ranging from maid to manicurist. The sweat in question is that of Delia Jones, a laundress with a shiftless philanderer for a mate. Always ready to beat or desert Delia, he finally attempts to kill her by planting a snake in her laundry basket. In an ending even more punitive of rural male gadabouts than "Spunk," Delia leaves the snake where its fangs will sink into her husband's flesh. She listens, unmoved, to his dying pleas for aid. Shifting the locale of female self-subordination, unreliable men, and women's need for a living wage from the metropolitan black North to the southern backwater, Hurston reverses the migration plot to castigate the masculine flamboyance touted in the Great Migration fiction of male authors.

Hurston's version of the Pullman maid, all but invisible in the male labor novel, acts with surprising ferocity. Not so the Chicago migrant washerwoman who appears in Marita Bonner's *Crisis* story "Drab Rambles" (1927). An emblem of the intertwining of sexual and economic debasement, Madie's work is at one of "thirty tubs and [as one of] the thirty women at the tubs."[97] Elsewhere in the story Bonner recognizes that Madie's suffering is shared with no-hope janitors and ditchdiggers. But what scars her life is her white employer's sexual assault, her silence about it to keep her job, and the difficulty of supporting the child born of that rape. The work destiny of the mulatta character Helga Crane in Nella Larsen's *Quicksand* (1928) is also gender-defined, although she is far better educated than the heroine of Edith Summers Kelley's *Weeds* (1923). Helga plummets to a similar kind of undesirable childbearing, a loveless marriage, and rural poverty, concluding, like Bonner's Madie, that endurance alone will be her triumph.

However women authors rearrange the fictions of their male counterparts, they find no Harlem antidote to blasted aspirations, and no escapist culture to soothe the soul of the laundress, the Black Belt mother harassed sexually at work, or the southern woman returned from the North. What they offer instead is a vision of salvation through economic freedom from men. This message is not articulated, as in white women's 1920s texts, as the toll taken by white-collar female success. Rather, looking backward to a Crane or Norris and forward to the Depression-era experience (Bonner was included in *Writing Red*, a 1987 anthology of women's fiction from the 1930s and 1940s), these proto-feminist work fables do not so much sing the blues as herald the female proletarian. Discarded are men's terms like "crude" ("Cordelia the Crude") or "ginned-up" (*Home*, 109). What has not killed these women has indeed made them stronger.

The View from the Mid-1930s: Notes on the Great Migration in William Attaway and Ralph Ellison

The early years of the Depression not only brought a close to the Harlem Renaissance era but laid the groundwork for the formation in 1935 of the Committee for Industrial Organization (CIO; later Congress of Industrial Organizations), which made it a policy to organize black workers. Linking the Locke circle and the mass organizing drives was the prolabor critique that a writer like Richard Wright brought to his scathing reconsideration of *The New Negro*. His 1937 essay "Blueprint for Negro Writing" called on the new black writers to replace the art of Locke's circle with "writing for the Negro masses" that reflected their drive toward unionism and reaction against the "harsh conditions of their lives."[98]

William Attaway and, in two recently discovered stories, Ralph Ellison, later of *Invisible Man* (1952) fame, were two of the new African American writers who looked back to the previous decade in order to tell a 1930s story. From the vantage point of the Committee for Industrial Organization era, their representations of black labor during the Great Migration offer a perspective not only on the Harlem Renaissance constructions of the folk at work but also on the oppositional plots of McKay and others.

In 1927 Attaway rebelled against the aspirations of his parents, Talented Tenth Chicago migrants, rebelling in 1927, by attending vocational high school; he continued his association with working-class people into the Depression era.[99] With the goal of being an eyewitness historian of the economic upheaval, he was by turns a mechanic, vagabond, seaman, salesman, and labor organizer. To professionalize his writing, he was also a college graduate, and an employee of the Chicago Federal Writers' Project (through which he met Richard Wright). Attaway celebrated his dual allegiance to class and to literature in 1939 when, on a grant, he wrote a historical novel of the Great Migration.

At once factual and dramatic, *Blood on the Forge* (1941), set in a western Pennsylvania mill town in 1919, is a social realist backward look at the Great Steel Strike of 1919 and the traditional divisions between white workers and black strikers. Except for a black local of the Amalgamated Association of Iron and Steel Workers, blacks not only were excluded from but shunned steelmen's unions for decades before and after the strike. As Attaway well knew, however, by 1939 thousands of blacks had joined the AFL splinter group the

Congress of Industrial Organizations and the left-led Steel Workers Organizing Committee (SWOC).[100] From the vantage point of the New Deal era, then, Attaway rewrote the early labor history of the Great Migration. In the factory story no writer of the Harlem Renaissance era told, he exploded the chimera of opportunity, revealed the corruptions of leisure culture, and argued for the interracial working-class solidarity that eluded even the most committed 1920s author.

The novel locates a world of migrant history in the story of the Mosses (suggesting their reluctance to join the move northward), three Kentucky half-brothers, recruited by a labor agent and hired by a mill for the most dangerous work. All are impoverished, unskilled, gullible, and ready to leave. The fugitive Big Mat (he killed a white overseer in a rage) symbolizes those pulled into interracial confrontation and flight from the lynch mob. Violence will be his lot in the North as well as he moves through identities as an interloper, a quasi-friend of nonunion Irish, a scab deputy for management, and, in his dying moments, a man awakened to the good fight. His half-brother, a Chinatown musician, stays out of work and out of the strike but later falls victim to an industrial accident, so common in the mills, and is blinded. Melody, also a musician, brings his blues heritage north but permanently injures his guitarist's hand. Other racial or ethnic figures carrying psychic wounds include a Mexican prostitute, who loves and leaves Mat, and the white Slav strikers who fall to company guns.

As a revision of the Pullman-to-Harlem labor fiction of the Harlem Renaissance era, *Blood on the Forge* presents a far grimmer landscape. But the industrial picture is more complex than in the earlier fiction. By venturing out of a ghettoized Harlem or a self-ghettoizing Pullman world, black workingmen make themselves as vulnerable as in the interracial South. There is another way to read the interracial emphasis in the novel. The acceptance of blacks in nonunion ethnic circles and Mat's awakening, though too late, to his manipulation by management suggests interracial labor interests, an analysis bolstered by the Party's high point in recruiting blacks, including Attaway himself.[101]

The novel opens a new chapter in texts of black labor's response to racism. As a "bottom dogs," or down-and-out novel, it is informed by a sense of both 1930s privations for all workers and black labor problems in basic industry. By looking backward, however, it adds a retrospective dimension to the post-war New Negro movement. Refusing to treat black workers in Harlemite isolation from the white labor movement, Attaway turns earlier work into precursory text even as it adds a needed finale to the work of McKay and his contemporaries.

Ralph Ellison viewed Attaway's novel through a post-Depression lens, finding the book powerful but insufficiently optimistic about the course of interracial unionism after the Great Migration.[102] Nevertheless, in selections from his own retrospective fiction Ellison provides a post-Migration coda to Attaway. In the late 1930s, Ellison wrote two important stories (only published in 1996) set in the 1920s, "Boy on a Train" and "I Did Not Learn Their Names."[103] Briefly summarized, in the first one, a migrant family, riding in a

Jim Crow baggage car with a coffin, represents the defeated hopes of all migrant families. In the second, an interracial hobo tale set in the Depression, the Great Migration has been replaced by the aimless movement of the nation's unemployed. Taken together, the two signal an irony crucial to the Great Migration: blacks in transit should place little hope in their destination.

The Black 1920s and the Representation of Work

The most laudatory rereadings of the Harlem Renaissance find it a social and cultural movement that attempted to understand the new black urbanization without denigrating Harlem as the new home of a peasant proletariat. Yet it is telling that such revisioning elides the contributors to *The New Negro* with those who soon became its opponents.[104] For it was, I argue, only those renegades who created the first real African American urban labor fiction prior to the Great Depression.

Even so, their body of work revealed an uneasy literary balance between race and class issues. To varying degrees, the new black authors admired the vibrant Harlem, always in transit, disdaining the time clock and the bourgeoisie, even as they experienced the marginalization such a philosophy generated. Ambivalent about their characters' adjustment to industrial time, McKay, Fisher, and Thurman focused not on black assembly-line workers wed to the rigid certainties of Fordism but on a working class in motion: Pullman porters, Harlem roustabouts (or wild women), southern refugees, or all three. Others, such as Toomer, Hurston, and Bonner, bypassing the lure of Harlem, wrote of workers encoiled in the dead-end South or the no-hope midwestern Black Belt. Thus rather than addressing the black proletariat, these writers created worker figures whose very ambiguity—rebels or marginals, role models or outlaws—was both a metaphor for the African American labor situation of the time and a projection of their own difficulties in according the black masses full respect.

Jon-Christian Suggs observes that the struggle to define and ensure their legal status—to be allowed the full participation of citizens—dwarfs all other existential dilemmas in literature by and about American blacks before the Harlem Renaissance period.[105] If one applies that generalization to the labor text prior to the rise of black trade unionism, what emerges is a predictably alienated black working class. Yet it is equally clear that these texts give voice to a new social type, the streetwise urban workingman and -woman of the urban Black Belt, who carves or craves a dignified self from peers that he (or, less often, she) cannot find in the larger world of whites. Their resentment of white employers stymied or forbidden, they displace their frustration onto sometimes violent social interactions.

In flight themselves from the aestheticism of Locke, the creators of these restless urbanites neither paper over the migrant "folk" nor romanticize their psychic displacement in northern ghettos. These authors, distrusting the "new" black as much as traditional whites, neither transform their migrants economically nor advance them politically. Variously rejecting or adding complexity to white writers' sensual, exotic, or subservient black, they offer no Noble Migrant. As their porters, furniture haulers, janitors, cooks, and prostitutes put on and take off the servile mask, they urge their characters to forgo the masquerade altogether.

To an extent, black male authors joined female authors to break down dichotomies between honest versus well-paid feminine labor, between womanly virtue and sexual waywardness. From McKay to Fisher, portraits of urban men's assertiveness and search for identity did not, though, produce a corollary scrutiny of the female urban proletariat. There were only a few proto-feminist women writers, with Hurston in the vanguard. As self-exiles from a masculinist Harlem, they widened the definitions of "home" and "work" to include exploitive child rearing as well as demeaning service work, unstable husbands as well as harsh employers.

Not before the new decade would labor fiction truly break down oppositions between "Negro" and "workingman" or acknowledge that women's wages, not their morals, were often the bedrock of the family. The African American worker as a literary subject would take a new direction after the American entry into World War II. Old issues of disenfranchisement and deprivation, dreams deferred and hopes dashed, would be energized by texts in which anger intensified to rage. For decades to come, the migration to new homes and new jobs woven into the labor texts of Harlem Renaissance fiction would be the cornerstone of an increasingly confrontational fiction about the African American dream.

CHAPTER 9

Heroic at Last
Depression Era Fictions

The compulsion of these men [Gold, Conroy, and others] to write of the life of the working class was rooted in the memory of their own life in it.

—ALFRED KAZIN, *ON NATIVE GROUNDS* (1942)

"There ain't any more Alger heroes now."

—JACK CONROY, *THE DISINHERITED* (1933)

"I'm just a black guy with nothing."

"All I do is work [she cried], work like a dog! From morning to night. I ain't got no happiness. I ain't ever had none. I just work! . . . I just work. I'm black and I work and don't bother anybody."

—RICHARD WRIGHT, *NATIVE SON* (1940)

William Gropper. *Automobile Industry*. Mural study, Detroit, Michigan, post office, 1940–1941. Oil on fiberboard, 20⅛ x 48 in. National Museum of American Art, Smithsonian Institution.

Working-class discontent, comments Robert S. McElvaine in his important study of America between 1929 and 1941, "ebbs and flows with prosperity and depression."[1] One of the ironies of the Depression period was that it gave rise to a more inclusive mass unionism than the country had ever witnessed. A brief review of a work history already much recounted is in order. Among those agitating in the early 1930s, the jobless Bonus Marchers of 1932, the Latino and Asian California migrant workers of the Cannery and Agricultural Workers' International Union (CAWIU), and the black and white members of the Southern Tenant Farmers' Union (STFU). They and groups like them helped pave the way for protest during Roosevelt's first New Deal.[2] In heavy industry as early as 1931, United Mine Workers' protesters in pinched Pennsylvania and Kentucky heralded the early decade's dramatic Amalgamated Clothing Workers strike in 1932 in New York City's garment center. Though not yet infused with the energy lent by section 7(a) of the 1933 National Industrial Recovery Act (NIRA), 1934 saw general strikes on the docks of San Francisco and impressive protests in midwestern trucking and southern textiles.[3] Such activity was obviously also bolstered by the Communist Party's militant Third Period (1928–1934) work among white as well as black small farmers and tenant farmers. Party organizers often worked effectively with the unemployed and as dual unionists in coal, auto, steel, and textiles.[4]

By 1935 the Communist Party, though building on its participation in the wave of strikes that marked the first half of the decade, followed the new Comintern policy and shifted to the United or Popular Front (1935–1939). Such cooperation with non-Communist organizations, a transient partnership best fictionalized in Ruth McKenney's *Industrial Valley* (1939), would usher in the far more permanent Congress of Industrial Organizations. Formed in a breakaway spirit from the American Federation of Labor, the CIO's new unionism enveloped the old issues of shop-floor control and speedups in a dedication to a militant pragmatism. In its increased efforts to organize workers on an industrywide basis, the CIO spearheaded drives to erase the old distinctions between skilled and unskilled, white and black, male and female. There were important strikes in the rubber-making industry in Akron, Ohio, in 1935–1936, the next year in Illinois steel, and the year after that in automotive Detroit in the Flint Sit-Down Strike.[5] These and allied labor protests in glass, electrical appliances, and textiles during the second New Deal gained mightily from the newly established collective bargaining of the 1935 Wagner Act and the National Labor Relations Board (NLRB). For the first time workers found government on their side against employers.[6] Revisionist historians point out that only 7 percent of American workers engaged in militant protest at the height of the Depression. But it was the perception of rank-and-file unionism that mattered to government, big business, and the rising new constituencies gathered under the CIO umbrella—four million strong by the late 1930s—as well as to the many labor novelists of the day.[7]

As the onrush of unionism met the economic maelstrom—one-quarter of American workers unemployed, and the same number underemployed at its lowest ebb—authors paid the working class a long overdue homage. This brief historical moment was an unprecedented occasion for worker-writers to turn their own lived experience into an art that privileged a host of other labor figures as well. Such storytellers wrote themselves and their class into what was loosely termed proletarian fiction. Jack London, writing in the socialist journal *The Comrade,* had employed the term "proletarian fiction" as early as 1901.[8] But for decades it largely referred to prolabor novelists and storytellers with some allegiance to the middle class or to authors of more ephemeral pieces (see chapters 5 and 7). But the 1930s saw a true "school" of literature in which individualist was replaced by the group ethic, and practitioners included prolabor novelists from the middle class. Race, ethnicity, gender, and politics joined class to divide a Mike Gold from a John Steinbeck, a Richard Wright from a Zora Neale Hurston, a Thomas Bell from a D'Arcy McNickle, and a Ruth McKenney from all of them. Whatever their class origins, this new generation acknowledged debts to predecessors like Rebecca Harding Davis, Stephen Crane, Theodore Dreiser, and Upton Sinclair while shedding the condescension that had characterized a century and a half of U.S. labor fiction.[9] Now texts riveted on the economic crisis of the 1930s could look back to formative labor events and forward to a workers' world.

Cultural representation, from the early decade's manifestos and congresses of Party-affiliated writers to the unionist musical theater of the United Front era, had never before been so intimately involved in promoting labor struggle. Examples abounded. The devoted CP journalist Tillie Lerner Olsen, at work on a labor novel herself, passionately described the San Francisco longshoremen who in 1934 fomented confrontation with the repressive authorities on the Embarcadero.[10] If not all observers were so awed by militant workers, gone was the philanthropic Protestant morality that had guided the Progressive Era's Pittsburgh Survey of heavy industry. A driving prolabor spirit infused worker-writers like Jack Conroy, who wrote and published bulletins during actual strikes. Meridel Le Sueur, under the Works Progress Administration (WPA), produced writing pamphlets and gave group lessons for Minneapolis workers.[11] Tom Tippett covered mine strikes for the *American Mercury* and authored the mining novel *Horse Shoe Bottoms* (1935).[12]

A far cry from John Reed's meticulously stage-managed Paterson strike pageant of 1913, another workers' college, Commonwealth, performed class-based music in its traveling road shows. So did garment trades' locals on Broadway itself, and even in the White House, in the CIO era.[13] Collaborations of a sort issued from professional novelists of the 1929 Gastonia Textile

Strike (which also inspired a worker-produced film). Mary Heaton Vorse, for instance, like the CP literary organ the *New Masses,* reprinted the folk poetry of Ella May Wiggins in her novel *Strike!* (1930). And a now-forgotten University of Michigan graduate student taught writing to the 1937 Flint strikers, who wrote their own plays during the course of the strike.[14] Finally, by the late 1930s, writers like Nelson Algren, Richard Wright, and Zora Neale Hurston had formalized still other interactions. They conducted WPA interviews in urban and rural sites with everyone from prostitutes to tenant farmers.

These and other prolabor writers shared the realization that the term "worker," even when prefaced by a racial, ethnic, or gender descriptor, could no longer be monolithic. For the first time in American literature, a truly wide landscape emerged, peopled by sharecropping blacks, Mexican farmworkers, Dust Bowl migrants, Detroit autoworkers, men in lumber, men in sweatshops, and women in canneries, peafields, homes, and commercialized sex venues.

Then and now, definitions of this elusive subgenre have focused less on depictions than on authorial credentials for revolutionary art. There were but a few years between Mike Gold's groundbreaking call for worker-writers and the lengthy 1935 manifesto of the American Writers' Congress. During that time, Party regulars, leftist critics, and labor authors from the rough-hewn to the sophisticated searched for a form and content that would animate the new ideology of collective goals, pragmatic militance, and the growth of working-class consciousness. As Edwin Seaver wrote approvingly in the *New Masses,* one of the chief journals dedicated to advancing proletarian fiction, these groups urged writers to use the novel to "accelerate the destruction of capitalism and the establishment of a workers' government."[15]

Such a dictum, which privileged novels of men in heavy industry, was at odds with the CP's emphasis on inclusive treatments of labor oppression. The critic and publisher Harold Strauss even argued that so doctrinaire an agenda propelled the proletarian novel into a sterile photographic realism, a dreary pessimism, or the antipuritanism of the disillusioned bourgeois. Strauss gave a much broader definition of the form. "Proletarian literature," he urged, rather than offering political representatives of the working class and its revolutionary aspirations, "must recognize all forms of human motivation." Thus it "should not be any particular kind of novel at all in respect to technique, but simply a novel that expresses a specific world view."[16] There should be a distinction, however, between the proletarian novel and the social novel. David Peeler aptly classifies the latter form, practiced by Steinbeck and others, as one that celebrates the common man but is resistant to "politically dogmatic solutions to workers' problems."[17] For the purposes of this chapter, proletarian novels, in contrast, advocate class consciousness. They also encompass the various strike, coming-of-age, conversion, bottom dogs, middle-class decay, and hybrid versions of Walter Rideout's still-valid categories in *The Radical Novel in the United States* (1956), just as these forms were hardly restricted to the white male factory worker.

In the hands of a Steinbeck, Le Sueur, or many lesser lights, working folk were far from the walking clichés of proletarianism derided by naysayers from the New Deal era to the post–cold war present.[18] Carla Cappetti points out that the 1930s writers, who worked within a loosely naturalistic form and contributed to this important chapter of American literary tradition, continue to be treated dismissively.[19] To this day, proletarian fiction provokes condescension, scorn, or erasure in most critical quarters, and even a 1972 essay praising a writer of the caliber of Gold makes the astonishing statement that he is "a wart on the buttocks of American literature."[20] But a new group of revisionists has arisen to reread the work novels of the 1930s rather than engage in a taxonomy.[21] To Paul Lauter, 1930s fiction is an "art of hunger and fear, of protest and search, of old anger and fresh hope."[22] Barbara Foley and Alan Wald argue that fiction by leftists liberates as much as it delimits, transforming a shifting CP doctrine to give rise to local expression.[23] And to Michael Denning, the bulk of 1930s protest fiction is regional narrative, the occasion for ethnography and an excavation of working-class values. Finally, Marcus Klein asserts that the very indeterminacy of the "forgotten man" made for almost infinite literary possibilities.[24]

All of these interpreters, furthermore, reject the old charges that left fiction is eviscerated by doctrine, that it bypasses race, gender, and ethnicity, or that it is at odds with literary experimentation. Thus the best explicators of the 1930s work novel steer clear of both pre- and post-HUAC denunciations, on the one hand, and exaggerated claims for proletarian authenticity, on the other. Yet there remains a need to widen their discussion. For one thing, texts are now engaged in a variety of appropriations of earlier plots, devices, and labor events with a new awareness that novels must no longer neglect or suppress the voices of the workers themselves. How did the best social realist art both incorporate and transcend narrative devices and favored tropes of the past? In many 1930s novels, mentor figures appear.[25] To what degree do they break with the elitist participant-observer of so much previous fiction? Particularly in novels by or about racial minorities and women, the representations of earlier decades had recapitulated other elitist prejudices or come to impasses. To what extent did the new authors, whether they issued from the group described or not, now enable the protagonists to tell their own stories?

American exceptionalism, with ideologies of mobility that were so central to a long line of fiction prior to the Depression, raises a final set of questions: How well did the decade's literary defenses of laboring people reorganize the working-class experience? Could plots integrate the revolutionary energies of the Left into a New Deal context? Did these novels rely on or make up for the dearth of a proletarian literary tradition? Did they echo the working-class voices or the Proletcult ones? If American writers never fully imitated Soviet models, what fiction arose to recast a fragmentary U.S. radical literary tradition to democratize class struggle and reshape old visions of rising?

Attempts to answer all of these questions must begin with the earliest pair of writers to transform the worker sketch into the proletarian bildungsroman, Mike Gold and Jack Conroy.

Tradition and the Proletarian Talent:
Honoring the Fathers in Depression Era Storytelling,
1930–1935

In July 1928 the new editor of the *New Masses,* Mike Gold, issued a call in his journal for the "working men, women, and children in America to do most of the writing."[26] Even before the Great Crash of 1929, Gold was aware that social protest texts by American workers would have a far more populist and even sentimental ring than Russian models.[27] Certainly, U.S. authors would find little inspiration in classics of socialist realism like Fyodor Gladkov's *Cement.* Issued serially in Russian in 1925 and available in translation a few years later, it brought deadly earnestness and Proletcult energy to the story of a 1920s workers' takeover of a cement factory. Bypassing models he knew to be inapplicable, Gold called for stories by and about revolutionary workers in America.

However much the ensuing months proved a "bonanza for worker literature," the early writers from labor origins were few on the ground.[28] To be sure, there was a flowering of militant worker-correspondents in journalism. As early as 1929, H. H. Lewis and Joseph Kalar intertwined Wobbly and CP philosophies in their labor-lore contributions to the Party organ, the *New Masses.*[29] But it was Sherwood Anderson, who was middle class in background, not T-Bone Slim, who influenced worker-correspondence pieces. Among these were M. L. Batey's *American Mercury* piece, "One American's Story" (September 1929); short stories such as those collected in George Milburn's *Oklahoma Town* (1931); and novels like Idwal Jones's *Steel Chips* (1929), clearly derived from D. H. Lawrence and the U.S. literary tradition of the gentleman worker. Of the early worker-writers, with the possible exception of Louis Colman, there were very few who could make the transition from the journalistic to the fictionalized piece.[30] Chief among them were two vastly different men of working-class origin, Mike Gold and Jack Conroy.

The two quickly amassed impressive Communist Party militant or Third Period (1928–1934) credentials. By 1930 Gold had participated in the important Charkov Conference, whose purpose was to form a program for a proletarian cultural movement in the United States, and he had been published under Comintern auspices. Conroy's "Hoover City" (1935) would soon be published by the English-language magazine of the International Union of Revolutionary Writers (IURW), *Literature of the World Revolution.*[31]

Though not so stated, the literary issue was how to write oneself into the narrative without sacrificing what Mike Gold called "rebel things" and the "hard facts of proletarian life."[32] It is not so much that autobiography requires or engenders a certain sentimentality. But its focus on the vicissitudes of the self can be at odds with a more revolutionary agenda. Gold's *Jews without Money,* joined by Jack Conroy's *The Disinherited,* soon became models for pieces by actual working-class writers in U.S. Proletcult circles such as the John Reed Clubs and ancillary networks of worker-writers from New York to Chicago to San Francisco. Selected early versions of *Jews without Money,* parts of which Gold, heeding his own call, had published in the *New Masses* in the late 1920s, seemed in many ways ideal.[33] Overlaid with a spiritual ethnography of his parents' shtetl generation, Gold's novel captured popular attention, and the publisher ordered eleven printings between February and October of 1930.[34] The novel met acclaim in the *New York Times* and the *Saturday Review,* both prestigious periodicals moved by Gold's poetic treatment of poverty.[35] Conroy's *The Disinherited* was also one of the most successful responses to Gold's call for worker art, witnessed by its partial publication in the *New Masses* in the early 1930s as well. Published in book form in 1933, in its positive reception by the mainstream and CP press it too seemed to herald a golden age as "one of the first memorable proletarian novel[s] of the decade," even though its sales were modest.[36] But to what extent had their novels solved the formidable problem of dispensing with a bourgeois narrator and his ascensionist values?

In his fictive recovery of the father by the proletarian son, Gold spent the bulk of his story on the same working-class milieu of his own youth and of his father's maturity. This semiautobiographical coming to terms with his own working-class origins required that he understand the tyranny of the success ethic on working people. Herman, a sympathetic and vocal stand-in for Gold's own parent, reiterates, "twenty years in America and poorer than when I came" (301). As an organizing device, the father's very lament for the lost promise of America enables the proletarian bildungsroman to place the Other center stage. Proletarian authorship now required a strong emotional connection to the worker-father and a movement toward solidarity with labor rather than economic and psychic superiority to it. The plot of the fallen patriarch, dreaming of a comeback, had been a vestige of the labor novel as far back as George Lippard's urban Gothics. What is dramatically altered is the exploration of downward (and later, for the son, lateral) mobility at the core of the book.

To fulfill goals both aesthetic and ideological, the novel's formal properties involved placing the labor remembrances of the father in the son's narrative. Thus the beginning vividly looks back on "Mikey's" observations of his milieu. The conclusion is his hard-won militance in the early Depression. In the rest of the novel, by constant shifts from son's to father's perspective, counterpointed by vignettes of the saintly mother, the novel demonstrates both the continuity of class affiliation and the ideological shifts from one generation to the next.

Gold found his literary front line in the sweatshops and tenements of the Lower East Side, whose grinding predictability made for spiritual restlessness and conflicts between foolishly ambitious Old World fathers and their more streetwise sons. In 1930 he defended his autobiographical father character, Herman, a pushcart peddler attacked by reviewers for his bourgeois psychology. He argued for the father's dramatic disillusionment as "precisely the point of the book."[37] The aesthetic decision to anchor the novel in the story of the father is only given added layers when Herman tells Old World stories of mythic riches to his son.

Like his prototype, Herman began as a small entrepreneur, not a laborer. But as Beth Wenger points out in *New York Jews and the Great Depression*

(1996), both in the 1910s and during the Depression, this figure lived on the economic edge and, in the words of one Gold biographer, "knew what work was."[38] Certainly Herman's business role is short-lived, as, cheated by his partner, he ekes out a proletarian living. The man who by day is an anonymous Jewish housepainter by night helps create the oral culture of smoky cafés and becomes his children's troubadour of Yiddish folk culture. In this fervid atmosphere of "talk . . . Jewish talk, [h]ot, sweaty, winey talk" (116), the only guide is the child who experienced it, now grown to the adult who remembers it and the artist who records it. Vanished is the need for a William Dean Howells reporting on the Jewish socialists or the spirit of the ghetto. Herman himself weaves tales with his lodge brothers (21), tells his children of Roumanian Golden Bears who talk (81), and is sent into ecstasies over Shakespeare performed in Yiddish (87). The pathos of the character issues from his warring identities. By night, the artist, he is eloquent. By day, the proletarian, he is confused by the double vision of the New World as Promised Land and as economic prison that accompanies his attempts to imitate competitive individualism.

The sense of the story as humanizing and individuating, rather than as one that turns the father into the merely pathetic, extends to many of the novel's characters. From Crane to J. W. Sullivan until Gold, most novelists and short-story writers portrayed Jewish working people as laughably avaricious oddities or tragic outcasts. Only with Abraham Cahan and Anzia Yezierska did a liveliness of spirit begin to leaven the portraits of driven and self-driving sweatshop drones. Gold took the next step and infused a life force, lacking in all previous representations, into "ordinary" Lower East Side Jews unable or unwilling to rise. Decoupling the emotionally important character from the conventionally ambitious one, he offered the life of his childhood and adolescence as an argument with God, a debate about the Messiah. His miserly Fyfka, sociopathic Louis One Eye, danger-courting Joey Cohen, and vulnerably holy Reb Samuel the umbrella maker are people whose psychic damage is laid at the door of a fiercely competitive society.

At the end of *Jews without Money*, Mikey simultaneously finds the answer to his father's economic despair and his own political awakening, reconciling the Messiah of his pious mother to fit the economically straitened world his father cannot navigate. Of the Depression era struggle on the Lower East Side, though, he only remarks at novel's end, "it went on for years" (309). The final paragraph, with its shift to 1929, has been criticized as too abrupt.[39] The incident on which the ending is based, an Elizabeth Gurley Flynn rally in Union Square in 1914 when Gold was fifteen, becomes in the finished novel an unnamed political rally of the Depression era. By tying the troubles of one labor generation to another's, the book can reconcile them. Gold was also building on his rather utopian depiction of the CP summer paradise for garment workers depicted in his 1926 *New Masses* sketch, "At a Workers' Vacation Camp." The the finished novel does not detail the idyllic environment of Camp Nitgedaiget or Camp No Worry (later advertised in the *Daily Worker*).[40] But Gold's refrain "O workers' Revolution. . . . O great Beginning!" (309) clearly predicts it.

Conroy also expanded the unitary emphasis of previous worker fiction by sympathizing with as well as transcending the imagined/remembered father's failed relation to financial success. He anchored his otherwise episodic narrative in the psychodrama of the son wrestling with the wishes of a father both economically doomed and fixated on middle-class respectability. Like Gold, Conroy based his character on his own father, a coal miner martyred in an industrial accident. In contrast to the petit bourgeois Herman Gold, Conroy's Tom Donovan is a UMW stalwart.[41] Conroy's protagonist, Larry Donovan, makes peace with his father by undergoing a workingman's odyssey that takes him through a swath of the industrial heartland. There he strives to understand the difficulty of applying his dead father's rigorous moral vision to the labor history of his own time. Compiling a varied manual work history, he travels the country looking for mentors to fill the void left by Tom Donovan's mine death a decade before. His encounters school him in the labor history of the early 1920s. A youthful apprentice in the yards, identifying with the older shopmen who befriend him, Larry observes but cannot fully comprehend the disappointment occasioned by the failure of the great railroad strike of 1922. Midway through the episodic novel, as a novice in a Midwest rubber factory, he asks his seasoned coworker Ed Saunders to help him make sense of this ninth circle of industrial hell.

Just pages before the closing he looks to the last of a series of mentor figures for the restoration of dignity for labor that his father envisioned but did not live to see.[42] In the end, Larry is still completely unformed. As the bewildered young man searches for and listens to a series of flawed mentor figures, they apply a weary cynicism to jobs in the Midwest auto, rubber, and bootleg liquor industry. Larry strives to meet his father's expectations, to be met with the hard truths of the early 1930s:

> "Will I have to work in a factory all my life?" I asked [Saunders]. "What can I build up to in a factory?"
>
> "You might get t' be a foreman. That pays higher that most white collar jobs you'd likely wait years for. I know you got ambitious ideas, kid, but it'll only be an accident if you ever get out of your class. You might as well make up your mind you're a workin' stiff and that you'll stay one unless lightning happens t' strike you—some kind of luck that hits only one out of a million workin' men. You'll work a while, maybe raise a mess of kids, get too old t' work in the factories and hafta sponge offen your kids the rest of your life. It's in the cards, kid. You might as well get used to it and enjoy yourself as much as you can."
>
> I had an uneasy feeling that he was right about this.

Only near the novel's end has Larry finally understood the import of his childhood promise to his father "to be a thief, a murderer, anything, but [never] a scab!"[43]

Ethnography in Conroy generates a small army of flat labor characters that is nothing less than a chorus of worker voices. It is as if he is as much interested in the ancestry of laboring people as in his own father.[44] The novel moves from the paternalistic experience of a pre–World War I Missouri mining camp to the strike-torn Midwest railyards of 1922 to the Fordist Detroit factory. In an experimental spirit, Conroy combines aspects of the previous century's novels of gentlemen workers thrust into real-life industrial strife with this series of work and road stories. Among the Wobblylike travelers, mining camp fixtures, are two eccentrics who serve to link Larry's adolescent surroundings with his factory experience years later. Mike Riordan, given to drunken sprees in Kansas City, returns to the mining camp to sit atop a peg leg, which he uses as a conversation piece when he is not railing at strikers. Joe Vash is similarly strange and almost as feisty. Vash, a Midwest steel-mill worker consigned to crutches ever since a pile of steel careened into him, hobbles after Larry and their fellow workers, "croaking warnings and prophecies of doom like a dyspeptic raven" (144). In contrast to Mike, who is a soothing presence for all his excesses, Joe is a crazed creature whose industrial victimization alienates rather than instructs. Thus is the father-son dynamic of Larry's youth distorted and warped by the transit from mining camp, hard as it was, to the urban factory surround.

At the end of the search for salvation at the heart of so much 1930s fiction, Larry cannot leave his fellow workers behind. He utters the memorable phrase that he will "rise with [his] class" (265). Yet if by so doing he rewrites his father's plans for him, it is to honor him more effectively. In this he is in direct contrast to the spiritually fatherless protagonists of the "bottom dogs" subgenre.[45]

By mid-decade even writers like Edward Anderson and Tom Kromer were distancing themselves from the labor past in a way that Gold and Conroy did not. It is no accident that this shift occurred around the time of the American Writers' Congress. Although it was called, ironically, to celebrate the "revolutionary spirit," Conroy's talk, "The Worker as Writer," was not well received. Gold and Conroy became synonymous with literary primitivism in some quarters and were deemed insufficiently revolutionary in others.[46] Novelists like Isidor Schneider and Daniel Fuchs, loosely following Gold's model, and Robert Cantwell and, to a far greater extent, Tom Tippett, writing in the mode of Conroy, respectively found the debt to the father paid or the paternal legacy far less certain. Schneider's Lower East Side tenement saga *From the Kingdom of Necessity* (1935), in which its Mikey figure vows to renew his ties to the workers, condescended to the old Jewish immigrants for denying their "class destiny."[47] Fuchs's trilogy of teeming ethnic Brooklyn, *Summer in Williamsburg* (1934), reads like a parody of *Jews without Money*. Children inherit a kind of will to despair from their immigrant fathers, an aimlessness only heightened by the harpy-matriarchs who, replacing Gold's benevolent Katey, threaten to castrate and destroy. The Cantwell wood-factory novel *Land of Plenty* (1934) alternates between deploring the activist father's work lot and demonstrating the pitiable heritage he leaves his son, who closes the novel weeping at the failure of the strike. *Horse Shoe Bottoms* is Tippett's historical novel of British coal miners transplanted to Kickapoo Creek, Illinois. Tippett retains Conroy's immense respect for and sadly elegiac memories of a father sacrificed to the greed of capitalist management. Yet the novel is more a hagiography set in an ambiguous coal-mining past of early UMW congresses than a rousing call to 1930s action. The novel addressed the deskilling that had been so central to industrial fiction from antebellum times. If in the post-Gold novel the father was shorn of respect, in the post-Conroy novel the death of the blue-collar union autodidact marked the passing of an artisanal unionism that could not return.

With its melding of potency and despair, *Horse Shoe Bottoms* provided a bridge between the worker-writers of the early decade and those who reshaped proletarian literature in the CIO era. By the New Deal period, the bourgeois desires of the father had melded, however temporarily, with radical interests.[48] It has often been argued that FDR, by using agencies like FERA (Federal Emergency Relief Administration) and the WPA and by implementating the 1935 Wagner Act, enacted many of the utopian proposals of the CP. To a considerable extent it seems that the goals of the CPUSA were those of the American Dream, a secure job, happy family, and assurances against sickness, death, and old age.[49]

In a related development, it was perhaps inevitable that this literary period saw the demise of the father as muse. With the downplaying of authorship and the privileging of perspective as the key distinguishing feature of proletarian literature, the novel of the CIO era was far less interested in following the life script of its creator.[50] The old emphasis on art that roused workers to decisive action now took the form imposed by authors who did not come from the labor class but were pro–New Deal. To be sure, some of these writers reiterated the Gold-Conroy theme of socialist activism as class mobility. In this second phase of the proletarian renaissance, the forgotten man is now remembered, the strike is often victorious, and anger, once unleashed, cannot be deflected.

The Union Makes Us Strong:
The Fiction of the Mass Strikes in the CIO Era

In the years prior to the second New Deal, the CP's militant Third Period disappeared in the United or Popular Front (1935). Leftists joined forces with the proponents of the New Deal and with antifascist groups. With membership on the rise, the Party tried to meld its urgent effort to determine the needs of a largely unorganized working class. They undertook New Deal–style research into the needs of everyone from the jobless to the workers on the speeded-up assemblyline.[51] In this period, before Communists were expelled from many unions, both the CIO and the unaffiliated strikers tolerated CP organizers.

Novels of pre-CIO industrial cities like Detroit, such as Catharine Brody's *Nobody Starves* (1932) and James Steele's *The Conveyor* (1935), follow the despair-or-agitate model endemic to so much Party-allied strike fiction. Ruth McKenney was also a left-leaning novelist, in fact, a Party member. But in *Industrial Valley* (1939), as in the protracted strike she dramatizes, the CIO brand of union is "the answer."[52] After years of dress rehearsals, the workers in Akron had finally gathered strength in February 1936 for a massive occupation of the General Tire and Rubber Company as well as the giant Goodyear factory itself.[53] Some of their demands, such as for a six-hour day to enable more workers to be employed, were identical to those in the CP platform. Others, such as the right to bargain collectively and abolish company unions, were on the CIO agenda.

Despite the influence of both CP and CIO activists, the Akron strike was in many ways a leaderless one. Spontaneous activity on the line shut down the plants. *Industrial Valley* acknowledges what a wide spectrum of strike novels, from Clara Weatherwax's *Marching! Marching!* (1935) to Steinbeck's *In Dubious Battle* (1936), could not. Weatherwax, the Party devotee, altered the facts of a successful Washington State lumber-mill strike to make martyrs of her worker characters. Steinbeck cast his farm laborers as easily manipulated by Party organizers imported for the California labor protest. McKenney subordinated agitprop, whether CP or, for that matter, CIO, to the rare period narrative in which workers discover their own power and events race ahead of union leaders' plans.

McKenney's strategy in her heavily journalistic account is to interweave fictive Everymen with names like Bill Lister and Job Hendrick into events in which anonymous workers spontaneously take the helm. "I ain't no talker" (239), one unnamed rubber worker begins a brief speech. Neither types nor individuals, McKenney's strikers, both invented and observed, interest the reader by their sincerity and situational pragmatism. None of them is impressed by doctrine, and some of them, though veterans of years of job actions, enter the 1936 sit-down strike steadfastly anti-union. From the ordinary tire builders who "stepped back from their machines" (261) to the picket captains on the march outside the factories, McKenney captures the excitement and the uncertainty that so often accompany landmark protests. The narrative does give ample space to the self-satisfied Akron elite, management strategists, workers' anxious wives, Party agitators, and John L. Lewis's UMW and ACW men, come to represent the CIO. All play their parts in this drama of the people of Akron (*Industrial Valley*, 379). But the leading actors are the workers who transform themselves from the disconsolate laborers of the early New Deal to more assertive participants. They weather the sporadic job actions of the ensuing years to become the confident rank and file of the month-long winter 1936 sit-down.

McKenney's admiration for the vox populi has its limits. In her coverage of the strike for the *New Yorker*, she described the most recently hired men as mountaineers unused to shoes and city ways.[54] Her lengthier narrative, however, omits potentially condescending details. Yet new arrivals or not, the Appalachians–turned–Ohio rubber workers are completely unsophisticated compared with their real-life counterparts in the many period oral histories commissioned by the Roosevelt administration. Pittsburgh-area steelworkers, another powerful CIO cadre, were sympathetic to the Akron cause. Unlike the rubber workers, they were Slavic immigrants and their sons. Yet like the Appalachian migrants to Ohio, these men forged factory-floor protest with considerable support from their families and with a pre-union worldview, which generated a similar independence in their relations with the unsatisfactory AFL leadership. As one Braddock, Pennsylvania, mill worker remembered, the old AAISW "wouldn't give us credentials."[55] Both the steelworkers and the Akron strikers, with whom they shared a history of discontent and tough bargaining posture, gave themselves political lessons far more than they learned them from their CIO leaders. And, in final contrast to McKenney's brief agit-prop section, these assembly-liners perceived the CP as insultingly anti-American.

In *Out of This Furnace* (1941), Thomas Bell used such insights about Braddock's stolid Slavic steelworkers and their native-born children to expand the possibilities of the CIO novel. The bulk of his novel explores social stratification, gender relations, and deep fear of American unions, from the 1880s to the Depression era. In so doing, Bell fictionalized the story of three generations of his own immigrant family. His novel honors patriarchs who as a group were far more vivid and far less defeated by industrial life than those of earlier proletarian novelists. Veterans of the nativism of their corrupt Irish American foremen and the horrific conditions of Carnegie's steelworks, they adopt blue-collar philosophies eloquently summarized by Mike Dobrejcak, the novel's stand-in for Bell's own father: "If they'd let me I could love that mill like something of my own. It's a terrible and beautiful thing to make iron. It's honest work, too, work the world needs. They should honor us."[56]

The novel's lengthy final reportorial section details the rise of the CIO and of the Steel Workers Organizing Committee in the Pennsylvania mills. It also narrates how the son of the long-dead Mike, John Doberjack, the family name now Americanized, becomes the kind of workers' representative that McKenney had depicted: a man who does not so much rise from the rank and file as embody it. Yet the novel as a whole is a tribute to CIO ideals. Fifty years of working-class history, rather than an authorial interpreter, seem to dictate its authenticity. Bell is that rare worker-writer who is far less interested in preaching trade unionism than in showing the development of industrial democracy on the work floor.

The novel's final part does pay familiar late-Depression homage to organized labor. Bell celebrates the "C.I.O.! C.I.O.! C.I.O.! . . . [as] a chant, a battle cry shaking the country from coast to coast" (354). Still, John Doberjack, the great-grandson, grandson, son, and nephew of steelworkers and their hard-working wives, summons up their spirits before he leaves for Washington to testify at a Senate hearing on conditions in his plant. Like the novel as a whole, the passage neither romanticizes these forebears nor judges them for their mistakes. It neither satirizes their dedication to upward mobility nor labels as passivity their inability to join political parties of a revolutionary nature. And, though not referring directly to the CIO's drive to organize women workers, it reiterates the feminism of the narrative by commemorating the bravery of the Doberjack women in the face of fatiguing caregiving and the privations of "Hunkietown." In the book's best paean to the CIO, John reflects that his people should have been there to testify because they would have known "what the words meant" and "what was being fought for here" (394).

Honoring the Mothers: Women's Literary Radicalism

Whether one's chronology is first and second New Deal or Third Period and Popular Front, alternative radical fiction by more marginalized groups in the 1930s eludes such sharp periodization—and its thematic movement from bitter outsider to optimistic striker. This is true for women writers in part because of timing. The prominent radical journalists Tillie Olsen and Meridel Le Sueur published parts of their novels throughout the 1930s, while Agnes Smedley saw a reissued edition of her work after 1934. There is a more telling reason, though. Olsen's apprentice warm-ups for an unfinished 1934–1937 manuscript of *Yonnondio;* Le Sueur's short fiction, later collected in *Salute to Spring* (1940), and her published sections of *The Girl* (1939–1945) and related short stories; and Smedley's *Daughter of Earth* disrupt the earth mother myth of their (predominantly) masculine colleagues.

In many of the novels of the era's representative male writers, women are in the home sphere. This was so much the case that feminist critics now see the female working class as a subject not recognized within proletarian realism.[57] By making women invisible members of the workforce, or denying the family the locus of the site of struggle and thus minimizing the importance of marriage, the family, and sexuality, such texts in effect remove women from history. Barbara Foley finds that while some male texts attend to gender issues, other male writers offer a (masculine) bildungsroman of bourgeois individualism. In the conversion to radicalism many of the worker-hero's "exemplary traits express his superior personal qualities rather than the formation of a militant consciousness."[58] When the subject is the coming of age of the hero or group, as is more often the case in 1930s plots, there is little room for a discussion of women's oppression within the family or the workplace. Amy Godine, who adds the social novelist to the proletarian novelists discussed in Rabinowitz and Foley, finds a search for the father in which there is a corresponding resentment of female hegemony.[59]

Rereadings of women writers have discovered that some of the most important texts of worker fiction came from the three radical women writers who told the mother's—and their mothers'—story. For Olsen and Smedley, who came from the working class, their own mothers' burdens provided inspiration. For Le Sueur, inspiration was less personal but no less derived from experience. She taught the female unemployed under the WPA in St. Paul, Minnesota. Whatever their leftist biographies, Olsen, Smedley, and Le Sueur radicalized the maternal plot by documenting the work conditions of the blue-collar domestic sphere.

The CPUSA officially advocated the complete liberation of women as well as men as a culmination of the proletarian struggle. In fiction by male (and some female) authors, woman's domestic chores are seen as a necessary sacrifice until the Soviet model of maternal protection can be put in place in America. Elizabeth Gurley Flynn in *New Masses* called every housewife a heroine.[60] Yet she was always a secondary character in representative male texts such as Edward Newhouse's strike novel *This Is Your Day* (1937). The good

Communist housewife, a bourgeoise with a radical overlay, sees her house-keeping and her Party involvement as twinned duties.[61]

In stark contrast, Olsen questioned the heroine housewife's role by portraying her as psychically scarred and angrily despondent. *Yonnondio* is a vision of the hard-luck Holbrook family's life that wove a pessimism about working-class change with an optimism about the human spirit's resilience. Set in the 1920s, the novel is also a bleak exploration of the blue-collar 1930s. Set in a Wyoming coal-mining town, it moves to a disastrous Dakota farm, and finally the satanic conditions of an urban Midwest, possibly in an Omaha slaughterhouse.

Olsen was a veteran of the slaughterhouse, the food-processing factory, and the hash house who knew the paid work of the woman laborer firsthand.[62] Her very notes for *Yonnondio* list the lower rates of pay women received for meatpacking jobs such as eardrum cutter and head splitter, jobs that in the novel itself are matter-of-factly dubbed those "men will not take."[63]

But the most hopeless job site of all in *Yonnondio* is the home front, where Olsen explores a more troubling form of labor exploitation. Some critics contend that the stay-at-home Anna has the satisfaction of being needed while Jim, frustrated by his out-to-work day, "only needs." They scant the fact that Jim, no stranger to the camaraderie of the neighborhood barroom, can escape the 106-degree factory and Anna's kitchen.[64] His wife is the imprisoned caretaker who cooks the family meals, puts up preserves, possibly to sell, and does other people's laundry in stifling conditions. Jim at least can imagine a strike or another job; Anna cannot plan for herself, and can do so in only a vague way for her children, because she exists in an anguished present. Applying the male focus on paid work to the laborer's own home, Olsen analyzes Anna's house as an unending workplace. In fact, she has the worst of both worlds. Unassisted child tending combines with home laundering, a thankless occupation easily categorized, as well as with her industrial piecework at home, as "bottom-of-the-barrel wage earning."[65]

From Olsen's maternal thwarting and constricted daughterhood it is a relief to turn to the economy of scarcity depicted in Le Sueur. Her published sections of *The Girl* focused on a young waitress's hard-luck lover. The bulk of the manuscript, still incomplete by decade's end, joined other fiction and reportage to center on female strikers, factory, store, and domestic service workers, women on relief, and unwed mothers. Le Sueur is aptly described as the muse of hard-luck midwestern women who form a support system, a sororal network of the disenfranchised. Her 1920s fiction and 1930s reportage describe the problem of the male laborer whose energies are taken up, and frequently depleted, by killing toil; her more famous 1930s fiction invokes a manless solution.

In Le Sueur's more enduring stories, collected in the 1940 *Salute to Spring,* she extolls mothers who never punish their children for their own miseries. "My grandmother raised her own children, my mother hers, and I mine," she wrote in a memoir, an accomplishment that informed much of her writing.[66] Le Sueur's artistic celebration of the solo mother represented its own kind of rebellion against Ma Joadism.

If Le Sueur relocated motherhood outside the patriarchal family, she also indicted a morally intrusive social service bureaucracy. She extolled mothers whose parenting role the patriarchal state tried to usurp ("Sequel to Love," 1935, and "Salvation Home," 1939). And she praised women and children who lived without men in communities or extended families of mothering women ("I'm Going, I Said," 1940; "The Dead in Steel," 1935) or had sometimes been deserted through widowhood ("The Laundress," 1927), though more often through male frailty ("Annunciation," 1935). Finally, in "Biography of My Daughter," a rare but important story of the proletarian daughter as working girl published in the 1935 *American Mercury*, the title character perishes for want of a supportive, not to say militant, women's community.

Daughter of Earth, published in 1929 and reissued in shortened form at the height of the Depression six years later, also balances the heroisms of and mistakes made by working-class mothers.[67] Unlike Olsen and Le Sueur, however, Smedley cast a cold eye on motherhood, both personally and politically, even in a future socialist state. When her early marriage was failing, she chose abortion over childbearing. Both at home and, throughout the 1930s, abroad, she campaigned for birth control, not a central concern of the other two women's texts. Prior to and during the Depression, when Olsen and Le Sueur were covering American labor unrest, Smedley waged her battle for class justice outside the United States, first in Germany and India, then in revolutionary China.

In her occasional ideological skirmishes with left-wing men on her brief visits home, she was less dependent on their good opinion than were Le Sueur and Olsen, who in their Party activities worked closely with male functionaries. Most important, except in some propagandistic pieces to further the cause of the Chinese Revolution, Smedley's fiction and reportage repudiated the mother-daughter bond. Although she acknowledged the emotional cost of this repudiation, her daughter figures wage a battle for separateness that Olsen's and Le Sueur's simply did not.[68]

Daughter of Earth, following Smedley's pre-China life fairly closely, charts Marie Rogers's formative years on a joyless northern Missouri farm and in a squalid Trinidad, Colorado, mining camp. She holds a succession of low-level teaching, sweatshop, and office jobs from New Mexico to New York City. Building on her past, she emerges a radical journalist with an impassioned involvement in the cause of Indian independence. The original novel catalogs Agnes/Marie's emotional and political ties to Indian revolutionaries. The abridged one excises the lengthy Indian section. In both versions, however, the deepest imperatives of the protagonist's life, as of Smedley's own, were to overcome the imprisoning conditions of her mother's existence and, in so doing, shed the negative self-image that the parents had imposed on her. Smedley created in Mrs. Rogers a maternal figure who, despite her ability to pierce through her own suffering to show concern for her daughter's future, is at once manipulative and insidious. Marie, the autonomous worker-daughter, must look to herself for a Good Mother. And so she does, finding herself as a self-supporting journalist committed to revolutionary politics. By the end of both versions of the novel, she considers her own life proof that "a woman who made her own living, and would always do so, could be as independent as men" (189). In the saga of Marie Rogers, selfhood is not only battling the limitations of the mother's life but also choosing the rebel's identity rather than the Good Daughter's.

Nevertheless, the women novelists of the Gastonia Textile Strike also sought to reinvent their relation to a male Left that could accept only a Mother Jones or a rebel girl and otherwise relegated the woman radical to the good comrade, the helpmeet wife, or the picket-line adjunct. The strike itself generated new models. In the mill economy women performed all the household tasks while raising children and plying the night shift at the mill. In fact, the ability to "work like men" and still meet maternal responsibilities was a twinned source of pride.[69]

Yet by 1929 the layoffs, speedups, and protests ushered in by the Depression had already hit the Piedmont South, those remote little towns of Tennessee and the Carolinas where much of the textile industry was concentrated and where women dominated. In Gastonia, for instance, on the morning of April 1, 1929, eighteen hundred of the Manville-Jenckes's Loray Mill's more than two thousand workers left their jobs.[70] Ultimately thirteen mills were affected, and the strike, though lost, garnered international sympathy. Although both the Party organizers who participated in the strike and the male novelists who reported on it saw it as basically a male enterprise, women not only helped spearhead the Loray Mill walkout to unionize the plant that ignited the strike but provided crucial support in their continued activism. The *Daily Worker,* for instance, featured women in front-page photographs as they did battle with "deputy thugs."[71]

When they took up the strike cudgel, Gastonia women fought for more than their family economy. They were also protesting substandard working conditions. The long textile day snatched them and later their teenage children from school to employ them as child labor. No chivalry toward southern womanhood leavened these women's burden. Instead they were at risk of illness from malnutrition to pellagra, the latter a disease that attacked the brain and body functions. Perhaps the unkindest cut was the mill's refusal to let the mothers off of night work, which robbed them of time to tend to their children. Gastonia's white female strikers did not discover a desire for self-definition, pursue individual aspirations, or aspire to a cross-race sisterhood. But precisely because it was a strike in which, though excluding disfranchised blacks, white women could marshal their energies on behalf of the working class, Gastonia appealed powerfully to more doctrinaire, non-Smedleyan exponents of proletarian realism, including the four established female radical writers in question. Their novels fit the flourishing fiction of left-wing thought. The typical Gastonia protagonist, like the heroines of the Communist periodical fiction of the time, "did not seem interested in . . . 'being somebody yourself.' "[72]

The women novelists of the female Gastonia—Mary Heaton Vorse in *Strike!* (1930), Grace Lumpkin in *To Make My Bread* (1932), Dorothy Myra Page in *Gathering Storm: A Story of the Black Belt* (1932), and Fielding Burke (Olive Tilford Dargan) in *Call Home the Heart* (1932)—filtered it through the story of the martyred mill mother and organizer Ella May Wiggins. This real-life woman, felled by a stray bullet as she rallied the poor-white mill hands of the Loray Mill, became known as the "minstrel of the strike."[73] Men's accounts of the Gastonia Strike, fictive and journalistic, represented Wiggins in this fashion because she fit the Mother Jones mold. Otherwise, the focus shifts to Gastonia's supposedly oversexed mill girls, noted in passing in Sherwood Anderson's *Beyond Desire* (1932) and William Rollins's *The Shadow Before* (1934).[74] Yet the women novelists of the strike, seeking a deeper truth, would have to balance this hagiography with Wiggins's unorthodox sexuality as well as her split between parenting her three children, earning a living, and being a strike leader. Feminizing class consciousness, far from swelling men's marches with rebel girls, comrade wives, and women martyrs, led to questioning the very sexual division of labor that seemed to preclude truly communal action.

Whether strictly or loosely following the events, all four, in contrast to the masculine imaginers of the strike, transform a backward handful of worn-out female workers into a corps of women participating eagerly in the revolt of the millhands. The fierce resistance of the women workers inspired descriptions of those like the alternately scratching and cajoling Mrs. (Ma) Gilfillin, "a tiny brown wisp of fury" (141), in Vorse's *Strike!* "Never you mind. We'll be bailed out by tomorrow, 'n back on the picket line," choruses Page's women striker.[75]

Gastonia women writers rebut the familiar period accusations of wage-earning women's censurable conduct in another way. Their mill women see no contradiction between being strikers and mothers. "Come on, women, we're walkin' out for more food for our chillen," proclaims Page's Marge Crenshaw (*Gathering Storm*, 280). But these mother/strikers soon take on an ideological sameness. A faceless group poised for the assault on the National Guard, the mothers are rarely individuated. In fact, it is only with the Ella May Wiggins character or, in a variant, a similarly mythic figure that the four female novelists crystallize women's central contribution to the strike.

Instead, by focusing on the class oppression of the southern mill worker, *Strike!* and the other novels imagine a genderless commitment to labor protest. In so doing, they scant a reality that was inconsistent with the solidarity. Because an elaborate system of male employees controlled the largely unskilled female workplace, in the mill women did not advance.[76] In recollections of mills like Loray, women admitted that "if we had demanded to be supervisors or anything like that, we would have been laughed out of there."[77] This is an awareness apparently denied those like Page's Marge Crenshaw. But there is a push in Gastonia fiction for feminine solidarity via the Ma Joad model. The image of the fiercely determined woman striker founders because of the ideological baggage these novels had to carry. In place of the revolt-minded mill woman was a female militant palatable to the dominant culture.

In 1936, many of the Gastonia novels by women and substantial amounts of fiction by Olsen, Le Sueur, and Smedley had already appeared. That year too the leftist journalist Leane Zugsmith published the once well known *A*

Time to Remember, set in a New York City department store about to erupt in a strike. By the Depression, sales was no longer a career path. Pictured as late as 1929 as a complacent feminine work world it had, at least for nonimmigrant women, lost the luster of its vocational appeal. A victorious strike was waged largely by women employees at Ohrbach's in 1935. Zugsmith might also have found copy in the protests against Macy's and Gimbel's in the early 1930s. Disappointingly, Zugsmith rewards her primary female characters Doni and Aline with the prospect of romantic involvements with union men. Interestingly, the minor female characters Ettie and Maxine, who coauthor the successful collective bargaining agreement that wins the strike (and in an imaginary sequel to the novel might have questioned the sexual division of labor still operating in the stores), are not so rewarded. If Zugsmith's message is that a wage-earning woman must shed psychic dependency in the job and home spheres to become a force for political change, she joins many of the radical women novelists of the day in the difficulty of balancing feminist and leftist aspirations.

No Relief: Richard Wright's Blacks without Money

In an essay describing the protagonist of *Native Son,* "How 'Bigger' Was Born," Richard Wright describes his furious, black, inner-city protagonist, Bigger Thomas, as representing all of the "dispossessed and disinherited."[78] Whether he was alluding to Conroy's novel is unclear, although he was friendly with Conroy and shared his disillusionment with the CP's dogmatic insistence on an inspiring revolutionary art.[79] Wright further defined Bigger's relationship to the exploited of the Great Depression by commenting that he was "not black all the time; he was white, too, and there were literally millions of him, everywhere" (xiv). Yet Wright's novel, though it has been called a proletarian bildungsroman and a novel of the independent Left, acquires crucial clarity as a radical treatment of work and race in the 1930s. In fact, the very reason that Bigger, unlike a Mikey or a Larry Donovan, does not experience a radical political coming of age has everything to do with how Wright both saw and constructed black working-class heroism.

As *Native Son* opens, an unnamed Chicago agency under the umbrella of the New Deal has arranged a job interview for its unhappy protagonist, Bigger Thomas. His mother warns that if he does not take the job, "the relief will cut us off. We won't have any food"(16). Bigger is no stranger to the beginnings of the welfare state. Wright alludes to his time spent at relief stations (60). At the interview for what Bigger terms the "damn relief job" (32), his future employer, the wealthy Mr. Dalton, alludes to a file kept on Bigger by the "relief people" (51). Thanks to the extensive records kept on jobless black youth by Chicago social service agencies, Mr. Dalton knows a great deal of Bigger's case history. The file would have detailed the family's transit from Mississippi five years before in the aftermath of the father's death in a southern race riot, and Bigger's eighth-grade education (74). He would also have known of his theft charge, his stint in reform school, and the agency's optimistic assessment that "you were a very good worker when you were interested in what you were doing" (51). When Bigger is hired for a chauffeur job, he learns that his predecessor "took a job with the government" (56) after years of going to night school. Bigger himself is uninterested in schooling, but his sister Vera is following the job training extended by the local YWCA to impoverished black women in 1930s Chicago: she is learning to sew (12).

Wright, of course, knew about Bigger before Mr. Dalton, and even identified with him to an extent. Wright's 1930s job life did not begin with the clerical, interviewing, and Federal Writer's Project (FWP) assignments of the later 1930s.[80] Depending on the biographical account, like Bigger, he spent some time on relief and did the dirty Chicago jobs of porter and stockyards worker for which Bigger might have been hired.[81] Yet by the time he was at South Side Boys' Club in Chicago's Black Belt, where he himself was "doing a kind of dressed-up police work" (xxvii), he was studying Bigger rather than emulating him. In 1945, when he wrote the introduction to the pioneering *Black Metropolis: A Study of Negro Life in a Northern City* by the University of Chicago–trained sociologists St. Clair Drake and Horace A. Cayton, he was at pains to draw parallels between *Black Metropolis* and his own novel. He characterized the book as one that pictured "the environment out of which the Bigger Thomases of our nation come."[82]

Wright distanced himself from Bigger to explore better the issue of black job dissatisfaction. As the allusion to the Daltons' first chauffeur suggests, white-collar skills could be learned by blacks, and Wright was not the only one to benefit from the public-service jobs given to blacks under the New Deal administration of the National Recovery Act. The fact remains that throughout the thirties there were three or four times as many blacks as whites on relief.[83] Integrationists charged that the New Deal discriminated against black workers in a variety of ways. Under what was nicknamed the "Negro Removal Act," blacks were given more aid than actual jobs. When they did receive relief work, it was not equal to their skills. Southern white landowners were often wrongly allowed to distribute money and jobs in the rural South and to exclude from the purview of government overseers fields of work performed by blacks, preventing them from receiving minimum wage.[84] Interestingly, in Wright's own *New Masses* sharecropping story, "Silt," published in August 1937, when the federal government was well aware of landlord chicanery, his dirt-poor southern black characters might as well have lived in the South of a half century before.

The same critics may well have applauded the CIO organizing drives aimed at blacks in steel, on the docks, and in meatpacking.[85] They would, however, have pointed out that in the historic 1937 Flint Sit-Down Strike, black participation was minimal, and in 1939 both Ford and Chrysler used black strikebreakers to defeat the United AutoWorkers.[86] Such halting progress no doubt issued from the old enmities and continuing discrimination by most AFL unions, if not in the new union movement itself.[87] More modest initiatives, such as the Jobs-for-Negroes movement in the Midwest and the Northeast (its motto was "Don't Buy Where You Can't Work") and the CP drives among the black unemployed in Pennsylvania and Illinois steel, had limited activist successes.[88] Of special relevance to *Native Son* is that CIO recruitment and Party work emanated from Bigger's home city, the home of the Pullman Company, which as late as 1937 held off granting full recognition to the black Brotherhood of Sleeping Car Porters.[89]

Chicago, considered the greatest labor exchange of any city in the United States, had industrialized waves of southern blacks since the days of the Great Migration. But it is no accident that Bigger has no more awareness of the CIO, the BCSP, and the boycott than of the good jobs at Swift or at International Harvester, much less than of the unionist blacks competing for them. Nor, because he has never heard of the NAACP, can Bigger understand the irony when the paternalistic Dalton describes himself as a supporter of the black organization (54–55). Instead, Bigger's life mirrors what Wright presents as the daily contradictions encountered by poor blacks. By the late 1930s the dire job situations of the city's blacks had been partly addressed, and they did come in frequent contact with white employers. Yet this Chicago is like any segregated American city, a place where James T. Farrell's Irish American homeowners think of a "nigger" as a pimp or a criminal.[90] In this context, Bigger's new service job driving a rich white college girl to and from campus and ferrying other members of the family around, while fairly well paid, is in a direct line from the often degrading Pullman portering of his father's generation, or even his own. And although Bigger does not name the BSCP, he instinctively recognizes the "black man's job" as one of servility. Furthermore, it is Bigger's allegedly promising but actually bitter job experience that structures the massive novel. He feels no eagerness at being hired because the job, which he considers reserved for black men, cannot raise his self-esteem. Perhaps, following an earlier pattern, that is why his ambition reaches no further than stealing from affluent whites while coercing his beaten-down lover, Bessie Mears, to fence the stolen goods.

Wright so structures the plot that Bigger's murderous crime is the culmination of a day in which Mary Dalton and her CP boyfriend Jan urge him to throw off the servant's yoke. In their arrogant naïveté, the two young people assume that Bigger will cease to be their chauffeur on command, just as, also at their bidding, he will be transmuted into their new friend and equal. Bigger's bewilderment erupts into rage when, back in the servant's role, he carries his drunken employer to her bedroom. In his fear at being found in Mary's bedroom, he suffocates her and disposes of her body.

The job continues to structure Bigger's experience in grotesque ways. There is a second interview with his employer the day after the murder. In many ways it is a parody of the first. The rich white man again interrogates the black servant, who is supposed to confine his replies to exactly what is asked of him. Bigger wishes to keep the job and presumably tell the truth in so doing, or at least as much truth as the employer needs to feel reassured. Dalton once again takes the "massa" role, though with a mounting anxiety. What he does not know, of course, is that he is questioning not his own servant but his daughter's murderer. It is only Bigger's well-learned ability to play the role expected of him that enables him to retain a job whose description has so radically altered.

Bigger's job, then, is in no way relief work. He never experiences anything but desperation in the telescoped time he is working for the Daltons. Jan and Mary in a sense kidnap Bigger and pelt him with their false egalitarianism. On another level it is when he commits the violent act that inevitably terminates his employment that Wright deepens the symbolic inquiry into the nature of black work.

The rest of this lengthy narrative, based on the actual case of the execution of the murderer Robert Nixon, concerns flight, capture, trial, and inevitable punishment. Yet it is the Bigger on the run or, in prison, describing his deed to his CP lawyer, who repudiates the docile workaday life of the 1930s black underclass. Bigger is no less a case history as a convicted murderer than as a young black man looking dispiritedly for a relief job.

A few years before *Native Son*, Wright published a condemnatory review of Zora Neale Hurston's novel of the black folk heritage, *Their Eyes Were Watching God* (1937). Because her book bypassed the social protest mode, it earned Hurston his scornful charge that she continued in the tradition of the singing and dancing Negro.[91] What may have fueled his anger is that Hurston's optimistic Eatonville, Florida, characters reside in an all-black incorporated village, the first in the nation. There they have far more control than Bigger over their work and emotional lives.

To write Bigger's story Richard Wright first had to find out what his own was.[92] The result of his soul-searching was to stress his protagonist's aloneness. Bigger never has the opportunity of a Tom Joad or a Larry Donovan to take hold of his life, much less make it an activist one. He is an alternative proletarian, an antihero of a disturbing kind.

Forgotten Families and Apparitional Migrants: *Grapes of Wrath* and Depression Era Multiculturalism

The Grapes of Wrath was a hugely popular novel that resurrected the Forgotten Family. Demoralized by Depression indignities but reluctant to sign up for New Deal relief programs, the Joads are able to retain their self-respect only by remaining faithful to family values. Neither overwhelmed by misfortune nor unpatriotically angry, they are decent rather than ambitious. When their farm fails and this proletarian Holy Family is tractored off their land, they undertake a migrant pilgrimage to find fruit-picking work in California. Humble and good, Ma Joad and her pregnant daughter are both versions of Dorothea Lange's famous 1936 "Migrant Mother" photograph. The Joad men, the son Tom, his father, and his uncle, are less successful than their women at fighting off feelings of unworthiness prompted by their tragic economic status. Yet they too symbolize the compassionate responsibility for one another central to the whole clan, mourning equally their lost rural work life and their aged grandparents, who die during the harsh journey to the fruit fields. In the tortured migration of the hard-luck Okie Joads, a wide readership found that the yeoman ideal, while bruised, had not been tarnished. Describing the Joads in a journal he wrote while composing the novel, Steinbeck praised them as people who are "much stronger and purer and braver than I am."[93]

The book has not been included in discussions of the radical collective novel, for it privileges self-reliance, the small rural entrepreneur, and the ability of people of different political allegiances to form migrant networks. Steinbeck was distrustful of the Communist Party. Although he observed the 1936 Salinas Lettuce Strike sympathetically, he shied away from too much involvement with the CIO when it asked him to support a cannery workers' union.[94] His tellingly titled pamphlet on white migrants, "Their Blood Is Strong" (1938), exposed their plight in Nipomo and other camps by focusing, as does its cover, on the resonance of one American family victimized by economic conditions. Steinbeck's novel *The Grapes of Wrath* (1939) continues the familial narrative, as Okie migrants and their children pick fruit together and pool their earnings. They understand their roles in the social unit that is greater than any one of them.[95] Thus, by novel's end, Ma Joad urges her daughter, whose baby dies in childbirth, to suckle a starving man in the name of a universal human family.[96]

As the Joads encounter this ever-wider population of migrants, they nevertheless meet people with a common racial and religious inheritance. The bulk of the Dust Bowl's displaced white refugees were southerners from Texas and Arkansas—states where the Ku Klux Klan had burgeoned as late as the 1920s—as well as Oklahoma.[97] The very American adaptiveness that is the best of the Joads and the many white migrants they encounter does have ethnic and racial limitations. Steinbeck's praise for the "strong blood" of the displaced U.S. small-farming population borders on a dream of a common racial inheritance.[98] It could not have escaped Steinbeck's notice that the Mexicans and Filipinos were, far more than the Okies, among the most impoverished groups in the United States. They labored in nearby canneries and even agitated over their exploitation in the lettuce fields near his own hometown of Salinas.[99] Because he disliked CP novelists, he probably was unacquainted with Clara Weatherwax's briefly praised but soon forgotten novel *Marching! Marching!* (1935). In what recent revisionists have lauded as a dramatic example of the collective novel, Weatherwax privileges a number of narrative voices and ethnic viewpoints.[100] Extending the protest novel in a way Steinbeck chose not to, she highlights a Filipino organizer, Mario, who is brutalized in a management attempt to stop a Washington State lumber strike. Closer to the publication date of the Steinbeck epic is Sanora Babb's novel-in-progress, *Whose Names Are Unknown* (1937–1938), which was inspired by her stay with migrant workers in California's San Joaquin Valley. Babb, who includes sections on Filipino field workers, was eventually turned down for publication because of her work's alleged similarities to Steinbeck's *Grapes of Wrath*. The decision is especially ironic in that, glossing over their well-known period militance, Steinbeck mentions Filipinos only in passing in the pamphlet *Their Blood Is Strong*. Years after the Depression, he does no more than allude to them in the opening pages of his aptly titled novel *Cannery Row* (1945).

Steinbeck may not have realized that Filipinos accounted for nearly 20 percent of the agricultural workforce in some parts of California. Chinese working people had also forged a notable presence in the Los Angeles International Ladies' Garment Workers Union. (Nevertheless, a rare Chinese American proletarian novel of 1937, *And China Has Hands,* by H. T. Tsiang, looks outside the United States to the Chinese Communists for a brighter future.) Although Steinbeck appears to have had limited knowledge of the Asian as well as the Latino population, he certainly knew that they were part of a much wider population of Latino and Asian farmworkers at the core of the United Cannery, Agricultural, Packing, and Allied Workers of America (UCAPAWA), an organization for which he at times expressed sympathy.[101] The Okies themselves were "regarded as a despised racial minority" by many white Californians.[102] It is as if Steinbeck decided that including the many Filipino ethnics visible in the labor barracks, union halls, and picket lines of California would dilute the "American" association of the native-born Joad men.

Thus in *Grapes of Wrath* there are only minimal references to the other people of color who routinely worked and struck in the fruit and vegetable fields of California. One occurs as the Joads swap gossip in the fruit fields about the woman who had sex with a "nigger" and gave birth to a child. She is remembered as a good picker (521). The other is a comment about an Oklahoma farm wife who is part Cherokee and therefore difficult and crazy (254). Although the U.S. government enacted a policy of repatriation for Mexican laborers in order to give whites like the Joads field and cannery work, the real-life counterparts of Steinbeck's American migrants would certainly have met and even worked with Filipino and Mexican people.[103]

In his need for a compelling saga, however, Steinbeck believed that he had to treat the heroism of a marginalized but white male group. In service of that vision he renders ethnics invisible. Nor does he treat women of various races with literary justice. Whether deliberately or not, he displaces a dubious sexuality onto the single, divorced, or widowed woman who bent over in the fields alongside whole families. Indeed, the book's unrelenting emphasis on Ma Joad as an earth mother implicitly reinforces the unnaturalness of the nonpatriarchal family. This deviance is then allied to racial difference—the "nigger," the crazed Cherokee. How much these people are excised from *The Grapes of Wrath* becomes obvious if one contrasts it with Charlie May Simon's *The Sharecropper* (1937), about an Arkansas sharecropper's multiracial tenant farmers' union, or Arnold Armstrong's *Parched Earth* (1934), on Native American farmworkers in California. To the latter group we now turn.

Depression Era Time Warp: Fiction, Native Americans, and the New Deal

In all of the subgenres of 1930s labor fiction, whatever the variations on heroic conduct, proletarian anger fuels the revolt against perceived injustice. From Conroy to Vorse, Wright to Steinbeck, Gold to McKenney, the protagonist seeks to undo the Depression wrongs of unemployment, eviction, pinched family economy, and cutbacks in the workweek. Bigger Thomas could not make common cause with a southern white mill woman, an Okie, or a Lower East Side Jewish socialist. But he joins them in projecting his considerable frustration onto a society he views as both complacent and cruel. Bigger, of course, parts company with white workers over the searing issue of race. Ironically, although novels by and about another racial minority, Native Americans, have been included under the proletarian literary umbrella, they are no closer to Wright's mental universe than they are to Conroy's or McKenney's.

New Deal policy created a vast new interest in reconstructing American Indian life and addressing the injuries of a half century of forced assimilation. There was an Indian bureau under FDR's New Deal, headed by John Collier: people as liberal-minded as Mary Heaton Vorse worked for him. It was no historical accident that the first full year of the Roosevelt administration saw the official death of the Capital Wild West Show. Since the early 1880s it had offered more lucrative, if still demeaning, employment than most Indian work.[104] Yet if we look to the novels, we find that the majority of Native Americans in the 1930s were doing menial jobs, cut off from their own anger and imprisoned in a history not their own.

D'Arcy McNickle's *The Surrounded* (1936) is that rare novel by and about Native Americans. Its 1930s publication was no doubt fueled by the New Deal scavenger hunt for diverse folklores. Reconstructed oral remembrances of nineteenth-century Native Americans included John G. Neihardt's *Black Elk Speaks* (1932), Ruth M. Underhill's *The Autobiography of a Papago Woman* (1936), and the American Indian John Joseph Mathews's 1900 Osage reservation novel, *Sundown* (1934). Despite—or because of—the period's passion for ethnography, McNickle's representative novel of the clash between Indian and white realities seems a continuation of Helen Hunt Jackson's turn-of-the-century *Ramona* plot. As if fifty years had not intervened, McNickle's protagonist, Archilde, is unable to connect to an antiquated Indian past. Yet also unable to buy into the local Catholic missionary's plan for his religious and cultural assimilation, he is beset by the same harsh truths that bedeviled Jackson's protagonists. Just as *Ramona* ends with a death, McNickle's tale closes with the living death of imprisonment in a white man's jail.

In actuality, the novel's treatment of Native American possibility is drawn in a time warp. By the 1930s federal officials had a renewed respect for Native American customs and even began to accept the role of tribal medicine.[105] Within this context, McNickle's fable of debasement and preempted identity seems a belated response to the notorious Bureau of Indian Affairs. Armstrong's *Parched Earth* also provided retrospection. Its opening section, set in mid-nineteenth-century California, features a bigoted Spanish grandee. He believes that "one [loses] caste by performing an Indian's task," an attitude toward Native American migrant workers that persisted well into the next century.[106] Yet the Armstrong novel, written by someone outside of the cultures described, filters its analysis of poorly treated Native Americans and other racial minorities through the lens of class. It is both McNickle's strength and limitation that he saw no intersection between the Native American novel and the proletarian novel.

Nipped in the Bud: Depression Era Work Fictions

American workers brought much experiential baggage to the tumultuous 1930s. Theirs was frequently a heritage of ethnic kinship, nonmilitant paternal organizations, and the sporadic, and often failed, strike. To a greater extent than ever before, U.S. writers recognized this lived history of accommodation and protest, bourgeois notions and working-class self-activity.

The best of these Depression era narratives, attempting to separate the striker from the strike, at the very least shared authority with workers, even if they could not give it over to them completely. Following up on the IWW worker-correspondent sketch, they imbued their texts with a new orality, anecdotal, vernacular, and defiant. More ambitiously, they transformed conservative tropes to meet radical goals.

In her benchmark study of the politics of form in proletarian fiction of the Great Depression, Barbara Foley finds that the most influential Marxist critics were "committed to the view that literary texts should make their politics felt through implicit, concrete, and nondidactic means."[107] The debate continues on the didacticism of any 1930s writer with CP affiliations, especially worker-writers like Gold and Conroy. I concur with Foley that Gold and Conroy succeeded in making their politics felt. I have argued here that these two pioneering authors from the class of which they wrote attempted a people's history in literary form with the local representing the universal. This was a literary enterprise that, given the dearth of previous models, was necessarily experimental. Thus Gold and Conroy, writing novels that begin in their reinvented childhoods, begin as well in the early manhood of their own fictionalized fathers. To a great extent each son's radicalization is the alternative ending to the father's story. They thus inaugurated the working-class novel by engaging in a complicated dialogue with earlier texts of working-class eccentricity and conformity, nobility and bestiality, impoverishment and ascension. To move forward as proletarian artists, they found and remade the past.

Ironically, the novels by those such as Gold, Conroy, and Steinbeck ennobled the lived work past of immigrant Jews, Welsh coal miners, and salt-of-the-earth small farmers just as these cultures were facing economic trauma. A similarly lucid retrospection characterizes Josephine Herbst's trilogy, inaugurated by *The Executioner Waits* (1934), and in Louis Zara's *Give Us This Day* (1934), Meyer Levin's *The Old Bunch* (1937), and Beatrice Bisno's *Tomorrow's Bread* (1938). Pietro di Donato's father-homage, *Christ in Concrete* (1939), a wrenching industrial-accident novel often paired with *Out of This Furnace*, privileges the Italianate speech of Geremio, the martyred, bricklaying father, to stress the ethnic separateness of the "swarthy" Abruzzeze immigrant. But not until the postwar decades would ethnic authors use elements of the proletarian novel to address Latino, Asian, and Native American labor truths. With the notable exception of Richard Wright's timeless, tragic naturalism, the marriage of past and present in the Golden Age of proletarian fiction concerned white workers.

Although 1930s leftists eschewed the old animal metaphors of the Progressive labor novels, in most proletarian novels it is hard to tell the striker from the strike. By the late 1930s, in the CIO novel, the rank and file experienced strikes and mass movements as acts of confidence in their own authority. In Thomas Bell's work, the generations of steelworkers who looked to their inner resources were the unofficial founders of the labor movement. Nor is a union victory, ideally inclusive of minorities and women, the sole predictor of labor's future. Ruth McKenney's approval of working people may have been contingent on their trade unionism. Nevertheless, like John Steinbeck, she never denied the legitimacy of the individual aspiration to climb.

In the literary recovery of working-class history, for novelists of men's militancy the struggle was to contextualize workingmen's diversity within a critique of capitalism. The relationship between feminism and the proletarian novel was more complex. Much of the important leftist fiction by and about women told the story of the oppressed mother. Neither adulatory nor denigrating, Olsen, Le Sueur, and Smedley rewrote what male texts argued were the aspirations and ambitions of proletarian mothers and their worker-daughters.

Olsen, Le Sueur, and Smedley joined the radical female storytellers of the Gastonia Strike to crystallize the struggle of the working-class woman writer as well as her subjects. Writers from Vorse to Page struggled to be faithful to women's labor experience while advocating the collective ascension at the heart of the era's most radical fiction.

"Women writers were not burrowers from within against the 'official' doctrines of the 1930s left, but its visionary conscience."[108] If this is an accurate perception, radical women writers engaged in dialogue with not only their Party's expectations of women's subordinate roles but the culture's as well. All too often in the masculinist proletarian novel women are left behind in manless communities to endure and to survive. It is difficult for them to redefine rising with their class if they are left behind the lines of the class struggle. It is similarly difficult to reconcile the motherly ideal with women on the barricades, a task undertaken by female radical novelists. Like their male colleagues, they refer to a labor past, engaged in an ethnographic present, and experiment with decentering the narrator. Whether telling the oppressed parents' story or creating a liberating mentor figure, as did their male colleagues, they refigure the collective envisioned in the male proletarian novel.

Whether revisioning or reporting labor voices, 1930s authors experimented with strategies of representation that replaced the survey with collaborations across the class divide. Yet the question was whether such cultural production joined authentic worker art to erase that division altogether and lay American exceptionalism to rest. Even as the 1930s tried to represent, in both senses of the word, the working class, a new kind of worker was emerging, less predictable and more informed. With the coming of war, and with Taft-Hartley looming on the horizon, a new generation of working-class writers would encounter American exceptionalism in a form that few in the golden age of the proletarian novel could have anticipated.

PART III

After the Proletarian Moment

CHAPTER 10

What Was Your Crime?
Representing Labor in the HUAC Era

In my new retrospective on the cold war treatment of proletarian writers, I'm going to say outright what I said indirectly in the stories.

—PHILLIP BONOSKY, INTERVIEW, REFERENCE CENTER FOR MARXIST STUDIES, JULY 23, 1998

"Nothin's gonna come outa the goddam strike. [ILA president Joseph Ryan] Kelly's sittin' around. [The waterfront CP] can't organize nothin'. Nobody else is doin' a goddam thing."

—THOMAS MCGRATH, *THIS COFFIN HAS NO HANDLES* (WRITTEN 1947–1948; PUBLISHED 1984)

"Half the guys in here, including me and Zach, have made McGregor Steel. That's a fact, we made this here jail for them to put us in."

—LLOYD BROWN, *IRON CITY* (1951)

Dorothea Lange, *Café near Pinhole, California,* 1956. Photograph. Oakland Museum Art Department, California.

What the New Deal had built for labor, the postwar Congress all but dismantled with the passage of the 1947 Taft-Hartley Act. The act, in brief, gave the federal government a veto over union politics, greatly diluted collective bargaining, and mandated unionist conformity. In effect, it replaced earlier shop-floor militance with contractual agreements. Among its more ominous provisions was a loyalty oath for labor leaders. Having to swear that they were not Communists virtually ensured that their unions would police themselves in service to an anti-Soviet cold war spirit.[1] A harbinger of the newly strengthened House Un-American Activities Committee (HUAC) and the zealous red-hunter Senator Joseph McCarthy (his heyday was 1950–1954), the act signaled the devastation of the labor Left and had widespread social, cultural, literary, and labor-literary effects.[2]

As early as 1938, the U.S. Communist leader Jay Lovestone, one of the most notable of the anti-Stalinists to break with the Party, testified before HUAC about "red" labor. As if prophesying Taft-Hartley, he remarked that "a good deal of the problem which the committee handles can be best handled by the labor movement."[3] A decade later, Taft-Hartley, reinaugurating a red scare climate, "deradicalized the union movement," outlawed mass picketing, and contributed to the ascendancy of management power.[4] The Congress of Industrial Organizations and the most potent of the trade unions under the American Federation of Labor (shrewdly or expediently, they would merge in the mid-1950s), to forestall further government intervention on the side of employers, scrambled to enact their own blacklists. By 1949 they had expelled suspected leftists from a once "red" union like the United Electricians (UE), famous—and notorious—for its wildcat work stoppages in 1945 and 1946. Leaders as diverse as CIO president Philip Murray, an American Steelworkers Association (ASWA) linchpin and a devout Catholic, and the United Auto Workers firebrand Walter Reuther used their still-considerable bargaining power. The two men advanced workplace contractualism. They pushed the exchange of some of the benefits of shop-floor democracy and stricter control of working conditions for contract and pension provisions.[5] In the new "moderate" trade unionism, whatever their reservations, labor leaders cut back on any effort to organize nonunion workers, lest such activity be linked to leftist politics. In a similar vein, they responded to the national mood by trying to curtail "unpatriotic" wartime and immediate postwar wildcat strikes in, among other industries, automobiles, docks, oil refinery, coal, and trucking.[6] Whether labor was selling out or exercising a new bargaining power, it was clearly trading with the enemy.

Increasingly, the established heavy-industrial trade unions preached consumerism, suburbanization, and the embourgeoisement both terms implied. In the name of postwar gains, organized labor subtly seemed to reinstate the nineteenth-century ideology of a workplace elite. It is true that during the postwar decade, for the first and possibly last time in American history, the average production worker in a large manufacturing concern could count on a union contract.[7] To give a fuller dimension to the official truth of the affluent worker, there arose a rhetoric of a democratized workplace with secure jobs for people of color and, in the wake of a New Deal presidential order, at least a surface adherence to racial integration.[8] As VJ Day neared, what had shifted most noticeably after a series of inner-city interracial conflicts characterized by working-class mob violence was a new sense of entitlement among wage-earning African Americans.[9] They returned home from military duty in which they had been shunted into "black jobs." They could well understand the resentments of home-front blacks in relatively good jobs now summarily swept aside to make room for white veterans.[10]

Although such harsh truths were compounded by AFL craft union intransigence and a host of Jim Crow customs in the mass-industrial North, there was some advance in biracialism.[11] African Americans, who moved beyond the segregated union locals and the social separation of the military until 1948, either retained membership in largely white unions such as the UMW and the UAW or struggled to retain the job benefits they had enjoyed as wartime replacements. In the rough environment of the eastern docks, the International Longshoremen's Association (ILA) had an embattled past of biracial unionism, often in the name of left-wing agitation.[12] African Americans were in postwar industry but not of it. In that they joined other minorities such as Mexican Americans, whose resentments erupted briefly in events like the 1943 Los Angeles Zoot Suit Riots. The Latino undocumented, in particular, were shunted into the fringe jobs of the industries that had so tentatively received them.[13]

Women, whether white or of color, would also find the vocational boons of what was called the "good war" to be ephemeral after it.[14] The war emergency had plucked hundreds of thousands of women out of low-level food-service and domestic jobs. One retrospective Labor Department Women's Bureau survey could have stood for many. Former saleswomen, waitresses, stenographers, and seamstresses, as well as factory employees in the textile mills, now laid railroad tracks, built ships, riveted airplane wings, and developed skills in the wartime automotive industry.[15] The numbers of white married women in the workforce especially would be greatly reduced in the home-loving 1950s. Yet many remained at work, part of the nineteen million white and minority women who made up almost one-third of the nation's workers.[16]

Black women, who made up over half of the one million blacks who entered the job market after Pearl Harbor, were among those who benefited least from the work the war opened up to them. They were at a disadvantage when competing with their white counterparts for defense jobs, such as the more lucrative automotive plant work, during the war. But they joined them in the occupational segregation of the reconversion period. There is no record that they were part of the fairly small number of working-class women in essential industries.[17] They staged their own wildcat strikes to protest the rapid decrease in the postwar labor market for women autoworkers.[18] And they certainly shared the experience of being turned away from the same plants that had used them in the war. Rosie the Unemployed Riveter could have been black. She was not so pictured other than in texts by African American authors or by white leftists.[19] Remarked the *Detroit Free Press* in 1953, using the typical language of exclusion and punishment so often invoked in labor circles, "Rosie feels something like Typhoid Mary when she applies for a factory job."[20]

There was a symbolic parallel to dismissals of redundant or replacement workers, people not likely to fit the image of the patriotic white male worker. Restrictive suspicion of political, racial, and ethnic minorities, dissenting voices, whether black or white, female or male, increasingly marginalized them from the late 1940s onward. Even the most liberal advocates emphasized increased productivity in the name of economic expansion as an end to class struggle.[21] However opposed in all other respects, leaders from John L. Lewis to Reuther and Murray found themselves ideologically aligned with those who praised worker concessions to employers in the name of American individualism and even classlessness.[22] As the labor movement redefined itself in the cold war period, old ascension philosophies took new form. Inevitably there arose the figure of the "good unionist" who informed on workplace Communists and fellow travelers and moved toward white-class affluence or was already there. The novelist and short-story writer Harvey Swados satirically termed him, in his classic collection of Ford auto factory stories *On the Line* (1957), the "happy worker."[23] Just as inevitably, this variation on the nineteenth-century self-propelled worker figure spawned its antithesis, variously termed "wild," "criminal," "subversive," or "marginal."

Even without the many wildcat strikes of the immediate postwar years, and no matter how many radicals went underground, to prison, or were purged for alleged disloyalty by their own comrades, the heritage of the Great Depression could not be totally erased. A grim literary naturalism reminiscent of Dreiser and Crane was revived to respond to the bland individualism of the time. A surprisingly substantial body of fiction offered lower-depths treatments of workers who had few skills and little education, and were ethnically and racially stigmatized. Except during the most ardent McCarthy years, some authors, weathering the time despite an activist past, even continued to expand the "bottom dogs" fiction they had written in the 1930s. Yet the biographer of one of the most celebrated of the worker-writers, Jack Conroy, who suffered joblessness at this time, best described it as a period of hostile postwar critics and publishers fearful of blacklists.[24]

Stories of what one historian called the "American Inquisition" and the "graveyard of [writers'] careers" abound.[25] For instance, Conroy had left the

Party two decades before but still continued to write under the leftist imprimatur. Thus when he favorably reviewed *Burning Valley* (1953), a novel by his unreconstructed Communist friend Phillip Bonosky, in the *Chicago Sun-Times,* he could not even command a byline. In any event, had Conroy's name not been prudently omitted, linking it to Bonosky's would only have jeopardized his chances of further review work. Bonosky was a board member of both the journal *Masses and Mainstream* and its identically named publishing house. In a 1998 interview at the CP-allied Reference Center for Marxist Studies, on whose board he still sat, Bonosky recalled one of the many paradoxes for leftist writers. Friends like Thomas McGrath were producing some of the most stirring proletarian novels but "didn't want to be published by us." These authors either remained unpublished or engaged in less drastic forms of self-censorship.[26]

Whether they were published by prestigious firms like Putnam's and Appleton-Century-Crofts or had put their writing careers on hold, whether they admitted to being a Communist or only answered to the allegiance "progressive" or "independent radical," there was hardly a novelist who did not experience cold war hostility to labor authors and those the 1930s dubbed cultural workers.[27] Even though McCarthy's star was falling by the mid-1950s, the forces he had helped put in motion, including the Hollywood blacklist, remained in place until the early 1960s.[28] Those who had escaped his wrath, like Swados or Harriette Arnow, who had never affiliated herself with party politics, may well have been heterodox or attenuated radicals who published a distinctly post-HUAC kind of labor fiction. Nelson Algren, whose novel on gambling and drug addiction, *The Man with the Golden Arm* (1948), was well received, found no favor with his down-and-out labor tales.[29] Those published by mainstream presses echoed, in one way or another, the distrust of labor activism and working-class people encoded in the era of the "red menace." Thus at a boom time for mainstream labor, literature exudes an atmosphere of uncertainty and disillusionment.

Some modern commentators contend that World War II "brought an end to even the anachronistic production of class-based, worker-oriented literature."[30] Michael Denning in *The Cultural Front* and Alan Wald in his University of Illinois Lost American Fiction Series introductions have maintained that there are 1930s social protest continuities rather than disjunctures in the cold war novel. Such critics cite fiction published under the aegis of the leftist houses Masses and Mainstream Press, Citadel, International, and Blue Heron as well as better-known fiction that ideologically broadened rather than disowned the 1930s form.[31] The literary radicalism of the HUAC era text returns to the darkly deterministic naturalism of Dreiser and Crane. As Alan Filreis claims, these are "thirties text[s] set against the developments of the forties."[32] So too may the 1950s as well, particularly given the anxious desire of authors to put Proletcult orthodoxies behind them. Also, as we shall observe, the post-1930 novel clearly was more concerned with the effects of social and economic forces on the individual rather than on the group psyche. This thrust toward individuation reflected a new literary interest in the mind of the worker in an organized-labor boom time, but it may also have reflected a new caution about labor writing, even among its ardent practitioners. Whether published in the postwar or first cold war decade, even the more daring novels containing workingmen and -women sent allegorical or coded messages about them, deemphasized social class, or placed class struggle in an earlier decade.[33]

As those who did write on work sought to revivify a literary naturalism that skirted doctrinaire social realism, confusion arose about reconceptualizing working-class aspiration. Writers who treated wildcatting and workplace protest and invoked the Odetsian *Waiting for Lefty* scenario did so without the optimism about proletarian consciousness that had characterized art in the 1930s. Their texts registered the changes in working-class aspiration wrought by a period that the sociologist Daniel Bell characterized as the end of ideology. In the exhaustion of political ideas many labor authors had to contend with the cultural resurgence of self, status, and the renewed commitment to individual nobility.[34] The kinds of novels identified by Walter Rideout in *The Radical Novel in the United States, 1900–1954* (1956) as strike, proletarian bildungsroman, bottom dogs, and bourgeois decay did not vanish.[35] But battles with the corruptions of prosperity became dominant, forcing the worker to the margins of his own narrative.

In revisiting, however reluctantly, the old nineteenth-century ideologies of Franklinesque self-transformation, the most prolabor text acquired a cold war tone. The dignity of labor consistently ran up against its suspected criminality. The young hoodlum of a series of Nelson Algren works (initiated by the 1942 novel *Never Come Morning*) mouths success clichés. In a novel that revokes the ending of Algren's Hollywood screenplay, the battered but triumphant Terry Malloy of Budd Schulberg's moneymaking screen version is murdered. Literally and figuratively blacklisted or displaced proletarians appear in Willard Motley's *Knock on Any Door* (1947), Algren's *The Neon Wilderness* (1947) and *A Walk on the Wild Side* (1956), Norman Mailer's *The Naked and the Dead* (1948), Harriette Arnow's *The Dollmaker* (1954), and Ann Petry's *The Street* (1946). The literary ambivalence about worker self-activity so characteristic of American labor fiction prior to the 1930s returns in a disturbing new psychological form.

As the oppositional identity loses heroic form and corruption becomes a new kind of labor dissent, workers trapped by threatening circumstances suffer from cultural claustrophobia. Isolated, scattered, or psychically disorganized, they express a psychological individualism that repositions crime less as personal deviance than as the defiance of the bourgeois middle. Resistance culture takes on new dimensions in a time of the "golden handcuffs" of a lifetime factory job.[36] In the name of all the have-nots shut out from and by American society, a covert dialogue with the "labor-red" past emerges. It often transcends the racial, ethnic, gender, and political affiliations of its creators. The cultural thrust toward homogenizing and defanging the working class must now in one way or another ask the workingman: what was your crime?

Chimeras of Opportunity:
The Postwar Labor Texts of Swados and Arnow

Harvey Swados was born almost a generation after Jack Conroy, Richard Wright, and Tillie Olsen. By the later 1950s, he was one of the foremost imaginers of postwar labor. He began his literary apprenticeship around the time of his blue-collar one, writing about and working in skilled metalwork as early as 1940.[37] Better educated and more used to middle-class living than at least these 1930s writers, Swados was the son of a physician father and an artist mother. As a Trotskyite member of the 1940s then Socialist Workers Party, he joined the so-called New York anti-Stalinist intellectuals in opposing both capitalism and collectivist bureaucracy.[38] He chose blue-collar work during college, and intermittently for a time afterward, in wartime radio and a huge postwar Ford auto factory in Mahwah, New Jersey. There, too, the wartime and postwar workscapes were in many ways those of plenty rather than of the scarcity described and experienced by his respected predecessors. Swados thus lived a mode of life made possible by the relatively prosperous two decades after he came home from the merchant marine in 1943.[39]

Over a decade before Harvey Swados came to prominence as a literary voice of postwar labor, the austere Henry Holt and Company joined Atlantic Monthly Press, Farrar Straus, and Harcourt Brace in rejecting his working-class coming-of-age novel, *The Unknown Constellations*. Written in 1946 and 1947, it would remain unpublished until 1995. Of wavering literary quality compared with the beautifully crafted stories of *On the Line,* it nevertheless introduces the discontented worker narrative that the later book would develop. The manuscript's cold publishing reception may well have been due to its ideologically bereft laboring figures. Their workplace lassitude and stifled yearnings cut them off from their workmates' friendship or their wives and lovers' affection. One reads this story of Swados's returning veteran, Jack Rodenko, less for the character than for the attempt to solve the problem of the cold war labor novel. A semiautobiographical hero, he is as much college educated as blue collar, as disturbed by the mindless materialism of his postwar surroundings as by his inability to posit alternatives. He responds to the down-and-out workers in his shabby New Orleans lodging house by turning their lives into an occasion for self-reproach. Nor does he expiate this guilt by association in the name of solidarity. His decision at novel's end to inform on his union-busting employer is consistent with his characteristic self-absorption.

Ten years later Swados had neither lessened his interest in nor solved the social dilemma posed by the nonideological workingman. After the Mahwah years he became a college teacher who observed labor with his students, taking classes to New York and Boston factory districts and union halls. Swados's own cross-class work biography does not diminish his involvement. *On the Line* was his important 1957 collection: *Dubliners* transported to automotive America in the Eisenhower era. But in the context of these well-received eight interrelated stories about the five-thousand-worker Mahwah plant, built as part of Ford's postwar expansion program, his familiarity with embourgeoisement is significant. Always at odds with the Party hierarchy, first as a college

Trotskyite and then as a socialist, he continued to write critically. Holding the union accountable, in the carefully liberal *Nation* he decried the UAW's cultivation of the myth of the Happy Worker. With the HUAC era over, he continued to deplore in the socialist journal *Dissent* what he saw as the UAW's complacencies.[40]

Swados came closer than anyone, with the possible exception of the former leftist and later bitter antileftist John Dos Passos, to writing seriously about the financial letdowns attendant on Big Unionism. Rather than casting Dos Passos's cold eye on corruption or going the underclass route of an Algren, he found that both responses devalued the organized-labor movement. Instead, he sought the meaning of labor's coveted Ford mega-factory employment, seemingly the model for the auto industry and others as well. Without sermonizing, he quietly mirrored the new postwar laborscape. He peopled his low-key stories with black and white characters, native born and ethnic Irish or Slav. His fictive roster included those who planned to work in the auto plant for the duration, those with an eye on college, and those returning to Ireland. In the early pages of his eight interrelated tales, the financial rewards of working on the line seem close to middle-classness, or at least its badges. There are many mentions of homes without mortgages, televisions, and the investment as old as Fordism itself: a discount on the "gleaming newborn autos . . . fitted out with glittering chrome ornamentation" the Ford workers had helped manufacture ("Fawn, with a Bit of Green," 25). The knockabout world of the Wobbly, the Bonus Marchers, Unemployment Councils, and the angry bottom dogs novel now seemed irrelevant.

Flint, its sister Detroit-area complex River Rouge, and other Midwest auto cities had a well-known Second New Deal and wartime history of sit-downs by employees from Ford and General Motors. Swados's plant, however, is severed from the old Detroit-area militance not only by its very newness but by something else as well. Those who sell their souls to the company store are well paid to do so, but they experience the job as a life sentence that is "hard, dull, unremitting, and backbreaking" ("The Day the Singer Fell," 7). In the vision of his text, to report to work at this "vast, endless, steel and concrete world" (24) is to undergo a sort of voluntary imprisonment in which isolation, discontent, aimlessness, and self-minimization are givens. "They don't even know your name here, only your social security number and your time clock number" ("The Day the Singer Fell," 15).

Many stories contain segments similar to the one in "Fawn, with a Bit of Green," about an Irishman who quits and returns home rather than continue to pay off the already rusting Ford car he has purchased with his labor. In the midst of a secure job, he finds his fellow workers making contemptuous references to their jobs and lives (28). The older hands are represented as so disillusioned that they sink in the monotony and the grinding routine. They pause only to augment their scorn with slighting references to the younger ones, who are, or like to believe they are, passing through on the way to college.

In place of the sit-downs and skirmishes with police and hired thugs of 1930s strike novels, even the violence is pared down. Now workers are consumers, and their desire to acquire badges of passing for middle class has replaced the old fire. Yet some sort of self-destructiveness invades every sketch. Joe is an assembly-line Abraham who sacrifices his son to the god of manufacture; another character falls and punctures his throat and singing career; another works out his alcoholism by numbing himself on the line.

This language of labor-class ambition, given these alienating surroundings, is not 1930s reactive militance. The workplace remains a kind of proletarian prison. "His lungs were being choked with dust and his spirit with mindless monotony" ("The Day the Singer Fell," 8). The 1950s codicil is that the workers have sold their souls to the company store for a good price. Swados's intellectual colleague Daniel Bell explained it best in *The End of Ideology*. Bell defined this crisis in trade unionism—high wages at the cost of spiritual sterility—as the capitalism of the proletariat. He questioned the renewed postwar emphasis on the rising standard of living for industrial workers. For Swados as for Bell, the price tag of this craving for respectability was a morally direction-less ambition.[41] Thus in Swados's poignant "A Present for the Boy," a factory old-timer castigates the new workers for resenting the regimentation of the job. "Pop" explains away their reactions as laziness or prideful ambition for a college exodus from manual work (84–87). Yet when his own son, Rudy, asks why he can't follow his father onto the assembly line instead of going to college, Pop evinces the kind of working-class self-disgust that characterizes so many in the Swados workforce: "I don't know how to do nothing else. You got the head to do better" (81). In this 1950s text, the fidelity to rising, character-istic of so much labor fiction prior to the Depression, is hollow. Rudy dies in a car crash the day he receives an automobile, his father's graduation gift; the heritage of materialism Pop wishes to pass on is fatal. In the story's final irony, Pop finds contentment with a dog he names after his son, training him with the words: "If you do like I say there's . . . a juicy present in it for you" (102).

Swados muckraked the world of autoworkers in a time when their pay and benefits were among the best in organized labor. This was an era in which Reuther's UAW espoused policies of social democratic reform and resisted "Big Three" (Ford, General Motors, and Chrysler) attempts at bottom-line cost-effectiveness, government deregulation, and flight from inner-city factories employing people of color. Yet, curbed at every step by an antilabor Congress and a conservative White House, the liberalism of the UAW was cordoned off from influence and power.[42] These contradictions inform Swados's vision of the autoworker as a conformist in a blue-collar shirt. Cut off by virtue of his manual work from the status of the gray-flannel-suited business-man, he is equally aloof from the problems of the least secure segment of the UAW rank and file. He is numbed by materialism rather than secure in it. Swados's greatest irony is that Mahwah's workers seem pinioned by the era's selective financial security. Summoning up the ghost of prewar militance, Swados offers a lone former Wobbly as chorus when he says men make their own tragedies. But neither he nor his creator provides a militant way to surmount them.

To the 1950s white woman author who fell under the rubric of the independent radical like Harriette Arnow, workingmen made the lives of their wives tragedies, too. Arnow's *The Dollmaker,* published in the mid-1950s, animated the insight that the widespread female responsiveness to postwar pressures, whether muted or resistant, altered the form and scope of their wage earning. Informing her narrative was her lived understanding of a work world in which women, married or single, white or black, had to adapt to the loss of lucrative work when soldiers returned to the "men's jobs" they had been holding down. Those with high school educations continued the steady influx into clerical sectors begun in the early decades of the century. Many of the less educated were downsized from industrial to service jobs. In the decade after war's end, more married women than ever before were swelling the female labor force. At this ideological moment, though, the culture was rediscovering woman's maternal imperative.[43]

Arnow well understood that women continued to sew at low wages. Even in 1958, a few years after her novel appeared, 80 percent of ILGWU workers were women, but they received 8 percent of pay raises.[44] In feminizing Swados's fiction of postwar male proletarianism, Arnow therefore looked not to a burgeoning male jobscape but to the pinched choices experienced by the 1930s woman. *The Dollmaker* rewrites the male factory story. Arnow's is a feminist slant on Clovis Nevels, an unthinking assembly-line worker. No stranger to manual labor or the rural mother, Arnow brought a wealth of woman-centered job experiences to the task. She built on Steinbeck's secular saint Ma Joad, Olsen's Anna Holbrook, the Gastonia mill tales, and her own 1930s home-as-sweatshop fiction. Repudiating the possibilities of the job-rich 1950s, she built as well on her own earlier tales of unappreciated working-class women servitors, such as the story published in the *Southern Review* in 1936, "The Washerwoman's Day." Also informing her novel was her life as a participant-observer in a Detroit housing project.[45]

Seized by consumerism, the complacently pro-union Clovis Nevels thrives in Arnow's auto world, as he would have in Swados's. Yet to do so he requires that his wife Gertie be a domestic caretaker, all the while criticizing her for never having to "git out an work" (252). As it is, he walks off to morning factory work amid the wage-earning mothers who live next door and across the way from him. Had he been at the gigantic Detroit-area River Rouge auto factory during the war, he would have been working with women trade unionists, although that plant was occupationally segregated by sex.[46] His sexism, demonstrated in crucial work-related scenes throughout the novel, would have been particularly resonant to Arnow's readership when the novel appeared in the mid-fifties.

A displaced person in citified Detroit, Gertie is the voice of a preindustrial and rural time. Clovis in Kentucky is a like a Walker Evans figure, a would-be machinist in a hardscrabble landscape. Gertie is the artisan, a folk artist of wood sculpture. Wrenched from her farm life, in which she earned money, like many rural women, by selling produce, she is the one who suffers the loss of vocation in the move from a market to an industrial economy. Arnow understood better than Swados how to articulate the corruptions and question the complacency of commodity culture. Clovis may escape the industrial accidents and psychic ills that constitute the lot of Swados's protagonists. It is

Gertie who experiences trauma and loss. The engines of industrialism take her children from her as her little girl is killed in a railway accident and her son runs off, breaking with his family to disappear in the modern city.

The Dollmaker does far more for U.S. labor fiction than the condescending study by the University of Chicago sociologists Lee Rainwater, Richard P. Coleman, and Gerald Handel, *Workingman's Wife: Her Personality, World, and Life Style* (1959). In that survey, female oral history is mediated by extreme judgmentalism about the psychic aspirations of blue-collar wives, who join their husbands in craving money to spend and presumably would shed any ethnic, religious, or folk heritage to be like everyone else.[47]

Arnow thus deftly reorders Swados's crime and imprisonment tropes by having this raw mountain woman, ill at ease with embourgeoisement, defy her husband's edicts to forget home and kin. She is simultaneously the harried wife of a dictatorial blue-collar worker and a homemaker rewarded with shoddy housing, kitchen appliances, children's clothing, and all of the machine-made replacements for the artisan culture she has regretfully left behind.

In her Kentucky days, Gertie was a productive woman. Without consciously articulating it, she equated personal freedom with the manifold duties and dawn-to-midnight chores of a subsistence economy. Repeatedly Arnow recounts how Gertie experiences every aspect of her new urban life as a punishment that she must endure in silence. Whereas her unimaginative husband escapes guilt for unknown crimes by disavowing his stigmatized hillbilly past, his wife experiences Detroit blue-collar life as a tribunal. Constantly mocked by more assimilated Detroiters as an outsider, she forces herself to teach her children to get along in the North by hiding their country roots. Unable to engage in the charade of conformity to the prevailing ideology, she does not dare to teach subversion either, fearing for her children's futures. While she cannot suppress her private morality, neither can she escape her spiritual solitary confinement. Her flimsy apartment, subject to the noises and odors of the neighborhood, will never be the site of her revolt against incarceration for the "crime" of being a poor hillbilly white.

We should remember that Swados makes no reference to the women automobile workers he must have known at Mahwah and elsewhere. He is equally silent about the alternate labor reality experienced by women in a time of renewed indifference to gender equality, even in relatively enlightened unions like the UAW.[48] Arnow does not suppress these portraits. She shows us married women with children who are permitted to swell the family wage. But it is crucial to her artistic purpose that, like Gertie, her women workers cannot sustain a support system. They are powerless to control their family's fascination with gimcrack consumerism, either by admonition or by withholding their factory woman's weekly wages. Because the cultural ideal of feminine job security, much less promotion, was quiescent in a time when a folk artist like Gertie was variously misunderstood, ridiculed, or minimized, her reaction to what she sees as a chimera of plenty is discounted by all who interact with her. Gertie is, in fact, a 1950s Cassandra, though one stripped of children, out of touch with her husband, descending to madness—forced to give up her sense of morality, of mothering, of community.

The late-naturalistic rawness of the unhappy figures peopling the works of Swados and Arnow was little understood in a time when, in the words of one reviewer, it was "refreshing" to read about labor.[49] Yet there was a kernel of truth in that observation as well. Whatever their debt to the 1930s social protest novel, Swados and Arnow had produced culturally palatable labor novels of the worker's misdirected quest for consumerist fulfillment. In a HUAC Hollywood governed by anxiously Americanized studio heads, a revised working-class self-actualization would further personalize the "human interest" plot. In a time of few cinematic labor narratives, *Marty* (1955), doubly surprising as an international hit and an enduring work of film art, can be usefully analyzed as an allegory of the problems confronting 1950s labor representation for "real Americans."

Marty, A Streetcar Named Desire, and Performing the Blue-Collar Self

By the early 1950s the HUAC eye was fixed on Hollywood's former leftists, on studio heads of Jewish (and therefore suspicious) ethnicity, and on any artists or entrepreneurs hardy enough to transform Broadway labor productions into cinematic ones. The liberal but anti-Communist authors of *Marty* and *A Streetcar Named Desire* (1947), both works about individuals rather than about groups, did not incur McCarthy's wrath. Perhaps it was no coincidence that the marketability of these works by Paddy Chayefsky and Tennessee Williams rested on a rather melodramatic simplicity concerning the working-class psyche. The Hollywood of mass-consumed visual imagery about working folk became the era's most unlikely purveyor of cinematic narrative about the anxious yearnings for acceptance and normality characterizing the real-life workforce.

As the exemplar of the new Hollywood labor film, *Marty* enjoyed the same uncritical mass approval as had Edward Steichen's still photography exhibit at the New York City Museum of Modern Art, "The Family of Man," debuting a few months before *Marty* opened.[50] Like the curiously soothing international assortment of largely working-class people in Steichen's upbeat, cliché-ridden photos—lovable participants in the 1950s construction of the human drama—the humble butcher, Marty Pilletti, also seems to resist class analysis.

Marty is just individualistic enough to wish to be his own boss but is clearly working class in his lack of sophistication, conversational skill, larger life goals, and links to an immigrant (and Catholic) ethnic heritage. An unattractive but sensitive man who lives in the Bronx with his mother, he is genial, happy in his work, and apolitical: the quintessential working stiff. Neither prosperous nor actively ambitious, he straddles the boundary, as did many of the more skilled trades in the 1950s, between blue-collar and middle-class income.

His dilemma is that he has been "looking for a girl every Saturday night of my life."[51] His humanity and sincerity are so obvious that the audience finds it only fitting that, against the odds for a shy, ungainly man approaching lifetime bachelorhood, he should find a wife by film's end. His instinctive resistance to embourgeoisement might, in other decades, have linked him to a salt-of-the-earth type, a meat-cutting everyman. One reviewer rightly praised the film's sentiment.[52] There is much in Chayefsky's teleplay, turned into a full-length Hollywood film, reminiscent of the harmless ethnic worker figures of the sentiment-drenched *Saturday Evening Post* at the beginning of the century. The movie version conveys a similar frustration with inarticulateness, in Marty's case a second-generation proletarian wordlessness rather than a new immigrant's accented English. And there is the same devotion to kin and family. And, as in the more sanitized local-color stories of H. C. Bunner and William Dean Howells, in place of the dangerous proletarian, there stands a protagonist of such good-hearted, if unimaginative, friendliness (135) that his unlikely romanticism endears and softens.

Marty's ultimate social success, indeed his triumph, is a tribute to assimilation rather than a legitimization of class difference. While Clara is plain, she is a college graduate, teaches school, and speaks an educated English to Marty's ungrammatical one. Her colorless name is deliberately ambiguous. She has no ethnic markers or affiliations and could well be in the Protestant majority. (Other than marking the Pillettis and their friends as Catholics, the script bears no other ethnic references.) Clara's appreciation of Marty as the "kindest man I ever met" (161) signals his acceptance by respectable society. On another level, given the obsession with women's not working and with their having a pleasing appearance, she has to settle for a man of his class as he settles for a woman with her face. Thus does the scenario displace the more distinctive aspects of his laboring identity onto a culturally demeaned physical appearance: "I'm a little, short, fat, ugly guy" (161). In fact, the tale is so constructed that the viewer can bond with Marty while retaining prejudices about uneducated working people that Marty himself, even if he could articulate them, would do little to challenge.

The Tennessee Williams play-turned-film, *A Streetcar Named Desire,* would appear in 1947, just before the HUAC ascendancy (the film appeared in 1951). It too made clear the extent to which blue-collar ungainliness was a stand-in for a defanged proletarian identity. In the character of Harold Mitchell, or Mitch, it reappears juxtaposed with its more menacing antithesis, sexuality, personified by Stanley Kowalski. The successful Broadway play (directed by Elia Kazan, who would soon do *On the Waterfront*) was made into a popular Hollywood movie in 1951. The movie version retained the utterly convincing Karl Malden, in real life a coal miner's son, as the factory worker Mitch, and the explosively talented Marlon Brando for the principal male lead. Stanley is clearly the dominant personality, a crude, if ambitious, working-class, Polish American Catholic. If Stanley is psychically remote from the kind-hearted Marty, Kowalski's buddy Mitch resembles Chayefsky's gentle protagonist. Another bumbling everyman of goodwill, Mitch also lives with his aging mother, longs for and fears marriage to a nice girl, and tries in vain to separate himself from his lewd buddies.

Where Marty manages to separate, Mitch does not. A man hungry for neither job promotion nor a life of volatile sensuality, he cannot withstand the rough machismo of his friend and unwillingly joins in punishing Stanley's vulnerable sister-in-law, Blanche DuBois, who, like Clara Davis, is an educated woman. Refusing to marry the unstable Blanche, who has plummeted from schoolteacher to a kind of paid southern promiscuity, Mitch chooses almost unthinkingly to remain a good Catholic son, a blue-collar pal and one untainted by carnal knowledge.

In his own way, Mitch buys into the normality of the working-class 1950s ethnic, satisfied to earn a decent living, anxious to fit in, and afraid to rebel. Stanley, whom materialism and sexual desire have made almost satanic, is entirely other. Whereas in a Group Theater production like Odets's *Waiting for Lefty* (in which Elia Kazan acted in the mid-1930s) he might have channeled his class rage and sexual energy into a cause, he is narcissistically bent on wresting Blanche's property for himself. Furious that she has used it up to maintain the facade of gentility, in a defining moment that fuses his gender and class rage, he makes her his property by raping her and throwing her out of "his" house.

Let it not be forgotten either that Kowalski had done war service as a noncom in the Engineers' Corps. While Mitch sits on the precision bench in the spare parts department, Stanley has a vague sales job which involves traveling for the same plant (52). Both his animality and his superior job status empower him to be violent with Blanche and seductively proprietary with his wife. Streetwise in the name of upward mobility, he is a dormant volcano. Had the play been developed, like *On the Waterfront*, into a novel after its movie version, Stanley might have fallen victim to working-class hubris, damned by his aggressiveness and acquisitiveness. But it was in another role tailor-made for Brando, that of Terry Malloy, that a humanized Stanley Kowalski would make an unlikely peace with the Marty/Mitch of his own nature.

Naming Names: Joe Docks and Representing Labor in the Cold War Labor Story

The relative 1940s risk taking of *Streetcar* was replaced by the reassurance of *Marty*, so that by the mid-1950s, when Hollywoodizing labor was a perilous enterprise, Arthur Miller's commissioned Brooklyn docks screenplay *The Hook* (written in 1947) was shelved. (Miller used it, much shorn of references to militance, as a basis for *A View from the Bridge* in 1955. It was not made into a film until 1961.) From the early years of the film industry through the war, independent producers and directors had made proworker features, many taken from the fiction of the day. But by 1954, when the New Mexican zinc-strike film *Salt of the Earth*, directed by the blacklisted Michael Wilson and featuring workers as actors, was made, virtually no one would distribute it.[53]

Far more in tune were the former Party adherents, the writer Budd Schulberg and the onetime Group Theater actor and director Elia Kazan. They had publicly reviled their former leftist associates and soon received the Hollywood imprimatur for a worker screenplay. Reversing the era's more common sequence, Schulberg later turned it into a novel. To sustain a more complicated labor narrative in the cold war, including one that inspired a full-length novel, Schulberg intuitively understood that it was crucial for prolabor writers to re-create the atmosphere of political menace surrounding trade unionism.

To that end they adapted the *Waiting for Lefty* scenario, the murder of an honest labor organizer and the collective decision to act assertively on the 1950s docks.

While the docks had a long association with illegal activity, in the era's shrinking labor-literary environment, the "crime-ridden" docks achieve prominence and a certain perverse fashionableness. Public fascination with the criminal exploitation of the rank and file played into a film noir scenario of moral ambiguity in which no one was innocent. Those hoping to rid the piers of leftist and industrial racketeers permanently personified the workingman by using the figure of "Joe Docks," the longshoreman of the New York and New Jersey piers, a play on the terms "GI Joe" and "an average Joe." Muckraking reporters like Malcolm Johnson in *Crime on the Waterfront* (1950), originally published in the *New York Sun,* and Budd Schulberg in his *Harper's* and *New York Times* articles (he would soon borrow Johnson's title for his original screenplay)[54] sympathized with the little guy. Now he was victimized not by pre-1930s management greed or Great Depression impoverishment but by the mob-infested union, the International Longshoremen's Association.

A disillusioned, passive, but decent type, Joe Docks settled for survival but privately seethed at dockside labor racketeers. More likely to feel a kinship with the American Catholic Trade Union (ACTU) than with the "red" dockworkers unable to find work,[55] he was nevertheless a man with strong loyalties to his work group. To comprehend the odd literary situation of a Joe Docks gaining both moral stature and the promise of a decent existence by naming names, one must understand the cultural associations of the Northeast docks. Guided by the "men on the docks who gave me a hand" and the labor priest Father John Corridan, fictionalized as Father Barry, Schulberg entered what was considered a labor-class jungle by mainstream America. By virtue of the strenuous and isolated nature of the work, even by 1959 there were enduring bourgeois prejudices against the atavistic world of the waterfront.[56] Layered with historic associations of political wildness, the ILA was one of the most radical labor organizations created by the working-class insurgency of the 1930s, and it retained an association with an enduring proletarianism. The dock was also a contested working-class terrain: the battle for loyalty was waged by the mob, the ACTU and its labor priests, a dwindling waterfront section of the CP, and government watchdog committees formed under the umbrella of Taft-Hartley.[57]

The reputation of maritime labor's West Coast red International Longshoremen's Warehouse Union (ILWU) was countered by the realpolitik of the 1950s and, particularly on the East Coast, by the anti-Communist policies of its rival the ILA.[58] The ILA's lifetime racketeer president, Joseph Ryan, was caricatured as "Johnny Friendly" in *On the Waterfront.* Ryan used red-baiting to consolidate his hold on the longshoremen, many of whom lived near the docks, had ethnic ties, and, as working-class Catholics, were suspicious of leftist organizers.[59] In fact, periodic strikes against the corrupt ILA leadership, even during the war, enlisted Jesuit "labor priests," who were as pro-CIO as they were antileft.[60] Yet as the choice of Marlon Brando for the film version implied, the bestial Stanley Kowalski, with whom the actor was linked in the popular mind, could have merged his toughness with that of Schulberg's featherbedding dockworker and thug Terry Malloy.

When Schulberg wrote *On the Waterfront,* he was all the while aware, as he wrote in his 1955 preface to the novelistic version, that he would "put [his] waterfront experience in perspective, with Terry [Malloy] finding his Calvary in a Jersey swamp."[61] The Calvary to which Schulberg refers is a step along the way to Terry's crucifixion. At the beginning of both the screenplay and the subsequent novel, Terry sees himself as a has-been fighter. By doing the bidding of Johnny Friendly (ILA chief Joe Ryan), he is on the run from his own sense of decency.[62]

The film version, as is well known, Hollywoodizes Terry's decision to be an informant and cooperate with federal anticrime lawyers; his martyrdom nevertheless leaves him alive, honorable, and ready for a new chapter in ILA history. Schulberg may have been infusing this ending with the recent accession to power of the reform candidates John Dwyer and Jackie Mullins. However, the bleak ending of the novel, which Schulberg wrote without the imprimatur of the studio boss Darryl F. Zanuck or the director Elia Kazan, was far more faithful to actual events. These unfolded after a brief reform period, or what was variously labeled reform without change or with the cover of respectability.[63] Like many real-life dockers whose defiance of Ryan was almost a suicidal act, this second Terry Malloy, his creator may well have realized, paid a price for informing. Naming names, whether talking to the "Feds" of the Waterfront Crime Commission or appearing before McCarthy himself, was, after all, an enterprise fraught with danger.

The Hollywood version of the Joe Docks plot reestablished working-class legitimacy by rescuing the workingman from disloyalty. In Schulberg's screenplay, the victory was over reds as much as gangsters. He writes the CP out of its ancillary role in the wildcat dock strike of 1948 on which the filmplay is loosely based. Instead the Catholic Church, united with a handful of ILA dissidents, saves the day. The novelized version, Schulberg's solo effort, was more ambiguous. Terry Malloy informs, is heroic, and dies. A film noir touch is added when Ryan, soon released from jail (282), takes up where he left off. The emphasis is on one martyred figure who single-handedly fights the dock mob.[64] This also played into the preference for a David and Goliath plot in which the little guy, with no "foreign" agitators assisting, rouses himself from the postwar labor stupor and attendant isolation of the little guys and wins, by his own efforts.

Without the electric presence that Marlon Brando projects in the film, Terry Malloy in the novel becomes intent on exchanging survival for salvation, a soft waterfront job for an unmarked grave in a New Jersey swamp (274). By associating Malloy with martyrdom, the novel both Christianizes and makes contemporary the *Waiting for Lefty* plot. In the lawless world of manual labor, the worker can atone for corruption only by dying to be reborn.

Schulberg's alternate *On the Waterfront* ends on a pessimistic note. At least, though, the novel was a sacrifice-for-normality plot in step with the melodramas of G men and crime-busters so popular in the early 1950s. By contrast, there was another plot that the period neither read nor wished to see filmed.

Though the novel was not to be published until 1984, Thomas McGrath's *This Coffin Has No Handles* was written in 1948, when its author was just feeling the chill of Taft-Hartley. The leftist ILWU had recently been trounced by Ryan and by Murder Incorporated boss Albert Anastasia's mob-controlled ILA.

McGrath extends a favored technique of the decentered 1930s proletarian novel. He moves into and out of the minds of his characters during one of the feebler wildcat strikes to hit the New York City waterfront a few years before the rise of McCarthy. The unfolding action is a threnody for the waterfront section of the CP and the unsung efforts of the 1945 wildcat strike agitator Sam Madell.[65] It is understandable that McGrath, himself soon to be called before HUAC, did not lobby with prestigious publishers for his pro-Party story, and even its 1984 publication was by a small press.[66]

As the novel's dour title suggests, it boasts no Terry Malloy to play the proletarian everyman, only a burnt-out leftist. Deliberately named Joe Hunter, he was an articulate waterfront organizer before he went off to war. He returns to find his fellow activists completely subdued and the rank and file they once ignited variously hostile or apathetic. As a film noir novel, it lets no character escape the criminal label or the guilt of self-incrimination. Hunter knows a prison term awaits him for his Communist involvement, and for the bulk of the novel he curses himself for leading the inactive life of an underground Party member. McGrath's version of Joe Ryan, Kelly, torments himself far more than does the government seeking to indict him. His prison sentence, like the real-life Ryan's, is short. But he is punished by the spiritual and moral bankruptcy of his existence. Nor can Terry be found in the twisted mind of Cock-Eye Dunn, a real mob thug eventually executed for thirteen murders. Terry is similarly absent from the character "Blackie" Carmody, a longshoreman who trades in his honesty for a good job with his crooked union. Equally unpromising are the minor characters: an alcoholic ex-Wobbly named Conn, a pun on the era's obsession with convicting the Left, and the various other drunks, hoods, and society types who fail to change the "lousy world" of the urban workingman (63). Father Barry is likewise absent, replaced by the ACTU, which does nothing to thwart Kelly "so long as he was competent to keep the Communists out" (25). Nor is there any relief on the desolate West Side avenues and sinister-looking dock streets or the fetid tenements and rundown hiring halls, where spies and informers contribute to the menace.

For all its homage to the 1930s—in the last, brief, Odetsian scene of the book, Joe rises from his own ashes and exhorts a small CP fraction to begin again in the name of a slain dock leader—McGrath's treatment of dock-strike realities anticipated the criminalized longshoreman of the 1950s. In that sense, the novel heralds the conflation of reds and racketeers in the HUAC period. McGrath spends most of the novel showing that the worker, caught between a discredited idealism and vibrant corruption, is stigmatized whatever he does. With the former workingman Blackie now turned hood rather than leftist to survive, the battle of creeds is not the Manichaean one of the communism-versus-capitalism novel. Rather, there is a Dantesque landscape in which the Party offers only the sacrifice of individualism to a misguided creed, on the one hand, or, on the other, individualism criminalized by gangsters in a world where "it's every man for himself" (190). In this dead-alive environment, no wonder the ghostlike characters seem to exist only at night.

By 1958, when the red-baiting had lessened somewhat and McGrath had published *Gates of Ivory, Gates of Horn,* a Masses and Mainstream novel rebuking cold war thinking, a few hardy CP writers revived his leftist-in-danger waterfront plot. One was Benjamin Appel in *The Raw Edge* (1958), published by Random House. Even more boldly than *This Coffin,* it focuses on blacklisting as a form of violence against the working class. But within those ten years, even the perception that violence in the U.S. workplace and mill town was an American rather than a subversive phenomenon took forms in CP texts that relied on popular models while dismantling them.

Texts from Underground: The Fiction of the Un-Americans

The year 1946 was when McGrath worked on the bulk of his manuscript, the largest number of wildcat strikes were called since the war had begun, and HUAC became a standing committee of the House of Representatives.[67] In 1955, the first volume of a two-volume HUAC report, covering 1938 to 1954, appeared, naming most of the authors mentioned in this chapter, some of whom also gave testimony. Other literary figures appeared in the pages of the second volume, published in 1970, covering the years from 1955 to 1968. By then, fifteen years after the first volume had been published, with McCarthy and the old HUAC dead, the American people received the document far more ambivalently.

Given this climate, it is not surprising that McGrath shelved his fine 1947–1948 waterfront manuscript. He thereby joined an important group of prolabor writers with Party affiliations, such as Tillie Olsen (*Tell Me a Riddle,* 1961, and *Yonnondio,* 1974) and Meridel Le Sueur (*The Girl,* 1978), or Party pasts like Richard Wright (*Lawd Today,* 1963), whose novels "lay unpublished for a generation."[68] The pro-Soviet journal *PM* was gone by 1948, and the intellectuals of the mid-1930s American Writers' Congress years were engaged in reconciling anti-Stalinism with a measure of embourgeoisement.[69] Those still involved in the literary Left only could have published reviews and articles in Party journals, principally *Masses and Mainstream,* as did the dispirited Jack Conroy, his more resilient Midwest literary colleague Meridel Le Sueur, McGrath, Phillip Bonosky, Howard Fast, and Lloyd Brown.[70] Unwilling to "attenuate . . . [their] radicalism" to compromise with political realities, for a time in their careers all of these writers formed part of a literary underground of silenced, culturally invisible proletarian writers.[71]

Phillip Bonosky, who was on the editorial board of *Masses and Mainstream* through the 1950s, recently recalled that he had to ask for contributions even to have his novel *Burning Valley* (1953) published by the journal's book publishing arm.[72] Yet such activity was more likely to be rather abbreviated: stories and poems in *Masses and Mainstream* (1948–1963), which was formed by fusing the Depression era *New Masses* and other Party organs.[73] Editorial board members included some of the few novelists who were publishing or trying to publish left-labor fiction outside its pages as well. Howard Fast's most allegorical "slaves of ideology novel," *Spartacus* (1951), which found popular acclaim, was excerpted the summer before in the July issue.[74]

Another contributor was Alexander Saxton, whose texts were published and buried by Appleton-Century-Crofts. They were not widely circulated in their time, or, for that matter, have they been reprinted in ours. But they were among the few cold war texts to acknowledge what Truman's attorney general, J. Howard McGrath, in 1949 pilloried as the "many communists in America . . . in factories . . . butcher stores, [and] on street corners."[75] Remembered Bonosky (whose own son was shadowed by the FBI), the "rawness of the struggle became debilitating . . . you're in the midst of a trauma."[76] Added to the heavy burden of the period's anxiety was the pressure on CP representations of fictive laborers to refute the "criminal" charges they had already acknowledged as true.

As much as any other labor fiction of the time, that of the CP was interwoven with the fears and rhetoric of the HUAC era. Whether they saw print or languished, used futurist or historical plotting, Party texts of the late 1940s and the 1950s continued the Popular Front goal of balancing communism and Americanism. Redefining these terms for the cold war era prompted the boldly repeated assertion that "reds," far from being criminals, were patriots unjustly maligned. In so doing, these authors located the suspended or stymied ambitions of the Left in an America corrupted, losing direction, and bowing down to bourgeois respectability.

Bonosky, one of the foremost authors to carry on the proletarian bildungsroman, a *Daily Worker* contributor, and a blacklisted U.S. steel activist, drew on Jack Conroy's *The Disinherited*, representing labor in and often by a bleak 1920s Pittsburgh-area Slavic and black steel town.[77] As Bonosky well knew, the nativist conscription of opportunities for the ethnic Slav was by now familiar enough in American letters. The Pittsburgh Survey era and the 1930s had contributed mightily to that discourse. Like his publisher, who refused to market the book, a hostile era could easily have seen subversion in the novel's references to the dawning militance of the young, first-generation Lithuanian American Benedict Bulmanis (Bonosky's family name was Baranauskas). In his psychic odyssey, the vulnerable son of poverty comes to see the heroism of Dobrik (which means "good" in Polish), a composite IWW/CP organizer jailed and savagely beaten for his activism.

Bonosky himself, however, provides an alternative interpretation of the novel. He notes that unlike his later novel *The Magic Fern*, a 1960 critique of the cold war witch-hunt in Pittsburgh, *Burning Valley* is far more ambiguous— "there is a certain indirection," in his words, about its protagonist's ideology.[78] Bonosky was well aware of the obvious era conflicts between communism and Catholicism played out in another blue-collar venue, the waterfront. Yet he still resolved the conflict of Benedict by having him be devoted to a Christianity politicized, but no less Christian for that. Even at novel's end, when the steel mill is evicting ethnic Slavs and migrant blacks to make room for corporate greed, Benedict still struggled with channeling his outrage into spiritual support for his people rather than, like Dobrik, making it manifest in the world.

Benedict's ideological conflict is to be torn between a purist Catholicism, symbolized by the elitist company informer, Father Brumbaugh, and that of a labor priest, Father Dahr, flawed, alcoholic, aged, and prolabor. The novel can be read allegorically, but it is as if by substituting another "suspect" creed, Bonosky tried for the lesser evil.

Alexander Saxton's Chicago novel of striking railroad workers, *The Great Midland* (1948), is a rare example of a pro-Party book published, reluctantly, by a noted publishing house (Appleton-Century-Crofts). One way it may have passed muster was its reaffirmation of marriage in the face of the re-arrangement of gender relations caused by wartime separation. An incisive, if "red," romance, it integrates the old Fannie Hurst disappointed-love plot into the story of a working-class comrade-wife. Stephanie Kovaks, a Workers' School teacher, is dedicated to the Communist struggle almost as much as to her unstable organizer husband, Dave Spaas, for "any dream that gave the strength to fight of men like . . . Dave was a dream to hold on to" (352).[79]

Despite such lapses into Proletcult rhetoric, Saxton's careful delineation of Stephanie's inner life manages to challenge Party injunctions against a trivializing romanticism while transcending Hurstian soap-opera sentimentality as well. What is more likely to have enabled one of the more liberal Appleton editors to recommend it, however, was the careful treatment of Spaas's ideological impasse in the face of Stalinist expediency. For, like Bonosky and so many period writers on the left, Saxton contextualizes earlier U.S. history, in this case the crucial time between the Nazi-Soviet Pact (1939) and the German invasion of Stalinist Russia (1941), in a leftists-in-trouble plot. Saxton even puts a labor-class argument against U.S. Communists in the mouth of Dave's apolitical coworker named (ironically?) Red Brogan. "What's wrong with you commies, anyhow?" he taunts Dave as they face military service. "[N]ow I guess we'll all be out beating the drums because Joe Stalin got his ass in the hot water" (304).

Like many pro-CP novels of the late 1940s and the next decade, Saxton prudently ends on an ideologically indecisive note. Dave, leaving the neighborhood branch of the Party far behind, is off to fight "Roosevelt's war" while bracing himself for the confusion over Stalin's war that will, as his creator was well aware, mark his postwar return. Saxton further acknowledges the looming ambiguity in Dave's riposte to Red: "A position that's right today may be wrong tomorrow" (305). The irony of the remark is twofold. However little a turncoat Stalin measures up today, the "patriotic" Americans who come to bail him out may be found wanting tomorrow.

By the mid-1950s the pro-Party novel with subject matter like Saxton's railroad protest was unpublishable outside the CP presses, and even then it was advertised as "giving typically American roots to the story."[80] A novel by the Party adherent Margaret Graham, *Swing Shift* (1956), published by Citadel Press, revisits the well-trod literary terrain of the labor movement from the Wobbly agitations of the 1920s through the birth of the CIO in the late 1930s. Despite such a setting, her presentation includes bows to the

McCarthy period. The protagonist is ethnic but not ethnic: the son of nineteenth-century mining Scots, the generically named "Mac," has come to this country to work hard and loyally. He leads a strike as do "red-blooded men in the tradition of Debs" (473). The conclusion only heightens the atmosphere of defensive militance. Unskilled railroad workers locked in opposition to the organized labor movement "win" the right to be represented by the skilled AFL unions.

The Popular Front in its cold war manifestations was at its most American in the many novels and fictive historical works of Howard Fast.[81] All of these works were produced or republished while Fast was a member of the Communist Party, which he joined immediately after the war and remained with in the early 1950s while he was under subpoena or in prison from 1950 to 1951. (He did not break with the Party until 1956.) Labeled a Communist, he redoubled his patriotic output, reactively producing biographical novels about U.S. history with titles like *Freedom Road* (1944), *The American* (1946), and *Citizen Tom Paine* (1943). Determined not to permit his banishment to the pages of his own Blue Heron Press or a year in prison prevent him from serving up a critique of capitalist materialism, he explored the fascism of red-baiters and the patriotism of reds in a number of historical novels. He prefaced the chapter from *Spartacus* (1951), his allegorical novel of Romans and Christians, reprinted in *Masses and Mainstream,* with a reminder that he had been in prison for his belief.

The chapter itself made an implicit connection to the clandestine survival culture of the Thracians, prisoners of a class war. The lengthy novel, true to that goal, gives a minute description of the exploited toil of Spartacus and his fellow slaves. Yet Fast is so allegorical about the slave masters that they could represent anyone from Hitler to the red-hunters.

Each of Fast's novels, in Alan Wald's phrase, uses historical analogies or nightmare landscapes as it struggles for ways for workers and their advocates to live in the 1940s and 1950s.[82] One novel in particular provides a revisionist reading of cold warriors. Drawing with tigerish tenacity on the survival skills of his urban working-class childhood, Fast wrote of the 1950s in *The Story of Lola Gregg* (1950), a Jack London *Iron Heel* sequel of sorts and the first in a series. In it, a CP Joe Docks "organizer" is hounded, chased, imprisoned, and put to death in and by a fascistic United States. Inevitably, to describe so dystopian a USA, Fast reasserts the criminalization trope. When Gregg is executed for his beliefs, the narrative comments: "for every pimp, crook, gangster, dope peddler, murderer, there is mercy, but no mercy for him."[83]

While new readings of Fast have argued that his cold war literary resistance effort was to excavate history from the bottom up, Fast himself has denied a conscious leftist intent, arguing that he added a complex dimension to official U.S. history. A fictionalized biography of George Washington, *Freedom Road,* carefully submerges Party language under the cloak of extolling the protagonist, who, if not a populist, much less a proletarian, emerges humanized, demythified, and dedicated to a revolutionary fight to end an eighteenth-century precursor of fascism (315). Returning to literary proletarianism, another novel, *The Proud and the Free* (1953), supplies a worker's-eye view of the common man's hardships in the Revolutionary War. Such works, while they convey messages about the complexity of patriotism, never reject the cherished image of the land of opportunity. Indeed, there seemed so few un-American surprises in Fast's voluminous output that an early one, *The Unvanquished* (1942, republished in 1946 and 1947), was billed by the ad on the back cover as literary entertainment on the order of Raymond Chandler, Ellery Queen, and Pearl Buck.[84]

Whatever the ostensible subject matter, those who continued the tradition of proletarian radical fiction subordinated a challenge to capitalist ethics to a coded critique of patriotic fervor. The titular subjects ranged from Pearl Harbor (Ben Appel, *The Fortress in the Rice*, 1951) to a miners' strike (Stephen Heym, *Goldsborough*, published in Germany in English in 1953). Other novels addressed the values confusion of Mexican American miners shut out from the American way (Lars Lawrence's novels, especially the 1956 *Out of the Dust*). Finally, fragmented tales concern young Chicano men, the sweepers and errand boys who are heavy after-hours drinkers. They find status and meaning in the Zoot Suit Riots rejection by more affluent Mexicans and whites alike ("El Hoyo," 1947, and the other 1947–1950 *Arizona Quarterly* stories of Mario Suarez).

The McCarthy era had a predictably devastating impact on the lives and fiction of white women writers on the left from working-class origins, with labor or feminist affiliations, or all three. It should be remembered that as late as the 1960s the onetime Progressive labor journalist and women workers' advocate Betty Friedan found it expedient to conceal her "UE Fights for Women Workers" (1952). Thankful that the pamphlet had been published under her maiden name, Friedan found it better to "strengthen" her feminism through a middle-class appeal.[85] At the beginning of the fifties, death had stilled the voice of the author of *Daughter of Earth*, Agnes Smedley, and censorship that of Meridel Le Sueur. She placed on hold her evolving 1930s novel, *The Girl*, parts of which she had published in the 1930s and early 1940s. It would not see print in book form until 1978.

The publishing environment for unrepentant white female Communists was, if anything, even more unpromising than for men. The reasons are complex. Women labor writers of the caliber of Olsen, Le Sueur, Smedley, and Ruth McKenney (discussed in chapter 9) had to struggle for recognition from male Party members and left-literary peers even during the brief vogue of proletarian fiction. As we have seen, their 1930s writings reflect their difficulties balancing Party loyalty and fictive explorations of the oppressed, homebound workingman's wife.

By the 1950s these women writers faced much starker choices as the battle to survive financially and support or help support their children collided once more with their fictive inquiries into the working lives of labor-class women on the home front as well as in the waged job. Heightening the pressure was the question of whether they could support their children and still remain engaged, if blacklisted, Communists. This was a choice that interrupted Olsen's fiction for twenty-two years. Le Sueur, who also scrambled for a living, proclaimed her radical politics by publishing in *Masses and Main-*

stream when she could not get published anywhere else. But she too sacrificed her most ardent plot, centered on a semi-utopian collective of labor-class women and children.

With crushing irony, Ethel Rosenberg, convicted with her less colorful husband, Julius, of spying for the Soviet Union and electrocuted in 1953, was the only prominent Communist woman of the 1950s to narrate, through her prison letters, the housewife rebellion story. With the possible exception of Ethel Rosenberg and those who fit her unwelcome archetype, white, immigrant, ethnic, working-class women capitulated to the cultural expectations surrounding what the title of one well-received centrist sociological study termed the "workingman's wife."[86] Conventional photojournalists were hostile to her public persona as an unregenerate comrade-wife. Nor, caught up in the attack on red-baiting, did the Party use the cause célèbre of the Rosenbergs to publicize Ethel's sexual vitality, psychic conflicts, wage-earning past, and personal ambitions, none of which figures in the avalanche of leftist publicity about her. There simply was no Ethel Rosenberg fiction, whether to deplore her comradeship or enshrine her for giving it new meaning.

Martyr or Lilith, it remains unclear what dissatisfactions with the blandness of 1950s womanhood accounted for Ethel's disruption of the happy housewife myth. The paradox remains. So famous and notorious a woman and one at the center of cold war cultural controversy, was, in her erasure from the labor fiction of working-class femininity, marginalized by the HUAC era—including its women.

On the Wild Side: Stand-ins and Displacements in Skid Row and Military Fiction

Algren and Mailer, though associated with 1940s postwar naturalism, the first loosely leftist and the second loosely socialist, are not yoked as writers, much less as labor writers. In opposite ways, their subject matter avoids much of the rural-industrial proletarian experience: Algren by concentrating on the fluid world of Skid Row and petty criminality, Mailer by his detailed analysis of a military hierarchy as regimented and focused as Algren's is chaotic and undisciplined. Algren, older by almost fifteen years, used his 1930s picaresque on-the-road and living-hard experience and his WPA stint interviewing marginal people for much of his postwar urban fiction. His stories are set either in the Depression or in an ambiguous time period with elements of the 1930s and its own day. Mailer's World War II novel, *The Naked and the Dead,* in contrast, is anchored in a specific battle in the Pacific, issues from his post-1930s military experience, and places its lower-class characters in a detailed mosaic of middle-class conscripts and aristocratic officers and the hierarchy of military life itself. On closer inspection, there is a worker subtext in each writer's fiction, and one that, despite obvious variations, says much about the ways that white writers with leftist backgrounds acceded to and rebelled against cold war constructions of working-class lawlessness.

In our era, Algren's books have been perceived as everything from Beat to postmodern. Yet few still position him in the tradition of the working-class novel, and in his own time he was termed a proletarian novelist by those who wished to denigrate him.[87] In his response to the antilabor complacencies of the 1950s, however, he is an important voice for the 1950s disinherited, whose wavering work ethic defined personalities already discouraged by low skills and demeaning surroundings. Not many authors, including those in Party circles, welcomed a visceral association with the disenfranchised. Algren continued to refine the bottom dogs plot of his 1930s fiction culled from WPA interviews with low-functioning people whose woes preceded the breadline era. The early 1940s saw Algren embellishing his understanding of his *Somebody in Boots* protagonists, the luckless hoodlum Cass McKay and his sad prostitute lover, Norah Egan. He extended his range in his experience as a migratory casual, hobo, carnival worker, and prisoner convicted of petty theft.[88] To that he added boilermaker's assistant and union work. Yet his postwar fiction, still vaguely set in the Depression years, did more than revitalize the vision of the hard-luck transient lured by low-level crime, hard drugs, or easy sex. It pointed to the labor irrelevance of the underdog in a time of full employment.[89]

Looked at from the perspective of his late 1940s short stories and his mid-1950s novel, Nelson Algren redefined the bottom dogs form in an affluent time. Though the underclass tale was consistently Algren's, it is thus anchored in his response to this period. Although he no longer did menial work or lived as much by necessity as by predilection near the skid rows and seedy bars of Chicago, he responded to what he considered the increasingly repressive atmosphere of America by exploring his fascination with the men and women who moved in and out of low-wage, kitchen, factory, and picking jobs. Whether his texts were cautiously praised or rejected by period critics as a tour of the "American annex of Dante's inferno," reviewers concluded that Algren's misfits had little to teach the reader.[90]

Algren's characters do not even embody negative ambition. As they sever themselves from trade union culture or blue-collar work, quitting wage-earning jobs for lives of self-destruction, addiction, petty crime, and prison stints, they are proof that jobs are no answer for them, and only in part because they are spiritual knockabouts. The postwar stories, though, completely disrupt the economic mobility plot at the very time when city jobs were plentiful. In place of the scrambling to survive is the wildness of the directionless individual. The atmosphere of hard luck or scarcity is, if anything, leavened with the delusional activities of the unapologetic figures who stumble from one mishap to another—never finding in the various barrooms, boxing rings, gambling halls, or freight cars cause for either hope or despair. His characters, in fact, exist in an existential void—believing neither in themselves nor in a deliberate rebellion, but only in the futility of sustained action.

Instead of the logic of poverty, Algren's postwar figures can offer no logic at all to their actions or life choices. In "Stickman's Laughter," a story in *The Neon Wilderness,* a day in the life of Banty Longobardi, Banty's greatest achievement is to get home in one piece, however incoherent and defeated, as he gambles and drinks away his week's pay in Chicago. Jailings replace Hoovervilles in "So Help Me." There 1930s denizens of hobo jungles botch a robbery and shrug off the heist gone bad, seeing it neither as retribution nor even as accident. In "Depend on Aunt Elly" women stumble from defense plant work to jail for soliciting to brothels.

A Walk on the Wild Side, misread as a languid reprise of 1930s literary proletarianism,[91] actually vibrates with mockery of both the gravity of the 1930s down-and-out protest novel and the hostility of postwar critics. In place of Steinbeck's vernacular *vir bonus,* Algren offers a father-and-son pair who comically invert Tom Joad's rural honesty and peripatetic militance. Fitz Linkhorn is a half-demented alcoholic who stands on soapboxes in 1930s California (the Joad family's disappointing "Promised Land") and rants about the AFL conspiracy with Wall Street to defraud the working stiff (39). His son, Dove, roams the country seeking a creed and exuding a back-country manliness, but unlike Tom, the only politics he believes in is sexual. With a phallus much larger than his working-class consciousness—Algren's slap at HUAC prudery—this Dove seeks no peace. He becomes a pimp and peep-show regular.

In all of these texts, Algren seems not so much to invert the postwar consumption and success ethic as to find it absurd. In pursuit of an aesthetics of dysfunctionalism, Algren makes poetic prose of the interiority of characters so oblivious to their surroundings that they float in and out of jails, encounters with the law, violence, drunkenness, and soliciting. Their avoidance of work as the human scrap heap of an orderly postwar society is one that no amount of HUAC autocracy can eradicate.

Had the more functional members of Algren's white underclass served in the wartime military, many no doubt would have experienced the chastening brutality inflicted by noncoms on their nonconformist platoon members. In what Mailer depicts as a hierarchical class structure—officers come from privileged backgrounds to make those below them feel their double superiority—the noncommissioned officers act out class rage. The brutal sergeants who inhabit not only *The Naked and the Dead* but also James Jones's *From Here to Eternity* (1951) take out their status insecurity on people like Mailer's hard-bitten IWW-type Red Valsen, Jones's hillbilly outsider Robert E. Lee Prewitt, or his streetfighting Italian from Brooklyn, Angelo Maggio. The man who torments Valsen was a National Guardsmen–protected company scab in the oil fields and killed strikers.[92] The Valsens and Maggios respond in kind. Valsen vows to "take no crap . . . he never had" (14). On patrol in the rain, he strengthens his resolve with the 1930s labor lament "Brother Can You Spare a Dime?" (101); Maggio taunts an MP, "Go ahead. Hit me again, you son of a whore" (450).

Ultimately Mailer's and Jones's poor-white subalterns succumb to what is presented as the militarily sanctioned sadism of vengeful sergeants in the name of wartime discipline. As but one strand in these complex military landscapes, the Valsens, Prewitts, and Maggios are swallowed up in immense plots with dominant ideas of spiritual malaise, evil, brutality, sadism, and sexual obsession and dysfunction. Yet, as countermilitary texts, they deplore the corruption of authority that drives enlisted men to wildness.[93]

Mailer's subplot particularly reinforces the larger theme of individual self-abasement rather than rank-and-file solidarity, as the route to working-class military survival. In fact, Mailer underscores the military as a dubious escape from an economically impoverished background and the burden of class prejudice. An important if secondary character, Julio Martinez, a Mexican American from San Antonio, can in the civilian world be "counterman in hash house; he can be bellhop; he can pick cotton in season; he can start store; but he cannot be a doctor, a lawyer, big merchant, chief" (65). When the draft begins, he makes corporal and then sergeant. Comments the narrator, "little Mexican boys also breathe the American fables" even if they do not "make you white protestant, firm, and aloof" (67). As the novel closes, such a working-class success story is undercut by Red Valsen's death. Unlike Martinez, and at peace with his IWW/coal-mining heritage, he resists the excesses of regimentation. For his defiance, he dies as a casualty not of war but of his sadistic sergeant, who refuses to protect him in battle.

Antilabor sentiment in the era's military fiction was as much a part of a myriad of prejudices against minorities or vulnerable figures as social indifference to a transient working underclass in the period's skid row stories. As the years have passed, Mailer has erased his own class critique, calling *The Naked and the Dead* a quest for God;[94] Algren's achievement has been likened to the efforts of Beat authors like Kerouac to escape the middle class.[95] Their involvement in a liberal critique, in the naturalist tradition of Jack Conroy, James T. Farrell, and John Steinbeck, and their liberal-left contribution to what Alan Wald in another context has called the Un-American Renaissance have yet to be recovered.[96]

Imprisoning Blackness:
African American Work Fiction and Urban Pathology

African American cold war authors, leftists or disillusioned ones, are a crucial authorial group to place under the Un-American Renaissance umbrella. White authors with Party affiliations, like Saxton (*The Great Midland*, 1948; *Bright Web in the Darkness*, 1958) and Bonosky (*Burning Valley*), presented poor working blacks holding on in a hostile white ethnic labor surround. Those anti-Stalinist leftists like Swados who were committed to a racially diverse workplace acknowledged some of the postwar strides of blacks in the auto industry. Yet, as in *On the Line*, even these skilled workers experience violent industrial accidents and stymied ascensions.

African American authors had harnessed the captivity trope to carry on the Richard Wright inquiry into social constructions of black lawlessness. This enterprise inevitably propelled them into symbolic associations in the HUAC era. African American authors who were or had been Communists or had served leftist literary apprenticeships, when called to testify, were faced with the choice of exile at home or relocation abroad. Lloyd Brown, one of Wright's spiritual heirs, had worked with a famous McCarthy target, the great actor and singer Paul Robeson, on the journal *Freedomways*, had been featured in *Daily Worker* articles on black CP writers, and also wrote for and served on the board of *Masses and Mainstream* during Bonosky's tenure.[97] The veteran Communist and son of former slaves, Harry Haywood, like so many of his white Party colleagues, would often "find two characters from the FBI waiting for me at my doorstep" in mid-1950s New York City.[98]

The African American component of cold war Marxist literary resistance, exemplified by Lloyd Brown, brought together the numerous disillusioned black leftists, who included Willard Motley, Chester Himes, James Baldwin (*Go Tell It on the Mountain*, 1953), John Oliver Killens, and Ann Petry. They skirted the sort of bitter revelations that the black Left memoirist Charles Denby included in his anti-UAW chronicle *Indignant Heart* (1952). Instead, playing on the jailhouse image, these writers used a variety of stand-ins for the incendiary topic of black working-class oppression.

A transitional text, Motley's crime novel *Knock on Any Door* (1947) attempted what would not be possible a few years later for African American authors: to reposition the racial naturalism of Wright in the wider context of the classic naturalism of Farrell and Dreiser. Instead of the later heroic black convict of Chester Himes or Lloyd Brown, Motley employs a white protagonist, the low-level Chicago career criminal Nick Romano, in what Bernard Bell in *The Afro-American Novel and Its Tradition* (1987) has termed a nonracial novel.[99]

In this story of the electric-chair execution of a white street tough whose pathological anger was nurtured by reform school and by hardened police, Motley provides continuity to the plot of the hard-case, unskilled, white, blue-collar ethnic who peoples work narratives from *Maggie* through *Studs Lonigan*. Nick's short, violent life, terminated in the electric chair, resembles that of another reform school product, Bigger Thomas. In its trial by rage and then by jury, the Motley novel suggests that in a post-Wright literary era the white protagonist can somehow empower the black narrative. In early 1940, in "The Almost White Boy," Motley had struggled with the racial problems of half-white men rejected by whites as uncivilized, a plot deemed too controversial to be published until the HUAC era had largely passed.[100] But it was only with *Knock on Any Door* that he further complicated the theme of the dangerous black by offering a lawless white who in all other respects seems to mirror Bigger Thomas as an environmental product. This is not to argue that Motley displaced the black rage plot onto working-class whites. Nick Romano is a parody of blue-collar assimilation in the early cold war. He walks out on good steel mill jobs (jobs blacks could only long for), has sex indiscriminately, except with his adoring wife Emma, and "works nights" stealing so he can be home with her during the day (291). In every way, Motley inaugurated the "whiteness studies" approach to urban working-class pathology that the cold war novel would explore so fully. But by so doing, he signaled the workplace (or prisonscape) interdependence of black and white laboring or politically militant figures.

Chester Himes brought to his jailhouse and labor narratives experiences that Motley could not. A prewar menial laborer and a member of the underworld who had served jail terms for burglary, he wrote early stories about white and black inmates and about his wartime defense-plant experience.[101] He raises the same question, despite the plot differences, in *If He Hollers Let Him Go* (1945*)*, on racial tensions in the Los Angeles defense industry. *If He*

Hollers was reissued the same year as Himes's *Lonely Crusade* (itself reissued three years later) appeared, the latter concerning a black defense worker/trade unionist used and discarded by the CP. Himes asks: do whites betray or befriend the black working class? Ironically, only in prison *(Cast the First Stone,* 1952) does he find viable interracial friendship, though in the name of homoerotic love.

Lloyd Brown provides perhaps the era's most thorough treatment of the black prisoner by amplifying the labor and militance themes of Motley and Himes. Brown himself was a working-class black conversant with resistance culture among black steelworkers in prewar Pittsburgh, the veteran of three years in a Jim Crow squadron in the army air force, and a committed leftist journalist who befriended blacks consigned to Death Row.[102] When the Communist Party's Masses and Mainstream Press published his novel *Iron City* in 1951, Brown boldly drew on his own experience. He had been a twenty-year member of the CP arrested during an early sweep of Communists in 1941. *Iron City* interlaces stories of white CP members arrested on "criminal syndicalism" charges with those of black convict converts to the Party. Without denying that some of the prisoners had preferred larceny to labor, Brown constantly juxtaposes the "white jobs" denied blacks who were law-abiding to underscore the incarceration of young black men on trumped-up charges, in particular Lonnie James (in real life Willie Jones), a laid-off steelworker accused of murder.

Tied in with these assessments of Lonnie's real work and alleged criminal life is a prison taxonomy that catalogs other young black inmates' former jobs. Brown drives the "lawful black" point home by inserting Lonnie's vita into the text, from orphanage to high school to laid-off tinplate worker to welfare recipient (125), providing news clippings that suggest the slanted reportage of the white press. In "The Legacy of Willie Jones" (*Masses and Mainstream,* February 1952) the author himself presents a coda to the squelched opportunities symbolized by Lonnie's execution. Brown characterizes him as "this doomed young Negro—a laborer in Carnegie Steel, framed by the implacable masters."[103]

No assessment of the legacy of *Native Son* in the HUAC era would be complete without mention of the brilliant fiction of indignation by Ralph Ellison and James Baldwin. Paradoxically this brilliance singles them out as exceptional figures. Displaying an eloquent sensitivity to race-based praise and insult, Ellison's transit-to-Harlem novel, *Invisible Man,* and Baldwin's escape-from-Harlem novel, *Go Tell It on the Mountain* (1953), reveal the precocity of an atypical but alienated black youth. Ellison's 1946 essay "Twentieth-Century Fiction and the Black Mask of Humanity" joins Baldwin's incendiary first essay series on the "rage of the disesteemed" in *Notes of a Native Son* (1949; rev. ed., 1953). Though published prior to these authors' best-selling novels, and reissued in the decade after the fiction, these pieces act as sequels of sorts to their novels.[104] While both Baldwin and Ellison expand the black otherness metaphor beyond U.S. borders, they argue for the double outsiderness of the African American *succès d'estime* with an international reputation. Ellison's lynching-witness southern migrant and Baldwin's vituperation victim and city boy express a rage at racist poverty born of their experience as African Americans. But they are also invested in joining a meritocracy of intellect closed to all but the most talented. The soul-searching of the protagonists is far removed from that of Saul Bellow's speculative Augie March, Budd Schulberg's brashly arriviste Sammy, and Sloan Wilson's 1955 bourgeois everyman in the gray flannel suit. Yet, in their own way, the work of Ellison and Baldwin joins such explorations of the ironies of 1950s success.

The shadow of Bigger Thomas hovers over fiction from Motley to Baldwin. The story of Bigger's unheralded murder victim, the maid Bessie Mears, a tale given short shrift at his trial for murdering a wealthy white woman, also haunted the texts of liberal-minded African American women writers. Some of the strongest New Deal voices were silent in the postwar era: Marita Bonner, curiously unproductive, and Zora Neale Hurston, in legal and spiritual trouble, were no longer writing fiction. The esteemed poet Gwendolyn Brooks, veering between helpful tour guide and outraged black intellectual, published a strange 1951 local-color tour of her South Side Chicago "Bronzeville" neighborhood in *Holiday* magazine. The poetic, fragmented *Maud Martha* (1953), her only novel, was also set in Bronzeville, where dwell Maud Martha Brown, her janitor father, and her grocery-clerk husband. But there is no fictive dialogue with either the black rage or the underemployment experience. Other African American women, such as the playwright and biographer Shirley Graham, contributed articles to Party journals like *Masses and Mainstream*. So too the now-forgotten Beulah Richardson, a poet in the Hughes tradition of "No Crystal Stair," who published domestic-work poems like "A Black Woman Speaks."[105] Party-affiliated fiction by black women was a rarity. Yet in a way this is rather reductive. The former maid and would-be clerical worker at the center of Ann Petry's *The Street* joins the iron-willed Bahamian matriarch of Paule Marshall's *Brown Girl, Brownstones* (1958), grooming her Brooklyn-born daughter for college and for property owning. Both women leave a legacy of violence to the very children they are trying to mother.

Published at opposite ends of the postwar downsizing of black workers, each novel, set during the war, rings with outrage that what was important about the war experience for black women was the extent to which doors remained closed.[106] For all her beauty, drive, and talent, Petry's Lutie Johnson can give her son only a Harlem slum flat. All attempts at careers other than domestic service are thwarted; prostitution is the sole vocation offered her by a harridan madam living in her building. What was Bessie Mears's passivity is Lutie's rage. Reversing the Bigger plot, she explodes in fury at a black hustler intending her harm, an eruption of violence that ends in his death. With her life in ruins and her preteen son held without bail for having stolen at the behest of another corrupt black man, Lutie ends up a fugitive from white justice.

The scenario of thwarting black manhood and the reactive violence of black women who see their ambitions frustrated was also found in a world very different from Lutie's gangster-ridden Harlem. In fact, Paule Marshall's fictive ethnography of struggling Caribbean property owners empowers the tireless factory worker/landlady Silla Boyce to commit domestic violence. In the name of her relentless ambitions and bewildered children, Silla mounts a campaign to wrest legal control from her insouciant husband, Deighton, which results in his deportation. To the emotional devastation of their children, unmanned, drained, disinherited, he creeps home to the West Indies to die.

Unlike many of their male colleagues, some of the chief African American women writers of the 1940s and 1950s who contribute to the Un-American Renaissance neither wrung forced confessions from their female characters nor sent them to prison. Yet their heroines partook of the punishment trope encircling myriad other cold war labor texts. In the end, they would find no parole from the remorse attendant on the mother's crime of the heart: the failure to establish a future for her children.

(Dis)placing Labor in the Literary 1940s and 1950s

The two-volume HUAC report on subversion published both in the mid-1950s and a decade and a half later included the most venerable labor organizations and leaders of the century. Many names and organizations completely alien to labor also appeared. But placed in the context of the era's labor fiction, "named" union leaders fed the period distrust of laboring people, even by themselves. The Left unwittingly blurred the boundary between guilt and guilt by association, loyalty and subversion, crime and hypocrisy, the unhappy worker and the true blue blue-collar American.

Though unable to detach current truth from governmental and media scandal spin, our era is, at the very least, more critical of HUAC than of the misguided reds. Hindsight reveals that the very overkill of the FBI files defeated their documentary purpose. Somewhere in the avalanche of data were serious charges against a limited number of Party zealots. Inevitably included were those with labor backgrounds and goals. The larger group was criminally misguided, placing Moscow directives above their goals as American citizens and willfully deaf to Khrushchev's 1956 revelations about Stalin's crimes against humanity. The former Soviet Union is making previously hidden archival material about the Rosenbergs and many other U.S. fellow travelers, including those devoted to the working class. The resultant debate about the degree of the executed spy couple's guilt continues. The fate of that quasi-proletarian couple may well be the cornerstone of a new field with labor ties, blacklist studies. The 1990s saw powerful arguments in memoirs by those who named names or were blacklisted as well as the efforts of impressive scholars such as Harvey Klehr arguing for complicity and Ellen Schrecker debunking conspiracy fantasies.[107]

Hemmed in by indirection in the dangerous years of the 1940s and 1950s, prolabor writers nevertheless challenged the assumption that the only way to dignify labor was to decriminalize it. The message was not new to U.S. labor fiction. Any social documentary reading of George Lippard, Rebecca Harding Davis, and Stephen Crane reveals that people in an economy of scarcity did cross the line between work and criminality. The marginalized workers who were celebrated in so many 1930s tales viewed it as a necessity to engage in politically lawless acts, often out of the conviction that there was also something rotten in the state of organized labor.[108] Not until the cold war, however, had labor and its literary defenders been summoned to atone for the Depression era "crimes" of civil disobedience, by marching for a veterans' bonus, agitating for collective bargaining, and closing down whole factory complexes. No wonder the disaffected soldiers, embittered convicts and ex-convicts, sexual rebels, and African American prisoners are haunted by the labor ghosts of the 1930s.

However differentiated in other ways, the workers of Schulberg and Algren, McGrath and Motley, Arnow and Petry walk alone, tormented in the midst of plenty. As the 1960s, a decade every bit as confrontational as the HUAC era, dawned, a widespread literary recidivism seemed to return workers to their Progressive Era "prisons" of inarticulateness: bit players in the dramas of their own simple, violent, or would-be middle-class lives.

Beneath what seemed a simple postwar ideology of hard work for good pay, the issues of American exceptionalism and worker ascension took on the confused coloration of the time. In the most prosperous labor circles, red-baiting the un-American, unhappy left-wing worker was counterpointed by the critique of working-class success and the ravages of consumerism. A resilient naturalism struggled against minimizing worker figures or assuming the only alternative to acquisitive individualism was to be a loner in a crowd. There was no return to the historical moment that gave birth to the golden age of worker art in the roughly two decades before the Left lost the culture wars to McCarthy and HUAC. But the Algrens and Browns and Petrys, shifting the workspace to the fleabag hotel, the prison cell, and its Harlem housing equivalent, left a legacy of sympathy for workers as people as well as members of a class. As so often in U.S. protest literature, authors could better show how to die nobly in a money-hungry land than to live there collectively.

"Proletarians were fashionable during the New Deal," a John Dos Passos soured on leftism and labor commented retrospectively of the 1950s in his pessimistic novel *Mid-Century* (1960).[109] In so doing, he unwittingly launched a new battle to define the worker narrative. The 1960s labor text would have little to say on the perils of prosperity. Cynicism about upward mobility would deepen treatments of labor's internecine struggles. There would be little praise for either individuality or the isolation of the honorable worker. As once again in U.S. literature native-born, white skilled workers' esteem came to replace self-transformation, the validity of a labor-oriented American whiteness would be at its lowest ebb. But in other ethnic, gender, and racial quarters, powerful, young, working-class writers were about to unveil the last of the hidden injuries of class.

CHAPTER 11

The Usable Past
Jobs, Myths, and Three Racial-Ethnic Literatures of the Civil Rights Era

The whole so-called Chicano movement seems to me nothing but another splinter from the old Civil Rights era. . . . I'd been around for the early Negro pushes for more jobs with car lots and banks.

[Yelling] viva Cesar Chavez! . . . we swell through [the barrio] of dogs and cats and trash.

—OSCAR ZETA ACOSTA, *THE REVOLT OF THE COCKROACH PEOPLE* (1973)

As you know, any plain person you chance to meet can prove to be a powerful immortal in disguise come to test you.

—MAXINE HONG KINGSTON, *CHINA MEN* (1977)

"These young boys who went to the Bureau school, they run their love life on white time. Now me, I go on Indian time."

—LOUISE ERDRICH, *LOVE MEDICINE* (1984)

Ronnie Farley, *Judy K. Buffalo,* Portland, Oregon, 1991. Photograph. Courtesy of Ronnie Farley.

I n the mid-1960s the cold war assault on labor and the Left began to ease, and a new alliance of blacks and Latinos renewed labor's postwar challenge to a broadened Taft-Hartley Act. The act's union-busting section 14, the "right to work" laws, which permitted business to exploit the racial and racial-ethnic minorities constituting a cheap force who earned less than the minimum wage, now came under fire.[1] Frequently joining forces with the civil rights forces led by Martin Luther King, Jr., in the South, where the "Negro broth-ers"[2] were protesting racism and job discrimination in Montgomery, Birming-ham, Selma, and Memphis, was the Chicano (a self-naming by the 1960s Mexican American) voice of the field migrants' United Farm Workers (UFW), Cesar Chavez, who called for the repeal of the anti-unionist section.[3] The veteran labor organizer did so in the name of the dignity of the black share-croppers and minimum-wage workers and of his own constituency. American-born Chicanos formed the largest underclass of Mexican heritage. Barrio menials and migrant farmworkers, they were descendants of the waves of World War I–era Mexicans who had arrived in the Southwest and on the West Coast to join Asians among the ranks of migrants.[4]

It was an impoverished class indeed. Two full decades after the Chavez "Huelga" movement, nine million of the twenty-five million Americans be-low the poverty line were Mexican Americans. For "the equality of a living wage," Chavez led quasi-religious protests against the grape industry in De-lano, California, in 1965 and again in 1968.[5] In spearheading important strikes of California migrant workers in 1968, he identified his formidable op-ponents as "industrialists and corporation farmers."[6]

The historic 1964 Civil Rights Act, though linked to poor southern blacks' agitation for the vote and against Jim Crow, had the potential to aid mass unionism among Chavez's Chicanos as well as among Asians, the vocation-ally fragmented Native Americans, and other racial-ethnic minorities. These were the working people caught in the secondary job market of field, restau-rant, hotel, laundry, hospital, and sweatshop work.[7] Under the civil rights aegis, a series of labor-related rights initiatives were undertaken. They ranged from the African American South to the Chicano barrios of Los Angeles and the migrant villages of the Imperial Valley to the congested Chinatowns of Asian pieceworkers on both coasts.[8] Moreover, by the end of the decade Na-tive Americans were emboldened by the birth of the 1968 American Indian Movement (AIM) and the 1972–1973 commemorative "occupation" of Wounded Knee, South Dakota.[9] They too rebelled against what they saw as their economic dead end of reservation impoverishment uncorrected by the Bureau of Indian Affairs (BIA).[10] In her irritated lament "I'm tired of finding two-bit jobs," one grudgingly assimilated woman speaks in a 1987 short story by Michael Dorris (himself part Modoc) for many other Native American tribes.[11]

For Chicanos, Chinese, and American Indians to alter their century-old situations as racialized cheap labor, they hoped as well to counteract the widespread perceptions of docility, passivity, and fecklessness that were their respective hallmarks of a century as laborers in the United States. From the Progressive Era onward, whether as field workers or as the "latest newcomers to industrial work," Mexicans—and soon, their Chicano descendants—had traditionally been the day laborers perceived as difficult to organize.[12] As pre–World War II strikebreakers in the smokestack industries, they were branded job-stealers and inevitably consigned to substandard steel, mining, packingtown, or citrus company towns.[13]

In the eight decades of their own tortured work history on rails and in fields, Asians had sometimes made common cause with Latinos.[14] Mexicans and pueblo mixed-bloods had also often worked together on railroad jobs in the very New Mexican towns that were home to barely subsisting Indians.[15] Yet far more often all of these racially coded groups, encased in the odd-jobs, subsistence-farming, or market economy, experienced the race labels and job segregation that remained after the demise of the Great Society and its uneven compliance with affirmative action.

As the 1970s dawned and the government ceased to be receptive to the economic demands of minorities, ethnic labor could look neither to widespread economic self-transformation nor to labor solidarity. Rather than celebrate a rediscovered labor heritage, each group saw it as only part of a broader agenda of social activism. The push to end racially segregated work was subordinated to the confrontational politics of Chavez's La Causa and of AIM.[16] Rare were the Chinese American labor organizers. Despite some New York City attempts in the Depression era to end the industrial isolation of the Chinese laundryman, even by the civil rights era, few outside left-wing garment-trades circles of expatriate Chinese seemed publicly concerned with working-class Chinese Americans.[17] One exception was the worker-activist Ben Fee, rediscovered in the 1970s by the working-class playwright Frank Chin. The grandson of a Southern Pacific steward, Chin owed his own early brakeman's job to the fair employment legislation of the 1960s.[18] Chin's plays deplored the Chinese American tendency to write the coolie-level Chinaman out of U.S. history and to contemptuously dub Chinatowns "game preserves."[19] Nevertheless, as Louis Chu's prophetic 1961 novel *Eat a Bowl of Tea* suggested, it would be honoring one's family rather than acknowledging one's working-class status that would shape ambition. Working-class Chinatowns bypassed mass unionism to engage in a quietly entrepreneurial push to raise living standards and make their children professionals if they could not rise to that level themselves.

Authors who came of age in the civil rights era and its wake, born between the Depression and the beginning of the cold war, were likewise chronologically and psychically distanced from the methods and goals of the Old Left. This was certainly not a group of writers who came down to the streets to fight the revolution or to indict the social inertia of the ethnic workingman and -woman. They were not strictly worker-writers or even working-class writers. Revealing no orthodox left-wing sympathies or inclination to engage in such activities, they certainly did not use the phrase "ethnic labor class" to distinguish their worker characters from the bourgeois who also inhabit their stories. These writers were often far more concerned with the broad themes of Chicano and Asian U.S. identity, or with Indianness, than with class and economic distinctions within each group. Still, as socially concerned authors immersed in community and family organizations, they deplored the economic and social borderlands that ghettoized working-class migrants and their American-born children. In 1998 the Arizona-born Luis Alberto Urrea, a university writing instructor, remembered from his childhood "the [names] they called dad and me—like *wetback. Spic, Beaner. Greaser, Pepper-belly. Yellow-belly. Taco-bender. Enchilada breath.*"[20]

Such candor does not come easily. Two generations of chroniclers of a labor-class ethnic childhood paved the way for Urrea's unsparing assessment. The post–civil rights wave included the "Chicano Renaissance" authors Tomas Rivera (*And the Earth Shall Not Devour Them,* 1971), Oscar Zeta Acosta (*The Revolt of the Cockroach People,* 1973), and Raymond Barrio (*The Plum Plum Pickers,* 1969). Among the important Chinese American writers with labor themes were Maxine Hong Kingston, the author of a fictionalized narrative (*China Men,* 1977), and the playwright Frank Chin (*The Chickencoop Chinaman,* 1971). Prominent Native American storytellers of work included Ted Williams (*The Reservation,* 1976) and Jim Welch (*The Death of Jim Loney,* 1979). The 1980s saw the emergence of authors of the caliber of Denise Chavez (*The Last of the Menu Girls,* 1986), Dagoberto Gilb ("The Death Mask of Pancho Villa," 1991), Leslie Marmon Silko (*Ceremony,* 1986), Louise Erdrich (*Love Medicine,* 1984), and Fay Myenne Ng ("A Red Sweater," 1986).

These writers all chronicled their own or closely observed labor-class hardships. Yet all of them only loosely fell under the rubric of ethnic proletarianism. This was in part because they followed the path of what their colleague Richard Rodriguez in his up-from-hardship memoir *Hunger of Memory* (1982) generically termed "the scholarship boy."[21] Rodriguez focused on the embourgeoisement that allegedly alienated ethnic writers from the very cultures they were seen as representing. He became for them, however, an oppositional rather than a representative model. A variety of other authors perceived their own upward mobility in mythic terms other than those of Franklinesque self-forging. They recognized in their "remade modes of being" as articulators of their cultural heritage a kinship with the uprooted "folk."[22]

This is not to imply that the authors bundled by literary criticism into ethnic groups concurred about the myths that constituted a usable past, or that one writer's ethnic hero was not another's fool or dupe.[23] But one can risk certain generalizations about and even among groups of writers. Appropriating the voices of factory workers and maids, urban itinerants and downwardly mobile immigrant parents, these authors placed such narrators in a quasi-mythical surround of "magical realism." Latino work narratives were often dominated by stream-of-consciousness narration; Asian talk stories (story-episodes) told of relatives' history or ancestors' magic; and American Indians of legends, charms, and portents. All were in some sense restructurings of the 1930s collective novel.[24] In its place is a chorus of working-poor sages and mentors who layer folktale narratives with their lived experiences in the United States.

To express the inner worlds of their working, and often impoverished, protagonists, these dual-identity writers departed from the linear, teleological Way-to-Wealth narrative associated with U.S. labor fiction since its inception (see chapter 2).[25] This chapter cannot hope to treat the many non-European multicultural literatures that have flowered since the civil rights era.[26] It can assess three important groups of racial-ethnic literary artists who make visible a trio of erased labor histories. In so doing, they engage in a long overdue struggle with ethnic labor caricatures. To that end, they ethnicize the tropes of otherness and compliance, nobility and atavism, work culture and work strictures, that have informed over a century of U.S. labor fiction. As with so many labor authors before them, representing working-class voices by challenging the ideal of classlessness propels them into struggles with the dominant culture in ways both familiar and new.

Representing Chavez and Novelizing Chicano Labor

From midwestern auto factories to California agricultural and domestic labor, job caste meant a depressingly consistent horizontal mobility for Mexican and Mexican American workers.[27] The barrio was perforce a cultural enclave, but it was also a ghettoized residential enclave for low-wage laborers in manufacturing, service industries, and migrant farmwork.[28] In his classic memoir, *Barrio Boy* (1971), Ernesto Galarza made a point of remembering a fiery leader named Duran, a veteran of Mexican mine strikes who balanced IWW sympathies, farmwork, and family duties in a World War I barrio in Sacramento, California.[29] But when the California remnants of the Old Left, veterans of the migrant workers' struggles of the 1930s, turned out to support Chicano protesters, they were lost in the radical chic crowd supporting Cesar Chavez's Causa and his well-publicized march from Delano to Sacramento.[30] Whether or not the downplayed labor themes were a result of the redirection of energies implied by barrio-based ethnic pride, as late as the 1960s fiction had not captured the factory or field-as-factory experience of Mexican migrants and their American-born children. Nor was there any account of the way a minority of such working people had participated in 1930s packinghouse, car, and steelworking unionization.[31] The mute peons and wordless conformists of Sinclair's unflattering *King Coal* (all of them the labor antitheses of Mexican organizers in Progressive Era mining towns) anticipate a more subtle though no less deliberate silencing in Steinbeck's *Tortilla Flat* (1935).[32] In his migrant plot, Steinbeck celebrated displaced rural Americans who fought against labor conditions in the California fruit and vegetable fields. But he directed New Deal attention away from the Mexican Americans or Filipinos who were also crucial to the labor protest in California's Imperial Valley.[33] Even by the late 1940s the Arizona stories of Mario Suarez's directionless if amiable braceros seem to depart little from the 1930s paisanos.[34] Many were the links, in fact, to Steinbeck's feckless characters, living on mañana time.

Such disparagement was consistent with the attitudes that accompanied the repatriation of Mexican industrial workers in the 1930s, and then in the 1940s the bracero program to import cheap agricultural labor back from across the border.[35] It was not until the rise of the UFW protests against "factories in the field" that radical-ethnic artists engaged in an agitprop agenda with links to the HUAC-silenced 1930s theater of Clifford Odets and the film *Salt of the Earth* (1954). Produced by nonethnic Hollywood leftists, *Salt of the Earth* was a homage to striking New Mexican zinc miners. The film honored their principled resistance to coercion, their religious faith, their wives' hard-won feminism, and their group defiance of their ethnic segregation. The art of a resurgent Chicano trade unionism awaited an ethnic worker-playwright, Luis Valdez, who founded the teatro camposino, a strikers' theater that served as the cultural base of the UFW on picket lines, at barrio and field rallies, and at union meetings. Performing playlets like "Huelga!" and satirizing their commodified status by wearing shirts covered with dollar bills, Valdez's picketers evolved what they called "actos," short scenes melding spirituality and agitprop and dealing with a specific element of the strike.[36] By April 1966, the teatro groups had joined the great company of strikers under the Chavez aegis in the march from Delano to Sacramento.[37]

Valdez soon shifted from political activism to celebration of Chicanos' roots in pre-Columbian history, music, and myth.[38] Chavez himself, with the UFW at times seeming his personal platform, increasingly stage-managed the Chicano labor movement, cleverly drawing on Mexican radical models. During the Mexican revolutionary epoch, 1910–1917, Emiliano Zapata's soldiers had carried banners to the "Zapatista Virgin of Guadalupe," and Pancho Villa's revolutionaries had displayed a similar religious devotion.[39] Chavez invoked the Mexican Revolution through the UFW's religious processions, especially a pilgrimage in which strikers carried the Virgin of Guadalupe, "patroness of the Mexican people." He played as well on the revolutionary quest for an Aztec Indian heritage, or Aztlan, mythically linked with the Promised Land.[40] During strikes like those in Delano in 1965 and again in 1968, Chavez was charismatic enough to reconcile an anti-Communist Catholicism with a decidedly secular dedication to the honor of workers. His station wagon was complete with a portable shrine to the Lady of Guadaloupe.[41] Labor movement expediency necessitated Chavez's eclecticism; he took religious, economic, political, and artistic help where he could.

The early 1970s, when the Chavez charisma was fading somewhat and UFW membership along with it, coincided with the efforts of the most militant generation of Chicano writers yet to try to voice the lived experience of migrant farmworkers. The dilemma of representing Chicano work, whether in field or hotel kitchen, was only heightened by these authors' controversial preference for magical realism and for a mythic, cyclical sense of time. Nowhere was this more evident than in the literary division of opinion on portraying Chavez himself.

Rudolfo Anaya's mystical rural-poverty novel *Bless Me, Ultima* (1972), set retrospectively in a New Mexican farm village much like the one of Anaya's own 1940s childhood, contains no direct reference to Chavez. Nonetheless, it anticipates the contradictions in that mixture of Chicano folk religiosity and Mexican Roman Catholicism on which the processions of Chavez's migrant strikers drew. In Anaya's rendering, the timeless, otherworldly Aztlan is an uneasy fit with the educational ambitions fueled by a hierarchical Catholic schooling. Rather than redefine the church in terms of the Virgin of Guadalupe or Christ figure, both central to the Chavez processionals, Anaya chooses to "purify" his young protagonist, Antonio, pulling him away from Christian teleology and toward mysticism.

While an unaccustomed task for writers with labor agendas, it remained for the Chicano Renaissance to place Anaya's quest for the mythical fatherland within the context of a usable working-class past. Dual-identity writers of the Chicano Renaissance, whether from privileged backgrounds, like Raymond Barrio, or impoverished ones, like Oscar Zeta Acosta and Tomas Rivera, seized the ethnic day. They too acknowledged migrants' beaten-down or angered responses to the plight of the "wetback" and their disappointments with the exclusionary myth of American exceptionalism. Most of Acosta's *The Revolt of the Cockroach People* is a cynical send-up of radical chic. Only the protagonist's brief audience with—or visitation by—Chavez reasserts the leader's spirituality. He appears as both a mythical father of Chicanos and a son of the Mexican radical tradition of Pancho Villa and his peasant revolutionaries.[42]

This construction of Chavez is out of step with the savage satire on the Chicano cultural movement embedded in the novel. Acosta deliberately skirts the frequent labor movement charge that Chavez had a messiah complex and was too distant from his rank and file. But he sets the Los Angeles barrio uprising in a sell-out, hypocritical milieu. Swiftly co-opting the Chicano Law Center is the Ford Foundation, which donates money to quiet the people chanting trendy ethnic awareness slogans.[43] La Causa's very political clout seems to challenge the mystification of Chavez for militant purposes.[44] Acosta casts a cold eye on that collaboration of barrio militants, artists, trade unionists, priests, Old Left radicals, and intellectuals, all rallied under the Chavez banner, a new generation fighting against factories in the fields.[45] Viewed this way, Cesar Chavez, the guru-father of Chicanos, is a shrewd labor activist, averse neither to cloaking himself in sacredness nor to throwing 1960s strobe light fund-raisers for his UFW.[46]

Barrio and Rivera continued to ask questions about the mythic Chavez and his actual victories over the Anglo growers. Their novels lament exploited pickers looking in vain for economic salvation, whether in prayers to the Virgin of Guadalupe or in the real-life Delano boycotts and job actions that constituted Chavez's politicized version of the Virgin. In Barrio's *The Plum Plum Pickers,* Ramiro Sanchez, a Chavez stand-in leading his fellow braceros in rebellion against the 1960s fruit industry, is swiftly humbled.[47] He who "would make California his own" (193) in the name of Chicanos finishes drunken and ineffectual.

Barrio conveyed the strike momentum in fictive news articles about it while he underplayed Chavez's Delano march to commemorate the Virgin of Guadalupe, the mother of Mexico (77). Though *The Plum Plum Pickers* was published at the height of Chavez's UFW and reissued in 1971, when the union's fortunes were waning, Barrio is really writing a post-UFW novel. He filters the techniques of Ruth McKenney's CIO fictive documentary *Industrial Valley* (1939) through the generational disempowerment captured by the sociologist Oscar Lewis in his classic *The Children of Sanchez: Autobiography of a Mexican Family* (1961). Nothing stirs Ramiro's fellow migrants to radical action after he loses his own fragile political selfhood in alcoholism. Nor does Barrio model his Chicano family after the self-reliant types of *The Grapes of Wrath* (1939). Barrio settles old scores with Steinbeck's Okies, whose real-life racism antagonized Chicano migrants. He portrays their representatives, the Zeke Johnsons, as baby-killing degenerates. No compassionate Tom or Rosasharn Joad inhabits this world.

Barrio does recall Steinbeck's Earth Mother character, Ma Joad, in this social protest threnody for a leaderless people. Devoted to her family's survival, Barrio's Lupe sees her prayers to the Virgin of Guadalupe for laboring people answered for her family alone. Her husband finds employment in a tree nursery far from the strike and the fields. In happy praise of her husband's chances for a raise and more status, Lupe distances herself from the Chicano struggle. At novel's close, she reflects on the prospect of entering the mainstream of California consumerism and buying a house.

Tomas Rivera, like Chavez the son of a migrant laborer, was born during the toughest years of the Texas depression. After receiving a doctorate near the end of the Chavez era (1969), he climbed to capitalist success as the chancellor of the University of California at Riverside.[48] But even as he rose from the scholarship boy to the highest-ranking Chicano in the nation in education, Rivera gave voice to his pre-ascensionist migrant childhood in arguably the most powerful ethnic revisionist bildungsroman of the time, *And the Earth Shall Not Devour Them* (1971). Viewed through the eyes of a young Chicano field worker in Texas, the events of this autobiographical novel are set in the 1950s, when Chavez himself was undergoing his first political awakening.

Unlike Barrio, Rivera tells a pre-UFW story. As such, it is structured largely as "a sort of community journal spoken aloud."[49] The intellectual rebel at its center seeks a way to throw off the predictability of migrant camp poverty, family misfortune, growers' brutality, and even the passivity of his family's Christian acceptance of it all. To that end, the protagonist daringly invokes not Christianity but its antithesis, embodied in this novel by his bold call on the devil. When the devil does not appear, nor does the earth swallow him up for blasphemy, the boy comes to realize his unused power to effect change by secular means.[50]

Rather than sacralizing or unfrocking the Chavez figure, Rivera thus deftly remakes the Faust myth to symbolize the Chicano quest for self-determination in the punitive field-factories of the Southwest. Viewed allegorically, the story introduces a self-inventing labor-class figure, on the brink of a manhood that will test his ideological rupture with the passivity of his field working parents. In the changeless world and oral tradition of the 1950s braceros, Rivera acknowledges that there was no vehicle yet for UFW proletarianism. Bridging the mythic and the mundane, his protagonist learns that in the ideological struggle for working-class selfhood, religion and myth are only as useful as the worker who derives strength from them.

In their literary struggle for a rhetoric of Mexican American laboring life, some of the other important male authors of the Chicano Renaissance portrayed a mythic Chavez whose radicalism was nevertheless preempted or premature. Rolando Hinojosa-Smith, no stranger himself to the anti-Mexicanism of the American 1950s and 1960s, explored such prejudice through an alternative reduction of mythic perspective. His pickle factory night watchmen, barflies, and overburdened mothers all seem caught between the waning moral force of community tradition and the banality of the new Tex-Mex lifestyle.

The thwarted or inchoate nature of resistance culture was certainly a preoccupation with those who, in the wake of the 1970s women's movement, brought Chicana feminism to Chavez's cause. Portraying the daughters of the people was as crucial to their 1980s texts as were the portraits of the sons in prefeminist texts by male authors. It should be noted that Chavez had his trusted women advisers, including Dolores Huerta and his own wife, Helen.[51] And there is the same vocational division as in male literary discourse: the scholarship girl versus the field hand in the Anglo-ruled house, the Mexican maid.[52] The 1980s continued to see pleas for migrant justice in texts such as *Another Land* (1982), by the seasoned Chicano popularizer Richard Vasquez, just as the decade before had witnessed texts on Chicana womanhood like Isabel Rios's *Victim* (1976). That such texts have not been reprinted points to a shift in subject in the years that the UFW lost support and Chicana feminism gained it.

The mission in 1980s women's texts is to bridge that gap in the name of resistance to Latino patriarchy, even at the cost of cultural estrangement. Herself the daughter of a tenant farmer, Gloria Anzaldúa earned a master's degree. The lesbian author of the poetic memoir-credo *Borderlands/La Frontera* (1987), she redefines the artistic mission of Barrio and Rivera. "I feel perfectly free, " she declares, "to rebel and to rail against my culture."[53] She seeks to resurrect the female deities of a folk Catholicism with pagan elements. Her pantheon would reestablish the links between the pre-Christian fertility goddesses and the Virgin of Guadalupe. In her allied artistic and spiritual quests, there is no distinction between the "dark" sensuality of the deities and the Christian "good mother" of the Virgin. Rather, both exist in a mythic pantheon to challenge the servitor identity she feels is imposed on all Chicana women, regardless of class (27–31). Using this schema, she bypasses the male-dominant Aztec-Mexican culture of the Delano marchers. In her feminist resistance, the Mexican serving woman, the cannery workers, and the undocumented woman, "la mujer indocumentado" (13), are in a kinship with the educated woman, the professional writer.

So idealized a vision of feminist rediscovery works well in the mythic weave of words that Anzaldua has at her command. Denise Chavez is as well acquainted as Anzaldúa with the rebellion implicit in the Chicana artist's fidelity to the inner life. Chavez finds 1980s artistic inspiration in contemporary women's low-waged work culture, shorn of deities and crossed-class borderlands. To give metaphorical power to the opening line of her alter ego, Rocio Esquivel, "I never wanted to be a nurse,"[54] Chavez utilizes the poignant vocational discoveries of an impressionable hospital maid. In the title story of her experience-based collection *The Last of the Menu Girls,* the imaginative sympathy of this youthful narrator brings humanity to her observations of doomed patients, irritable floor nurses, and the "list on the menu of all the people I'd worked with" (37). With measured irony, Rocio offers her own girlhood in a New Mexican extended family of elderly female relatives as that "previous experience with the sick and dying" (13) requisite for the Chicana caretaking role, whether mandated by Latin machismo or poorly paid by Memorial Hospital in Altavista, California. But in the defiance characteristic of feminist art following the male-centered Chicano Renaissance, those borders between child rearing, wifework, and subsistence-wage work blur.

Denise Chavez restores visibility to the menu girl's servitude. In her hands that servitude is both the barrio woman's fate and an essential Chicana writer's apprenticeship. Such Latina fiction knowingly departs from the labor assertiveness of California cannery women to present an alternative feminism. Sandra Cisneros's acclaimed *The House on Mango Street* (1983) builds on her working-class Mexican American experience in a largely Puerto Rican inner-city Chicago neighborhood. Alma Gomez's sweatshop tale "El Sueño Perdido" (1983) is situated in Denise Chavez territory. Yet Cisneros resembles Gomez, as she does other recent Latina authors, in finding both literary inspiration and cause for feminist lament in her protagonist's vocational woes. These authors' patriarchal providers, who are humiliated, unreliable, or adversarial, further supply the counterfeit machismo explored by Gloria Anzaldúa.

From fiction on Cesar Chavez to fiction by Denise Chavez, Chicano work literature has sought to capture the migrant's ways of knowing. It has defined that collision between a Mexican folk religion with pagan elements and a mercilessly practical El Norte (the immigrant renaming of the United States) that an embattled labor movement was just beginning to reconcile as the Reagan-Bush era dawned.

Mining Ore on Gold Mountain: China Men

As late as the 1930s, when it was the rare proletarian author who pointed to the promise of revolution in China and activism in New York, the familiar "Chinaman's story" appeared in that ode to the underdog, *Jews without Money* (1930). In one of the multicultural tenement novel's many ethnic asides, Mike Gold referred to the drunken Chinese laundryman patronizing blind Lower East Side prostitutes who could not know his race.[55] Gold might in part have been reacting to the antistrike ideologies of the laundryman's profession. By 1930, when leftist students in New York City tried to organize the largest Chinese labor organization, the Chinese Hand Laundry Alliance, it had only three thousand members.[56] In any case, his unflattering thumbnail sketch harked back to the "laundryman's story" of over half a century before, one that the editor of the 1993 anthology *Charlie Chan Is Dead* pilloried as "grotesque representations."[57] As launderers to the miners but never miners themselves, the "chinks" in such works provided the comedy of ethnic servitude.[58]

By the civil rights era, the Chinese American writer established a counterhistory in which upward mobility was the Pyrrhic victory of the submissive small businessman offering a service to the white world. One who restored a lost labor heritage was David Henry Hwang in his two-character strike play *The Dance and the Railroad* (1981). It overturned the "coolie" stereotype by returning to the long-overlooked activism of the 1867 Chinese Central Pacific railroad workers on the transcontinental project. Hwang's Ma and Lone represent the many strikers who, trying to reverse the labor movement prejudice against them as scabs, called for white men's wages and hours.[59] Hwang joined Maxine Hong Kingston, who incorporated the key labor strike into "The Grandfather of the Sierra Nevada Mountains" in *China Men,* a section of her hybrid nonfiction-novel as family saga. The strike slogan was "Eight hours a day good for white man, all the same good for China Man."[60]

In rediscovering this long-erased strike in which the Chinese men's demands were met by a slight rise in wages, Hwang never sheds the ironist's perspective. Ma is so elated by their victory over the "white devils"—railroad management and the wider society—that he composes a celebratory proletarian folk opera with the help of Lone. Thus buoyed up by his own glorification of the strike, he dispenses with Chinese culture and U.S. radical-labor ideology alike. Immersing himself in Yankee practicality, he rushes back to join the laborers and become Americanized and tough (85–86). Lone, as his name implies, is left to practice traditional Chinese opera dances that Ma had recycled and then discarded.

Hwang's play was reacting against post-HUAC works like Louis Chu's waiter's novel, *Eat a Bowl of Tea,* which, though with light comedy, rehearses submission and reverence for Old World customs and wives. Hwang, however ironically, restored the striker's story. Frank Chin, equally aware of what his 1988 book of short stories by the same name termed the Chinaman Pacific & Frisco R.R. Co., is fueled by outrage to rewrite Harte and Twain's racially segregated Chinese labor history.[61] Tam in Chin's early 1980s play *The Chickencoop Chinaman* acknowledges the "Heathen Chinee" stereotype.[62] Aware of his relatives' toil and now seeking the American Dream for himself and his family, Tam invokes Chinese talk story. This traditional Chinese narrative form fusing legend with vernacular storytelling is filtered through the unlikely medium of the American tall tale. Tam speaks English reminiscent of the comic American "ring-tailed" roarer of Twain and Harte, but he does so to lay blame for his relatives' historic mistreatment at the door of American racism. In his essay "Confessions of the Chinatown Cowboy," Chin similarly melds Chinese and American Western lore in the person of the labor activist Ben Fee, a type at once evocative of Chinese samurai and western loners.[63]

Hwang and Chin are in the vanguard of writers who reestablish Chinese working-class heroism by satirizing Americanness. They have determinedly resisted the "fake Chinese American dream."[64] Maxine Hong Kingston, however, made by far the most ambitious 1970s attempt to explore the dichotomies between Asian spirituality and Western materialism. Better known for *The Woman Warrior* (1976), her poetic homage to women's ways of knowing and the visionary lore of her mother's immigrant generation, Kingston is rarely viewed as an author who privileges labor themes, although she has said she preferred *China Men*, her "better book," to *The Woman Warrior*.[65] Yet in *China Men*, again juxtaposing Chinese and Western time, she provides a multigenerational saga of toiling male relatives and explores the metaphoric meaning of both railroad and laundry work.

Hwang did much to explore the way Chinese menials tried to meld a cultural inheritance with an alienating labor environment. Kingston frames a narrative with lengthy sections on heroic dreamers, including her "coolie" great-grandfather, Ah Goong, who traveled to Gold Mountain three times to work for the white "demons" on the transcontinental railroad. In restoring him to both family and public history, Kingston reclaims her self-silencing, alienated laundryman father. She interlaces scenes and recollections of her father's drab but increasingly profitable Stockton, California, laundry shop. *China Men* intertwines this spiritually comfortless place with the "timeless, stylized realm of heroic history."[66]

Perhaps anticipating the dancer-railroad toilers of Hwang, Kingston depicts her ancestors as evidence of the Chinese maxim "Any plain person you chance to meet can prove to be a powerful immortal in disguise come to test you" (119). The "plainness" includes labor actualities. Kingston carefully inserts an annotated labor chronology from the railroad years to the publication date of her book (152–159). But the same ancestors are simultaneously "yellow peril" day workers and powerful mythmakers. Even during the corrosive ten-hour workday, they move imaginatively out of linear, historical time into sacred time in which they are, in Mircea Eliade's phrase, "indissolubly connected with the Cosmos and the cosmic rhythms."[67] Thus does Ah Goong, in drilling a granite mountain for three years, transcend the sweated job. He participates in his own legend:

He worked in the tunnel so long, he learned to see many colors in black. When he stumbled out, he tried to talk about time. "I felt time," he said, "I saw time. I saw world. . . . I saw time, and it doesn't move. If we break through the mountain, hollow it, time won't have moved anyway. You translators ought to tell the foreigners that." (135)

Talk story such as this is also illustrated in the section about her other great-grandfather, Bak Goong, an 1850s Hawaiian cane-field laborer. Storytelling here acts as a labor protest. In this way Kingston frames these men's elaborately imaginative acts: "the men plowed circles instead of furrows and shouted down into them as if reaching home by a primordial cable system" (117). They liberated themselves by transforming the unpromising white foremen and apathetic local prostitutes into stories of passive-aggressively defying the "dead white demon" with the "glass eyes," an exorcism in their own language (104).

As "Oriental" as all this is, in her mixture of workaday and mythical worlds, Kingston's laborer is both nobody and mythmaker. In telling a Chinese tale, she knowingly tells a classic immigrant American one as well. The many references to the status ambiguity of her disappointed father seem a response to proletarian fiction of the 1930s. Like Mikey's immigrant parent Herman in *Jews without Money*, Kingston's father, beleaguered by thieving partners as Kingston's fictionalized narrative opens, is a gold mine of Old World parables. This figure of storytelling wisdom and monetary woes is just one in a long line of downwardly mobile literary predecessors. He laments, "They can't tell a teacher's body from a laborer's body" (145).

"How could they not go to the Gold Mountain again, which belonged to them, which they had invented and discovered?" asks Kingston's narrator about those long-dead China men (43). Mining ore on Gold Mountain is also her literary restaging of the Chinese American labor experience. Themselves the well-educated first-generation products of postwar assimilation, Kingston and fellow authors such as Gus Lee in his autobiographical novel of 1940s Chinese in working-class San Francisco, *China Boy* (1991), subordinate class to ethnicity. Yet only by conjuring the ghosts of once-despised coolies and launderers and invoking the mid-nineteenth-century Chinese ethnic divisions between angry and cowed workers, railroad strikers and laundry-shop entrepreneurs, can they generate the texts their more comfortable lives could not.

Carlisle Jobs, Wounded Knee Rebellions: Native American Fiction in the AIM Era

A final exemplar of a literature in which racial ethnic-writers with prolabor sympathies enlist a rich non-Christian oral tradition and a mythic sense of time to challenge white superiority and a technological work culture is neatly identified in the title *The American Indian and the Problem of History* (1987). One prong of the offensive to remake indigenous peoples of the United States was the Dawes Allotment Act of 1887. The act empowered the federal government to displace various tribes onto individual rather than tribal reservation allotments in exchange for valuable ancient lands. In a parallel development, the boarding-school system, synonymous with the Carlisle, Pennsylvania, Indian-Industrial School (1879–1918), slotted young people into tribal teaching jobs and the service sector of the larger world of whites.[68] Even by the 1960s mission schools were still fragmenting memory, language, and cultural tradition.

The cumulative sense of social and economic injustice expressed in three generations of fiction writers issued from the aftermath of what has rather ironically been termed the "last militant mass protest of the sixties," the early 1970s American Indian Movement.[69] AIM occupied the Bureau of Indian Affairs office Washington, D.C., in 1972. That same year and well into the next in Wounded Knee, South Dakota, witnessed the last gasp of Indian resistance on the Great Plains at the site of the 1890 massacre of Lakota (Sioux) Indians by the U.S. 7th Cavalry. Eighty years later, AIM was vividly aware of the Euro-American reportage of that event in its day.[70] Led by the charismatic, politically savvy Russell Means, AIM issued a manifesto couched in military terms.

Largely lost in news coverage of AIM's 1972 Wounded Knee demonstrations and subsequent courtroom acquittals was the movement's accompanying cry against almost a century of labor that was reservation-subsistence or off-reservation-menial.[71] Means's fellow militant Mary Crow Dog amplified the work plight some years later with the publication of her memoir *Lakota Woman* (1990). She describes living "Indian style on Boston's skid row" and in "poverty houses" where those who were unable to subsist as farmers "worked as berry picker[s] and spud picker[s] at one dollar an hour" as late as the mid-1960s.[72]

For period versions of tribal work anomie and joblessness as a form of rebellion, there were as usual ample 1970s census data on the poverty, alcoholism, and crime rates of the varied tribes. But a truer representation of the legacy of Dawes, Carlisle, and Wounded Knee was provided by the novels and shorter fiction.

In 1968 Russell Means was still seeking to apply to modern circumstances the principles of Chief Joseph of the Nez Perce to be "free to travel, free to stop, free to work . . . free to choose my own teachers."[73] The same year, set in Navajo-California locales, Scott Momaday's *House Made of Dawn* appeared. The conscripted wartime assimilation of its veteran central character, Abel, gave a literary dimension to Chief Joseph's principles. Abel is left estranged from his own culture, wounded psychologically, and unable to hold a job in the world of whites. His life, viewed broadly, is an allegory of the uncertain acolyte years of AIM, when leaders held down "white jobs" while demonstrating and being arrested: Abel himself cannot effectively search for origins. By the time James Welch's *The Death of Jim Loney* (1979) was published, that work's Blackfoot title character had taken on a richer symbolic dimension.[74] A nonperson (41) to the BIA, this figure is a jobless Montana veteran of war, of small-town bars and housing projects (106), and of itinerant work on railroad, highway, and farmhand jobs (3). He resembles his mother, a post–mission school menial (his ambitious sister has long since departed and become acculturated to white professionalism). Loney searches for a better release from the burden of job time than the oblivion of bar time. Like Momaday's Abel, he cannot sustain the journey and his life collapses in violence.

Welch articulated the urgent loneliness produced by the need for an American Indian spiritual life. Though it appeared before the rather despairing Welch text, Ted Williams's Tuscarora text, *The Reservation* (1976), in contrast, was an attempt to impose Indian time on the lives of the characters.[75] Williams, in fact, seems to downplay the western New York State Native American poverty of his traditional characters, who are scholars of medicines and ancient prayers. On closer inspection, however, these ill-housed, ill-clad sages are as physically handicapped as they are temporally liberated. Nor have their low-level jobs ceased to be the emblem of cultural tensions. The region has an alarming number of cripples and people missing limbs, possibly lost to the ravages of diabetes, which Indians suffer from disproportionately. In symbolic terms, this is the former warrior's dismemberment, the price of being Indian.

By the 1980s an author like Louise Erdrich seems remote from the "Indian rage" school of her AIM-era male predecessors. But it is not because she is unfamiliar with the impoverished conditions of the Turtle Mountain Reservation in North Dakota, which she threads into her novel *Love Medicine* (1984, expanded in 1993).[76] Erdrich's Chippewa mother may have observed the oppression of reservation life at one remove as the daughter of a tribal chairman. Yet Erdrich's saga of four intertwined families whose lives move in and out of the reservation-as-skid row is filled with understanding of the social problems attendant on economic stagnation. Her fiction, in fact, spends pages on the familiar conflicts between assimilated "white" work ("I looked good. And I looked white"), low-level "Indian" work, and government schools that teach the difference.[77] Erdrich excels in imagining dirt-poor allotments on which families like the Lazarres, "horse-thieving drunks"(63), and the Kashpaws scrape by, stretching "last year's cream money" (102). But even as the narrative rehearses the pinched lives of American Indians it enthrones larger-than-life forest dwellers like the anchorite Moses Pillager, and his oft-recounted journey to town to buy green coffee beans for twelve nickels (87).

Erdrich's greatest virtue as an imaginer of Native American life is to endow her characters with the ability to recapture, however transiently, a mythic identity in the time before mission schools and sadistic nuns imposed a cruel vision of self-abnegation. This alternative self is explored in a key chapter describing the relationship between the young, convent-bred Albertine Johnson and a devil-hunting lunatic nun, Sister Leopolda. Erdrich's men and women frequently experience transformative moments in which they feel propelled into sacred time. Theirs is the trance-producing contemplation of nature to conjure up the "Manitous, the invisible ones who lived in the woods" (89); the memory of parental lore, itself passed down through generations; or even that state of drunkenness that produces visions of walking on water. The most common inspiration, however, is "the love that would be a medicine." The more disenfranchised her characters feel, the more they seek mental flight.

Erdrich excels at finding the extraordinary beneath the ordinary. Her government and mission school graduates interpret their scrubbing and kitchen jobs with spirited acerbity. As one declaims, "If this is God's work, then, I've done it all my life "(51). The narrative particularly hovers over June Kashpaw, a "magician and a nothing-and-nowhere person at the same time" (92), and over "Lulu the scrubber[,] a sorceress of sex" (82). Little, illegitimate June Lazarre, to survive, "had sucked on pine sap and grazed grass and nipped buds like a deer" (87): a Native American returned to the world of the forest spirit.

Leslie Marmon Silko, a part-Laguna Indian who began her education at the local BIA school and later went to Catholic schools in Albuquerque, is as eloquent and visionary as Erdrich in reconstructing an Indian identity. Yet Silko has criticized Erdrich's mythmaking for being her own rather than the Native American's.[78] *Ceremony* (1986), which re-visions the male writers of the decade before, is Silko's troubling novel of Tayo, a returning warrior on a spiritual quest for sanity. He returns home to Gallup, New Mexico, from World War II silent, wounded.

It is not Tayo's memories of imprisonment by the Japanese that bind him in the wordlessness of the traumatized veteran. Aware of his mixed-breed heritage, he is an overdetermined cultural misfit denied the dignity accorded white soldiers and cut off from the historic bravery of his tribal ancestors. As other returning American Indian veterans, once his pueblo friends, lapse into the "Indian way" of alcoholism, violence, and rage, the wage-earning but assimilated women on the Native American home front endure sorrows born of their service-oriented schooling: offered theater-scrubbing jobs when they know how to type (162). "The Gallup people," writes Silko bitterly, "didn't have to pay good wages . . . because there were plenty more Indians where these [warehouse haulers and motel maids] had come from" (115).

As in Erdrich's intricate plotting, mythic and narrative time in *Ceremony* often converge. But in this moneyless, emotionally battered surround, the jobless and the underclass lose the endearing qualities that enabled them to taste Erdrich's love medicine. As holding on to his sanity, much less earning a living, becomes increasingly irrelevant, Tayo goes through a series of cleansing mystical experiences mentored by a tribal healer, Betonie, which put him in touch with his tribe's "usable past" (87). While ultimately he builds on the mystical to provide an economic base for his family, he can only regain a sense of reality through this Native American "cycle of restoration" (196).

In 1990, years after the Wounded Knee agitations, Mary Crow Dog reminisced about AIM. She urged the Sioux to join other Indian nations and reclaim Indianness by rejecting "approved rising," the embourgeoisement of a settled career, a house off-reservation, and a host of other mission-inspired values.[79] *Interior Landscapes*, a midwestern memoir by the part-Indian writer Gerald Vizenor, published the same year, advised taking on the trickster identity as a way to stave off economic humiliation and cultural anomie.[80] Another meditation, the part-Maidu Indian Janice Gould's 1992 essay "The Problem of Being 'Indian,'" rings changes on an old plaint: every college in the United States was built on native land.[81] What all of these memoirists suggest as well is that in over two decades of Native American fiction prior to the 1990s, the jobs remain the same. In Welch as in Silko, the hand-to-mouth reservation Indian is a hapless BIA pawn. The mission one is a forced convert or an establishment sell-out. And the protester is the variously thwarted warrior, trickster, or exile driven mad by disparagement from whites in command of the jobs and the money. It would take the next decade's writers to attempt to reconcile the contradictions between the aimlessly unemployed and the securely "Indian."

Lest Stereotypes Define Us: Three Hyphenated Literatures

Recent scholarship on ethnicity, labor-class or not, has demonstrated a trio of major attitudes. One vague approach is to define it loosely as "memory, response, attitude, mood . . . transmitted through generations."[82] A second school has concentrated on the way the dominant white society constructed ethnicity to fit its own expectations. A third group of scholars, many of them recent, has pointed firmly to ethnicity's fluid nature. Applied to the literatures under study, these contested ways of defining "Chicano," "Chinese American," and the varied "Native Americans" complicate the task of dual-identity authors who seek to give validity to these respective labor experiences.

Representing ethnic labor was a formidable task for the writers under scrutiny here. A first wave of 1960s authors sought clarity and authenticity in the strong oral traditions of their cultural heritages. In the second wave, from the late 1970s to the decade of the 1990s, writers incorporated the scholarship boy and girl into work-centered plots and subplots, picturing a highly problematic assimilation. Powered by technique, these texts reawaken the 1930s debate regarding "orthodox" art about workers.

As social protest participants in a U.S. labor-literary tradition, these writers were also responsive to another ethnic-labor legacy, one likely to ridicule heroic, much less magical, racial-ethnic laborers. Whether they hailed from the working class or not, all of these authors were implicitly conscious of the discriminatory messages encoded in one hundred years of nativist fiction fostered in texts by western humorists (see chapter 4), northeastern local colorists, literary naturalists, Progressives, and Socialists as well as Communists. This is not to deny that they borrowed from the European immigrant portraits of Mike Gold and Thomas Bell, in which environmental violence, weakened father figures, bleak childhoods, and the need to move beyond parental—and ancestral—belief figured prominently. But these writers used their own journeys across class boundaries to highlight the problems of dual identity.[83]

Ethnic authors substituted their characters' insularity and attachments to turbulent neighborhoods and battling families for lengthier scrutinies of class struggle or odes to the labor stalwart. Theirs was not the anticapitalist agit-prop consciousness of so many 1930s labor writers, but was an alternative proletarianism. By the 1990s, the storytelling laborer had receded in the face of a pervasive postmodern cynicism. In the new Asian texts, hardworking people shed their class stigmata or, as in the Chicano and Native American texts, are still hostages to the truncated legacy of the Great Society.[84] Work, though a constant, is almost an afterthought. There is as much irreverence about identity politics as about improving labor conditions among the new bards of the barrio, the bicoastal Chinatowns, and the reservation.

An important new Chicano author in this new tradition is Dagoberto Gilb. His *The Magic of Blood* (1993), a collection of stories, like his earlier *Winners on the Pass Line* (1985), centers on working people. Gilb's narrators are Los Angeles union men, some facing eviction, or West Texas nonunion workers with solid drug habits.[85] Disavowing, by their dispiritedness, the Chavez legacy as a "son of the revolution," none finds a usable past in the Mexican Revolution of 1910. By the early 1990s in "The Death Mask of Pancho Villa," the assassinated leader's facial cast is supposedly for sale on the black market.[86]

For the new Chinese American author, the central drama still lies in the vexed relationship to capitalistic whiteness. Fay Myenne Ng in "A Red Sweater" (1986), a short section from an early version of her 1993 novel *Bone*, gives a wryly humorous reflection on the cultural gap between Chinese-born parents and their first-generation children, who have good jobs and prefer *I Love Lucy* to talk story.[87] By the time Ng completed the novel, the bitter parents had become more bitter, the work histories more inclusive but less distinguished.[88] The middle-class children are even more unable to benefit from the sufferings of their elders who survived Gold Mountain even if they did not climb it. The new ghosts are far from warriors. Ona, the drug-taking young woman in *Bone* who haunts her older sister's narrative imagination, jumps out of a San Francisco window. Her ghost leaves no legends and no answers.[89]

The 1990s also saw Native American authors transmuting the crisis narrative of AIM-era protest into meditations on the complete absurdity of reservation life. In Greg Sarris's interlocking Pomo Indian stories in *Grand Avenue* (1994), the underemployed southern California inner-city characters are as disgusted by the dull, constraining reservation as by the alienating white culture on the wrong side of the tracks. Sherman Alexie, who was not born until 1966, a decade and a half after Sarris, is equally conscious of the cultural blows to Indianness. He writes knowledgeably of the legacy left by BIA mismanagement of the Washington State Spokane Indian reservation, where he sets his novel *Reservation Blues* (1995).[90] No balanced discussion can avoid mention of the novel's careful respect for its characters' family histories and its appreciation of U.S. "blues" culture. But Alexie consistently brings an ironist's eye to the economic situation. He produces familiar hapless characters who seek a way out of dead-end odd jobs only to remain connected to "Indian time" (51). But Alexie jokes about Indian time as laziness as his characters make pop songs out of Indian history.[91]

As the 1960s began, Michael Harrington, in *The Other America: Poverty in the United States* (1962), reminded the affluent whites who supported the Great Society platform that low wage earning was not restricted to people of color.[92] Not surprisingly, the poor white, often viewed as dangerously racist, had received neither attention nor sympathy from most racial-ethnic authors. In the wake of the civil rights era, U.S. authors sympathetic to the white ethnic poor returned to the Steinbeck plot of bottom dogs whites. But as the Depression era cynicism about rising took a distinctly post–Great Society form, working-class whiteness became the contested literary terrain it had always been in the nation's labor fiction.

CHAPTER 12

Working-Class Twilight
White Labor Texts of the Civil Rights and Vietnam Decades

He moved his drinking time up to early afternoon, while he was still supposed to be working. . . . He'd go to work with a thermos bottle of vodka in his lunch pail.

—RAYMOND CARVER, "WHERE I'M CALLING FROM" (1981)

"My God, I'm going to blow up, my life's all wrong, everything's all wrong."

—RUSSELL BANKS, *CONTINENTAL DRIFT* (1985)

Being dead here [in a Catholic cemetery in Albany] would [at least] situate a man in place and time.

—WILLIAM KENNEDY, *IRONWEED* (1979)

Edward Hopper, *Pennsylvania Coal Town,* 1948. Oil on canvas, 28 × 40 in.
The Butler Institute of American Art, Youngstown, Ohio.

I n *Which Side Are You On?: Trying to Be for Labor When It's Flat on Its Back* (1992), a former United Mine Workers lawyer looks back at the curiously reactionary working-class conservatism of the late 1960s.[1] By 1967 even the labor liberal Walter Reuther, though a onetime CIO president himself, was a foe of the entrenchments of the AFL-CIO and had curbed his own UAW's wildcat strikes. There were pockets of resurgent militance in the desperate Appalachian coal regions and in ennui-laden postal work. But the industrial decade's end saw fewer and fewer affluent workers in stable unions, more lapses in democracy, increased concessions to management, declines in membership, and a turning away from on-the-job resistance.[2] In the new, postindustrial environment, between the plant-closing recession of 1974–1975 and that of 1982–1983, millions of manufacturing jobs—including many of those in the already pinched economy of the textile-driven South—were lost, "replaced" by service-sector work at far lower pay (see the conclusion).[3]

By contrast, members of labor's upper tier enjoyed middle-class affluence. The elite craft unions of the AFL, especially in job-rich venues like New York City's construction trades, experienced the fruits of American exceptionalism in the only industrialized democracy without a labor or socialist base. Acting as a conservative political force rather than a syndicalist one, AFL-branch unionist plumbers and pipefitters, to name two venerable building-trades crafts, were more likely to demonstrate in support of the Vietnam War than in solidarity with unorganized or low-wage U.S. labor.

From the early Vietnam years through the war's end in the mid-1970s, hard-hat feeling against the student Left's antiwar demonstrations allied the members of Big Labor with the status quo, whether military or economic. (The 1970s and 1980s would see a similar drawing of battle lines between lower-middle-class "Nixon Democrats," and later "Reagan Democrats," and student activists over environmental issues.)[4] By the early 1970s, the late Walter Reuther's pro-King, pro-Chavez UAW finally came out against escalating the war, but not in favor of halting it.[5] The white-dominated labor movement was in fact waging a public relations war with a widespread public perception of the skilled white trade unions as hawkish and bigoted. That sentiment continued to build in the 1970s and 1980s. These post–Kennedy/Johnson years saw reversals for unionized minorities such as blacks in Pittsburgh steel, Mexican American men in southwestern copper mining, and the Chicana and Latina sweatshop women in the New York City garment trades.[6] Social violence, including the 1967 riots, abounded in minority ghettos. The National

Commission on the Causes and Prevention of Violence, analyzing racial antipathies in densely populated urban areas, singled out the exceptionalism myth for criticism.[7] It found two Americas, one white and the other black.

In broad terms, the next two decades also saw a humbling economic slump for white working-class people, one that affected even those affluent blue-collar unionists in the "golden handcuff" industries such as automobile and steel. By 1981, the year when the Reagan administration permanently replaced striking air traffic controllers en masse, there were redoubled efforts to undermine labor's political influence and culture, which had been in place since Taft-Hartley and the HUAC era.[8] In what prolaborites saw as an "attack on working people," steel mills and coal mines curbed production. Pennsylvania's onetime giant Homestead closed in 1986, for instance. They pared down the workweek preparatory to abandoning that onetime regional giant of manufacturing, the Midwest, which was prophetically, and later ruefully, called the Rust Belt.[9]

In a frequent trope of the new labor fiction, Russell Banks's searing novels *Continental Drift* (1985) and *Affliction* (1989) speak to the insecure status of Euro-American whites. As if at any moment they might be downsized, they radiate an angry resentment that marks them as cultural icons of blue-collar bellicosity and racial bigotry. The media used tags such as "white backlash" to describe the kind of blue-collar alienation that fueled support for the segregationist governor George Wallace. Such jargon had just enough validity to brand a far larger group of male white workers experiencing a complex working-class resentment.[10] In his noisiest Hollywood manifestation, the volatile working-man of no discernible ethnicity became the profane, hard-drinking, hippie-hating factory worker popularly encapsulated in Hollywood films like *Joe* (1970). Instead of expressing outrage at being thus pilloried, Big Labor, overwhelmingly led by white men (and in the case of Teamsters and miners, often under congressional probe itself), deplored the union decertification and the diminution of seniority that eroded the position of the old membership. It made at best an ambivalent assault on discriminatory hiring practices and was routinely accused of holding on to whiteness.[11]

Ironically, then, just at the time when the white worker was feeling embattled and fearing loss of control, there was a hardening of leftist intellectuals' views about the bourgeois lifestyle of the privileged sector of the white working class labeled "blue-collar aristocrats."[12] Richard Price's naturalistic *Bloodbrothers* (1976) summarizes the type as riding high on "forty thou [and] all the union benefits you can eat."[13] A bevy of studies scrutinized the foreign mindset of these frequently profane men with the fascination and occasional ambivalence that had characterized the "lower-depths" studies of the sociological 1890s (see chapter 4).[14]

Blue- and pink-collar white women might have inspired similar studies had they not been battling occupational segregation, token levels of participation in the best craft jobs, and the feminization of poverty produced by their relegation to the low-paying, nonsupervisory service-sector work.[15] In the sewing and textile trades, working-class white women did make common cause across the racial divide, yet the attention paid to them from the middle-class feminist movement never seemed on a par with that accorded minority women of color.[16] The routinized day of breadwinning white women did dominate works such as *Nobody Speaks for Me* (1976), edited by Nancy Seifer, Elinor Langer's *Inside the New York Telephone Company* (1970), and *Dignity: Lower-Income Women Tell of Their Lives and Struggles* (1985), edited by Fran Leeper Buss. Yet despite the fact that so many women's movement titles were published in the decade separating these books, such studies were comparatively sparse.[17] As spiritually isolated from the boons of male-led unionism as from those of middle-class feminism, white working women received short shrift even in articles devoted to them.[18]

There were searching inquiries into blue-collar life and masculine work culture. "White Workers, Blue Mood," "The New Ethnicity and Blue Collars," and "Old Working Class, New Working Class" argue that the workingman had grounds for discontent about his limited class options or, if solidly middle class, his minimal psychic satisfactions.[19] The period saw bold denials of blue-collar ascension that attempted to revivify Marxism. Sociological classics, such as Stanley Aronowitz's *False Promises: The Shaping of American Working-Class Consciousness* (1973), Richard Sennett and Jonathan Cobb's *The Hidden Injuries of Class* (1972), and Harry Braverman's *Labor and Monopoly Capital: The Degradation of Work in the Twentieth Century* (1974) located in a critique of the capitalist mode of production the betrayal of workers whose lives were (mis)shaped by their "degraded" work.[20] But of all the period surveyors of the white everyman it was Studs Terkel's best-selling 1972 interview compilation, *Working*, that captured the public mind. Terkel focused on the private and nonradical ways in which workers respond to workplace realities. He offered a host of white men (women workers, like racial-ethnic men and women, were significantly underrepresented), from the poorly paid to the well paid, who complained far more about the psychic than the physical dangers of their jobs. They shared only an isolation from the larger society even as they sought to advance within it. To a wide variety of observers, then, the late 1960s onward seemed to witness what might be termed the twilight of the white work ethic.

Given the old craft divisions and rivalries that even the merging of the AFL and the CIO did not extinguish, it had always been difficult to speak monolithically of white labor. Many of the original AFL unions were dominated by the "Nordic" bias of the Progressive Era. They thus refused to recognize the fluid and interactive nature of all ethnic identities, especially those located between "whiteness" and "blackness."[21] However unwieldy, the turn-of-the-century eugenicists' ideology of the "Nordic white" as "successful white," which had fed into intrawhite resentments and hatreds for 150 years, continued to thrive. Contemporary labor fiction corroborated the fact.[22] Railroad men with German Catholic roots ridiculed Italian Catholics and Protestant West Virginians as "white trash."[23] Russell Banks's unraveling New Hampshire repairman, migrating entrepreneurially to Florida, reveals his own status insecurity in culturally bigoted disdain for the "crackers" he sees there.[24]

The subgenre of the metropolitan tough-guy novel disseminated unflattering representations of mainstream white labor as well. Jimmy Breslin's

Yonkers picaresque *Table Money* (1986) addresses blue-collar urban ethnics with poor impulse control and unenlightened racial views. The protagonist, Owen Morrissey, a sandhog (tunnel worker) returned from Vietnam, may seem muted in his conduct compared with the havoc-wreaking of Sylvester Stallone's vet in the period blockbuster *Rambo: First Blood: Part II* (1986). Still, Owen acts up and acts out in a series of barroom, union hall, and marital spats.[25] So too the Bronx-based pipefitters, the Italian American De Cocos, of Richard Price's Swiftian *Bloodbrothers* (1976). Price's near obsession with working-class profanity reveals not only the fear that " 'niggers' are almost like us" (18) but an animus toward the ethnic groups with whom ethnic workers like the De Cocos most often competed. These groups were white Euro-Americans of Italian or Slavic descent whose urbanization from the turn of the century onward included "becoming white" in order to distance themselves from the historical associations of their ethnic groups with bestiality and "debased" blackness (see chapter 5).[26]

Many other intrawhite labor rivalries continue to appear. Denise Giardina's *The Unquiet Earth* (1992) is the story of a Harlan County–like company town on the skids. (The "Bloody Harlan" strike of 1931 would be a touchstone for protests there decades later.) The "hillbillies of the hollow," former mountain people who work in the mines, hurl racial epithets at the blacks with whom they mine. They are in turn routinely spurned as "white trash" by the relatively respectable lower-middle-class whites.[27] As Dorothy Allison's writings point out, these people were all too aware of the charges put forth by eugenicists since the 1880s about the degeneracy of country life and the "survival of the unfittest."[28] These poor whites not only shun the black miners who live on "Colored Row" but also routinely shun other white workers, such as the Slavs and their American-born children dwelling in Hunkie Hill (*Unquiet Earth*, 106). (When poor whites live on bad terms with Native Americans, they invoke the term "Indian trash.")[29] Eager to hold on to what Neil Foley terms "the whiteness of manhood" rather than be spurned as the "bad-gened whites" of eugenicist theory, they pride themselves on being the "purest whites" in Appalachia.[30]

Writing about the continued white rural sharecropping culture in Texas (where the Ku Klux Klan maintained a presence) prior to World War II, Foley posits that the "pore whites" clung to not being black, Mexican, or foreign born.[31] If, at least in this regard, white boyishness was a collective identity, sustaining it involved a posture of defiance in regions so impoverished that there were no jobs for either whites or people of color.

During the civil rights era and the dismantling and aftermath of the Great Society in the 1970s and 1980s, talented new writers with worker roots and sympathies such as Raymond Carver, Joyce Carol Oates, and Russell Banks probed the "problem" of whiteness in an array of stories concerning Euro-American ethnics. With a surprising consistency of portraiture, they complicated the 1930s novelistic ode to the common man with a vision of labor-class whites trashing themselves by trashing others. Far less noticed was *To the Bright and Shining Sun* (1970) by the future best-selling suspense and crime author James Lee Burke, who foregrounds a coal miner, oblivious to the irony, sporting a tattoo with a UMW logo and a Confederate flag. Joyce Carol Oates's portrait of a displaced Appalachian migrant, Loretta Wendell, in the white minority in explosive 1960s Detroit, similarly locates the character as "so conscious of being white!"[32] These characters joined a wide range of working-class whites from the inbred, incestuous, and often racist families in the regions that spawn the low-functioning subjects—half-imagined, half-observed—of Carolyn Chute's *The Beans of Egypt, Maine* (1985) and Dorothy Allison's *Trash* (1988), later reworked and artistically strengthened as *Bastard Out of Carolina* (1992). Superficially at least, the lives of these authors recalled those of the participant-artists of the 1930s, such as Mike Gold and Jack Conroy.[33] John Sayles (*Union Dues*, 1977) worked as a hospital orderly, plastic molder, and meatpacker; Russell Banks was at various times a carpet installer and plumber. Raymond Carver (*Cathedral*, 1981) made a living of sorts in a sawmill and later did janitorial work. John Yount (*Hardcastle*, 1980) labored on construction sites, and Charles Bukowski was well qualified to write *Post Office* (1971) after more than a decade of postal work. Carolyn Chute, before a journalist's education enabled her to begin breaking out of her family's Maine poverty, was for a time a potato farm worker trying to make ends meet as a single mother.[34] Like Denise Giardina, who was the daughter of coal-mining folk, Chute returned from college to her native region as an activist.[35]

Dorothy Allison, looking back over two decades, still believed herself to be "the one who got away, who got a job from Lyndon Johnson's War on Poverty and went to college on a scholarship."[36] But Banks dropped out of college after a few weeks to make his way to Florida, and Carver left graduate school to become a janitor. Their biographies suggested the larger conflicts of work, identity, and status anxieties that their fiction was also to work out.[37]

Taken together, all of these writers had difficulty isolating the particular qualities of working-class experience.[38] Inheritors of the more radical-minded U.S. labor author's long-standing critique of American exceptionalism, they struggled to work out the triangular relationship between traditional myths of classless self-advancement, the erased legacy of the mass-unionist 1930s, and the puzzling new apolitical working-class self-involvement. As the return to a 1930s vision of solidarity becomes increasingly irrelevant to a working-class identity, there emerges an unlikely spokesman for labor, the economically immobilized poor white. In a varied set of approaches to the ossification of so symbolic a workforce, the storyteller of (and often from) impoverished whiteness has two overriding labor concerns: Who is trashing? Who is trashed?

Framing the Common Man:
The White Working-Class Fiction of the Carver Generation

In the 1970s and 1980s, a crew of sociologists and political commentators examined the "world" of the white blue-collar male worker in ways reminiscent of the Progressive Era Pittsburgh Survey.[39] Like their predecessors, these sociologists saw working-class attitudes as amoral territory to be traversed under the guidance of their own moral compasses. With varying degrees of condescension, they probed the mentality of those whose income and street address (in a whites-only neighborhood) nominally qualified them for middle-class status. Archie Bunkers without the comedy, these men's views on race, politics, and gender, however, separated them from their liberal interviewers. Moreover, the subjects sometimes prompted their interviewers to construct a kind of taxonomy of rage. Such classifications were based on the degree of hostility to the Department of Labor's affirmative action initiatives to make women and minorities into journeyman apprentices in ironwork, carpentry, and electrical work and to create the Equal Employment Opportunity Commission (EEOC).[40]

In literature, the apathy and discontent of this suburbanized blue-collar manual worker resembled that of the trapped "organization man" in the vise of middle-class discontent.[41] In search of distinguishing features, sociologists of class pointed to the public nature of blue-collar drinking, womanizing, and vocal anger at the powers-that-be.[42] The implication was that middle-class men fleeing desperation were somehow less crude, if more hypocritical. Novelists like John Updike and John Cheever overlay the plot of the self-involved commuter from the managerial classes—Sloan Wilson's "gray flannel suit" for the 1970s and 1980s—with the eloquence of disengagement. In the hands of a writer like the southern-born sometime carpenter Larry Brown, whose lower-middle-class characters in the story collection *Facing the Music* (1988) and the more ambitious *Joe* (1991) exemplify flattened affect, there is a leap in subject rather than tone. Brown thus joins the blue-collar anomie school of which Raymond Carver is the chief example.[43]

As the service sector became a site from which to probe the intersection between self and work, novels examined nine-to-five figures like postal workers and repairmen on the prowl for spiritual meaning. One disappointed reviewer in the progressive journal *Mother Jones* pointed to Raymond Carver's "intensely private focus,"[44] another way of saying that Carver steers clear of linking debilitated psyches to oppressive social conditions. Carver's explicator could just as well have been describing "common man" authors such as Leonard Gardner, whose poignant ex-boxer novel *Fat City* (1969) is an elegy for unskilled American manhood on the decline.

But it is Carver who is the consummate observer and re-creator of his characters' emotional minimalism. As one character remarks, their mantra seems to be "[things] didn't matter much one way or the other."[45] Because his people seem so directionless, carpenters fired from their jobs are as flooded with anomie as prosperous businessmen on benders. In rare displays of energy, they occasionally reaffirm their whiteness by labeling blacks "spades" ("Vitamins," *Cathedral*, 99) when they go drinking in black jazz clubs. There is no added irony besieging Carver's blue-collar types because they experience the predictability of their days with an obliviousness that makes boundaries between white-collar and blue-collar work seem porous. The anomie besieging unemployed roofers, substance-abusing electricians, and others living from one paycheck to the next grants them entry into the "Carverville" community of desperation, imminent loss of control, ferocious self-destructiveness, and the deadened self. In one representative collection, *Cathedral* (1981), dead-voiced characters leave or lose the "nothing job" (91), their psyches mired in boredom.

For the quick-change artists of Banks's oeuvre, too, despair is not a classless country. His perennial subject is the structure and psychology of white proletarian life.[46] But Banks, replacing minimalism with neo-naturalism, has an alternative interpretation of the U.S. workingman who cannot as facilely combat the not-so-quiet desperation of the Carver character. Banks's figures of working-class aloneness, whose job descriptions have strayed off the beaten trade-unionist path, keep worrying about what they see as the "life-as-ladder" problem (*Continental Drift*, 15) without recognizing that the quest itself is not for money or status but for relief from their own resentments at cultural devaluation. In *Affliction*, Wade Whitehouse, plying two jobs as laborer and lawman in a small New Hampshire town, is a pure product of America who goes murderously crazy.

In *Continental Drift*, an even more representative Banksian man, Bob Dubois, an oil burner repairman, has little but his own prideful whiteness to mark his connection to the respectable artisan of the early trade unions, who had often moved from employment to entrepreneur. Like so many of the post–Taft-Hartley workers in labor literature, he is in an emotional pressure cooker. He knows what he does not like: the taxing work he does is at the top of the list. He votes with his feet to retain his right to white man's work and migrates to Florida to manage his brother's store and a black man who does the sweeping. But he cannot combat the social invisibility he had experienced in his New Hampshire town, with the appropriately burdensome name of Catamount. As he moves through a Byzantine plot, a prey to his own poor impulse control, he looks for salvation in all the wrong places.

Bob's self-made businessman brother Eddie is an updated Way-to-Wealth advocate, a gun-owning, vulgar, drunken, and affluent racist. Faced with Eddie's credo of the importance of money and consumer goods, Bob is unable to keep the faith. When Bob accidentally kills a black man and lives out his new sense of criminality by becoming a backwater smuggler, he embraces crime with the energy of narcissistic despair.

Another neo-naturalist, Charles Bukowski, writes as if to rebuke the edgy Banks workingman. It is difficult to classify in labor terms an author whose 1970s storytelling, under the aegis of the Beats' iconoclastic City Lights Press, included *Erections, Ejaculations, and General Tales of Ordinary Madness* (1972). The hedonistic counterculturalism—though seeking "beatitude," the Beat literary movement denounced capitalist greed—acquires a blue-collar overlay in Bukowski's fictionalized autobiography *Post Office* (1971). (Like his main character, Chinaski, Bukowski was a postal worker for twelve years.)[47] Richard Wright, in the Chicago-based *Lawd Today* (1963), completed in 1937 but not published until the civil rights years, had charted the marginality of black postal workers. While Wright's central figure does not think in terms of a collective will to change a stifling workplace culture, his anger is a precondition for the militancy of real-life postal employees in the decades to come.[48] But Chinaski, always writing the Great American Novel or Poem, is part of a white, male, California postal-work majority.[49] In fact, he aestheticizes his disaffection and celebrates his own ennui. He insists that the predictability of his post-office assembly line mirrors his beat-artist vision of the "straight" world. From his endlessly secure vantage point, he can aspire to be a "good hustler."[50] The king of the put-on, he reduces wage earning to a boring intrusion on the pursuit of sensation, and intimate relationships to "the best ride in months" (45).

One way to read Bukowski is to see the worker-writer projecting and displacing self-ridicule to the point where he is a self-appointed antitype. Exceptional because he can savage the average employee, the Carver-Banks-Bukowski figure is survivalist, near psychotic, and passively aggressive. Given the negative work ethic inspired by orders barked over loudspeakers (48) and union rules as bureaucratized as work ones (74), the Bukowski "hero" trades an oppositional consciousness for the "artistic" fruits of chronicling his own apathy.

Two of their most important fellow writers contextualize white laboring men within a lost radical UMW tradition in the coalfields of eastern Kentucky and nearby West Virginia.[51] (It was not accidental that the end of the civil rights era saw "the demise of the black miner" in these regions peopled by an economically weak and racially divided workforce.)[52] James Lee Burke's *To the Bright and Shining Sun* and John Sayles's *Union Dues* link the common man's erosion of spirit to the twilight of their worker fathers, reduced to a white-trash subsistence when they rightly belong in the artisan tradition of the dignified workingman. The Burke novel's opening chapter harks back to the aggressive prewar protest years of Harlan to stress the minimal news coverage of 1970s wildcat Appalachian coal strikes. Elegiac homage disappears in light of the realpolitik of the "union's near-criminal neglect of men and health safety practices after 1968."[53] Burke's is a threnody for the skilled men replaced and used up by machines. The miner is a played-out everyman on welfare whose land has been sold out from under him and strip-mined by the corporations that are now laying him off. When with unconscious irony the local sheriff says, "My county ain't going to turn into no war like Harlan" (27), he is tragically correct.

Of the writers who link the skilled workingman's erosion of spirit to the betrayal of the trade union movement, the writer-novelist-filmmaker John Sayles is possibly the most eloquent.[54] In *Union Dues*, his displaced West Virginian Hunter McNatt is admiringly described by his dispirited fellow miners as "someone out of the same mold as the people [who] founded the union."[55] McNatt is urged to reenter union politics just as in 1969 the real-life Jock Yablonski began a campaign to unseat Tony Boyle from the UMW presidency on a reform slate. What is in store for Hunter and his family in the course of the narrative is a spiritual version of the fate of Yablonski, who was murdered with his wife and daughter by Boyle henchmen as he slept.[56] One of Hunter's sons, Darwin, has survived the "working-class war" in Vietnam.[57] But hardly fit, he is instead traumatized and cut off. Depressed by Darwin's remoteness, Hunter is squeezed on all sides by hazardous work conditions, his coworkers' mixture of fear and apathy, and the UMW corruption that was headline news in the late 1960s.[58]

Hunter thus clings to the history of the early organizers killed by company thugs in the 1930s and tells a bored Boston interviewer that he had "been

UMW since he was workin'" (164). The phrase speaks volumes for what the labor lawyer Thomas Geoghegan's *Which Side Are You On?* terms "UMW Appalachian and Southern West Virginia and Southern Illinois culture."[59] But it is incomprehensible to his son Hobie, who flees his father's dim economic prospects and runs away to Boston and the cul-de-sac of day labor.

Deadpan irony thus runs up against Dreiserian social indignation. *Union Dues* lays the blame for the sorry state of labor at the door of the narcissistic New Left, whose agenda officially included a new radical alliance with labor. This was supposedly an improvement on the grassroots Old Left symbolized by Hunter's generation.[60] Like a unionist Job, Hunter is assailed by occupational illness and poor medical care that results in his wife's death. Sayles juxtaposes Hunter's dead end with the pontificating about radical theory by overindulged students who drop out of their expensive colleges. It is the New Left, a folksong army living in communes, singing trendily of the 1913 Ludlow Massacre (220) and mining history, that trashes the McNatt family. In a grotesque parody of anarchists' "propaganda by the deed," Hobie McNatt is sent to bomb a factory. As the most impassioned labor author of his generation, Sayles defrocks the hippie activist whose so-called liberalism was the most pernicious example of contempt for the white working class. In a valiant attempt to remake the old proletarian novel, he rises to a moral indignation blunted in his fellow anomie writers.

Mining History: The UMW Novelists and Others

Although Sayles was aware of the often effective union busting in which the mining companies had engaged for over a century, even a decade after *Union Dues* he continued to position West Virginia's UMW history in terms of doomed individualism. Thus he deliberately placed *Union Dues* within the context of his 1920s coal strike film *Matewan* (1987), set in the nativist and racist era of the Palmer Raids (see chapter 7) and the beginning of the 1920s "Great Coalfield Wars."[61] In it he returns African Americans, as imported scabs to unionists, into the mining surround from which he had omitted them in the 1977 novel. In the preface to his account of the *Matewan* filming, Sayles paid homage to the real-life West Virginia coal workers of Mingo County. They had provided him with the inspiration and background material both for his historical film on the bloody shoot-out with company thugs in *Matewan* and for his fictive portrait of Hunter McNatt.[62]

Sayles is so persuasive that it almost escapes notice how deftly he individuates strikers in a departure from a more traditional interpretation, including that underlying *Harlan Miners Speak* (1931). Compiled by Theodore Dreiser and other leftist intellectuals who visited Harlan, that work gives voice to descendants of the old mining brotherhoods and new recruits to the agitational Communist Party rival to the UMW, the National Miners Union.[63] Sayles, in contrast, carries forward a novelist's concern shared with Giardina, Burke, and others. As a recorder and, given his liberties with the actual events, a creator of labor history, his subtext is the personal loss experienced by his key characters.[64]

If, as Freud observed, no memory is without motive, the mining novels of the 1970s and 1980s did more than recover an erased labor history in a period of comparative national prosperity or lament that Tony Boyle represented a venal alternative to the forceful if controversial John L. Lewis days.[65] This white mining retrospection was no literary accident. By the 1970s coal miners were little better off—and in some ways worse off—than in the days when the Wagner Act had permitted what Taft-Hartley subsequently outlawed. The songwriter Florence Reese stood up at a 1972 convention and sang the protest song she had composed for the 1930s protest, "Which Side Are You On?"[66] Even as late as 1988, in Pittston, West Virginia, a coal company, in the best anti–New Deal style, cut off health benefits to widows and disabled miners in retaliation against the UMW.[67]

John Yount's unfairly neglected novel *Hardcastle* (1980) is set in the violent coalfields of eastern Kentucky in the waning months of the Hoover presidency. He brings an angle of vision to the pro-unionism of these men that resonates far more in the modern era than does the Depression era novel of a Lauren Gilfillan (*I Went to Pit College,* 1934) or a Jack Conroy (*The Disinherited,* 1933). The bonds among Yount's figures, in fact, are based far more on the mysteries of friendship than on the vagaries of union affiliation. In that spirit, the novel even redraws the boundaries between oppressed miners and Baldwin gun thugs that seemed so uncrossable in the era itself. (Artistic decisions such as these also aroused the wrath of a prestigious reviewer when the book first appeared.)[68]

In brief, the action concerns Regus Bone, a mine company guard who befriends a thieving traveling musician and finds him a guard's job. Only the curious friendship between the two seems to propel their drift over to the union side. Furthermore, in the novel's lengthy final account of the failed strike, the union itself recedes as a moral center. "A few months later, when it was clear the union was broken, the organizers and lawyers and all the rest of the [CP] National Miners Union people vanished like smoke."[69]

Another mining protest novel in which the 1930s can be read through the 1970s by subordinating the strike novel to the kinship one is Denise Giardina's strongly written *The Unquiet Earth.* Her novel opens with Dillon Freeman, a prototypical coal miner's son, summoning up Depression era courage by tapping the spirit of his long-dead union organizer father. Giardina takes him and the other Blackberry Creek, West Virginia, denizens of Mining Camp Number 13 through fifty years of draining wildcat labor strife characterized by 50 percent wage cuts, lockouts at rifle point, and retaliatory industrial sabotage. Decades later, the new union strategies, in a concession-filled time, will be "nonviolent civil disobedience" (309) in response to the new M16s of the company guards (105). When a now-aged Dillon hears this news, his dilemma epitomizes that of the post–Taft-Hartley labor militant. He is too old to go back, however ineffectual he finds the new workers who are taking cues from the international union.

The mining camp, of course, was but one of the Depression era venues resurrected in the historical novel of the 1970s and 1980s. William Kennedy's *Ironweed,* to cite a prominent example, also intertwines a fully developed character with the vagaries and violence of labor history. It approaches the rueful 1930s militant through the consciousness of Francis Phelan, an alcoholic derelict who superficially rekindles the persona of the ubiquitous Depression era forgotten man. Phelan's proletarian vita includes participating in antiscab violence, riding the rails, smiling crookedly on breadlines, and camping in hobo jungles.[70] All are activities covered in novels by Tom Kromer, Edward Dahlberg, and Edward Anderson (see chapter 9).

A recycling of this kind of fiction was hardly fashionable enough to win, as did the Kennedy novel, the 1984 Pulitzer Prize. A closer analysis reveals that Kennedy's Francis Phelan parts company with any labor-literary fixture, whether survivalist hobo or mining-camp martyr. Phelan neither reproaches society for the injustice of unemployment nor echoes the old IWW hobo refrain "Hallelujah on the Bum."[71] His constant question is the self-absorbed "How will I get through the next twenty minutes?"(23–24). Kennedy plays his skewed but lively survival instinct against his customary deadness of spirit. Phelan drinks neither to quench widely shared economic despair nor to expiate whatever personal guilt is merited for not realizing his youthful promise and disappointing, even injuring, his family. No simple 1970s descendant of the "road novel" hobo of the 1930s, Phelan seems to derive a perverse satisfaction from a cult of self-deadening in which he visits ghosts of iron factories (140) and finds graveyard jobs to talk to his long-dead family members.

Even in such "historical" fiction, Yankee individualism and New Deal crusading fervor vanish. All that remains is self-defeating narcissism. Throughout the narrative Kennedy evokes Phelan's favored state of self-involved nostalgia, which centers on scripting scenes with the ghosts of those he betrayed long ago. When he conjures the ghost of a scab he accidentally killed years before, Francis engages in a rare display of political radicalism by taunting the scab about taking food out of the Phelan family's mouths. But even when he thus rescripts his past, what emerges is "odd logic coming from a man who abandoned his own family every spring and summer thereafter, when baseball season started . . . and [in time] permanently" (26). In Kennedy's modernization of the on-the-skids experience, Phelan recalls the diminished self of Carver, Bukowski, and their contemporaries. A survivor, Phelan writes his own labor history, but it is one in which he does little work and takes less responsibility. Despite his proletarian credentials, Phelan's fall is willed, not economically determined.

Outsider Art and White Trash Individualism

For decades prior to and following the Job Corps, mainstream white society perceived Appalachia, the South, and the more remote regions of New England as geographical-cultural outbacks. Describing the cut-off inhabitants, the term "white trash" as a "classed form of Otherness" lingered far past the civil rights era as a name for the inheritors of a kind of social and economic immobility.[72] In the southern Snopeses, a "sorry white" sharecropping family, William Faulkner erased even the humanity of the poor white farming classes.[73] In novels like *The Hamlet* (1940), the predatory Flem Snopes and his tribe, including Mink, Lump, and I.O., live up to their morally empty names. Much post–civil rights era fiction written in the wake of incomplete anti-poverty initiatives in Appalachia and the tenant-farming South sought to balance Steinbeck and Faulkner's antithetical visions.

The circumstances bedeviling Steinbeck's Joads or Dorothea Lange's "Migrant Mother" singled out the victims of the Dust Bowl as classic survivors of economic catastrophe, too proud to seek out the government aid programs of the New Deal. The grandchildren of the 1930s generation, in contrast, by the 1970s and 1980s were "white trash" welfare recipients scratching out an existence or inhabiting slum neighborhoods still marked by postwar unemployment. The aftermath of the 1964 Civil Rights Act, however much it aroused the public conscience about the treatment of minorities of color, did little to soften a long-standing cultural impatience with the white marginality of which the residents of Appalachia were a convenient symbol. They were deemed shiftless, difficult to organize, rural, or migrant urban tricksters wedding their welfare checks to the profits of dodgy pickup-truck jobs. "Lazy," "predatory," "incestuous," "criminal," and "violent" were descriptors that blackened the reputation of poor whites from West Virginia to Maine.[74]

James Dickey's backcountry Georgia novel *Deliverance* (1970), later a successful Hollywood film, and Harry Crews's *A Feast of Snakes* (1976) breathed fictive life into these stereotypes. So did Cormac McCarthy's customarily brutal first novel *The Orchard Keeper* (1965), set in a Tennessee of mountain folk and bootleggers. For the white trash plot as the distorted mirror of "normative" working-class whiteness, however, we must look to the alternatively deviant work ethic in Oates, Allison, and Chute.

As a writer who has always located pathology squarely in family systems, Joyce Carol Oates seems an unlikely "up from trashiness" author. In the 1969 National Book Award–winning *Them*, her Detroit characters shed self-contempt and shame, though not the "right" to violence or criminality. The title refers literally to Jules and Maureen Wendell, the ambitious children of the hillbilly migrants who declined from fairly well paid Midwest auto work to welfare. Jules and Maureen, suffering no aversion to thievery or prostitution, respectively, determinedly lift themselves up. If, as is often the case in Oates's oeuvre, their vitality borders on the psychotic, they move on and up in a white trash variant of a familiar modern American plot (see chapter 10).

Read within the racialized labor history of Detroit, which was three-quarters black by the civil rights era, Oates's title refers also to the many "us/them" dichotomies of the working class. Unless they met with some workplace accident, like Jules Wendell's father, Howard, who is crushed to death on the line at Chrysler, whites could rise to foreman. Blacks quite simply could not.[75] Oates makes peripheral the League of Revolutionary Black Workers style of agitation in the Chrysler factory captured so ably in the interviews composing Dan Georgakas's *Detroit: I Do Mind Dying* (1975; reprint, 1999).[76] Her inner city, from which "respectable" whites have long since fled, is a site of black-white riots and Darwinian racism. To launch themselves, the discontented

Wendells hold on to their sense of white entitlement. In their hunger to rise by using others, the brother and sister are ruthless dreamers.

Members of the Boatwright tribe, who people Dorothy Allison's world, are without the prospect of Oates's unscrupulously achieved upward climb. Set squarely in a nonurban economy, her early collection *Trash,* later revised as *Bastard out of Carolina,* rings changes on the theme of survivalism. Taking pride in their separateness, their liquor, and their womanizing, many of the Boatwright men, impatient with the limits of textile mill routine, scrounge up odd jobs or pursue self-employment. These men are hell on wheels in more than one sense. In the culture of the open southern road, they are the wild ones at a time when Carver and Banks are depicting exhaustion in the U.S. workforce.

Allison's retrospectively autobiographical narrator, the ten-year-old Bone, is caught between her admiration for her uncles' untamed individualism and her shame at the draining identity of an otherness welded to poor-white hardship. Early on she learns that rebellion against servitude does little to mitigate the Boatwright heritage. It is one of bare dirt yards, plank porches, and being looked at as if they came from the photojournalistic pages of James Agee and Walker Evans's *Let Us Now Praise Famous Men* (1941). Worse, some of them, like the hereditarily marred Jukes or Kallikaks, are promising subjects for eugenics "science" (*Bastard,* 14).[77] Viewed in labor terms, these men lack the opportunities to forge either an artisan or a skilled-trades identity.

Carolyn Chute's title characters, the Bean family of Egypt, Maine, lack both the class cachet of Glen and the vital attractiveness of the Boatwright men. From the outsider viewpoint of Earlene, a comparatively refined young woman who marries into their tribe, they bear a "CroMagnon look."[78] As atavistic as they are haphazard, the Beans collectively flesh out the tacky, outsider lives that take such comic form in Charles Booth's celebrated cartoons for the *New Yorker.*

Like the white trash novelists in the serio-comic mode of William Faulkner and Erskine Caldwell, Chute deconstructs the eccentricity of the impoverished. Unlike her predecessors, Chute charts an unsparing ethnography that becomes a "brother's keeper" catechism of her (liberal-minded) reader. In modern psychological parlance, the Beans perform their lives by combining a frontier self-reliance with a dependence on government handouts. Impossible to idealize, they are the sum of their junk-filled lawns, broken-down pickups, casual child rearing, and hygiene practices as limited as their ambitions. But the more one reads in the novel, the more the Beans' twinned obliviousness and ignorance seem to be, not evidence of genetic inferiority, but voiceless stridency against being labeled bestial. Although her reviewers find no poetry in the Beans' recalcitrant poverty, Chute argues that Maine white trash actually subvert the normative categories of "jobless," "employed," and "dependent." Strange as it is, the Beans' caginess, while economically futile, jettisons economic incentive in the name of emotional survival.

From Standing by Your Man to Standing Alone: Gender in the White Trash Novel

The Great Society's response to women's economic and social subordination was the fitfully implemented Equal Pay Act of 1963, the 1964 Civil Rights Act prohibiting gender discrimination in employment, and the 1966 formation of the assimilationist National Organization of Women (NOW).[79] The bleak reality was that poor-white women, when they did work outside the home, worked in separate labor forces with separate pay scales.[80] From coal camp to textile mill, the old "pin money" and "family wages" theories of women in paid labor work held devaluative sway.

The Gastonia radicalism of Ella May Wiggins may have lived on in the women who attended the Southern School for Union Women in the 1970s and 1980s—the "Norma Raes" of textile organizing—but they were a rarity.[81] Like their male coworkers, these poor-white women accepted the owner's vision of opportunity, however minimal, over a unionist promise of collective security.[82] Nor, in a parallel development, was there any fundamental challenge to the ideology of the home among the most militant of the modern Ella Mays, such as those in the Harlan County Strike of 1973–1974.[83] In the North, the mid-1970s had witnessed increases in women at work and even the formation of the Coalition of Labor Union Women (CLUW), whose greatest strength and/or flaw was to work within the traditional labor movement.[84] But industrial women workers, having fallen short of the "comparable worth" compensation promised under affirmative action, suffered with men from the widespread deindustrialization. Throughout the 1960s and 1970s, CLUW had little if any success in unionizing southern women's "sewing jobs." They made no headway in the world of the pink-collar and fast-food worker to which Allison's mother and her fictive counterpart, Anney Boatwright, belonged when, as single heads of household, they were trying to support their children.[85]

In her introduction to *Trash,* Allison made this distinction between the sexes in the South's persistent culture of poverty. "The characters," she wrote, "became eccentric, fascinating—not . . . cold-eyed, mean and nasty bastards . . . [but] dangerous frightened women and the more dangerous and just as frightened men"(10). If Allison's women carry on the tradition of inner strength found in the Kentucky novelist Harriette Arnow's *Dollmaker* (1954; see chapter 10), they share a less dubious honor as well. Whether staying home or working outside of it, the self-subordination of standing by one's man is clearly a sexual-political sacrifice.[86] As a lesbian writer, Allison brings an alternative gendered labor perspective to the quest for feminine identity in such an environment. She calls her Lambda Literary Award– and Best Small Press–winning *Trash* "the condensed and reinvented experience of a cross-eyed working-class lesbian" (*Trash,* 12).[87] In *Bastard* (published by the mainstream Dutton), she privileges the adolescent Bone of the 1950s and shifts away from a declared lesbianism. Yet in both texts, Allison transforms the search of her mother's generation for a husband/father figure into a seizing of "male" self-reliance and economic independence.

In *Thinking Class: Sketches from a Cultural Worker* (1996), Joanna Kadi has observed, "The word *queer* [as oddly different] captures not only my sexual identity but my class identity as well."[88] Yet Allison has denied that *Bastard* is a lesbian bildungsroman.[89] Placed in the context of Kadi, Allison's statement, while literally true, points to the late 1980s gay activist–writer's difficulty balancing class and gay concerns.[90] Allison details the bellicose lesbianism of her precollege years, but she is never a "gay worker" in the sense recently documented by historians of the interwar logging camps, shipyards, and Chicago urban wage-earning scene.[91] Thus, in *Trash*, a grown-up Bone/Allison is alternately guilty about "passing" as middle class and cosmetizing her southern poor-whiteness for her bourgeois lovers. In *Bastard* there are no working-class gay alliances such as in the 1995 film *Out at Work*. Nor is there a branch of Pride at Work, the recent national organization against homophobia and discrimination on the job and within unions.[92]

There is instead the organizing theme of the search to be legitimate, that is, respected in the larger white world as the self-transformation from feminine "weakness" to manly authenticity is accomplished. Almost instinctively, Bone finds the book's rare manly female to free herself from the insulting state of bastardy (the very word connotes debased maleness). This mentor is her rough-hewn aunt Raylene Boatwright, a mannish textile mill veteran who prefers repairing machines to loom work. Like her niece, Raylene, plain-looking (unfeminine) and never married, denies any interest in men. She lives alone and free on her pension, near the river in a home she owns. Although Raylene is not permitted to take on sexual discrimination in the workplace—she is consigned to the looms—in her thinking and lifestyle she exemplifies the masculinized woman's work alternative.

Figures like Raylene prophesy a lesbian alternative to the South's petrified code of standing by one's man. (Linda Niemann's 1990 literary memoir, *Boomer*, about a lesbian railroad brakeman, also participated in this challenge to traditional manhood.)[93] It is Raylene's comparatively successful rebellion against gender prescriptions that enables her to combat the stigmatization of "trash" with which the Boatwright men and their subordinate if resilient wives are branded. Raylene's time preceded the period when black and white women began working together in mills like J. P. Stevens, as well as the renewed organizational efforts of the CIO in that regard.[94] Given her time and place, Raylene directs her energies, in any event, away from the violence and self-defeating wildness of Bone's uncles. In so doing, Raylene does better than any other woman in the "white trash" texts of Allison or Chute.

Every Man Is an Island: White Working-Class Literature on the Eve of the 1990s

Anger at class invisibility is not new to representations of Euro-American or native-born white workers. This book has charted how the self-destructive type, taking on the ideological coloration of the period and the political convictions of his creators, was never out of literary fashion. What is new about the novels published in the 1970s and 1980s is that the writers provide little sense that they have any programs for reform. Although they produce a fiction filled with rage, they do not seem to be radicals with authority.

Defying belief in a once-mythically resonant social mobility, labor fiction, from the "anomie" school of Carver and Banks to the last individualists of Sayles and Yount, remained faithful on the eve of the 1990s to a lost ideal of collectivity. But it did so only to the extent that it deplored working-class characters who had bartered both solidarity and creativity for a measure of embourgeoisement. Their jobs, not arranged to tap human potential, neither sustained their identity nor inspired them to make a commitment to any form of work, lucrative or otherwise. Yet these writers brought no crusading fervor to their insights, or even minimalist introspection. Instead, they partook of an enduring cultural impatience with 1930s art, as if the common man trope had lost its power to communicate. In this landscape of white-collar underachievers, assembly-line Willy Lomans, and burned-out drifters, these post-1960s novels, taken together, conveyed an "intense and frozen sadness."[95]

It is not surprising that the 1970s, although the word had not been in use for decades, found the discredited "proletarian" in a literary preoccupation with the ebbing vitality of the rural working poor. Caught in an eternal Walker Evans photo, he sharecropped much as he had tried to do during the New Deal years. In symbolic terms, such a figure plays out the fears of a besieged white workforce vulnerable to its own kind of Appalachianization.

Like Allison and her colleagues, the playwright Robert Schenkkan recognized the vitality beneath the deadpan. He even provided the afterword on bottom dog whiteness as a mirror of the nation's fixation on race in his Pulitzer Prize–winning *The Kentucky Cycle* (1992). As much epic as play, it revises white working-class history from Revolutionary War days to the end of the 1980s by restoring the truths about Appalachian mistreatment of and colonizing intermarriage with Native Americans and blacks.[96] Yet, as there is no admission of the multicultural heritage, so there is no biracial unity or justice for minorities. The audience climbs from branch to branch of three interlocking family trees, those of the land-grabbing, parricidal Rowens, the equally venal Talberts, and the once enslaved and later bootlegging Biggses.

In the play's final scene, the UMW flunky Rowen, the Blue Star Mine owner Talbert, and the conscienceless liquor purveyor Biggs are still feuding. Prosperous yet morally trashy, the three seem oblivious that the land on which they bicker has been strip-mined and—like the people who once farmed it—trashed indeed.

Enduring racial tensions and occasional harmonies marked much labor fiction after the pre–World War II era. Nevertheless, it remained for the new decade of authors to fashion a new labor fiction from the injuries of and by the white working class. The phoenixlike trope of the self-made man rose to energize a postindustrial landscape of ascension, alienation, and despair.

Everything Old Is New Again

Working Through Class in the Literary 1990s

What is most exceptional about America is its abiding belief in its exceptionalism.

—HENRY LOUIS GATES, JR., PACE UNIVERSITY, NEW YORK, OCTOBER 4, 1998

We still don't admit there are classes in this country. I've never met an average person. "I'm a bit above average," people say of themselves.

—PHILLIP BONOSKY, REFERENCE CENTER FOR MARXIST STUDIES, NEW YORK, JULY 23, 1998

[Working-class art is concerned with] creating spaces for a discourse of the working body in a context where machines and technology and market forces matter most.

—JANET ZANDY, "GOD JOB," *WRITING WORK: WRITERS ON WORKING-CLASS WRITING* (1999)

Honoré Sharrer, *Workers and Paintings,* 1944. Oil on composition board, 11⅝ × 37 in. The Museum of Modern Art, New York. Gift of Lincoln Kirstein. Photograph © 1998 The Museum of Modern Art, New York.

The 1980s and 1990s witnessed a series of mass firings, plant closings, and concessionary postindustrial strikes that more often than not were futile efforts to prevent jobs from going "offshore" and overseas.[1] During these twenty years, employers in the industries that once fueled the labor movement—steel, coal, rubber, automobiles—cut jobs, pensions, and health coverage.[2] They were aided by a spate of labor laws that, as the onetime UMW reformer Rich Trumka remarked in 1990, are essentially antilabor.[3] Employers took full advantage of their right to replace striking workers. Before using that expedient, management often blocked workplace organizing, weakened laws permitting free speech, and even, in a burst of 1990s Taylorism, installed automated monitors to survey efficiency and performance.[4]

From a business viewpoint, these initiatives to stop Big Labor in its tracks and stunt further unionism are solidly grounded in the notion of U.S. classlessness and the individualist ethos.[5] The New York Times claimed that the 1990s witnessed the rise of a different class structure: "The new class consciousness makes less distinction between workers and management."[6] Phrased differently, given the recent prosperity and low unemployment in growth industries from construction to skilled electronic maintenance, management frequently woos the skilled worker away from the closed shop.[7] Employers as diverse as electrical contractors and the service-work outsourcers on which many public institutions rely have augmented these efforts to outbid the union's benefit package. They have also mounted aggressive campaigns to convince employees and the public that the company "family" functions as a cooperative unit intent only on "quality assurance." Similarly Orwellian language covers over the truths behind "fully employed part-timer," "capitalist restructuring," and that catchall term beloved of minimum-wage payers, the "sales associate." These developments have not escaped the satiric lens of Ben Hamper's novelistic Flint, Michigan, Rivethead: Tales from the Assembly Line (1991) or the ironic surface resignation of the New Jersey Ford Company wife in Agnes Rossi's "The Quick" (1992).[8] In the post–cold war tradition of Carver and his colleagues (see chapter 12), they discard the language of class for that of (elusive) self-fulfillment. Yet like any unionist, they can easily spot the old paternalism under the new public relations.

Exchanging unified labor militancy for a job-security pragmatism, "realistic" union leaders over the past twenty-five years have engaged in their own unfair labor practices by their obliviousness to work-floor and retirement inequities.[9] Leaders from the old AFL craft trades to the CIO-forged mass-industrial ones have disappointed, though not surprised, the rank and file with their perennial mismanagement and greed.[10] Nevertheless, there is a sense of empowerment among labor's loyal dissidents, who agree on little else. Included on this roster are insurgent Teamster activists, advocates for the rights of undocumented alien workers, academic historians, and the more pessimistic labor authors joining Hamper, such as James Carroll in his Boston-Irish waterfront *The City Below* (1994) and Thomas Kelly in the Bronx tunnel-work saga *Payback* (1997). The Kelly novel, successfully marketed as a thriller, is set in the 1980s, when he spent three of his ten years in construction work as a sandhog in the Bronx. Kelly is particularly acute in depicting the proletarian dystopia of construction-trade racketeers and ineffectual unions. As the new millennium approached, the author of "Who's Sticking to the Union?" (1999) predicted that there was "no respite in sight for the ordeal of American unionism."[11]

Yet, like reports of the disappearance of the working class as a recognizable entity, accounts that ring the death knell for the labor movement have been exaggerated. In the late 1990s, with an economy more prosperous than it had been in the decade's first half, the *New York Times*, not known for its positive attention to labor, ran front-page articles on the ample coffers, political clout, and successes of the AFL-CIO.[12] In contrast to their minimal attention to a host of failed strikes in the early 1990s, many mainstream papers gave unusually complete coverage to the United Parcel Service strike's relative victory in 1997 and to the UAW's 1998 partial victory over General Motors. The UPS couriers won most of their demands, particularly in their fight against the scourge of the service sector, full-time work downgraded to part-time status; more ominously, the UAW strike gave the company the power to use temporary workers.[13] Several other *Times* pieces admitted, however grudgingly, that from the streets of Manhattan to the Newark docks, union workers make 20 percent more than nonunion ones.[14]

As if exorcising the ghosts of Homestead and Youngstown, new combinations of unions are scrambling to forge alliances to meet the challenges posed by the rush of U.S. companies to benefit from global economic competition. In a perennial effort to rekindle garment-trades solidarity, the AFL-CIO is downplaying its own crafts-elite image. The joint labor council has marched against the kind of Third World sweatshops in New York City, Florida, and California that are so reminiscent of the Jacob Riis era and were limned in the stories of Dorothy Richardson and Anzia Yezierska.[15] Under the AFL-CIO aegis, there have also been unionist mergers, such as those of the Paper Workers (themselves a combination of older unions) and the Oil, Chemical, and Atomic Workers. The United Auto Workers now includes locals and sublocals of the National Writers Union (NWU); the similarly hydra-headed Teamsters Union is seeking to sign up everyone from oil burner repairmen to migrant Chicano apple pickers, Hispanic women cosmetic factory hands, and adjunct college teachers.[16]

It is a complicated question whether "credentialed laborers" such as part-time instructors are indeed workers, though some have engaged in unionizing and other forms of labor activism (teaching assistants at the University of

California and at Yale, for instance). Stanley Aronowitz is certain that they man a corporate knowledge factory, but their transient situations as acolyte educators await labor studies clarification in the new millennium.[17] A group of activist academics, many associated with Scholars and Writers for Social Justice (SAWSJ) would agree. (See the provocatively titled essays of Cary Nelson, Barbara Ehrenreich, and many others in Nelson's 1997 collection *Will Teach for Food: Academic Labor in Crisis*).[18] The Aronowitz book *The Knowledge Factory: Dismantling the Corporate University* (2000) extends the category to full-time college professors as well. There is an allied SAWSJ initiative, "teach-ins" in which left-liberal senior professors have joined John Sweeney, the media-savvy AFL-CIO president, on the dais.[19] Such events have raised the hope of rekindling the intellectuals' enthusiasm for allying themselves with the working class in a way reminiscent of the 1930s.

Yet what marks the labor movement's entry into the millennium is the vague rubric service work, which stands for 80 percent of all nonagricultural employment. Organized labor, despite divisions, scandals, and attacks from prominent politicians, understands well that the decade's best track record on mass unionism is found outside the factory world in the rise of service-sector unionism, now 40 percent of organized labor. Add to that the fact that nearly 9 million white women and black and Hispanic union members, compared with 8.3 million white male union members, swelled the ranks of Big Labor in the mid-1990s.[20]

Consider the municipal unions of the American Federation of State, County, and Municipal Employees (AFSCME), with potent (if perennially investigated) locals like New York City's DC 37, which includes clerks, school aides, and municipal hospital workers.[21] (The watershed 1968 Memphis Sanitation Workers' Strike, supported by Dr. King, was led by Local 1733 of AFSCME.)[22] An even more powerful force is the Health and Hospital Workers' Union. The proactive, multistate Local 1199, under its savvy leader, Dennis Rivera, can muster the rank and file for traffic-halting strike marches through the streets of New York.[23] Equally important are the successes of the Service Employees International Union (SEIU) in organizing so-called marginal sectors such as janitors. Now that 1199 and SEIU have merged, there is a viable movement to transform local cultures of solidarity into something far more powerful.

The twenty-first-century factory may well be relocated to the computer terminal (whether at the workplace or at home), the cubicle, the discount-store cash register, the nighttime cleaning stint, the home-health visit, the microwave counter, and the wrapping department.[24] Many of those on the line may be, in Aronowitz's pessimistic assessment, contingent, temporary, or part time, and the term may even encompass the economically slavish labor of southern prison workers.[25] These laborers will compose the "just-in-time" workforce of a new postwork culture whose hallmark will be the expendability of the most skilled technicians.[26] In practice, the entire workforce could be "replaceable, effaceable, utterly contingent, without commitment to any job, skill or place."[27]

Just as in the days of antebellum artisan republicanism, the skilled craftsman may belong to a technological guild elite with the power to lead or secede from the ranks of other service-labor workers, organized or unorganized. What is more certain is that a whole new work fiction remains to be written on the daily lives of working people inside and outside the old-fashioned factory. Today's labor fiction, while it critiques the "live white-collar or die" mentality, chooses not to decipher the class ambiguities of the American 1990s. It does not enshrine a Dennis Rivera the way its predecessors did the UFW's patron saint, Cesar Chavez.

A rare exception is the Chicana author Helena Maria Viramontes (*Under the Feet of Jesus*, 1995).[28] Her text is the "Harvest of Shame" protest that ignited the Chavez reforms. Her imagery, evocative of *The Grapes of Wrath*, is of Hoovervilles, masquerading as farmworker housing, in a California landscape of selfish Anglo plenty. In fact, her novel takes up where Tomas Rivera (*And the Earth Shall Not Devour Them*, 1971; see chapter 12) left off. In the 1990s there is even more indifference from agribusiness, more cruelty from overseers, and younger child labor: a central character, Estrella, has accompanied her mother to the fields since she was four years old (51). Viramontes's message is unsparing: the illegals who survive will never prosper. Yet her prose on what the *Washington Post* reviewers called an "appalling life" is eloquent.[29] Thus does Viramontes pay respectful homage to Mexican strawberry pickers and, by implication, to the black midwestern chicken-processing workers and the Asian, Arab, or Hispanic sweatshop seamstresses. Nevertheless, the fact that recognized ethnic novelists seem to have left Viramontes alone to continue the proletarian literary tradition suggests, if anything, that the term "working class," when applied to the new labor imaginers, seems more repressed than ever.

In the rapid turnover of authors claiming authority to represent labor, the newest breed to revisit the world of hard work seems even more remote from the laboring experience than the generation before. Because these writers' own lives recapitulate the tensions between marginal and privileged status so common to U.S. exceptionalist thought, their allegiances are tangled and ambivalent. Like their predecessors, these veterans of odd jobs, heavy labor, and (condescendingly) bestowed scholarships are no populists. Many of them wish to look without being seen, to bring the lives of one group before the scrutiny of another, to be working-class from a distance. It is instructive, too, that some of the authors whose allegiance to their working class heritage is more straightforward customarily appear in esoteric small-press editions.

Yet mainstream or art press, if these authors bypass the language of class struggle, they cleverly deconstruct the prevailing work ethic. The earliest labor organizations crusaded for the nobility of hard work as much as for higher wages and the control of artisanal and industrial time, for self-help and against moral engineering. Now easy money and the search for escapes from wage-earning work inform the quest for a working-class identity. The frequent alternative, articulated by other ethnic authors of color, is to play out in Franklinesque style the El Norte ideology by not going home again and minimizing solidarity with the common people, the unified ethnic crowd from which one has distinguished oneself. With the rise of the literature of the "discouraged worker," whether of the inner city or the service sector, a new, nonfiction narrative of disgruntlement—a loosely woven series of irreverent anecdotes—has arisen to which it is hard to apply the more familiar labels of working-class, labor relations, or traditional labor studies.

This chapter can but touch on the way these self-defeating alternatives have reformulated the American Dream. It is the province of a separate book to explore how the most pressing social issues of juvenile crime, drugs, abusive parenting, and their intersection with the era's easy-work gospel inform the new work fiction and narrative. But this book cannot end without a brief discussion of this oddly reformulated competitive individualism, this literary reenvisioning of "men's work" and "women's work," "white work" and "black work," "easy work" and "hard work."

Let us begin with a quintet of well-known writers whose characters report to factories and offices and include those more fortunate baby boomers with working-class origins: Ben Hamper, Michael Dorris, Ralph Lombreglia, Agnes Rossi, and Claudia Shear. Their stories and narratives deconstruct and reinforce the stereotypes associated with white steelworkers (rivetheads) as well as with those less remarked in the U.S. literature of labor: nurses, short-order cooks, deejays, clerks, in short, every worker from the mainstream unionist to the completely disaffiliated. Other 1990s writers continued the neurotic self-involvement of the largely Euro-American labor-literary 1980s (see chapter 12). Such an author is Richard Russo, who centers his upstate New York novel *Nobody's Fool* (1993) on a colorful construction hand confronting age by dramatically bemoaning his bad luck. Like others who deplore their "nigger wages"[30] with loud comedy, this misfit laboring man seems intent on living out the stereotype of the blue-collar oaf.

Premier among these portrayals is Ben Hamper's flippantly comic *Rivethead: Tales from the Assembly Line*. Reading like a novel, it embellishes his years at the General Motors factory in Flint, Michigan, as a riveter. The critics, hungry for the creative work of a "proletarian journalist" like Hamper, enthusiastically praised the no-holds-barred wit. But they were reading against the grain, belying the way Hamper vitiated the activist legacy of the United Auto Workers that had so strengthened the New Deal's social safety net.

For Hamper's version of identity politics is a (self-)doomed search for the meaning of modern industrial work. From the very beginning, he both acknowledges and disclaims his blue-collar UMW heritage. He is highly disapproving of the father in whose footsteps he followed for a job and the grandfather who survived the Depression and, presumably, the sit-down strikes of the 1930s. Both men are lambasted as working-class Know-Nothings: passive, unimaginative, and lacking ambition. Included in this blast is the union that in its heyday (c. 1940–1965) negotiated for the Hamper men some of the highest salaries in organized labor. He is particularly critical of the union's successes, most vividly its ability in the plushier 1970s to garner sizable unemployment pay (73), which, he notes with the satirist's eye but not his moral outrage, paid members well not to work.

Scanted too are the historic efforts of white male craft and industrial workers to assert control over organized labor that had occupied the U.S. novel for decades. The union, in fact, ends up as the villain for the oddest of reasons. It has made work so easy that the task of Hamper's generation and those that follow is to escape a 1990s update on alienation. "Fuckin A," Ben's friend Roy remarks, "do you realize we just grossed about $100 for standin' around and doin' absolutely nothin'?" (*Rivethead*, 35). The cult of lazy work for easy money is bolstered by the escapism of substance abuse in the factory washroom. It has replaced both the artisan pride of some of the earliest industrial work and the Taylorist rush for efficiency of the Ford era and legacy. "Gary and Bud worked their jobs together so that one of them read the paper or did a crossword. This form of combo workmanship was a time-honored tradition throughout the shop that helped alleviate much of the boredom" (35).

Hamper's self-mockery keeps pace with his vitriolic humor about the rivet-work. "It was the $12.82 cents an hour and the benefits package and the opportunity to swill a cold one in between breaks in the madness," he remembered in the mid-1980s. Such work "doomed us to trudge into convenience stores looking like Spam patties in wet suits" (58). That this is an economically charmed—or cursed—proletarianism Hamper well knows. He narrates the Reagan-era layoffs (117), the rehirings after years out of work, and the new round of layoffs. He stops before the most dramatic downsizing devolution of his industry, although he peppers his book with a nonchalance and trickster mentality about his own checkered work life, his various hirings and firings, that overturns the 1980s world-weariness of Raymond Carver, Russell Banks, and Charles Bukowski.

At a 1999 conference on working-class studies held in the dying steeltown, Youngstown, Ohio, the keynote speaker, Stanley Aronowitz, validated Hamper's view of a rebelliously shiftless factory floor when he observed, "The great impulse of the working class . . . is to do as little work as they can."[31] Yet other steeltown ethnography provides a more balanced and serious study of the "us-versus-them" mentality beneath the surface of basic industrial work.[32] Hamper himself is not nearly as perturbed by the potential decline of the U.S. auto industry, whose workers pridefully thought they were immune to attrition in the face of global competitors, as by the futility of the U.S. working-man's search for the dignity of labor.

Rivethead, then, presents a white male work culture that responds at most with rage recycled as boredom, or leavened by practical jokes on the foremen, to the oppressions of the factory. By his own departure from the factory, Hamper signaled that a riveter too can find a separate peace. (A similar message, conveyed with more explicit understanding of the social contract canceled by this act, is in David Mamet's 1992 story-essay "The Truck Factory.") But Hamper's blue-collar jeremiad leaves his fellow workers no path to follow once they are out the door.

Before his premature death, Michael Dorris, who in other fiction drew on his Native American heritage, provided a philosophy of change. He acknowledges Thoreauvian longings in those who hold down clerical, construction, maintenance, and even white-collar jobs. In "The Benchmark" (1993), he does so in the name of the old Euro-American nineteenth-century pride in workmanship:

My dad taught me the trade, and more often than not I used his words when I work because they still apply. He instructed my eye. One morning the year I became his journeyman, we were driving to a job in his Chevy. I was twenty, twenty-one at the time, when he called my attention to an abandoned field on the right.

What do you see, Frank, he asked me, and stopped the car.

I'd sink a test at about thirty feet, I told Dad. Another halfways to the bank. We could conduct the overflow through a four-inch. . . . Five, he corrected, but . . . [he was] satisfied that my imagination could now fill an empty space with water. . . .

He worked up to the week he died. . . . It bothers me, when I let it, that I've apprenticed no successor.[33]

The passage is beautiful for a number of reasons, both literary and philosophical. Dorris creates the fiction and thus fills his story with water as skillfully as his protagonists. Yet though Dorris lifts malaise into self-realization, for his characters the joy of work is compromised by modern times. To recapture the lost beauty of craftwork, he has to take the worker out of the workplace. (A kindred philosophy informs the fine Tess Gallagher story "Met a Guy Once," set in IWW territory in her 1997 collection *At the Owl Woman Saloon*.)[34] Also, the Dorris story, so dedicated to the joy and fulfillment of work, is no philosopher's stone: it is told by a grieving father whose child drowned in a half-constructed pool. The same work that is so satisfying is in reality a threnody for a lost son.

Ralph Lombreglia, the author of the savagely ironic "Make Me Work" (1994), gives a kind of uneasy closure to the white working-class male indecision about quick money or spiritual meaning. A college student glimpsed by Anthony, the bewildered central figure of the story, conveys a version of the Hamper message by wearing a T-shirt decorated with the logo of the story.[35] The shirt also calls up the working-class chic that has developed of late: ads appear on Labor Day for Tiffany's sterling silver wrenches and "Nuts and Bolts" cufflinks. Children of the suburbs sport labels like "Workers for Freedom" and "Laundry Industry." And the *New York Times* runs photo spreads with weathered laborers costumed in designer "work clothes."[36]

This complexly co-opted proletarianism is at the heart of the Lombreglia story, for beneath Anthony's race to be fashionable is a deep class insecurity that no amount of easy work will conceal. Balding and inauthentic (covering up his Boston Italian North End origins), Anthony is a self-styled "veteran" of Woodstock who is well paid at his sound-engineering television work. His profession serves as a metaphor for the man who, like Anthony, isn't seen, but is always in search of an attractive "image" and girlfriend. Inevitably, he is used by the slick types who people his shallow, performative world. The story accretes irony in an encounter between Anthony and a vengefully successful work and love rival in which Lombreglia explores the class-based source of Anthony's outsiderness. Anthony's fast-lane friend takes them to the very cafeteria-society type of restaurant where young Anthony spent his youth. Now a café, it is glitzed up for the in crowd. As his friend throws his weight around and successfully makes a big show of being on friendly terms with the owners (an inductee into the Sons of Italy), Anthony's final liability emerges: he has known the owners all of his life. In this café-proletarianism for sale, the prosperous, self-invented proprietors and customers agree loudly that Anthony doesn't fit in; he lacks style. He is too reminiscent of the old-fashioned, hardworking working class.

Agnes Rossi, like Dorris and Lombreglia, is commended by sophisticated reviewers as a writer of "ordinary life," a term now interchangeable with the view described by writers who widen the lens beyond blue-collar life but never forget classed borders and frustrations. Work relations join strange encounters to blur the borders between taxing work doing someone's accounts and emotional work comforting troubled people. Rossi writes to the situation of bookkeepers, tellers, waitresses, cashiers, telephone operators, professional nurses and caregivers, secretaries, nonadministrative librarians, and clerks, the last her heroine's reluctant occupation. Informing her art is the knowledge that women's numbers are now doubling and even tripling in law, chemistry, industrial engineering, and political office.[37] Thus for Rossi the effort to represent women's labor, that is, white women's labor, is set neither in the sweatshop nor under the glass ceiling, but in the various landscapes of the 75 percent of all workingwomen who make under $25,000 a year where the secret griefs of the overqualified are played out.[38]

Marriage in this world becomes a desperate antidote to office boredom, and domestic divisions of labor that overload working and non–wage-earning wives alike shape the dissatisfactions of Rossi's female protagonists. The setting of the title story of her collection *The Quick* (1992), working-class Paterson, New Jersey, a former anarchist silk town sympathetic to Sacco and Vanzetti, is too limiting for the heroine. She eventually escapes but not before experiencing a few reverses, symbolized by bad jobs: "That night I lay on my bed and wondered what the hell had happened. One minute, it seemed, I was a fairly hip college student with a boyfriend and the next I was meditating in the aisles at Woolworth's" (53).

Nonempowering work may never plumb the depths of Rossi's women, who manage to find a poetry in their discontents, but it certainly reins them in. A variation on this theme is provided in Claudia Shear's picaresque work monologue, in which tricking the bosses is a highlight of the job. Shear later pulled *Blown Sideways through Life* (1994) into an acclaimed one-woman show in Greenwich Village. Like the witty, less well known Lucy Honig (*The Truly Needy and Other Stories*, 1999), Shear plays with many of the themes in recent work fiction: the erratic movement between "uneducated" and "educated" jobs, the private rebellions, the eccentric workers who all have stories worthy of a blue-collar Dostoevski.[39]

White labor writers respond to the contradictions of the late twentieth and early twenty-first century, in which there is expansion for some, retrenchment for others, and, whatever the present financial package, job insecurity forever.[40] The joyless, passive-aggressive persona, armed largely with sarcasm against the two formidable enemies of the working class, stigmatization and monotony, seems a modern, white, working-class way of being. As fiction continues to chronicle the strategies people have devised for coping with their working-class position, increasingly what remains is posture.

If this is the remnant of the old labor movement's white workplace entitlement, downsizing plays out in alternative ways in the African American inner-city narrative that recognizes the racist sentiments of white industrial workers.[41] It will be remembered that, inaugurating the divided stream of the African American captivity narrative, Frederick Douglass remarked that it was easier for a black man to be a lawyer than a blacksmith, a skilled craftsman. He may have thus established the transformation of the fugitive into the professional. But it could also be that Douglass was predicting a long-lived discouraged worker narrative, to use the economic euphemism for the chronically laid-off, in which each generation of the black proletariat would fight the vocational battle anew with the labor unions, with management, and with social devaluation.[42]

Recent short-story collections, most notably the stories set in the black section of contemporary Pittsburgh's post-steel Homestead by John Edgar Wideman (*All Stories Are True,* 1993), and the novels of the Chicago naturalist Ronald L. Fair (*Hog Butcher,* 1966; *We Can't Breathe,* 1972), in recounting African Americans' history, are of necessity concerned with their work experience as well. Yet it is to the heirs of Douglass's *Narrative,* his progress-report autobiography, that one must look for the most recent imaging of modern black mass work. Today's many memoirs reveal a species of Douglassian self-madeism and a conviction that it is honorable to oppose an imprisoning system.

These former ghetto youths, convicts, dealers, and marginals write with precision and polish of their often-successful attempts to fight for a sense of economic and emotional well-being. Yet, though like Douglass in the New Bedford shipyards they perceive a racial division of labor, they obviously part company with Douglass in their attitude toward what the *Narrative* called the dignity of all nonslave work.[43] By the late 1990s black unemployment rates were consistently two to three times those of whites.[44] More black men were in prison than in college, one in three in their twenties was in trouble with the law, and the percentage of drug arrests involving blacks was even higher than the percentage of drug users who were black.[45] Such replacement of work by crime or alleged crime can be contextualized in terms of what the sociologist William Julius Wilson has called a disappearance of work owing to the collapse of a low-wage economy, global economic reorganization, and the abolition of non-"offshore," unskilled factory jobs.[46]

The inner-city coming-of-age story embodied by Nathan McCall's memoir *Makes Me Wanna Holler: A Young Black Man in America* (1994) tries to fuse the Douglass and Wilson models. McCall is of particular interest not so much because his ascension to journalistic potency personifies the transit from an antiwork to a work ethic, but because his is both a defiance of and a return to the dignity-of-work argument. He picks up the argument where Douglass left it: in a shipyard. But he is nothing if not scornful that as a security guard his stepfather lived a life controlled by work.[47]

In many ways, McCall turns Douglass's *Narrative* into Wilson's disappearance-of-work narrative. For one thing, McCall redefines black work so that it is inevitably lesser: "White people pursue careers; black people pursue jobs" (214). Thus the only alternatives to poorly paid menial or apprentice work are the lucrative entry-level positions in the drug trade. McCall is certainly not alone in today's culture in rejecting manual work. But, unlike those interviewed in *No Shame in My Game: The Working Poor in the Inner City* (1999) by Katherine S. Newman, in which the sentiment is often "I hate this damn job but it's a job," his disdain for menial work is boundless.[48] Many are the statements that ghettoized work is real only if illegal. Again the shipyard image surfaces: "As for the risks, dealing drugs seemed no more risky than working a thankless job at the shipyard . . . always under the fear of being laid off" (103).

The first two-thirds of the book privilege his decision to quit apprentice construction work in 1971 (89), a time when Equal Employment Opportunity Commission programs were aimed at getting minority men into the building trades. McCall moved out of that work world well before achieving journeyman status and, returning to a youthful pattern of behavior, dealt drugs until he was apprehended seven years later. During his stay in prison, McCall continues to reconcile contradictions between the classed experience of the white middle and the black underclass by questioning the work ethic itself as a model for blacks. In a trope of black rebellion reminiscent of earlier texts by Chesnutt, McKay, and Wright, it is morally better to be a "baad-ass nigger" (89). To be a working-class black, then, is an insult for the bulk of the narrative. Indeed, McCall rebukes those who found him impatient with his working-class status. One of his few references to it is that "working-class black people" visited relatives in prison (287, 407).

The braggadocio that offers the crime skills on a prison rap sheet like a vita, as a kind of alternative to low-wage jobs (233), changes when McCall, in a postmodern version of the Douglass narrative, wins a scholarship from prison. He harnesses his in-your-face anger to confront an intimidating white world by working harder than it (239, 254). Ten years after prison, he has transformed himself into the city hall bureau chief of the *Atlanta Journal-Constitution*. Providing closure to the work-crime dilemma, only when he covers trials does he see former friends, being led in chains from one area to another (287). These men inspire ambivalence: they are those he had called "baad-ass niggers" and tried to emulate, those whose down payment on their materialist aspirations was living the ghetto fast life (371). Only now can he also revise his vision of the working-class black (407)—"hardworking, right-doing" men like his once-reviled security guard stepfather. But he seems oblivious to the irony, for he is as angry at the two-tier job system at narrative's end as he was hollering mad in the beginning.[49]

If black journalists excel at reconstructing their own odds-against-it rise, white journalists see no redemption for blacks in the drug-infested ghetto or for the whites who try to discipline them. Madison Smartt Bell's deterministic thriller *Ten Indians* (1996) explores the death of a well-off therapist who seeks to expiate his social indifference by teaching martial arts in a storefront gym.[50] Richard Price has based a number of volumes on the collisions between careerist haves and public assistance have-nots. His portrait of inner-city tragedy is brutal to whites and blacks alike.

Black violence produces jobs for whites in Price's 1998 hit, *Freedomland*.[51] He builds on *Clockers* (1984), a novel about the drug entrepreneurs who spend the "working day" (38) among the seven hundred families and potential customers of the Henry Armstrong Houses, a Newark-like environment.[52] The projects are located in the fictional Dempsy, a pun alluding to the neighborhood as a dumping ground for black welfare families. Compared with the earlier *Clockers*, the projects are now even grimier. Nor are there any references to white customers, only the hair-trigger youth who have the misfortune to live there.[53] Price's landscape, the result of "municipal contempt for the underclass" (303), is a completely Wilsonian disappearance-of-work environment. The only products are poverty and drug transactions. Roving gangs of blacks, as well as Asians, Latinos, and Native Americans, have changed from social to economic units.[54] The only reference to education is made by a former crack addict with a college degree who is out of work and often delusional (483).

Class does not fade from the narrative. The paradox at the heart of this novel is that there is fairly lucrative work for whites in this hellhole: crime produces livelihoods for the largely white police force and the army of reporters. The most assiduous newshound, a woman named Jesse Haus, snoops in the Armstrong Houses to be the first to report a rape, a murder, the reaction to the shooting of a black son or niece. The irony is that she is a Red Diaper baby (9) who finds the story in every apartment (452) no cause for the 1930s style cultural work of exposing evils. She makes a good living and, when the day's work is done, escapes over the line to white Gannon (Price's barb at suburban enclaves like the right side of the Teaneck and Tenafly tracks). In so doing, she replicates the lifestyle of the police whom she dogs when she is not sniffing out news on the streets. Disaster for blacks is opportunity for this white.

Jesse may well represent the white woman's unnerving ambitiousness, but Price, like Bell, routinely casts the women who are not drugged-out prostitutes (and some who are) as angrily defending their relatives. This is not the case with African American writers like John Edgar Wideman. His long-suffering women living in a Pittsburgh neighborhood of broken curbs and garbage-strewn gutters are saddened that their own sons and those of their neighbors have become addicts.[55] But these respectable women, veterans of a life of hard paid work, do not scruple to term them all "sorry-assed junkies" (7). McCall is slightly more ambiguous. He subordinates his disdain for shiftless men who live off welfare mothers (407) and his resentment that his grandmother was an exploited maid to a reactive misogyny: "We hated them," he writes of the black women who could often find jobs more easily than their men, "because they were black and we were black" (50), a sinister herald of the family violence issue in African American family life.[56] In contrast, Ellease Southerland and the memoirist Patrice Gaines, whose heroines belong to a tradition of black female professionalism best studied elsewhere, call on black men, with varying degrees of sympathy, to get back to work.[57]

In labor terms, African American women writers chart how this hatred is directed at single-mother breadwinners. Such hostility from their men underscores their devaluation in the wider society. Viewed that way, the paid workplace, even if menial, is the site of relative stability as much as of low-waged exploitation. One of the dead-end alternative escapes from such hateful influences is to be herself criminal. The inability to escape hateful influences is also the subject of a variant plot, violence against one's own child. In Toni Morrison's *Beloved* (1987), inspired by the antebellum Margaret Garner case, a woman kills her child and tries to kill three others to keep them from being returned to slavery.[58]

While drawing some strength from the techniques of white portrayers of the female underdog such as Joyce Carol Oates, Joan Didion, and the psychic casualty Sylvia Plath, black women write violence narratives in which the black woman's job is to escape criminally abusive relationships. In what might be called the Alice Walker tradition of the novel of relationship abuse, the men practice sexism against black women even though the women are vocationally oppressed by the larger society.[59] In Walker's case, that society is the enduringly Jim Crow South. Her heroine's husband, named Mister in the spirit of the white master's mentality, symbolically lives off the fruits of her domestic service to him. He certainly sanctions the ideology that in the home only women work.[60]

Eva's Man (1987) by Gayl Jones, is a novel fraught with, and wrought by, antitheses. Its anchoring, often first-person narrative comprises the recollections of a psychotic young black Kentucky woman who has been institutionalized for murdering and then gruesomely castrating her lover. Crossing class lines, Jones could have encountered young working women like Eva in rural Kentucky, where she lived until she attended Connecticut College and Brown University.[61] Twenty-four when she wrote the novel, Jones observed Eva, with Toni Morrison as a friend and editor, from a privileged yet eerily prophetic angle of vision. In the years that followed, Jones herself entered into angry relationships with abusive working-class men, and experienced institutionalization in the wake of one of them.[62]

Eva's work history is as confused as her psychic one: "I've been going from one tobacco factory to another. You get tired and try another. In the summer, though, most of the times you get laid off anyway."[63] The factory is but one of the worlds Eva drops into and out of, and her affectlessness makes her even more baffling. Is she, as she claims, the veteran of tobacco farm and factory jobs in Connecticut, West Virginia, New Mexico, and Kentucky, as well as of a failed marriage and a sexually abusive childhood? What is meant by her comment about working at the Southwestern Tobacco Company and at P. Lorillard: "I forget" (171)?

Jones's Eva, despite the biblical association, conforms least of all to the patriarchal vision of a temptress. Eva, it turns out, not only had a sexually abusive childhood but has supported herself and had two years of college at Kentucky State (75). It is difficult to reconcile these atypical details, embedded in Eva's case history, with the promiscuous black woman bouncing from bar to lower-class hotel and spinning finally out of control.[64]

What Jones has produced is a will-to-die narrative that undoes vocation and progress to return to the scarred childhood of the borderline personality. It is a text that illustrates the single black woman down on her luck who lashes out in sexual violence against men's symbolic castration of her. These tropes, furthermore, only gain in power when joined to that of the 1990s: getting the sexually abused black woman back to work.

The charged—and overused, given the percentage of white women in that category—subject of the promiscuous black welfare mother surfaced in fiction as early as Saul Bellow's Depression era story "Looking for Mr. Green."[65] In women's texts there is more sympathy for the facade of promiscuity. While the title character of Terry McMillan's *Mama* works as a household worker, unskilled factory worker, and prostitute before going on welfare for a time, she is a complicated person and the matriarch of a family of female professionals and male ne'er-do-wells.[66] As is common in 1990s labor fiction, she has no connection to the nonwhite women workers currently taking the strike-hall mike or forging wins in HERE (Hotel Employees and Restaurant Employees Union) and SEIU/1199.[67]

Black women's fictive labor history, unionist or otherwise, is particularly hard to find.[68] There is the occasional text, such as *Blue Collar Blues* (1999) by Rosalyn McMillan, set in an auto factory. But alcoholism, masculine marital sadism, and reactive feminine promiscuity wrench the focus from ghetto unemployment and economic hopelessness. As with previous novels about women escaping ghetto abusiveness, Ramona Lofton's (pen name Sapphire) *Push* (1997) is tangentially a labor book. Yet there is a difference. Lofton builds on two sets of work sources: her experience teaching writing to teenagers and adults throughout the 1980s and early 1990s, and the new workfare programs designed to get young, and in the inner city, black mothers into jobs. Thus the novel reprints a letter from the Human Resources Administration in which Precious, the protagonist, with two illegitimate children to keep and a reading program and incest survivors' groups to attend, is ordered to report for workfare upon reaching eighteen lest her money be cut off. The voice of the caseworker appears as well: "Precious is capable of going to work now."[69]

Push is a will-to-live novel for the 1990s. It plays off against the cultural emphasis on getting the black welfare mother into the workforce. But in a challenge to official speech, it interprets "going to work now" quite differently. Updating *Maggie: A Girl of the Streets,* Precious is the product of two sexually, psychologically, and verbally abusive parents. At one point a neighbor says to her mother, "Mary, what you doin'! You gonna kill that chile" (10). Precious had two children by her father, one, when she was twelve, a child with Down syndrome, the other probably infected with HIV, as is Precious, from her drug-addicted father. For six years her parents acted as her employers: she "serviced" her father, cooked and cleaned and gave sex to her mother, and gave over her welfare check to her. All that time an illiterate Precious got passing grades in school and planned in her fantasies to get a job and "out HER house" (23).

This quest for a job and a paycheck (81) becomes more real when she relocates to a shelter for young mothers and begins learning to read and write.

But she also soon learns the gap between aspiration and the job world as the city presses her to pay back her social debt as a live-in home attendant and to place her children in care. As in McCall and others, Precious shuns the menial (127) as not worth the effort. As one of her reading group members charges,

> "I wanna work, but not for no . . . welfare check. And I be displacing brothers and sisters who really got jobs cleaning up 'cause I'm there working for free. And what kinda shit is it for someone like Precious to have to quit school before she gets her G.E.D. to work at some live-in job. She'll never make a rise she get stuck in some shit like that!" (123)

The actual jobs these women land, though, are indeed menial. The feisty Precious, studying to be someone, will soon die of AIDS.

The urban ethnographer Sherry Ortner has presciently remarked that a class framework is invoked through the very language of ethnicity.[70] The multicultural up-from-poverty tale is home to a multiplicity of working-class ethnic cultures. The previous chapter studied the storytelling of Asian, Native American, and Chicano writers fueled by their legacies and empowered by the resilient self to cross the class divide. The 1990s fiction of Lan Samantha Chang (*Hunger,* 1998) and Sherman Alexie (*Reservation Blues,* 1995) and Luis Alberto Urrea's novelistic memoir (*Nobody's Son,* 1998) join a variety of memoirs, often bittersweet, that retrace the means of ascent.

To understand ethnic interactions with the search for an easy work culture in a contingent worker environment, however, it is instructive to consider another working-class ethnicity with a recent flowering in literature. The Puerto Rican author Irene Vilar wrote in *The Ladies' Gallery* (1998), translated from the Spanish, an acknowledgment that the Puerto Rican transit to Americanism is particularly representative: "New York is harsh, everybody knows that. And getting ahead means so many things: Latin rebelliousness . . . a lot of Anglo-Saxon triumphalism. Getting ahead, at all costs."[71]

In 1968 Piri Thomas, now considered the dean of working-class Puerto Rican memoirists, asked rhetorically, "Where are the books by Puerto Ricans?"[72] He himself had just assessed the New York City Latino work, barrio, and prison experience in the groundbreaking *Down These Mean Streets* (1967). Eliding memoir and fiction and covering Hispanic East Harlem of the 1940s through the mid-1960s, Thomas was the self-acknowledged child of those "forgotten workers," women who did piecework and men out of work. By the 1950s, he had turned to an increasingly disaffected, gang-oriented drug culture. In the book's sweatshop sewing segment, Thomas remarks that under oppressive conditions, such as those endured by his mother, at times the sole breadwinner, the boundaries between individual and collective experience blur in memoir and fiction alike. When Thomas declared that he was born into a criminal world, he was writing as the Other. He was indicting not only the criminalization of the poor, especially people of color, but also the criminal justice system for dispensing unequal justice to people of color. Foreshadowing the fact that by century's end for every Hispanic man with a college degree twenty-four would be behind bars,[73] Thomas was sounding the theme that *Mean Streets* would elaborate by exploring the many meanings of imprisonment. For one who hated the system, prison became a metaphysical environment in which one shed the criminal label to forgo anger and rage and fight for a sense of being.

In his afterword to the thirtieth anniversary edition of the book, however, Thomas recasts his own ethnic labor narrative for the 1990s. Rather than point to the Puerto Rican presence in new labor unions as well as in the old labor sweatshops, Thomas urges a Rainbow Coalition response to underclass poverty: less anger, no sole ethnicity, an end to arrogance and greed. "Viva the children of all the colors!" (337). He stresses a recognition of universality, of common humanity, that renders class irrelevant. Steering clear of the language of interethnic struggle, he points to the need to lift up the poor, declares that "minority" is a racist term, and carefully avoids linking class to ethnic issues.

Esmeralda Santiago, a memoirist for a newer generation (she was born in 1948), also sent a mixed message in *When I Was Puerto Rican* (1993). Her memoir carries on the Thomas tradition of paying passionately eloquent attention to the injustices of the Puerto Rican work experience. In this case, it was an intimate knowledge of the employment difficulties of her mother, who came to the United States in the 1970s to help her eleven children appropriate success and assimilate. The memoir is filled with scenes in which her mother celebrates Esmeralda's rites of passage by bringing home bras she herself sewed in the factory.[74] But the daughter also receives her mother's fear that she will become a "blanquito," passing for white. In the effort to integrate rebellion and ascension, Santiago's memoir is marked by the sense of irony that is so often reiterated in memoirs of working-class roots.

At a public lecture in 1998, Santiago too swerved around ethnic struggle. When asked about the Puerto Ricanness of her adolescent experience, she commented that she was discriminated against for being poor, not Puerto Rican. She followed with the surprising assertion that her rise through education had been "enabled by the hierarchy of talent," on which there was no place, apparently, for her siblings, who "lacked the sophistication to rise."[75] In this are echoes of the intellectual superior to the masses, the artist-hero who, in Santiago's phrase, had realized her hope that "one day I would never go back" (*When I Was Puerto Rican*, 263).

D. H. Lawrence cautioned, of course, that we should never trust the teller but trust the tale. Reading Santiago through her public persona, however, can illuminate the divided allegiances of many a modern ethnic author. In the finale of *When I Was Puerto Rican*, she details her sortie onto WASP terrain. She auditioned before prim lady judges—stifling, she recalled, the impulse to curtsy (264) for a coveted entry into the Performing Arts High School, then largely peopled by rich kids. (She became one of three Puerto Rican and four black students among the almost two hundred students.)[76]

Her audition, a rehearsal for acceptance by the white majority, is cast more as a journey than as a performance. She begins weakly, reciting a monologue with a thick accent almost incomprehensible to the ladies. That talent will out is the message, for her auditors ask her to mime decorating a Christmas tree, in essence to use sign language to express her Americanization because she cannot yet speak English properly. Her mimicry of the dominant culture is also a working-class experience of humiliation. She must pass from ethnic silence to American voice. She will rise, but only after being remade.

No Latino writer wrestling with the dignity and vulnerability of ethnic working people seems more opposed to this view than the young short-story writer Junot Diaz. This Dominican literary craftsman quickly made the leap into market visibility; early versions of his stories appeared in the mid-1990s in the *New Yorker* and the *Paris Review* before being issued in the collection *Drown* (1996).[77] The resolutely Latino inhabitants of Diaz's "hood" in Edison, New Jersey, veer between dreams of making it big in a "nice easy job" (195), being "normal" (65), and enduring the institutionalized life of the welfare family. Defending against the sneers of everyone from middle-class blacks (145) to Anglo drug customers (129) to the wider white society, Diaz's characters wear the armor of fatalist machismo: live fast, die young. In Diaz's closest reference to the Left, Old or New, his characters reactively sneer at reform-minded people whose parents were in the peace movement.

Essentially Diaz is working with the sense of dislocation produced by *la migra*. His people, from overworked parents in low-wage jobs to underage drug couriers, emulate assimilation through their particular parodies of the American Dream. The optimistic rubric of "Aurora," the most extreme story, is belied by its narrative; one section, "A Working Day" (50), also uses upward-mobility buzzwords. Here the familiar emphasis on the salesmanship of drug dealing builds to an even more outlandishly capitalist finale. The dealer and his junkie prostitute girlfriend, who is just out of jail, hole up in a condemned apartment. There they fantasize about "a big blue house, hobbies, the whole fucking thing" (65).

Just as in fiction by whites and African Americans, there is no rapprochement between ethnic wage earning and a metropolitan workforce. Ethnic writers themselves feel little interest in "labor," as if it is either debased or co-opted.[78] What does surface, as in writings by African Americans, is the disjunction between success and failure, between drug money and welfare poverty, in the same family. Neither pole empowers people to retain what is best in their cultural legacy. By the mid-1990s, the legacy of ethnic working-class storytelling (see chapter 11) seemed to bring neither spiritual enrichment nor oppositional empowerment to the fully assimilated writers of a racial-ethnic identity. The key Whitmanesque passage from the Chicano writer Luis Alberto Urrea's *Nobody's Son* registers a shift from class- and ethnic-based identity to a New Age vagueness. After detailing the indignities experienced by his proud father in "beaner"-hating Arizona, he pays homage to him by widening the reference: "I am Other. I am you. . . . Every one of us, everybody, all of you reading this. Each border patrol agent and every trembling Mexican peering through a fence. Every Klansman."[79]

Such indiscriminate ecumenism, whether hopeful or disturbing, informs fictive working-class portraits. Already by the mid-1980s, the figures of wisdom often embodied in the grandmothers and mothers in fiction by Sandra

Cisneros and Denise Chavez, Leslie Marmon Silko, Maxine Hong Kingston, and Tomas Rivera have been driven insane by memories of brutality in their home countries. Helena Maria Viramontes's frightening story "The Cariboo Café" (1995), which addresses the tragedy of dictatorships that "disappear" their children, is hardly an American-refuge story. A Salvadoran woman, delusional with grief over a child disappeared from her home country, steals the children of illegal aliens who are themselves too busy working and running from immigration officials or authority to care properly for them. Although these American children do not vanish, the old woman is herself killed by American policemen. However mystical the fable, the inference is that the "everyday horror" of one country is replicated in another.[80]

This theme of destroyed expectations in the United States, so counter to the perennial self-transformation trope, finds studied exploration in the literary children of Piri Thomas discussed earlier. In writings that reflect on their opportunities as well as their failures, these scholarship boys and girls share with Euro-American ethnics and whites from the South and Appalachia the sense of co-optation: "It is a contradiction of our culture that [public] intellectuals who speak and articulate positions for their class frequently get tracked out of their milieu as quickly as society can arrange it."[81] Another way of putting it is that ethnic authors who treat labor themes in service to their roots retain an antibourgeois consciousness. But they do not write in a spirit of partisanship with the SEIU and the ILGWU. Theirs is at best a restrained resistance to the present-day illegal sweatshops in the old neighborhoods and the new offshore Nike, Calvin Klein, and Liz Claiborne factories of the Third World global village.[82]

As the Reagan cutbacks were in full force, the critic Morris Dickstein, in "Hallucinating the Past," a tribute to Mike Gold, deplored the wavering federal implementation of job and welfare programs since the New Deal. Yet Dickstein, nostalgic for Gold's generation, was referring as well to the literary response to a probusiness political climate after the golden age of working-class literature. He was writing in *Grand Street,* an independently published journal, that has endured despite the vicissitudes in the mainstream press of work fiction.[83] Few creative authors appearing in the alternative presses today espouse the politics associated with the still-extant socialist publishing house Charles H. Kerr, founded in 1886 in Chicago, or American Communist International Publishers, of 1924 New York City vintage.[84]

The Appalachia-born novelist Barbara Kingsolver has remarked of her down-home heroine Taylor Greer in the novels *The Bean Trees* (1988) and *Pigs in Heaven* (1993) that she wanted these books to be read by "the guy that runs Rex and Paul's Service Station" in Carlisle, Kentucky, as much as by the sophisticated, highly educated reader.[85] Kingsolver's richly metaphorical abilities as a spinner of labyrinthine kinship sagas, far more than her wryly pragmatic heroine, has won her the HarperCollins imprimatur. Labor fiction in the 1990s is more commonly published by presses ranging from small to tiny. These include West End (Albuquerque), Bottom Dog (Huron, Ohio), Arte Publico (Houston), Milkweed (Minneapolis), and The Crossing Press (Trumansburg, N.Y.), publishing authors who thereby become more visible but invisible.[86] Their works grant recognition to people whose jobs are not glamorous, who barely make it from payday to payday, and who have stories to tell. Unlike mainstream fiction—sometimes by the same authors in more successful stages of their careers—this fiction fights against the conviction that the chief duty of the working class is to abolish itself. Here, there is an outpost of the working-class aesthetic. Here, despite the still-fragmentary history of U.S. working-class culture, there is an investment in retaining or reclaiming a working-class identity rather than fixating on the social-estrangement or up-from-poverty story.[87]

Some authors, including academics from (and some still in) the working class, do not see their working-class origins as the absence of bourgeois values.[88] Such writers balance class injustice with class pride. They manifest a "bone deep knowledge of what it mean[s] to be shut out" with a certainty that working people bear the seeds of their own redemption.[89] While many of them enjoy the professional-teacher fruits of competitive individualism, they pin their hopes for a better world on a remembered world of working-class kinship and hard-earned wisdom. Lennard Davis recalls, in the tradition of Gold, that "there were many sages amongst us in the Bronx."[90] These little-known writers try not to find glory in working to exhaustion—getting lost in the anonymity and the grind.[91] They seek to coax out memory, not revive nostalgia.[92] Such is the richness of remembrance in the recently reissued fiction of Tina de Rosa (*Paper Fish,* 1980) and Tony Ardizzone's ethnic memories of Italian working-class Chicago, *Taking It Home* (1996). Both reclaim working-class Chicago from Farrell's and Algren's dark visions.

Others, particularly Latino authors, remain faithful to the lower-depths tradition of working-class poverty, the illicit and hidden black market literature of America in which "no life and no place is destitute."[93] Consider, for instance, two texts in which the lives of the poor have their own sources of pride and pleasure, the seamstress's daughter Nicholasa Mohr's bittersweet prosuccess collection *El Bronx Remembered* (Arte Publico, 1986) and Abraham Rodriguez's survivalist *Boy without a Flag* (Milkweed Press, 1992).[94]

Then there are those writers who take *Rivethead* to a logical conclusion: the retail store or fast-food job as neither a rite of passage nor a temporary situation, but as a likely work fate. Lacking the idiosyncratic interest that a Claudia Shear brings to the vagaries of the behind-the-counter or at-the-terminal world, these eyewitness historians post their interpretations in a disturbing phenomenon of the small (and tiny) press world, the vocational zine. Serving up a quasi-journalistic diatribe, in both real space and cyberspace, these publications have their roots as much in science fiction and punk rock cults as in a radical labor underground.[95] In their fury at normal society, more laborite periodicals like *Temp Slave* preach the gospel of the slacker.[96] To date there has been no fictional narrative that complements the cinematic one of the intentionally tasteless 1994 convenience-store movie *Clerks*.[97]

Cyber-publications like *Z Magazine* offer serious studies of organizing approaches and rank-and-file labor struggles online.[98] But although many work zines make screed a kind of literary subgenre and reflect plenty of anger, alienation, and bitterness, the writers rarely make the jump to unionism or at least some sort of collective action as a possible, partial solution. They revel in the aesthetics of complaint. A prime example is the webzine *Disgruntled* (www.disgruntled.com), with its tone of soured entitlement.[99]

Finally, a related small-press phenomenon of the 1990s is the story of poor-white reentitlement. It is rehearsed in the lesser-known fiction of the southern "poor-white" Dorothy Allison and that of newcomers like Paula K. Gover. Allison's *Trash* (see chapter 12), a series of interlocking short stories narrated by the girl Bone/Allison grown to retrospective womanhood, includes descriptions of violent white lesbian lovemaking in the Deep South. (Lesbian narratives, including racial-ethnic ones, are also the subject of small-press attention. Valerie Miner established a small-press precedent of sorts in her 1984 novel *Winter's Edge,* concerning a love relationship between two older San Francisco women, a waitress and a news-shop clerk.)[100] Clearly Allison has taken liberties that she chose to bypass in the Dutton-published *Bastard out of Carolina.* But *Trash* also tries to excavate, albeit in less detail, another repressed southern working-class experience. In the story "The Meanest Woman Ever Left Tennessee," Allison's fictive title character, Shirley Boatwood, recalls battles with her own sadistic mother over unionizing the mill where Shirley and her daughter Mattie Boatwood both worked. As the narrative closes with Mattie's fantasy of unionizing the children she would have one day, Allison fuses trade unionism with the redemptive love of family so foreign to Shirley Boatwood.

Paula Gover's *White Boys and River Girls,* published in 1995 by the small, selective Algonquin Books of Chapel Hill, appropriately enough a division of New York's Workman Publishing, is less sanguine.[101] Set in backward Georgia, welfare checks and illegal liquor stills (8) are alternatives to laying tar on runways. Gover displays a kind of courage in writing these "white trash" stories, in which the ethic of rising is continually undercut. Interestingly, another Georgian's small-press publication, Janisse Ray's memoir, *Ecology of a Cracker Childhood* (1999), tells a "scholarship-girl" success story and cleverly appeals to current fascination with environmental issues. Ray's book won the recognition denied Gover.[102] An even more telling example is provided by James Lee Burke, the author of the fine Appalachian novel *To the Bright and Shining Sun* (see chapter 12). Burke widened his work to a commercial audience when he wrote *Half of Paradise* (1965), a mixed-genre transitional text that balances excellent poor-white fictive biography with a rather stereotyped chain gang narrative. After that, to earn six- and seven-figure advances, he redirected his analysis of working-class violence to novels with white trash local color.[103] The Kentucky-born playwright Naomi Wallace boldly experiments in *Slaughter City* (1995) with late Renaissance satiric drama on the uneasily biracial meatpacking floor. But the play, influenced by her interviews with workers in hazardous jobs, lacks *Rivethead*'s humor and its production is hardly lucrative outside the highbrow world of the play festival and the off-Broadway stage.[104] Rare indeed is the best-sellerdom accorded *Rocket Boys,* made into a Hollywood film that tried to position the hero as a coal miner's son. Homer Hickam's 1998 memoir is indeed set squarely in a coal-mining context: Hickam's friends, as their fathers did, will work for the Company. But as the son of the benevolently dictatorial mine superintendent, Hickam can rein-vent himself as a NASA engineer without disavowing his roots, which are not really working class. More predictable a "hillbilly" success was Tracy Letts's trailer camp play, produced on Broadway in 1998, the black-humored *Killer Joe*. This in-your-face parody of lowlife poor relations who work as Pizza Hut waitresses and two-bit drug dealers and conspire to murder their mother for the insurance melds Erskine Caldwell's grotesqueries with Quentin Taran-tino's (*Pulp Fiction*, 1994).[105]

Today the small-press tradition makes up in seriousness what it lacks in mass appeal. As evidenced by the newest generation of writers from the work-ing class, the problem of bridging the gap between awareness of separateness and the wish to assimilate lives on. But so does the vitality of those workers who challenge that social distance.

As with the earliest labor texts of valiant mechanics on the rise or driven mad by downward mobility, the labor margins have once again become the center. Except among writers of color and women regionalists, even the post-"classical" worker novel seems to have come to an exhausted halt. Ilan Stevens remarked that no neighborhood is ever real until a writer touches it.[106] The lived-experience novel of Mike Gold to this day makes the veiled au-tobiography *Jews without Money* fiction in the best sense of the word: a fully realized world of the working-class imagination. In the 1990s, seventy-five years after the fact, an aged Henry Roth tried to revivify a similarly immigrant-Jewish ethnic surround. But Roth's *Call It Sleep* (1934) could not be transformed into the four volumes of *Mercy of a Rude Stream*, all published between 1994 and 1998.[107] There was no imaginative space in which to over-lay *Call It Sleep*'s fearful but impassioned attachments to immigrant relatives with the two later novels' account of Ira Seligman's incest and guilt. Paradox-ically, the very candor and modernity of the protagonist's long-buried sexual story created only two linked memoirs striving to recapture a lost historical moment.

Yet Roth's conflation of fiction and autobiography reveals a truth about today's working-class memoir. Its spiritual descendant is another form, al-lied to fiction, the escape memoir, which bids fair to become the new worker representation at the start of the new century. Once again American authors pin their hopes on the individual, reviving proletarian memory to inspire the worker to recognize that he has within himself the seeds of his own redemption.

If the memory of labor's hardships rather than the new voice of struggling or empowered labor is taking over the fiction of today, the memoir is creating a space for working-class people to represent themselves. It may well be, whether sadly or comically, that in this postmobility era marked with the de-sire for easy, lucrative work, the memoir is ideally suited for a labor narrative that is less about reinvented working people than about strategies for mer-chandising a working-class identity. One hopes not.

Since the disappearance of the blue-collar working stiff, work has (re)ap-peared elsewhere, from the old Way-to-Wealth narratives in a more enlight-ened multicultural dress to the discourse of those disaffected, credentialed laborers in the knowledge industry disclaiming any identification with the masses but liable to the historic insecurity of manual wage earners. In fact, the historic and artistic difficulties in linking skilled work, much less noncraft labor, with embourgeoisement have infused the literature of labor for 150 years. There is a clear line of development from Mose, the hard-drinking, womanizing "wild man," from his antebellum origins to his *Rivethead* incarnation. Whatever the period, U.S. literature couples a recurring stance of tourism with a wariness about the working-class subject or the role of social crusader. The late nineteenth century's slum tours in the lowest depths of the urban wilderness become the late twentieth century's forays into understanding the psychically fragmented worker.

This study has sought to establish the literary relationship of labor to upward mobility in the allied contexts of periodization and working-class history. It has also asked what it feels like to be described by other people and erased by them at the same time.[108] Clearly the workingman and -woman are radically revised with every shift in social ideology, with every conception of race, ethnicity, or gender. Thus working-class consciousness is a slippery term indeed, for it cannot be welded to the hopes of the Left any more than to the fears of the Right.

So many U.S. writers have made their own convictions about the dream of mobility those of the workingman and -woman they themselves have imagined. Thus worker figures dubbed shiftless, low-functioning, dispossessed, or even criminal still rightly belong in the company of George Lippard's desperate, jobless carpenters; Rebecca Harding Davis's ironworkers; John Hay's subversive mob; the dime novel's ferocious Molly Maguires; Frank Norris's mindless throng of Polk Street clerks; Reginald Wright Kauffman's commercialized sex-traders; Mary Heaton Vorse's pathetic mill children; Jack Conroy's dispossessed ditch-diggers, truckers, bridge-builders, and hoboes; Thomas Bell's heroically tragic steelworkers; Harriette Arnow's World War II Kentuckians flooding munitions-plant Detroit; Chester Himes's brooding black war workers; Thomas McGrath's cynical longshoremen; John Sayles's played-out miners; Jimmy Breslin's barfly tunnel workers; Sherman Alexie's self-deceiving tricksters; Sapphire's eloquently profane workfare candidates; and the proactive drug dealers of Richard Price's and Junot Diaz's job-poor ghettoes.

If American history teaches us anything, it is that our fiction cannot bear too much proletarian reality. With each new decade, workers change less than the narratives that represent them. In a nation that too often denigrates or masks workers' achievements, a century and a half of fiction about working people has fixed a restless, often flickering gaze on labor's enduring struggles. Such conflicts are played out in a country that, denying class and continually reinventing itself, refuses to acknowledge the resultant co-optations and hidden injuries.

The very characteristics that have rendered the best work literature controversial have ignited its strengths: a critical engagement with the classism of the everyday; an insistence that identity dwells apart from economic gain; and a humanity that issues from acknowledging rather than disowning working-class origins.

Notes

Preface

1. Daniel Horwitz, "Going East: A Novel of Proletarian Life," serialized in the *Daily Worker*, 22 August 1934, 5; 28 August 1934, 5; 29 August 1934, 5; 30 August 1934, 5; 31 August 1934, 5; 1 September 1934, 7; 4 September 1934, 5; 5 September 1934, 5; 6 September 1934, 5; 7 September 1934, 5; 8 September 1934, 7; 10 September 1934, 5; 11 September 1934, 5; 12 September 1934, 5; 14 September 1934, 5.

2. Kevin Baker, "Ballplayers Are Workers, Too," *New York Times*, 10 February 1995, A29. Ironically, mention of the real workers thrown out of jobs, the ushers, vendors, and clubhouse waiters, is relegated to a Sports Sunday piece by George Vecsey, "Sympathy for the Real Labor Force," *New York Times*, 7 August 1994, 8:1. This strange new version of the old crusading fervor has no room for the many native- and foreign-born workers squeezed by corporate retrenchment, NAFTA, and, despite recent rallying, the uncertain future of organized labor.

3. Lawrence Buttenweiser and Raymond Horton, "A Leaner New York in Thirty Minutes a Day," *New York Times*, 10 February 1995, A29. See also, for this latter-day Taylorism, George Varinaktarakis and Janice Kim Winch, "Cross-Training in Paced Assembly Lines," *informs,* pub. the Institute for Operations Research and the Management Sciences, Lubin School of Business, Pace University, 2000. The authors recommend a system in which "every worker of the assembly line follows a simple rule of what to do next." They castigate asynchronous movement, which "allows workers to 'hide' in the crowd. . . . As a result, a great amount of worker capacity is lost." See also "Why America Needs Unions but Not the Kind It Has Now," *Newsweek*, 23 May 1994, 70–74.

A short, factual article buried in the middle of the *Times* helped commemorate a recent Labor Day by noting that the Occupational Safety and Health Administration (OSHA) had cut costs by conducting fewer inspections of workplaces than at any time since 1971. See "Study Finds Decline in Workplace Inspections," *New York Times*, 6 September 1999, A13.

4. Although this piece appeared before the jobless rate fell dramatically, note the headline: Sylvia Nasar, "Jobless Rate in August Again Dipped to a 29-Year Low: Labor Market Was Tight but Wages Barely Rose," *New York Times*, 4 September 1999, C1; "For Your Information," *UA* [United Association of Plumbers and Pipe Fitters] *Journal* (January 1995): 11. "The labor movement is a diminished force amidst hostile seas. . . . "[T]hreatened with extinction [is a] skilled and resourceful industrial working class." Bruce Laurie, "A Class Threatened with Extinction," *Chronicle of Higher Education*, 5 April 1996, B64.

5. Paul Solman, report, *McNeil/Lehrer Newshour*, WNET, 17 January 1995. Quite contrary statistics are cited in Rebecca P. Heath, "The New Working Class," *American Demographics* 9 (January 1998): 51–55. But Heath acknowledges that there was no

category for lower middle class, nor were respondents asked why they answered as they did; such a question would have elicited more salient definitions of working class. I am indebted to Paul Lauter for the Heath reference. See also an article arguing that as early as 1945, working-class Americans misperceived themselves as middle class, in John Cassidy, "Who Killed the Middle Class?" *New Yorker*, 16 October 1995, 114.

Added to the problem of defining who belongs to the working class these days is that people do not accept the designation "working class." As much consumers as producers who labor, they use lower-middle-class and middle-class blue-collar worker almost interchangeably to indicate white middle-class belonging. In a lecture at the Tamiment Library, New York University, on April 13, 1999, Daniel Walkowitz commented that people making anywhere from $20,000 to $200,000 call themselves middle class but might not call one another that.

6. Constance Coiner provided an excellent summary of Paul Lauter's view in "Literature of Resistance: The Intersection of Feminism and the Communist Left in Meridel Le Sueur and Tillie Olsen," in *Radical Revisions: Rereading 1930s Culture*, ed. Bill Mullen and Sherry Lee Linkon (Urbana: University of Illinois Press, 1996), 144, 164n.

7. Sherry Lee Linkon of the Youngstown Center for Working-Class Studies finds three contending models of class: Marxist (relation to the means of production), Weberian (triad of education/occupation/income), and "discursive" (media-driven influences). On the partial validity of each model, and the difficulty of defining the term "working class," see Sherry Lee Linkon, "Introduction," in *Teaching/Working/Class*, ed. Sherry Lee Linkon (Amherst: University of Massachusetts Press, 1999), 2–4. Martin J. Burke seems bemused by the varied and contradictory classifications of class structure in a book rightly called *The Conundrums of Class: Social Order in America* (Chicago: University of Chicago Press, 1995). See, especially, xii. See also Steven Greenhouse, "The Rise of the Working Class," *New York Times*, 3 September 1997, D1, 2; Terence Rafferty, "Accept No Substitutes," *New Yorker*, 17 May 1993, 112.

8. Richard Sennett, "Back to Class Warfare," op-ed page, *New York Times*, 27 December 1994, A21. See also Reeve Vanneman and Lynn Weber Cannon, *The American Perception of Class* (Philadelphia: Temple University Press, 1987), and Benjamin DeMott, *The Imperial Middle: Why Americans Can't Think Straight about Class* (New Haven: Yale University Press, 1990).

9. Janet Zandy, "Introduction," in *Liberating Memory: Our Work and Our Working-Class Consciousness*, ed. Janet Zandy (New Brunswick, N.J.: Rutgers University Press, 1995), 1. The epigraph above, "Jude remains obscure," is in David Joseph, "Breaking through the Sounds of Silence," in Zandy, *Liberating Memory*, 139.

Introduction

1. In 1996 Labor Studies faced the Death and Dying bookcase in a flagship New York City Barnes & Noble superstore, and clerks questioned on labor books directed customers to the childbirth section. Throughout this book, the term "American" refers to North America, not to the United States only.

2. Dirk Johnson, "Rank and File's Verdict: A Walkout Well Waged," *New York Times*, 20 August 1997, D19, and "Settlement at UPS" (editorial page), ibid., A22; Nichole M. Christian, "3,400 Strike at G.M. Plant; Assembly Put at Risk," *New York Times*, 6 May 1998, A7.

3. Steve Lohr, "Accepting the Harsh Truth of a Blue-Collar Recession," *New York Times*, 25 December 1991, 1. See also James Bennet, "Mere Hint of Jobs Draws Crowd in Detroit," *New York Times*, 11 November 1991, 1; and Andy Vazac, "The Forgotten Worker," letter to the editor, *New York Times*, 12 September 1994, A14. The article "UAW Members Vote Down Contract with Caterpillar" (*New York Times*, 23 February 1998) reports on a contract that describes the "unfair labor practices" of the union, not of the company that hired temporary and replacement workers (A3); see also Andrew Hacker, "Who's Sticking to the Union?" *New York Review of Books*, 18 February 1999, 45.

4. See Monique P. Yazigi, "So Hard to Find Good Employers These Days," *New York Times*, 15 August 1999, A1, 2.

5. "Labor Federation Expresses Its Vulnerability in Hostile Times," *New York Times*, 26 February 1995, A23; "Union Movement Loses Another Big One," *New York Times*, 19 April 1992, 4:1; "'Good Jobs in Hard Times," *Crain's Business Weekly*, 3 October 1992, 3:1, 6. On the hatred of company unions, see *Labor Notes* 191 (February 1995): 1. See also the labor organizer George Biderman's letter to the editor, *New York Times*, "Labor Gains Nothing in Company Unions," 19 January 1995, A22. See also Charles V. Bagli, "Latest Construction Bottleneck: Shortage of Skilled Workers," *New York Times*, 15 August 1999, 29.

6. "Millions of Casualties on Business Battlefields" (*New York Times*, 3 March 1996), speaks of the "most acute job insecurity since the Depression" (26).

7. Howard Risher, "Behind the Big Picture: Employment Trends in the 1990s," *Compensation and Benefits Review* 29, no. 1 (January-February 1997): 8. See also "Productivity Up 0.7% in '96," *Minneapolis Star Tribune*, 12 March 1997.

8. Morris Dickstein, "Hallucinating the Past: *Jews without Money* Revisited," *Grand Street* 9 (Winter 1989): 163.

9. While the 1980s and 1990s have witnessed an erosion in traditional blue-collar jobs and newer forms of white collar drudgery have burgeoned, Patricia Cayo Sexton's assertion that the new definition of working class should encompasses all "those who are neither top executives nor self-employed—that is, the vast majority of employed people," seems overstated. See Patricia Cayo Sexton, *The War on Labor and the Left* (Boulder, Colo.: Westview Press, 1991). In the higher work echelons, workers like legal aid lawyers and major league ballplayers can now claim union affiliations, but their professional identities define them far more than their laboring ones. So too full-time college professors and schoolteachers, even though the leftist term "cultural workers" certainly applies to both groups. Farmers are somewhat more problematic. While they swelled the Populist (or People's) Party of the 1890s, entered the Farmer-Labor Party, and demonstrated with miners and unemployed factory workers during the Depression, their alliance with labor was uneasy. This study includes fiction on agrarian radicalism, migrant farmworkers, and tenant farmers and sharecroppers, but not the entrepreneurial farmer, however circumscribed his independence as a businessman. Women's unpaid child rearing and housework are not a focal point here. I place this unremunerated feminine work in discussions of texts on women's (customarily low-) paid labor.

10. Reeve Vanneman and Lynn Weber Cannon, *The American Perception of Class* (Philadelphia: Temple University Press, 1987), 2. See the section "American Class Conflicts" for a clarifying discussion (4–7).

11. For a severe repudiation of American exceptionalism as an applicable theory, see Paul Buhle, [Review of *American Exceptionalism: U.S. Working-Class Formation in an International Context*], *Journal of American History* 85 (September 1998): 641.

12. Paul Buhle, "American Exceptionalism," in *The Encyclopedia of the American Left*, ed. Mari Jo Buhle, Paul Buhle, and Dan Georgakas (New York: Garland, 1990), 20. Paul Buhle's brief essay provides an excellent overview of the ideas associated with the term and the revisionist scrutiny of it. For other summaries of American historians' debates on working-class exceptionalism, traditionalism, and resistance to the bourgeois ethos, see Alice Kessler-Harris, "A New Agenda for American Labor History: A Gendered Analysis and the Question of Class," in *Perspectives on American Labor History: The Problems of Synthesis*, ed. J. Carroll Moody and Alice Kessler-Harris (De Kalb: Northern Illinois University Press, 1990), 217–223; and David Montgomery, "To Study the People: The American Working Class," *Labor History* 21 (Fall 1980): 485–512. James Guimond lucidly explains liberal and conservative versions of exceptionalism as interpretations of the American Dream in *American Photography and the American Dream* (Chapel Hill: University of North Carolina Press, 1991), 1–16. On the labor movement's linguistic departures from the exceptionalism idea, see David R. Roediger, *The Wages of Whiteness: Race and the Making of the American Working Class* (London: Verso, 1991), 66.

13. Janet Zandy, "In the Skin of a Worker." Modern Language Association session on "What Makes a Text Working-Class?" San Francisco, December 1998. A similar definition of working-class literature is in Paul Lauter, "American Proletarianism," in *The Columbia History of the American Novel*, ed. Emory Elliott et al. (New York: Columbia University Press, 1991), 334–335.

14. For a recent best-seller mourning the lost masculinity once characteristic of the blue-collar male, see Susan Faludi, *Stiffed: The Betrayal of the American Man* (New York: Alfred A. Knopf, 1999). For more analytical comments on the "beefy" worker, I am indebted to Renny Christopher.

15. See, for an excellent example, a coal-mining memoir of sorts by a mine superintendent's son, Homer Hickam, Jr., *Rocket Boys* (1998). It was reissued in 1999 as *October Sky* after the movie of that name was released.

16. Zandy, "In the Skin of a Worker."

17. See Janet Zandy, "Introduction," in *Calling Home: Working-Class Women's Writings—An Anthology*, ed. Janet Zandy (New Brunswick, N.J.: Rutgers University Press, 1990), 7n; and Nicholas Coles, "Democratizing Literature: Issues in Teaching Working-Class Literature," *College English* 7 (November 1986): 668. Space constraints permit me to name only a few of the new labor poets. They include Marge Piercy, *My Mother's Body* (New York: Alfred A. Knopf, 1985); Sue Doro, *Blue Collar Goodbyes* (Watsonville, Calif.: Papier-Mâché Press, 1992); Jim Daniels, *Punching Out* (Detroit: Wayne State University Press, 1990); and Sonia Sanchez, *Homegirls and Handgrenades* (New York: Thunder's Month Press, 1984).

18. See Clark D. Halker, *For Democracy, Workers, and God: Labor Song-Poems and Labor Protest, 1865–1895* (Urbana: University of Illinois Press, 1991); Robbie Lieberman, *"My Song Is My Weapon": People's Songs, American Communism, and the Politics of Culture, 1930–1950* (Urbana: University of Illinois Press, 1989); and Archie Green, "American Labor Lore: Its Meanings and Uses," *Industrial Relations* 4 (February 1965): 51–69.

19. Peter Conn, *The Divided Mind: Ideology and Imagination in America, 1898–1917* (Cambridge: Cambridge University Press, 1983), 15.

20. Emory Elliott, "Introduction," in *The Columbia History of the American Novel*, ed. Emory Elliott et al. (New York: Columbia University Press, 1991), xvi.

21. Christophe Den Tandt, *The Urban Sublime and American Literary Naturalism* (Urbana: University of Illinois Press, 1998), 12–13; "Three Ways to Study Culture,"

in *A Handbook of Critical Approaches to Literature*, 4th ed., ed. Wilfred L. Guerin et al. (New York: Oxford University Press, 1999), 239–245, 247–253.

22. Carolyn Porter, "Are We Being Historical Yet?" *South Atlantic Quarterly* 87 (Fall 1988): 743–759.

23. John Higham, "Opinion," *Chronicle of Higher Education*, 28 July 1993, B6. For the new scholars of fiction by Asian and African Americans and related racial fiction who hold up an ethnic and cultural mirror to the works, see Elaine Kim, Preface, in *Charlie Chan Is Dead: An Anthology of Contemporary Asian American Fiction*, ed. Jessica Hagedorn (New York: Penguin, 1993); and essays by various hands in the "Critical Essays" section in Alice Walker, *"Everyday Use"* (New Brunswick, N.J.: Rutgers University Press, 1994). Constance Coiner makes a similar point in "Class," in *Oxford Companion to Women's Writing*, ed. Cathy N. Davidson and Linda Wagner-Martin (New York: Oxford University Press, 1995), 194. I concur with Coiner that "far broader categorical parameters than many people recognize" define working-class writing, "even though readers and critics usually identify the texts in other terms" (194).

24. Qtd. in William J. Puette, *Through Jaundiced Eyes: How the Media View Organized Labor* (Ithaca, N.Y.: ILR Press, 1992), 8. For a 1960s update of this view and the New Left's denial that it found the (white male) blue-collar workers reactionary and even racist, see Maurice Isserman's disclaimer in "Left Out" [review of John Patrick Diggins's *The Rise and Fall of the American Left*], *New York Times Book Review*, 6 March 1992, 9. Conversely, for a scathing appraisal of the New Left's idealization of the "politically correct" proletariat of the 1930s, see William Phillips, "Histories of the Left," *Partisan Review* 60 (1993): 337–340.

25. Carla Cappetti, *Writing Chicago: Modernism, Ethnography, and the Novel* (New York: Columbia University Press, 1993), 149.

26. Qtd. in ibid.

27. Paul Lauter, *Canons and Contexts* (New York: Oxford University Press, 1991), 112.

28. See, for, example, the Feminist Press reissues of lost women writers of the radical 1930s, the University of Illinois Press reprints of novels by the radical Left, the ILR Press Literature of American Labor reprints, the Northeastern University Press Library of Black Literature, and the Schomburg Library of Nineteenth-Century Black Women Writers.

29. Elaine Scarry, "Work and the Body in Hardy and Other Nineteenth-Century British Novelists," *Representations* 3 (Summer 1983): 121n.

30. A sampling of the best of this scholarship is Alan Wald, "The 1930s Left in U.S. Literature Reconsidered," in *Radical Revisions: Rereading 1930s Culture*, ed. Bill Mullen and Sherry Lee Linkon (Urbana: University of Illinois Press, 1996), 13–28; Michael Denning, *The Cultural Front: The Laboring of American Culture in the Twentieth Century* (New York: Verso, 1996); Bill Mullen and Sherry Linkon, "Introduction: Rereading 1930s Culture," in *Radical Revisions*, 1–12; Cary Nelson, *Repression and Recovery: Modern American Poetry and the Politics of Cultural Memory, 1910–1945* (Madison: University of Wisconsin Press, 1989).

31. Paula Rabinowitz, *Labor and Desire: Women's Revolutionary Fiction in Depression America* (Chapel Hill: University of North Carolina Press, 1991), 21; Julia Stein, "Tangled Threads: Two Novels about Women in the Textile Trades, *Call the Darkness Light*, by Nancy Zaroulis and *Folly* by Maureen Brady," *Women's Studies Quarterly* 26, nos. 1/2 (Spring/Summer 1998): 98–102. Stein offers a number of titles to augment reading lists of proletarian fiction.

32. Walter B. Rideout, *The Radical Novel in the United States, 1900–1954: Some Interrelations of Literature and Society* (Cambridge: Harvard University Press, 1956); Fay M. Blake, *The Strike in the American Novel* (Metuchen, N.J.: Scarecrow Press, 1972). See also Jon-Christian Suggs, "The Proletarian Novel," in *Dictionary of Literary Biography*, vol. 9, pt. 3, ed. James J. Martine (Detroit: Gale Research, 1981), 231–245; Virginia Prestridge, *The Worker in American Fiction: An Annotated Bibliography* (Champaign: University of Illinois Institute of Industrial and Labor Relations, 1954). The scant number of these early surveys contrasts with the numerous past studies of proletarian fiction, including essay collections such as *The American Writer and the Great Depression*, ed. Harvey Swados (Indianapolis: Bobbs-Merrill, 1966); *Years of Protest*, ed. Jack Salzman and Barry Wallenstein (New York: Pegasus, 1967); *Proletarian Writers of the Thirties*, ed. David Madden (Carbondale: Southern Illinois University Press, 1968); and *Literature at the Barricades: American Writers in the 1930s*, ed. Ralph Bogardus (Tuscaloosa: University of Alabama Press, 1982). On the continued critical reappraisal of the 1930s, see note 13.

33. For positive appraisals, see Michael Rogin, "The Cultural Front," *Journal of American History* 84 (September 1997): 712–715; Adam Schatz, "The Cultural Front," *The Nation* 264, no. 9 (10 March 1997): 25–29; Karen Winkler, "A Scholar Mixes History and Culture to Argue for a New Look at the 1930s," *Chronicle of Higher Education*, 21 March 1977, A17–21.

34. A preview of Alan Wald's forthcoming two-volume study is offered in his important essay "Culture and Commitment: U.S. Communist Writers Reconsidered," in *New Studies in the Politics and Culture of U.S. Communism*, ed. Michael E. Brown et al. (New York: Monthly Review Press, 1993), 281–306.

35. Douglas Wixson, *The Worker-Writer in America: Jack Conroy and the Tradition of Midwestern Literary Radicalism, 1898–1990* (Urbana: University of Illinois Press, 1994); Barbara Foley, *Radical Representations: Politics and Form in U.S. Proletarian Fiction, 1929–1941* (Durham, N.C.: Duke University Press, 1993); Rabinowitz, *Labor and Desire*; Paul Lauter, "Working-Class Women's Literature: An Introduction to Study," *Radical Teacher* 15 (March 1980): 16–26; Zandy, *Calling Home*.

36. *Writing Red: An Anthology of American Women Writers, 1930–1940*, ed. Charlotte Nekola and Paula Rabinowitz (New York: Feminist Press, 1987). Jon-Christian Suggs has edited a documentary collection of (masculine) literary pronouncements during the Proletcult era of the late 1920s and 1930s. *American Proletarian Culture: The Twenties and the Thirties*, Dictionary of Literary Biography Documentary Series, vol. 11, ed. Jon-Christian Suggs (Detroit: Gale Research, 1993).

37. Nicholas K. Bromell, *By the Sweat of the Brow: Literature and Labor in Antebellum America* (Chicago: University of Chicago Press, 1993); David Sprague Herreshoff, *Labor into Art: The Theme of Work in Nineteenth-Century American Literature* (Detroit: Wayne State University Press, 1991); Michael Denning, *Mechanic Accents: Dime Novels and Working-Class Culture in America* (London: Verso, 1987).

38. Foley, *Radical Representations*; Rabinowitz, *Labor and Desire*; Constance Coiner, *Better Red: The Writing and Resistance of Tillie Olsen and Meridel Le Sueur* (New York: Oxford University Press, 1995).

39. Some prominent examples are Ruth Geller, "The American Labor Novel, 1871–1884" (Ph.D. diss., State University of New York at Buffalo, 1980); Dorothy S. Pam, "Exploitation, Independence, and Solidarity: The Changing Role of American Working Women as Reflected in Working-Girl Melodrama" (Ph.D. diss., New York University, 1980); Suzanne Sowinska, "American Women Writers and the Radical Agenda, 1925–1940" (Ph.D. diss., University of Washington, 1992); and Kenneth Brown, "The Lean Years: The Afro-American Novelist during the Depression

(1929–1941)" (Ph.D. diss., University of Iowa, 1986). See also the annotated listings in Wald, "Culture and Commitment," 302n, 303n; Bill V. Mullen, *Popular Fronts: Chicago and African-American Cultural Politics, 1935–1946* (Urbana: University of Illinois Press, 1999).

40. On this omission, see, for instance, George Chauncey, "Skimming the Cream of a Half-Century of Name-Brand Gay Life and Gossip," *New York Times*, 30 December 1997, E12. His own recent book, save for nods to the hobo encounters chronicled mainly in Depression era memoirs, is virtually silent on fiction by and about working-class gay men. See George Chauncey, *Gay New York: Gender, Urban Culture, and the Making of the Gay Male World, 1890–1940* (New York: BasicBooks, 1994). Useful social-historical references appear on 390n, 397n, 409n, 414n, and 450n.

41. The omission of gay and lesbian labor concerns is evident in *Not Your Father's Labor Movement: Inside the AFL-CIO*, ed. Jo-ann Mort (New York: Verso, 1998) and in the many "public intellectuals'" essays in the less mainstream *Audacious Democracy: Labor, Intellectuals, and the Social Reconstruction of America*, ed. Steven Fraser and Joshua B. Freeman (Boston: Houghton Mifflin, 1997). See, by way of contrast, the film *Out at Work*, dir. Kelly Anderson and Tami Gold, Frameline Productions, 1997, which aired at the 1997 Sundance Film Festival. See also James B. Stewart, "Coming Out at Chrysler," *New Yorker*, 21 July 1997, 38–48. Some attention, however, is given to the subject in the monthly quasi-organized labor broadside *Labor Notes*. See Desma Holcomb, "Unions Join Fight against Anti-Gay Job Bias," *Labor Notes*, no. 187 (October 1994): 7.

42. John Loughery, *The Other Side of Silence: Men's Lives and Gay Identities, a Twentieth Century History* (New York: Holt, 1998); Jillian Sandell, "Telling Stories of 'Queer White Trash': Race, Class, and Sexuality in the Work of Dorothy Allison," in *White Trash: Race and Class in America*, ed. Matt Wray and Annalee Newitz (New York: Routledge, 1997), 223.

43. Joanne Kadi, *Thinking Class: Sketches from a Cultural Worker* (Boston: South End Press, 1996), 144. See also David P. Becker, "Growing Up in Two Closets: Class and Privilege in the Lesbian and Gay Community," in *Queerly Classed*, ed. Susan Raffo (Boston: South End Press, 1997), 227–234.

44. Gilgun, though critical of the dominant culture, is not himself a gay red writer. Although I did not have the time to give Gilgun's texts as thorough a reading as I would have wished, I am grateful that Wendell Ricketts directed me to his out-of-print novel *Music I Never Dreamed Of* (1989). In a letter to the author lamenting the small-press limitations on gay and lesbian authors, Ricketts noted, "breaking through [the mainstream publishing] ceiling is virtually impossible—every year roughly one queer writer seems to do it." He also observes, "There is [virtually nothing] written by or for working-class gay men [except for] isolated stories in "GM fiction anthologies." E-mail to author, 8 October 1999.

45. See, for instance, Leslie Feinberg, *Stone Butch Blues* (1994), on a lesbian factory worker "passing" as a man, and the textile factory novel by the textile activist Maureen Brady, *Folly* (1994). For a discussion placing *Folly* in the context of lesbian working-class feminism, see Stein, "Tangled Threads," 100–102.

46. A recent study on cowboys in American culture claims that these western workingmen "authored language by inventing brands" as a way of "denying their disenfranchisement" by the ranchers. Thus their folk poems on heaven are viewed as "writing[s] [of] holy discourse." See Blake Allmendinger, *The Cowboy: Representations of Labor in an American Work Culture* (New York: Oxford University Press, 1992), 4–5. See also Carl Freedman and Christopher Kendrick, "Forms of Labor in Dashiell

Hammett's *Red Harvest*," *PMLA* 106 (March 1991): 220. Remarks one caustic observer of the new theorists: "The tendency is to theorize class in order to prove that it has a place at the university." See Carol Faulkner, "My Beautiful Mother," in *Liberating Memory: Our Work and Our Working-Class Consciousness*, ed. Janet Zandy (New Brunswick, N.J.: Rutgers University Press, 1995), 201. Conversely, for a strong essay theorizing race, class, and labor literature, see Eric Schocket, " 'Discovering Some New Race': Rebecca Harding Davis's 'Life in the Iron Mills' and the Literary Emergence of Working-Class Whiteness," *PMLA* 115, no. 1 (February 2000): 46–59. It appears in a special issue of the journal, "Rereading Class."

47. Janet Zandy, "God Job," in *Writing Work: Writers on Working-Class Writing*, ed. David Shevin, Janet Zandy, and Larry Smith (Huron, Ohio: Bottom Dog Press, 1999), 175–191. Her work in progress is "Hands: Working-Class Bodies Speak."

48. Bromell, *By the Sweat of the Brow*, 178.

49. George Gonos, "Workplace Communities and Moral Exclusion: The Contingent Workers of Academe," in *Contingent Work: American Employment Relations in Transition*, ed. Kathleen Barker and Kathleen Christensen (Ithaca, N.Y.: ILR Press, 1998), 197–201. On likening journalistic to police labor, see Christopher P. Wilson, "True and True(r) Crime: Cop Shops and Crime Scenes in the 1980s," *American Literary History* 4 (Winter 1997): 718–743.

50. Bromell, *By the Sweat of the Brow*, 176.

51. George Orwell, "Marrakech," in *A Collection of Essays by George Orwell* (1946; reprint, New York: Harcourt, Brace, 1953), 183.

52. Lise Vogel, "Hearts to Feel and Tongues to Speak: New England Mill Women in the Early Nineteenth Century," in *Class, Sex, and the Woman Worker*, ed. Milton Cantor and Bruce Laurie (Westport, Conn.: Greenwood Press, 1977), 72.

53. See Montgomery, "To Study the People," 504–505, and Halker, *For Democracy, Workers, and God*, 10–11, for brief summaries of the debate on whether there is an American working-class culture. For a representative defense of work culture, see Patricia A. Cooper, *Once a Cigar Maker: Men, Women, and Work Culture in American Cigar Factories, 1900–1919* (Urbana: University of Illinois Press, 1987). See also Louise Lamphere, "Bringing the Family to Work: Women's Culture on the Shop Floor," *Feminist Studies* 11 (Fall 1985): 519–540.

54. On class and gender formation and workingwomen's rebellions (and failures to rebel) against traditional economic and sexual hierarchies, see writings by the dean of the women's labor historians, Alice Kessler-Harris, especially her *Out to Work: A History of Wage-Earning Women in the United States* (New York: Oxford University Press, 1982). See also Christine Stansell, *City of Women: Sex and Class in New York, 1789–1860* (New York: Alfred A. Knopf, 1986); Ardis Cameron, *Radicals of the Worst Sort: Laboring Women in Lawrence, Massachusetts, 1860–1912* (Urbana: University of Illinois Press, 1993); and essays by various hands in *A Needle, a Bobbin, a Strike: Women Needleworkers in America*, ed. Joan M. Jensen and Sue Davidson (Philadelphia: Temple University Press, 1984).

Recently some scholars, such as Paula Rabinowitz, have resurrected the 1930s Communist Party debate on the productive nature of housework and widened traditional definitions of work to include the female home-front and child-rearing experience, whether urban or rural, white or black. Female proletarian authors writing on the homesite put "sexuality and maternity into working-class narrative" (Rabinowitz, *Labor and Desire*, 182), but such authors did not equate these activities with waged work. Although I address Olsen, Le Sueur, and their colleagues on the exploitation of working-class wives, my concern is with domestic womanhood's breadwinning counterpart, the female wage earner.

55. An excellent summary of the schism between the two versions of labor history, the Commons (or Wisconsin) School, which focused on the struggle to organize unions and engage in collective bargaining and saw workers as economic pragmatists, and the Gutman School, which focused on the community and on working-class culture, is in John Schacht, "Labor History in the Academy: A Layman's Guide to a Century of Scholarship," *Labor's Heritage* 5 (Winter 1994): 4–21. Schacht further distinguishes between the Gutman school approach and David Montgomery's. While both see labor history in class terms that are neither color-blind nor accent-mute, the latter studies shop-floor control. See David Montgomery, *The Fall of the House of Labor: The Workplace, the State, and American Labor Activism, 1865–1925* (Cambridge: Cambridge University Press, 1987). For a closely reasoned critique of Gutman's strengths and limitations as a historian of working-classness, a summary of his New Left disciples, and an often ungenerous rebuke of oppositionalist interpretations of workers, see Nick Salvatore, "Herbert Gutman's Narrative of the American Working Class: A Reevaluation," *International Journal of Politics, Culture, and Society* 12, no. 1 (1998): 43–80, esp. 72–79. For other developments among the new labor historians, see Schacht, "Labor History in the Academy."

56. See Sean Wilentz, *Chants Democratic: New York City and the Rise of the American Working Class, 1788–1850* (New York: Oxford University Press, 1984); Bruce Laurie, *Artisans into Workers: Labor in Nineteenth-Century America* (New York: Noonday/Farrar, Straus and Giroux, 1989), chaps. 1 and 2; and Ronald L. Lewis, *Iron and Slaves: Industrial Slavery in Maryland and Virginia, 1715–1865* (Westport, Conn.: Greenwood Press, 1979).

57. Groundbreaking studies of such worker contestations include Roy Rosenzweig, *Eight Hours for What We Will: Workers and Leisure in an Industrial City, 1870–1920* (Cambridge: Cambridge University Press, 1983), and Kathy Peiss, *Cheap Amusements: Working Women and Leisure in Turn-of-the-Century New York* (Philadelphia: Temple University Press, 1986). Examples, however, abound.

58. Suggs, "Proletarian Novel," 233.

59. Rideout, *Radical Novel,* 181–182.

60. Melvin P. Levy, "Michael Gold: *Jews without Money*," *New Republic*, 26 March 1930, 161. See also Gold's reply, "A Proletarian Novel," *New Republic*, 4 June 1930, 74.

61. See, for instance, Carol Snee, "'Working-Class Literature' or Proletarian Writing?" in *Culture and Crisis in Britain in the Thirties*, ed. Jon Clark et al. (London: Lawrence, 1979), 167–168.

62. Qtd. in Rideout, *Radical Novel*, 167; Snee, "'Working-Class Literature?'" 167–168.

63. Coles, "Democratizing Literature," 668.

64. On the leftist literary tradition, see Wald, "Culture and Commitment," 281–306. Such was certainly the consensus of the participants at the most recent Youngstown Conference on Working Class Studies, 9–12 June 1999, Youngstown State University, Youngstown, Ohio; see *Proceedings of the Fourth Biennial Conference: Class, Identity, and Nation*, ed. Clyde Moneyhun (Youngstown, Ohio: Center for Working-Class Studies, 1999).

65. Remarks Janet Zandy, "a collectivist rather than individualistic sensibility is a key difference between bourgeois art and working-class art"; "Introduction," in *Calling Home*, 12.

66. Schacht, "Labor History," 18.

67. Cameron, *Radicals*, 4.

68. Ibid.

69. Alan Trachtenberg, Foreword, in Guimond, *American Photography and the American Dream*, viii. Trachtenberg continues: "Its terminology and imagery have been employed to . . . blame the poor and disadvantaged as responsible for themselves or to side with the losers against the rich, the comfortable, the smug, and the institutions they control" (viii).

70. Denning, *Cultural Front*, 244.

71. Zandy, "Introduction," in *Calling Home*, 12.

Chapter 1. Workers in the Wings

1. A railroad, outwork, and milltown technology of sorts existed in the 1820s and 1830s. Widespread awareness of mechanization, however, is rightly located in the 1840s, as Leo Marx does in *The Machine and the Garden: Technology and the Pastoral Ideal in America* (New York: Oxford University Press, 1964). Although the factory did not dominate manufacturing before the Civil War, Lowell in the 1840s inaugurated the factory system, a mass industrial workforce, and a new industrial morality. See, for example, Gary Kulik et al., "Introduction," in *The New England Mill Village*, ed. Gary Kulik et al. (Cambridge: MIT Press, 1982), xxii–xxv. The 1840s, not coincidentally, was the first decade of the industrial problem novel. Contrast the novels discussed herein and Sarah Bagley's *The Factory Girl* (Boston: Monroe, 1814), a New England imitation of Henry Fielding's *Amelia* with a painted-on industrial venue. For similar pre-1840s urban underclass heroines (but few heroes), see Janis P. Stout, *Sodoms in Eden: The City in American Fiction before 1860* (Westport, Conn.: Greenwood Press, 1979), 24–25. The labor historian David Montgomery not only finds wage labor the "productive normative relation" but also argues against viewing the previous decade as preindustrial, observing that large-scale outwork prefigured the advent of the textile factory. See David Montgomery, "To Study the People: The American Working Class," *Labor History* 21 (Fall 1980): 489.

2. Daniel T. Rodgers is eloquent on the "strain between the mobility ideal and the reality of widespread wage earning" in *The Work Ethic in Industrial America, 1850–1920* (Chicago: University of Chicago Press, 1978), 37. On the fading dream of self-employment, see Rex Burns, *Success in America: The Yeoman Dream and the Industrial Revolution* (Amherst: University of Massachusetts Press, 1976), chap. 3.

3. On the honorable trades, see Bruce Laurie, *Artisans into Workers: Labor in Nineteenth-Century America* (New York: Noonday/Farrar, Straus and Giroux, 1989), 27.

4. Leslie Fiedler, "Introduction," in George Lippard, *The Quaker City; or, The Monks of Monk Hall* (1844; reprint, New York: Odyssey Press, 1970), xii; hereafter cited in text. Class formation in antebellum America continues to generate much controversy. Paul Buhle joins the many labor historians who see no true working class until after the Civil War. His *Marxism in the United States: Remapping the History of the American Left* (London: Verso, 1987) begins with 1860. But Sean Wilentz, *Chants Democratic: New York City and the Rise of the Working Class, 1788–1850* (New York: Oxford University Press, 1984), adds clarity to the debate. While no "single entity" emerged, "a new order of human relations did emerge . . . defined chiefly . . . by the subordination of wage labor to capital" and causing people to act in new "class" ways (18).

5. Laurie, *Artisans into Workers*, 63. On threats to the free labor ideal, and antebellum melding of freeborn toil and the Protestant ethic, see Rodgers, *The Work Ethic*, chap. 1, and 32–33.

6. "He that hath a Trade hath an Estate," explains Benjamin Franklin, *Poor Richard's Almanack* [1756], in *The Autobiography of Benjamin Franklin* (New York: Modern Library, 1944), 218; Laurie, *Artisans into Workers*, 50.

7. On a working-class and, especially, a mechanics' institute self-education that included novel reading, see Ronald Zboray, *A Fictive People: Antebellum Economic Development and the American Reading Public* (New York: Oxford University Press, 1993), 129–132.

8. See Norman Ware's chapter on the degradation of the worker in his excellent study *The Industrial Worker, 1840–1860* (1924; reprint, Gloucester, Mass.: Peter Smith, 1959), 26–70. The term "mechanic" became more diffused as the century progressed. For a succinct discussion of what it meant in the 1840s and 1850s, see Nicholas K. Bromell, *By the Sweat of the Brow: Literature and Labor in Antebellum America* (Chicago: University of Chicago Press, 1993), 257n. In the early 1800s it referred to skilled manual workers, usually owning the tools of their trades. By the late antebellum decades it meant any skilled worker, although in genteel quarters the term retained its association with the old craft-based trades as late as the 1880s and 1890s. See the reference to an "industrious mechanic," a skilled iron moulder, in Charles Loring Brace, *The Dangerous Classes of New York* (New York: Wynkoop and Hallenbeck, 1880), 166. As the term became diffused, the adjective "honest" often preceded it, as if to combat the prejudice against manual laborers. To this day, however, in trades such as construction, the highest praise a skilled worker can receive is to be called a "good mechanic." See Richard Schneirov, *Pride and Solidarity: A History of the Plumbers and Pipefitters of Columbus, Ohio, 1889–1989* (Ithaca, N.Y.: ILR Press, 1993), 5.

9. David R. Roediger, *Our Own Time: A History of American Labor and the Working Day* (London: Verso, 1989), chap. 4. On both the scattered triumphs of the Ten-Hour Movement and the widespread ineffectiveness of early trade unions, see Richard O. Boyer and Herbert M. Morais, *Labor's Untold Story*, 3d ed. (Pittsburgh: United Electrical Workers, 1988), 16–17; and Thomas R. Brooks, *Toil and Trouble: A History of American Labor* (New York: Delta Books, 1964), chap. 3. Brooks even terms the 1840s the "era of lost causes" (32). See also Ware, *The Industrial Worker*, passim. On scattered Irish dockers' protests, see Peter Way, *Common Labour: Workers and the Digging of the North American Canals, 1780–1860* (New York: Cambridge University Press, 1993).

10. Laurie, *Artisans into Workers*, 46–63; T. D. Seymour Bassett, "The Secular Utopian Socialists," in *Socialism and American Life*, vol. 1, ed. Donald Drew Egbert and Stow Persons (Princeton, N.J.: Princeton University Press, 1952), 155–209; David Sprague Herreshoff, *American Disciples of Marx from the Age of Jackson to the Progressive Era* (Detroit: Wayne State University Press, 1967), chap. 1. "It would be foolish," notes Jon-Christian Suggs, "to argue that any of these [communal] attempts or any of the literary expressions of the same impetus, was Marxian"; see Suggs, "The Proletarian Novel," in *Dictionary of Literary Biography*, vol. 9, pt. 3, ed. James J. Martine (Detroit: Gale Research, 1981), 232. Leslie Fiedler, *Love and Death in the American Novel*, rev. ed. (New York: Laurel/Dell, 1966), reaches a similar conclusion: "It was a long time . . . before socialism penetrated deep enough into the American mind to make a modern version of class struggle possible" (73).

11. Jon-Christian Suggs, Preface, in *American Proletarian Culture: The Twenties and the Thirties*, ed. Jon-Christian Suggs (Detroit: Gale Research, 1993), suggests that Douai's never-translated *Fata Morgana* (1859) was revolution-minded (5). Far more common was the completely diluted socialism of the German-language versions of the antiurban novel. One such critique of American capital, translated soon after its

1851 German-language publication, was Henry Boernstein, *Mysteries and Miseries of St. Louis*. Translated by Friedrich Munch in 1852, it has been published in a modernized edition, edited by Steven Rowman and Elizabeth Sims (Chicago: Charles H. Kerr, 1990). See also Michael Denning, *Mechanic Accents: Dime Novels and Working-Class Culture in America* (London: Verso, 1986), 85–86.

12. Ralph Waldo Emerson, "The American Scholar," in *Selections from Ralph Waldo Emerson: An Organic Anthology*, ed. Stephen Whicher (Boston: Houghton Mifflin, 1960), 78. See, too, despite his animadversions on the factory system, Thoreau's dismissive attitude in *Walden* toward Irish laborers like Michael Collins. He elevates the woodcutter Therien, but it could be argued that a forest worker did not represent the modern industrial workforce so much as the "simple and independent mind [who] does not toil at the bidding of any prince." Henry David Thoreau, *Walden and Resistance to Civil Government* [1854], 2d ed., ed. William Rossi (New York: W. W. Norton, 1966), 39.

13. Such radicals spun nonconfrontational agrarian and property reform plans, again with reference to the skilled white crafts.

14. On western emigration, see Laurie, *Artisans into Workers*, 66; George Loring Brace applies period thinking in *The Best Method of Disposing of Paupers and Vagrant Children* (New York: Wynkoop and Hallenbeck, 1859).

15. Smith, Arthur, and Lippard, as well as E.Z.C. Judson and William Wells Brown, were all dime or cheap story novelists, known to both bourgeois and working-class readers. But these three authors' respective fidelity to Christian, temperance, and urban exposé themes are, to my mind, far more germane. On the dime novelist's mass appeal, see Denning, *Mechanic Accents*, pt. 1. Biographical information on Smith and Arthur delineating their literary foci appear in, respectively, Ann Douglas, *The Feminization of American Culture* (New York: Alfred A. Knopf, 1977), 101, 128; and C. Hugh Holman, "Introduction," in T. S. Arthur, *Ten Nights in a Bar-Room* (New York: Odyssey Press, 1966), passim. From a wealth of Lippard assessments, see, for instance, David S. Reynolds, *George Lippard* (Boston: G. K. Hall, 1982), 56–63.

16. Fay M. Blake, *The Strike in the American Novel* (Metuchen, N.J.: Scarecrow Press, 1972), finds no 1840s novel that addresses the strike. The most authoritative source on the urban labor novel of the day, Adrienne Siegel's *The Image of the American City in Popular Literature, 1820–1870* (Port Washington, N.Y.: Kennikat Press, 1981), locates (but does not give titles of) three novels that include glancing references to such labor protest (77). Yet her claim that sixty-five novels dealt extensively with urban labor seems exaggerated. See, for example, one of her representative examples, Augustine Duzanne, *The Tenant-House* (New York: Robert M. De Witt, 1857), with its sparse allusions to seamstresses and others "who toiled obsessively" (11).

17. Howard B. Rock, *Artisans of the New Republic: The Tradesmen of New York City in the Age of Jefferson* (New York: New York University Press, 1979), 13; Bruce C. Levine, "In the Heat of Two Revolutions: The Forging of German-American Radicalism," in *"Struggle a Hard Battle": Essays on Working-Class Immigrants*, ed. Dirk Hoerder (DeKalb: Northern Illinois University Press, 1986), 19–45; Roediger, *Our Own Time*, chap. 4.

18. Robert Ernst, *Immigrant Life in New York City, 1825–1863* (New York: King's Crown/Columbia University Press, 1949), 69–72.

19. Ibid., 69.

20. Even as skilled northern freedmen and except as hated strikebreakers, blacks were obviously denied white labor opportunities. See Leon F. Litwack, *North of Slav-*

ery: *The Negro in the Free States, 1790–1860* (Chicago: University of Chicago Press, 1961), 153–179. On black scabs, see Ernst, *Immigrant Life*, 105.

21. Southern racist antebellum slave tales and proslavery orations by those like Zebulon Baird Vance and Richard Malcolm Johnson plied images of contented, comically devoted darkies. See that literature's admirer Carl Holliday, *A History of Southern Literature* (1906; reprint, Port Washington, N.Y.: Kennikat Press, 1969), 251. There is no space here to enter the debate on Stowe's racist slave stereotypes. For a brief discussion of the issue, see John William Ward, "Afterword," in Harriet Beecher Stowe, *Uncle Tom's Cabin* [1852] (New York: Signet, 1966), 492–493. Among those attacking the novel are James Baldwin, "Everybody's Protest Novel," *Notes of a Native Son* [1949] (Boston: Beacon Press, 1967), 16; defending, Jane Tompkins, *Sensational Designs: The Cultural Work of American Fiction, 1790–1860* (New York: Oxford University Press, 1985), 123–134. On differences between white- and black-authored slave narratives, the critical tendency seems to be to study the genre itself or narratives by black authors. Compare the approach, for example, of Robert S. Levine, "Fiction and Reform I," in *The Columbia History of the American Novel*, ed. Emory Elliott et al. (New York: Columbia University Press, 1991), 140–142, and that in the essays by various hands in *Slavery and the Literary Imagination*, ed. Deborah E. McDowell and Arnold Rampersad (Baltimore: Johns Hopkins University Press, 1989).

22. Nellie McKay, "Autobiography and the Early Novel," in Elliott et al., *Columbia History*, 45.

23. Wilentz, *Chants Democratic*, 263.

24. Writes Bruce Laurie, *The Working People of Philadelphia* (Philadelphia: Temple University Press, 1980): "The same workers who endorsed strikes pressed for cooperation and even land reform" (193). On the (nonsocialist) ideological amalgam that was on the agenda of the Workingmen's Party and informed the *Voice of Industry*, see Lewis S. Feuer, "The North American Origin of Marx's Socialism," *Western Political Quarterly* 16 (March 1963): 53–56.

25. *Voice of Industry*, Paper of the New England Workingmen's Association, 29 May 1845, 2.

26. Ibid., 12 June 1845, 12.

27. Ibid., 2.

28. Qtd. in Burns, *Success in America*, 117.

29. For contrasting discussions on what "escape" literature meant to working-class readers, see Zboray, *A Fictive People*, 128–132, and Denning, *Mechanic Accents*, pt. 1. The former contends, as I will, that the form reinforced the status quo; the latter argues that by empowering workerist themes, the form subtly challenged bourgeois hegemony.

30. Frederick Douglass, *The Heroic Slave* [1853], in *Three Classic African-American Novels*, ed. William L. Andrews (New York: Mentor Books, 1990), 33; hereafter cited in text.

31. Women's function as minor characters in the male urban Gothic form, and quasi-heroic labor helpmeets in the postbellum Knights of Labor novel is the subject of chapter 3, which examines gendered (and sexualized) literary and cultural reactions to female industrial work.

32. Marcus Klein, *Easterns, Westerns, and Private Eyes: American Matters, 1870–1900* (Madison: University of Wisconsin Press, 1994), 3.

33. On the attempts to form national labor organizations that espoused closed shops, minimum wage, and the like, see Brooks, *Toil and Trouble*, 33–36. The debate on whether American workers ever achieved working-class consciousness continues

to this day and is addressed in later chapters; see, for instance, Herreshoff, *American Disciples of Marx*, 15. On the antebellum working class, even if, as Wilentz, *Chants Democratic*, contends, there was a "glimmer . . . of a language of class" (59), there is little evidence of militant or even collective resistance to the demands of a rising industrialism, although there was clearly a tension between it and preindustrial modes of work and thought. David Brody, *In Labor's Cause: Main Themes on the History of the American Worker* (New York: Oxford University Press, 1993), has identified one true "shift in industrial consciousness" (33) by the Civil War: the demand for payment in units of time rather than by the day.

34. *Who Built America?*, vol. 1, Bruce Levine et al. (New York: Pantheon Books, 1989), 240.

35. Elliot J. Gorn, " 'Goodbye Boys, I Die a True American': Homicide, Nativism, and Working-Class Culture in Antebellum New York City," *Journal of American History* 74 (September 1987): 408. More key, if somewhat inconsistent, information on the Mose figure appears in Stuart M. Blumin, "George G. Foster and the Emerging Metropolis," in George G. Foster, *New York by Gaslight and Other Urban Sketches*, ed. Stuart M. Blumin (Berkeley: University of California Press, 1990), 55–60, hereafter cited in text; Wilentz, *Chants Democratic*, 299–301; and Eric Lott, *Love and Theft: Blackface Minstrelsy and the American Working Class* (New York: Oxford University Press, 1993), 81–84. Mose was the first in a line of alienated city toughs that runs through his Irish successors, Stephen Crane's Jimmie and James T. Farrell's Studs Lonigan.

36. Frank Rahill, *The World of Melodrama* (University Park, Pa.: Pennsylvania State University Press, 1967), 254; George Odell, *Annals of the New York Stage* (New York: Columbia University Press, 1949), 634. Mose was even portrayed by a son of the Bowery himself, the actor Frank Chanfrau.

37. Writes Stuart Blumin, he "represented the young, single, native-born white workers of the city; or, rather, a particular sub-community of such workers who were evolving distinctively high-spirited styles of life and dress." Blumin, "George G. Foster," 55.

38. Eugene Sue, *The Wandering Jew* (1842); G. M. Reynolds, *The Mysteries of London* (1845–1848). Lest my allusion to these authors and the urban Gothic flatten a complicated melodramatic form, see the provocative discussion of the subgenre's social commentary, and of Sue, Reynolds, and Lippard as ambiguously Marxian authors, in Denning, *Mechanic Accents*, chap. 6.

39. To Wilentz (*Chants Democratic*, 9), he is a butcher; in Arthur Hobson Quinn, *A History of the American Drama* (New York: Harper and Brothers, 1923), a printer at the *New York Sun* (305); a stonecutter or carpenter to Alexander Saxton, "Blackface Minstrelsy and Jacksonian Ideology," *American Quarterly* 27 (March 1975): 9; to David R. Roediger, *The Wages of Whiteness: Race and the Making of the American Working Class* (London: Verso, 1991), either unemployed or an apprentice artisan (99).

40. E.Z.C. Judson, *The Mysteries and Miseries of New York: A Story of Real Life*, pt. 2 (New York: Berford and Co., 1848), 31–34.

41. George G. Foster, *New York in Slices* (New York: William H. Graham, 1849), 44; hereafter cited in text.

42. Janet Zandy, "Introduction," in *Liberating Memory: Our Work and Our Working-Class Consciousness*, ed. Janet Zandy (New Brunswick, N.J.: Rutgers University Press, 1995), 2. She also observes, "[Working people] are perceived as too loud, too direct, too 'uneducated' "—Mose before his whitewash by Foster. Critics continue to reread Foster's hostility as an inattention to detail, and his ambiguity as a response to the

evolving language of social differentiation in the 1840s. See Stuart M. Blumin, "Explaining the New Metropolis: Perception, Depiction, and Analysis in Mid-Nineteenth-Century New York City," *Journal of Urban History* 11 (November 1984): 23. Blumin also defends Foster's vacillation between a proletarian Mose and a middle-class Mose as part of the period's lack of clarity about social differences.

43. David Reynolds, in his reading of Foster, has observed that Mose remains the representative workingman of the antebellum era. But if so, why must Mose be, in Reynolds's own Fosterlike term, "wicked but lovable"? David S. Reynolds, *Beneath the American Renaissance: The Subversive Imagination in the Age of Emerson and Melville* (New York: Alfred A. Knopf, 1988), 285, 464.

44. See, in this regard, Michael Feldberg, *The Philadelphia Riots of 1844: A Study of Ethnic Conflict* (Westport, Conn.: Greenwood Press, 1975), esp. chap. 3.

45. Levine et al., *Who Built America?*, vol. 1, 245.

46. Mechanization was the process whereby employers changed costly skilled labor into smaller, less expensive tasks, enabling them to replace skilled journeymen with female and child labor.

47. B. Levine, "In the Heat of Two Revolutions," 25; Siegel, *Image of the American City*, 85. See Cornelius Mathews's *Big Abel and the Little Manhattan* (1845; reprint, New York: Garrett Press, 1970): "Idle jobless men are no longer men" (56–57).

48. Cornelius Mathews, *The Career of Puffer Hopkins* (1842; reprint, New York: Garrett Press, 1970), 95; hereafter cited in text. Mathews himself may have resembled Fob's employer more than he knew.

49. It should be added that at a time when the majority of urban skilled tailors, German-born at that, were increasingly receptive to workingmen's congresses, Fob anticipates the pinched attic and cellar workers found on visits by Jacob Riis, William Dean Howells, and the journalistic tenement novelists of the 1890s. See B. Levine, "In the Heat of Two Revolutions," 27.

50. Solon Robinson, *Hot Corn* (New York: De Witt and Davenport, 1854); and John Denison Vose, *Seven Nights in Gotham* (New York: Bunnel and Price, 1852). See also Siegel, *Image of the American City*, 43–44.

51. See Herbert Gutman's title essay in *Work, Culture, and Society in Industrializing America: Essays in American Working-Class History* (New York: Vintage Books, 1977), 19–21. Another good discussion of workplace drinking and attempts to control it is in Paul Faler, "Cultural Aspects of the Industrial Revolution: Lynn, Massachusetts, Shoemakers and Industrial Morality, 1826–1860," *Labor History* 15 (Summer 1974): 379–384.

52. Evans, in fact, is stalking the ideal of being "well-bred," although Whitman resists making a connection between drinking and snobbery, much as he did any link between drinking and nonurban proletarianism. Walt Whitman, *Franklin Evans; or, the Inebriate* [1842], ed. Jean Downey (New Haven, Conn.: College and University Press, 1967), 67.

53. Indeed, the novel's original subtitle, *The Merchant's Clerk*, suggests that the greater tragedy is not drinking among the lower orders. It is among the middling ones, which is curious, given the period's stereotypical associations of Irish hod carriers and drunkenness. Downey, "Notes on the Text," in Whitman, *Franklin Evans*, n.p.

54. Dion Boucicault's *The Poor of New York* is, however, somewhat misnamed. The play concerns an affluent family swindled, impoverished, and restored to wealth, reflecting the typical period distaste for proletarian characters.

55. Bromell, *By the Sweat of the Brow*, 69.

56. Montgomery, "To Study the People," 504.

57. Lippard was an early representative of the journey to the working-class heart of darkness, including, however briefly, descents into substandard housing, which would be a staple of fiction about the worker and lives on in autobiographies of 1930s leftists and in sections of modern memoirs of public housing projects.

58. Qtd. in Roger Butterfield, "George Lippard and His Secret Brotherhood," *Pennsylvania Magazine of History and Biography* 74 (July 1955): 297.

59. Butterfield, "George Lippard," 286. Lippard's rhetoric of oppression and uprising was weakened by a fanciful plan to eradicate all factories, and a reluctance to spell out the steps between granting free land to urban workers and the revolutionary reconstruction of capitalist economic relations.

60. George Lippard, "Social Divisions," in David S. Reynolds, *George Lippard: An Anthology* (New York: Peter Lang, 1986), 280–281.

61. The terms, reiterated in the book, form the subtitle of Lippard's novel *New York: Its Upper Ten and Lower Million* (1853; reprint, Upper Saddle River, N.J.: Gregg Press, 1970); hereafted cited in text.

62. Reynolds, *George Lippard*, 57. George Lippard, *The Quaker City; or, The Monks of Monk Hall* [1844], intro. Leslie Fiedler (New York: Odyssey Press, 1970); hereafter cited in text.

63. Ibid., 58.

64. The "walking dead" theme is pervasive, for instance, in *Working Classics: Poems on Industrial Life*, ed. Peter Oresick and Nicholas Coles (Urbana: University of Illinois Press, 1990), particularly Lorna Dee Cervantes's "Cannery Town in August" (37). The issue is addressed in detail in chapter 12 below.

65. Lippard's prose writings supported trade unions and cooperative stores for workers, but he was completely opposed to strikes or, it would seem, any nonrevolutionary labor-confrontational activity. See Butterfield, "George Lippard," 297–299. It is ironic in this regard that he does see a future in which labor might have to "go to War . . . with the Rifle, Sword and Knife!" (qtd. in Fiedler, "Introduction," in Lippard, *Quaker City*, viii).

66. Denning, *Mechanic Accents*, 111; Elizabeth Oakes Smith, *The Newsboy* (New York: J. C. Derby, 1854), 480, hereafter cited in text; Sylvester Judd, *Richard Edney; or, The Governor's Family* (Boston: Phillips, Sampson, and Co., 1850), 12, hereafter cited in text.

67. Denning sees Dermoyne's missed inheritance as an allegory of the country's failure to give the artisan republican his due (*Mechanic Accents*, 111).

68. Fiedler, *Love and Death in the American Novel*, 238. George G. Foster's *Celio; or, New York above Ground and Under-Ground* (New York: Dewitt and Davenport, 1850), 143, tacks on a worker exodus to a pastoral arcadia, but it is even less credible than Lippard's Dermoyne-led western trek. For the Arthur Dermoynes to be enfranchised, they can only bow out of the economic struggle—which the money men are so clearly winning—almost as if they are too refined to soil themselves by such contact.

69. Fiedler, *Love and Death in the American Novel*, 237.

70. Denning, *Mechanic Accents*, 28.

71. Eric H. Monkkonen, "Nineteenth-Century Institutions: Dealing with the Urban 'Underclass,'" in *The "Underclass" Debate: Views from History*, ed. Michael B. Katz (Princeton, N.J.: Princeton University Press, 1993), 357.

72. The Newsboy's Lodging House, founded that year, had space for fifty. See Charles Loring Brace, *Short Sermons to Newsboys: With a History of the Formation of the Newsboy's Lodging House* (New York: Charles Scribner and Co., 1866), 215. For another typical period description of the lumpen-proletarian-to-capitalist trajectory, see John Morrow's seminovelistic *A Voice from the Newsboys* (n.p., 1860).

73. Lisa N. Peters, "Images of the Homeless in American Art, 1860–1910," in *On Being Homeless: Historical Perspectives*, ed. Rick Beard (New York: Museum of the City of New York, 1987), 43.

74. Brace, *Short Sermons to Newsboys*, 217, 28, 215.

75. Qtd. in Michael B. Katz, "The Urban 'Underclass' as a Metaphor of Social Transformation," in Katz, *The "Underclass" Debate*, 9.

76. Others more explicitly linked the newsboy to antisocial behavior, labeling him a thief, depraved, and a child-father of the deviant, discontented subproletarian. See William F. Howe and Abraham Hummel, *In Danger! or, Life in New York* (1872; reprint, New York: J. S. Ogilvie, 1888), 16–25.

77. Although it focuses on middle-class children, Anne Tropp Trensky's "The Saintly Child in Nineteenth-Century American Fiction," *Prospects* 1 (1975): 389–413, delineates the ideology that her title names.

78. Douglas, *The Feminization of American Culture*, chap. 3.

79. Stout, *Sodoms in Eden*, 32.

80. On the increasingly outmoded mechanic-turned-merchant formula in period fiction, see Siegel, *Image of the American City*, 84.

81. Ibid., 84, 85.

82. Judd seems to move toward these truths in a series of brief scenes in which workers use shop talk and complain about increased workloads. See Bromell, *By the Sweat of the Brow*, 56.

83. Ian Tyrell, *Sobering Up: From Temperance to Prohibition in Antebellum America* (Westport, Conn.: Greenwood Press, 1979), 167; Laurie, *Artisans into Workers*, 52, 56.

84. Montgomery, "To Study the People," 486; Gutman, *Work, Culture, and Society*, 19–21.

85. On the New England Great Awakenings, see Faler, "Cultural Aspects of the Industrial Revolution," 370.

86. Laurie, *Working People of Philadelphia*, 52.

87. Ibid.

88. Judd provides the Christianized answer to the secular "nature's nobleman," the old labor radicals' and mechanics' institutes' emphasis on education and personal advancement. [An anonymous review of Herman Melville's *Redburn* (1849)], *New York Sunday Times*, 18 November 1849, n.p. Melville himself both disdained and craved a popular readership. Contrast his comments on "a beggarly *Redburn*!" with his anxious question to his publisher on copies sold. (At 4,300, *Redburn* had outsold *Moby-Dick* by 1,500 as of December 1853.) See, respectively, the letters to Evert A. Duyckinck, 14 December 1849, and to Harper Brothers, 6 December 1853, in *The Letters of Herman Melville*, ed. Merrell R. David and William H. Gilman (New Haven, Conn.: Yale University Press, 1960), 95, 165.

89. Richard Henry Dana, Jr., *Two Years before the Mast* [1840] (New York: Penguin Books, 1986). If the book influenced Melville, Dana, another sometime sailor sans labor-class origins, admired *Redburn* as well. On Melville's autobiographical links to the *Redburn* voyage, see Tyrus Hillway, *Herman Melville* (New York: Twayne, 1963), 72–73.

90. Dana recalled ruefully, "Jack Tar is a slave aboard ship" (*Two Years before the Mast*, 120). Herman Melville, *Redburn, His First Voyage* [1849], in *Melville: Redburn, White-Jacket, and Moby-Dick* (New York: Library of America, 1983), 263, 76; hereafter cited in text.

91. See Briton Cooper Busch, *"Whaling Will Never Do for Me": The American Whaleman in the Nineteenth Century* (Lexington: University Press of Kentucky, 1994), 7. Busch's analysis extends to nonwhaling ships like Redburn's. See also Bruce

Nelson, *Workers on the Waterfront: Seamen, Longshoremen, and Unionism in the 1930s* (Urbana: University of Illinois Press, 1990), 25.

92. *White-Jacket's* antiflogging message seems separated from those flogged. The class divisions between shipboard officers and men, "peers and underlings" (the title of chapter 6), are more urgently rendered.

93. For a brief, astute discussion of Steelkilt's superiority to the *Town Ho* crew he unsuccessfully attempts to radicalize, see David Sprague Herreshoff, *Labor into Art: The Theme of Work in Nineteenth-Century American Literature* (Detroit: Wayne State University Press, 1991), 34. On the glancing work references in *Moby-Dick*, see Bromell, *By the Sweat of the Brow*, 88.

94. If he invokes the victim trope, he also plays with a version of Mose in the figure of Jackson, who combines the Bowery b'hoy (*Redburn*, 66) with the sinister qualities of a corrupt Lippard servitor. Also, the novel's Liverpool sections borrow from the "mysteries and miseries" form. Redburn takes on a guidebook persona when touring the "cellars, sinks, and hovels" (205) of British poverty. Bromell, *By the Sweat of the Brow*, 67. Demonizing Jackson does not, as one critic has suggested, make him a victim of the social order. If anything, it shows the underside of the Mose character, the angry prole whom Foster and his contemporaries so feared.

95. They even praised Melville's ability to show the shipboard version of the urban lower depths. [Anonymous review of *Redburn*], *New York Literary American*, 24 November 1849, 419.

96. Larzer Ziff, *Literary Democracy: The Declaration of Cultural Independence in America* (New York: Penguin Books, 1982), 98.

97. Laurie, *Artisans into Workers*, 27. A common racist phrase of the day, Roediger finds it in an 1844 issue of the craft-connected periodical *The Mechanic* (See *Wages of Whiteness*, 44).

98. On Melville's contradictory racial attitudes, see Eric J. Sundquist, *To Wake the Nations: Race in the Making of American Literature* (Cambridge: Harvard University Press, 1993), 152–154. For a provocative discussion of *Moby-Dick's* skilled black workers, see Herreshoff, *Labor into Art*, 40–42.

99. Busch, *"Whaling Will Never Do for Me,"* 33; Philip S. Foner and Ronald L. Lewis, "Introduction," in Foner and Lewis, *Black Workers: A Documentary History from Colonial Times to the Present* (Philadelphia: Temple University Press, 1989), 4.

100. See Herreshoff's comment on "preindustrial" psychology (*Labor into Art*, 43); Busch, *"Whaling Will Never Do for Me,"* 32.

101. That image did not even embrace the known, if seldom acknowledged, truths of African American labor. The majority of the half a million freed blacks were relegated to menial and unskilled tasks in northern cities. Their four million enslaved brothers and sisters, an abused, unpaid rural-industrial labor pool, fared even worse. See John Hope Franklin and Alfred A. Moss, Jr., *From Slavery to Freedom: A History of African Americans*, 7th ed. (New York: Alfred A. Knopf, 1994), 123; Charles H. Wesley, *Negro Labor in the United States, 1850–1925* (New York: Russell and Russell, 1927), 43–68.

102. Saxton, "Blackface Minstrelsy and Jacksonian Ideology," 8–9; Roediger, *Wages of Whiteness*, 100. For an alternative interpretation, see Lott, *Love and Theft*, 83–85.

103. Lott, *Love and Theft*, 149; Roediger, *Wages of Whiteness*, 96–110.

104. See essays by various hands in *The Other Slaves: Slave Mechanics, Artisans, and Craftsmen*, ed. James E. Newton and Ronald L. Lewis (Boston: G. K. Hall, 1978); Franklin and Moss, *From Slavery to Freedom*, 132.

105. Qtd. in Foner and Lewis, "Introduction," in *Black Workers*, 2. From the white artisan opposed to teaching trades to blacks to the poor unskilled southern white, many had a vested interest in keeping black Mose just that. See Franklin and Moss, *From Slavery to Freedom*, 132.

106. Frederick Douglass, "A Plan for an Industrial College . . ." [1853], in Foner and Lewis, *Black Workers*, 120; Foner and Lewis, "Introduction," in *Black Workers*, 3.

107. Litwack, *North of Slavery*, 159–160; Wilentz, *Chants Democratic*, 236. No blacks were admitted to antebellum labor unions.

108. Frederick Douglass, *The Narrative of the Life of Frederick Douglass: An American Slave* (1845; reprint: New York: Signet, 1968), 57.

109. Roediger, *Wages of Whiteness*, 86. Apart from a cadre of followers of the vacillating George Evans and other utopian socialists, and some emigré Marxists writing in German, even radical thinkers were strangely silent on the slavery issue and seemed to prefer using plantation enslavement as a metaphor for white laboring people's oppression (ibid., 77). The antiabolitionism of native socialist experiments is contrasted with the emigrant socialism of the less visible German abolitionists in Philip S. Foner, *American Socialism and Black Americans from the Age of Jackson to World War II* (Westport, Conn.: Greenwood Press, 1977), chap. 1.

110. Robin Winks, *The Blacks in Canada* (New Haven, Conn.: Yale University Press, 1972), 186–195.

111. William Wells Brown, *The Narrative of William Wells Brown, A Fugitive Slave*, in *From Fugitive Slave to Free Man*, [1848], ed. William L. Andrews (New York: Mentor, 1993), 27. On continuities and discontinuities with real-life slaves' work ethic, see Eugene D. Genovese, *Roll, Jordan, Roll: The World the Slaves Made* (New York: Vintage Books, 1972), 309–324.

112. There were typically two hundred pounds of cotton picked, with an assured whipping if the quota was not met; and farm chores after the field day was over. See Henry Bibb, 339–342, and Solomon Northup, 314–322, in *Puttin' On Ole Massa: The Slave Narratives of Henry Bibb, William Wells Brown, and Solomon Northup*, ed. Gilbert Osofsky (New York: Harper and Row, 1969); hereafter cited in text.

113. William Wells Brown, *Clotel* [1853], in Andrews, *Three Classic African-American Novels*, 119, 140.

114. Bernard Bell, *The Afro-American Novel and Its Tradition* (Amherst: University of Massachusetts Press, 1987), 29.

115. Osofsky, "Introduction," in *Puttin' On Ole Massa*, 29.

116. Frederick Douglass, "Learn Trades or Starve!" [1853], and "A Plan . . . ," in Foner and Lewis, *Black Workers*, 119, 121.

117. Josia Henson, *The Life of Josiah Henson* [1849] (New York: Corinth Books, 1962), 176–210. On the legal, financial, and political difficulties with Henson's settlement in Dawn, Canada, see Winks, *Blacks in Canada*, 196–204.

118. Such settlements fared poorly. On Delany's multilayered emigration thinking, see Floyd J. Miller, *The Search for a Black Nationality: Black Colonization and Emigration, 1787–1863* (Urbana: University of Illinois Press, 1975), 115–133. On the thwarted black communities in Ohio, see Winks, *Blacks in Canada*, 156, 179–182.

119. Charles T. Davis and Henry Louis Gates, Jr., "Introduction," in *The Slave's Narrative*, ed. Charles T. Davis and Henry Louis Gates, Jr. (New York: Oxford University Press, 1985), xvi.

120. Litwack, *North of Slavery*, 176–178; Franklin and Moss, *From Slavery to Freedom*, 147.

121. Foner and Lewis, "Introduction," in *Black Workers*, 2.

122. William L. Andrews, *To Tell a Free Story: The First Century of Afro-American Autobiography, 1760–1865* (Urbana: University of Illinois, 1986), 131.

123. Miller, *Search for a Black Nationality*, 106, 128, 124.

124. On Delany's difficulties with discrimination at Harvard and elsewhere, see Miller, *Search for a Black Nationality*, 122–123.

125. Floyd J. Miller, "A Note on This Edition," in Martin R. Delany, *Blake; or, the Huts of America* (Boston: Beacon Press, 1970), n.p.; hereafter cited in text. The serialized novel was not published in book form in its time.

126. See, in a rare slave memoir yoking mental and manual work, James W. C. Pennington, *The Fugitive Blacksmith* (1850; reprint, Westport, Conn.: Negro Universities Press, 1971): "It cost me two years' hard labour after I fled, to unshackle my mind" (56).

127. Cited in Litwack, *North of Slavery*, 158.

128. Denning, *Mechanic Accents*, 105–112.

129. Bell, *Afro-American Novel*, 29.

Chapter 2. I'm Looking through You

1. The NLU advocated an eight-hour day and, like the WBA and IMU, believed in the walkout. Norman J. Ware, *The Labor Movement in the United States, 1860–1895* (1929; reprint, Gloucester, Mass.: Peter Smith, 1959), chap. 1. By 1873, reports Michael Serrin, there were more industrial workers in the United States than farmers. Michael Serrin, *Homestead: The Glory and Tragedy of a Steel Town* (1992; reprint, New York: Vintage Books, 1993), 33.

2. On militant period strikes, see, for example, James E. Wolfe, "Iron Moulders' Lockout of 1883–1884," in *Labor Conflict in the United States: An Encyclopedia*, ed. Ronald L. Filippelli (New York: Garland, 1990), 263–266. On cooperatives, see George E. McNeill, "Co-operation," in *The Labor Movement: The Problem of Today*, ed. George E. McNeill (Boston: A. M. Bridgman and Co., 1887), 508–531; and Daniel T. Rodgers, *The Work Ethic in Industrial America, 1850–1920* (Chicago: University of Chicago Press, 1978), 40–64. A key exponent of the "new" working-class history who widens the focus beyond the official labor movement without scanting workers' protests is Herbert G. Gutman, "The Worker's Search for Power: Labor in the Gilded Age," in *The Gilded Age: A Reappraisal*, ed. H. Wayne Morgan (Syracuse, N.Y: Syracuse University Press, 1963), 38–68.

3. There was even limited support for all-black locals, if not integrated union membership. On early (1868–1872) gains and difficulties, see the still-timely article by Herman D. Bloch, "Labor and the Negro, 1866–1910," *Journal of Negro History* 50 (1965): 163–184. See also David M. Corbin, *Life, Work, and Rebellion in the Coal Fields: The Southern West Virginia Miners, 1880–1922* (Urbana: University of Illinois Press, 1981), 225; John Hope Franklin and Alfred A. Moss, Jr., *From Slavery to Freedom: A History of African Americans*, 7th ed. (New York: Alfred A. Knopf, 1994), 232–237.

4. On an uncharacteristically effective cross-trade alliance between trade union males and female unionists in the sewing trades, see Carole Turbin, *Working Women of Collar City: Gender, Class, and Community in Troy, 1864–1886* (Urbana: University of Illinois Press, 1992), 162–166. By the postwar 1860s, the Knights of Labor had granted women a form of helpmeet labor equality. Those like the powerful iron moulders' president and National Labor Union advocate William Sylvis advocated the admission of (white) women into the trade union movement. But, comment Boyer and Morais, "most men and most trade unions regarded women

workers . . . as a menace who drove wages down." See chapter 3 below, and Richard O. Boyer and Henry M. Morais, *Labor's Untold Story* (Pittsburgh: United Electrical Workers, 1955), 33n. See also Philip S. Foner, *Women and the American Labor Movement from Colonial Times to the Eve of World War I* (New York: Free Press, 1979), 126–130, 185–212.

5. Richard L. Ehrlich, "Immigrant Strikebreaking Activity: A Sampling of Opinion Expressed in the *National Labor Tribune*, 1878–1885," *Labor History* 15 (Fall 1974): 528–542. Comments Ehrlich, "Throughout the later 1870s and well into the 1880s unskilled jobs were at a premium, and the continued influx of immigrant workmen only served to intensify this problem" (530). By 1865 there were three million immigrants in the United States and four million African Americans.

6. Stuart Creighton Miller, *The Unwelcome Immigrant: The American Image of the Chinese, 1785–1882* (Berkeley: University of California Press, 1969), 175, 195–199, 235n.

7. *Who Built America?: Working People and the Nation's Economy, Politics, Culture, and Society*, vol. 2, ed. Joshua Freeman et al. (New York: Pantheon, 1992), 30; David Montgomery, "William Sylvis and the Search for Working-Class Citizenship," in *Labor Leaders in America*, ed. Melvyn Dubofsky and Warren Van Tine (Urbana: University of Illinois Press, 1987), 3–24.

8. Fixing output quotas themselves, in some cases they secured privileged positions without union rules or accommodation to employers. David Montgomery, "Workers' Control of Machine Production in the Nineteenth Century," *Labor History* 17 (1976): 489, 492.

9. Philip S. Foner, *The Labor Movement in the United States from Colonial Times to the Founding of the American Federation of Labor*, vol. 1 (New York: International Publishers, 1947), 439–450.

10. Ostreicher argues for a "working-class subculture of opposition." Yet he defines the term in a way that suggests cooperating with one another rather than opposing the capitalist way: "an interlocking network of formal institutions and informal practices based on an ethic of social equality." Richard Jules Ostreicher, *Solidarity and Fragmentation: Working People and Class Consciousness in Detroit, 1875–1900* (Urbana: University of Illinois Press, 1986), xv.

11. They also published proceedings and editorialized on prolabor candidates. See, for example, the front-page references to the proceedings of the National Labor Union, *Workingman's Advocate*, 10 October 1868; "The Strike Spreading," *National Labor Tribune* 3 (24 April 1875): 1; "Trade Unionism," *The Toiler*, 29 August 1874, n.p.; and "Co-operation," *Journal of United Labor* 6 (10 January 1886): 1172.

12. The strike spread to fourteen states from coast to coast and involved battles with militia. Solid discussions of the Railway Strike appear in Samuel Yellen, *American Labor Struggles, 1877–1934* (1936; reprint, New York: Pathfinder Press, 1974), chap. 1; and Jeremy Brecher, *Strike!* (Boston: South End Press, 1972), chap. 1.

13. Freeman et al., *Who Built America?*, vol. 2, 558.

14. Rodgers, *Work Ethic in Industrial America*, 46; on Haymarket, see Yellen, *American Labor Struggles*, and Ware, *The Labor Movement in the United States*, 314–316.

15. The Knights espoused a cooperative commonwealth alternative to narrow trade unionism that was dedicated to the eventual emancipation of labor through education, and disseminated vague plans for land reform and the abolition of the wage system. A brief but balanced discussion of the Knights of Labor and their journals is provided by David Brody, "Journal of United Labor [and] Journal of the Knights of Labor," in *The American Radical Press*, vol. 1, ed. Joseph R. Conlin (Westport, Conn.: Greenwood Press, 1974), 25–31.

16. For a representative listing of trade assembly members in the Knights' own journal—including housewives, paper-box makers, machinists, glove makers, and steamfitters—see "Monthly Summary," *Journal of United Labor* 6 (10 January 1886): 1172.

17. Fay M. Blake, *The Strike in the American Novel* (Metuchen, N. J.: Scarecrow Press, 1972), 18.

18. Unlike the Knights, the AFL pragmatically excluded the unskilled to consolidate union gains. The two organizations were in harmony, however, in their opposition to the tremendous concentration of wealth and power.

19. Nonetheless, upheavals such as the Uprising of 1877—a date coincident with the founding of the Socialist Labor Party, made up largely of immigrants—prompted the establishment of at least one strike-based St. Louis "commune." See Jonathan Grossman, "Co-operative Foundries," *New York History* 24 (1943): 196–209. Paul Buhle, *Marxism in the United States: Remapping the History of the American Left* (London: Verso, 1987), finds even immigrant socialism "primitive in the 1870s and unsuccessfully mass revolutionary in the 1880s" (32).

20. See Paul Buhle, "Socialist Labor Party," in *The Encyclopedia of the American Left*, ed. Mari Jo Buhle, Paul Buhle, and Dan Georgakas (New York: Garland, 1990), 713.

21. Labor biracialism occurred unevenly, for example, on the New Orleans docks, in the Alabama coalfields of the 1870s and 1880s, and in St. Louis strike processions during the Uprising of 1877. On the NCLU, see Philip S. Foner, *Organized Labor and the Black Worker, 1619–1973* (New York: Praeger, 1974), 30–46. On labor protest biracialism, see Eric Arnesen, *Waterfront Workers of New Orleans: Race, Class, and Politics, 1863–1923* (New York: Oxford University Press, 1991). On the illustration at the beginning of this chapter, John George Brown's *The Longshoremen's Noon*, as a representation of dockworkers' biracialism, see Judith A. Schomer, "New Workers in a New World: Painting American Labor," *Labor's Heritage* 3 (1991): 41. See also Ronald Lewis, *Black Coal Miners in America: Race, Class, and Community Conflict, 1780–1980* (Lexington: University Press of Kentucky, 1987); and David Roediger, " 'Not Only the Ruling Classes to Overcome, but Also the So-Called Mob': Class, Skill, and Community in the St. Louis General Strike of 1877," *Journal of Social History* 19 (1985): 214–215, 230–232. See also Brecher, *Strike!*, 17. On the Knights' enlightened racial policies and some exceptions to it, see the documents in "The Black Worker during the Era of the Knights of Labor," in *Black Workers: A Documentary History from Colonial Times to the Present*, ed. Philip S. Foner and Ronald L. Lewis (Philadelphia: Temple University Press, 1989), 209–236.

22. Franklin and Moss, *From Slavery to Freedom*, 234; William H. Harris, *The Harder We Run: Black Workers since the Civil War* (New York: Oxford University Press, 1982), 16–26.

23. Public interest in the threat of the miners, the power of their regional Workingmen's Benevolent Association (WBA), and the specter of the Molly Maguires' alleged (but never reliably proved) responsibility for labor sabotage during the strike all helped promote Cornwall's postbellum novel of labor penitence through accommodation. See Curtis Seltzer, *Fire in the Hole: Miners and Managers in the American Coal Industry* (Lexington: University Press of Kentucky, 1985), 26.

24. Cornwall's primary character even alludes to Avondale. Also factored in were the 1870 WBA strike for the eight-hour day, the 1873 formation of the Miners' National Association (MNA), and the arrested but not yet tried and hanged Mollies. On Avondale as well as the WBA, see Seltzer, *Fire in the Hole*, 25. See, as well, on the Molly Maguires, ibid., 27; Anthony Bimba's (overly) exculpatory *The Molly Maguires*

(New York: International Publishers, 1932); and a jaundiced view of "the dreaded Mollie Maguires," Allan Pinkerton, *The Mollie Maguires and the Detectives* (1877; reprint, New York: Dover Books, 1973), 254.

25. Erhlich, "Immigrant Strikebreaking Activity," 54; Herbert G. Gutman, "Reconstruction in Ohio: Negroes in the Hocking Valley Coal Mines in 1873 and 1874," *Labor History* 3 (1962): 243–264.

26. C. M. Cornwall, *Free, Yet Forging Their Own Chains* (New York: Dodd, Mead, 1876), 53; hereafter cited in text.

27. On the control-minded, company-town mentality of coal operators and its ill effects on miners, see, for example, Corbin, *Life, Work, and Rebellion in the Coal Fields*, chap. 1. On the mining policy of Pennsylvania's border state, West Virginia, Corbin comments: "Coal companies were free from prosecution for safety violations. Until 1904 there was not a single prosecution in the entire state" (17).

28. This contented worker will magically resolve tensions among strikers and scabs, and restore and enact mine safety laws. And he will protect his men against any further fraudulent owners, such as the one who, cutting wages while making profits, helped precipitate the outbreak.

29. Blake, *Strike in the American Novel*, 37–39.

30. Remarks Cawelti, unsound financiers thus shared with economic misfits both a low moral threshold and an inability to follow "the older pattern of self-help." See John G. Cawelti, *Apostles of the Self-Made Man: Changing Concepts of Success in America* (Chicago: University of Chicago Press, 1965), 131.

31. Cornwall adopted the female novelist George Eliot's expedient of the male pseudonym to be taken seriously as an imaginer of workingmen. [Anonymous review of *Free, Yet Forging Their Own Chains*], *Saturday Review* [London] 42 (28 October 1876): 552.

32. On the background, events, and reprisals, see Daniel J. Walkowitz, *Worker City, Company Town: Iron and Cotton-Worker Protest in Troy and Cohoes, New York, 1855–1884* (Urbana: University of Illinois Press, 1972), 183–186, 191–192, 198–199, 208–210.

33. Thomas Bailey Aldrich, *The Stillwater Tragedy* (1880; reprint, Ridgewood, N.J.: Gregg Press, 1968), 172, 176, 180, 182; hereafter cited in text.

34. Issues such as this joined those of establishing closed shops and gaining wage increases. See Walkowitz, *Worker City, Company Town*, 184.

35. Montgomery adds that by the early 1880s skilled tradesmen also shifted from a group ethical code to formal rules and sanctions, and from resistance to employers' pretensions to control over them. Montgomery, "Workers' Control," 493; Grossman, "Co-operative Foundries," 200–201.

36. It is important to remember that Aldrich was already known for *The Story of a Bad Boy* (1870), an autobiographical novel on the order of *Tom Sawyer*. His paternalism, like that of fellow novelists John Hay and Charles Joseph Bellamy, is a mixture of satire on the "bad boy" worker's exploitation by Irish and Italian troublemakers.

37. Robert Grant, *Face to Face* (1886), Charles Benjamin, *The Strike in the B——— Mill* (1887), and, an immigrant variant, Katherine Pearson Woods, *Metzerott, Shoemaker* (1889).

38. Biographical information on Hay appears in Charles Vandersee, "Introduction," in John Hay, *The Bread-Winners* (New Haven: College and University Press, 1973), 28–34.

39. The Knights were hitting their stride during the early 1880s. For his savagely satiric depiction of the "brothers," see John Hay, *The Bread-Winners: A Social*

Study (1883; reprint, Ridgewood, N.J.: Gregg Press, 1967), 82–85; hereafter cited in text.

40. Hay was a prominent Clevelander. On Cleveland as Buffland, see Vandersee, "Introduction," in Hay, *The Bread-Winners*, 28–30.

41. Hay prefers these self-righteous cadres to those of the real-life strike, when state militia and federal troops were sent in to large cities of the Midwest.

42. President Hayes admitted to his diary that the strikes were no rebellion against government power. See Gerald G. Eggert, "Railroad Strikes of 1877," in Filippelli, *Labor Conflict in the United States*, 444.

43. For a provocative discussion of visual representations such as Thomas Anshutz's *The Ironworkers' Noontime* (1880) and subversions of the turn-of-the-century association between manliness and skilled manual labor, see Melissa Dabakis, "Douglas Tilden's *Mechanics Fountain*: Labor and the 'Crisis of Masculinity' in the 1890s," *American Quarterly* 47 (June 1995): 204–235. On wifely militance, see, for instance, Foner, *Women and the American Labor Movement*, 172, 238–239. See also Serrin, *Homestead*, on steelworkers' women in the 1892 Homestead Strike, beating Pinkertons who fired on their husbands and sons (80).

44. Qtd. in Vandersee, "Introduction," in Hay, *The Bread-Winners*, 31.

45. The cross-class match elicited this acid summation from the rather conventional *Nation*: "The heroine of the love-story is an impossible creature, who elopes with an eloquent 'workingman's orator,' lives with him for more than a year, and then returns to . . . [the mill owner] Philip Breton." See "Recent Novels," *Nation* 743 (25 September 1879): 213. [An anonymous review of *The Breton Mills*], *Harper's* 59 (October 1879): 792, fulsomely found the novel to be concerned with abolishing the "evils of our industrial system . . . by presen[ting] suggestive ideas for their amelioration."

46. Charles Joseph Bellamy, *The Breton Mills* (New York: G. P. Putnam, 1879), 230; hereafter cited in text.

47. As Vandersee aptly observes, "A new age had dawned in America, when poor but honest Americans were to remain contented at the bottom of the social heap so as not to hinder the rapacity of the upper levels" ("Introduction," in Hay, *The Bread-Winners*, 14).

48. For a good discussion of the genesis of (nonliterary) labor mutualism, see Sean Wilentz, *Chants Democratic: New York City and the Rise of the American Working Class, 1788–1850* (New York: Oxford University Press, 1984).

49. Even novels focused on economic reform, while filled with exchanges between unethical financiers plotting new corporate depredations, largely bypassed the troubles of these underpaid workers. See Walter B. Rideout, *The Radical Novel in the United States, 1900–1954* (Cambridge: Harvard University Press, 1956), 10.

50. Ibid., 36.

51. Henry F. Keenan, *The Money-Makers: A Social Parable* (1885; reprint, Ridgewood, N.J.: Gregg Press, 1968), 265–266, 275, 291–302.

52. Rideout, *Radical Novel*, 36.

53. Harriet Boomer Barber, *Drafted In: A Sequel to "The Bread-Winners"* (New York: Bliss Publishing, 1888), 54; hereafter cited in text.

54. Martin Foran, *The Other Side* (Washington, D.C.: W. A. Ingham, 1886), 337; hereafter cited in text.

55. Montgomery, "Workers' Control," 495.

56. Boyer and Morais, *Labor's Untold Story*, 69; Blake, *Strike in the American Novel*, 41.

57. Even such a mercantile pillar as Andrew Carnegie spoke of profit sharing in a speech to his employees, although in reality he used a somewhat higher sliding-

pay scale to make his men forgo an eight-hour day. Rodgers, *The Work Ethic in Industrial America*, 42–48; "Profit-Sharing," *Annual Report of the U.S. Commissioner of Labor* (Washington, D.C.: Government Printing Office, 1886), 279–289.

58. Serrin describes a Carnegie plan that gave with one hand what it took away with the other. *Homestead*, 51–53. In fiction, period moderates (like Warner) as well as those allied to the labor movement (like Foran) linked profit sharing to a guardianship that delegated power to worker surrogates and trustees whose own rise, if not prefiguring that of the proletarians they represented, at least guaranteed an improved living standard. Foran envisioned a trustee determined to guarantee employee involvement. Warner was wedded to a less enlightened goal: keeping class lines distinct while offering modest pay increases.

59. See Beverley Warner, *Troubled Waters* (Boston: J. B. Lippincott, 1885), who sounds a common compromise note. In the revised profit sharing, profits would be "in proportion to faithfulness and ability" (318). He makes no mention of workers' participation in decision making.

60. For a sample of such poetic exhortation in the workingmen's press, see Mrs. S. A. Yates, "The Victory," *Workingman's Advocate*, 8 May 1875, n.p. On Doyle and Aiken, see Michael Denning, *Mechanic Accents: Dime Novels and Working-Class Culture in America* (London: Verso, 1987), 125–137.

61. Denning, *Mechanic Accents*, 169–173; Mary C. Grimes, "Introduction," in *The Knights in Fiction: Two Labor Novels of the 1880s: T. Fulton Gantt, Breaking the Chains (1887) and Frederick Whittaker, Larry Locke, Man of Iron (1883–1884)*, ed. Mary C. Grimes (Urbana: University of Illinois Press, 1986), 14; both hereafter cited in text.

62. Denning, *Mechanic Accents*, 179.

63. Harry's voice is almost identical to that in countless articles in the Knights' newspaper, the *Journal of United Labor*. Oblivious to the irony of representing workingmen's voices in a completely formal way, one anonymous worker opined in the *Journal of United Labor*, "There is no institution so democratic as the centre in which a group of workmen exercise their activity." See "The Superior Workman," *Journal of United Labor* 6 (10 February 1886): 1190.

64. Richard Bridgman, *The Colloquial Style in America* (New York: Oxford University Press, 1966), 61, 65.

65. Franklin and Moss, *From Slavery to Freedom*, 282; Julie Saville, *The Work of Reconstruction: From Slave to Wage Laborer in South Carolina, 1860–1870* (Cambridge: Cambridge University Press, 1994).

66. Foner, *Organized Labor and the Black Worker*, 40, 63.

67. Franklin and Moss, *From Slavery to Freedom*, 281; Philip S. Foner and Ronald L. Lewis, "The Knights Organize Black Labor," in Foner and Lewis, *Black Workers*, 15; Bloch, "Labor and the Negro," 175.

68. But their vacillating racial policies did little to aid the AAISW's minuscule black lodge membership. There were only twenty members in Pittsburgh by the early 1880s. See Dennis C. Dickerson, *Out of the Crucible: Black Steelworkers in Western Pennsylvania, 1875–1980* (Albany: State University of New York Press, 1986), 12.

69. Ibid., 8–10. On blacks' even more blocked access to skilled work in the southern iron and steel industries, see Henry M. McKiven, Jr., *Iron and Steel: Class, Race, and Community in Birmingham, Alabama, 1875–1920* (Chapel Hill: University of North Carolina Press, 1995), chap. 3.

70. Philip S. Foner and Ronald L. Lewis, "Black Labor Militancy and the Knights' 1887 Sugar Strike," in Foner and Lewis, *Black Workers*, 17–18.

71. David M. Katzman, *Before the Ghetto: Black Detroit in the Nineteenth Century* (Urbana: University of Illinois Press, 1973), 105.

72. Franklin and Moss, *From Slavery to Freedom*, 282.

73. Ibid., 280. In Richmond, Virginia, 80 percent of unskilled workers were blacks; and few New York blacks worked outside the menial labor fields of domestic and personal service. See Leon Fink, *Workingmen's Democracy: The Knights of Labor and American Politics* (Urbana: University of Illinois Press, 1983), 150; Seth Scheiner, *Negro Mecca: A History of the Negro in New York City, 1865–1920* (New York: New York University Press, 1965), 49.

74. Booker T. Washington, *Up from Slavery* [1901], in *Three Negro Classics* (New York: Avon Books, 1965), 65–66.

75. Donal F. Lindsey, *Indians at Hampton Institute, 1877–1923* (Chapel Hill: University of North Carolina Press, 1995), 9.

76. At least, the implication was, they had countered the antebellum southern conviction that blacks would make inept workers outside the reins of slavery. See Scheiner, *Negro Mecca*, 47.

77. Frederick Douglass, *Life and Times of Frederick Douglass* (Hartford, Conn.: Park Publishing, 1882), 384–386, associates his life with the ethic of the self-made man. These pages form a stark contrast to the low expectations and dialect self-presentations of southern black turpentine workers in Stephen Powers, *Afoot and Alone: A Walk from Sea to Sea* (Hartford, Conn.: Columbia Book Co., 1884), 22–31.

78. Douglass, *Life and Times*, 211–213, 252–255. Briefly Douglass sharpens his attack on the New Bedford racism that, as a skilled caulker, he had endured so many years before.

79. Foner, *Organized Labor and the Black Worker*, 24.

80. Douglass, *Life and Times*, 213.

81. Frances Smith Foster, "African American Progress-Report Autobiographies," in *Redefining American Literary History*, ed. A. LaVonne Brown Ruoff and Jerry W. Ward, Jr. (New York: Modern Language Association, 1990), 273–274. Howard himself belonged to the professions.

82. W.E.B. Du Bois, *Black Reconstruction in America, 1860–1880* (1935; reprint, New York: Atheneum, 1982). Chapter 10, for instance, is titled "The Black Proletariat in South Carolina." The South's hard-working sharecropper/farmworker blacks were underrepresented in postbellum black fiction and narrative. Poor whites, though represented literarily, if only as vicious, squalid, and/or grotesque and sunk in economic and moral apathy, were essentially perceived as nonworkers. See Sylvia Jenkins Cook, *From Tobacco Road to Route 66: The Southern Poor White in Fiction* (Chapel Hill: University of North Carolina Press, 1976), 5–13, 115, 124.

83. While such figures were present in *Clotel*, here, on the other side of slavery, they come in for particular attack. William Wells Brown, *Clotel; or, The Colored Heroine* (1867; reprint, Miami: Mnemosyne Publishing, 1969), 119–121.

84. Adds Brown, to "deceive whites" was now "a religious duty." William Wells Brown, *My Southern Home* (3d ed.), in *From Fugitive Slave to Free Man: The Autobiographies of William Wells Brown*, ed. William L. Andrews (1882; reprint, New York: New American Library, 1993), 149.

85. Brown, *My Southern Home*, 282, 267.

86. Interestingly, the one workman whose education in a trade is delineated is a shoemaker. Though Brown does not note it, the profession was well represented in the Knights of Labor assembly and associated with a great deal of labor activism. But Brown's unnamed figure learned his trade, almost as part of his punishment, in state prison, where he had been confined for ten years. Indeed, he abandons that skill to seek easier work as a waiter.

87. Brown, *My Southern Home*, 297. It should be added, however, that Brown and Douglass disliked the Hampton Institute's program, run by white administrators to groom southern blacks for subordinate roles in the New South.

88. Land allocation, the agricultural rights of freed slaves, and other problems reflecting the volatile and confusing black role in the postplantation system inspired Brown, Douglass, and Howard to reject the accommodationism symbolized by the passivity of blacks in the face of both southern racism and their own ignorance of voting and property rights.

89. Lindsey, *Indians at Hampton Institute*, 24.

90. Michael Dorris, "Introduction," in Helen Hunt Jackson, *Ramona* (1884; reprint, New York: Signet, 1988), v; hereafter cited in text. For a rare 1880s Indian-authored critique of government land appropriation, see Sarah Winnemuca Hopkins, *Life among the Piutes* (1883; reprint, Bishop, Calif.: Sierra Medina Publishing, 1969).

91. A few years after Jackson's novel, white settlers, tacitly empowered by the 1887 Dawes Allotment Act, whittled away at redistributed reservation lands, as Jackson had predicted. By 1880 the Lakota Sioux Reservation had been split into six agencies, and nine million acres of Indian land had been signed away to the federal government. On both detribalization and the surrender of Sitting Bull, see Dee Brown, *Bury My Heart at Wounded Knee: An Indian History of the West* (New York: Holt, Rinehart and Winston, 1971), 420–430.

92. Lindsey, *Indians at Hampton Institute*, xi.

93. By the time *Ramona* appeared, a small but symbolic number of Indians had been studying alongside blacks at Virginia's Hampton Institute for seven years. See Lindsey, *Indians at Hampton Institute*, 51, 58, 267.

94. Blacks, also emerging from a benighted if far more oppressive communal situation, were given slightly more ambitious training in manual trades. For a modern indictment of Hampton's industrial education program in the early postbellum decades, however, see Donald Spivey, *Schooling for the New Slavery: Black Industrial Education, 1868–1915* (Westport, Conn.: Greenwood Press, 1978), 20–24.

95. Harte also co-authored an unsuccessful 1877 play with Mark Twain, *Ah Sin*, which even found loyalty in a Chinese camp servant. Mistaken for another salvo in the culturally pervasive anti-Asian attacks, the play was a flop. Harte's own plentiful short fiction, as if in recoil from censure, offers servants who, to judge by the few lines accorded them, were ciphers and mutes. A sampling of *Ah Sin*'s dialogue suggests why audiences found anti-Chinese portraiture in its title character: "Walkee bottomside hillee-stage bloke down-plenty smashy upee." Mark Twain and Bret Harte, *Ah Sin* (1877; reprint, San Francisco: San Francisco Book Club, 1961), 10. See also the dialect characters in Atwell Whitney's appalling *Almond-Eyed: A Story of the Day* (San Francisco: A. L. Bancroft, 1878), with its "locust of Chinese" (9), and Bret Harte, *A Phyllis of the Sierras* (Boston: Houghton Mifflin, 1887), 22, 42, 104, 119. For a modern critique, see William Wu, *The Yellow Peril: Chinese Americans in American Fiction, 1850–1940* (New York: Archon Books, 1982), 20, 213n.

96. Joaquin Miller, a literary huckster, paid a great deal more attention to a waning cultural stereotype, the warpath Indian. See his *Life amongst the Modocs* (1873; reprint, San Jose, Calif.: Urion Press, 1987). On Bierce, see Wu, *Yellow Peril*, 22.

97. Only foes of unionism such as Thomas Bailey Aldrich found such works the lesser of two evils. He inserted a satiric passage in *The Stillwater Tragedy* in which the hapless Han-Lin's laundry becomes the target of crazed strikers whose idea of socialism does not, Aldrich satirically reminds his readers, extend to the Chinese (190). But even Aldrich found little to praise in worker obedience when it bore a Chinese

name, offering no true rebuttal to the sinophobia that the organized labor movement shared with manufacturing interests. Yet it was labor that led the charge. See Wu, *Yellow Peril*, 35, and Stuart Creighton Miller, *The Unwelcome Immigrant: The American Image of the Chinese, 1785–1882* (Berkeley: University of California Press, 1969), 151–175.

98. Miller, *Unwelcome Immigrant*, 180. See also Richard A. Fitzgerald, "Illustrations in the San Francisco *Wasp* and Chinese Labor in the 1870s," *Southwest Economy and Society* 5 (Winter 1981): 3–9.

99. Serrin, *Homestead*, 55.

100. On the Ute Indian Peter Johnson's refusal to perform manual labor, see Lindsey, *Indians at Hampton Institute*, 20.

Chapter 3. Labor's Ladies

1. For the early nineteenth-century origins of "worker versus woman" ideologies, see Gerda Lerner, "The Lady and the Mill Girl: Changes in the Status of Women in the Age of Jackson," in *A Heritage of Her Own: Toward a New Social History of American Women*, ed. Nancy F. Cott and Elizabeth H. Pleck (New York: Touchstone/Simon and Schuster, 1979), 182–196. An excellent analysis of hardening prejudice against unwomanly wage earners in the late antebellum period is Alice Kessler-Harris, *Out to Work: A History of Wage-Earning Women in the United States* (New York: Oxford University Press, 1982), chap. 3.

2. On Lowell's centrality to women's labor history, see Thomas Dublin, *Women at Work: The Transformation of Work and Community in Lowell, Massachusetts, 1826–1860* (New York: Columbia University Press, 1979).

3. Mary H. Blewett, *We Will Rise in Our Might: Workingwomen's Voices from Nineteenth-Century New England* (Ithaca, N.Y.: Cornell University Press, 1991); Carole Turbin, *Working Women of Collar City: Gender, Class, and Community in Troy, 1864–1886* (Urbana: University of Illinois Press, 1992); *Out of the Sweatshop: The Struggle for Industrial Democracy*, ed. Leon Stein (New York: Quadrangle/New York Times Book Co., 1977), pts. 1–2. See also Adrienne Siegel, *The Image of the American City in Popular Literature, 1820–1870* (Port Washington, N.Y.: Kennikat Press, 1981), 81; and Phillip S. Foner, *Women and the American Labor Movement from Colonial Times to the Eve of World War I* (New York: Free Press, 1979), 139.

4. On Wright, see Sean Wilentz, *Chants Democratic: New York City and the Rise of the American Working Class, 1788–1850* (New York: Oxford University Press, 1984), 176–183. On Susan B. Anthony's *Revolution* and the suffragists' limited support for female laborers, see Foner, *Women and the American Labor Movement*, 134–140, and Margaret Marsh, *Anarchist Women, 1870–1920* (Philadelphia: Temple University Press, 1981), 21, 70–71. On journals like *Woodhull's*, see Paul Buhle, *Marxism in the United States: Remapping the History of the American Left* (London: Verso, 1987), 37.

5. Claudia Goldin, "Female Labor Force Participation," *Journal of Economic History* 37 (March 1977): 91–92, 96–97. See also Sharon Harley, "Northern Black Female Workers: Jacksonian Era," in *The Afro-American Woman: Struggles and Images*, ed. Sharon Harley and Rosalyn Terborg-Penn (Port Washington, N.Y.: Kennikat Press, 1978), 7.

6. Foner, *Women and the American Labor Movement*, 105.

7. Mrs. M. P. Handy, "In a Tobacco Factory," *Harper's Monthly* 47 (October 1873): 713–719; Donna Franklin, "Black History," *New York Times*, 16 October 1995, A23; Jacqueline Jones, *Labor of Love, Labor of Sorrow: Black Women, Work, and the Family from Slavery to the Present* (1985; reprint, New York: Vintage Books, 1986), 74.

8. Jones, *Labor of Love*, 63.

9. Nancy Woloch, *Women and the American Experience* (New York: Alfred A. Knopf, 1984), 227; David M. Katzman, *Seven Days a Week: Women and Domestic Service in Industrializing America* (1978; reprint, Urbana: University of Illinois Press, 1981), 196–197.

10. Thomas Dublin, "Women, Work, and Protest in the Early Lowell Mills: 'The Oppressing Hand of Avarice Would Enslave Us,'" *Labor History* 16 (Winter 1975): 99–116; Blewett, *We Will Rise in Our Might*, pt. 2 passim; Daniel J. Walkowitz, "Working-Class Women in the Gilded Age: Factory, Community, and Family among Cohoes, New York, Cotton Workers," *Journal of Social History* 5 (Summer 1972): 464–490; Turbin, *Working Women of Collar City*, 1–28.

11. Blewett, *We Will Rise in Our Might*, 106–112; Ardis Cameron, *Radicals of the Worst Sort: Laboring Women in Lawrence, Massachusetts, 1860–1912* (Urbana: University of Illinois Press, 1993), chaps. 1–3; Susan Levine, *Labor's True Woman: Carpet Weavers, Industrialization, and Labor Reform in the Gilded Age* (Philadelphia: Temple University Press, 1984), chap. 2.

12. On the Illinois Women's Alliance, and particularly the labor activist Leonora Barry's role in it, see Meredith Tax, *The Rising of the Women: Feminist Solidarity and Class Conflict, 1880–1917* (New York: Monthly Review Press, 1980), 65–89.

13. Foner, *Women and the American Labor Movement*, 124, 176, 188.

14. David R. Roediger, *Our Own Time: A History of American Labor and the Working Day* (London: Verso, 1989), 196.

15. On the wage-earning women's support for the ten-hour day, see ibid., 53–61; for the eight-hour day, also see ibid., 92, 96, 98.

16. Turbin, *Working Women of Collar City*, 162–166. On planned female cooperative ventures paralleling those of the ironworkers, see 163.

17. Levine, *Labor's True Woman*, chap. 5. On breadwinning white women's racism, see ibid., 106. Further sources on racism include Robert L. Ernst, *Immigrant Life in New York City* (1949; reprint, Port Washington, N.Y.: Ira J. Friedman, 1965), 67; and Katzman, *Seven Days a Week*, 195. A resentfully anti-Chinese laundress, probably based in part on fact, appears in Atwell Whitney, *Almond-Eyed: A Story of the Day* (San Francisco: A. L. Bancroft, 1878), 26.

18. W.E.B. Du Bois, *Black Reconstruction in America, 1860–1880* (1935; reprint, New York: Atheneum, 1982), 417, 508.

19. Susan A. Mann, "Slavery, Sharecropping, and Sexual Inequality," in *"We Specialize in the Wholly Impossible": A Reader in Black Women's History*, ed. Darlene Clark Hine et al. (Brooklyn, N.Y.: Carlson Publishing, 1995), 281–302.

20. Kessler-Harris, *Out to Work*, 82.

21. Levine, *Labor's True Woman*, 10. On the Knights of Labor precursor, the National Labor Union, and its minimal support for workingwomen, see Foner, *Women and the American Labor Movement*, chap. 8.

22. Bruce Laurie, *The Working People of Philadelphia* (Philadelphia: Temple University Press, 1980), 82, 86; Jeanne Boydston, *Home and Work: Housework, Wages, and the Ideology of Labor in the Early Republic* (New York: Oxford University Press, 1990), 152–155. Unpaid home labor, not considered real work, produced everything from slighting references to the work of women to manifestos on women's physical unfitness for paid labor.

23. Benita Eisler, "Introduction," in *The Lowell Offering: Writings by New England Mill Women (1840–1845)*, ed. Benita Eisler (Philadelphia: J. B. Lippincott, 1977). References to the mill girls' essays in the *Offering* are hereafter cited in text.

24. In addition to *Charlotte Temple* and *Monima*, see also the anonymously authored *Laura* (1809). In none of these cousins of Samuel Richardson's ur-novel of

betrayed purity, *Clarissa* (1748), is there a poor girl who must ply the needle or tread the loom. Even Read's Monima, though briefly reduced to beggary, is restored to former affluence.

25. Janis P. Stout, *Sodoms in Eden: The City in American Fiction before 1860* (Westport, Conn.: Greenwood Press, 1979), 25.

26. Ariel Ivers Cummings, *The Factory Girl; or, Gardez La [sic] Coeur* (Lowell, Mass.: J. E. Short, 1847), 165; hereafter cited in text. Such heroines also people Osgood Bradbury's pulp novella *The Mysteries of Lowell* (Boston: Edward T. Williams, 1844) and the clergyman Day Kellogg Lee's *Merrimack; or, Life at the Loom* (New York: Redfield, 1854); both hereafter cited in the text.

27. Caroline Dall, *Woman's Right to Labor* (Boston: Walker, Wise and Co., 1860), 5. See also Virginia Penny, "How Women Can Make Money," in Stein, *Out of the Sweatshop*, 11. T. S. Arthur's hapless title character joins that of Mrs. C. W. Denison's *Edna Etheril, the Boston Seamstress* (1847).

28. Nina Baym, "Melodramas of Beset Manhood: How Theories of American Fiction Exclude Women Writers," *American Quarterly* 33 (1981): 130.

29. Dublin, "Women, Work, and Protest in the Early Lowell Mills," 99. Dreiser's lament appears in his novel *Sister Carrie* (1900).

30. See the title essay in Herbert Gutman, *Work, Culture, and Society in Industrializing America: Essays in American Working-Class History* (New York: Vintage Books, 1977), 26. See also Gary Kulik, *The New England Mill Village, 1790–1860*, ed. Gary Kulik et al. (Cambridge: MIT Press, 1982), xxxi. On the shoebinder as "lady stitcher," a counterpart of the Lowell factory lady, see Blewett, *We Will Rise in Our Might*, 93.

31. Michael Paul Rogin, *Subversive Genealogy: The Politics and Art of Herman Melville* (New York: Alfred A. Knopf, 1983), 203.

32. Lise Vogel, "Hearts to Feel and Tongues to Speak: New England Mill Women in the Early Nineteenth Century," in *Class, Sex, and the Woman Worker*, ed. Milton Cantor and Bruce Laurie (Westport, Conn.: Greenwood Press, 1977), 66.

33. On regulations at Lowell, see Eisler, "Introduction," in *Lowell Offering*, 24–26.

34. Harriet Hanson Robinson, *Loom and Spindle; or, Life among the Early Mill Girls* (Boston: T. Y. Crowell and Co., 1898), 40–41. For a diametrically opposed, and suitably anonymous, view of Lowell as "dirty work," see "The Lowell Factory Girl" [c. 1830s], in Philip S. Foner, *American Labor Songs of the Nineteenth Century* (Urbana: University of Illinois Press, 1995), 43.

35. Eisler, "Introduction," in *Lowell Offering*, 34.

36. Ibid., 34, 40–41.

37. Eisler, "Introduction," in *Lowell Offering*, 29.

38. On the increased proletarianization of Lowell women's work, see Dublin, *Women at Work*, 194–196.

39. On Lowell memoirist Lucy Larcom's 1881 idealization of the sanctity of work at the antebellum mills, see Shirley Marchalonis, *The Worlds of Lucy Larcom, 1824–1893* (Athens: University of Georgia Press, 1989), 223–224. The durability of the myth was such that, well into the 1880s, roseate retrospection about Lowell's early mill girls reinforced the moral finishing-school ideology.

40. Herman Melville, "The Paradise of Bachelors and the Tartarus of Maids" [1855], in *Herman Melville: Selected Tales and Poems*, ed. Richard Chase (New York: Holt, Rinehart, and Winston, 1966), 216; hereafter cited in text.

41. Robert S. Levine, "Fiction and Reform I," in *The Columbia History of the American Novel*, ed. Emory Elliott et al. (New York: Columbia University Press,

1991), 138; David S. Reynolds, *Beneath the American Renaissance: The Subversive Imagination in the Age of Emerson and Melville* (New York: Alfred A. Knopf, 1988), 352–353.

42. Strangely enough, this is a novel. See Reynolds, *Beneath the American Renaissance*, 88.

43. Rogin, *Subversive Genealogy*, 206.

44. Ibid., 203.

45. On the European factory of Melville's time as an alleged promiscuous, and lesbian, world, see the midcentury sexual historian A.J.B. Parent-Duchatelet, excerpted in Havelock Ellis, *Studies in the Psychology of Sex*, vol. 2 (1905; reprint, New York: Random House, 1942), pt. 4, 212–213; and the discussion of Parent-Duchatelet in Alain Corbin, *Women for Hire: Prostitution and Sexuality in France after 1850* (Cambridge: Harvard University Press, 1990), 6. On actual homoeroticism among prostitutes, see A.J.B. Parent-Duchatelet, *De la Prostitution dans la Ville de Paris* (Paris: J.-B. Bellière et fils, 1857), vol. 1, 159–167. On its prevalence among workingwomen-turned-prostitutes, see Corbin, *Women for Hire*, 69, 81, 84, and 108. See also Ruth Rosen, *The Lost Sisterhood: Prostitution in America, 1900–1918* (Baltimore: Johns Hopkins University Press, 1982), 104, 197n.

46. On the inconsistencies in Victorian ideologies of female passionlessness, see E. J. Sigsworth and T. J. Wyke, "A Study of Victorian Prostitution and Venereal Disease," in *Suffer and Be Still: Women in the Victorian Age*, ed. Martha Vicinus (Bloomington: Indiana University Press, 1972), 82–83. The "discourse of prostitution" is studied in Mary Poovey, "Anatomical Realism and Social Investigation in Early Nineteenth-Century Manchester," *Differences: A Journal of Feminist Cultural Studies* 5 (Fall 1993): 5. Poovey contends, intriguingly, that rather than impose sexual segregation, factories "challenged the sexual division of labor" (5).

47. William Sanger, *The History of Prostitution* (1858; reprint, New York: Medical Publishing Co., 1906), 535. Sanger had a horror of lesbianism, evident when he refers to the sexual preferences of prostitutes in ancient Greece (52). Unlike European historians of prostitution, he could not consciously acknowledge lesbian existence in the nineteenth-century city.

48. Reynolds, *Beneath the American Renaissance*, 353.

49. [Horace Greeley], "Labor in New-York," *New York Daily Tribune*, 19 August 1845, 2.

50. Ibid., 3.

51. Christine Stansell, *City of Women: Sex and Class in New York, 1789–1860* (New York: Alfred A. Knopf, 1986), 127.

52. Harriet Beecher Stowe, "The Seamstress" [1840], in Harriet Beecher Stowe, *The Mayflower; or, Sketches of Scenes and Characters among the Descendants of the Pilgrims* [1853] (New York: Hurst and Co., n.d.), 225, 254.

53. Stansell, *City of Women*, 94.

54. Ibid., 94.

55. Qtd. in Alice Kessler-Harris, *Women Have Always Worked: A Historical Overview* (New York: Feminist Press, 1981), 68.

56. Wilentz observes that even in the skilled trades, women were often hired more cheaply than men and given simpler tasks (*Chants Democratic*, 31).

57. Robert Ernst, *Immigrant Life in New York City, 1825–1863* (New York: King's Crown/Columbia University Press, 1949), 125.

58. Kessler-Harris, *Out to Work*, 75.

59. Jane Atterbridge Rose, *Rebecca Harding Davis* (New York: Twayne Publishers, 1993), 7–8.

60. For recent nonlaborist interpretations of Davis's characters as allegories of the female artist, see ibid., 21, 176n-177n.

61. For an alternate interpretation of *Margret Howth* as an unrelenting critique of industrial capitalism, see Jean Fagan Yellin, "Afterword," in Rebecca Harding Davis, *Margret Howth: A Story of Today* (1862; reprint, New York: Feminist Press, 1990), 271–302.

62. Jean Pfaelzer, "The Common Stories of Rebecca Harding Davis," in *A Rebecca Harding Davis Reader: "Life in the Iron-Mills," Selected Fiction, and Essays*, ed. Jean Pfaelzer (Pittsburgh: University of Pittsburgh Press, 1995), calls the Korl woman the era's "most forceful attack on the cult of the true woman" (xix).

63. Pfaelzer, "The Common Stories," argues that Hugh Wolfe as a feminized male is symbolic of women's resistance (xix). Yet such a reading seems to scant his male labor-class identity.

64. Peter Conn, *Literature in America: An Illustrated History* (Cambridge: Cambridge University Press, 1989), 264.

65. Ibid. Davis skillfully constructs a polluted labor-life environment reminiscent of the popular Gothicist George Lippard's *Nazarene* (1846) and *Adonai* (1851). Like Davis, Lippard was unusual in his allusions to the gendered nature of industrial slavery. Yet what he sketched from his visits to Philadelphia's prisonlike textile mills and subterranean sweatshops, Davis imaginatively enters and expands.

66. Rebecca Harding Davis, *Life in the Iron Mills*, in *Life in the Iron Mills and Other Stories*, ed. and intro. Tillie Olsen (1861; reprint, New York: Feminist Press, 1985), 19; hereafter cited in text.

67. To appreciate Davis's verisimilitude, see the excellent discussion of the night shift's effect on iron mill Pittsburgh, and on the gendered labor lives of the men and women who lived nearby, in Susan J. Kleinberg, *The Shadow of the Mills: Working-Class Families in Pittsburgh, 1870–1907* (Pittsburgh: University of Pittsburgh Press, 1989), chap. 1. Most Davis critics, however, inaccurately assume that the Bessemer process, allied with night work, was in place before the Civil War. See Pfaelzer, "The Common Stories," 236. In contrast, see the historians Thomas H. Pauly, "American Art and Labor: The Case of Anshutz's The Ironworkers' Noontime," *American Quarterly* 40 (1988): 348; and Henry Dickerson Scott, *Iron and Steel in Wheeling* (Toledo, Ohio: Carlson Publishing Co., 1929).

68. Pfaelzer, "The Common Stories," assumes the narrator is female (xviii). I agree with Jane Atterbridge Rose that because the narrator is of "indeterminate sex," one should assume he is male (*Rebecca Harding Davis*, 15).

69. Jailhouse atonement, in Davis's depiction, prompts a consciousness of one's failings that can lead to a better life. Such is the case with Deborah. Visited in her cell by a non–labor-class Quaker woman who had followed the trial, Deborah is given the promise that she will "begin thy life again . . . by God's help" (63).

70. Yellin, "Afterword," in Davis, *Margret Howth*, 285.

71. Foner, *Women and the American Labor Movement*, 153; Cameron, *Radicals of the Worst Sort*, 25–26, 42, 55.

72. For a strange early novel more like *Little Women* than *The Silent Partner*, see Phelps's *Up the Hill; or, Life in a Factory* (1865). Information on Phelps's cross-class interactions appears in Mari Jo Buhle and Florence Howe, "Afterword," in Elizabeth Stuart Phelps, *The Silent Partner* (1871; reprint, New York: Feminist Press, 1983), 372, hereafter cited in text; and Carole Farley Kessler, "Elizabeth Stuart Phelps," in *Oxford Companion to Women's Writing*, ed. Cathy N. Davidson and Linda Wagner-Martin (New York: Oxford University Press, 1995), 660. On her participation in the 1869 women's labor conference, see "Opening Address by Miss Phelps" (1869) and "The

Working Women: White Slavery in New England" (1869), both in *America's Working Women: A Documentary History, 1600 to the Present*, rev. ed., ed. Rosalyn Baxandall and Linda Gordon (New York: W. W. Norton, 1993), 105–108. Finally, a more critical view of Phelps's dealings with mill women is in Cameron, *Radicals of the Worst Sort*, xvi.

73. It is curious that Phelps, as if doubting that Sip's real-life counterparts could speak without a Phelps/Perley as intermediary, gives only factory men validation outside the text. "Mr. Mell's testimony may be found in the reports of the Massachusetts Bureau of Labor," she appends to a page of the text (111). The report itself contained workingwomen's testimony.

74. Laurie, *Artisans into Workers*, 93.

75. Ibid.

76. Gutman, *Work, Culture, and Society*, 93.

77. Clark D. Halker, *For Democracy, Workers, and God: Labor Song-Poems and Labor Protest, 1865–1895* (Urbana: University of Illinois Press, 1991), 136, 140. See also Gutman, *Work, Culture, and Society*, 16.

78. Nancy A. Walker, *The Disobedient Writer: Women and Narrative Tradition* (Austin: University of Texas Press, 1995). On Perley Kelso as a disappointingly sentimental heroine, see Judith Fetterley, "'Checkmate': Elizabeth Stuart Phelps's *The Silent Partner*," *Legacy* 3 (1986): 17–29. See also Michael Denning, *Mechanic Accents: Dime Novels and Working-Class Culture in America* (London: Verso, 1986), 186, who classifies Phelps as a domestic novelist. For the opposite view, see Mari Jo Buhle, *Women and American Socialism, 1870–1920* (Urbana: University of Illinois Press, 1981), 98n.

79. Louisa May Alcott, *Work: A Story of Experience*, ed. Sarah Elbert (1873; reprint, New York: Schocken Books, 1977), 442; hereafter cited in text. On Alcott's unhappy experience with her father's male-oriented utopia, Fruitlands, see Elbert, "Introduction," in Alcott, *Work*, xiii.

80. Elbert, "Introduction," in Alcott, *Work*, xxxii.

81. On workingwomen's interracial separateness, see Foner, *Women and the American Labor Movement*, 105; Jacqueline Jones, *The Dispossessed: America's Underclass from the Civil War to the Present* (New York: Basic Books, 1992), 146; and Katzman, *Seven Days a Week*, 175. Even the enlightened female Knights had racially distinct locals. See Levine, *Labor's True Woman*, 108. One account of turn-of-the-century laundry work suggests that white women were willing to work with black men on tasks inferior to theirs, but not with black women. See Dorothy Richardson, *The Long Day: The Story of a New York Working Girl*, ed. Cindy Aron Sondik (1905; reprint, Charlottesville: University Press of Virginia, 1990), 235–236.

82. Andrea Starr Alonso, "A Study of Two Women's Slave Narratives: *Incidents in the Life of a Slave Girl* and *The History of Mary Prince*," in Hine et al., *"We Specialize in the Wholly Impossible,"* 143–146.

83. Winifred Morgan, "Gender-Related Difference in the Slave Narratives of Harriet Jacobs and Frederick Douglass," *American Studies* 15 (Fall 1994): 73–94. See also Frances Foster, "'In Respect to Females': Differences in the Portrayal of Women by Male and Female Narrators," *Black American Literature Forum* 15 (Summer 1981): 66–70.

84. Jones, *Labor of Love*, 22, 143.

85. Harriet Jacobs, *Incidents in the Life of a Slave Girl* (1861; reprint, New York: Oxford University Press/Schomburg Library, 1988), 82; hereafter cited in text.

86. Jean Fagan Yellin, "Introduction," in Harriet Jacobs, *Incidents in the Life of a Slave Girl*, ed. Jean Fagan Yellin (Cambridge: Harvard University Press, 1987), xv. I

am indebted to this source for information on Jacobs's relations with Norcom and Sawyer as well as on her northern work life after freedom.

87. Hazel V. Carby, *Reconstructing Womanhood: The Emergence of the Afro-American Woman Novelist* (New York: Oxford University Press, 1987), 47.

88. William L. Andrews, "The Changing Moral Discourse of Nineteenth-Century African American Women's Autobiography: Harriet Jacobs and Elizabeth Keckley," in *De/Colonizing the Subject: The Politics of Gender: African American Women's Autobiography*, ed. Sidonie Smith and Julie Watson (Minneapolis: University of Minnesota Press, 1992), 236–237.

89. Elizabeth Keckley, *Behind the Scenes; or, Thirty Years a Slave, and Four Years in the White House* (1868; reprint, New York: Oxford University Press/Schomburg Library, 1988), 32; hereafter cited in text.

90. Andrews, "The Changing Moral Discourse," 263.

91. William L. Andrews, "Introduction," in *Three Classic African-American Novels*, ed. William L. Andrews (New York: Mentor Books, 1990), 19. References to *Our Nig* are to this edition and are cited in text.

92. Carby, *Reconstructing Womanhood*, 43.

93. Henry Louis Gates, Jr., Foreword: In Her Own Write, in *Collected Black Women's Narratives* (New York: Oxford University Press/Schomburg Library, 1986), xvi.

94. Francis Greenwood Peabody, *Education for Life: The Story of Hampton Institute* (Garden City, N.Y.: Doubleday, Page, and Co., 1918), 117–118; Booker T. Washington, *Up from Slavery* [1901], in *Three Negro Classics* (New York: Avon Books, 1965), 68.

95. Research on women at Hampton remains sparse. See the brief reference in Donald Spivey, *Schooling for the New Slavery: Black Industrial Education, 1868–1915* (Westport, Conn.: Greenwood Press, 1978), 20l. On the spartan living arrangements, see the excerpt from the autobiography of Della Irving Hayden [1917], in *We Are Your Sisters: Black Women in the Nineteenth Century*, ed. Dorothy Sterling (New York: W. W. Norton, 1984), 378.

96. Katzman, *Seven Days a Week*, 206.

97. Black women graduates supervised Indian women students. See Robert A. Trennert, "Educating Indian Girls at Nonreservation Boarding Schools, 1878–1920," *Western Historical Quarterly* 13 (July 1982): 278. See also Linda M. Perkins, "The Impact of the 'Cult of True Womanhood' on the Education of Black Women," *Journal of Social Issues* 39 (1983): 17–28; and "Iron Teeth," in *With These Hands: Women Working on the Land*, ed. Joan M. Jensen (Old Westbury, N.Y.: Feminist Press, 1981), 62.

98. On the white superintendent of postbellum Hampton, General Armstrong, and his view that only white women were "ladies," see Donal F. Lindsey, *Indians at Hampton Institute, 1877–1923* (Chapel Hill: University of North Carolina Press, 1995), 9.

99. By the 1880s articles within the black press had begun expressing a conservative view of women. See Linda M. Perkins, "The Education of Black Women in the Nineteenth Century," in *Women and Higher Education in American History*, ed. John Mack Farragher and Florence Howe (New York: W. W. Norton, 1968), 76–77.

100. Carroll D. Wright, *The Working Girls of Boston* (1884; reprint, New York: Arno/New York Times Book Co., 1969). No African American women are included in the survey. The conclusions were reinforced in an 1889 tabulation of seventeen thousand Boston working girls, and in New York City reformer Helen Campbell's anecdotal *Prisoners of Poverty: Women Wage-Workers, Their Trades and Their Lives*

(1887; reprint, New York: Garrett Press, 1970), chap. 2, where Campbell tells the story of the fallen seamstress Rose Haggerty. See, for example, Commissioner of Labor, *Fourth Annual Report, 1888,* 22–24. In the 1888 report, black women are mentioned slightingly (19); they are excluded from the Campbell survey.

101. Lillian Sommers, *For Her Daily Bread* (Chicago: Rand, McNally, 1887), 13. For contrasts between middlebrow and working-class texts, see the discussion of *Bertha the Sewing Machine Girl* in Dorothy S. Pam, "Exploitation, Independence, and Solidarity: The Changing Role of American Working Women as Reflected in the Working-Girl Melodrama" (Ph.D. diss., New York University, 1980); and the Bertha excerpt in Stein, *Out of the Sweatshop,* 18–19.

102. On the 1880s and 1890s transformation from "salesgirl" to (still nonimmigrant) "saleslady," see Susan Porter Benson, *Counter Cultures: Saleswomen, Managers, and Customers in American Department Stores, 1890–1940* (Urbana: University of Illinois Press, 1988), 24–27, 134–135. Benson notes that there were eight thousand saleswomen in 1880; by 1890, fifty-eight thousand (23). On the absence of blacks, see page 209. On the mid-nineteenth-century ideological origins of the morally dubious salesgirl, see Amy Gilman Srebnick, *The Mysterious Death of Mary Rogers: Sex and Culture in Nineteenth-Century New York* (New York: Oxford University Press, 1995), 47.

103. Walkowitz, "Working-Class Women in the Gilded Age," 465.

Chapter 4. Taking to Their Streets

1. The 1890 U.S. Census, writes John Graham in an essay on monopoly capitalism, "reported that one percent of the population took for itself more of the national wealth than the remaining population owned." See his Preface, in *"Yours for the Revolution": The Appeal to Reason, 1895–1922* (Lincoln: University of Nebraska Press, 1990), x. A good discussion of 1890s reactive labor militance appears in *Who Built America?: Working People and the Nation's Economy, Politics, Culture, and Society,* vol. 2, ed. Joshua Freeman et al. (New York: Pantheon, 1992), 132–144. See also David Montogomery, "Strikes in Nineteenth-Century America," *Social Science History* 4 (February 1980): 81–104.

2. Thomas R. Brooks, *Toil and Trouble: A History of American Labor* (New York: Delta Books, 1964), 84. See also Samuel Yellen, *American Labor Struggles, 1877–1934* (1936; reprint, New York: Pathfinder Press, 1974), chap. 4.

3. David Montgomery, *The Fall of the House of Labor: The Workplace, the State, and American Labor Activism, 1865–1925* (Cambridge: Cambridge University Press, 1987), chap. 1.

4. See Marie Boltin, "The Homestead Strike, 1892," in *Labor Conflict in the United States: An Encyclopedia,* ed. Ronald L. Filippelli (New York: Garland, 1990), 241–246 and Freeman et al., *Who Built America?,* vol. 2, 132–137. Montogomery, *Fall of the House of Labor,* reports that the Amalgamated Association of Iron and Steel Workers, to which Homestead's strikers belonged, was the largest union of its kind in the world (35).

5. On the limited strike role of Slavic immigrants, see David Montgomery, "Afterword," in *The River Ran Red,* ed. David P. Demarest, Jr. (Pittsburgh: University of Pittsburgh Press, 1982), 226. On biracialism and its limits, see Ronald Lewis, *Black Coal Miners in America: Race, Class, and Community Conflict, 1780–1980* (Lexington: University Press of Kentucky, 1987), 86–87, 102. See also Herbert G. Gutman's still-controversial "The Negro and the United Mine Workers of America: The Career and Letters of Richard L. Davis and Their Meaning, 1890–1900," in his *Work, Culture,*

and Society in Industrializing America: Essays in American Working-Class and Social History (New York: Vintage Books, 1977), 121–208. On blacks' underrepresentation in Homestead, see John E. Bodnar, "The Impact of the 'New Immigration' on the Black Worker: Steelton, Pennsylvania, 1880–1920," *Labor History* 17 (Spring 1976): 214–229. On the numerous southern blacks in (unskilled) iron and steel work in the 1890s, see Henry M. McKiven, Jr., *Iron and Steel: Class, Race, and Community in Birmingham, Alabama, 1875–1920* (Chapel Hill: University of North Carolina Press, 1995), chap. 3. Finally, on the plight of skilled black workers in the 1890s, see Lucian B. Gatewood, "The Black Artisan in the U.S., 1890–1930," *Review of Black Political Economy* 5 (Fall 1974): 19–44.

6. [Mrs.] Nico Bech-Meyer, *A Story from Pullmantown* (Chicago: Charles H. Kerr, 1894), 75. Kerr was a socialist publishing house, making this unchallenged anti-immigrant comment all the more telling.

7. The depression of 1893 left three million unemployed. On such joblessness and strikes, see Freeman et al., *Who Built America?*, vol. 2, 138, 144. On a related event, the 1894 march on Washington of Jacob Coxey's jobless "army," scattered by militia and corporate power, see Donald McMurry, *Coxey's Army: A Study of the Industrial Movement of 1894* (Boston: Little, Brown and Co., 1929). Dispersed, some returned to the labor market; others became part of the growing "tramp problem." For a vignette on New York derelicts, see Stephen Crane's "An Experiment in Misery" (1894).

8. James P. Cannon, "Introduction," in Eugene V. Debs, *Eugene V. Debs Speaks* (New York: Pathfinder Press, 1970), 12–13.

9. Paul Avrich, *Sacco and Vanzetti: The Anarchist Background* (Princeton: Princeton University Press, 1991), 98.

10. Irving Howe, *World of Our Fathers* (New York: Touchstone/Simon and Schuster, 1976), 288. By 1890, of the 200,000 Jews in New York City, 60 percent worked in the needle trades (Howe, 80). See also Ronald Sanders, *The Downtown Jews: Portraits of an Immigrant Generation* (1969; reprint, New York: Dover Books, 1987), 287–288; Paul Buhle, *Marxism in the United States: Remapping the History of the American Left* (London: Verso, 1987), 49–57; and Paul Buhle, "Socialist Labor Party," in *The Encyclopedia of the American Left*, ed. Mari Jo Buhle, Paul Buhle, and Dan Georgakas (New York: Garland, 1990), 714. On, for example, the much more limited anarchist presence in the United States, see Avrich, *Sacco and Vanzetti*, chaps. 1–4.

11. Bernard Mergen, "'Another Great Prize': The Jewish Labor Movement in the Context of American Labor History," *YIVO Annual of Jewish Social Science* 16 (1975–1976): 400; Howe, *World of Our Fathers*, 82.

12. Montgomery, *Fall of the House of Labor*, 2, describes the "shared presumption that individualism was appropriate only for the prosperous and well born." He cites the telling statistic that 40 percent of all workers were day laborers in the 1870s compared with 20 percent in the 1890s (64).

13. See also ibid., 85. On Gompers and prudential unionism, see Bruce Laurie, *Artisans into Workers: Labor in Nineteenth-Century America* (New York: Noonday/Farrar, Straus and Giroux, 1989), 198–199. For a more severe assessment, see Philip S. Foner, *History of the Labor Movement in the United States from the Founding of the AFL to the Emergence of American Capitalism* (1955; reprint, New York: International Publishers, 1980), 185–188.

14. Founded in 1892 without AFL support, the People's or Populist Party excluded blacks, "new ethnics," and Catholics and cobbled together a brief alliance of farmers, railroad men, and rural migrants to steel mills. See Freeman et al., *Who Built America?*, vol. 2, 147–148, and Normal Pollack, *The Populist Response to Indus-*

trial America (Cambridge: Harvard University Press, 1962). Edwin Markham's poem "The Man with the Hoe" (1899) has Populist overtones.

15. See Jacob A. Riis, "Jewtown," in Riis, *How the Other Half Lives: Studies among the Tenements of New York* [1890] (rev. ed., 1902; reprint, New York: Dover Books, 1970), 85–96. The famous photographs, though the subject of Riis's lantern-slide lectures, were not available in halftone reproductions until 1900.

16. Thomas Kessner, *The Golden Door: Italian and Jewish Immigrant Mobility in New York City, 1880–1915* (New York: Oxford University Press, 1977), 136. See also Allen F. Davis, *Spearheads for Reform: The Social Settlements and the Progressive Movement, 1890–1914* (New York: Oxford University Press, 1967), 43.

17. Comments Howe: "The Jewish socialists could not find a path that would lead them out of the miseries of sectarian life" (*World of Our Fathers*, 288). See also Arthur Mann, "Samuel Gompers and the Irony of Racism," *Antioch Review* 13 (June 1953): 206.

18. Mergen, " 'Another Great Prize,' " 401.

19. Montgomery, *Fall of the House of Labor*, 83; see also Kessner, *The Golden Door*, chap. 7.

20. Kessner, *The Golden Door*, ix.

21. Walter A. Wyckoff, *The Workers, an Experiment in Reality*, vol. 1, *The West* (New York: Charles Scribner's Sons, 1898), 200.

22. Sol Cohen, "Foreword," in Robert A. Woods et al., *The Poor in Great Cities: Their Problems and What Is Doing* [*sic*] *to Solve Them* (1895; reprint, New York: Garrett Press, 1970); Roy Lubove, *The Progressives and the Slums: Tenement House Reform in New York City, 1890–1917* (Pittsburgh: University of Pittsburgh Press, 1962). See also Alan M. Kraut, *Silent Travelers: Genes, Germs, and the "Immigrant Menace"* (New York: Basic Books, 1994), 143. Remarked Rose Cohen of the period in her autobiography, *Out of the Shadow: A Russian Jewish Girlhood on the Lower East Side* (1918; reprint, Ithaca, N.Y.: Cornell University Press, 1995): "I did not know that the part of the city where I was living was called . . . the Slums . . . or [that it] was still new and a curiosity to the people in the [rich] part of the city" (240–241).

23. Hamlin Garland, "Homestead and Its Perilous Trades," *McClure's* 111 (June 1894): 3–20. Although a few hundred blacks lived in Homestead, Garland apparently did not "see" them. Garland's comment on "strange beasts" is quoted in Walter Fuller Taylor, *The Economic Novel in America* (Chapel Hill: University of North Carolina Press, 1942), 187. So too in *The Workers* (1898), the economics professor Walter Wyckoff, a participant-observer of manual laborers, both immigrant and native born, spent more time describing their lodgings and customs than their work.

24. Theodore Dreiser, "Fall River," c. 1899, unpub. ms., Theodore Dreiser Papers, Van Pelt-Dietrich Library, University of Pennsylvania. On Homestead, see Theodore Dreiser, *Newspaper Days*, ed. T. D. Nostwich (Philadelphia: University of Pennsylvania Press, 1991), 498–501.

25. Attitudes toward lower-depths fiction are revealed in negative reviews of *Maggie: A Girl of the Streets* in the *New York Tribune*, 31 May 1896, 31; the *Nation* 53 (2 July 1896): 15; and the *Home Journal* (New York), 8 July 1896.

26. Kessner, *The Golden Door*, 48.

27. For a good discussion of period views on domesticating immigrant strangeness, see, for example, Anne E. Goldman, *Take My Word: Autobiographical Innovations of Ethnic American Working Women* (Berkeley: University of California Press, 1996), 117–123.

28. John Cumbler, "Immigration, Ethnicity, and the American Working-Class Community: Fall River, 1850–1900," in *Labor Divided: Race and Ethnicity in United*

States Labor Struggles, ed. Robert Asher and Charles Stephenson (Albany: State University of New York Press, 1990), 154.

29. Literary contributions to labor journals were conventional in the extreme. See, for example, "Mary's Career," *National Labor Tribune*, 6 October 1898, 6, or "An Awkward Mistake," 7. The radical dailies, weeklies, and monthlies of the 1890s paid minimal attention to fiction. Thus when the Midwest socialist journal *The Appeal to Reason* chose a Crane story in 1898 it is not surprising that it selected "An Ominous Baby" (1894), an allegorical tale of a tenement boy who wanders into and steals from a rich neighborhood. Yet it suggests less Crane's critique of capitalism than the dearth of 1890s prolabor and radical fiction. On the purported anticapitalist message of the story, see Graham, Preface, in *"Yours for the Revolution,"* 218. For a more balanced assessment of Crane's politics, drawing on his *McClure's* article on the mines, see Joseph Katz, "Stephen Crane: Muckraker," *Columbia Library Columns* 17 (1968): 2–7.

30. Peter Gottlieb, "Migration and Jobs: The New Black Workers in Pittsburgh, 1916–1930," *Western Pennsylvania Historical Quarterly* 61 (January 1978): 3. Despite the increase, in the 1890s migrants in industrial cities like Buffalo, Cleveland, and Pittsburgh still numbered in the thousands.

31. I. K. Friedman, *The Lucky Number* (Chicago: Way and Williams, 1896), 19.

32. Julian Ralph, "Love in the Barracks," in Ralph, *People We Pass: Stories of Life among the Masses of New York City* (New York: Harper and Brothers, 1896), 65; E. W. Townsend, *A Daughter of the Tenements* (New York: Lovel, Coryell, 1895), 223; both hereafter cited in text. See also the reference to the Chinaman's "cynical sneer" in William Dean Howells, *A Hazard of New Fortunes* (1890; reprint, New York: Signet/ New American Library, 1965), 161; hereafter cited in text.

33. Julian Ralph's essay "The Bowery" (*Century Illustrated* [December 1891]: 237) refers to the "red men" of an earlier America. It would be another decade before the publication of Riis's photo of Iroquois bead workers, living in Lower East Side squalor, in the 1901 edition of *How the Other Half Lives*. In the 1890s, the era of the posed reservation photograph and the more than one hundred Wild West shows featuring stage battles between cowboys and Native Americans, only Stephen Crane among New York City tenement novelists expressed journalistic sympathy for the Indians' "centuries of oppression and humiliation"; see Stephen Crane, "Harvard University against the Carlisle Indians," *New York Journal* (1 November 1896): 5. See also *Partial Recall: Photographs of Native Americans*, ed. Lucy Lippard (New York: New Press, 1996).

34. Carlos Baker, "Delineation of Life and Character," in *The Literary History of the United States*, 3d ed. rev., ed. Robert E. Spiller et al. (New York: Macmillan, 1969), 843. This work is still a valuable resource on regionalist literature.

35. Benedict Giamo, *On the Bowery: Confronting Homelessness in American Society* (Iowa City: University of Iowa Press, 1989), 54.

36. Good analyses of tenement tales and novels appear in ibid., *On the Bowery*, 54–64, and Alan Trachtenberg, "Experiments in Another Country: Stephen Crane's New York City Sketches," *Southern Review* 10 (Spring 1974): 265–285.

37. Giamo, *On the Bowery*, 32.

38. See "Edward W. Townsend Dies," *New York Times*, 17 March 1942, 21.

39. On one level, Chimmie is the spiritual grandfather of the confrontational toughs of Depression-era gangster films like *Angels with Dirty Faces* (1938) and *Public Enemy* (1931). On another, he is a clever update of the antebellum Mose figure, with an overlay of Elizabeth Oakes Smith's good-hearted newsboy.

40. E. W. Townsend, *Chimmie Fadden* (1895; reprint, New York: Garrett Press, 1969), 177; hereafter cited in text. A similar character appears in the popular cartoons of the period. See Michael Angelo Woolf, *Sketches of Life in a Great City* (New York: G. P. Putnam's Sons, 1899); and R. F. Outcault's *"The Yellow Kid": A Centennial Celebration of the Kid Who Started the Comics*, intro. Bill Blackbeard (Northampton, Mass.: Kitchen Sink Press, 1995).

41. "The Variety Stage," *Harper's Weekly* 29 (March 1902): 414. See also Paul Antonie Distler, "Ethnic Comedy," in *Conference on the History of American Popular Entertainment*, ed. Myron Matlaw (Westport, Conn.: Greenwood Press, 1979), 35.

42. Robert W. Snyder, *The Voice of the City: Vaudeville and Popular Culture in New York* (New York: Oxford University Press, 1989), 43.

43. Ibid., 137; David M. Fine, "Abraham Cahan, Stephen Crane, and the Romantic Tenement Tale of the Nineties," *American Studies* 14 (Spring 1973): 100.

44. *A Daughter of the Tenements* was generally far better received than other tenement fiction. See *Bookman* 1 (March 1895): 110–112; Edward Al [Theodore Dreiser], "The Literary Shower," *Ev'ry Month* 1 (February 1896): 10. A more critical review is in *The Literary World* 26 (30 November 1895): 428.

45. Maren Stange, *Symbols of Ideal Life: Social Documentary Photography in America, 1890–1950* (Cambridge: Cambridge University Press, 1989), 17.

46. "Jacob Riis," in *American Reformers*, ed. Alden Whitman (New York: H. W. Wilson, 1985), 689–690.

47. Marianne Doezema, *George Bellows and Urban America* (New Haven: Yale University Press, 1992), 140.

48. James W. Sullivan, "Not Yet," in Sullivan, *Tenement Tales of New York* (New York: Henry Holt and Co., 1895), 192; hereafter cited in text.

49. For an interpretation of the tale as prefiguring the next century's radical novel, see Giamo, *On the Bowery*, 64.

50. See, for example, the reference to a "big mulatto" in Frank Norris, *McTeague: A Story of San Francisco* [1899], Norton Critical Edition, ed. Donald Pizer (New York: W. W. Norton, 1977), 366; hereafter cited in text. Stephen Crane's portraits of small-town black servitors in *Whilomville Stories* (1900) are addressed in my next chapter.

51. Jacob A. Riis, "The Color Line in New York," in Riis, *How the Other Half Lives*, compares good blacks (116) with lawless ones (119).

52. W.E.B. Du Bois, *The Philadelphia Negro: A Social Study* (1899; reprint, New York: Benjamin Blom, 1967), 313. On Du Bois's moral disapproval of the Seventh Ward's Submerged Tenth, see Arnold Rampersad, *The Art and Imagination of W.E.B. Du Bois* (1976; reprint, New York: Schocken Books, 1990), 51; and Joseph P. DeMarco, *The Social Thought of W.E.B. Du Bois* (Lanham, Md.: University Press of America, 1983), 48–50.

53. Du Bois finds Seventh Ward "libertines" "larcenous" and "pleasureseeking" (*The Philadelphia Negro*, 313) and a "desperate" class (312).

54. Du Bois, *The Philadelphia Negro*, 313.

55. Nancy Woloch, *Women and the America Experience* (New York: Alfred A. Knopf, 1984), 235.

56. Ibid., 230–231; Elizabeth Ewen, *Immigrant Women in the Land of Dollars: Life and Culture on the Lower East Side, 1890–1925* (New York: Monthly Review Press, 1995), 23–25.

57. Riis, "The Working Girls of New York," in Riis, *How the Other Half Lives*, 183, 184.

58. Ibid., 184, 187.

59. Magdalena J. Zaborowska, *How We Found America: Reading Gender through East European Immigrant Narratives* (Chapel Hill: University of North Carolina Press, 1995), 146. By the 1920s, a Jewish writer with ghetto origins like Anzia Yezierska could debunk the "stereotype of the exotic other's superior sexuality" (146).

60. Kathy Peiss, *Cheap Amusements: Working Women and Leisure in Turn-of-the-Century New York* (Philadelphia: Temple University Press, 1986), 50, 89. See also John F. Kasson, *Amusing the Million: Coney Island at the Turn of the Century* (1977; reprint, New York: Hill and Wang, 1991), 29.

61. Jacob R. Riis, *Out of Mulberry Street: Stories of Tenement Life in New York City* (1898; reprint, Upper Saddle River, N.J.: Gregg Press, 1970), 122; hereafter cited in text.

62. Other tenement vamps appear in Riis's "Spooning in Dynamite Alley" (*Out of Mulberry Street*) and Ralph's "Love in the Barracks" (*People We Pass*). For a fuller discussion of these and allied texts, see Laura Hapke, *Tales of the Working Girl: Wage-Earning Women in American Literature, 1890–1925* (New York: Twayne/Macmillan, 1992), chap. 2.

63. Jacqueline Jones reports that by 1900 less than 3 percent of black women worked in manufacturing; Jacqueline Jones, *Labor of Love, Labor of Sorrow: Black Women, Work, and the Family from Slavery to the Present* (1985; reprint, New York: Vintage Books, 1986), 166.

64. Francis Hopkinson Smith, *Tom Grogan* (Boston: Houghton Mifflin, 1895), 7, 36.

65. *Bookman* (May 1896): 264.

66. On the publishing history of *Maggie*, see Joseph Katz, "Art and Compromise: The *Maggie* Nobody Knows," *Modern Fiction Studies* (Summer 1966): 203–212. See also Hershel Parker and Brian Higgins, "Maggie's 'Last Night': Authorial Design and Editorial Patching," *Studies in the Novel* 10 (Spring 1978): 64–75.

67. Giamo, *On the Bowery*, 163.

68. Milton Cantor, "Bibliographic Essay," in *American Working-Class Culture: Explorations in American Labor and Social History*, ed. Milton Cantor (Westport, Conn.: Greenwood Press, 1979), 424.

69. Stephen Crane, *Maggie: A Girl of the Streets* [1893], Norton Critical Edition, ed. Thomas Gullason (New York: W. W. Norton, 1979), 28. Future references, hereafter cited in text, are to this original, unexpurgated edition.

70. Hamlin Garland, "An Ambitious French Novel and a Modest American Story," *The Arena* 8 (June 1893): xi. Elsewhere in the piece he defends the book.

71. William Dean Howells, "New York Low Life in Fiction," *New York World*, 26 July 1896, 18) makes the comparison to Greek tragedy. A good summary of period critics defending the realism of *Maggie* is in Robert Wooster Stallman, *Stephen Crane: A Biography* (New York: George Braziller, 1968), 539–545.

72. Mark Peel, "On the Margins: Lodgers and Boarders in Boston, 1860–1900," *Journal of American History* 72 (March 1986): 314.

73. Helen R. Crane, "My Uncle, Stephen Crane," *American Mercury* 31 (January 1934): 26. An important article addressing Crane's Bowery period is Christopher P. Wilson, "Stephen Crane and the Police," *American Quarterly* 48 (June 1996): 273–325.

74. Crane's famous comment that "the root of Bowery life is a sort of cowardice" remains ambiguous. See his letter to Catherine Harris, 12 November 1896, reprinted in Stephen Crane, "Letters," in Crane, *Maggie: A Girl of the Streets*, 139.

75. A telling anecdote on bourgeois resentment of New York's wild "micks" is in Lewis A. Erenberg, *Steppin' Out: New York Nightlife and the Transformation of American Culture, 1890–1930* (Chicago: University of Chicago Press, 1984), 8.

76. Giamo, *On the Bowery*, 150.

77. For this revisionist interpretation of Libbey's working-girl literature, see Michael Denning, *Mechanic Accents: Dime Novels and Working-Class Culture in America* (London: Verso, 1986), 196–200.

78. Trachtenberg, "Experiments in Another Country," 273; Peter Brooks, *The Melodramatic Imagination: Balzac, Henry James, Melodrama, and the Mode of Excess* (1976; reprint, New Haven: Yale University Press, 1995), ix.

79. On factory immigrants' difficulties with the 1890s industrial ethic, see Daniel T. Rodgers, *The Work Ethic in Industrial America, 1850–1920* (Chicago: University of Chicago Press, 1978), 174–175. A good discussion of 1890s crusades against working-class drinking is in Roy Rosenzweig, *Eight Hours for What We Will: Workers and Leisure in an Industrial City, 1870–1920*, (Cambridge: Cambridge University Press, 1983), chap. 4.

80. See Stallman, *Stephen Crane*, 76; and Richard Chase, "Introduction," in Stephen Crane, *The Red Badge of Courage* (Boston: Houghton Mifflin, 1895), xxv.

81. Stephen Crane, "George's Mother," in *Stephen Crane: Stories and Tales*, ed. Robert Wooster Stallman (1952; reprint, New York: Vintage Books, 1955), 146; Jon M. Kingsdale, "The 'Poor Man's Club': Social Functions of the Urban Working-Class Saloon," *New England Quarterly* 23 (October 1973): 476.

82. Giamo, *On the Bowery*, 166.

83. Francis G. Couvares, *The Remaking of Pittsburgh: Class and Culture in an Industrializing City, 1877–1919* (Pittsburgh: University of Pittsburgh Press, 1984), 32–34. One period observer of factory workers of the Johnson family's class might have been describing Crane's characters: "They know no interest in their work nor pleasure in its doing. . . . With sullen perseverance they endure the torment of labor, with pay-day in view and then Saturday night . . . with their mad revels in what they call life"; see Wyckoff, *The Workers*, 1:184–185.

84. On Cahan's negative reception, see Fine, "Cahan, Crane, and the Romantic Tenement Tale," 86. On positive reviews, see Bernard G. Richards, "Abraham Cahan Cast in a New Role," in Abraham Cahan, *"Yekl" and "The Imported Bridegroom"* (1896, 1898; reprint, New York: Dover Books, 1970), vii.

85. Sanders, *The Downtown Jews*, 205; Howe, *World of Our Fathers*, 538.

86. Qtd. in Howe, *World of Our Fathers*, 210. A description of the *Forward*'s own (politically correct) annual ball appears in Howe (211).

87. On the actual charwoman's murder, see Robert Lundy, "The Making of *McTeague* and *The Octopus*" (Ph.D. diss., University of California at Berkeley, 1956), 121–122. For another labor-class news story on which Norris possibly drew, see Donald Pizer, "The Genesis of *McTeague*," in Norris, *McTeague: A Story of San Francisco*, 301.

88. Carl Smith, *Urban Disorder and the Shape of Belief* (Chicago: University of Chicago Press, 1995), 195. Though billed as an industrial utopia, there was neither profit sharing nor home ownership. Smith observes of the rigidly controlled company town that its overseers thought the "culture of labor was inherently debased" (196).

89. Taylor, *The Economic Novel in America*, 108. For a variant on the old workers' surrogate novel of the 1870s and the 1880s, see Daniel Carter Beard, *Moonblight and Six Feet of Romance* (1892). A miner with a deep brogue does appear in Mary Hallock

Foote's conservative *Coeur d'Alene* (1894), on the embattled Idaho silver mine region, but in addition to being a management mouthpiece he belongs to the old-immigrant Irish of the pre-1890s migrations.

90. Edward King, *Joseph Zalmonah* (1893; reprint, Ridgeway, N.J.: Gregg Press, 1967), 57. See also a character's reference to "the American boys" versus "our people" (20).

91. Howells's knowledge of period rail strikes is discussed in Kenneth E. Eble, *William Dean Howells*, 2d ed. (Boston: Twayne Publishers, 1982), 116–117. Further information on Howells's limited involvement in labor, including his shock on visiting Lowell's immigrant mills in 1887 and his opposition to the stiff Haymarket sentences, is in Michael Spindler, *American Literature and Social Change: William Dean Howells to Arthur Miller* (Bloomington: Indiana University Press, 1983), 76.

92. Howells's politics in *A Hazard of New Fortunes*, finds Daniel Borus, in *Writing Realism: Howells, James, and Norris in the Mass Market* (Chapel Hill: University of North Carolina Press, 1989), 159, evinces an intellectual concern for labor. Giamo sees more of a balance between an old moralism and a new program for social justice (*On the Bowery*, 236n). Kenneth S. Lynn, *William Dean Howells: An American Life* (1970; reprint, New York: Harcourt Brace Jovanovich, 1971), 289–302, views him and the novel as emotionally unable to identify with the powerless or draw meaningful conclusions from labor unrest. In another novel touching on workers, *A Traveler from Altruria* (1894), Howells preaches socialism but in a comfortably distant utopian future.

93. On, for example, the more skilled sectors of the working class as reformulating dominant bourgeois standards by embracing sexual respectability and female domesticity but repudiating industrial capitalism, see Mary E. Odem, *Delinquent Daughters: Protecting and Policing Adolescent Female Sexuality in the United States, 1885–1920* (Chapel Hill: University of North Carolina Press, 1995), 46. On workers' temperance drives employing similar reformulations, see Rosenzweig, *Eight Hours for What We Will*, 94.

94. Qtd. in Spindler, *American Literature and Social Change*, 75. Walter Rideout begins *The Radical Novel in the United States, 1900–1954* (Cambridge: Harvard University Press, 1956) in the new century. Presumably by then the novel form was more committed to a close study of workers.

95. Couvares, *The Remaking of Pittsburgh*, 34.

96. Although Depression era social protest fiction like John Dos Passos's *USA* (1938) satirized American condescension toward the poor, Michael Denning finds a continuation of the slumming tradition described in this chapter. *USA* "is not finally a depiction of the working-class districts; it is a depiction of those who seek them out." Michael Denning, *The Cultural Front: The Laboring of American Culture in the Twentieth Century* (London: Verso, 1996), 198.

Chapter 5. Beastmen and Labor Experts

1. Michael P. Weber and Ewa Morawska, "East Europeans in Steel Towns: A Comparative Analysis," *Journal of American History* 11 (May 1985): 284.

2. N. Sue Weiler, "The Uprising in Chicago: The Men's Garment Workers Strike, 1910–1911," in *A Needle, a Bobbin, a Strike: Women Needleworkers in America*, ed. Joan M. Jensen and Sue Davidson (Philadelphia: Temple University Press, 1984), 113–145.

3. *Who Built America?: Working People and the Nation's Economy, Politics, Culture and Society*, vol. 2, ed. Joshua Freeman et al. (New York: Pantheon, 1992), 167. See

also Ronald L. Filippelli, "The Youngstown, Ohio, Steel Strike of 1915–1916," in *Labor Conflict in the United States: An Encyclopedia,* ed. Ronald L. Filippelli (New York: Garland, 1990), 578–579.

4. Tamara K. Hareven and Randolph Langenbach, eds., *Amoskeag: Life and Work in an American Factory City* (New York: Pantheon Books, 1978), 10, 20–21. This is a classic oral history text.

5. Freeman et al., *Who Built America?,* vol. 2, 171.

6. On the African American migration from the South prior to 1917, see Gilbert Osofsky, *Harlem: The Making of a Ghetto—Negro New York, 1890–1930,* 2d ed. (1966; reprint, Chicago: Ivan R. Dee, 1996).

7. See Ronald Takaki, *A Different Mirror: A History of Multicultural America* (Boston: Little, Brown and Co., 1993), 311–324 and 201–202, respectively; and Freeman et al., *Who Built America?,* vol. 2, 170.

8. Irving Howe, *World of Our Fathers* (New York: Touchstone/Simon and Schuster, 1976), 323. Howe applies the term to international socialism, but it is just as applicable to the American working class.

9. David Montgomery, *The Fall of the House of Labor: The Workplace, the State, and American Labor Activism, 1865–1925* (Cambridge: Cambridge University Press, 1987), 109–110.

10. Filippelli, "Packinghouse Workers' Strike of 1904," in Filippelli, *Labor Conflict,* 389.

11. Elizabeth Gurley Flynn, *The Rebel Girl, an Autobiography: My First Life (1906–1926)* (1955; reprint, New York: International Publishers, 1986), 128.

12. Carl I. Meyerhuber, Jr., "The McKees Rocks, Pennsylvania, Strike of 1909," in Filippelli, *Labor Conflict,* 318–321. For a useful, if partisan, source on the era's mining strikes, see Mother Jones, *The Autobiography of Mother Jones,* 3d ed. rev., ed. Mary Field Parton (Chicago: Charles H. Kerr Publishing, 1977).

13. Writes Montgomery, *The Fall of the House of Labor,* 109–110, in a stirring passage: "Striking Italian building laborers in Buffalo, Providence, and New York marched through the streets behind red banners and bands playing the 'Garibaldi March'; Slovak and Polish laborers walked out of steel mills in McKeesport, Duquesne, and Bethlehem, also accompanied by marches, music, and Socialist rhetoric; track laborers of a dozen nationalities halted work on the Canadian Northern under the leadership of IWW job delegates. These struggles blended with the more famous militancy of unskilled factory operatives in Lawrence, Paterson, and Passaic and of immigrant coal miners from Westmoreland County, Pennsylvania, to Ludlow, Colorado."

14. See, for example, George Rawick, "Working-Class Self-Activity," in *Workers' Struggles, Past and Present: A "Radical America" Reader,* ed. James Green (Philadelphia: Temple University Press, 1983), 141–150.

15. James R. Barrett, "Introduction," in Upton Sinclair, *The Jungle* (1906; reprint, Urbana: University of Illinois Press, 1988), xxxvi.

16. Gerald Sorin, *The Prophetic Minority: American Jewish Immigrant Radicals, 1880–1920* (Bloomington: Indiana University Press, 1985), 87. See also Howe, *World of Our Fathers,* 311–324.

17. See, in this regard, Philip S. Foner, *History of the Labor Movement in the United States: The Policies and Practices of the American Federation of Labor, 1900–1909* (1964; reprint, New York: International Publishers, 1981), 78, chap. 4 passim.

18. Moses Rischin, "The Jewish Labor Movement in America: A Social Interpretation," *Labor History* 4 (Fall 1963): 231. On Mexican and Asian minorities and socialism, see Takaki, *A Different Mirror;* on agrarians, see James R. Green, *Grass-Roots*

Socialism: Radical Movements in the Southwest, 1895–1943 (Baton Rouge: Louisiana State University Press, 1978). See also R. Lawrence Moore, "Flawed Fraternity: American Socialist Response to the Negro, 1901–1912," *The Historian* 32 (1969): 1–18. AFL prejudice was not always so clear. See Barrett, "Introduction," in Sinclair, *The Jungle* (1988), xxxin.

19. *Letters from a Workingman* (Chicago: Fleming H. Revell, 1888), 35. While the anonymously authored book may have been that of a professional writer, the nativist and antisocialist convictions were those of many in the U.S. workforce.

20. Paul Buhle, *Marxism in the United States: Remapping the History of the American Left* (London: Verso, 1987), 192. See also Paul Buhle, "The Socialist Party," in *The Encyclopedia of the American Left*, ed. Mari Jo Buhle, Paul Buhle, and Dan Georgakas (New York: Garland, 1990), 717.

21. These agrarian or migrant labor bodies were often at odds with or ignored by organized labor and the Socialist Party hierarchy alike. See also note 18.

22. S. J. Kleinberg, *The Shadow of the Mills: Working-Class Families in Pittsburgh, 1870–1907* (Pittsburgh: University of Pittsburgh Press, 1989), 14.

23. See John Bodnar, *Steelton: Immigration and Industrialization, 1870–1940* (1977; reprint, Pittsburgh: University of Pittsburgh Press, 1990), 107–110, and Ronald L. Lewis, *Black Coal Miners in America: Race, Class, and Community Conflict, 1780–1980* (Lexington: University Press of Kentucky, 1987), 191. An exception to black nonparticipation is the Chicago meatpackers' strike of 1904; see Barrett, "Introduction," in Sinclair, *The Jungle* (1988), xxii–xxiii.

24. John Fitch, "Old at Forty," *American* 67 (March 1911): 654.

25. See John F. McClymer, "The Pittsburgh Survey, 1907–1914: Forging an Ideology in the Steel District," *Pennsylvania History* 41 (April 1974): 169–186.

26. See the excellent piece by Maurine W. Greenwald, "Visualizing Pittsburgh in the 1900s: Art and Photography in the Service of Social Reform," in *Pittsburgh Surveyed: Social Science and Social Reform in the Early Twentieth Century*, ed. Maurine W. Greenwald and Margo Anderson (Pittsburgh: University of Pittsburgh Press, 1996), 141–143. Greenwald admits that Hine's photographs remain contested ideological terrain, seen by some modern critics as fitting "comfortably" the Kellogg Survey philosophy (143).

27. Steven Fraser, *Labor Will Rule: Sidney Hillman and the Rise of American Labor* (Ithaca, N.Y.: Cornell University Press, 1991), 72. See also Allen F. Davis, *Spearheads for Reform: The Social Settlements and the Progressive Movement, 1890–1914* (New Brunswick, N.J.: Rutgers University Press, 1967), 111–116.

28. Barrett, "Introduction," in Sinclair, *The Jungle* (1988), xix; Charles L. Leinenweber, "The American Socialist Party and 'New' Immigrants," *Science and Society* 32 (Winter 1968): 21.

29. For similar titles, see Davis, *Spearheads for Reform.*

30. McClymer, "The Pittsburgh Survey," 169.

31. Maren Stange, *Symbols of Ideal Life: Social Documentary Photography in America, 1890–1950* (Cambridge: Cambridge University Press, 1989), 49.

32. Roy Lubove, "Introduction," in John A. Fitch, *The Steel Workers* (1911; reprint, Pittsburgh: University of Pittsburgh Press, 1989), xiii.

33. Stange, *Symbols of Ideal Life*, 64.

34. Fay M. Blake, *The Strike in the American Novel* (Metuchen, N.J.: Scarecrow Press, 1972), 82.

35. Walter B. Rideout, *The Radical Novel in the United States, 1900–1954* (1956; reprint, New York: Columbia University Press, 1992), 61.

36. Werner Sollors, "Introduction," in *The Life Stories of Undistinguished Americans as Told by Themselves,* ed. Hamilton Holt (1906; reprint, New York: Routledge, 1990), xiii.

37. Osofsky, *Harlem,* 26.

38. Michael B. Folsom, "Upton Sinclair's Escape from *The Jungle:* The Narrative Strategy and Suppressed Conclusion of America's First Proletarian Novel," *Prospects* 4 (1979): 238.

39. Christine Scriabine, "Upton Sinclair and the Writing of *The Jungle,*" *Chicago Historical Quarterly* 10 (Spring 1981): 31.

40. A good discussion of the relationship between *The Jungle* and *The Appeal* is in John Graham, Preface, in *"Yours for the Revolution": The "Appeal to Reason," 1895–1922,* ed. John Graham (Lincoln: University of Nebraska Press, 1990), ix–xii.

41. On these splits in the Socialist Party, see Peter Conn, *The Divided Mind: Ideology and Imagination in America* (Cambridge: Cambridge University Press, 1983), 277; Richard W. Fox, "The Paradox of Progressive Socialism: The Case of Morris Hillquit, 1901–1914," *American Quarterly* 26 (March 1974): 127–140.

42. Eugene V. Debs, "Working Class Politics," in *Eugene V. Debs Speaks*, ed. Jean Y. Tussey (New York: Pathfinder Press, 1972), 175.

43. A brief but solid account of Socialist Party factionalism is in Buhle, "The Socialist Party," 716–723. Wobbly leader Bill Haywood called the IWW "socialism with its working clothes on." See Buhle, *Marxism in the United States,* 87.

44. Buhle, *Marxism in the United States,* 90.

45. Qtd. in Folsom, "Upton Sinclair's Escape," 244.

46. Barrett, "Introduction," in Sinclair, *The Jungle* (1988), lxiii.

47. Upton Sinclair, *The Jungle* [1906] (New York: Penguin, 1985), 24; hereafter cited in text.

48. I am indebted to Leon Harris, *Upton Sinclair: American Rebel* (New York: Thomas Y. Crowell Co., 1975), 9, 15, 34, 376, for information on Sinclair's upbringing.

49. Folsom, "Upton Sinclair's Escape," 257.

50. Ibid., 254.

51. Ibid., 253.

52. James Oppenheim, *Pay Envelopes: Tales of the Mill, the Mine, and the City Street* (New York: B. W. Huebsch, 1911), 122; hereafter cited in text.

53. See Jim Seymour, "The Dishwasher" [1913] and "Out in the Breadline" [1910], in *Rebel Voices: An IWW Anthology*, exp. Ed., ed. Joyce L. Kornbluh (Chicago: Charles H. Kerr Publishing, 1988), 77.

54. Douglas Wixson, *Worker-Writer in America: Jack Conroy and the Tradition of Midwestern Literary Radicalism, 1898–1990* (Urbana: University of Illinois Press, 1994), 211.

55. Jonathan Auerbach, *Male Call: Becoming Jack London* (Durham: Duke University Press, 1996), 3.

56. Mark Pittenger, "A World of Difference: Constructing the 'Underclass' in Progressive America," *American Studies* 49 (March 1997): 43; Jack London, letter to Anna Strunsky Walling, 5 January 1902, in Anna Strunsky Walling, "Memoirs of Jack London" [July 1917], in *Echoes of Revolt: "The Masses," 1911–1917*, ed. William L. O'Neill (1966; reprint, Chicago: Ivan R. Dee, 1989). London externalizes animality in much of his period prose, most notably in *The People of the Abyss* (1902). Jack London, *Martin Eden* [1909] (New York: Penguin, 1984), 119; hereafter cited in text.

57. No longer is he "weighted down by the incubus of his working-class station." See Conn, *The Divided Mind,* 76.

58. Ernest Poole, *The Harbor* (New York: Macmillan Co., 1915), 15.

59. Christopher Wilson, "The Making of a Best Seller," *New York Times Book Review*, 22 December 1985, 25.

60. The patrician transiently experimenting with work (see chapter 4), outworn even by the Progressive Era, continues to make an appearance in such "orthodox" proletarian fiction as Mike Pell, *S.S. Utah* (New York: International Publishers, 1933), 15–19, set in the pre–New Deal years.

61. Upton Sinclair, *King Coal* (1917; reprint, New York: Penguin, 1984), 417.

62. David Graham Phillips, *The Conflict* (New York: D. Appleton and Co., 1911), 269; hereafter cited in text.

63. Winston Churchill, *The Dwelling-Place of Light* (New York: Macmillan, 1917), 286; hereafter cited in text.

64. Nor, when they ask Janet to join their march, does a Haywood figure emerge to say, as he did during the Lawrence protests, "There is no foreigner here except the capitalist." Qtd. in Melvyn Dubofsky, "Lawrence, Massachusetts, Textile Strike of 1912," in Filippelli, *Labor Conflict,* 79.

65. H. P. Boynton, [review of *The Dwelling-Place of Light*], *Bookman* 46 (17 November 1917): 339. See also the Boynton review in *The Nation* 195 (11 October 1917): 403.

66. Fraser, *Labor Will Rule,* 87.

67. Ernest Poole, "Abraham Cahan: Socialist—Journalist—Friend of the Ghetto," *The Outlook* 49 (29 October 1991): 476.

68. Abraham Cahan, *The Rise of David Levinsky* [1917] (New York: Harper and Row, 1960), 274; hereafter cited in text.

69. John Higham, "Introduction," in Cahan, *The Rise of David Levinsky*, vi.

70. Irving Howe, *World of Our Fathers* (New York: Simon and Schuster, 1976), 526.

71. Ibid., 525.

72. Sorin, *The Prophetic Minority,* 55.

73. "Editorial Notice," *The Masses* (December 1912): 3.

74. Robert A. Rosenstone, *Romantic Revolutionary: Biography of John Reed* (New York: Alfred A. Knopf, 1975), chap. 8; Cary Nelson, *Repression and Recovery: Modern American Poetry and the Politics of Cultural Memory, 1910–1945* (Madison: University of Wisconsin Press, 1989), 77–78.

75. Nelson, *Repression and Recovery*, 23.

76. Rebecca Zurier, "Introduction," in Zurier, *Art for* The Masses*: A Radical Magazine and Its Graphics, 1911–1917* (Philadelphia: Temple University Press, 1988), 3.

77. See Max Eastman, "Class War in Colorado [*Masses*, July 1914]," reprinted in O'Neill, *Echoes of Revolt,* 149–159.

78. John Reed, "Another Case of Ingratitude," *The Masses* (July 1913): 17; hereafter cited in text.

79. Mary Field, "Bums—A Story," *The Masses* (May 1913): 172.

80. Nelson, *Repression and Recovery*, 135.

81. "I ain' no w'ite folks' nigger": Charles W. Chesnutt, *The Marrow of Tradition* [1901], in *The African-American Novel in the Age of Reaction: Three Classics,* ed. William L. Andrews (New York: Mentor, 1992), 301; hereafter cited in text. W.E.B. Du Bois quoted in Robin D. G. Kelley and Paul Buhle, "W.E.B. Du Bois (1868–1963)," in Mari Jo Buhle et al., *The Encyclopedia of the American Left*, 203.

82. Mary White Ovington, "The White Brute" [October-November 1915], in O'Neill, *Echoes of Revolt*, 237.

83. For a good discussion of Dixon, see Sandra Gunning, *Race, Rape, and Lynching: The Red Record of American Literature, 1890–1912* (New York: Oxford University Press, 1996), chap. 4. Recent rereadings of Crane stories like "The Monster" (1897), later published as part of the Whilomville collection, find his racial attitudes more ambiguous. See Lee Clark Mitchell, "Face, Race, and Disfiguration in Stephen Crane's 'The Monster,' " *Critical Inquiry* 17 (Autumn 1990): 174–192. Yet to this reader a Crane servant character like Peter Washington is another of his underclass grotesques, at once pitiable and ludicrous.

84. Herbert Gutman, "Black Coal Miners and the American Labor Movement," in Herbert Gutman, *Work, Culture, and Society in Industrializing America: Essays in American Working-Class and Social History* (New York: Vintage, 1977), 122–123, 145. Although the presence of blacks in Pittsburgh's steel mills was slight, the Pittsburgh Survey included pieces on racial harmony by the black sociologists Helen Tucker and Richard Wright.

85. Charles W. Chesnutt, "Peonage, or the New Slavery," *The Voice of the Negro* 4 (1904): 394–397; Thomas J. James, "The Negroes of the Southern States," *The Southern Workman* 41 (August 1912): 459–472.

86. For a sense of how African American writers avoided describing the type dubbed the "shiftless, dirty Negro," see Gloria T. Hull, "Introduction," in Alice Dunbar-Nelson, *The Works of Alice Dunbar-Nelson* (New York: Schomburg Library/Oxford University Press, 1988), xl–xli.

87. On period assumptions, see Osofsky, *Harlem*, 38.

88. Gunning, *Race, Rape, and Lynching*, 47.

89. Douglass deplored the "vicious dissipation" thrust upon the slaves. Frederick Douglass, *Narrative of the Life of Frederick Douglass: An American Slave* (1845; reprint, New York: Signet, 1968), 85. For a discussion of the different versions of the text and Douglass's representations of black labor, see chapter 2 above.

90. Ernestine Williams Pickens, *Charles W. Chesnutt and the Progressive Movement* (New York: Pace University Press, 1994), 123.

91. Montgomery, *The Fall of the House of Labor*, 88, 100, 103, 108; Eric Arnesen, *Waterfront Workers of New Orleans: Race, Class, and Politics, 1863–1923* (New York: Oxford University Press, 1991).

92. John Hope Franklin and Alfred A. Moss, Jr., *From Slavery to Freedom: A History of African Americans*, 7th ed. (New York: Alfred A. Knopf, 1994), 263.

93. Greg Robinson, "Wilmington, North Carolina, Riot of 1898," in *Encyclopedia of African-American Culture and History*, vol. 5, ed. Jack Salzman et al. (New York: Macmillan, 1996), 2857.

94. On Josh's revolutionary potential, see Eric S. Sundquist, *To Wake the Nations: Race in the Making of American Literature* (Cambridge: Harvard University Press, 1993), 442.

95. Ibid., 438. See Arnesen, *Waterfront Workers of New Orleans*, on the militance of southern black dockers; Montgomery, *The Fall of the House of Labor*, 103, 108.

96. On the stereotype, see Ivan Light, "The Ethnic Vice Industry," *American Sociological Review* 42 (June 1977): 472. On its application to Josh, see Sundquist, *To Wake the Nations* (442).

97. W.E.B. Du Bois, "The Black North," *New York Times*, 17 November 1901, recommended Dunbar's novel "to get an idea of the temptations that surround the young [black] immigrant."

98. Accounts of the galvanizing incident vary. In their August 16–17, 1900, coverage of the riot, the *New York Times* and the *New York Tribune* blamed Harris. Osofsky, *Harlem,* 46–47, in contrast, presented the killing as self-defense.

99. Arthur P. Davis, "Paul Laurence Dunbar," in *Dictionary of American Negro Biography,* ed. Rayford W. Logan and Michael R. Winston (New York: W. W. Norton, 1982), 200. I am indebted to this source for biographical details on Dunbar.

100. Paul Laurence Dunbar, *The Sport of the Gods* [1902], in Andrews, *The African-American Novel in the Age of Reaction,* 567.

101. Oscar Micheaux, *The Conquest: The Story of a Negro Pioneer* (1913; reprint, Lincoln: University of Nebraska Press, 1994), 18, 21, 26, 27, 28, 31, 38; hereafter cited in text.

102. On Chinese workers who "liked the IWW," see Flynn, *The Rebel Girl,* 145. On sinophobia, see Takaki, *A Different Mirror,* chap. 8.

103. Sollors, "Introduction," in Holt, *Life Stories,* xvii.

104. "The Transformation of the Alien into the American Citizen," *Arena* 36 (September 1906): 320–329.

105. Leinenweber, "The American Socialist Party," 8.

106. Complained the aging social protest author Rebecca Harding Davis, the "importance of success in money making is [always] given the first place." See Rebecca Harding Davis, *"Life Stories of Undistinguished Americans"* [1906], in *A Rebecca Davis Harding Reader,* ed. Jean Pfaelzer (Pittsburgh: University of Pittsburgh Press, 1995), 460.

107. He similarly passes over the kind of Asian/Mexican alliance that characterized the important 1903 farmworkers' strike in Oxnard, California. Two hundred Mexican farmworkers made common cause with hundreds of Japanese laborers. See Takaki, *A Different Mirror,* 187–188; "Story of a Chinaman," in Holt, *Life Stories,* 185.

108. "Story of a Chinaman," in Holt, *Life Stories,* 185.

109. A rediscovery of this important Chinese American writer has been prompted by the publication of Sui Sin Far, *Mrs. Spring Fragrance and Other Writings* (Urbana: University of Illinois Press, 1995). It reprints "Chinese Workmen in America," her July 3, 1913, *Independent* essay, as well as fiction praising Chinese diligence but in which her class biases are also revealed.

110. "The Life Story of an Indian," in Holt, *Life Stories,* 138.

111. See, in this regard, A. LaVonne Brown Ruoff, "American Indian Literature: A Bibliography," in *Redefining American Literary History,* ed. A. LaVonne Brown Ruoff and Jerry W. Ward, Jr. (New York: Modern Language Association, 1990), 327–352.

112. Edward Goodbird, *Goodbird the Indian: His Story* (1914; reprint, St. Paul: Minnesota Historical Society Press, 1985), chap. 8.

113. Sollors, "Introduction," in Holt, *Life Stories,* xxvii–xxviii.

114. Blake, *The Strike in the American Novel,* 57.

115. For a brief summary, see June Howard, *Form and History in American Literary Naturalism* (Chapel Hill: University of North Carolina Press, 1985), 78–79.

116. Rideout, *The Radical Novel in the United States,* 61.

Chapter 6. Facing the Unwomanly

1. Qtd. in Meredith Tax, *The Rising of the Women: Feminist Solidarity and Class Conflict, 1880–1917* (New York: Monthly Review Press, 1980), 220. Her chapter 8 is the most accurate modern account of the Shirtwaist Strike of 1909–1910. I am indebted to her discussion for the facts of the protest. See also Roger Waldinger, "Another Look at the International Ladies' Garment Workers' Union: Women, Industry

Structure, and Collective Action," in *Women, Work, and Protest*, ed. Ruth Milkman (London: Routledge and Kegan Paul, 1985), 86–109.

2. Elizabeth Gurley Flynn, *The Rebel Girl, an Autobiography: My First Life (1906–1926)*, rev. ed. (1955; reprint, New York: International Publishers, 1986), 127, 136, 143.

3. On both the continuity and the changing nature of purity crusades, see Laura Hapke, *Girls Who Went Wrong: Prostitutes in American Fiction, 1885–1917* (Bowling Green, Ohio: Bowling Green State University Popular Press, 1989), chap. 1.

4. Helen L. Sumner, *Report on the Condition of Woman and Child Wage-Earners in the United States,* vol. 9 (Washington, D.C.: Government Printing Office, 1910), 32; Edith Abbott, *Women in Industry: A Study in American Economic History* (New York: D. Appleton and Co., 1910), 309. On lesser pay for the same jobs, see "Terms of Employment and Shop Standards"; and [Appendix] in Elizabeth Hasanovitz, *One of Them* (Boston: Houghton Mifflin, 1918), 330.

5. See "Are Low Wages Responsible for Women's Immorality?" *Current Opinion* 53 (1913): 402; *Prostitution in America: Three Investigations, 1902–1914* (New York: Arno Press/New York Times, 1976); Annie Allen, "How to Save Girls Who Have Fallen," *Survey* (6 August 1910): 684–696, and Jane Addams, *A New Conscience and an Ancient Evil* (New York: Macmillan, 1912).

6. George J. Kneeland, Preface, in *Commercialized Prostitution in New York City*, 4th ed. (New York: D. Appleton and Co., 1917), xii. Kneeland chaired the Chicago Vice Commission, the most thorough and important of its day.

7. Clara E. Laughlin, *The Work-a-Day Girl: A Study of Some Present-Day Conditions* (New York: Fleming H. Revell Co., 1913), 154.

8. See the useful study by Joanne J. Meyerowitz, *Women Adrift: Independent Wage Earners in Chicago, 1880–1930* (Chicago: University of Chicago Press, 1988).

9. Lynn Y. Weiner, *From Working Girl to Working Mother: The Female Labor Force in the United States, 1820–1980* (Chapel Hill: University of North Carolina Press, 1985), 23. See also Laura Hapke, *Tales of the Working Girl: Wage-Earning Women in American Literature, 1890–1925* (New York: Twayne/Macmillan, 1992), chap. 1.

10. See Kathy Peiss and Christina Simmons, *Passion and Power: Sexuality in History* (Philadelphia: Temple University Press, 1980), 6.

11. David M. Katzman, *Seven Days a Week: Women and Domestic Service in Industrializing America* (1978; reprint, Urbana: University of Illinois Press, 1981), chap. 7, "White Mistress and Black Servant"; Alice Kessler-Harris, *Women Have Always Worked: A Historical Overview* (Old Westbury, N.Y.: Feminist Press, 1981), 83. See also Cindy Sondik Aron, "Introduction," in Dorothy Richardson, *The Long Day: The Story of a New York Working Girl* (1906; reprint, Charlottesville: University Press of Virginia, 1990), xvii.

12. See, respectively, "The Migration of Colored Girls from Virginia," *Hampton Negro Conference Bulletin* 1 (September 1905): 75–79; the (white) reformer Frances A. Kellor's "Opportunities for Southern Negro Women in Northern Cities," *Voice of the Negro* 2 (July 1905): 470–473; and "Employment of Colored Women in Chicago," *Crisis* 1 (January 1911): 24–25.

13. Ovington (who was white) was a NAACP luminary. For a discussion of Progressive studies of black women workers, I am indebted to Jacqueline Jones, *Labor of Love, Labor of Sorrow: Black Women, Work, and the Family from Slavery to the Present* (1985; reprint, New York: Vintage Books, 1986), 162–164, 371n, and 376n.

14. Clara Lemlich, "Life in the Shop" [1909], reprinted in *Out of the Sweatshop*, ed. Leon Stein (New York: Quadrangle/New York Times Books, 1977), 66.

15. Pauline E. Hopkins, *Contending Forces: A Romance Illustrative of Negro Life North and South* (1900; reprint, Carbondale: Southern Illinois University Press, 1978), 149; hereafter cited in text.

16. Mary E. Odem, *Delinquent Daughters: Protecting and Policing Adolescent Female Sexuality in the United States, 1885–1920* (Chapel Hill: University of North Carolina Press, 1995), 28–29. For fairly reliable statistics on black prostitutes in a large U.S. city, see Walter C. Reckless, *Vice in Chicago* (Chicago: University of Chicago Press, 1933), 26–27. A relatively rare white surveyor of black "employment agencies" as recruiting grounds for prostitutes was Frances Kellor. See Kellor, "Opportunities for Southern Negro Women," 470. On black reformers' attempts to protect female migrants, see, for instance, "The Migration of Colored Girls from Virginia," 75–79.

17. Gina Marchetti, *Romance and the "Yellow Peril": Race, Sex, and Discursive Strategies in Hollywood Fiction* (Berkeley: University of California Press, 1993), 3. In contrast to the filmic erasure of Chinese women, see the discussion of white women and white slavery in Shelley Stamp Lindsey, "Wages and Sin: *Traffic in Souls* and the White Slavery Scare," *Persistence of Vision* 9 (1991): 90–102.

18. Marlon Hom, "Songs of the Hundred Men's Wife," in *Songs of Gold Mountain*, ed. Marlon Hom (Berkeley: University of California Press, 1987), 310. See also Lucie Cheng Hirata, "Free, Indentured, Enslaved: Chinese Prostitutes in Nineteenth-Century America," *Signs* 5 (1979): 3–29; and Yuji Ichioka, "Ameryuki-San: Japanese Prostitutes in America," *Amerasia* 4 (1977): 1–22.

19. Odem, *Delinquent Daughters*, 49.

20. Ivan Light, "The Ethnic Vice Industry, 1880–1944," *American Sociological Review* 42 (June 1977): 468–472.

21. Maxine Schwartz Seller, "The Uprising of the Twenty Thousand: Sex, Class, and Ethnicity in the Shirtwaist Makers' Strike of 1909," in *"Struggle a Hard Battle": Essays on Working-Class Immigrants*, ed. Dirk Hoerder (DeKalb: Northern Illinois University Press, 1986), 254–279.

22. Annelise Orleck, *Common Sense and a Little Fire: Women and Working-Class Politics in the United States, 1900–1965* (Chapel Hill: University of North Carolina Press, 1995), 62.

23. Tax, *The Rising of the Women*, 218–220. Their other modest demands included an end to subcontracting and weekly instead of biweekly payments for work.

24. See, for example, "The Story of Rosalinda," *Collier's* 51 (10 May 1913): 16.

25. "Is White Slavery Nothing More than a Myth?" *Current Opinion* 55 (13 November 1913): 348. See also Brand Whitlock, "The White Slave," *Forum* 15 (February 1914): 193–216.

26. Emma Goldman, "The White Slave Traffic," *Mother Earth* 4 (January 1910): 4. See also A. T. Heist, "The Procurer's Assistant," *Mother Earth* 1 (1906): 31. On Socialist resolutions regarding white slavery, see Sally M. Miller, "Other Socialists: Native-Born and Immigrant Women in the Socialist Party of America, 1901–1917," *Labor History* 24 (Winter 1983): 89–90; Gustavus Myers, "The White Slave Traffic," *International Socialist Review* 11 (November 1910): 278–279.

27. Ruth Rosen, *The Lost Sisterhood: Prostitution in America, 1900–1918* (Baltimore: Johns Hopkins University Press, 1982), 133, finds that less than 10 percent of prostitutes had been forced into the trade.

28. George Kibbe Turner, "The Daughters of the Poor: A Plain Story of the Development of New York City as a Leading Center of the White Slave Trade," *McClure's* 34 (November 1909): 59. In addition to the titles listed in this chapter, see

also Ernest H. Bell, *Fighting the Traffic in Young Girls* (Chicago: Illinois Vigilance Association, 1910).

29. William Hard, "The Woman's Invasion," *Everybody's Magazine* 19 (November 1908): 579–591.

30. Ruth Alexander, *The Girl Problem: Female Sexual Delinquency in New York, 1900–1930* (Ithaca, N.Y.: Cornell University Press, 1995), 2. The phrase "putting on style" appears frequently in Kathy Peiss, *Cheap Amusements: Working Women and Leisure in Turn-of-the-Century New York* (Philadelphia: Temple University Press, 1986). On the new venues for working women, see Janet Staiger, *Bad Women: Regulating Sexuality in Early American Cinema* (Minneapolis: University of Minnesota Press, 1995), 45.

31. Qtd. in Hapke, *Tales of the Working Girl*, 1. See also Nancy Woloch, *Women and the American Experience* (New York: Alfred A. Knopf, 1984), 243.

32. Alice Kessler-Harris, *Out to Work: A History of Wage-Earning Women in the United States* (New York: Oxford University Press, 1982), 140.

33. On women's limited union membership, see ibid., 86, 152. On their marital aspirations, see Leslie Woodcock Tentler, *Wage-Earning Women: Industrial Work and Family Life in the United States, 1900–1930* (New York: Oxford University Press, 1979), chaps. 2 and 3.

34. See, respectively, Henry T. Finck, "Jobs Unsuitable for Women," *Independent* (11 April 1907): 834–835; Belle Lindner Israels, "The Way of the Girl," *Survey* (3 July 1909): 489–491.

35. See, respectively, Clifford Roe, *The Great War on White Slavery; or, Fighting for the Protection of Our Girls* (Chicago: W. Walter, 1911); Neil K. Basen, "Kate Richards O'Hare: The 'First Lady' of American Socialism, 1901–1917," *Labor History* 21 (1980): 155. An excellent brief discussion of the Socialist response to the war on prostitution, from pamphlet to lurid poem, is in Mari Jo Buhle, *Women and American Socialism, 1870–1920* (Urbana: University of Illinois Press, 1981), 253–256. The lurid headline appeared in the 1914 *National Rip-Saw,* and is quoted in Buhle, *Women and American Socialism,* 285n.

36. Jane Campbell, "Rediscovery: Pauline Hopkins," *Belles Lettres: A Review of Books by Women* (Spring 1992): 9. See also Abby Arthur Johnson and Ronald M. Johnson, "Away from Accommodation: Radical Editors and Protest Journalism," *Journal of Negro History* 62 (October 1977): 326–327.

37. See "The Day's Work in a Cannery: From a Factory Girl's Diary," *Life and Labor* 2 (November 1912): 326–328; Agnes Nestor, "A Day's Work Making Gloves," *Life and Labor* 2 (November 1912): 137–139; Rose Schneiderman, "A Cap Maker's Story," *Independent* 58 (27 April 1905): 935–938; Maud Younger, "The Diary of an Amateur Waitress: An Industrial Problem from the Worker's Point of View," *McClure's* 28 (March-April 1907): 543–552, 665–677.

38. Seller, "The Uprising of the Twenty Thousand," 259.

39. On these "stigmata of difference, " see Mark Pittenger, "A World of Difference: Constructing the 'Underclass' in Progressive America," *American Quarterly* 49 (March 1997): 47. He aptly terms *The Woman Who Toils* a "spy story" (47).

40. Marie Van Vorst, *Amanda of the Mill* (Indianapolis: Bobbs-Merrill, 1904), 250.

41. Kessler-Harris, *Out to Work*, 93.

42. Dorothy Richardson, "Trades Unions in Petticoats," *Leslie's Monthly Magazine* 57 (March 1904): 491, 489.

43. Dorothy Richardson, "The Difficulties and Dangers Confronting the Working Woman," *Annals of the American Academy of Political and Social Sciences* 37 (January-

May 1906): 624–626; Rose H. Phelps [Pastor] Stokes, "The Condition of Working Women, from the Working Woman's Viewpoint," *Annals of the American Academy of Political and Social Sciences* 37 (January-May 1906): 627–637. The year before, the journal *Independent*'s lifelets, including those of sweatshop and mill-town girls, had already interested its well-heeled liberal readership in how the working class lived.

44. Richardson's *New York Times* obituary (29 March 1955, 29) characterized her as the author of *The Long Day*, "who stirred the city with a book on the plight of the working girl in 1905."

45. Richardson, *The Long Day*, 281; hereafter cited in text.

46. That belief would inform her play *The Woman Who Wouldn't* [1916], about an artificial-flower maker who becomes a labor leader. See Rose H. Phelps Stokes, "The Condition of Working Women," 173. See also Herbert L. Shapiro and David L. Sterling, "Introduction," in Rose Pastor Stokes, *"I Belong to the Working Class": The Unfinished Autobiography of Rose Pastor Stokes*, ed. Herbert Shapiro and David L. Sterling (Athens: University of Georgia Press, 1992), xii–xiii. See, too, "Notable Books of the Day," *Literary Digest* 31 (1905): 835.

47. Magdalena J. Zaborowska, *How We Found America: Reading Gender through East European Immigrant Narratives* (Chapel Hill: University of North Carolina Press, 1995), 53. For a provocative analysis of Antin's "subversions," see Zaborowska's chapter 8.

48. Ibid., 53; Mary Antin, *The Promised Land* (1912; reprint, Boston: Houghton Mifflin, 1969), 360.

49. See, for example, Lizzie M. Holmes, "Not by Bread Alone," *American Federationist* 9 (January 1902): 11–14.

50. Qtd. in Ann Schofield, "Rebel Girls and Union Maids: The Woman Question in the Journals of the AFL and IWW, 1905–1920," *Feminist Studies* 9 (Summer 1983): 351.

51. Although mainstream reportage and case histories overlap somewhat, see the article in a popular journal by William Mailly, "The Working Girls' Strike," *Independent* 67 (23 December 1909): 1414–1420; and Sarah Comstock, "The Uprising of the Girls," *Collier's* (25 December 1909): 14. Case-history approaches are in Sue Ainslie Clark and Edith Wyatt, "Working-Girls' Budgets: The Shirtwaist-Makers and Their Strike," *McClure's* 36 (November 1910): 70–81, and Miriam Scott, "The Spirit of the Girl Strikers," *Outlook* 94 (19 February 1910): 394–395. For Socialist labor-press support, see Theresa Malkiel, "Socialist Women and the Shirtwaist Makers' Strike," *New York Call*, 8 February 1910.

52. Orleck, *Common Sense and a Little Fire*, 57.

53. Ann Schofield, "The Uprising of the 20,000: The Making of a Labor Legend," in *A Needle, a Bobbin, a Strike: Women Needleworkers in America*, ed. Joan M. Jensen and Sue Davidson (Philadelphia: Temple University Press, 1984), 172.

54. See Buhle, *Women and American Socialism*, 190–194.

55. Qtd. in Flynn, *The Rebel Girl*, 56.

56. Irving Howe, *World of Our Fathers* (New York: Touchstone/Simon and Schuster, 1976), 300.

57. For an excellent biographical discussion of Lemlich, see Orleck, *Common Sense and a Little Fire*, 48–50, 57–63.

58. Ibid., 5, 2.

59. A good account of the drama of that evening appears in Seller, "The Uprising of the Twenty Thousand," 254–255.

60. Qtd. in Schofield, "The Uprising of the 20,000," 167.

61. Fay M. Blake, *The Strike in the American Novel* (Metuchen, N.J.: Scarecrow Press, 1972), 62–63. On women's political and statistical power in the party structure prior to 1909, see Sally M. Miller, "Other Socialists: Native-Born and Immigrant Women in the Socialist Party of America, 1901–1917," *Labor History* 24 (Winter 1983): 85–87.

62. James R. Barrett, *Work and Community in the Jungle: Chicago's Packinghouse Workers, 1894–1922* (Urbana: University of Illinois Press, 1987), 52; Philip S. Foner, *History of the Labor Movement in the United States*, vol. 3 (New York: International Publishers, 1964), 251.

63. These categories are articulated in Schofield, "Rebel Girls and Union Maids," 335–358. I do, however, take issue with her view that Wobbly short fiction was less mired in True Womanhood ideology than, for instance, Barnum's Socialist press stories.

64. *Industrial Worker* (19 December 1917): 1.

65. See Schofield, "Rebel Girls and Union Maids," 351–353.

66. "On East Broadway" [review of *Comrade Yetta*], *New York Times*, 16 March 1913, 252.

67. Arthur Bullard [Albert Edwards], *Comrade Yetta* (New York: Macmillan, 1913), 78; hereafter cited in text.

68. I am indebted to Tax, *The Rising of the Women*, 177–178, for this biographical information on Lemlich.

69. Clark and Wyatt, "Working-Girls' Budgets: The Shirtwaist Makers and Their Strike," 81.

70. The heiress Mabel Train, for instance, is modeled on the founder of the WTUL, Margaret Dreier Robins.

71. Orleck, *Common Sense and a Little Fire*, 118–119. Later, however, Lemlich was given an honorary pension for her services to the ILGWU.

72. James Weinstein, *The Decline of Socialism in America, 1912–1925* (New York: Monthly Review Press, 1967), 6.

73. Ibid., 54; Walter S. Rideout, *The Radical Novel in the United States, 1900–1954* (Cambridge: Harvard University Press, 1956), 50.

74. Mari Jo Buhle, *Women and the American Left* (Boston: G. K. Hall, 1983), 113.

75. Miller, "Other Socialists," 89–101 passim. There may be nothing to reproach in Yetta's plea "to win Socialism for the babies" (445). Little remains of the woman who had wanted to empower the tubercular, slow-moving Mrs. Cohen, a widow whose children were more immediately threatened than future generations of Socialists. In her firebrand days Yetta had leapt to the sweatshop podium and commanded: "Nobody'll go back to work . . . unless [the boss] takes Mrs. Cohen" (120).

76. Rideout, *The Radical Novel in the United States*, 62. Blaine's factory is the site of a fictive version of the tragic 1911 Triangle Factory fire, an event that in Oppenheim's narrative precedes the Shirtwaist Strike. This rearrangement aside, it is true that Oppenheim includes everything from the Lemlich-charged Cooper Union meeting to the draconian judge who sentenced girl picketers for striking against God (265).

77. [Review of *The Nine-Tenths* by James Oppenheim], *Dial* (1 December 1911): 472. James Oppenheim, *The Nine-Tenths* (1911; reprint, Upper Saddle River, N.J.: Gregg Press, 1968); hereafter cited in text.

78. James Oppenheim, *Pay Envelopes: Tales of the Mill, Mine, and the City* (New York: B. W. Huebsch, 1911), 168.

79. Theresa S. Malkiel, *The Diary of a Shirtwaist Striker*, intro. Francoise Basch (1910; reprint, Ithaca, N.Y.: ILR Press, 1990), 11; hereafter cited in text.

80. Basch, "Introduction," in Malkiel, *The Diary of a Shirtwaist Striker*, 65–66.

81. See the memoir of Yvette Eastman, *Dearest Wilding*, ed. Thomas T. Riggio (Philadelphia: University of Pennsylvania Press, 1995). She was sixteen when they began an affair. See also Miriam Gogol, "A Psychoanalytic/Biographical/Feminist Reading of *Dearest Wilding*," in *New Approaches to Reading Theodore Dreiser*, ed. Yoshinobu Hakutani, forthcoming 2001.

82. Maurine Weiner Greenwald, "Introduction: Women at Work through the Eyes of Elizabeth Beardsley Butler and Lewis Hine," in Elizabeth Beardsley Butler, *Women and the Trades: Pittsburgh, 1907–1908* (1909; reprint, Pittsburgh: University of Pittsburgh Press, 1984), vii–xiv.

83. Butler, *Women and the Trades*, 306.

84. Ibid., 304.

85. Philip S. Foner, *Women and the American Labor Movement from Colonial Times to the Eve of World War I* (New York: Free Press, 1979), 309.

86. Compare Dreiser's Jennie with Jack London's low-level toiler, the cannery worker Lizzie Connolly in *Martin Eden* (1909), Jennie's precursor as a sacrificial working-class fallen woman. London's 1913 novel *Valley of the Moon* marries off its laundress breadwinner, thus shifting the focus to her domestic life with a teamster militant.

87. On the novel's instant fame, see a review in the *New York Times*, 17 September 1910, 511. Though not as committed to Socialist documentary as Sinclair in *The Jungle*, Kauffman did append the influential 1910 Rockefeller Grand Jury report on prostitution in New York City to further establish the authenticity of the novel.

88. "Reginald Wright Kauffman," *National Cyclopedia of American Biography*, vol. 48 (New York: James T. White, 1965), 531–532; "Writers and Their Work," *Hampton's* 23 (August 1909): 285.

89. Reginald Wright Kauffman, *The House of Bondage* (1910; reprint, Upper Saddle River, N.J.: Gregg Press, 1968). Estelle Baker's novel *The Rose Door* (1911), about a San Francisco brothel of that name, also uses the outraged orator, as does Virginia Brooks's *Little Lost Sister* (1914). In the former, an ex-inmate lectures a respectable bourgeoise on the life histories of the girls. In the latter, neither alcoholism nor a lack of education prevents the hardened Lou from rhetorical speeches on the limits of city government and vice commissions.

90. James H. Brower, *The Mills of Mammon* (Joliet, Ill.: P. H. Murray, 1909), 130.

91. Mark Thomas Connelly, *The Response to Prostitution in the Progressive Era* (Chapel Hill: University of North Carolina Press, 1980), 115.

92. Representative essays on what social purity advocates called the "common welfare" are "Anti-Vice Program of a Woman's Club," *Survey* 33 (October 1914): 81, and "Church Crusade on the Barbary Coast," *Survey* 37 (March 1917): 691–692. For a modern assessment, see Barbara Meil Hobson, *Uneasy Virtue: The Politics of Prostitution and the American Reform Tradition* (1987; reprint, Chicago: University of Chicago Press, 1990), chap. 6.

93. Sue Davidson, "Introduction," to *The Maimie Papers*, ed. Ruth Rosen and Sue Davidson (Old Westbury, N.Y.: Feminist Press, 1977), xxii.

94. In Kauffman's punishing scenario, Violet sinks to venereal disease and waterfront whoring; Katie Flanagan redirects her energies to her blue-collar marriage; and Carrie and her narrative simply disappear.

95. Margaret von Staden, "My Story" [c. 1910], unpub. ms., Harriet Laidlaw papers, Schlesinger Library, Radcliffe College. Her working-class autobiography appears in the first seven chapters.

96. Ibid., 152. She not only calls it "work" (156) and a "profession" (108), but describing, for instance, the bargaining that goes on between prostitute and customer (63), proclaims that "this is the only work a girl can get a living of" (108).

97. Rosen and Davidson, *The Maimie Papers*, letter 2, p. 4.

98. The IWW's economic rationale for prostitution was quite Victorian at times. A rare semifictional dissection of the prudishly termed "soiled sisters of the underworld," allegedly by a fallen cannery worker, the suggestively named "Madeline Faraway," is "Red Light Woman Gives Industrial Reasons for Prostitution," *Industrial Worker*, 23 September 1916, 4.

99. Schofield, "Rebel Girls and Union Maids," 350.

100. John Reed, "Where the Heart Is," *The Masses* 4 (January 1913): 8.

101. John Reed, "A Daughter of the Revolution," *The Masses* 6 (February 1915): 8. In variants, the defiant prostitute title character of Horatio Winslow's November 1911 *Masses* tale "A Daughter of Delight" (an unwed mother as well) succumbs poignantly to disease and death. But she remains to the end a slangy posturer.

102. Hutchins Hapgood, *An Anarchist Woman* (New York: Duffield and Co., 1909), 56.

103. Alfred Kreymbourg, *Edna: A Girl of the Streets* (New York: G. Bruno, 1915), 26.

104. Brand Whitlock, "The Girl That's Down," in Whitlock, *The Fall Guy* (Indianapolis: Bobbs-Merrill, 1912), 213–230.

105. David Graham Phillips, *Susan Lenox: Her Fall and Rise*, 2 vols. [the sole unexpurgated edition] (New York: D. Appleton and Co., 1917), II, 289; hereafter cited in text.

106. [Ad for *Susan Lenox*], *Hearst's*, June 1916.

107. For the publishing history of the novel, see Isaac Marcosson, *David Graham Phillips and His Times* (New York: Dodd, Mead and Co., 1932), chap. 8. Even bowdlerized, the text was condemned from the *New York Times* to the midwestern *Bellman* because its title character did not escape retribution.

108. Further biography of Hopkins can be found in Ann Allen Shockley, "Pauline Elizabeth Hopkins: A Biographical Excursion into Obscurity," *Phylon* 33 (Spring 1972): 22–26.

109. Sandra Gunning, *Race, Rape, and Lynching: The Red Record of American Literature, 1890–1912* (New York: Oxford University Press, 1996), 97.

110. "Employment of Colored Women in Chicago," 24. See also Meyerowitz, *Women Adrift*, 15; and John B. Reid, " 'A Career to Build, a People to Serve, a Purpose to Accomplish': Race, Class, Gender, and Detroit's First Black Women Teachers, 1865–1916," in *"We Specialize in the Wholly Impossible": A Reader in Black Women's History*, ed. Darlene Clark Hine et al. (Brooklyn, N.Y.: Carlson Publishing, 1995), 303–320.

111. Jones, *Labor of Love, Labor of Sorrow*, 179.

112. See Addie W. Hunter, "A Colored Working Girl and Race Prejudice," *Crisis* 6 (April 1916): 32–34; and "Employment of Colored Women in Chicago," 24.

113. Jones, *Labor of Love, Labor of Sorrow*, 179.

114. Dexter Fisher, "Introduction," in *Cogewea, the Half Blood: A Depiction of the Great Montana Cattle Range* (1927; reprint, Lincoln: University of Nebraska Press, 1981), vi. For a talented, if conflicted, exception, see two strongly worded essays by

Zitkala-Sa, "School Days of an Indian Girl," *Atlantic Monthly* 85 (February 1900): 185–194, and "Why I Am a Pagan," *Atlantic Monthly* 90 (December 1902): 801–803.

115. As *The Maimie Papers* reveals, Maimie did feel barred from success in the business world where, writes Ruth Rosen, she "encountered a great deal of cultural and institutionalized sexism" (xxx).

116. Reid, "A Career to Build," 312–313.

117. Hazel V. Carby, *Reconstructing Womanhood: The Emergence of the Afro-American Woman Novelist* (New York: Oxford University Press, 1987), 162.

118. Cathy Davidson, *Revolution and the Word: The Rise of the Novel in America* (New York: Oxford University Press, 1986), 19, 43.

119. Louise Montgomery, *The American Girl in the Stockyards District* (Chicago: University of Chicago Press, 1913), 69. See also Hilda Satt Polacheck, *I Came a Stranger: The Story of a Hull-House Girl*, ed. Dena J. Polacheck Epstein (Urbana: University of Illinois Press, 1983), 63–64.

120. Leon Stein, *The Triangle Fire* (New York: Carroll and Graf, 1962), 109. Schneiderman, qtd. in Meredith Tax, "Conditions of Working Women in the Late Nineteenth and Early Twentieth Centuries," *Women: A Journal of Liberation* 2 (Fall 1970): 20.

121. Basch, "Introduction," in Malkiel, *The Diary of a Shirtwaist Striker*, 23.

Chapter 7. The Hungry Eye

1. Douglas Wixson, *Worker-Writer in America: Jack Conroy and the Tradition of Midwestern Literary Radicalism, 1898–1990* (Urbana: University of Illinois Press, 1994), 127, 97.

2. Stephen Meyer, *The Five-Dollar Day: Labor Management and Social Control in the Ford Motor Company* (Albany: State University of New York Press, 1981), 144; Wixson, *Worker-Writer in America*, 105–106. For a discussion of how Chicago working-class communities filtered popular culture through ethnicity, see Lizabeth Cohen, *Making a New Deal: Industrial Workers in Chicago, 1919–1939* (Cambridge: Cambridge University Press, 1990), chap. 3.

3. Theodore Dreiser, *An American Tragedy* (1925; reprint, New York: Signet, 1964), 234; hereafter cited in text. At this writing, there is no scholarly edition of the novel.

4. James R. Green, *The World of the Worker: Labor in Twentieth-Century America* (New York: Hill and Wang, 1980), 111. See also his excellent discussion of the "new capitalism," 100–113; and Robert Kanigel, *The One Best Way: Frederick Winslow Taylor and the Enigma of Efficiency* (New York: Viking Press, 1997). While Taylorism, in honor of the speedup expert Frederick Taylor, is most often associated with the 1910s, devotion to scientific management became a fixture of industrial policy in the 1920s.

5. Wixson, *Worker-Writer in America*, 127, 96.

6. Steve Nelson, James R. Barrett, and Rob Ruck, *Steve Nelson: American Radical* (Pittsburgh: University of Pittsburgh Press, 1981), 39.

7. Wixson, *Worker-Writer in America*, 132.

8. On the black minority, see Nelson, Barrett, and Ruck, *Steve Nelson*, 50. On the Mexican minority, see Gilbert G. Gonzalez, *Labor and Community: Mexican Citrus Worker Villages in a Southern California County, 1900–1950* (Urbana: University of Illinois Press, 1994), 39, 42; and Cletus E. Daniel, *Bitter Harvest: A History of California Farmworkers, 1870–1941* (Berkeley: University of California Press, 1981), 101. On minority expectations, conditions, and literature in the 1920s, see chapter 8 below.

9. Frank Stricker, "Affluence for Whom? Another Look at Prosperity and the Working Classes in the 1920s," *Labor History* 24 (Winter 1983): 5–6.

10. Cohen, *Making a New Deal*, chap. 2 passim.

11. On this erosion of labor gains, see Wixson, *Worker-Writer in America*, 86.

12. Meyer, *The Five-Dollar Day*, 123.

13. "500 Reds at Ellis Island," *New York Times*, 4 January 1920, 1; see also "Still Hunting Uncaught Reds," on the same page of that issue. For an exaggerated tribute to the Bolsheviks and the Red Army, see the pamphlet by the Communist Party faithful William Z. Foster, *The Russian Revolution* (Chicago: Trade Union Educational League, 1921).

14. These events were recorded nervously, if with great fascination. Observers ranged from conservative U.S. policy analysts to the editors of the liberal-minded *Survey* magazine to contributors to *Soviet Russia Today* (the magazine of the Friends of the Soviet Union). On the Friends, and on visitors to Russia, partial and un-decided, see Peter G. Filene, *Americans and the Soviet Experiment, 1917–1933* (Cambridge: Harvard University Press, 1967), chaps. 2–5; Sylvia R. Margulies, *The Pilgrimage to Russia: The Soviet Union and the Treatment of Foreigners, 1924–1937* (Madison: University of Wisconsin Press, 1968), 36 and chaps. 4, 5. On Dubinsky's evolving view of Russia, see Steven Fraser, *Labor Will Rule: Sidney Hillman and the Rise of American Labor* (Ithaca, N.Y.: Cornell University Press, 1991), chap. 7. On his visit to Russia, see ibid., 183–184. Filene reports that by 1927 the American Communist Party wanted to build the Friends of the Soviet Union into a "mass organization" (41).

15. Alien radicals were summarily imprisoned for possession of anarchist litera-ture. A good account of purging the nation of them before and during the red scare is in Paul Avrich, *Sacco and Vanzetti: The Anarchist Background* (Princeton: Princeton University Press, 1991), 130–145, 164, 173–175. See also Donald Johnson, *Red Scare* (Lexington: University Press of Kentucky, 1955).

16. Qtd. in Theodore Draper, *The Roots of American Communism* (New York: Viking Press, 1957), 206. The headline is in *New York Times*, 4 January 1920, 1. See also the fine discussion of the red scare in Avrich, *Sacco and Vanzetti*, chap. 8.

17. International Harvester, fearing an outcry when the two men were finally executed in 1927, ran checks of employee opinion of the case. See Cohen, *Making a New Deal*, 175.

18. Upton Sinclair, *Boston*, 2 vols. (New York: Albert and Charles Boni, 1928), 206; hereafter cited in text.

19. On the railway strike, see David Montgomery, *The Fall of the House of Labor: The Workplace, the State, and American Labor Activism, 1865–1925* (Cambridge: Cambridge University Press, 1987), 399, 404. On docks and mines, see Ronald L. Filip-pelli, "The Seattle General Strike of 1919," 465–472, and "The Anthracite Coal Strike of 1922," 19–24, and for background on the United Mine Workers (UMW) in the early 1920s, see "The Bituminous Coal Strike of 1927," all in *Labor Conflict in the United States: An Encyclopedia*, ed. Ronald L. Filippelli (New York: Garland, 1990), 50–56.

20. The Communist Party, which published the story under its Daily Worker Press aegis, broke with the IWW in 1922. Gold tended to concur with their policy decisions, and his story, which concerned IWW political prisoners, was probably written well before 1926.

21. Meyer, *The Five-Dollar Day*, 193. See also *Who Built America?: Working People and the Nation's Economy, Politics, Culture and Society*, vol. 2, ed. Joshua Freeman et al. (New York: Pantheon, 1992), 261.

22. Foster, *The Russian Revolution*, 16.

23. On SP/CP factionalism, see Paul Buhle, "Red Scare," in *The Encyclopedia of the American Left*, ed. Mari Jo Buhle, Paul Buhle, and Dan Georgakas (New York: Garland, 1990), 646.

24. Michael Denning, "'The Special American Conditions': Marxism and American Studies," *American Quarterly* 38, no. 3 (1986): 357.

25. Upton Sinclair, *Oil!* (1927; reprint, Berkeley: University of California Press, 1996), 416, 430, 508–510; hereafter cited in text.

26. A good summary of the declining fortunes of the American Communist Party in the 1920s is in Paul Buhle and Dan Georgakas, "Communist Party, U.S.A.," in Buhle, Buhle, and Georgakas, *The Encyclopedia of the American Left*, 148–150. See also Fraser M. Ottanelli, *The Communist Party of the United States from the Depression to World War II* (New Brunswick, N.J.: Rutgers University Press, 1991), 15; and Walter B. Rideout, *The Radical Novel in the United States, 1900–1954* (Cambridge: Harvard University Press, 1956), 109. On the short-lived Farmer-Labor Party, see Freeman et al., *Who Built America?*, vol. 2, 295.

27. "The Outcast's Prayer," *Industrial Worker* (July 1921), reprinted in *Rebel Voices: An IWW Anthology*, ed. Joyce L. Kornbluh (1964; reprint, Chicago: Charles H. Kerr, 1988), 86.

28. Joseph R. Conlin, "William D. 'Big Bill' Haywood: The Westerner as Labor Radical," in *Labor Leaders in America*, ed. Melvyn Dubofsky and Warren Van Tine (Urbana: University of Illinois Press, 1987), 131.

29. Green, *World of the Worker*, 110.

30. There is no book-length biography of Gold, who responded to the red scare by changing his name from Irwin Granich. As one of those trying to piece together Gold's labor experiences in the 1920s, I am indebted to, among others, Michael Folsom, "Introduction," in *Mike Gold: A Literary Anthology*, ed. Michael Folsom (New York: International Publishers, 1972), 7–20; Michael Folsom, "Michael Gold," in *Dictionary of Literary Biography*, vol. 9, pt. 2, ed. James J. Martine (Detroit: Gale Research, 1981), 72–74; Richard Tuerk, "Michael Gold," in *Dictionary of Literary Biography*, vol. 28, ed. Daniel Walden (Detroit: Gale Research, 1984), 83–87; and Diane Levenberg, "Three Jewish Writers and the Spirit of the Thirties: Michael Gold, Anzia Yezierska, and Henry Roth," *Book Forum* 6, no. 2 (1982): 235–237.

31. See Daniel Aaron, *Writers on the Left* (1961; reprint, New York: Avon, 1965), 104–107; Morris Dickstein, "Hallucinating the Past: *Jews without Money* Revisited," *Grand Street* 9 (Winter 1989): 155–157; and James D. Bloom, *Left Letters: The Culture Wars of Mike Gold and Joseph Freeman* (New York: Columbia University Press, 1992), 71–72.

32. See, for instance, Louis Baury, "The Message of Proletaire," *Bookman* 34 (December 1911): 400–404. Isaac K. Friedman, "Fair Exchange," in Friedman, *The Lucky Number* (Chicago: Way and Williams, 1896), refers to "the proletarian children" (145). On preproletarian fiction, see Jon-Christian Suggs, "The Proletarian Novel," in *Dictionary of Literary Biography*, vol. 9, pt. 3, ed. James J. Martine (Detroit: Gale Research, 1981), 232–233. Prior to the Depression, even the nonleftist Jewish press used the word "proletariat" negatively. See Judah J. Shapiro, *The Friendly Society: A History of the Workmen's Circle* (New York: Judaica Press, 1970), 19–20.

33. Mike Gold, "Towards Proletarian Art," *Liberator* (February 1921), in Folsom, *Mike Gold*, 95.

34. See, for example, Mike Gold, "The American Famine," *Liberator* (November 1921), in Folsom, *Mike Gold*, 95. Gold's playlet in the Clifford Odets mold implicitly

praising the Russian system is Mike Gold, "Strike! A Mass Recitation," *New Masses* 1 (July 1926): 19–21.

35. On his correspondence, see his reprinted letters in *American Proletarian Culture: The Twenties and the Thirties*, Dictionary of Literary Biography Documentary Series, vol. 11, ed. Jon-Christian Suggs (Detroit: Gale Research, 1993), 85–88. On the workshop he conducted, see Marvin E. Gettleman, "New York Workers School, 1923–1944: Communist Education in American Society," in *New Studies in the Politics and Culture of U.S. Communism*, ed. Michael E Brown et al. (New York: Monthly Review Press, 1993), 266. On the influence of Russian theater, see Richard Tuerk, "Michael Gold's *Hoboken Blues*: An Experiment That Failed," *MELUS* 20 (Winter 1995): 3–16.

36. Martha Banta, *Taylored Lives: Narrative Productions in the Age of Taylor, Veblen, and Ford* (Chicago: University of Chicago Press, 1993); Michael W. Munley, "Stories of Work for the American Century: *Taylored Lives*," *American Quarterly* 46 (September 1994): 462–469.

37. Mike Gold, "Love on a Garbage Dump," *New Masses* (December 1928), in Folsom, *Mike Gold*, 18.

38. Eric Homberger, *American Writers and Radical Politics, 1900–39: Equivocal Commitments* (New York: St. Martin's, 1986), 119.

39. The latter journal was named for its eccentric socialist founder, who was known for his Little Blue Books, ten-cent editions of everyone from Charles Dickens to Clarence Darrow to Oscar Wilde. See William McCann, "Emanuel Haldeman-Julius," *Dictionary of American Biography: 1951–1955*, supp. 5, ed. John A. Garraty (New York: Charles Scribner's, 1977), 264–265; Wixson, *Worker-Writer in America*, 107–108.

40. Dreiser, very explicit about his protagonist's ignorance of birth control, by its mere mention ensured the book's banning in Boston, and a court battle, which he lost, about his "obscene" book. A good account is in Richard Lingeman, *Theodore Dreiser*, vol. 2, *An American Journey* (New York: G. P. Putnam, 1990), 321–322.

41. For a solid discussion on the similarities and differences between Clyde Griffiths and Chester Gillette, see Richard Lehan, *Theodore Dreiser: His World and His Novels* (Carbondale: Southern Illinois University Press, 1969), 146–151.

42. Influential reviewers in the *New York Times*, the *New York World*, and the *Saturday Review of Literature* (but not, given the obscenity proceedings, the *Boston Transcript*, which blasted the book) marveled at how well he had outlined the psychic landscape of a tormented young American ashamed of his missionary background. R. L. Duffus, *"An American Tragedy,"* *New York Times*, 10 January 1926, 1; J. W. Crawford, *"An American Tragedy,"* *New York World*, 10 January 1926, 6; Sherwood Anderson, *"An American Tragedy,"* *Saturday Review of Literature* 2 (9 January 1926): 475; E. F. Edgett, *"An American Tragedy,"* *Boston Transcript*, 9 January 1926, 3. Dreiser relied on the *New York World* for his knowledge of the Gillette trial.

43. A selection of reviewers who found *An American Tragedy* a book of greatness—while steering clear of the issue of class—includes Sherwood Anderson, "Dreiser," *Saturday Review of Literature* (9 January 1926): 475; Julia Collier Harris, "Dreiser's Long Expected Novel Depicts the Tragedy and Turmoil of Youth," *Columbus [Ohio] Enquirer Sun*, 3 January 1926, reprinted in *Theodore Dreiser: The Critical Reception*, ed. Jack Salzman (New York: David Lewis, 1972), 445; and Charles R. Walker, "Dreiser Moves Upward," *Independent*, 6 February 1926, reprinted in *Dreiser: The Critical Reception*, 468. For a standard negative appraisal, see Stuart Sherman, "Mr. Dreiser in Tragic Realism," *New York Herald Tribune Books*, 3 January 1926, 1–3.

44. Qtd. in Filene, *Americans and the Soviet Experiment, 1917–1933*, 188. By 1931, a few years after Dreiser's Soviet visit, the *New Masses* was celebrating his birthday. See the review *"The Titan," New Masses* 2 (September 1931): 533. Dreiser joined the Party in 1944, when he was seventy-four.

45. In their view, Clyde's very inability to explain the causes of his desperation or to curb its self-destructive consequences could be extended to the members of a vast American lower-middle class who, like Clyde, had not reached an awareness of their misdirected loyalty to their bosses. Louis Adamic, "Theodore Dreiser: An Appreciation," *Haldeman-Julius Quarterly* 1 (January 1927): 96. For Dreiser's Depression era journalism, see, for instance, "What the Proletariat Reads," *Saturday Review* 11 (1 December 1934): 321–322.

46. One letter to Dreiser is excerpted in Kenneth Payne, "Naturalism and the Proletarians: The Case of Michael Gold," *Anglo-American Studies* 3 (April 1983): 22. See also Lingeman, *Theodore Dreiser*, vol. 2, 353. Aaron's pronouncement in *Writers on the Left*, 105, that Gold found Dreiser middle class does not square with Gold's sentiments in his letter from the mid-1920s. See the excerpted letter in Payne, "Naturalism and the Proletarians," 26.

47. For a provocative discussion of the novel's multiple perspectives, see Caren J. Town, "Voicing the Tragedy: Narrative Conflict in Dreiser's *An American Tragedy*," *Dreiser Studies* 26 (Fall 1995): 12–29.

48. Robert Penn Warren, "Homage to Theodore Dreiser on the Centenary of His Birth," in *Critical Essays on Theodore Dreiser*, comp. Donald Pizer (Boston: G. K. Hall, 1981), 190. For a contrasting approach that finds psychic dwarfing rather than heroism in Clyde, see Philip Fisher, *Hard Facts: Setting and Form in the American Novel* (New York: Oxford University Press, 1985), 138–153.

49. Robert Elias, *Theodore Dreiser: Apostle of Nature* (Ithaca, N.Y.: Cornell University Press, 1970), 221.

50. Qtd. in Richard Lingeman, *Theodore Dreiser*, vol. 1, *At the Gates of the City, 1871–1907* (New York: G. P. Putnam, 1986), 186.

51. Recent critics have reformulated the doomed Aladdin as a compulsive materialist. They find in Clyde the fear of social anonymity, symbolized by his increasingly frantic acquisitiveness. Critics have argued that Clyde makes little distinction between people and objects, desiring to possess that which "promises to transform him." Lingeman, *Theodore Dreiser*, vol. 2, 265; Amy Kaplan, *The Social Construction of American Realism* (Chicago: University of Chicago Press, 1988), 151. To this reader, Clyde's upward rise is laced with pathology.

52. Rideout, *The Radical Novel in the United States*, 116.

53. See, for instance, Upton Sinclair, "Money Writes! A Study of the Economic Interpretation of Today's Literature," *Haldeman-Julius Quarterly* 4 (July–August, 1927): 3–19.

54. Wixson, *Worker-Writer in America*, 124.

55. Dos Passos's novel *USA* (1938) contains a Sacco and Vanzetti subplot. Denning provocatively claims for Dos Passos's version of the deathwatch scene in which crowds mass outside the prison the status of the "proletarian sublime" (rather than the culmination of an anti-Left posture). Michael Denning, *The Cultural Front: The Laboring of American Culture in the Twentieth Century* (London: Verso, 1996), 199. To this reader, Dos Passos's stance is more detached. See also chapter 4, note 96, above.

56. See, for example, K.S., *Boston Transcript* (1 December 1928): 4.

57. Reviewers deemed *Boston* well crafted, and the *Survey* compared it favorably to *The Jungle*. The respective remarks appear in Floyd Dell, *New York Herald Tribune*

Books (11 November 1928): 3; Horace Gregory, *"Boston,"* *New York Evening Post* (17 November 1928): 8; A. G. Hayes, *"Boston,"* *Survey* 61 (1 December 1928): 315.

58. Compare, for instance, Vanzetti's letters to Mrs. Thornwell in *Boston* (195, 262) with actual correspondence with Mrs. Elizabeth Glendower Evans in *The Letters of Sacco and Vanzetti*, ed. Marion Denman Frankfurter and Gardner Jackson (New York: Viking, 1928), 81, 287. Sinclair himself joined the group a few months before the executions. See also William A. Bloodworth, Jr., *Upton Sinclair* (Boston: Twayne, 1977), 115.

59. Donna Gabaccia, "Neither Padrone Slaves nor Primitive Rebels: Sicilians on Two Continents," in *"Struggle a Hard Battle": Essays on Working-Class Immigrants*, ed. Dirk Hoerder (DeKalb: Northern Illinois University Press, 1986), 296–297.

60. Sinclair even added an "appreciation" to the 1924 edition, a reprint of his *Boston Advertiser* piece the year before. Vanzetti originally wrote the pamphlet in his native tongue, though its prose was enhanced by a devoted translator. Its emphasis on poverty, self-improvement, and its sentimental lyricism about the potential beauty of existence appealed sufficiently to Sinclair to inspire him to term Vanzetti this "great man of Massachusetts." See Frederick J. Hoffman, *The Twenties: American Writing in the Postwar Decade*, rev. ed. (New York: Free Press), 115.

61. Sinclair, *"The Story of a Proletarian Life,"* 16 September 1923, *Boston Advertiser,* reprinted as "An Appreciation," in Vanzetti, *The Story of a Proletarian Life*, 5–7.

62. Bloodworth, *Upton Sinclair*, 115. See also Avrich, *Sacco and Vanzetti*, 41–45.

63. Those who knew him best emphasized his modesty, his fondness for children and flowers, and his sweet nature. Avrich, *Sacco and Vanzetti*, 41–43. Vanzetti certainly cast himself as a believer in "the concept of fraternity, of universal love," and a defender of "the weak, the poor, the oppressed." Qtd. in ibid., 43.

64. Ibid., 43.

65. Poetry, too, appeared in the *New Masses, New Republic*, and a collection devoted to the trial and execution, *America Arraigned* (1928). See, for instance, Michael Gold, " 'It's a Fine Day'—Said Governor Fuller," "New Magazine Section," *Daily Worker* (27 August 1927): 1; Alex Bittelman, "Sacco and Vanzetti Will Not Be Forgotten," ibid., 4. Bittelman edited the *Daily Worker's New Magazine*. A good discussion of the poets' responses to the trial is in Hoffman, *The Twenties*, 404–406.

66. See, for comparison, Frankfurter and Jackson, *The Letters of Sacco and Vanzetti*, 46, 53–54, 76, 112, 240–243.

67. Anzia Yezierska, *Bread Givers: A Struggle between a Father of the Old World and a Daughter of the New* (1925; reprint, New York: Persea Books, 1975), 142–143; hereafter cited in text.

68. Alice Kessler-Harris, *Out to Work: A History of Wage-Earning Women in the United States* (New York: Oxford University Press, 1982), 224. On the decline in foreign-born domestic servants, and for further statistics regarding working women in service, see David Katzman, *Seven Days a Week: Women and Domestic Service in Industrializing America* (1978; reprint, Urbana: University of Illinois Press, 1981), 48–51. Chapter 8 below analyzes statistics on black women's work, in which different patterns were evident.

69. "Women Workers Invade All Occupations," *New York Times*, 12 August 1923, 126; Chase G. Woodhouse, "The Status of Women," *American Journal of Sociology* 35 (May 1930): 1091–1096.

70. Seamstresses ("America and I," 1923, and *Salome of the Tenements*, 1923) and shopgirls (*Arrogant Beggar*, 1927), and as secondary characters, prostitutes ("Wild Winter Love," 1923) also figured in Yezierska's fiction.

71. Ellen Golub, "Eat Your Heart Out: The Fiction of Anzia Yezierska," *Studies in American Jewish Literature* 3 (1983): 58.

72. Anzia Yezierska, "Soap and Water," in *Hungry Hearts and Other Stories* (1920; reprint, New York: Persea Books, 1985), 175.

73. Educated WASP males were modeled on the writer's Columbia professor John Dewey. See Mary V. Dearborn, *Love in the Promised Land: The Story of Anzia Yezierska and John Dewey* (New York: Free Press, 1998), chaps. 4–5.

74. Yezierska succeeded to the extent that the era read Alger, not Lemlich, into her stories. For an interpretive summary of Yezierska criticism, see Magdalena J. Zaborowska, *How We Found America: Reading Gender through East European Immigrant Narratives* (Chapel Hill: University of North Carolina Press, 1995), 115–119.

75. Anzia Yezierska, "The Immigrant Speaks," *Good Housekeeping* (1920), reprinted in part in Anzia Yezierska, "Mostly about Myself," in Yezierska, *Children of Loneliness* (New York: Funk and Wagnalls, 1923), 9–31. Further material about her, although speculative at times, is in a book by her daughter, Louise Levitas Henriksen, *Anzia Yezierska: A Writer's Life* (New Brunswick, N.J.: Rutgers University Press, 1988).

76. Green, *The World of the Worker*, applies this truth to the era's clerical sector (108).

77. It should not be forgotten that Yezierska lived for a time at the socialist Rand School and that she researched the ethnography of the Philadelphia Polish community and of homeless workers both there and on the Lower East Side. See Levenberg, "Three Jewish Writers," 235–237.

78. Zaborowska, *How We Found America*, 131.

79. This reader has identified only two Cohen stories from the 1920s with New World settings, "Hands: A Few Sketches from Life," *The Touchstone* 7 (August 1920): 382–389, hereafter cited in text; and the similar "Voices of Spring on the East Side," *The Touchstone* 6 (January 1920): 195–199. For shtetl sketches, see, for instance, "Half a Dream," *Menorah Journal* 10 (August 1924): 373–380. Cohen stories with other settings are "The Laugh," *The Calendar* 1 (July 1925): 387–390; and "Natalka's Polka," in *The Best Short Stories of 1922*, ed. Edward J. O'Brien (Boston: Small, Maynard, 1923), 83–100. Information on Cohen and her unfinished 1922 memoir is in Lois Raider Elias, "Afterword," in Bella [Cohen] Spewack, *Streets, a Memoir of the Lower East Side* (New York: Feminist Press, 1995), 159–173; hereafter cited in text.

80. Omissions of rural labor routinely occur in pieces such as Mary Anderson, "Working Conditions," *American Federationist* 32 (October 1925): 946–949. See also "Women in Industry," *Monthly Labor Review* 12 (January 1921): 155. Lacunae for the 1920s woman farmworker exist as well in the important collection of writings (and its bibliographic endnotes) *With These Hands: Women Working on the Land*, ed. Joan M. Jensen (Old Westbury, N.Y.: Feminist Press, 1981).

81. Fannie Hurst, *Anatomy of Me* (Garden City, N.Y.: Doubleday, 1958), 179. Trotsky reportedly told Hurst, "I know [*Lummox*] so well that I can recite most of it from memory." Though not as involved as Sinclair, Hurst was also a member of the Sacco-Vanzetti Defense Committee.

82. Mike Gold, excerpt from a letter to V. F. Calverton, c. 1925–1926, in Suggs, *American Proletarian Culture*, 85. Suggs has informed me that the excerpt is complete in its reference to Kelley; letter to the author, 5 June 1997. See also Charlotte Margolis Goodman, "Afterword," in Edith Summers Kelley, *Weeds* (1923; reprint, New York: Feminist Press, 1996), 354–355; hereafter cited in text.

83. There is also a tie to the Gastonia school of women novelists, including Mary Heaton Vorse, Grace Lumpkin, and Dorothy Page, all of whom published Depression era novels about the mill women of the Gastonia Textile Strike of 1929. See chapter 9 below.

84. Joseph A. Hill, *Women in Gainful Occupations, 1870–1920* (Washington, D.C.: Government Printing Office, 1929), 43.

85. Willam Isaac Thomas, *The Unadjusted Girl* (1923; reprint, Montclair, N.J.: Patterson Smith, 1969), 4.

86. Annelise Orleck, *Common Sense and a Little Fire: Women and Working-Class Politics in the United States, 1900–1965* (Chapel Hill: University of North Carolina Press, 1995), 113, and chap. 4 passim. See also Susan Lehrer, *Origins of Productive Labor Legislation for Women, 1905–1925* (Albany: State University of New York Press, 1987), chap. 6.

87. The statistic is in William H. Chafe, *The American Woman: Her Changing Social, Economic, and Political Roles, 1920–1970* (New York: Oxford University Press, 1972), 68. The woman unionist was more likely to take the Mother Jones route and do most of her organizing in men's trades. See Alice Kessler-Harris, "Introduction," in Ann Washington Craton, "The Autobiography of Ann Washington Craton," ed. Alice Kessler-Harris, *Signs* 1 (Summer 1976): 1019–1022. Concerned with male unionists, the excerpt from Craton's previously unpublished 1944 autobiography refers (negatively) both to Sarah Conboy of the United Textile Workers and to the former suffragist Pauline Clark, a Bryn Mawr graduate (1031, 1024).

88. For a lucid discussion of the student body, curriculum, and journal *Shop and School*, see Karyn Hollis, "Liberating Voices: Autobiographical Writing at the Bryn Mawr Summer School for Women Workers, 1921–1938," *College Composition and Communication* 45 (February 1994): 31–60.

89. Brigid O'Farrell and Joyce L. Kornbluh, "Bryn Mawr Summer School for Women Workers in Industry," in *Rocking the Boat: Union Women's Voices, 1915–1975*, ed. Brigid O'Farrell and Joyce L. Kornbluh (New Brunswick, N.J.: Rutgers University Press, 1996), 21, and Carmen Lucia, "A Bryn Mawr Summer School Student," ibid., 40.

90. A group from the summer school went to a rally for the two men in 1927, shortly before the execution. See Hollis, "Liberating Voices," 40–41. The Sacco-Vanzetti rally is described in Lucia, "A Bryn Mawr Summer School Student," in O'Farrell and Kornbluh, *Rocking the Boat*, 40.

91. Hollis, "Liberating Voices," 39.

92. Mike Gold, "Go Left, Young Writers!" *New Masses* 4 (January 1929): 3.

93. Gold, letter to Calverton, c. 1925–1926, in Suggs, *American Proletarian Culture*, 85.

94. Mike Gold, *New Masses* (November-December 1917).

95. See the excerpt from the 1921 Eden and Cedar Paul translation of *Proletcult* in Suggs, *American Proletarian Culture*, 53–56. See also Vyacheslav Poliansky, "The Banner of the Proletcult" [trans. unknown], *Plebs* [London] (January 1921): 3–7. Information on the Comintern journals is from the author's interview with Jon-Christian Suggs, New York City, 27 March 1997, who noted that one story in *Literature of World Revolution* was a Japanese tale called "The Cannery."

96. There remains a division of opinion about the relationship between 1920s artistic modernism and the Left. Cary Nelson, *Repression and Recovery: Modern American Poetry and the Politics of Cultural Memory* (Madison: University of Wisconsin Press, 1989), argues for a close connection. Suggs, "Historical Overview," *American Proletarian Culture*, sees a more equivocal relation (12–13).

97. Alfred Kreymbourg, "Truck Drivers," *Liberator* 6 (April 1923): 12–13.

98. Floyd Dell, "Charlie in the Steel-Mills," *Liberator* 6 (February 1923): 5; Charles Rumford Walker, Foreword, in Charles Rumford Walker, *Steel: The Diary of a Furnace Worker*, n.p.

99. Elmer J. Williams, "The First Born," *Liberator* 6 (May 1923): 26–28.

100. Lauter, "American Proletarianism," 343. See also Peck, " 'The Tradition of American Revolutionary Literature,' " 390.

101. Homberger, *American Writers and Radical Politics*, 121.

102. John Dos Passos, "The New Masses I'd Like," 20, and Michael Gold, "Let It Be Really New!," both in *New Masses* 1 (June 1926): 20, 26.

103. Robin E. Dunbar, "Mammonart and Communist Art," *Daily Worker* (23 May 1925); G. Lelevitch, "Proletarian Literature in Soviet Russia," *Daily Worker* (21 March 1925).

104. Mike Gold, "Faster America, Faster! A Movie in Ten Reels," *New Masses*, November 1926, in Folsom, *Mike Gold*, 147.

105. Mike Gold, "On a Section Gang," *New Masses* 3 (July 1928): 8; hereafter cited in text.

106. Kornbluh, Preface to the First Edition, in *Rebel Voices*, ix.

107. William Z. Foster, *Pages from a Worker's Life* (1939; reprint, New York: International Publishers, 1978), 106–109. Reflecting the 1920s hostility of the CP to the IWW, Foster lamented that by the early 1920s the IWW was a "reactionary sect" (144).

108. Lloyd Thompson, "A Vag in College," *Liberator* (July 1923): 22.

109. Literary putdowns of the IWW were common. Marrying his effete protagonist off to a rich woman, Van Vechten, in *Peter Whipple* (1922), in part a satire on Bill Haywood and his wealthy friend Mabel Dodge, assumed that social climbing was standard Wobbly behavior. Variants on this plot include Harold Lord Varney's *Revolt* (1919), M. H. Hedges's *Dan Minturn* (1927), and *Venture* (1927), by Gold's one-time *Liberator* colleague Max Eastman. For other unabashedly anti-IWW novels, see Arthur Jerome Eddy, *Ganton & Co.* (1908) and the popular western author Zane Grey, *Desert of Wheat* (1918). Though they do not rebuke actual figures, they all novelize Wobblies who sell out.

110. On "hobohemia," see Nels Anderson, "Introduction," in Anderson, to *The Hobo: The Sociology of the Homeless Man* (1923; reprint, Chicago: University of Chicago Press, 1965), 15–16; see also pt. 1 passim. See also James Gilbert, *Writers and Partisans: A History of Literary Radicalism in America* (1968; reprint, New York: Columbia University Press, 1992), 14.

111. Joe Hill, "The Tramp," in *The Little Red Song Book: IWW Songs* (1923; reprint, Chicago: Charles H. Kerr, 1989), 20–21. Other "tramp" titles include Hill's "Scissor Bill" (16–17) and the anonymous "Where Is My Wandering Boy Tonight?" (42–43).

112. Anderson, *The Hobo*, xiv–xv. On *Hobo News*, see Lynne M. Adrian, "Introduction," in Charles Elmer Fox, *Tales of an American Hobo* (Iowa City: University of Iowa Press, 1989), xvii–xx.

113. Harry Clayton, "The IWW on a Full-Rigged Ship," reprinted in Kornbluh, *Rebel Voices*, 363.

114. Matilda Robbins, "My Story" [n.d.], unpub. ms., Matilda Robbins Papers, box no. 2, Walter P. Reuther Library, Wayne State University, Detroit, 103.

115. Matilda Robbins, "One of Ours," reprinted in Kornbluh, *Rebel Voices*, 360.

116. Walter Blair, *Native American Humor* (1957; reprint, New York: Harper and Row, 1960), 102–123.

117. William Akers, "Tightline Johnson Goes to Heaven," reprinted in Kornbluh, *Rebel Voices,* 93. The Akers story is actually a dream Johnson has after he breaks into a wealthy house. He wakes up to the sight of God's tears, which mirrors the story's political message: organized religion, like rich homeowners, is the comic foil of egalitarian irreverence.

118. Gerald V. Morris, "On the Skidroad: What One Sees on Los Angeles' Street of Forsaken Men," *Haldeman-Julius Quarterly* 2 (July-September 1928): 78.

119. O. W. Cooley, "The Damned Outfit: A Pair of Apple Pickers Fall into a Haywire Dump," *Haldeman-Julius Quarterly* 2 (April-June 1928): 157–161; hereafter cited in text.

120. Interestingly, Slim, the proselytizing CP protagonist of Mike Pell, *S.S. Utah* (New York: International Publishers, 1933), is initially mistaken for a Wobbly (27–28).

121. Richard Bridgman, *The Colloquial Style in America* (New York: Oxford University Press, 1966), 29; see also 35 and 210.

122. Wixson, *Worker-Writer in America*, 102.

123. Suggs interview, 27 March 1997.

124. See Mike Gold, "Write for Us!," *New Masses* 4 (July 1928): 2, and similarities between Ed Falkowski, "Miners' 'Progress,'" *New Masses* 4 (December 1928): 8, and his "Coal Miners' Children," *New Masses* 4 (October 1929): 6.

125. This quotation appears in Francis Russell, *Tragedy in Dedham: The Sacco-Vanzetti Case* (New York: McGraw-Hill, 1971), 386–388n; and Sinclair, *Boston*, 615. Hoffman, *The Twenties*, 405, erroneously reports that Vanzetti delivered these remarks in a speech to Judge Thayer at sentencing. On this and Strong's own later variations on the remarks, see Francis Russell, "Appendix A," *Sacco and Vanzetti: Case Resolved* (New York: Viking, 1986), 222. See also Bloodworth, *Upton Sinclair*, 166n. Three months after the speech, Mike Gold was arrested during a Sacco and Vanzetti protest demonstration.

Chapter 8. From Black Folk to Working Class

1. James R. Grossman, "The White Man's Union: The Great Migration and the Resonance of Race and Class in Chicago, 1916–1922," in *The Great Migration in Historical Perspective: New Dimensions of Race, Class, and Gender*, ed. Joe William Trotter, Jr. (Bloomington: Indiana University Press, 1991), 85.

2. Neil Fligstein, *Going North: Migration of Blacks and Whites from the South, 1900–1950* (New York: Academic Press, 1981), 135.

3. Jack Kirby Temple, "The Southern Exodus, 1910–1960," *Journal of Southern History* 49, no. 4 (1983): 591.

4. Ronald L. Lewis, *Black Coal Miners in America: Race, Class, and Community Conflict, 1780–1980* (Lexington: University Press of Kentucky, 1987), chap. 4; Eric Arnesen, "Following the Color Line of Labor: Black Workers and Miners in the Labor Movement before 1930," *Radical History Review* 55 (Winter 1993): 68–69.

5. Joe William Trotter, Jr., *Black Milwaukee: The Making of an Industrial Proletariat, 1915–1945* (Urbana: University of Illinois Press, 1985), 47.

6. Jacqueline Jones, *Labor of Love, Labor of Sorrow: Black Women, Work, and the Family from Slavery to the Present* (1985; reprint, New York: Vintage Books, 1986), 208; Darlene Clark Hine, "Black Migration to the Urban Midwest: The Gender Dimension, 1915–1945," in Trotter, *The Great Migration*, 130.

7. Trotter, *Black Milwaukee*, 58.

8. Alain Locke, "The New Negro," in *The New Negro: Voices of the Harlem Renaissance*, ed. Alain Locke (1925; reprint, New York: Touchstone/Simon and Schuster, 1992), 9.

9. August Meier and Elliott Rudwick, *Black Detroit and the Rise of the UAW* (New York: Oxford University Press, 1979), 8.

10. Ibid., 16.

11. Ibid., 5.

12. Locke, "The New Negro," 9.

13. Douglas Wixson, *The Worker-Writer in America: Jack Conroy and the Tradition of Midwestern Literary Radicalism, 1898–1990* (Urbana: University of Illinois Press, 1994), 137. See also the informative chapter 5, "Welfare Capitalism and Black Steelworkers, 1916–1930," in Dennis C. Dickerson, *Out of the Crucible: Black Steelworkers in Western Pennsylvania, 1875–1980* (Albany: State University of New York Press, 1986).

14. Dickerson, *Out of the Crucible,* 117.

15. Wixson, *The Worker-Writer in America,* 136–137. On the employer rationale for racial quotas, see Lizabeth Cohen, *Making a New Deal: Industrial Workers in Chicago, 1919–1939* (Cambridge: Cambridge University Press, 1990), 205. Cohen also discusses the practice of advancing selected blacks to skilled positions as "strike insurance" (205).

16. On Chicago's 1920 population, see Grossman, "The White Man's Union," 85. Stockyards job statistics are in Alma Herbst, *The Negro in the Slaughtering and Meatpacking Industry in Chicago* (Chicago: University of Chicago Press, 1932), xxi. On the black slums of Philadelphia and New York's Harlem, see Gilbert Osofsky, *Harlem: The Making of a Ghetto—Negro New York, 1890–1930*, 2d ed. (1966; reprint, Chicago: Ivan R. Dee, 1996), 140 and chap. 9.

17. Rick Halpern and Roger Horowitz, *Meatpackers: An Oral History of Black Packinghouse Workers and Their Struggle for Racial and Economic Equality* (New York: Twayne, 1996), 4; see also Rick Halpern, *On the Killing Floor: Black and White Workers in Chicago's Packinghouses, 1904–1954* (Urbana: University of Illinois Press, 1987), chap. 3.

18. Jones, *Labor of Love,* 177; Hine, "Black Migration to the Urban Midwest," 139–140; Herbst, *The Negro in the Slaughtering and Meatpacking Industry,* 157.

19. David M. Katzman, *Seven Days a Week: Women and Domestic Service in Industrializing America* (1978; reprint, Urbana: University of Illinois Press, 1981), 76–79.

20. Alice Kessler-Harris, *Out to Work: A History of Wage-Earning Women in the United States* (New York: Oxford University Press, 1982), 238. On Mexicans in meatpacking, see James R. Barrett, *Work and Community in the Jungle: Chicago's Packinghouse Workers, 1894–1922* (Urbana: University of Illinois Press, 1987), 50–51. The bulk of Mexicans were migrant laborers in California, however.

21. Barbara M. Posadas, "The Hierarchy of Color and Psychological Adjustment in an Industrial Environment: Filipinos, the Pullman Company, and the Brotherhood of Sleeping Car Porters," *Labor History* 23 (Summer 1982): 350. A good period source on the job stratification of Mexicans and Filipinos, and one that largely avoids the condescensions of the earlier decade, is *The Proceedings of the National Conference of Social Work, 1929* (Chicago: University of Chicago Press, 1930), 531–538; 573–579. See also Philip S. Foner, *Racism, Dissent, and Asian Americans* (Westport, Conn.: Greenwood Press, 1993), 12, 200; and Ronald Takaki, *A Different Mirror: A History of Multicultural America* (Boston: Little, Brown and Co., 1993), 264–276. On Mexican workers, see Gilbert G. Gonzalez, *Labor and Community: Mexican Citrus Worker Villages in a Southern California County, 1900–1950* (Urbana: Uni-

versity of Illinois Press, 1994), 20, 28–29, 40–42; and Takaki, *A Different Mirror*, chap. 12. See chapter 11 of this book for an exploration of U.S. work fiction on and by Asians and Chicanos, embryonic in the 1920s.

22. A good sampling of titles from the two periodicals appears in Jones, *Labor of Love*, 380n and 387n; and in James R. Grossman, *Land of Hope: Chicago, Black Southerners, and the Great Migration* (Chicago: University of Chicago Press, 1988), 368–369. Migrant correspondence is reprinted in Emmett J. Scott, "Documents: Letters of Negro Migrants, 1916–1918," *Journal of Negro History* 4 (July-October 1919): 290–340, 412–465. Though reflective of wartime job opportunities for blacks, the letters nevertheless sound themes of the postwar era.

23. Jean Toomer, *Cane* (1923; reprint, New York: Liveright/Norton, 1993), 71; hereafter cited in text.

24. Temple, "The Southern Exodus," 591–592.

25. Lewis, *Black Coal Miners in America*, 102.

26. Daniel P. Jordan, "The Mingo War: Labor Violence in the Southern West Virginia Coal Fields, 1919–1922," in *Essays in Southern Labor History*, ed. Gary M. Fink and Merl E. Reed (Westport, Conn.: Greenwood Press, 1976), 119–120; Jacqueline Jones, *The Dispossessed: America's Underclass from the Civil War to the Present* (New York: Basic Books, 1992), 143. Contestations by modern historians over the racial tolerance of the UMW are briefly discussed in Joe William Trotter, Jr., *Coal, Class, and Color: Blacks in Southern West Virginia, 1915–1932* (Urbana: University of Illinois Press, 1990), 263–267. On the poor conditions of black miners in that region, see E. Franklin Frazier, "Open Forum," *Messenger* 6 (November 1924): 362–363.

27. On meatpacking employers like the two giants, Swift and Armour, and their motives for creating interracial workplaces, see Cohen, *Making a New Deal*, 202–203. For a balanced discussion of union recruitment, though one focused on the CIO era, see Rick Halpern and Roger Horowitz, " 'The Strength of the Black Community': African American Workers, Unionism, and the Meatpacking Industry," in Halpern and Horowitz, *Meatpackers*, 1–26. On other Chicago biracial initiatives—by locals of the Janitors' Union, the Hod Carriers, and the ILGWU—see John B. Jentz, "Citizenship, Self-Respect, and Political Power: Chicago's Flat Janitors Trailblaze the Service Employees International Union, 1912–1921," *Labor's Heritage* 9 (Summer 1997): 16.

28. Grossman, "The White Man's Union," passim. On the black organizer, see Halpern, *On the Killing Floor*, 75–76.

29. Jones, *The Dispossessed*, 141–145; Eric Arnesen, "Charting an Independent Course: African-American Railroad Workers in the World War I Era," in *Labor Histories: Class, Politics, and the Working-Class Experience*, ed. Eric Arnesen, Julie Greene, and Bruce Laurie (Urbana: University of Illinois Press, 1998). On black unionism, see Eric Arnesen, "Following the Color Line of Labor: Black Workers and the Labor Movement before 1930," *Radical History Review* 55 (Winter 1993): 53–87 passim. A black repairman and his white apprentice appear briefly in the "1919" chapter section of the leftist Alexander Saxton, *The Great Midland* (1948; reprint, Urbana: University of Illinois Press, 1997), 16. On the Chicago riot and white labor, see William M. Tuttle, Jr., *Race Riot: Chicago in the Red Summer of 1919* (Urbana: University of Illinois Press, 1996), 44, 108–112.

30. William H. Harris, *The Harder We Run: Black Workers since the Civil War* (New York: Oxford University Press, 1982), 50. On sawmills and docks, see Melvyn Dubofsky, *We Shall Be All: A History of the Industrial Workers of the World* (Chicago: Quadrangle Books, 1969), 213, 448.

31. Meier and Rudwick, *Black Detroit*, 14.

32. Ibid., 30. On the minimal participation of blacks in the CP prior to the Depression, see Robin D. G. Kelley, *Hammer and Hoe: Alabama Communists during the Great Depression* (Chapel Hill: University of North Carolina Press, 1990), 25.

33. On McKay's *Liberator* years, his ABB membership, and his visit to Russia, see Wayne F. Cooper: *Claude McKay: Rebel Sojourner in the Harlem Renaissance* (Baton Rouge: Louisiana State University Press, 1987), chap. 6, chap. 5, 43, 175–178.

34. Frank R. Crosswaith, "The Pullman Porters Break All Records" (1926), in *The Black Worker: The Era of Post-War Prosperity and the Great Depression, 1920–1936*, ed. Philip S. Foner and Ronald L. Lewis (Philadelphia: Temple University Press, 1981), 206; Jervis Anderson, *A. Philip Randolph* (New York: Harcourt Brace Jovanovich, 1972) 96; and Philip S. Foner, *American Socialism and Black Americans from the Age of Jackson to World War II* (Westport, Conn.: Greenwood Press, 1977), 339.

35. Trotter, "Introduction," in *The Great Migration*, xi; see also Henry M. McKiven, Jr., *Iron and Steel: Class, Race, and Community in Birmingham, Alabama, 1875–1920* (Chapel Hill: University of North Carolina Press, 1995), chaps. 5–9.

36. Trotter, "Introduction," in *The Great Migration*, xi. See also Farah Jasmine Griffin, *"Who Set You Flowin'?": The African-American Migration Narrative* (New York: Oxford University Press, 1995), 19.

37. Grossman, *Land of Hope*, 224. On the relative radicalism of the *Messenger*, see Foner, *American Socialism*, 287, 295, 307, 311.

38. Crosswaith, "The Pullman Porters," 207.

39. Anderson, *A. Philip Randolph*, 171.

40. Harris, *The Harder We Run*, 59–60. For a possibly autobiographical account of portering in the Progressive years written in dime-novel fashion, see C. Anderson, *A Sleeping Car Porter's Experience* (n.p., 1916).

41. Harris, *The Harder We Run*, 60–61.

42. Griffin, *"Who Set You Flowin',"* 19.

43. Anderson, *A. Philip Randolph*, 159; Edward M. Swift and Charles S. Boyd, "The Pullman Porter Looks at Life," *Psychoanalytic Review* 15 (October 1928): 393–416.

44. Grossman, *Land of Hope*, 110, 74, 224.

45. Wallace Thurman, *The Blacker the Berry* (1929; reprint, New York: Collier/Macmillan, 1970), 210; hereafter cited in text.

46. Qtd. in Anderson, *A. Philip Randolph*, 161.

47. A valuable article on BSCP labor tactics is Frank R. Crosswaith, "Porters Smash a Company Union," *Labor Age* 17 (January 1928): 16.

48. On the "George" stereotype, see Bernard Mergen, "The Pullman Porters: From 'George' to Brotherhood," *South Atlantic Quarterly* 73 (Spring 1974): 224–235.

49. Claude McKay, "A Negro to His Critics," *New York Herald Tribune Books*, 6 March 1932, 1; see Anderson, *A. Philip Randolph*, 146, on McKay's links to the *Messenger*.

50. W.E.B. Du Bois, *Dark Princess: A Romance* (New York: Harcourt, Brace, 1928), 47. For similar condemnations of Pullman racism, see 48, 49, and 78.

51. Jack Santino, *Miles of Smiles, Years of Struggle: Stories of Black Pullman Porters* (Urbana: University of Illinois Press 1989), 120.

52. Philip S. Foner, *Women and the American Labor Movement from World War I to the Present* (New York: Free Press, 1980), 247. M. Melinda Chateauvert, *Marching Together* (Urbana: University of Illinois Press, 1988), addresses the women's auxiliaries of the BSCP and includes material on the maids.

53. Mattie Mae Stafford, "Ode to the Brotherhood," *Messenger* 9 (January 1927): 211. See also Crosswaith, "The Pullman Porters," 206–207.

54. Anderson, *A. Philip Randolph*, 189.

55. Thomas L. Dabney, "The Union in the Dining Car," *Locomotive Engineers Journal* 61 (July 1927): 517.

56. Anderson, *A. Philip Randolph*, 216; Robert W. Dunn, "Pullman 'Company Union' Slavery" (1926), in Foner and Lewis, *The Black Worker*, 210.

57. Dunn, "Pullman 'Company Union' Slavery," 210, 212.

58. A. Philip Randolph, "A New Crowd—A New Negro," *Messenger* 1 (May-June 1919): 27. Cartoons in the journal caricatured anti-union porters as Uncle Tom types. See, for example, *Messenger* 9, no. 3 (1928): 91.

59. Arnold Rampersad, "Introduction," in Locke, *The New Negro*, ix.

60. Wayne F. Cooper, *The Passion of Claude McKay* (New York: Schocken Books, 1973), 28, 222; Nathan Irvin Huggins, "Introduction," in *Voices from the Harlem Renaissance*, ed. Nathan Irvin Huggins (1976; reprint, New York: Oxford University Press, 1995), 8.

61. Meier and Rudwick, *Black Detroit*, 8. See also Paul Kellogg ("The Negro Pioneers," in Locke, *The New Negro*, 271–277), who was considerably more favorable to the black masses than was the Pittsburgh Survey, which he directed, in the Progressive years.

62. David Levering Lewis, "Introduction," in *The Portable Harlem Renaissance Reader*, ed. David Levering Lewis (New York: Penguin Books, 1994), xiii; Locke, "The New Negro," 3, 4, 7.

63. Alain Locke, "The Negro Intellectual," *New York Herald Tribune Books*, 29 May 1928, 12.

64. Lewis, "Introduction," in *The Portable Harlem Renaissance Reader*, xiii. See also Hazel Carby, "Policing the Black Woman's Body in an Urban Context," *Critical Inquiry* 18 (Summer 1992): 747.

65. Willam Stanley Braithwaite, "The Negro in American Literature," in Locke, *The New Negro*, 40; Henry Louis Gates, Jr., *Figures in Black: Words, Signs, and the "Racial" Self* (New York: Oxford University Press 1987), chap. 9. Among the wealth of texts on the cultural importance of the trickster as figure and strategy in the African American oral tradition are Geneva Smitherman, *Talkin' and Testifyin': The Language of Black America* (Boston: Houghton Mifflin, 1980), and Roger D. Abrahams, *Deep Down in the Jungle* (1964; reprint, Chicago: Aldine Publishing, 1969).

66. Tom Lutz, "Introduction," in *These "Colored" United States: African American Essays from the 1920s*, ed. Tom Lutz and Susanna Ashton (New Brunswick, N.J.: Rutgers University Press, 1996), 5.

67. Claude McKay, [review of *Shuffle Along*], *Liberator* 4 (December 1921): 24.

68. McKay, "A Negro to His Critics," 1.

69. Darwin T. Turner, "Introduction," in Toomer, *Cane*, xiv–xv. Biographical data are culled from Chidi Ikonné, *From Du Bois to Van Vechten: The Early New Negro Literature, 1903–1926* (Westport, Conn.: Greenwood Press, 1987), chap. 4.

70. It is instructive to compare Toomer's handling of the flight from southern forced labor to modern industrial society with the friend of the Harlem Renaissance and NAACP personality Walter White's treatment in his unfinished 1929 novel *Blackjack*. For a critique of White's difficulties integrating the new Harlem paid-work plot, see Jon Christian Suggs, " 'Blackjack': Walter White and Modernism in an Unknown Boxing Novel," *Michigan Quarterly Review* 38, no. 4 (Fall 1999): 514–540.

71. For a more optimistic reading of the novel, see Thadious M. Davis, "Race and Region," in *The Columbia History of the American Novel*, ed. Emory Elliott et al. (New York: Columbia University Press, 1991), 418–420.

72. McKay, "A Negro to His Critics," 1.

73. Peter Gottlieb, *Making Their Own Way: Southern Blacks' Migration to Pittsburgh, 1916–1930* (Urbana: University of Illinois Press, 1987), chaps. 2, 3.

74. Quoted in David Levering Lewis, *When Harlem Was in Vogue* (1979; New York: Oxford University Press, 1989), 127. On the novel's reception, see John Chamberlain, "When Spring Comes to Harlem," *New York Times*, 11 March 1928. See also James R. Giles, *Claude McKay* (Boston: Twayne Publishing Co., 1976), 24, and Cooper, *Claude McKay*, 245–248.

75. Anderson, *A. Philip Randolph*, 154.

76. Harris, *The Harder We Run*, 71–72.

77. Claude McKay, "How Black Sees Green and Red," *Liberator* 4 (June 1921): 17–21.

78. Claude McKay, *A Long Way from Home: An Autobiography* (1937; reprint, New York: Harcourt Brace Jovanovich, 1970), 228. Claude McKay, *Home to Harlem* (1928; reprint, Boston: Northeastern University Press, 1987); hereafter cited in text.

79. For a valiant defense of Gold's play as a paean to black preindustrial values, see William J. Maxwell, "The Proletarian as New Negro: Mike Gold's Harlem Renaissance," in *Radical Revisions: Rereading 1930s Culture*, ed. Bill Mullen and Sherry Lee Linkon (Urbana: University of Illinois Press, 1996), 91–119.

80. Eugene O'Neill, *Emperor Jones, Anna Christie, and The Hairy Ape* (1922; reprint, New York: Vintage Books, 1972), 12.

81. Lewis, *When Harlem Was in Vogue*, 228.

82. On subsistence wages tracked by the Labor Department, see Mary Elizabeth Pidgeon, *Women in Florida Industries*, Women's Bureau pamphlet no. 80 (Washington, D.C.: Government Printing Office, 1930), 48–49. On adaptations to domestic service, see Elizabeth Clark-Lewis, *Living In, Living Out: African American Domestics in Washington, D.C.* (Washington, D.C.: Smithsonian Institution Press, 1994).

83. Hine, "Black Migration to the Urban Midwest," 140.

84. Elise Johnson McDougald, "The Task of Negro Womanhood," in Locke, *The New Negro*, 378; Katzman, *Seven Days a Week*, 222; Kessler-Harris, *Out to Work*, 237–238; Lisa M. Fine, *The Souls of the Skyscraper: Female Clerical Workers in Chicago, 1870–1930* (Philadelphia: Temple University Press, 1990), 174.

85. Jean Collier Brown, *The Negro Woman Worker* (Washington, D.C.: Government Printing Office, 1938), 1. On black women professionals, see Gwendolyn Etter-Lewis, *My Soul Is My Own: Oral Narratives of African American Women in the Professions* (New York: Routledge, 1993), although the majority of women profiled began their careers in the 1930s.

86. Carby, "Policing the Black Woman's Body," 741.

87. Ibid. See, too, Adrienne Lash Jones, "Struggle among Saints: African American Women and the YWCA, 1870–1920," in *Men and Women Adrift: The YMCA and the YWCA in the City*, ed. Nina Mjagki and Margaret Spratt (New York: New York University Press, 1997), 171–177.

88. Jones, "Struggle among Saints," 171, 176.

89. Joanne J. Meyerowitz, *Women Adrift: Independent Wage Earners in Chicago, 1880–1930* (Chicago: University of Chicago Press, 1988), 14–15.

90. William I. Thomas, *The Unadjusted Girl* (1923; reprint, Montclair, N.J.: Paterson Smith, 1969), 107–108.

91. Carby, "Policing the Black Woman's Body," 739–740, prefers the term "moral panic." Reflecting a prevalent modern view, Ivan Light places 1920s northern black female prostitution in the "tourist-entertainment industry." See Ivan Light, "The Ethnic Vice Industry, 1880–1944," *American Sociological Review* 42 (June 1977): 472.

92. Daphne Duval Harrison, *Black Pearls: Blues Queens of the 1920s* (New Brunswick, N.J.: Rutgers University Press, 1988), 14, 22, 232. Perhaps it was no accident that one of the best-known blues singers had the red-light name "Chippie" Hill. By the 1930s, when Billie Holiday worked as a prostitute while learning to become a singer, the pattern was set. See Daphne Duval Harrison, "Billie Holiday," in *Black Women in America: An Historical Encyclopedia*, ed. Darlene Clark Hine (Brooklyn, N.Y.: Carlson Publishing, 1993), 565.

93. Jones, *Labor of Love,* 181; Meyerowitz, *Women Adrift,* 40.

94. McDougald, "The Task of Negro Womanhood," 370; Langston Hughes, "Luani of the Jungles," which first appeared in the sole issue of Wallace Thurman's *Fire!!* (1926).

95. Biographical information on Thurman is in Lewis, *When Harlem Was in Vogue,* 193–194, 277–281.

96. Willoughby Cyrus Waterman, *Prostitution and Its Repression in New York City, 1900–1931* (New York: Columbia University Press, 1932), 128.

97. Marita Bonner, "Drab Rambles," in *Frye Street and Environs: The Collected Short Stories of Marita Bonner*, ed. Joyce Flynn and Joyce Stricklin (Boston: Beacon Press, 1987), 98.

98. Richard Wright, "Blueprint for Negro Writing" (1937), in Lewis, *The Portable Harlem Renaissance Reader,* 197. By including the essay, the editor is obviously extending the term "Harlem Renaissance" beyond the traditional confines.

99. Samuel B. Garren, "William Attaway," in *Dictionary of Literary Biography*, vol. 76 (Detroit: Gale Research, 1988), 3–7. See also Richard Yarborough, "Afterword," in William Attaway, *Blood on the Forge* (1941; reprint, New York: Monthly Review Press, 1987), 298–300.

100. John Hope Franklin and Alfred A. Moss, Jr., *From Slavery to Freedom: A History of African Americans*, 7th ed. (New York: Alfred A. Knopf, 1994), 402–403.

101. Alan Wald, "Culture and Commitment: U.S. Communist Writers," in *New Studies in the Politics and Culture of U.S. Communism*, ed. Michael E. Brown et al. (New York: Monthly Review Press, 1993), 296.

102. Ralph Ellison, "Transition," *Negro Quarterly* 1 (Spring 1942): 87–92.

103. The stories appeared in the *New Yorker,* 29 April 1996, 110–115. See also William Grimes, "Treasures under Ralph Ellison's Dining Table," *New York Times*, 18 April 1996, C13.

104. Cary D. Wintz, *Black Culture in the Harlem Renaissance* (College Station: Texas A&M University Press, 1996), chap. 1.

105. Jon-Christian Suggs, *Whispered Consolations: Law and Narrative in African American Life* (Ann Arbor: University of Michigan Press, 2000).

Chapter 9. Heroic at Last

1. Robert S. McElvaine, *The Great Depression: America, 1929–1941* (New York: Times Book Co./Random House, 1984), 297.

2. Although the Bonus March was an isolated event, it was of a piece with the Unemployed Councils. See Lizabeth Cohen, *Making a New Deal: Industrial Workers in Chicago, 1919–1939* (New York: Cambridge University Press, 1990), 308–309; Ronald L. Filippelli, "California Farmworkers' Strikes of 1933," in *Labor Conflict in the United States: An Encyclopedia*, ed. Ronald L. Filippelli (New York: Garland, 1990), 79–83. A good brief discussion of the STFU, including black and white cotton pickers' strikes, is in William H. Harris, *The Harder We Run: Black Workers since the Civil War* (New York: Oxford University Press, 1982), 102–103. See also H. L. Mitchell,

Roll the Union On: A Pictorial History of the Southern Tenant Farmers' Union (Chicago: Charles H. Kerr, 1987).

3. On the cultural significance of the Harlan County, Kentucky, strike, see Michael Denning, *The Cultural Front: The Laboring of American Culture in the Twentieth Century* (London: Verso, 1996), 264. On ACW militance, see Steven Fraser, *Labor Will Rule: Sidney Hillman and the Rise of American Labor* (Ithaca, N.Y.: Cornell University Press, 1991), 255. On the dock strike, see Bruce Nelson, *Workers on the Waterfront: Seamen, Longshoremen, and Unionism in the 1930s* (Urbana: University of Illinois Press, 1990), chap. 5. On the Teamsters, see Elizabeth Faue, *Community of Suffering and Struggle: Women, Men, and the Labor Movement in Minneapolis, 1915–1945* (Chapel Hill: University of North Carolina Press, 1991), chaps. 4–6. On textile protests, see John A. Salmond, *Gastonia 1929: The Story of the Loray Mill Strike* (Chapel Hill: University of North Carolina Press, 1995), 181–185.

4. For a Party foot soldier's account of organizing among such groups, see Steve Nelson, James R. Barrett, and Rob Ruck, *Steve Nelson, American Radical* (Pittsburgh: University of Pittsburgh Press, 1981), chap. 6.

5. Akron was the first important CIO strike. See *How the Rubber Workers Won* (Washington, D.C.: Committee for Industrial Organization, 1936), and McElvaine, *The Great Depression*, 290. On related CIO organizing activities and strikes, see "C.I.O. Begins Drive in Textiles Today," *New York Times*, 19 March 1937, 3; Sydney Fine, *Sit-Down: The General Motors Strike of 1936–1937* (Ann Arbor: University of Michigan Press, 1969), and the novel *Little Steel* (1938) by Upton Sinclair.

6. "Congress of Industrial Organizations," in *Labor Unions*, ed. Gary M. Fink (Westport, Conn.: Greenwood Press, 1977), 65–71; McElvaine, *The Great Depression*, 258–259. On NIRA, section 7(a), see also Cohen, *Making a New Deal*, 302.

7. For the parameters of the debate, see James Green, "Working-Class Militancy in the Great Depression," *Radical America* 6 (November-December 1972): 1–36. The 7 percent statistic is in Melvyn Dubofsky, " 'Not So 'Turbulent Years': Another Look at the American 1930s," *Amerikastudien* 24, no. 1 (1980): 5. See also Sidney Verba, "Unemployment, Class Consciousness, and Radical Politics: What Didn't Happen in the Thirties," *Journal of Politics* 39 (1977): 292–323.

8. Julia Stein, "Tangled Threads: Two Novels about Women in the Textile Trades," *Women's Studies Quarterly* 26, nos. 1/2 (Spring/Summer 1998): 99.

9. On such literary homage, see Martin Russak, "Jack London: America's First Proletarian Writer," *New Masses* 4 (January 1929): 13; on 1930s writers' "left-wing naturalism," see Alfred Kazin, *On Native Grounds* (1942; reprint, Garden City, N.Y.: Doubleday/Anchor Books, 1956), 296. For a passage in Michael Gold's *Jews without Money* (1930) (1935; reprint, New York: Carroll and Graf Publishers 1996) that could have been written by Crane, see "The East Side, for children, was a world plunged in eternal war" (42); hereafter cited in text.

10. Tillie Olsen, "The Strike" [1934], reprinted in *Calling Home: Working-Class Women's Writings—An Anthology*, ed. Janet Zandy (New Brunswick, N.J.: Rutgers University Press, 1990), 275.

11. Douglas Wixson, *Worker-Writer in America: Jack Conroy and the Tradition of Midwestern Literary Radicalism, 1898–1990* (Urbana: University of Illinois Press, 1994), 391. On Le Sueur's WPA work, for instance, see biographical data in Neala Schleuning Yount, " 'America: Song We Sang without Knowing': Meridel Le Sueur's America" (Ph.D. diss., University of Minnesota, 1978), 28–34.

12. In another characteristic period endeavor, he taught for a time at the radical Brookwood, a workers' university in upstate New York with its own Labor Players. Denning, *The Cultural Front*, 71, 73. On the drama group at Brookwood and else-

where, see Colette A. Hyman, *Staging Strikes: Workers' Theatre and the American Labor Movement* (Philadelphia: Temple University Press, 1997).

13. Jon-Christian Suggs, "Editorial Introduction," in *American Proletarian Culture: The Twenties and the Thirties*, Dictionary of Literary Biography Documentary Series, vol. 11, ed. Jon-Christian Suggs (Detroit: Gale Research, 1993), 173; see also Laura Hapke, *Daughters of the Great Depression: Women, Work, and Fiction in the American 1930s* (Athens: University of Georgia Press, 1995), 111–112.

14. Mary Heaton Vorse, *Rebel Pen: The Writings of Mary Heaton Vorse*, ed. Dee Garrison (New York: Monthly Review Press, 1985), 185.

15. [Edwin Seaver], "Call for an American Writers' Congress," *New Masses* 14 (January-March 1935): 20. See also his "The Proletarian Novel," in *American Writers' Congress*, ed. Henry Hart (New York: International Publishers, 1935), 101.

16. Harold Strauss, "Realism in the Proletarian Novel," *Yale Review* 28, no. 2 (1938): 374.

17. David P. Peeler, *Hope among Us Yet: Social Criticism and Social Solace in Depression America* (Athens: University of Georgia Press, 1987), 155.

18. For representative vilification of the leftist writer, often by disillusioned leftists themselves, in the 1930s, see James T. Farrell, *A Note on Literary Criticism* (New York: Vanguard Press, 1936), passim. A good assessment of modern critical disdain for 1930s writers in general, and Gold in particular, is Jack Salzman, "Not M. Gorky but Still Mike Gold," *Nation*, 10 July 1972, 8. See also Alfred Kazin, "Introduction," in Gold, *Jews without Money*, who calls Gold a "primitive" (3).

19. Carla Cappetti, *Writing Chicago: Modernism, Ethnography, and the Novel* (New York: Columbia University Press, 1993), 2–3.

20. Salzman, "Not M. Gorky but Still Mike Gold," 24.

21. There are divisions within this group, though, on the CP's feminism. For a severe critique of the Party, see Paula Rabinowitz, "Women and U.S. Literary Radicalism," in *Writing Red: An Anthology of American Women Writers, 1930–1940*, ed. Charlotte Nekola and Paula Rabinowitz (New York: Feminist Press, 1987), 1–19. For a more generous view, see Barbara Foley, *Radical Representations: Politics and Form in U.S. Proletarian Fiction, 1929–1941* (Durham, N.C.: Duke University Press, 1993).

22. Paul Lauter, "American Proletarianism," in *The Columbia History of the American Novel*, ed. Emory Elliott et al. (New York: Columbia University Press, 1991), 335.

23. Foley, *Radical Representations*, passim; Alan M. Wald, "The 1930s Left in U.S. Literature Reconsidered," in *Radical Revisions: Rereading 1930s Culture*, ed. Bill Mullen and Sherry Lee Linkon (Urbana: University of Illinois Press, 1996), 21–22.

24. Denning, *The Cultural Front*, passim; Marcus Klein, *Foreigners: The Making of American Literature, 1900–1940* (Chicago: University of Chicago Press, 1981), 92.

25. For a good discussion of mentor figures, see Foley, *Radical Representations*, 373–376.

26. Mike Gold, "Write for Us!" *New Masses* 4 (July 1928): 2.

27. Eric Homberger, *American Writers and Radical Politics, 1900–39: Equivocal Commitments* (New York: St. Martin's Press, 1986), 126.

28. Peeler, *Hope among Us Yet*, 164.

29. H. H. Lewis, "Memoirs of a Dishwasher," *New Masses* 4 (February 1929): 7; Joseph Kalar, "A Miner's Kid," *New Masses* 5 (February 1930): 6. See also Ed Falkowski, "Miners' Progress," *New Masses* 4 (December 1928): 8. A good discussion of these early worker-writers is in Wixson, *Worker-Writer in America*, 190–209.

30. Colman's retrospective *Lumber* [1930], significantly, recounts IWW lumber-industry struggles in Washington State rather than their legacy for 1929.

31. Mike Gold, "The Charkov Conference of Revolutionary Writers," *New Masses* 6 (February 1931): 6–8. See also Homberger, *American Writers and Radical Politics,* chap. 5. On the revolutionism of the Third Period, see Foley, *Radical Representations*, 125–128. On Conroy's "Hoover City," see Wixson, *Worker-Writer in America,* 232.

32. Mike Gold, [review of *Shanty Irish*], *New Masses* 4 (February 1929): 26.

33. For a complete listing of these *New Masses* pieces, see Richard Tuerk, "*Jews without Money* as a Work of Art," *Studies in American Jewish Literature* 7, no. 1 (1988): 77n, 78.

34. Michael Folsom, "Introduction," in *Mike Gold: A Literary Anthology*, ed. Michael Folsom (New York: International Publishers, 1972), 15.

35. Leonard Ehrlich, "*Jews without Money*," *Saturday Review of Literature* 6 (19 April 1930): 944.

36. Daniel Aaron, "Introduction," in *The Disinherited* (New York: Hill and Wang, 1963), viii.

37. Mike Gold, "A Proletarian Novel?" *New Republic*, 4 June 1930, 74.

38. Folsom, "Introduction," in *Mike Gold*, 11.

39. For a good summation of criticism of the ending, see Tuerk, "*Jews without Money*," 77–78.

40. Advertisement for Camp Nitgedaiget, *Daily Worker* [whose slogan was "America's Only Working Class Daily Newspaper"], 20 September 1934, 3.

41. Wixson, *Worker-Writer in America*, 18–22, 66–77.

42. In "High Bridge," an April 1931 *New Masses* sketch later revised for inclusion in the novel, Conroy's Larry character had been the older and wiser one.

43. Jack Conroy, *The Disinherited* (1933; reprint, Columbia: University of Missouri Press, 1991), 190–191; hereafter cited in text.

44. I am indebted to Janet Casey for this observation.

45. The "bottom dogs" subgenre took its name from Edward Dahlberg's 1930 watershed novel of that name. Its best practitioners were Edward Anderson (*Hungry Men*), Nelson Algren (*Somebody in Boots*), and Tom Kromer (*Waiting for Nothing*), authors of post-Conroy works appearing in 1935.

46. [Edwin Seaver], "Call for an American Writers' Congress." Conroy's reception is (somewhat angrily) detailed in Wixson, *Worker-Writer in America*, 389. See also Foley, *Radical Representations*, 125–128.

47. Isidor Schneider, *From the Kingdom of Necessity* (New York: G. P. Putnam's, 1935), 450, 25. Even Henry Roth's Freudian *Call It Sleep* (1934) views the father figure with a kind of terrified scorn.

48. Letter from Janet Casey to author, 10 May 1999. I am indebted to her for this observation.

49. Rosalyn Fraad Baxandall, "The God That Flourished, an American Hero," *Radical History Review* 28–30 (1984): 409.

50. Foley, *Radical Representations*, 87.

51. Michael E. Staub, *Voices of Persuasion: Politics of Representation in 1930s America* (New York: Cambridge University Press, 1994), chap. 5.

52. The pro-CP novelist Ruth McKenney covered the important Akron Rubber Strike. See Ruth McKenney, *Industrial Valley* (1939; reprint, Ithaca, N.Y.: ILR Press, 1992), 376; hereafter cited in text. On its period reception, see, for instance, [review of *Industrial Valley*], *New York Times*, 5 March 1939, 14; Daniel Aaron, [review of *Industrial Valley*], *Books*, 19 February 1939, 6.

53. For an excellent account of the conflicts at Akron, see Jeremy Brecher, *Strike!*, rev. ed. (Boston: South End Press, 1997), 193–212.

54. Ruth McKenney, "Uneasy City," *New Yorker*, 19 December 1936, 83.

55. John Bodnar, *Workers' World: Kinship, Community, and Protest in an Industrial Society, 1900–1940* (Baltimore: Johns Hopkins University Press, 1982), 139.

56. Thomas Bell, *Out of This Furnace* (1941; reprint, Pittsburgh: University of Pittsburgh Press, 1976), 195–196; hereafter cited in text.

57. Paula Rabinowitz, *Labor and Desire: Women's Revolutionary Fiction in Depression America* (Chapel Hill: University of North Carolina Press, 1991), 69.

58. Barbara Foley, "Women and the Left in the 1930s," *American Literary History* 2 (Spring 1990): 163.

59. Amy Godine, "Notes toward a Reappraisal of Depression Literature," *Prospects* 5 (1979): 212.

60. Elizabeth Gurley Flynn, "Housewives—Our Country's Heroines," *People's Daily World* [formerly *Daily Worker*], 8 January 1939, 9.

61. Edward Newhouse, *This Is Your Day* (1937; reprint, New York: AMS Press, 1977), 39.

62. Marleen Barr, "Tillie Olsen," *Dictionary of Literary Biography*, vol. 28, ed. Daniel Walden, vol. 28 (Detroit: Gale Research, 1984), 197.

63. See Tillie Olsen, "General Notes for *Yonnondio*," folder 13, Berg Collection, New York Public Library.

64. Mickey Pearlman and Abby Werlock, *Tillie Olsen* (Boston: Twayne, 1991), 51.

65. Susan Porter Benson, "Women, Work, and the Family Economy: Industrial Homework in Rhode Island," in *Homework: Historical and Contemporary Perspectives on Paid Labor at Home*, ed. Eileen Boris and Cynthia R. Daniels (Urbana: University of Illinois Press, 1989), 71; Elsa Jane Dixler, "The Woman Question: Women and the American Communist Party, 1929–1941" (Ph.D. diss., Yale University, 1974), 129; Annie Gottlieb, "*Yonnondio*: From the Thirties," *New York Times Book Review*, 31 March 1974, 5.

66. Meridel Le Sueur, *Crusaders* (New York: Blue Heron Press, 1955), 39.

67. Agnes Smedley, *Daughter of Earth* (1929; reprint, Old Westbury, N.Y.: Feminist Press, 1987); hereafter cited in text.

68. For biographical data on Smedley, I am indebted to Janice R. MacKinnon and Stephen R. MacKinnon, *Agnes Smedley: The Life and Times of an American Radical* (Berkeley: University of California Press, 1988), chaps. 1–6.

69. Qtd. in Jacqueline Dowd Hall et al., *Like a Family: The Making of a Southern Cotton Mill World* (Chapel Hill: University of North Carolina Press, 1987), 18.

70. As is often the case in estimates of numbers of strikers, one source, in this case *The Encyclopedia of the American Left,* ed. Mari Jo Buhle, Paul Buhle, and Dan Georgakas (New York: Garland, 1990), 255, says that Manville-Jenckes employed thirty-five hundred. Another source, Draper, gives two thousand (14). Theodore Draper, "Gastonia Revisited," *Social Research* 38 (Spring 1971). Regarding the percentage of women strikers, most sources are mute, although Foner says they were in the majority (232). Philip S. Foner, *Women and the American Labor Movement from World War I to the Present* (New York: Free Press, 1980).

71. A front-page photo appears under the headline "Jailing a Woman Striker in Gastonia Strike Zone," with a caption about rough handling by a deputy-thug (*Daily Worker*, 12 April 1929). Another photo, on the 8 April front page, shows "one of the militant women textile workers in Gastonia, North Carolina, wresting a gun from a National Guardsman." Page 4 of the 15 April issue carries the headline "Gastonia Mill Girl Was Paid $20 since Christmas"; page 6 reprints a poem from Christene Patton, a "young Loray striker."

72. Dixler, "The Woman Question," 124.

73. Fred Beal, *Proletarian Journey* (New York: Hilman-Curl, 1937), 159.

74. See Hapke, *Daughters of the Great Depression*, chap. 5.

75. Dorothy Myra Page, *Gathering Storm: A Study of the Black Belt* (New York: International Publishers, 1932), 321; hereafter cited in text.

76. Mary E. Frederickson, "Heroines and Girl Strikers: Gender Issues and Organized Labor in the Twentieth-Century American South," in *Organized Labor in the Twentieth-Century South*, ed. Robert H. Zieger (Knoxville: University of Tennessee Press, 1991), 161.

77. Qtd. in *Hard Times Cotton Mill Girls: Personal Histories of Womanhood and Poverty in the South*, ed. Victoria Byerly (Ithaca, N.Y.: ILR Press, 1986), 76.

78. Richard Wright, "How 'Bigger' Was Born," "Introduction," in Richard Wright, *Native Son* (1940; reprint, New York: Harper and Row, 1989), xx; hereafter cited in text. For the shocked but still positive reception, see, for instance, [review of *Native Son*], *New York Times*, 8 March 1940, 2; Margaret Marshall, [review of *Native Son*], *Nation* 150 (16 March 1940): 367; and Milton Rugoff, "*Native Son*," *Books*, 3 March 1949, 5.

79. Wixson, *Worker-Writer in America*, 300.

80. A good brief account of Wright is in Constance Webb, "Richard Wright," in Buhle, Buhle, and Georgakas, *The Encyclopedia of the American Left*, 860–861. See also Ralph Ellison, "Remembering Richard Wright," *Delta* 18 (April 1984): 1–3. Socialism, it should be noted, was no alternative. Writes Foner, "There was nothing in the 1934 Socialist party election platform on the Negro" (342). Philips S. Foner, *American Socialism and Black Americans from the Age of Jackson to World War II* (Westport, Conn.: Greenwood Press, 1977).

81. Although Wright includes his boy's club job in "How 'Bigger' Was Born" (xxvi), on his relief stint, see Edward D. Clark, "Richard Wright," in *Afro-American Writers, 1940–1955*, ed. Trudier Harris (Detroit: Gale Research, 1988), 202. On portering, see Webb, "Richard Wright," 860, and on the stockyards, see Michael Fabre, *The Unfinished Quest of Richard Wright* (Urbana: University of Illinois Press, 1993), 133.

82. Richard Wright," Introduction" in J. G. St. Clair Drake and Horace A. Cayton, *Black Metropolis: A Study of Negro Life in a Northern City*, rev. ed. (1945; reprint, Chicago: University of Chicago Press, 1993), xviii.

83. Cheryl Lynn Greenberg, *Or Does It Explode?: Black Harlem in the Great Depression* (New York: Oxford University Press, 1991), 154, 163; Cohen, *Making a New Deal*, 512, 220, 279, 294. For a highly critical account of the New Deal and African Americans, see Jill S. Quadagno, *The Color of Welfare: How Racism Undermined the War on Poverty* (New York: Oxford University Press, 1994).

84. Harris, *The Harder We Run*, 104–106; Jacqueline Jones, *The Dispossessed: America's Underclasses from the Civil War to the Present* (New York: Basic Books, 1992), 105, 187, 222.

85. A telling study is Roger D. Horowitz, *"Negro and White, Unite and Fight!": A Social History of Industrial Unionism in Meatpacking, 1930–1990* (Urbana: University of Illinois Press, 1997), 115.

86. August Meier and Elliott Rudwick, *Black Detroit and the Rise of the UAW* (New York: Oxford University Press, 1979), 34–35. Much more progress in integrating auto unions, it should be noted, occurred in the early 1940s. See Ibid., chap. 2.

87. John Hope Franklin and Alfred A. Moss Jr., *From Slavery to Freedom: A History of African Americans*, 7th ed. (New York: Alfred A. Knopf, 1994), 404, 403.

88. Nelson, Barrett, and Ruck, *Steve Nelson*, 159.

89. Franklin and Moss, *From Slavery to Freedom*, 382, 402.

90. James T. Farrell, *The Young Manhood of Studs Lonigan* [1932], in *Studs Lonigan: A Trilogy* (New York: Vanguard Press, 1935), 331.

91. Richard Wright, "Between Laughter and Tears," *New Masses* 22 (5 October 1937): 25.

92. Cappetti, *Writing Chicago*, 189. A decade before, chronicling his own early years in the autobiographical novel *Not without Laughter* (1930), Langston Hughes wrote of a mother-headed household constricted by poor work and conditions that he went to Chicago to escape. But in Hughes, the city that defeats Bigger and his family is a testament to migrant family unity and economic optimism.

93. John Steinbeck, *Working Days: The Journals of "The Grapes of Wrath," 1938–1941*, ed. Robert DeMott (New York: Penguin Books, 1989), 36.

94. Jay Parini, *John Steinbeck: A Biography* (New York: Henry Holt and Co., 1995), 165; Steinbeck, *Working Days*, 42.

95. John Steinbeck, *The Grapes of Wrath* (1939; reprint, New York: Penguin Books, 1976); hereafter cited in text. The Joads are further inspired by a communitarian government camp for migrant families, even though they always prefer to help themselves rather than be helped. Steinbeck thus realized his goal "to make the people live" by empowering a collective group of Okie characters who also represent his populist philosophy. See John Steinbeck, *Working Days*, 38–39.

96. Peeler, *Hope among Us Yet*, 164.

97. Jones, in *The Dispossessed*, remarks that whereas blacks embraced the North, whites headed to the West Coast (219). On the Klan's influence in Dust Bowl regions, see Harris, *The Harder We Run*, 20–21.

98. For the literary dangers of such a racial vision, see Sean McCann, "Constructing Race Williams: The Klan and the Making of Hard-Boiled Crime Fiction," *American Quarterly* 49 (December 1977): 711.

99. For the Salinas workers, see the solid article on this still underresearched subject by Robert G. Lee, "The Hidden World of Asian Immigrant Radicalism," in *The Immigrant Left in the United States*, ed. Paul Buhle and Dan Georgakas (Albany: State University of New York Press, 1996), 280.

100. See Foley, *Radical Representations*, 412–414, and Jon-Christian Suggs, "Introduction," in Clara Weatherwax, *Marching! Marching!* (1935; reprint, Detroit: Omnigraphics, 1990), iii–xliv.

101. Steinbeck, *Their Blood Is Strong* (San Francisco: Simon J. Lubin Society, 1938), 32, 31; Robert DeMott, "Notes," *Working Days*, 149. On prejudice against the Filipino presence, particularly in the harvest fields of California, see Kevin Starr, *Endangered Dreams: The Great Depression in California* (New York: Oxford University Press, 1996), 63–64.

102. Starr, *Endangered Dreams*, 231.

103. Camille Guerin-Gonzales, *Mexican Workers and American Dreams: Immigration, Repatriation, and California Farm Labor, 1900–1939* (New Brunswick, N.J.: Rutgers University Press, 1994), 124–128. See also Vicki L. Ruiz, *Cannery Women, Cannery Lives: Mexican Women, Unionization, and the California Food Processing Industry, 1930–1950* (Albuquerque: University of New Mexico Press, 1987), 8, 45, and chap. 3.

104. For the argument that Native Americans regained some pride in the Wild West shows, see L. G. Moses, *Wild West Shows and the Images of American Indians, 1883–1933* (Albuquerque: University of New Mexico Press, 1997). A more convincing portrait of Indians as workers is in Randy Kennedy, "Mohawk Memories: An Indian Community Flourished and Faded in a Section of Brooklyn," *New York Times,*

28 December 1996, 29, 33. See also Joseph Mitchell, "The Mohawks in High Steel" [1949], in Mitchell, *Up in the Old Hotel and Other Stories* (New York: Pantheon Books, 1992), 179.

105. Kim Strosnider, " 'White Man's Medicine': Imposing Western Values on the Navajo," *Chronicle of Higher Education* (16 January 1998): A10.

106. Arnold B. Armstrong, *Parched Earth* (New York: Macmillan, 1934), 17.

107. Foley, *Radical Representations*, 139, 131–138.

108. Ibid., 239.

Chapter 10. What Was Your Crime?

1. The cold war lasted officially from 1945 to 1989, but for the purposes of labor fiction and U.S. culture, the most potent anti-Soviet period was from 1945 to the early 1960s. By the 1960s and 1970s, wrote the lifelong socialist Irving Howe, "we now began to think that the years of conservative doldrums were coming to an end." "Introduction," to Michael Harrington, *The Other America: Poverty in the United States* (1962; reprint, New York: Collier/Macmillan, 1993), v. On Taft-Hartley's anti-communism, see R. Alton Lee, *Truman and Taft-Hartley* (Lexington: University Press of Kentucky, 1966). Although Truman unsuccessfully opposed the act, he was a committed anticommunist. For a wealth of sources about labor in the Taft-Hartley years, see David M. Oshinsky, *Senator Joseph McCarthy and the American Labor Movement* (Madison: University of Wisconsin Press, 1976), chap. 5. In a 1998 talk, Ellen Schrecker observed that the prime target of red-hunters was labor. Ellen Schrecker, Tamiment Library talk on *Many Are the Crimes* [by Ellen Schrecker], New York University, 28 October 1998.

2. The committee had been in existence since 1938. Ellen W. Schrecker, "McCarthyism and the Labor Movement: The Role of the State," in *The CIO's Left-Led Unions*, ed. Steve Rosswurm (New Brunswick, N.J.: Rutgers University Press, 1992), 139. In the late 1940s, the old Rapp-Coudert Committee, which had gone red-hunting in schools, was disbanded. In the early 1950s, a revivified HUAC was just gathering steam in engineering a new "red scare." The debate on the threat posed to national security by fellow travelers still rages. The orders-from-Moscow theorists include Harvey Klehr, John Earl Haynes, and Kyrill Anderson, "Introduction," in *The Soviet World of American Communism* (New Haven: Yale University Press, 1998). Concise rebuttals are in Alan Wald, "Culture and Commitment: U.S. Communist Writers Reconsidered," in *New Studies in the Politics and Culture of U.S. Communism*, ed. Michael E. Brown et al. (New York: Monthly Review Press, 1993), 283–284; and Julia Dietrich, *The Old Left in History and Literature* (New York: Twayne Publishers, 1996), 159–161.

3. U.S. House of Representatives, Special Committee on Un-American Activities, testimony of Jay Lovestone, *Investigation of Un-American Propaganda in the United States: Hearing*, vol. 11 (Washington, D.C.: Government Printing Office, 1940), 7097.

4. *Who Built America?: Working People and the Nation's Economy, Politics, Culture, and Society*, vol. 2, ed. Joshua Freeman et al. (New York: Pantheon, 1992), 492.

5. Historians continue to disagree about the collective bargaining power inscribed in workplace contractualism. David Brody, *In Labor's Cause: Main Themes on the History of the American Worker* (New York: Oxford University Press, 1993), 221, sees empowerment. The contrary argument is in George Lipsitz, *Rainbow at Midnight: Labor and Culture in the 1940s* (Urbana: University of Illinois Press, 1981), 158. An excellent discussion of the strengths and weaknesses of Reuther's bargaining

methods is in Nelson Lichtenstein, *The Most Dangerous Man in Detroit: Walter Reuther and the Fate of American Labor* (New York: Basic Books, 1995), chap. 12.

6. Lipsitz, *Rainbow at Midnight*, 158. Lichtenstein (*The Most Dangerous Man in Detroit*, 50) makes a good case for the conservatism of CIO leaders, who "sought to channel working-class militancy into a stable and responsible unionism rooted in the AFL tradition" in "defending the No-Strike pledge."

7. David Montgomery, "Introduction," in K. B. Gilden, *Between the Hills and the Sea* (1971; reprint, Urbana: University of Illinois Press, 1989), xii.

8. The "affluent worker" phrase is in David Brody, *Workers in Industrial America: Essays on the Twentieth-Century Struggle*, 2d ed. (New York: Oxford University Press, 1993), 176. For fine oral histories of the halfway measures toward the integration of heavy industry prior to the civil rights movement, see John Hinshaw, "Perceiving Racism: Homestead from Depression to Deindustrialization," *Pennsylvania History* 63 (Winter 1966): 17–33. The continuity of Jim Crow policies in crucial industries was mirrored in the segregation policy of the wartime military.

9. J. G. St. Clair Drake, "The Negro in Chicago," *Sociology of Education* 17 (January 1944): 266–271. Blacks "made their feelings known" (266).

10. Quintard Taylor, "The Great Migration: The Afro-American Communities of Seattle and Portland during the 1940s," *Arizona and the West* 23 (Summer 1981): 126.

11. Harvard Sitkoff, "Racial Militancy and Interracial Violence in the Second World War," *Journal of American History* 58 (December 1971): 681. For a CP perspective on increased biracialism in the consistently leftist Marine Workers' Industrial Union's California locals, see Bill Bailey, *The Kid from Hoboken: An Autobiography* (San Francisco: Smyrna Press, 1993), 416.

12. With the Left in decline, black leftists were ejected from their jobs along with activist whites. They were segregated in "colored" locals, and particularly discriminated against in hiring. See Colin Davis, " 'All I Got's a Hook': New York Longshoremen and the 1948 Dock Strike," in *Waterfront Workers: New Perspectives on Race and Class*, ed. Calvin Winslow (Urbana: University of Illinois Press, 1998), 133. On black leftists' treatment by the CIO, see Harry Haywood, *Black Bolshevik: Autobiography of an Afro-American Communist* (Chicago: Liberator Press, 1978), 566–567, and Phillip Bonosky, "The Story of Ben Carreathers," *Masses and Mainstream* (July 1953): 34–44.

13. Montgomery, "Introduction," in Gilden, *Between the Hills and the Sea*, xvi n. On wartime and postwar Mexican labor in the United States, see Juan Gomez-Quinones, *Mexican American Labor, 1790–1990* (Albuquerque: University of New Mexico Press, 1994), 157–159. See also James R. Green, *The World of the Worker: Labor in Twentieth-Century America* (New York: Hill and Wang, 1980), 211.

14. Dominic J. Capeci, Jr., "Introduction," in *Detroit and the "Good War": The World War II Letters of Mayor Edward Jeffries and Friends,* ed. Dominic J. Capeci, Jr. (Lexington: University Press of Kentucky, 1996), 14–15, 29. For a less sanguine description by a Kentucky woman in a Chicago aircraft factory, see "Peggy Terry," in *"The Good War": An Oral History of World War II*, comp. Studs Terkel (New York: Ballantine Books, 1984), 105–110.

15. William H. Chafe, "World War II as a Pivotal Experience for American Women," in *Women and War: The Changing Status of American Women from the 1930s to the 1950s*, ed. Maria Diedrich and Dorothea Fischer-Hornung (New York: Berg-St. Martin's, 1990), 23.

16. Less than three million women were in unions by 1954. See Susan Estabrook Kennedy, *If All We Did Was to Weep at Home: A History of White Working-*

Class Women in America (Bloomington: Indiana University Press, 1979), 213–214. See also Alice Kessler-Harris, *Out to Work: A History of Wage-Earning Women in the United States* (New York: Oxford University Press, 1982), 300–311.

17. Nancy Gabin, " 'They Have Placed a Penalty on Womanhood': The Protest Actions of Women Auto Workers in Detroit-Area UAW Locals, 1945–1947," *Feminist Studies* 8, no. 2 (Summer 1982): 373–374.

18. In occupations such as New York City garment work, they did walk out. See the discussion of the women's militance in John C. Walter, "Frank R. Crosswaith and Labor Unionization in Harlem, 1939–1945," *Afro-Americans in New York Life and History* 7 (July 1983): 47–48.

19. Chester Himes's *If He Hollers,* published in 1945, was reissued only two years later; white leftists included Alexander Saxton, author of the interracial shipyard novel *Bright Web in the Darkness* (1958).

20. Qtd. in Nancy F. Gabin, *Feminism in the Labor Movement: Women and the United Auto Workers, 1935–1975* (Ithaca, N.Y.: Cornell University Press, 1990), 155.

21. On the strike wave of 1945–1946, see Lipsitz, *Rainbow at Midnight*, 105 and chap. 4. A good discussion of the ideological bind of the UAW, dedicated to liberalism but fenced off from it by government and management, is in Kevin Boyle, *The UAW and the Heyday of American Liberalism, 1945–1968* (Ithaca, N.Y.: Cornell University Press, 1995).

22. Qtd. in Montgomery, "Introduction," in Gilden, *Between the Hills and the Sea*, xviii.

23. Harvey Swados, "The Myth of the Happy Worker," in Harvey Swados, *On the Line* (1957; reprint, Urbana: University of Illinois Press, 1990), 235.

24. Douglas Wixson, *The Worker-Writer in America: Jack Conroy and the Tradition of Midwestern Literary Radicalism, 1898–1990* (Urbana: University of Illinois Press, 1994), 459; Freeman et al., *Who Built America?*, vol. 2, 501–502. I am indebted to Phillip Bonosky for the information on Conroy's no-byline review of his *Burning Valley*. Phillip Bonosky, interview with the author, New York City, 23 July 1998.

25. Griffin Fariello, *Red Scare: Memories of the American Inquisition—An Oral History* (New York: Avon Books, 1995), 144.

26. For the information about Conroy's literary erasure and the Masses and Mainstream Press in the 1950s, I am again indebted to Phillip Bonosky, interview, 23 July 1998.

27. A fine discussion of the crackdown on artists, writers, and other cultural workers is Jane De Hart Mathews, "Art and Politics in Cold War America," *American Historical Review* 81 (October 1976): 762–787. For a much-consulted period directory that included artists and writers in broadcasting, see *Red Channels: The Report of Communist Influence in Radio and Television* (New York: American Business Consultants, 1950). A recent memoir is Walter Bernstein, *Inside Out: A Memoir* (New York: Alfred A. Knopf, 1998).

28. Fariello, *Red Scare*, 289 (John Sanford interview).

29. Alan Wald, "Introduction," in Phillip Bonosky, *Burning Valley* (1953; reprint, Urbana: University of Illinois Press, 1998). Wald lists many, but not Arnow, among the attenuated (ix) and does consider Norman Mailer "heterodox" (xxx).

30. Jon-Christian Suggs, "The Proletarian Novel," *Dictionary of Literary Biography*, vol. 9, pt. 3, ed. James J. Martine (Detroit: Gale Research, 1981), 245. Blake ends her study in 1945. See Fay M. Blake, *The Strike in the American Novel* (Metuchen, N.J.: Scarecrow Press, 1972). Rideout found that radical novels were still in print at the time his own book appeared in 1956. But in a 1982 preface to the reissued edition,

he writes that the post-1950 novels of radicals "continued to come in a trickle and not in a stream." Walter B. Rideout, *The Radical Novel in the United States, 1900–1954* (1956; reprint, New York: Columbia University Press, 1982), xiv. More typical of more recent critical approaches is a study of cold war fiction that omits any mention of labor texts and terms Mailer a "revisionist liberal." Thomas Hill Schaub, Preface, in *American Fiction in the Cold War* (Madison: University of Wisconsin Press, 1991), vii.

31. For an example of "broadening" theorists, see Michael Denning, *The Cultural Front: The Laboring of American Culture in the Twentieth Century* (New York: Verso, 1996), 222–228.

32. Alan Filreis, "Introduction," in Ira Wolfert, *Tucker's People* (1943; reprint, Urbana: University of Illinois Press, 1997), xxv.

33. Lipsitz, *Rainbow at Midnight*, 280.

34. Daniel Bell, *The End of Ideology: On the Exhaustion of Political Ideas in the Fifties*, rev. ed. (New York: Free Press/Collier/Macmillan, 1962). See especially the introduction, 13–17.

35. Rideout, *The Radical Novel in the United States,* 171.

36. Jim Daniels, "Troubleshooting: Poetry, the Factory, and the University," in *Liberating Memory: Our Work and Our Working-Class Consciousness*, ed. Janet Zandy (New Brunswick, N.J.: Rutgers University Press, 1995), 87.

37. For biographical information on Swados, I am indebted to Neil D. Isaacs, "Introduction," in Harvey Swados, *The Unknown Constellations* [1947] (Urbana: University of Illinois Press, 1995), ix–xliv.

38. A good brief discussion of this group, including Swados, is in Jack Stuart, "Workers' Party," in *The Encyclopedia of the American Left*, ed. Mari Jo Buhle, Paul Buhle, and Dan Georgakas (New York: Garland, 1990), 852–853. Providing an extensive scrutiny is Alan Wald, *The New York Intellectuals: The Rise and Decline of the Anti-Stalinist Left from the 1930s to the 1980s* (Chapel Hill: University of North Carolina Press, 1987).

39. Swados sandwiched in labor stints between doing public relations for Israeli war bonds. He also wrote for American television and, living frugally but aesthetically, hammered out his writings in the south of France.

40. Swados, "The Myth of the Happy Worker," 235–237. The stories in *On the Line* are hereafter cited in text; see also Harvey Swados, "The UAW—Over the Top or over the Hill?" *Dissent* (Fall 1963): 321–342.

41. Bell, *The End of Ideology*, 223 and chap. 10.

42. Boyle, *The UAW and the Heyday of American Liberalism*, 99.

43. Chafe, "World War II as a Pivotal Experience," 21–33, acknowledges the renewed conservatism in cultural values but rather boldly concludes that the feminine presence in the 1950s workforce "helped to create a context in which another generation" could forge a coherent political movement (33). Chafe's view remains controversial.

44. Kennedy, *If All We Did*, 214. Further data are in Eugenia Kaledin, *Mothers and More: American Women in the 1950s* (Boston: Twayne Publishers, 1984), chap. 4.

45. Harriette Arrow, *The Dollmaker* (1954; New York: Avon Books, 1974); hereafter cited in text. Glenda Hobbs, "Harriette Simpson Arnow," in *Dictionary of Literary Biography,* vol. 6, 2nd ser., ed. James E. Kibler, Jr. (Detroit: Gale Research, 1980), 3. For biographical material, I am indebted to Glenda Hobbs, "Harriette Louisa Simpson Arnow," in *American Women Writers,* vol. 1, ed. Lina Mainiero (New York: Frederick Ungar, 1979), 67–70. See also Hobbs's essay, "Starting Out in the Thirties:

Harriette Arnow's Literary Genesis," in *Literature at the Barricades: The American Writer in the 1930s*, ed. Ralph F. Bogardus and Fred Hobson (Tuscaloosa: University of Alabama Press, 1982), 145–149.

46. Gabin, *Feminism in the Labor Movement*, 146–147.

47. Burleigh B. Gardner, "Introduction," in Lee Rainwater, Richard P. Coleman, and Gerald Handel, *Workingman's Wife: Her Personality, World, and Life Style* (New York: Oceana Publications, 1957), xi.

48. Kennedy, *If All We Did*, 213. She comments later on "working-class male distrust of women, wage earning or not" (222). Steinbeck's 1930s secular saint, Ma Joad, was now an object of suspicion.

49. A. J. De Filipps, "Review of *On the Line*," *Commentary* 67 (October 1957), 109.

50. Dorothy Grafly, "The Camera, Friend or Foe?" *American Artist,* 19 May 1955: 42; E. Rosskam, "Family and Steichen," *Art News*, March 1955, 34–37. A loud dissenting voice to challenge the exhibit's ideology was Hilton Kramer, "Exhibiting the Family of Man," *Commentary*, October 1955, 364–367.

51. Paddy Chayefsky, *Marty*, in *Television Plays by Paddy Chayefsky* (New York: Simon and Schuster, 1955); hereafter cited in text. The television version aired in 1953, and the same writer-director-producer trio worked on the film.

52. "Review of *Marty*," *The Nation*, 30 April 1955, 381.

53. For a chronology of the film's rejections by distributors, see Deborah Silverton Rosenfelt, "Making the Film: Documenting the Opposition," in Michael Wilson, *Salt of the Earth* (film prod. 1953) (New York: Feminist Press, 1978), 186–187.

54. See Thomas H. Pauly, *An American Odyssey: Elia Kazan and American Culture* (Philadelphia: Temple University Press, 1983), chap. 7, for a full discussion of the tortuous writing and production of the screenplay, which went through eight versions.

55. Michael Harrington, "Catholics in the Labor Movement: A Case History," *Labor History* 1, no. 3 (Fall 1960): 237–263. For an interesting CP assessment of "the foe" (the ACTU), see Bailey, *The Kid from Hoboken*, 390.

56. Daniel Bell, "The Racket-Ridden Longshoremen," *Dissent* 6 (Autumn 1959): 417. The article became chapter 9 of *The End of Ideology*.

57. For an excellent introduction to the proletarian complexities of the late 1940s and early 1950s New York, Brooklyn, and New Jersey waterfronts, see Davis, " 'All I Got's a Hook.' "

58. For an interesting pro-CP account of differences, see Hal Simon, "The Rank-and-File Strike of the New York Longshoremen," *Political Affairs* 24 (December 1945): 1088–1096.

59. "The Maritime Unions," *Fortune* 16 (September 1937): 128–132, 143, 137. On red-baiting, see Howard Kimeldorf, *Reds or Rackets?: The Making of Radical and Conservative Unions on the Waterfront* (Berkeley: University of California Press, 1988), chap. 5.

60. Steve Rosswurm, "The Catholic Church and the Left-Led Unions: Labor Priests, Labor Schools, and the ACTU," in *The CIO's Left-Led Unions*, 120. See also Vernon Jensen, *Strife on the Waterfront: The Port of New York since 1945* (Ithaca, N.Y.: Cornell University Press, 1974). On Jesuit labor schools and labor priests, again see Davis, " 'All I Got's a Hook,' " 140, 151n27.

61. Budd Schulberg, "Introduction," in Budd Schulberg, *Waterfront* (New York: Donald M. Fine, 1956), n.p.

62. For similarities between the real-life Ryan and the fictive Friendly, see Malcolm Johnson, *Crime on the Waterfront* (New York: McGraw-Hill, 1950), 143.

63. Bell, "The Racket-Ridden Longshoremen," 425, 427.

64. The figure was based in part on Pete Panto and Andy Hintz. See Vorse, "Pirate's Nest," *Harper's Magazine*, April 1952, 28.

65. On Madell, see David Montgomery, *The Fall of the House of Labor: The Workplace, the State, and American Labor Activism, 1865–1925* (Cambridge: Cambridge University Press, 1987), 143.

66. Writes Joe Doyle, "The narrator in *This Coffin* . . . is an extremely pessimistic man." "Introduction," in Thomas McGrath, *This Coffin Has No Handles* [1948] (New York: Thunder's Mouth Press, 1988), x; hereafter cited in text. On Anastasia and Ryan, see Davis, "'All I Got's a Hook,'" 137 and 142, respectively.

67. Richard Criley, "House Committee on Un-American Activities, AKA House Un-American Activities Committee (HUAC)," in Buhle, Buhle, and Georgakas, *The Encyclopedia of the American Left*, 334.

68. Denning, *The Cultural Front*, 228.

69. Philip Rahv, qtd. in Carla Cappetti, *Writing Chicago: Modernism, Ethnography, and the Novel* (New York: Columbia University Press, 1993), 149.

70. Le Sueur was among the approximately two thousand American Communists hounded out of work by the FBI. Shunned by the publishing world, she went "underground" in 1951. See Vivian Gornick, *The Romance of American Communism* (New York: Basic Books, 1977), 158. See also Dorothy Ray Healey and Maurice Isserman, *California Red: A Life in the American Communist Party* (Urbana: University of Illinois Press, 1993), 125.

71. Alan Wald ("Introduction," in Bonosky, *Burning Valley*, ix) lists these underground leftist authors.

72. Ibid., xv.

73. A great deal more needs to be done on the history of the journal. For positive, but hardly unbiased, period assessments, see K. Orlova, "Masses and Mainstream," *Soviet Literature Monthly* (1954): 143–147. See also Joseph North, "The Masses Tradition," *Masses and Mainstream*, September 1951.

74. Howard Fast, "Spartacus," *Masses and Mainstream* 4, no. 7 (July 1951): 21–36. See also Rideout, *The Radical Novel in the United States*, 300.

75. Qtd. in Fariello, "Introduction," in *Red Scare*, 27.

76. Bonosky interview, 23 July 1998.

77. It should be added that Bonosky drew on Joyce's *Portrait of the Artist as a Young Man* and Hardy's *Jude the Obscure*. I am indebted to Alan Wald, "Introduction," in Bonosky, *Burning Valley*, for biographical data on Bonosky.

78. Bonosky interview, 23 July 1998.

79. Alexander Saxton, *The Great Midland* (1948; reprint, Urbana: University of Illinois Press, 1997), 352; hereafter cited in text.

80. Margaret Graham [Lois McDonald], *Swing Shift* (New York: Citadel Press, 1956), inside jacket flap.

81. Years later, Fast, by then anti-CP for almost four decades, denied the cold war influence. See Alan Wald and Alan Filreis, "A Conversation with Howard Fast, March 23, 1994," *Prospects* 29 (1995): 520–521.

82. Alan Wald, letter to the author, 23 June 1998.

83. Howard Fast, *The Story of Lola Gregg* (New York: Blue Heron Press, 1956), 200.

84. Howard Fast, *The Unvanquished* (Cleveland: World Publishing Company, 1942), back cover.

85. For this convincing argument I am indebted to Daniel Horowitz, "Rethinking Betty Friedan and the Feminine Mystique: Labor Union Radicalism and Feminism

in Cold War America," *American Quarterly* 48, no. 1 (March 1996): 5–11. See esp. p. 11.

86. It is worth noting that Julius expected to support his wife while she remained home with their two young sons. But, lover more than mother, Ethel Rosenberg seems more authentic in her prison letters when she declares her devotion to her Party and her husband. Her laments for the forced separation from her children sound hollow in contrast. See Ethel's letter to Julius, 19 July 1951, in *The Rosenberg Letters: A Complete Edition of the Prison Correspondence of Julius and Ethel Rosenberg*, ed. Michael Meeropol (New York: Garland Publishers, 1994), 168–169.

87. For a revisionist discussion that summarizes the misreadings, and eloquently attempts to defend Algren's talent, see Cappetti, *Writing Chicago,* 149–155.

88. Martha Heasley Cox and Wayne Chatterton, *Nelson Algren* (Boston: Twayne/G. K. Hall, 1973), 14–17. See an often critical Bettina Drew, *Nelson Algren: A Life on the Wild Side* (New York: Putnam, 1989), 147, for the facts of his unionism.

89. For a contrasting interpretation, see R. W. Lid, "A World Imagined: The Art of Nelson Algren," in *American Literary Naturalism: A Reassessment*, ed. Yoshinobu Hakutani and Lewis Fried (Heidelberg: Anglistiche Forschungen, 1975), 195ff.

90. Budd Schulberg, *New York Times Book Review*, 21 October 1951.

91. Lid, "A World Imagined," 195. Nelson Algren, *A Walk on the Wild Side* (1956; reprint, New York: Penguin Books, 1986); hereafter cited in text.

92. Norman Mailer, *The Naked and the Dead* (New York: Modern Library, 1948), 160, 161; hereafter cited in text.

93. Eisinger finds an "enslavement" theme in the war novel of Mailer. Chester E. Eisinger, *Fiction of the Forties* (Chicago: University of Chicago Press, 1963), 33.

94. Michiko Kakutani, "Self-Portrait of an Artist," *New York Times*, 15 May 1998, E41. For biographical details on Mailer during the 1940s, see Philip H. Bufithio, "Norman Mailer," in *Dictionary of Literary Biography*, vol. 2, ed. Jeffrey Lelterman and Richard Lyman (Detroit: Gale Research, 1978), 278–279.

95. Kerouac, though working class, shed his origins with dispatch, and many period authors were unaware that he had them. Thomas McGrath offers a typically ambivalent leftist response to the "middle-class" Kerouac's *On the Road* in "Search for Kicks," *Masses and Mainstream* 11 (February 1958): 53–56.

96. Alan Wald, Foreword to the 1994 Edition, in Lloyd Brown, *Iron City* (1951; reprint, Boston: Northeastern University Press, 1994), xvi.

97. John Hudson Jones, "Problems of Negro Writers Discussed at Harlem Forum," *Daily Worker,* 3 March 1948; Lloyd L. Brown, "Which Way for the Negro Writer?" *Masses and Mainstream* 4 (March 1951): 53–62.

98. Haywood, *Black Bolshevik*, 591.

99. Bernard Bell, *The Afro-American Novel and Its Tradition* (Amherst: University of Massachusetts Press, 1987), defines the Motley novel as an "experiment with nonracial themes and protagonists" (190–191). For a period review by a prominent African American sociologist with the same opinion, see Horace A. Cayton, "The Known City," *New Republic*, 12 May 1947, 31. Certainly the popularity of this novel "by a Negro author" had much to do with the public's fascination with white Dead End kids and their grown-up hoodlum selves. See "Who Made This Boy a Murderer?" *Look* 11 (30 September 1947): 21–31. Willard Motley, *Knock on Any Door* (1947; reprint, DeKalb: Northern Illinois University Press, 1989); hereafter cited in text.

100. On Motley's difficulties with "The Almost White Boy," see Robert E. Fleming, "Willard Motley," *Dictionary of Literary Biography*, vol. 76, ed. Trudier Harris (Detroit: Gale Research, 1988), 114.

101. Chester Himes, "Crazy in the Stir," *Esquire* (August 1934); "To What Red Hell?" *Esquire* (October 1934); and "The Visiting Hour," *Esquire* (September 1936). For biographical information, see Ralph Reckley, "Chester Himes," *Dictionary of Literary Biography*, vol. 76, 89–103.

102. Biographical matter on Brown is in Alan Wald, Foreword, in Lloyd L. Brown, *Iron City* (1951; reprint, Boston: Northeastern University Press, 1994), xv–xvi; hereafter cited in text.

103. Lloyd Brown, "The Legacy of Willie Jones," *Masses and Mainstream* 5, no. 2 (February 1952): 46.

104. James Baldwin, "A Stranger in the Village" [1953], in James Baldwin, *Notes of a Native Son*, 2d ed. rev. (Boston: Beacon Press, 1957), 165.

105. See the poem by Beulah Richardson, "A Black Woman Speaks," *Masses and Mainstream* 4 (October 1951): 21. The playwright Shirley Graham, on the journal's board of directors, contributed book reviews as well.

106. Karen Tucker Anderson, "Last Hired, First Fired: Black Women Workers during World War II," *Journal of American History* 69 (June 1982): 97.

107. See note 2.

108. Gabin, *Feminism in the Labor Movement*, 152.

109. John Dos Passos, *Mid-Century* (1960; reprint, Cambridge, Mass.: Riverside Press, 1961), 89.

Chapter 11. The Usable Past

1. The term "racial-ethnic" refers to non-Euro-American people slotted into color categories other than African American. For a recent defense of the new term, see Karen Anderson, *Changing Woman: A History of Racial-Ethnic Women in Modern America* (New York: Oxford University Press, 1999). See also Cesar E. Chavez and Bayard Rustin, *"Right to Work" Laws: A Trap for America's Minorities* [c. 1972] (New York: A. Philip Randolph Institute, n.d.), 1–18; Janice Gould, "The Problem of Being 'Indian': One Mixed-Blood's Dilemma," in *De/Colonizing the Subject: The Politics of Gender in Women's Autobiography*, ed. Sidonie Smith and Julia Watson (Minneapolis: University of Minnesota Press, 1992), 83 and passim.

2. *Who Built America?: Working People and the Nation's Economy, Politics, Culture, and Society*, vol. 2, ed. Joshua Freeman et al. (New York: Pantheon Books, 1992), 565.

3. On Chicano self-naming, see Rudolfo Anaya, "Introduction," in *Growing up Chicana/o*, ed. Tiffany Ana Lopez (1993; reprint, New York: Avon Books, 1995), 6; Chavez and Rustin, *"Right to Work" Laws*, 1–18.

4. On these Chicano workers, as well as those in the Midwest, doing industrial work, see Gilbert G. Gonzalez, *Labor and Community: Mexican Citrus Worker Villages in a Southern California County, 1900–1950* (Urbana: University of Illinois Press, 1994), chap. 7.

5. Cesar Chavez, "The California Farm Workers' Struggle," *Black Scholar* (7 June 1976), 16–19. Evidence of Chavez's continuing broad appeal was the piece's appearance the same year in the *Los Angeles Times*, 8 April 1976.

6. Chavez and Rustin, *"Right to Work" Laws*, 8.

7. On the limited effectiveness of UAW support, see Nelson Lichtenstein, *The Most Dangerous Man in Detroit: Walter Reuther and the Fate of American Labor* (New York: Basic Books, 1995), 433. A discussion of AFL/CIO links via the United Auto Workers is in Maclovio R. Barraza, "Manana Is Too Late—Labor Standards," in *Aztlan: An Anthology of Mexican American Literature*, ed. Luis Valdez and Stan Steiner (New York: Vintage Books, 1972), 188–189.

8. James Diego Vigil, *Barrio Gangs: Street Life and Identity in Southern California* (Austin: University of Texas Press, 1988), 5.

9. A. LaVonne Brown Ruoff and Jerry W. Ward, Jr., *American Indian Literatures* (New York: Modern Language Association, 1990), 193. See also Robert Allen Warrior, "Recession and Regression: The Economics of Federal Indian Policy since 1900," *Christianity and Crisis* 52, no. 10 (22 June 1992): 223–224.

10. Juan Gomez-Quinones, *Mexican American Labor, 1790–1990* (Albuquerque: University of New Mexico Press, 1994), 204.

11. Michael Dorris, "Queen of Diamonds," [1987] in *Talking Leaves: Contemporary Native American Short Stories*, ed. Craig Lesley (New York: Delta Publishing, 1991), 55.

12. Zaragosa Vargas, *Proletarians of the North: A History of Mexican Industrial Workers in Detroit and the Midwest, 1917–1933* (Berkeley: University of California Press, 1993), 87; also 7, 80, and 86.

13. Francisco E. Balderrama and Raymond Rodriguez, *Decade of Betrayal: Mexican Repatriation in the 1930s* (Albuquerque: University of New Mexico Press, 1995), 2–3. Nor, despite the renaissance, termed "La Causa" by Chavez, did their scattered labor skirmishes in the California canneries and garment trades garner more than limited organized-labor support.

14. On late nineteenth-century interethnic alliances, see Alfredo Montoya, "A Brief Look at Latino Union History in the West and Southwest: A Mexican American Labor Leader's Perspective," *Journal of Hispanic Policy* 4 (1988–1989): 118. See also Jonathan Rosenblum, *Copper Crucible: How the Arizona Miners' Strike of 1983 Recast Labor Management Relations in America*, 2d ed. (Ithaca, N.Y.: ILR Press, 1998).

15. On Mexican section gangs in Native American towns, see Leslie Marmon Silko, *Ceremony* (1977; reprint, New York: Penguin, 1986), 160; hereafter cited in text. For biographical data on this important Laguna author as well as other writers discussed in this chapter see www.galenet.com.

16. John William Sayer, *Ghost Dancing the Law: The Wounded Knee Trials* (Cambridge: Harvard University Press, 1997); see chapter 1 for a good discussion of Wounded Knee in both political and economic terms.

17. Renqui Yu, "To Merge with the Mass: Left-Wing Chinese Students and Chinese Hand Laundry Workers in New York City in the 1930s," in *Asian Americans: Comparative and Global Perspectives*, ed. Shirley Hune et al. (Pullman: Washington State University Press, 1991), 49. He notes that they had some contempt for the masses of Chinese (50). See also John W. Tchen, *The Chinese Laundryman: A Study of Social Isolation* (1953; reprint, New York: New York University Press, 1987).

18. Dorothy Ritsuko McDonald, "Introduction," to Frank Chin, *The Chickencoop Chinaman* and *The Year of the Dragon*, in *Three American Literatures,* ed. Houston A. Baker, Jr. (New York: Modern Language Association, 1982), 231.

19. Ibid., 230.

20. Luis Alberto Urrea, *Nobody's Son: Notes from an American Life* (Tucson: University of Arizona Press, 1998), 1, 8. Elsewhere he observes: "My father [was] just another beaner [to them] . . . unable to touch the American Dream. Scrubbing the urinals used by white men who were far below him in every way" (42).

21. Richard Rodriguez, *Hunger of Memory: The Education of Richard Rodriguez* (1982; reprint, New York: Bantam, 1983). This is a term reminiscent of the Accidental Worker figures of Gilded Age labor fiction.

22. Henry Staten, "Ethnic Authenticity, Class, and Autobiography: The Case of *Hunger of Memory*," *PMLA* 113 (January 1998): 104.

23. Articles crystallizing the respective ethnic-literature controversies are Staten, "Ethnic Authenticity," 103–116, and Juan Bruce-Novoa, "Canonical and Noncanonical Texts: A Chicano Case Study," in *Redefining American Literary History*, ed. A. LaVonne Brown Ruoff and Jerry W. Ward, Jr. (New York: Modern Language Association, 1990), 196–209; Jeffrey Paul Chan, "Introduction," in *The Big Aiieeee!: An Anthology of Chinese American and Japanese American Literature*, ed. Jeffrey Paul Chan et al. (New York: Meridian Books, 1991); Susan Perez-Castillo, "Postmodernism, Native American Literature, and the Real: The Silko-Erdrich Controversy," *Massachusetts Review* 32 (1991): 287.

24. It is true that such ethnic variants dispensed with the "living newsreel" and with the kind of juxtaposition of documentary sections and those on groups of key characters that Barbara Foley finds central in, for instance, *The Grapes of Wrath*. Barbara Foley, *Radical Representations: Politics and Form in U.S. Proletarian Fiction, 1929–1941* (Durham, N.C.: Duke University Press, 1993), 398–402.

25. One recent scholar of Native American lore provides an elegant differentiation: "There are two types of time in operation in [fiction with mythic concerns]. The one is . . . a linear segment, remorselessly historical, profane, and anthropological. . . . [The other] . . . is eternal, cyclical, endlessly repetitive, powered by Nature, and cosmogonic." Calvin Martin, "Time and the American Indian," in *The American Indian and the Problem of History*, ed. Calvin Martin (New York: Oxford University Press, 1987), 194. Edward Dahlberg, a novelist-interpreter of proletarian fiction, adds the important observation that in sociological, proletarian literature there are no stars, nights or dawns, no nature to touch, soften, or elevate man.

26. Included in the new working-class literature are writers of Puerto Rican, Dominican, Colombian, West Indian, Japanese, Filipino, and diverse Native American background. To cite but one example: it is limiting to consign the new working-class writer, Lois-Ann Yamamaka, to an endnote, but mention must be made of her novel *Wild Meat and the Bully Burgers* (New York: Farrar, Straus and Giroux, 1995). The protagonist, Lovey, searches for a way to reconcile her family's myths of samurai with both American commerce and Hawaiian macadamia nut factory jobs.

27. Vargas, *Proletarians of the North*, 86.

28. Gonzalez, *Labor and Community*, 182.

29. Ernesto Galarza, *Barrio Boy* (Notre Dame, Ind.: University of Notre Dame Press, 1971), 240.

30. An interesting sidelight: The Old Left's support was most probably solicited, not for any purely labor issue, but for bilingual education.

31. Vargas, *Proletarians of the North*, 6, 80, 130, 165–170, 199.

32. Upton Sinclair, *King Coal* (1917; reprint, New York: Bantam Books, 1994), 226; David Montgomery, *The Fall of the House of Labor: The Workplace, the State, and American Labor Activism, 1865–1925* (Cambridge: Cambridge University Press, 1987), 335.

33. Mexican Americans are fleetingly visualized in a little-known Dorothea Lange photograph for the Farm Security Administration, "Mexican Worker, Imperial Valley, Ca., 1935." Carleton Beals, *The Crime of Cuba* (Philadelphia: J. B. Lippincott Company, 1933), provided a leftist indictment of the right-wing dictator Gerard Machado and featured Walker Evans's photographs of coal loaders, sugar workers, and breadlines (20).

34. John Steinbeck, *Tortilla Flat* (1935; reprint, New York: Penguin, 1973), writes with unintentional irony of "paisanos" (2). He also describes Monterey types "free

of the complicated systems of American business [who] live in old wooden houses set in weedy yards [with] the pine trees from the forest . . . about the houses" (2).

35. Richard Griswold Del Castillo and Arnold de Leon, *North to Aztlan: A History of Mexican Americans in the United States* (New York: Twayne Publishers, 1997), 104–108; Ronald Takaki, *A Different Mirror: A History of Multicultural America* (Boston: Little, Brown and Co., 1993), 391–392.

36. On Valdez's work as the "cultural arm of the UFW," see Colette A. Hyman, *Staging Strikes: Workers' Theatre and the American Labor Movement* (Philadelphia: Temple University Press, 1997), 145. On Valdez's innovations, see also Carlota Cardenas de Dwyer, "The Development of Chicano Drama and Luis Valdez's *Actos*," in *Modern Chicano Writers: A Collection of Critical Essays*, ed. Joseph Sommers and Tomas Ybarra-Frausto (Englewood Cliffs, N.J.: Prentice-Hall, 1979), 163.

37. On La Causa, see Freeman et al., *Who Built America?*, vol. 2, 565; Cletus E. Daniel, "Cesar Chavez and the Unionization of California Farm Workers," in *Labor Leaders in America*, ed. Melvyn Dubofsky and Warren Van Tine (Urbana: University of Illinois Press, 1987), 366–370.

38. "Luis Valdez," in *Hispanic Literature Criticism*, vol. 2, ed. Jelena Krstovic (Detroit: Gale Research, 1994), 1281.

39. John M. Hart, *Anarchism and the Mexican Working Class, 1860–1931* (Austin: University of Texas Press, 1987), 61, 131, 103.

40. On Guadalupe as patroness, see Valdez and Steiner, *Aztlan*, 198. On definitions of this elusive "Aztlan," see Luis Leal and Pepe Barron, "Chicano Literature: An Overview," in Baker, *Three American Literatures*, 9, and Raymond A. Paredes, "The Evolution of Chicano Literature," ibid., 61.

41. Daniel, "Cesar Chavez," 366.

42. Editorial introduction, "Walkout in Albuquerque," in Valdez and Steiner, *Aztlan*, 211.

43. Daniel, "Cesar Chavez," 350.

44. Ibid., 374.

45. Chavez and Rustin, *"Right to Work" Laws*, 14.

46. Oscar Zeta Acosta, *The Revolt of the Cockroach People* (San Francisco: Straight Arrow Books, 1973), 33; hereafter cited in text.

47. Raymond Barrio, *The Plum Plum Pickers* (1969; reprint, New York: Harper/Colophon Books, 1971), 122; hereafter cited in text.

48. Biographical information on Rivera and on the background of his book is in "Tomas Rivera," in *Hispanic Writers*, ed. Bryan Ryan (Detroit: Gale Research, 1991), 402–403. See also the excellent resource by Del Castillo and de Leon, *North to Aztlan*, 145.

49. Barbara Kingsolver, *Holding the Line: Women in the Great Arizona Mine Strike of 1983* (Ithaca, N.Y.: ILR Press, 1999), xiii.

50. Tomas Rivera, *And the Earth Did Not Devour Him*, trans. Evangelina Vigil-Pinon (1971; reprint, Houston: Arte Publico Press, 1992). Rivera's reiterated phrase "nothing has been lost" echoes that of Hemingway's Nick Adams in "Big-Two-Hearted River."

51. Daniel, "Cesar Chavez," 364.

52. Evelyn Nakano Glenn, "Servitude to Service Work: Historical Continuities with the Racial Division of Paid Reproductive Labor," in *Unequal Sisters: A Multicultural Reader in U.S. Women's History*, 2d ed., ed. Vicki L. Ruiz and Ellen Carol DuBois (New York: Routledge, 1994), 412.

53. Gloria Anzaldúa, *Borderlands/La Frontera* (San Francisco: Aunt Lute Books, 1987), 21; hereafter cited in text.

54. Denise Chavez, *The Last of the Menu Girls* (Houston: Arte Publico Books, 1986), 13; hereafter cited in text.

55. Michael Gold, *Jews without Money* (1930) (1935; reprint, New York: Carroll and Graf, 1996), 33.

56. On the business focus of Chinatown working people, see Paul M. Ong, "Chinese Labor in Early San Francisco: Racial Segmentation and Industrial Expansion," *Amerasia* 8, no. 1 (1981): 67–74. On the CHLA, see Renqui Yu, *To Save China, to Save Ourselves: The Chinese Hand Laundry Alliance of New York* (Philadelphia: Temple University Press, 1992).

57. Elaine Kim, Preface, in *Charlie Chan Is Dead: An Anthology of Contemporary Asian American Fiction*, ed. Jessica Hagedorn (New York: Penguin, 1993), ix.

58. For a discussion of ethnic service and gender, see Glenn, "Servitude to Service Work," 410–418.

59. David Henry Hwang, "Introduction," in *FOB and Other Plays* (New York: New American Library, 1990), xi.

60. Maxine Hong Kingston, *China Men* (1977; reprint, New York: Vintage/Random House, 1989), 140; hereafter cited in text. See also David Henry Hwang, *The Dance and the Railroad* (New York: New American Library, 1990), 65; hereafter cited in text.

61. Frank Chin, *The Chinaman Pacific & Frisco R.R. Co.* (San Francisco: Coffeehouse Press, 1988); see also his lengthy essay "Come All Ye Asian American Writers of the Real and the Fake," in Chin et al., *The Big Aiiieeeee!* 1–93.

62. For a diatribe against the Chinese American, see Jeffrey Paul Chan, "Introduction," in Chin et al., *The Big Aiiieeeee!*, xi.

63. Frank Chin, "Confessions of the Chinatown Cowboy," *Bulletin of Concerned Asian Scholars* 4 (Fall 1972): 58.

64. Chin, "Introduction," in Chin et al., *The Big Aiiieeeee!*, iii, xiii.

65. Qtd. in letter to author from Janet Zandy, 21 December 1999.

66. Linda Ching Sledge, "Oral Tradition in Kingston's *China Men*," in Ruoff and Ward, *Redefining American Literary History*, 145.

67. Mircea Eliade, *The Myth of the Eternal Return or Cosmos and History*, trans. Willard R. Trask (1954: reprint, Princeton, N.J.: Princeton University Press, 1974), xiii.

68. See the fact-filled article by Mary Kay Morel, "Captain Pratt's School," *American History* 32 (May/June 1997): 26–34. See also my chapter 4 discussion of Carlisle and Hampton institutes.

69. Sayer, *Ghost Dancing the Law*, 3.

70. The *New York Tribune* of 31 December 1890 carried the headline "Treachery of the Indians in Attacking the Troops." Qtd. in Michael Robertson, *Stephen Crane, Journalism, and the Making of Modern American Literature* (New York: Columbia University Press, 1997), 220.

71. See Sayer, *Ghost Dancing the Law*, 7.

72. Mary Crow Dog, *Lakota Woman* (New York: HarperCollins, 1990), 188, 173, 178.

73. Qtd. in Russell Means, *Where White Men Fear to Tread: The Autobiography of Russell Means* (New York: St. Martin's Press, 1995), 160.

74. James Welch, *The Death of Jim Loney* (New York: Harper and Row, 1979); hereafter cited in text.

75. Ted L. Williams, *The Reservation* (Syracuse, N.Y.: Syracuse University Press, 1976), 20.

76. An acute analysis is in Julie Maristuen-Rodakowski, "The Turtle Mountain Reservation in North Dakota: Its History as Depicted in Louise Erdrich's 'Love Medicine' and 'Beet Queen,'" *American Indian Culture and Research Journal* 12, no. 3 (1998): 33–48.

77. Louise Erdrich, *Love Medicine* (1984; rev ed., New York: Harper Perennial, 1993), 48; hereafter cited in text.

78. Perez-Castillo, "Postmodernism, Native American Literature, and the Real," 287. It is instructive to contrast Erdrich with Leslie Marmon Silko, *Ceremony* (1977) (New York: New American Library, 1986); hereafter cited in text.

79. Crow Dog, *Lakota Woman*, 56–57.

80. Gerald Vizenor, *Interior Landscapes: Autobiographical Myths and Memoirs* (Minneapolis: University of Minnesota Press, 1990).

81. Gould, "The Problem of Being 'Indian.'" 81.

82. Amritjit Singh, Preface, in *Memory, Narrative, and Identity: New Essays in Ethnic American Literatures*, ed. Amritjit Singh et al. (Boston: Northeastern University Press, 1994), vii.

83. Such dual identity encompassed the assimilated, upwardly mobile ethnic or the vast majority in the racialized, marginalized ethnic workforce. See Michael Denning, *The Cultural Front: The Laboring of American Culture in the Twentieth Century* (London: Verso, 1996), 235.

84. On the impoverishment of these respective groups, see "CBS News Revisits Migrants 35 Years Later," *New York Times*, 20 July 1995, C16; Wesley Macawili, "Chinatown Workers Organize," *The Progressive* 58, no. 2 (1995): 14; Fred H. Schmidt, *The Simpleminded Children: Spanish Surnamed Employment in the Midwest* (Washington, D.C.: Government Printing Office, n.d.), 70–71; and Seth Mydans, "New Frontier for Gangs: Indian Reservations," *New York Times*, 18 March 1995, A1, A7.

85. See the union laborer in Gilb's story "Nancy Flores," the unemployed unionist in "Look on the Bright Side," in *The Magic of Blood* (Albuquerque: University of New Mexico Press, 1993), 3, 27, and the disaffected construction hands/heroin addicts in "Down in the West Texas Town," in *Winners on the Pass Line* (El Paso: Cinque Punto Press, 1985), 9–19. Gilb seems all too aware of how memories of the powerful revolutionary have been reduced to a bogus souvenir.

86. In 1994, under Chavez's original cofounder Dolores Huerta, the UFW began a new effort to rebuild its strength and power. On a commemorative march from Delano to Sacramento, Huerta and other leaders called for a regeneration of the union. The story marks the literary distance between an early Chicano novelist like Jose Antonio Villareal, whose 1959 historical novel *Pocho* romanticized a valiant, if jobless, soldier in Villa's army. In "The Death Mask of Pancho Villa" Gilb implicitly rejects the Villa legacy of general strikes for poor fieldworkers and agrarians and implicitly reveals the need for the kind of revivified UFW that would once more march from Delano to Sacramento.

87. Fay Myenne Ng, "A Red Sweater," in Hagedorn, *Charlie Chan Is Dead*, 359, 362.

88. One key Ng character, Leon, has been, among other things, a fry cook, bus boy, steward, and steelworker.

89. Much new Chinese American fiction joins other Asian American works in exploring neurotic confusion and affluent guilt among the younger generation, the key subjects of Amy Tan's *The Joy Luck Club* (1989).

90. He refers ironically, too, to its 1881 creation. See Sherman Alexie, *Reservation Blues* (New York: Atlantic Monthly Press, 1995); hereafter cited in text. What heralds a new literary phase of conceptualizing labor (to be treated in the conclu-

sion), however, is that the "hyphenated" identity bypasses pre-1990s literary struggle between shame and pride. Nor is there need for the forced disappearance of claims to ethnic authenticity.

91. A clarifying piece about Alexie is Timothy Egan, "An Indian without Reservations," *New York Times Magazine*, 18 January 1998, 16–20.

92. Michael Harrington, *The Other America: Poverty in the United States* (1962; reprint, New York: Collier/Macmillan, 1963).

Chapter 12. Working-Class Twilight

1. Thomas Geoghegan, *Which Side Are You On?: Trying to Be for Labor When It's Flat on Its Back* (New York: Plume/New American Library, 1992), 55.

2. For a good discussion, see Jeremy Brecher, *Strike!*, rev. ed. (Boston: South End Press, 1997), chap. 9.

3. See, for instance, Ruth Milkman, *Farewell to the Factory: Auto Workers in the Late Twentieth Century* (Berkeley: University of California Press, 1997); and Judith Modell and Charlee Brodsky, *A Town without Steel: Revisioning Homestead* (Pittsburgh: University of Pittsburgh Press, 1998). Oral history on the loss of northern manufacturing jobs is in "Child of the Shutdown" and "Eulogy," in *Amoskeag: Life and Work in an American Factory City*, ed. Tamara K. Hareven and Randolph Langenbach (New York: Pantheon Books, 1978), 359–361, 362–363. On the southern textile mill downsizing, see John Gaventa and Barbara Ellen Smith, "The Deindustrialization of the Textile South," in *Hanging by a Thread: Social Change in Southern Textiles*, ed. Jeffrey Leiter et al. (Ithaca, N.Y.: ILR Press, 1991), 181, 188.

4. Joanna Kadi, *Thinking Class: Sketches from a Cultural Worker* (Boston: South End Press, 1996), provides a logical discussion (150).

5. The degree of labor movement antiwar protest remains fiercely debated. For dove views, see Philip S. Foner, *U.S. Labor and the Vietnam War* (New York: International Publishers, 1989), and the useful anecdotal "evidence" in Joe Mackall, "The Stories of Working-Class Lights," in *Writing Work: Writers on Working-Class Writing*, ed. David Shevin, Janet Zandy, and Larry Smith (Huron, Ohio: Bottom Dog Press, 1999), 15, and "Labor, the Working Class, and the Vietnam War," in H-Labor Digest Listserv, December 1997, H-Labor@H-Net.MSU.edu. See also Peter B. Levy, *The New Left and Labor in the 1960s* (Urbana: University of Illinois Press, 1997). Robert Zieger summarizes the more common approach in *American Workers, American Unions*, 2d ed. (Baltimore: Johns Hopkins University Press, 1994), chap. 6. On veterans from labor backgrounds perceiving antiwar protest as personal rejection, see Christian G. Appy, *Working-Class War: American Combat Soldiers and Vietnam* (Chapel Hill: University of North Carolina Press, 1993), 257–269.

6. An excellent oral history of African American steelworkers without labor or management support is the documentary *Struggles in Steel*, dir. Ray Henderson, California Newsreel, 1996. See also Jonathan D. Rosenblum, *Copper Crucible: How the Arizona Miners' Strike of 1983 Recast Labor-Management Relations in America*, 2d ed. (Ithaca, N.Y.: ILR Press, 1998); "Women at Farah: An Unfinished Story," in *A Needle, a Bobbin, a Strike: Women Needleworkers in America*, ed. Joan M. Jensen and Sue Davidson (Philadelphia: Temple University Press, 1984), 261–275.

7. Richard Slotkin, *Gunfighter Nation: The Myth of the Frontier in Twentieth-Century America* (New York: Atheneum, 1992), 556–557.

8. Raymond L. Hogler, "Air Traffic Controllers' Strike of 1981," in *Labor Conflict in the United States: An Encyclopedia*, ed. Ronald L. Filippelli (New York: Garland, 1990), 5.

9. *Who Built America?: Working People and the Nation's Economy, Politics, Culture, and Society*, vol. 2, ed. Joshua Freeman et al. (New York: Pantheon Books, 1992), 656; Zieger, *American Workers, American Unions*, 173.

10. Richard F. Hamilton, "Liberal Intelligentsia and White Backlash," in *The World of the Blue-Collar Worker*, ed. Irving Howe (New York: Quadrangle Books/New York Times, 1972), 227–238. On Wallace and "white backlash," see Zieger, *American Workers, American Unions*, 188–190.

11. See especially Zieger's succinct, lucid discussion in *American Workers, American Unions*, 187–192; see also Freeman et al., *Who Built America?*, vol. 2, 600–603.

12. E. E. LeMasters, *Blue-Collar Aristocrats: Life-Styles at a Working-Class Tavern* (Madison: University of Wisconsin Press, 1975). The author's uncertain stance is evidenced in his preface acknowledgment of these "men . . . who tolerated his middle-classness" (ix).

13. Richard Price, *Bloodbrothers* (New York: Penguin, 1976), 99; hereafter cited in text.

14. Such studies began in the mid-1960s but did not prompt the attention of those such as Arthur B. Shostak and William Gomberg, eds., *Blue-Collar World: Studies of the American Worker* (Englewood Cliffs, N.J.: Prentice Hall, 1964), and the misleadingly titled *The White Majority: Between Poverty and Affluence*, ed. Louise Kapp Howe (New York: Random House, 1970). See the important essays on the liberal intelligentsia and the white backlash, the importance of social class, and the like in the socialist journal *Dissent* essays, edited by the journal editor, Irving Howe, and republished as *The World of the Blue-Collar Worker*.

15. Rosalyn Baxandall and Linda Gordon, "1955 to the Present: An Introduction," in *America's Working Women: A Documentary History, 1600 to the Present*, rev. ed., ed. Rosalyn Baxandall and Linda Gordon (New York: W. W. Norton, 1993), 289–309. See also Amy Walshok, *Blue-Collar Women: Pioneers on the Male Frontier* (New York: Anchor/Doubleday, 1981); and Joan Smith, "The Paradox of Women's Poverty: Wage-Earning Women and Economic Transformation," *Signs* 19, no. 2 (Winter 1984): 291–310.

16. Sara Evans, *Born for Liberty: A History of Women in America* (New York: Free Press, 1989), offers the common argument that more attention was paid to racial diversity among working-class than middle-class white feminists (299).

17. See also the essays by various hands in *Women and Unions: Forging a Partnership*, ed. Dorothy Sue Cobble (Ithaca, N.Y.: ILR Press, 1993).

18. Judith Buber Agassi, "Women Who Work in Factories," in Howe, *The World of the Blue-Collar Worker*, 239–248. It is constructive to contrast this essay, the sole one on women in the volume, to the earlier sociological classic by Mirra Komarovsky, *Blue-Collar Marriage* (New York: Random House, 1964). Komarovsky, however, also privileges white men's work rather than that of their homemaker wives. On the persistence of white working women's exclusion from women's studies, see Alison Bernstein and Jacklyn Cock, "A Troubling Picture of Gender Inequity," *Chronicle of Higher Education*, sec. 2, 15 June 1994, B2.

19. Gus Tyler, "White Workers, Blue Mood" (198–209), Andrew M. Greeley, "The New Ethnicity and Blue Collars" (285–296), and Michael Harrington, "Old Working Class, New Working Class" (135–158) all appeared in Howe, *The World of the Blue-Collar Worker*. These authors—Socialist Old Left, Catholic, and New Left—have little else in common.

20. Chief among the studies arguing that efficiency was a "new Fordism" in that unions and management seemed to collaborate in pushing workers though in-

creasing their pay is Stanley Aronowitz, *False Promises: The Shaping of American Working-Class Consciousness* (New York: McGraw Hill, 1973). See also the review article by Nicholaus Mills, "Work and the System," *Yale Review* 63 (June 1974): 566–572.

21. John Hartigan, "Name Calling: Objectifying 'Poor Whites' and 'White Trash' in Detroit," in *White Trash: Race and Class in America*, ed. Annalee Newitz and Matt Wray (New York: Routledge, 1997), 47.

22. For an excellent account of negative historical attitudes toward poor whites, see Sylvia Jenkins Cook, *From Tobacco Road to Route 66: The Southern Poor White in Fiction* (Chapel Hill: University of North Carolina Press, 1976), especially the preface (ix–xiv).

23. Richard Hague, *Milltown Natural: Essays and Stories from a Life* (Huron, Ohio: Bottom Dog Press, 1997), 6.

24. Russell Banks, *Continental Drift* (New York: Ballantine Books, 1985), 93; hereafter cited in text.

25. The Vietnam narrative does not fit easily into working-class fiction. While depictions of killing machines and psychic casualties are not presented in class terms, soldiers do share the labor trope of alienation from technology. See novels as otherwise divergent as Tim O'Brien, *Going After Cacciato* (1975), James Webb, *Fields of Fire* (1981), Robert Stone, *The Dog Soldiers* (1973), and John M. Del Vecchio, *The 13th Valley* (1981). For a survey of two hundred such Vietnam War novels, see Donald Ringnalda, "Fighting and Writing: America's Vietnam War Literature," *Journal of American Studies* 22, no. 1 (1988): 25–42.

26. Neil Foley, "Introduction," in Foley, *The White Scourge: Mexicans, Blacks, and Poor Whites in Texas Cotton Culture* (Berkeley: University of California Press, 1997), 6. The introduction provides a penetrating overview of the color line and racialization of poor whites. See also studies such as Noel Ignatiev, *How the Irish Became White* (New York: Routledge, 1995); and Luis Alberto Urrea, *Nobody's Son: Notes from an American Life* (Tucson: University of Arizona Press, 1998): "We won't have our boy speaking like white trash" (54).

27. Denise Giardina, *The Unquiet Earth* (New York: Ivy/Ballantine, 1992), 9, 40, 16; hereafter cited in text. For pertinent biographical information, see Lillian S. Robinson, "The Coal Miner's Daughter," *Nation* 255, no. 22 (27 December 1992): 816–817.

28. The apt quotations are from Nicole Hahn Rafter, "Introduction," in *White Trash: The Eugenic Family Studies, 1877–1919*, ed. John Summers and Nicole Hahn Rafter (Boston: Northeastern University Press, 1988), 7, 5. See also Hahn's critique of the "genetic virtue" of the middle class (6). For a novelist who internalizes these critiques, see Harry Crews, *A Feast of Snakes* (1976).

29. Annalee Newitz and Matt Wray, "Introduction," in *White Trash*, 4.

30. Foley, *The White Scourge*, 12, 6. For a factual West Virginia mining-town memoir describing more pacific racial relations on the job but segregated houses off of it, see Homer Hickam, Jr., *October Sky* [originally titled *Rocket Boys*] (1998; reprint, New York: Island/Dell, 1999). See especially page 3.

31. Foley, *The White Scourge*, 7.

32. Joyce Carol Oates, *Them* (New York: Fawcett/Crest, 1969), 322; hereafter cited in text. Oates has carefully distanced herself from her own working-class roots. Standard biographies like Joanne V. Creighton, *Joyce Carol Oates* (Boston: Twayne, 1979) follow her lead.

33. On working-class participant-artists, see Tom Wayman, *Inside Job: Essays on the New Work Writing* (Madeira Park, B.C.: Harbour Publishing, 1983), 74.

34. Bertha Harris, "Holy Beauty or Degradation: *The Beans of Egypt, Maine*," and "Caring about the Working Poor," *New York Times Book Review*, 13 January 1985.

35. See Denise Giardina, "Coalfield Women," in *Women of Coal*, ed. Randall Norris and Jean-Philippe Cypres (Lexington: University Press of Kentucky), 2–4.

36. Dorothy Allison, *Trash* (San Francisco: Firebrand Books, 1988), 7; hereafter cited in text.

37. Robert Niemi, *Russell Banks* (New York: Twayne, 1997), xv; "The *Paris Review* Interview: Raymond Carver," in Raymond Carver, *Fires: Essays, Poems, Stories* (New York: Vintage Books, 1984), 187–216, esp. 189, 193, and 206. For otherwise scarce biographical data on Yount, see "John Yount," *Contemporary Authors*, ser. 47, ed. Pamela S. Deer (Detroit: Gale Research, 1995), 481–483. See also Harry Crews's autobiographical "white trash" migration novel *The Hawk Is Dying* (1979).

38. Paul Lauter, "American Proletarianism," in *The Columbia History of the American Novel*, ed. Emory Elliott et al. (New York: Columbia University Press, 1991), 331.

39. See note 14.

40. That taxonomy was still extant by the time of Sue Cobble's 1993 anthology *Women and Unions*. See Brigid O'Farrell and Suzanne Moore, "Unions, Hard Hats, and Women Workers," in Cobble, *Women and Unions*, 71–84; and the oral testimony in Susan Eisenberg, *We'll Call You If We Need You: Experiences of Women Working Construction* (Ithaca, N.Y.: ILR Press, 1998). On the EEOC, see Heidi Hartmann, "Roundtable on Pay Equity and Affirmative Action," in Cobble, *Women and Unions*, 50; on blacks and minorities hired in construction under affirmative action, see Cobble, *Women and Unions*, 67.

41. The 1980s saw such revisionism as David Halle, *America's Working Man: Work, Home, and Politics among Blue-Collar Property Owners* (Chicago: University of Chicago Press, 1984). Although Halle probes the intermixture of middle- and lower-class aspects of blue-collar life, he skips over unionism.

42. LeMasters, *Blue-Collar Aristocrats*.

43. See, for instance, Ewing Campbell, *Raymond Carver: A Study of the Short Fiction* (New York: Twayne, 1992): "Carver's compositions are [the] reshaped experience of blue-collar despair" (xi).

44. Adam Hochschild, "Life through a Close-Up Lens," *Mother Jones* (October 1988): 50. See also Tony Eprile's comment about "sameness of narrative tone" in the work of Carver's contemporary Michael Dorris, in "We Are What We Do: *Working Men*," *New York Times Book Review*, 17 October 1993, 12.

45. Raymond Carver, "A Small, Good Thing," in Raymond Carver, *Cathedral* (New York: Vintage Books, 1981), 113; hereafter cited in text.

46. Niemi, *Russell Banks*, x. Janet Zandy suggests that Banks carried this theme into the 1990s with novels about the failure of community like *The Sweet Hereafter* (1992).

47. Dan Georgakas, "The Beats and the New Left," in *The Encyclopedia of the American Left*, ed. Mari Jo Buhle, Paul Buhle, and Dan Georgakas (New York: Garland Publishers, 1990), 77.

48. Freeman et al., *Who Built America?*, vol. 2, 598.

49. A number of Bukowski novels trace Chinaski's artistic mishaps and sneering responses. He permits himself post-hangover workdays, fights with his boss, and unpleasantness to customers on a mail route, all the while deliberately congratulating himself on his superiority to his circumstances.

50. Charles Bukowski, *Post Office* (Santa Barbara, Calif.: Black Sparrow Press, 1971), 38; hereafter cited in text.

51. A good discussion of the decline of the older miners who fought the organizing battles of the 1930s is in John Gaventa, *Power and Powerlessness: Quiescence and Rebellion in an Appalachian Valley* (Urbana: University of Illinois Press, 1980), 155–186.

52. In this regard, see Ronald L. Lewis, *Black Coal Miners in America: Race, Class, and Community Conflict, 1780–1980* (Lexington: University Press of Kentucky, 1987), chap. 9.

53. James Lee Burke, *To the Bright and Shining Sun* (New York: Hyperion, 1970), 209; hereafter cited in text.

54. There should, for example, be more familiarity with his 1992 film *City of Hope*. In contrast, despite Sayles's immense sympathy for the Rosenbergs' sons, the Meeropols, whom his *Book of Daniel* (1971) novelizes into a brother and sister, they come across as spoiled products of the counterculture.

55. John Sayles, *Union Dues* (New York: Harper Perennial, 1977), 40; hereafter cited in text.

56. Lewis, *Black Coal Miners*, offers a succinct account of Boyle's regime and Yablonski's murder (184–187).

57. See Appy, *Working-Class War*, esp. chap. 1.

58. For an extreme vision of UMW crookedness, complete with a racketeering union local, robbed in revenge by its disgruntled members, see Paul Schraeder's first film, *Blue Collar* (1978). An important reading of this film as an attack on non–AFL-CIO unions by Hollywood is in William J. Puette, *Through Jaundiced Eyes: How the Media View Organized Labor* (Ithaca, N.Y.: ILR Press, 1992).

59. Geoghegan, *Which Side Are You On?*, 39.

60. For a brilliant short story on the vitality of the octogenarian urban Jewish left in the 1960s, see John Sayles, "At the Anarchists' Convention," in John Sayles, *The Anarchists' Convention* (1975; reprint, New York: HarperPerennial, 1979), 23–34.

61. On the particulars of the Matewan strike and its parallels to the 1980s, see James R. Green, " 'Tying the Knot of Solidarity': The Pittston Strike of 1989–1990," in *The United Mine Workers of America: A Model of Industrial Solidarity?*, ed. John H. M. Laslett (University Park: Pennsylvania State University Press, 1996), 514, 516, 519.

62. John Sayles, *Thinking in Pictures: The Making of the Movie "Matewan"* (Boston: Houghton Mifflin, 1987), 9–11.

63. Ibid., 10–11. See also Theodore Dreiser et al., eds., *Harlan Miners Speak* (New York: Harcourt, Brace, 1932), 141.

64. Sayles, *Thinking in Pictures*, 11. A highly critical article on *Matewan* is Stephen Brier, "A History Film without Much History," *Radical History Review* 41 (1988): 120–128.

65. Laslett, "Introduction," in *United Mine Workers*, clarifies the pro- and anti-Lewis factions (1–29).

66. Tom Zaniello, *Working Stiffs, Union Maids, Reds, and Riffraff: An Organized Guide to Films about Labor* (Ithaca, N.Y.: ILR Press, 1996), 106–108.

67. Green, " 'Tying the Knot of Solidarity, '" 516.

68. Julian Moynihan, "How Green Was My Kentucky Valley," *New York Times Book Review*, 27 July 1980, 12.

69. John Yount, *Hardcastle* (Dallas: Southern Methodist University Press, 1980), 284; hereafter cited in text.

70. William Kennedy, *Ironweed* (1979; reprint, New York: Penguin, 1983), 208; hereafter cited in text.

71. "Hallelujah on the Bum" [later Hollywoodized as "Hallelujah, I'm a Bum"], in *Rebel Voices: An IWW Songbook* ed. Joyce L. Kornbluh (1964; reprint, Chicago: Charles H. Kerr, 1988), 71–72.

72. Hartigan, "Name Calling," 49.

73. On Faulkner's "sorry whites," see Foley, *The White Scourge*, 6, 7, and chap. 6; and Frederick J. Hoffman, *William Faulkner* (Boston: Twayne, 1961), 84–86.

74. Roxanne A. Dunbar, "Bloody Footprints: Reflections on Growing up Poor White," in Hartigan, *White Trash*, 75, 78.

75. On the racial divisions built into Chrysler assembly-line work in that period, see Jacqueline Jones, *American Work: Four Centuries of Black and White Labor* (New York: W. W. Norton, 1998), 367; and Dan Georgakas, "The League of Revolutionary Black Workers," in Buhle, Buhle, and Georgakas, *The Encyclopedia of the American Left*, 415–419.

76. Dan Georgakas, *Detroit: I Do Mind Dying*, rev. ed. (Boston: South End Press, 1999); Ze'ev Chafets, *Devil's Night: And Other True Tales of Detroit* (New York: Random House, 1990), 23–24, 68–69.

77. On the Jukes and Kallikaks, see Rafter, "Introduction," in Summers and Rafter, *White Trash* , 10–11. Bone learns from her roguish uncles to think like a man and to meet the injuries of class through a cult of personality. Neither attitude helps her in coping with sexual abuse at the hands of her stepfather, Glen, the bad-seed scion of an elitist town family. Allison is not oblivious to the irony that "legitimacy" is conferred on Glen, the personification of normality as the new husband of Anney Boatwright, through his job doing steady Teamsters' work driving an RC Cola truck. For Glen is the book's most poisonous character: he rapes his stepdaughter Bone and demonizes her to deflect attention from his own trashy conduct.

78. Carolyn Chute, *The Beans of Egypt, Maine* (New York: Ticknor and Fields, 1985), 60; hereafter cited in text. Earlene is a distinct literary throwback to David Graham Phillips, *Susan Lenox: Her Fall and Rise* (Carbondale: Southern Illinois University Press, 1977). Phillips, a Gilded Age "success novelist," frees his title character from an unsavory backwoods marriage. Chute, however, is more realistic.

79. Lise Vogel, "Socialist Feminism," in Buhle, Buhle, and Georgakas, *The Encyclopedia of the American Left*, 709.

80. See Sally Ward Maggard, "From Farm to Coal Camp to Back Office and McDonald's: Living in the Midst of Appalachia's Latest Transformation," *Journal of the Appalachian Studies Association* 6 (1994): 14–38. An impressive summary of women's situation is in Ruth Rosen, "Women's Liberation," in Buhle, Buhle, and Georgakas, *The Encyclopedia of the American Left*, 834–841. On women's pre–World War II participation in textile work and protest, see Laura Hapke, *Daughters of the Great Depression: Women, Work, and Fiction in the American 1930s* (Athens: University of Georgia Press, 1995), 145–147.

81. On schooling in the 1970s and 1980s, see Betty Tsang, "Better than B-12," in *Sisterhood and Solidarity: Workers' Education for Women, 1914–1984*, ed. Joyce L. Kornbluh and Mary Frederickson (Philadelphia: Temple University Press, 1984), 316–317.

82. Randall J. Patton, " 'A World of Opportunity within the Tufting Empire': Labor Relations in North Georgia's Carpet Industry," *Georgia Historical Review* 81, no. 2 (Summer 1997): 426–451.

83. Sally Ward Maggard, "Women's Participation in the Brookside Coal Strike: Militance, Class, and Gender in Appalachia," *Frontiers* 9, no. 3 (1987): 19.

84. On CLUW, see Evans, *Born for Liberty*, 300; and Kornbluh and Frederickson, *Sisterhood and Solidarity*, 294–297.

85. Evans, *Born for Liberty*, 303–310.

86. On these ideas as central to the of mountain-woman southern fiction, see Charlotte Goodman, "Images of American Rural Women," *University of Michigan Papers in Women's Studies* (June 1995): 57–70.

87. Dorothy Allison, *Trash* (Ithaca, N.Y.: Firebrand Books, 1988). Biographical data on Allison and her awards appear in Ann E. Imbrie, "Dorothy E. Allison," in *The Gay and Lesbian Literary Heritage: A Companion*, ed. Claude J. Summers (New York: Henry Holt, 1995), 22.

88. Kadi, *Thinking Class*, 145.

89. Jillian Sandell, "Telling Stories of 'Queer White Trash': Race, Class, and Sexuality in the Work of Dorothy Allison," in Newitz and Wray, *White Trash*, 223.

90. On the difficulty of balancing gay and class concerns, see Susan Raffo, "Introduction," in *Queerly Classed*, ed. Susan Raffo (Boston: South End Press, 1997), and the essays by various hands in this worthwhile collection.

91. See the H-labor online postings of July 1998 on homosexuality in logging camps; Alan Bérubé's work-in-progress on marine stewards and cooks (Karla Jay, letter to author, 17 November 1996); and Joanne J. Meyerowitz, *Women Adrift: Independent Wage Earners in Chicago, 1880–1930* (Chicago: University of Chicago Press, 1988), 95–96, 111–114.

92. See "Lesbian/Gay Labor Conference Set for June in California," *Labor Notes* (May 1996). For a provocative critique of the bourgeois, materialistic gay, see Donald Morton, "Birth of the Cyberqueer," *MLA* 110, no. 3 (May 1995): 369–381.

93. Linda Niemann, *Boomer: Railroad Memoirs* (Boston: Cleis Press, 1990). See Lillian Faderman, *To Believe in Women* (Boston: Houghton Mifflin, 1999), on lesbian contributions to the labor movement.

94. On black women at the J. P. Stevens southern mill, consult Fran Leeper Buss, ed., *Dignity: Lower-Income Women Tell of Their Lives and Struggles* (Ann Arbor: University of Michigan Press, 1985), 203; on prototypes for "Norma Rae," see ibid., 221–224, and Jones, *American Work*, 367.

95. Steven Marcus, *The Other Victorians: A Study of Sexuality and Pornography in Mid-Nineteenth-Century England* (1964; reprint, New York: New American Library, 1974), 11.

96. So controversial remains the Schenkkan portrait of the backward Appalachian that a 1999 series of essays refutes it still. See *Confronting Appalachian Stereotypes: Back Talk from an American Region*, ed. Dwight B. Billings, Gurney Norman, and Katherine Ledford (Lexington: University Press of Kentucky, 1999). The three editors join twenty other contributors to oppose pejorative images of Appalachia.

Conclusion

1. See Jo Ann E. Argersinger, *Making the Amalgamated: Gender, Ethnicity, and Class in the Baltimore Clothing Industry, 1899–1939* (Baltimore: Johns Hopkins University Press, 1999), 1–7; and Karen J. Winkler, "A 'Heartbreaking' Look at the Death of an American Factory," *Chronicle of Higher Education*, 18 March 1998, A18.

2. See Jonathan Rosenblum, *Copper Crucible: How the Arizona Miners' Strike of 1983 Recast Labor-Management Relations in America*, 2d ed. (Ithaca, N.Y.: ILR Press, 1998), ix.

3. Interview with Rich Trumka, *Out of Darkness: The Mine Workers' Story*, dir. Barbara Kopple, prod. Labor History and Cultural Foundation, 1990—a classic documentary. Trumka is now secretary-treasurer of the AFL-CIO.

4. Michael D. Yates, *Why Unions Matter* (New York: Monthly Review Press, 1987), 137; Michael Kazin, "In Scabs There Is Strength" [review of Jonathan Rosenblum, *Copper Crucible*], *New York Times Book Review,* 15 January 1995, 11.

5. Nelson Lichtenstein, e-mail, H-Labor Digest, 17 August 1998 to 18 August 1998, H-Labor@H-Net.MSU.edu.

6. Louis Uchitelle, "The Rise of the Losing Class," *New York Times,* sect. 4, 20 November 1994, 1, 5.

7. Author's interview with striking IBEW worker, in front of 41 Park Row, New York City, 15 August 1999.

8. Ben Hamper, *Rivethead: Tales from the Assembly Line* (New York: Warner Books, 1991), 117, hereafter cited in text; and Agnes Rossi, *The Quick* (New York: W. W. Norton, 1992), 57, hereafter cited in text.

9. A recent worker-philosopher riposte is Reg Thericault, *How to Tell When You're Tired: A Brief Examination of Work* (New York: W. W. Norton, 1995). An appendix gives updates on working-class history and progress, the international labor movement, and the knowledge industries.

10. Elliott Kotler, interview on the United Federation of Teachers, Co-op City, the Bronx, 1 July 1998.

11. Andrew Hacker, "Who's Sticking to the Union?" *New York Review of Books,* 18 February 1999, 45–46. Hacker reviewed current labor books, including Stanley Aronowitz's *From the Ashes of the Old: American Labor and America's Future* (Boston: Houghton Mifflin, 1999).

12. "Labor Successes Mark Turning Point for Unions, Experts Say," *New York Times,* 1 September 1997, A1, A13; Jill Abramson and Steven Greenhouse, "Labor Victory on Trade Bill Reveals Power," *New York Times,* 14 November 1997, A1. See also Steven Greenhouse, "Union Wins a Long Battle at an Investment Bank's Cafeteria," *New York Times,* 17 May 1999, 28.

13. Hacker, "Who's Sticking," 45; "UAW Members Vote down Contract with Caterpillar," *New York Times,* 23 February 1998.

14. Steven Greenhouse, "A Victory for Labor, but How Lasting Will It Be?" *New York Times,* 20 August 1977, A1, D18; David Cay Johnston, "On Payday, Union Jobs Stack Up Very Well, but Will Anyone Be Listening?" *New York Times,* 23 May 1999, business section 1:9. See Johnston, "On Payday, Union Jobs Stack Up," for *New York Times* coverage of the UPS strike. See also Douglas Century, "Still a Contender on the Waterfront," *New York Times,* 12 March 1999, 50.

15. Jane H. Lii, "Week in Sweatshop Reveals Grim Conspiracy of the Poor," *New York Times,* 12 March 1995, A1, A40; Daniel Jacoby, *Laboring for Freedom: A New Look at the History of Labor in America* (Armonk, N.Y.: M. E. Sharpe, 1998), 149.

16. The NWU is part of the UAW's Technical, Office, and Professional Division (TOP). Discussion of this labor alliance is on the H-Labor Listserv, 2 January 2000, H-Labor@H-Net.MSU.com; I am particularly grateful to Daniel Bender, Ellen Schrecker, and Rob Weir for their contributions to that exchange. On the UFW see Timothy Egan, "Teamsters and Ex-Rival [UFW] Go After Apple Industry," *New York Times,* 19 August 1997, A10. In a similar spirit, the International Longshoremen's Association has been recruiting workers in sugar factories.

17. For a still timely article laying out the issues surrounding the future of union organizing in higher education, see Courtney Leatherman and Denise K. Magner, "Faculty and Graduate-Student Strife over Job Issues Flares on Many Campuses," *Chronicle of Higher Education,* 29 November 1996, A12–13.

18. One recent letter to supporters noted that the organization was dedicated to "re-establishing a connection between the labor movement and the cultural and in-

tellectual community." There is some irony in the statement. Another source for the link between academics and labor is the Cincinnati-area video *Degrees of Shame* (Barbara Wolf Video Work, 1997), in which the producer/director, Barbara Wolf, tried to dramatize how the situation of adjuncts is reminiscent of that of migrant farmworkers in the 1960 farmworkers' documentary, *Harvest of Shame*. See Cary Nelson, *Will Teach for Food* (Minneapolis: University of Minnesota Press, 1997). On the perception of underemployed Ph.D. and graduate student adjuncts as part of an academic labor crisis, see also Cary Nelson, *Manifesto of a Tenured Radical* (New York: New York University Press, 1997).

19. The essays issuing from the 1996 Columbia University "Teach-In with the Labor Movement," including one by John Sweeney, are in *Audacious Democracy: Labor, Intellectuals, and the Social Reconstruction of America*, ed. Steven Fraser and Joshua Freeman (New York: Mariner Books, 1997). SAWSJ also posts general calls such as the one to picket wealthy Metropolitan Opera patrons, who exploit the immigrant workers serving them, on opening night; Dahlia Ward, online posting, 21 September 1999; dahlia_llama@hotmail.com. For a relatively rare instance in which organized labor, in this case the building tradesmen working on campus, has joined the faculty's "general strike," see Robin Wilson, "Faculty Union Strikes at Wayne State University," *Chronicle of Higher Education*, 24 September 1999, A18. More typical is the University of Tennessee Teach-in, 3–4 March 2000, "Labor Rights as Human Rights at Home and Abroad," sponsored by student groups and local union organizations, with imported AFL-CIO speakers. An early call to interested parties was in the H-Labor Listserv of 31 December 1999, H-Labor@H-Net.MSU.edu. The website http://www.workplace-gsc.com/ is the site for *workplace: a journal for academic labor*.

20. The reliable source for these 1995 statistics is Robin D. G. Kelley, "Colloquy," *Chronicle of Higher Education* webpage, chronicle.com/colloquy/99/workingclass/29.htm.

21. Robert Zieger, *American Workers, American Unions*, 2d ed. (Baltimore: Johns Hopkins University Press, 1994), 163. Corruption and theft in AFSCME by a cadre of officials recently resulted in a theft of $4.6 million from the membership, as noted in Jim Lehrer, report, Lehrer News Hour, PBS, 21 January 2000.

22. Ronald L. Filippelli, "Memphis Sanitation Strike," in *Labor Conflict in the United States: An Encyclopedia*, ed. Ronald L. Filippelli (New York: Garland, 1990), 321–324; Joan Turner Beifuss, *At the River I Stand*, rev. ed. (Memphis: St. Luke's Press, 1990), contains a fast-paced account, although it is often difficult to pinpoint names and dates.

23. Leon Fink and Brian Greenberg, *Upheaval in the Quiet Zone: A History of Hospital Workers' Union, Local 1199* (Urbana: University of Illinois Press, 1994).

24. See Jacoby, *Laboring for Freedom*, 152–156, on service-sector workers as the new factory workers.

25. South Carolina prisons, for instance, deal with CorCraft to use prison assembly lines to make furniture—not a skilled career after jail either. On prison labor for companies, see a 1999 cable television program on BCAT with Annemarie Polinsky, industrial director of the AFL-CIO, and Edward Cleary, president of the New York State AFL-CIO, 14 July 1999.

26. Stanley Aronowitz and Jonathan Cobb, eds., *Post-Work: The Wages of Cybernation* (New York: Routledge, 1997). Richard Vigilante writes, "The transit from an industrial to a post-industrial society that comes when we make our machines not only augmenters of muscle but extensions of mind . . . has promised to eliminate the phrase 'working-class' from the American vocabulary," *The Daily News Strike and the Future of American Labor* (New York: Simon and Schuster, 1994), 12. For a pre-

dictably entrepreneurial vision see "'Office Economy' Found to Boost Jobs and Incomes," *Deloitte and Touche Review*, 16 March 1998, 2.

27. Jean Bethke Elshtain, "Lost City," *New Republic*, 4 November 1996, 25. Any municipality in a state can ask for prison labor, and, with little or no OSHA oversight, the prisoner's safety is not protected.

28. Helena Maria Viramontes, *Under the Feet of Jesus* (Houston: Arte Publico Press, 1995); hereafter cited in text.

29. Joanne Omang, "Book World," *Washington Post*, 14 May 1995, also available at Lexis/Nexis, Galenet.

30. Richard Russo, *Nobody's Fool* (New York: Random House, 1993), 371.

31. Qtd. in Jeff Sharlet, "Seeking Solidarity in the Culture of the Working Class," *Chronicle of Higher Education*, 23 July 1999, A1.

32. Robert Bruno, *Steelworker Alley: How Class Works in Youngstown* (Ithaca, N.Y.: Cornell University Press, 1999).

33. Michael Dorris, "The Benchmark," in Michael Dorris, *Working Men* (New York: H. Holt, 1993), 2–4.

34. Tess Gallagher, "I Met a Guy Once," in Tess Gallagher, *At the Owl Woman Saloon* (New York: Scribner's, 1997), 27–41. Gallagher's central character calls himself a "gyppo," a logger appellation common to IWW fiction by Ralph Winstead (see chapter 9).

35. Ralph Lombreglia, *Make Me Work* (New York: Penguin Books, 1994), 157.

36. Tiffany and Co. advertisement, *New York Times*, 5 September 1994, 3; "Working Men," *New York Times*, 3 September 1994. See also the Tennessee tar-shack recasting in Michael Perry, "Creating a Home on the Margins," *New York Times Magazine*, 7 March 1999, 64; "Status in a Class-Free Society," *New York Times Magazine*, 15 November 1998, entire issue; and "Visit a Virtual Steel Mill," www.pbs.org, *The American Experience*: "The Richest Man in the World" [flattering biography of Andrew Carnegie], produced by WGBH, Boston, 1997, and funded in part by the NEH.

37. Sam Roberts, "Women's Work: What's New, What Isn't," *New York Times*, 27 April 1995, B6.

38. Ibid. Women of color make less customarily. Jacqueline Jones, *American Work: Four Centuries of Black and White Labor* (New York: W. W. Norton, 1998), 372, 379, 485. For a counterview, see Charmeynne D. Nelson, "Myths about Black Women Workers in America," *Black Scholar* (March 1975): 8.

39. See especially Lucy Honig, "No Friends, All Strangers," in Lucy Honig, *The Truly Needy and Other Stories* (Pittsburgh: University of Pittsburgh Press, 1999), 1–19, which contains the memorable line, "I give shampoos and sweep up, they don't know me from Adam" (1). For Shear's nonchalantly profane response to a boss, see Claudia Shear, *Blown Sideways through Life* (New York: Dial Press, 1995), 11; and Laura Mansnerus, "A Conversation with Claudia Shear," *New York Times*, 6 April 1994, C1.

40. Peter T. Kilborn, "In New Work World, Employees Call All the Shots," *New York Times*, 3 July 1998, 1–7; *Contingent Work: American Employment Relations in Transition*, ed. Kathleen Barker and Kathleen Christensen (Ithaca, N.Y.: ILR Press, 1998).

41. For some compelling anecdotal evidence on such continuing attitudes, see the on-line posting about the National Steel Company's white workforce, William Lynn Watson, 9 June 1998, Center for Working-Class Studies Listserv, CWCS-L@ysub.ysu.edu.

42. On the "black failure" narrative as a trope, see Daniel Walkowitz, *Working with Class: Social Workers and the Politics of Middle-Class Identity* (Chapel Hill: University of North Carolina Press, 1999).

43. Frederick Douglass, *The Narrative of the Life of Frederick Douglass: An American Slave* (1845; reprint, New York: Signet, 1968), 177.

44. J. Jones, *American Work*, 372, 374–375.

45. Fox Butterfield, "More Blacks in Their Twenties Have Trouble with the Law," *New York Times*, 5 October 1995, A18.

46. William Julius Wilson, *When Work Disappears: The World of the New Urban Poor* (New York: Alfred A. Knopf, 1996). On the controversy surrounding Wilson's assertions that a WPA program needs to be revived for the inner-city poor, see "A Prominent Scholar's Plan for the Inner Cities Draws Fire," *Chronicle of Higher Education*, 5 September 1997, A21; and Sean Wilentz, "Jobless and Hopeless: *When Work Disappears* by William Julius Wilson," *New York Times Book Review*, 29 September 1996, 7.

47. Nathan McCall, *Makes Me Wanna Holler: A Young Black Man in America* (1994; reprint, New York: Vintage Books, 1995), 85; hereafter cited in text.

48. Qtd. in Nina Ayoub, "New Scholarly Books," *Chronicle of Higher Education*. On the disdain for menial work among inner-city youths, see Michael Massing, "Ghetto Blasting," *New Yorker*, 16 January 1995, 36. On the rejection of menial jobs, see the various essays in *Social Forms/Human Capacities: Essays in Authority and Difference*, ed. Philip Richard Corrigan (London: Routledge, 1990). For sentiments mirroring McCall's among black prisoners, see Jerome Washington, "Diamond Bob" (1994; reprinted in *Prison Writing in Twentieth-Century America*, ed. H. Bruce Franklin [New York: Penguin Books, 1998]), 320.

49. For a piercing critique of the inconsistencies in McCall's philosophy, see Adam Hochschild, "A Furious Man," *New York Times Book Review*, 7 February 1994, 11.

50. For an accurate review of the novel as a naturalist work at a breakneck pace, see Kai Maristed, *"Ten Indians," Los Angeles Times Book Review*, 15 December 1996, 9.

51. Praise for the Price novel from middle- and highbrows can be found in, respectively, John Skow, "Fishy in New Jersey?" *Time*, 18 May 1998, 93, and Gene Seymour, *"Freedomland," The Nation*, 20 July 1998, 25.

52. Richard Price, *Clockers* (1984; reprint, New York: Avon Books, 1993), 38.

53. Richard Price, *Freedomland* (New York: Broadway Books, 1998), 485; hereafter cited in text.

54. Bruce Schneider, *Vampires, Dragons, and Egyptian Kings: Youth Gangs in Postwar New York* (Urbana: University of Illinois Press, 1999); George Hudson, "Jury Gets Federal Racketeering Case against Latin Kings," *New York Times*, 24 September 1995. See also Franklin, *Prison Writing in Twentieth-Century America*, passim. On racial-ethnic laboring versus criminal gang activity in 1970s Los Angeles, see Luis J. Rodriguez, *Always Running: La Vida Loca—Gang Days in L.A.* (New York: Simon and Schuster, 1993), 8, 17, 38, 40–41.

55. John Edgar Wideman, "All Stories Are True," in John Edgar Wideman, *All Stories Are True* (New York: Vintage Books, 1993), 4; hereafter cited in text.

56. J. Jones notes that black women historically have found work more often than have black men. See *American Work*, 372, 379.

57. To best contextualize Gaines, Southerland, and McMillan, however, see studies noting the erosion of black women's job gains such as Natalie J. Sokoloff, *Black Women and White Women in the Professions: Occupational Segregation by Race and*

Gender, 1960–1980 (New York: Routledge, 1992); and Augustin Kwasi Fosu, "Occupational Gains of Black Women since the 1964 Civil Rights Act: Long-term or Episodic?" *American Economic Review* 87 (May 1997): 311–314.

58. Novels like *Beloved* and *Mama Day* rightly belong to a discussion of African American women's spirituality. In this regard, see G. Michelle Collins, "There Where We Are Not: The Magical Real in *Beloved* and *Mama Day*," *Southern Review* 24 (1988): 681.

59. A fruitful perspective from the wealth of articles on Walker's portrait of female mistreatment is Emma Waters-Dawson, "From Victim to Victor: Walker's Women in *The Color Purple*," in *The Aching Hearth: Family Violence in Life and Literature*, ed. Sara Munson Deats and Lagretta Tallent Lenker (New York: Insight/Plenum, 1991): 255–268.

60. Alice Walker, *The Color Purple* (New York: Washington Square Books, 1982), 29. Few black male critics have attempted to reverse Walker's reputation as determinedly anti–black working (or nonworking) male. A standard piece in that regard is Robert Towers, "Good Men Are Hard to Find," *New York Review of Books*, 12 August 1982, 35–36. See the contradictions in even one rare attempt, J. Charles Washington, "Positive Black Male Images in Alice Walker's Fiction," *Obsidian* 3, no. 1 (1983): 23–48.

61. Claudia Tate, "Introduction" to Gayl Jones interview in *Black Woman Writers at Work* (New York: Continuum, 1983), 89.

62. Jones is claimed as both an African American and a Caribbean author; see Stellamaris Coser, *Bridging the Americas: The Literature of Paule Marshall, Toni Morrison and Gayl Jones* (Philadelphia: Temple University Press, 1995), chap. 4.

63. Gayle Jones, *Eva's Man* (Boston: Beacon Press, 1987), 111; hereafter cited in text.

64. An impressive countertradition of African American women's (working-class) empowerment writing preceded Sapphire's novel *Push* (1997). It includes Sarah E. Wright, *This Child's Gonna Live* (1969), Louise Meriwether, *Daddy Was a Number Runner* (1970), Alice Walker's "Everyday Use" (1983), Gloria Naylor, *The Women of Brewster Place* (1988), and Toni Morrison, *The Bluest Eye* (1970), the lesbian feminist Audre Lorde's autobiographical *Zami: A New Spelling of My Name* (1982), and the writer-activist Toni Cade Bambara's novel *The Salt Eaters* (1980). Recent Caribbean women's literature updates female work situations in Paule Marshall's *Brown Girl, Brownstones* (1959), particularly works by Jamaica Kincaid (*Lucy*, 1990) and Edwige Dantikat (*Krik! Krak!*, 1994). Yet Jones's Eve can enter no world, including the factory, but that of the mentally ill. She cannot be a touchstone for the black woman's paid work narrative in the tradition of Zora Neale Hurston, Ann Petry, or Jones's fellow Caribbean Paule Marshall (see chapter 10).

65. Saul Bellow, "Looking for Mr. Green" [1951], in *The Urban Muse: Stories on the American City*, ed. Ilan Stevans (New York: Delta Books, 1998), 260–282. In this Chicago tale it is significant that the white welfare mother is depicted as a successful con artist, unlike the beaten-down black ghetto matriarch. On modern misconceptions of black women on welfare, see Valerie Polakov, *Lives on the Edge* (Chicago: University of Chicago Press, 1997). See also "Income Gap Persists for Blacks and Whites," *New York Times*, 23 February 1995, A21.

66. Terry McMillan, *Mama* (New York: Washington Square Press, 1987).

67. J. Jones provides a "race watch" context for black women hotel workers in *American Work*, 369–370. See also Mary C. King, "Black Women's Labor Market Status: Occupational Segregation in the United States and Great Britain," *Review of Black Political Economy* 24, no. 1 (1995): 23–41, and Roberts, "Women's Work," B6.

68. Barbara F. Reskin and Camille Z. Charles, "Now You See 'em, Now You Don't: Race, Ethnicity, and Gender in Labor Market Research," in *Latinas and African American Women at Work: Race, Gender, and Economic Inequality*, ed. Irene Browne (New York: Russell Sage Foundation, 1999), 380–407, and Femi I. Ajanaku et al., "Underdevelopment in the U.S. Labor Market: The Case of African American Female Workers," *Urban League Review* 14 (Winter 1990–1991): 29. The rare fictionalized autobiography is Ruthie Bolton, *Gal: A True Life* (New York: Harcourt, Brace, 1994). Interestingly, Bolton dictated it to the prominent white writer Josephine Humphreys.

69. Sapphire [Ramona Lofton], *Push* (New York: Random House, 1997), 119; hereafter cited in text.

70. Sherry Ortner, "Reading America: Preliminary Notes on Class and Culture," in *Recapturing Anthropology: Working in the Present*, ed. Richard G. Fox (Santa Fe: School of American Research Press, 1991), 182.

71. Irene Vilar, *The Ladies' Gallery: A Memoir of Family Secrets*, trans. Gregory Rabassa (New York: Vintage Books, 1998), 12.

72. Piri Thomas, lecture, Pace University, New York City, 8 April 1999. See also Piri Thomas, "Afterword to the Thirtieth-Anniversary Edition," in Piri Thomas, *Down These Mean Streets* (1967; reprint, New York: Vintage Books, 1997), 333–337; hereafter cited in text. El Taller Boricua, the artists' collective of "Spanish Harlem," the founding community of what later became El Museo del Barrio, had just been funded in the late 1960s to provide a cultural corridor in East Harlem. But groundbreaking Puerto Rican prison art dealing with, for instance, sexuality followed Thomas; the poet and playwright Miguel Pinero did not publish his drama *Short Eyes* until 1975.

73. For a recent study of the links between poverty for blacks and Hispanics, see Sam Roberts, *A Portrait of America Based on the Latest U.S. Census* (New York: Times Books, 1994).

74. Esmeralda Santiago, *When I Was Puerto Rican* (New York: Addison-Wesley, 1993), 233; hereafter cited in text.

75. Esmeralda Santiago, lecture, Pace University, April 9, 1998. Santiago's memoir, *Almost a Woman* (Reading, Mass.: Perseus Books, 1998), addresses this notion of the hierarchy of talent.

76. Santiago lecture, Pace University, 1998.

77. Junot Diaz, *Drown* (New York: Riverhead Books, 1996); hereafter cited in text. In an interesting transit, Diaz moved through poverty to scholarship boyhood to steel mill work to an MFA. See Amalia Duarte, "Junot Diaz: Eye of a Journalist, Tongue of a Poet," *Hispanic Outlook*, 7 April 1997, 13–15.

78. See Carmen Rivera, "Julia," in *Nuestro New York: An Anthology of Puerto Rican Plays*, ed. John V. Antush (New York: Mentor, 1992).

79. Luis Alberto Urrea, *Nobody's Son: Notes from an American Life* (Tucson: University of Arizona Press, 1998), 58.

80. Yvonne Yarbo-Bejarano, "Introduction," in Helena Maria Viramontes, *The Moth and Other Stories*, 2d ed. (1988; Houston: Arte Publico Press, 1995), 21.

81. Janet Zandy, ed., *Liberating Memory: Our Work and Our Working-Class Consciousness* (New Brunswick, N.J.: Rutgers University Press, 1995), 57.

82. "Labor Abuses in NIKE Factories Exposed," *Sweatshop Watch* (Winter 1997): 1. A passionate new social document is *No Sweat: Fashion, Free Trade, and the Rights of Garment Workers*, ed. Andrew Ross (New York: Verso, 1997). For a contrasting assessment of well-off young people's attitudes toward the usefulness of sweatshop protests, see Martin Van Der Werf, "Sweatshop Protests Raise Ethical and Practical Issues," significantly placed in the Money and Management section of the *Chronicle*

of *Higher Education*, 5 March 1999, A38–39. The *New York Times* labor reporter Bob Herbert has been doggedly contributing op-ed columns on the subject for years. See Bob Herbert, "In Deep Denial," *New York Times*, 13 October 1995, A33; "A Sweatshop Victory," *New York Times*, 22 December 1995, A39; "From Sweatshops to Aerobics: How Nike Defends Women's Rights," *New York Times*, 24 June 1996, A15; "Brutality in Vietnam," *New York Times*, 3 March 1997, A29. See also Don Van Natta, Jr., "Exploitation Is Worsening, [California] Garment Workers Tell Labor Chief," *New York Times*, 13 September 1995, B1; and Van Natta, "Seamstresses Protest Factory Conditions" [on Donna Karan International], *New York Times*, 1 July 1999, B8.

83. Morris Dickstein, "Hallucinating the Past," *Grand Street* 9 (Winter 1989): 163–170.

84. For examples of the new worker-writing that is less "radical" than the crusading journalism that appears in the journal, see the occasional stories in *Southern Exposure: A Journal of Politics and Culture*, published by the (pro–civil rights) Institute for Southern Studies.

85. Donna Berry, "An Interview with Barbara Kingsolver," in *Backtalk: Women Writers Speak Out,* ed. Donna Berry (New Brunswick, N.J.: Rutgers University Press, 1993), also available at Gale Literary Databases, www.galenet.com.

86. See also the small-press edition of Dorothy Langley's 1940s southeastern Missouri hillbilly novel, *Swamp Angel*. See Helen Bugbee, "Introduction," in Dorothy Langley, *Swamp Angel* (Chicago: Academy Chicago, 1982), n.p. The novel was originally turned down by publishers for its "depressing" content (and reissued by Simon and Schuster when it was completely revised). West End Press, begun in 1976 by John Crawford, is far better known than the others listed, both as Meridel Le Sueur's publisher and that of multicultural literature. To date, though, Le Sueur's unfinished Depression novel, *The Girl* (see chapter 9), continuously in print since 1978, has sold less than twenty-five thousand copies. West End also published an "underground" steelworker-writer anthology, *Overtime: Punchin' Out with the Mill Hunk Herald (1979–1989)* (1990). In contrast to such American small-press constrictions, under the aegis of the Federation of Worker Writers and Community Publishers (known as FEDS) (ourworld.compuserve.com/homepages/working press), the "Incite to Write" movement in Great Britain, formed in 1976 to further working-class writing and community publishing, has to date no real U.S. counterpart.

87. Joe Mackall, "The Stories of Working-Class Lights," in *Writing Work: Writers on Working-Class Writing,* ed. David Shevin, Janet Zandy, and Larry Smith (Huron, Ohio: Bottom Dogs Press, 1999), 8. On the manifold difficulties of working-class representation and the need to theorize an aesthetic, see Peter Hitchcock, "They Must Be Represented?: Problems in Theories of Working-Class Representation," *PMLA* 115, no. 1 (February 2000): 20–31.

88. Wayne Rapp, "Lessons from the Underground," in *Writing Work,* 30.

89. Zandy, *Liberating Memory,* 67.

90. Lennard Davis, "A Voyage Out," in ibid., 57.

91. Heidi Shayla, "Working Poor," in *Writing Work,* 19.

92. Janet Zandy, "Introduction," in *Calling Home: Working-Class Women's Writings—An Anthology,* ed. Janet Zandy (New Brunswick, N.J.: Rutgers University Press, 1990).

93. Paul Christensen, "Failing," in *Writing Work,* 50; qtd. in Richard Hague, *Milltown Natural: Essays and Stories from a Life* (Huron, Ohio: Bottom Dog Press, 1997), 9.

94. See also Nicholasa Mohr, *In My Own Words: Growing Up in the Sanctuary of My Imagination* (New York: Julian Messner/Simon and Schuster, 1994), a memoir

contrasting her search for self-esteem with the depressing effects of her brother's imprisonment for drug dealing. On Rodriguez's view of the South Bronx and his debt to Piri Thomas, see Ian Fisher, "Chronicler of Bleak Truths in South Bronx: Novelist Finds His Muse Close to Home and Perhaps, Ultimately, His Escape," *New York Times*, 9 August 1993, B3.

95. An important new study is Stephen Duncombe, *Notes from Underground: Zines and the Politics of Alternative Culture* (London: Verso, 1997), esp. chap. 4, "Work," 44–70.

96. Ibid., 85. "Repent! Quit Your Job! Slack Off!" from the zine *Exformation* (1994).

97. *Clerks*, 1994, written and directed by Kevin Smith, produced by Scott Mosler and Kevin Smith.

98. Two shining examples are by the iconoclastic radical historian Jeremy Brecher, "Labor Update," *Z Magazine*, July/August 1998, and "American Labor on the Eve of the Millennium," *Z Magazine*, October 1998 (www.zmag.org/zmag/ articles).

99. Such zines on work life join movies in satirizing service-sector work. A sample of the zine: "Summertime and the livin' is easy, unless it's a really nice day and you have to work," Daniel S. Levine online posting, 27 July 1999 (dslevine@ disgruntled.com). In this the clerks resemble their white-collar betters from Silicon Valley to Washington, D.C., whose recent credo is "Consider the quit at every juncture" quoted in Michael Lewis, "The Joy of Quitting," *New York Times Magazine*, 5 September 1999, 21.

100. Valerie Miner's novel *Winter's Edge* was, however, first published with a more prominent press outside the United States (London: Methuen, 1984) and later by Crossing Press (Freedom, Calif., 1987). See also Maureen Brady's *Folly* (Trumansburg, N.Y.: Crossing Press, 1982), an interracial, work-stoppage story set in 1970s North Carolina that concerns lesbian textile workers. Praised by Audre Lorde and Tillie Olsen, it was reprinted in 1994 under the (more prestigious) Feminist Press imprimatur. See also the short story collection on ethnic working-class women in London by Barbara Burford, *The Threshing Floor* (published in 1982 by the small San Francisco press Firebrands, and reissued in 1998).

101. Paula Gover, *White Boys and River Girls* (Chapel Hill, N.C.: Algonquin Books, 1995); hereafter cited in text.

102. Janisse Ray, *Ecology of a Cracker Childhood* (Minneapolis: Milkweed Editions, 1999); Tony Horwitz, "In Praise of the Blue-Tailed Mole Skink" [*sic*], *New York Times Book Review*, 9 January 2000, 16.

103. For some fine labor passages, see James Lee Burke, *Half of Paradise* (New York: Hyperion, 1965), 36–37, 264–266, 277–278, 296–297. See also, in this regard, Dannie Martin's semiautobiographical mystery novel *The Dishwasher* (New York: W. W. Norton, 1995). It moves in and out of his Lompoc, California, prison memories, describing menial work and comparing the protagonist to a John Travolta lookalike. A more recent, commercialized novel by James Lee Burke is *Sunset Limited* (1998).

104. Naomi Wallace, *Slaughter City* (Boston: Faber and Faber, 1998). "High-art" poems on Appalachia, perhaps because of a poetry-loving audience, do find favor with highbrow readers. See Charles Wright, *Appalachia* (New York: Farrar, Straus and Giroux, 1998). Wright's work, though, consciously "elevates" its subject. See also the labor Rust Belt poet Philip Levine, *What Work Is* (New York: Alfred A. Knopf, 1991). For a related text, that of a hobo intellectual who transforms the underclass narrative into a witty tour de force, see Lars Eighner, *Travels with Lizbeth: Three Years on the Road and on the Streets* (1992; reprint, New York: Fawcett Columbine, 1993).

105. See, for instance, Peter Marks, "The Cream Still Rises, Even from Barrel Bottom," *New York Times*, 2 February 1999, E1. On the rationale for the parodic success of such "white-trash" plays, see Michiko Kakutani, "Critic's Notebook: With Reality Reeling, Pity the Poor Realist," *New York Times,* 22 June 1994, C13, C18.

106. Ilan Stevens, "Introduction," in *The Urban Muse: Stories of the American City*, ed. Ilan Stevens (New York: Delta Books, 1998), xviii.

107. Henry Roth, *Mercy of a Rude Stream* (New York: St. Martin's Press): vol. 1, *A Star Shines over Mount Morris Park* (1994); vol. 2, *A Diving Rock on the Hudson* (1995); vol. 3, *From Bondage* (1996); vol. 4, *Requiem for Harlem* (1998). For a generous assessment of the tetralogy, see Allegra Goodman, "About Time: *Requiem for Harlem*," *New York Times Book Review*, 5 January 1998, 16.

108. Janet Zandy, "In the Skin of a Worker," paper presented at a meeting of the Modern Language Association, December 1998.

Index

Page numbers in italics refer to illustrations.

447

Index

474

About the Author

Laura Hapke is Professor of English at Pace University in New York. She is the author of *Daughters of the Great Depression: Women, Work, and Fiction in the American 1930s* and other books and articles. She has published widely on labor fiction and working-class studies.